Women Warriors
in History

Also by Mary Ellen Snodgrass and from McFarland

Edwidge Danticat: A Companion to the Young Adult Literature (2022)

Octavia E. Butler: A Literary Companion (2022)

Asian Women Artists: A Biographical Dictionary, 2700 BCE to Today (2022)

Television's Outlander: A Companion, Seasons 1–5 (2021)

Rachel Carson: A Literary Companion (2021)

Marion Zimmer Bradley: A Companion to the Young Adult Literature (2020)

Lee Smith: A Literary Companion (2019)

Coins and Currency: An Historical Encyclopedia, 2d ed. (2019)

Gary Paulsen: A Companion to the Young Adult Literature (2018)

Brian Friel: A Literary Companion (2017)

World Epidemics: A Cultural Chronology of Disease from Prehistory to the Era of Zika, 2d ed. (2017)

Settlers of the American West: The Lives of 231 Notable Pioneers (2015)

Isabel Allende: A Literary Companion (2013)

Leslie Marmon Silko: A Literary Companion (2011)

Peter Carey: A Literary Companion (2010)

Jamaica Kincaid: A Literary Companion (2008)

Kaye Gibbons: A Literary Companion (2007)

Walter Dean Myers: A Literary Companion (2006)

World Shores and Beaches: A Descriptive and Historical Guide to 50 Coastal Treasures (2005)

Barbara Kingsolver: A Literary Companion (2004)

August Wilson: A Literary Companion (2004)

Amy Tan: A Literary Companion (2004)

Who's Who in the Middle Ages (2001; paperback 2013)

Encyclopedia of World Scriptures (2001; paperback 2011)

Women Warriors in History

*1,622 Biographies Worldwide
from the Bronze Age to the Present*

MARY ELLEN SNODGRASS

McFarland & Company, Inc., Publishers
Jefferson, North Carolina

LIBRARY OF CONGRESS CATALOGUING-IN-PUBLICATION DATA

Names: Snodgrass, Mary Ellen, author.
Title: Women warriors in history : 1,622 biographies worldwide from the Bronze age to the present / Mary Ellen Snodgrass.
Description: Jefferson, North Carolina : McFarland & Company, Inc., Publishers, 2023 | Includes bibliographical references and index.
Identifiers: LCCN 2023025237 | ISBN 9781476693057 (paperback : acid free paper) ∞
ISBN 9781476650326 (ebook)
Subjects: LCSH: Women soldiers—Biography. | Women and war—History. | Women in war—History.
Classification: LCC UB416 .S626 2023 | DDC 355.0082—dc23/eng/20230628
LC record available at https://lccn.loc.gov/2023025237

BRITISH LIBRARY CATALOGUING DATA ARE AVAILABLE

ISBN (print) 978-1-4766-9305-7
ISBN (ebook) 978-1-4766-5032-6

© 2023 Mary Ellen Snodgrass. All rights reserved

No part of this book may be reproduced or transmitted in any form or by any means, electronic or mechanical, including photocopying or recording, or by any information storage and retrieval system, without permission in writing from the publisher.

Front cover images: *from top left clockwise* T'ang Qunying (unknown author, public domain); Subaltern Mary Spencer-Churchill of the British Auxiliary Territorial Service, with members of the U.S. Women's Army Corps (Library of Congress); Empress Taytu Betul of first Italo-Ethiopian war (ilbusca/iStock); Juana Azurduy (unknown author, public domain); The women of '76: "Molly Pitcher," Currier & Ives (Library of Congress); Deborah from The Holy Scriptures, Old and New Testaments book collection published in 1885 (Nicku/Shutterstock); Calamity Jane, Gen. Crook's scout, no. 2, circa 1895 (Library of Congress)

Printed in the United States of America

McFarland & Company, Inc., Publishers
Box 611, Jefferson, North Carolina 28640
www.mcfarlandpub.com

For my sisters,
Audrey and Frances

Acknowledgments

Aaron LaFromboise, Director of Library Services, Blackfeet Community College, Browning, Montana
Anderson Academic Common, University of Denver, Colorado
Davidson College Library, Davidson, North Carolina
Davis Library, University of North Carolina at Chapel Hill
Duke University, Durham, North Carolina
Enrica Dente degli Scrovegni, office assistant, Consulate General of Italy, Los Angeles, California
Gramley Library, Salem College, Winston-Salem, North Carolina
High Point University Library, High Point, North Carolina
Iva Croff, Chair of Liberal Studies & General Education Core, Blackfeet Community College, Browning, Montana
J. Murray Atkins Library, University of North Carolina at Charlotte
Maxwell Library, Bridgewater State University, Bridgewater, Massachusetts
Moye Library, University of Mount Olive, North Carolina
Z. Smith Reynolds Library, Wake Forest University, Winston-Salem, North Carolina

Extra thanks to Martin Otts, reference librarian at the Patrick Beaver Library, to publicist Mary Canrobert, a reliable champion of my work, and to Steve Baker, who diagnoses the moods of my computer. I love you all.

Table of Contents

Acknowledgments	vi
Preface	1
Introduction	3
Bronze Age, 3300–1200 BCE	7
Iron Age, 1200 BCE–500 CE	10
Middle Ages, 400–1400	45
Viking Age, 770–1066	61
High Middle Ages, 1000–1300	69
The Crusades, 1096–1291	72
Late Middle Ages, 1300–1500	95
Renaissance, 1400–1600	122
Early Modern Era, 1600–1750	152
Early Modern Civil Wars, 1640–1804	159
Colonial Wars and Revolutions, 1700–1850	178
Napoleonic Era, 1793–1815	211
Wars of Independence, 1815–1825	235
American Civil War, April 12, 1861–April 9, 1865	261
The Great War, 1914–1918	297
World War II, September 1, 1939–September 2, 1945	326
Afghan War, October 15, 1999–September 11, 2021	404
Glossary	437
Appendix A: Warriors by Birthplace and Time	441
Appendix B: Warriors by Role	464
Bibliography	493
Index	499

Who is she that looketh forth as the morning,
 fair as the moon, clear as the sun, and
 terrible as an army with banners?
                              —Song of Solomon 6:10

Preface

Women Warriors in History compiles the names and deeds of known female fighters and their aggressions, from archers with bronze arrow points and Viking raiders to helicopter pilots and commanders of aircraft carriers. Listed by seventeen periods of world history, the entries summarize heroes the likes of the Old Testament judge Deborah, Joan of Arc, Elizabeth I, Aisha, Mary Spenser-Churchill, Calamity Jane, Cleopatra VII, Molly Pitcher, and Julia Child. Along with the famous are myriad unheralded scrappers and risk-takers swept up in fierce crises. The full panoply of sixteen hundred twenty-two names taps an under-reported strand of women's history—the females who have armed themselves for threats to self, family, home, civil rights, and country.

As an aid to women's historians, feminists, students, teachers, and researchers, this book provides an appendix alphabetized by birthplace and time, a means of surveying global efforts by age and nationality from Aceh to Zimbabwe. The itemizing of combat roles in the second appendix divides achievers by ninety-two specifics—those who excelled at martial arts and sharpshooting, rebels, the medal winners, the ones who spent time in prison, wounded veterans, and martyrs.

A glossary familiarizes the reader with obscure items, places, weapons, transport, and military concepts:

> *Items:* standard, citadel, moat, chatelaine, Crusades, gumbe, contraband, atlatl
> *military terms:* vanguard, MI5, jihad, daimyo, Luftwaffe, mole, OSS, ranger, blitz
> *places:* Moghulistan, Guinea, Frisia, Catalonia, Bengal, Media, Peloponnesus
> *transport:* wherry, gunboat, white buses, sloop, fireship, howdah, man-o'-war
> *weapons:* arquebus, urumi, sten, tribuchet, musket, kampilan, gae bolg, naginata

Explanations clarify the use of the gumbe drum for signaling Afro-Caribbean revolutionaries and the Swedish lineup of white buses to rescue refugees and death camp escapees.

The bibliography introduces primary sources dating from early history to current times. The compilation stresses first-person memoirs and historical accounts of revolt and combat as well as newspaper and magazine articles from around the world. Valuable compendia cite a mix of authors:

- French army officer Jean Beague's 1556 history *The Scots War*
- The 1330 Japanese epic *The Tale of the Heike*
- U.S. feminist editor Sarah Josepha Hale's 1853 overview *Woman's Record; or, Sketches of All Distinguished Women, from "the Beginning" till AD 1850*
- Mughal emperor Babur's 1530 memoir *Baburnama*
- Montana fur trader James Willard Schultz's 1916 anthology *Blackfeet Tales of Glacier National Park*
- Zhao Ye's ten-volume compilation *Spring and Autumn Annals of Wu and Yue* from 479 BCE
- Franciscan friar Pedro Simón's 1627 chronicle *Noticias Historiales de las Conquistas de Tierra Firme en las Indias Occidentales*
- Han chronicler Sima Tan's *Records of the Grand Historian* from 110 BCE
- U.S. Civil War cavalryman Henry Norton's 1889 collection *Deeds of Daring*

Survey texts cover significant writings in Latin, Sanskrit, French, Arabic, Russian, Chinese, and Spanish. Notable authors range over the globe:

- *Chronicles of Froissart*
- *Hit*, by Mary Edwards Walker, a U.S. civil war surgeon and wounded veteran
- *The Hymns of the Rigveda*
- Port-au-Prince native Thomas Madiou's *Histoire d'Haïti: 1799–1847*
- Roman historian Appian's *Foreign Wars*
- *The Travels of Ibn Battuta, AD 1325–1354*
- U.S. Indian superintendent A.B. Meacham, author of *Winema and Her People*
- Venezuelan military officer and historian José de Oviedo's 1723 *Historia de la Conquista y Población de la Provincia de Venezuela*.

Thorough indexing identifies specifics, as with Al Qaeda, Simón Bolívar, First Indochina War, Paraguayan War, Zapatistas, shield maidens, Iroquois Confederacy, Idi Amin, Warsaw Ghetto Uprising, Afrika Korps, Chiang Kai-shek, and Minutewomen.

Introduction

Humankind has no lack of viragos to admire. Drawing on accounts of the Trojan War from 1200 BCE, Virgil's *Aeneid* lauded Penthesilea, the Thracian Amazon commander described in oral lore whose "martial eye/flamed on from troop to troop … a warrior-virgin braving mail-clad men" (I:490–493). Her example refused to die in the arts for the appeal of a virtuoso equestrienne who sprinted into a doomed clash of Trojans with Greeks. The stereotype of the elegant, bare-breasted rider, beautiful to behold, continued to impact ancient reinventions of the one outstanding *belletrix* (female soldier)—typically royal, semi-divine, or aristocratic—audacious enough to face the vaunted slayer Achilles.

The image endured in the Middle East with grand battle scenes of Arab princesses who obscured their gender with veiling and astounded males with prowess, camel riding, and the saber expertise usually denied girls in training. In their youth, exemplary girls emulated fathers, husbands, and brothers to acquire skill at sword fighting, in particular, the Jewish Yemenite hitman Zaynab bint al-Harith and Syrian champion Khawla bint al-Azwar. A bright upsurge in realism highlighted Afra 'Bint Ghifar al-Humayriah, an Arab who liberated captive women by demonstrating how to outfox Byzantine sentries. Her savvy at turning tent poles into pikes resounded through Jordan and Palestine.

A comprehensive study of female warriors demands inclusion from global sovereignties that no longer exist, including Siam, Lycia, Argos, Scythia, and Bohemia. Because of the absence of women's history in the epochs of preliterate civilization, research must investigate pictorial and symbolic records from pyramids, sculpture, coinage, and pictographs and scan tapestry, bas relief, mural, calligraphy, and painting. Among autobiographies and eyewitness accounts of amazons and their war dynamics, secondhand reportage derives from specialists, as with Caradoc's *History of Wales,* a translation of Vietnamese surgeon Dang Thuy Tram's *Last Night I Dreamed of Peace,* Ari the Learned's *The Book of the Settlement of Iceland*, Abraham Foenander's *An Account of the Polynesian Race,* Thom Haywoode's *Gynaikeion,* and Captain Carette's article "Algérie."

Those soldiers on the list of 1,622 female fighters whom historians tend to ignore or downplay extend over multiple nationalities:

- British marine Jane Townsend, a defier of Napoleon at the battle of Trafalgar, Spain, on October 21, 1805
- Guatemalan queen K'abel, who commanded forces in 672 against the Central American city of Tikal
- four librarians—Agnes Dorothee Humbert, Yvonne Suzanne Oddon, Germaine Tillion, and Lucie Boutillier du Retail—who initiated the French Resistance at the Musée de l'Homme after the fall of Paris on June 14, 1940
- sea rover Alfhild of Geatland, a Scandinavian marine raider of the 400s CE
- a seductive Chinese spy in 472 BCE, Xi Shi from Zhiji south of Shanghai, who aided the king of Yue to annex the state of Wu
- Buffalo Calf Road Woman, the Northern Cheyenne brave from Montana who unseated General George Custer from his steed at the battle of Little Big Horn on June 24, 1876
- Ahhotep, an Egyptian warrior-queen of 1530 BCE and the world's first deployer of national forces

The older the account, the more likely that hard-edged chroniclers challenge its reliability. Misogynistic doubters prefer to label epic or literary characterization as myth or legend, the fate of Lady Fu Hao, a Chinese army recruiter from the Shang dynasty; Mongol unifier Mandukhai Khatun, a relative of Genghis Khan; Freydís Eiríksdóttir, an Icelandic explorer and pacifier of Vinland; and her sister-in-law Gudrid Thorbjarnardóttir, a battler of the New World's "red man." Less likely to be discounted, scriptural figures command respect in history, literature, and art, especially. These women include Vishpala, the Bronze Age warrior-queen from the Indus Valley lauded in the Hindu Rigveda; Jael, the lone Kenite assassin noted in Judges 5:24 for nerve; Assyrian warrior-monarch Shammuramat, a ninth-century BCE defender of Assur; and Aisha, Muhammad's widow and Koranic heroine, who led Islam's first civil war. Oral tradition and verse receive another form of skepticism, as with the deeds of Numidian charioteer Asbyte, decapitated during a one-on-one bout with the Cretan mercenary Mopsus; the celebrated Trung sisters, Vietnamese skirmishers exterminated in the first century CE; and Kushite queen Amanirenas, who went head-to-head with the Roman legions of Augustus Caesar. Further deflating feminist truths, variants of outcomes muddy the facts, for example, in 61 CE, Boudicca, the East Anglian commander of the Iceni of Britannia, rumored to have died of disease or by suicide.

Crucial to the text, diction tends toward grim action verbs. The most menacing feature means of torment and murder: starve, garrot, flay, scourge, throttle, dismember, stake, waterboard, crush, behead, disembowel. A glimpse of the suffering awaiting saboteurs, spies, and guerrilla warriors alerts readers to the daring of female soldiers who enter confrontations with no illusions about the fate of the loser. Because the captives are women, they add to the list of outcomes the possibility of sexual mutilation and rape, two war crimes that continue into the twenty-first century with no change in motivation or intent.

Biographies of women warriors stress normal feminine circumstances. Models exemplify young girls, single maidens, brides, and mothers. Among the females disguised in sailor suits or chain mail stand crones, widows, and parturient women, including rebel Kathleen Clarke, who lost a pregnancy in Dublin during the 1916 Easter Uprising, and General Li Zhen, who miscarried a fetus while assembling recruits for China's communist army in 1927. The reason for a soldier's enthusiasm could be vengeance, religious fanaticism, unemployment, homelessness, the spirit of adventure, or the absence of a father or husband, who could be posted far from home or marching with zealots to the Crusades or Iraq War. Scenes of chatelaines and their daughters and maidservants atop castle ramparts dramatize make-do armaments—stones, masonry, flaming combustibles, or kettles of boiling water or oil. Even in surrender, wonder-women the stature of Nur Jahan, Roxana of Bactria, and Anita Garibaldi maintained dignity as they ceded their lands and manses and awaited judgment.

The shift of individual combat during the Napoleonic age to sisterhood exemplified a female buddy system in the camaraderie of grenadiers, Eidelweis Pirates, "black widows," and the "night witches." Spanish and Filipina resisters shared the tasks of surveillance, lookout, and swordswoman alongside more familiar domestic jobs of feeding and supplying regiments and ferrying casualties to medical centers. Lacking the indoctrination of a professional infantry, defiers of invading Frenchmen and German, Italian, and Japanese fascists easily switched to the traditional female skills of herbalism, nutrition, debriding and bandaging wounds, and protection of noncombatants against atrocities.

The days of wearing men's clothes and adopting male names ended with upfront soldiery. The onset of *Realpolitik* during the world wars aroused battlefield sodalities dedicated to needs as unfamiliar as ambulance driving, arson, assassination, cartography, and smuggling. World War I introduced the female combat pilot and bombardier; World War II infused urban battle zones with commando raids, sabotage, parachuting, and cryptoanalysis. Women formulated Molotov cocktails and packaged TNT to deny German Nazis reliance on depots, troop trains, telegraph, telephone, and power grids. Women uninitiated into forgery produced reams of phony ID papers and passports for distribution to refugees and downed air crew. Those women unskilled at surveillance and disguise adopted practical means of changing hair color and wardrobe and altering their social standing from wartime volunteers to apartment maids, nannies, and laundresses. By the late 1900s and early 2000s, chicanery lost out to straightforward enlistment in global armies that recognized the value of women in the military police, underwater reconnaissance, terrorism, and drone strikes.

Bronze Age, 3300–1200 BCE

The appearance of female fighters during the Bronze Age coincided with advances in writing and the first recorded women's history. Beginning at Sumer, advances in metallurgy enabled warcraft by replacing Stone Age weapons with bronze lance points and arrowheads. Both projectiles were lightweight and suitable for women's use.

ca. 1900 BCE

A legendary female warrior-queen of north central India around 1900 BCE in the late Bronze Age, **Vishpala (also Vispala, fl. 1200 BCE)**, the defender of a tribal settlement near the Kurukshetra region, became the first wounded veteran in world history to receive a prosthetic limb. Alongside her husband Khelraja, she drove a chariot and wielded a sword. The loss occurred in a border war, in which she entered a night battle. Rescuers carried the queen to an ashram (religious retreat) hospital to stop the bleeding, but the foot and leg bones were so severely smashed they couldn't be mended.

According to the Rigveda, a collection of sacred Hindu hymns compiled in Sanskrit from 3500 to 1800 BCE, the twin Ashvin physicians intervened in the Dasarajan, the battle of Ten Kings on the Parusni (modern Ravi) river on the border of eastern Pakistan and northwestern India. After a holy sacrifice and priestly prayers, they examined the injury. The duo contributed an iron orthotic replacement as a reward for the queen's probity and virtue. The operation enabled Vishpala to stand immediately and to continue functioning on two feet to gain dominance over the enemy.

1760 BCE

A legendary archer and warrior queen of Lycia (modern Turkey) during the rule of Sin-Muballit, **Eurypyle (fl. eighteenth century BCE)** obliterated the Amorites in 1760 BCE and seized their capital of Mari in western Mesopotamia (modern Syria). In the estimation of the Anatolian writer Arrian, compiler of *Fragmenta Historicorum Graecorum* (Fragments of Greek History), she earned respect from the ancients for leading a contingent of mounted female archers against the Semitic idol-worshipping nomads who occupied Canaan and opposed the Israelites. The campaign destabilized the Amorites and their hold on Babylon.

Her name survives as the identity of a brush-footed leafwing butterfly.

ca. 1530 BCE

An admired militaristic monarch of the Theban royal house, around 1530 BCE during Egypt's golden age, **Ahhotep I (fl. 1560–1530 BCE)**, wife of her brother Seqenenre Tao II and daughter of Senakhtenre Ahmose the Elder and Queen Tetisheri, suppressed a rebellion in Upper Egypt. Three centuries before Lady Fu Hao of China's Shang dynasty mustered soldiers, Ahhotep I was the first female warrior mentioned in history to have deployed national forces and put down uprisings. Her son, Pharaoh Ahmose I, with the regent-queen's aid, ended conflict against the Hyksos, a Nile Valley tribe ruled by King Apepi.

At Memphis around 1554 BCE, Ahhotep's husband/brother died in battle of axe and dagger wounds on the face. A column honoring Amon at Karnak on the upper Nile marked her skill at rallying the national army and retrieving deserters. Her troops defended the kingdom against immigrant Asiatic Hyksos at a time when the royal family suffered a dearth of male leaders. By corralling fugitives and exiling protesters, she restored order, unified Egypt, and earned a combat pendant, the Order of the Golden Fly. After Ahmose I founded the eighteenth dynasty, the queen mother lived to age ninety. A dagger and axe accompanied Ahhotep to interment.

1479 BCE

In the late Bronze Age in 1479 BCE during Egypt's eighteenth dynasty, **Hatshepsut (1507–January 16, 1458, BCE)**, a productive pharaoh from Thebes, led aggressive campaigns against pre-Hebrew Canaan and along the Nile River against the nomadic Medjay of Nubia (modern Al Dabbah, Sudan). She began the Egyptian outreach with a trade expedition to Punt (modern Somalia and Eritrea) to secure wild animals, ebony, ivory, frankincense, gold, and myrrh. Subsequent expeditions involved army raids by her stepson Tuthmose to the north on the Mediterranean port of Byblos (in modern Lebanon) and east to Sinai, a peninsula rich in turquoise.

1250 BCE

During China's Shang Dynasty in 1250 BCE, Lady **Fu Hao (1250–1200 BCE)**, a Bronze Age high priestess and third wife of emperor Wu Ding, commanded thirteen thousand soldiers in a significant ambush against the Ba tribe, fishers and hunters of Sichuan in southwestern China. A trusted consort and the earliest female general, she occupied a border fief chosen as a bulwark against aggressors. She advanced in power alongside first imperial wife **Fu Jing (1250–1200 BCE)**, a prophet and military adviser. Fu Jing wore a general's helmet and bore bronze halberds or axe-bladed pikes in army expeditions against the Long tribe. For her prowess, she earned ten fiefs.

According to oracle bones from the ancient capital of Yinxu in northeastern China, Fu Hao outranked generals Zhi and Hou Gao during combat against the Ba tribe. She recruited three thousand men in a campaign against the Mongolic Tu and twice obeyed the king's order to attack the Yi of Vietnam and

Siam. Her victories included routing the Qiang cavalry with her ten thousand soldiers. At her death, Wu Ding interred Fu Hao at Anyang, Henan, alongside one hundred weapons, bridles and chariot ornaments, arrowheads, curved bronze knives, and the style of battle axe modeled on her tomb statue. He continued to offer prayers for her protection during a campaign against the Gong state.

ca. 1200 BCE

A Libyan monarch who invaded Asia around 1200 BCE at the end of the Bronze Age, **Egee (fl. 1200 BCE)** led a fighting force across North Africa to Troy (Hissarlik, modern Turkey) to battle King Laomedon, a famed horse breeder and founder of the Trojan dynasty. Her army won numerous skirmishes and seized costly plunder. As reported by Greek chronicler Diodorus Siculus in his *Library of History*, on her voyage home in jubilation, she and her combat loot disappeared in a sea storm. Her name identified the place of death as the Aegean Sea. Judy Chicago honored her two-continent march to war with a depiction in the artwork *The Dinner Party*. A Libyan province bears Queen Egee's name.

Iron Age,
1200 BCE–500 CE

An increase in female soldiery paralleled an advance in metallurgy and weaponry such as pikes, crossbows, and longbows. As communities produced abundant crops, they could afford standing armies. Although enlistment denied women professional military positions, those obtaining power through royal or aristocratic birth or marriage gained credence as leaders of armed men.

1075 BCE

Britain's first ruling queen, **Gwendolen of Cornwall (1130–1065 BCE)** secured the kingdom in 1075 BCE during the early Iron Age after invading her own realm and winning the battle of the River Stour. Because of marital betrayal, her husband, King Locrinus, heir of Brutus of Troy, took as his lover Estrildis, a Saxon princess rescued from the Hun invader Humber. Gwendolen gained military acumen from her father Corineus, a model warrior and wielder of the battle axe, and retreated to his realm at Cornwall to recruit an army of mercenaries for a retaliatory war.

According to the Welsh priest Geoffrey of Monmouth's *History Regum Britanniae* (History of the Kings of Britain), during a confrontation at the River Stour on Cornwall's eastern boundary from Wiltshire to the English Channel at Bournemouth, Locrinus died in combat from an arrow wound. At the River Severn on the Welsh border, Gwendolen ordered Estrildis drowned. Execution of Locrinus's illegitimate daughter Habren freed the queen for fifteen years of stable rule. The historical drama *Locrine* survives in the apocrypha of William Shakespeare. Poet William Blake honored her as a Daughter of Albion.

1070 BCE

During the early Iron Age, **Deborah (also Debora, Debbora, D'vorah, or Dvora, 1107–1067 BCE)**, a charismatic Israelite seer, infantry strategist, and combat hymnographer in the Old Testament book of Judges, restored liberty to Hebrew refugees pressing northwest from Egypt. The only female jurist in a period of failed law and order, she held court in 1070 BCE under a palm tree at Ephraim between Bethel and Ramah. For two decades, oppression by Jabin (or Yavin), the despot of upper Canaan, depended on advanced ironworkers who made plows, swords, spears, and javelins. Deborah chose an auspicious point in hostilities to unite disparate Hebrew tribes.

Deborah seized leadership of army bowmen and slingers and goaded King Barak to fight the battle of Kedesh (or Qedesh), Jabin's citadel. In a holy war, the Israelites moved against the capital of Hazor, Canaan, the idol-worshipping forerunner of Phoenicia, Palestine, Lebanon, Syria, Transjordan, and Israel. Deborah stirred the Benjamite and Ephraimite shock troops to action against the Canaanites amassed to the southwest at Megiddo. At the time, forty thousand Israelites in Meroz and men of the Asher, Dan, Reuben, and Gilead clans failed to recruit a coalition because of a dwindling faith in Yahweh.

Appointed commander-in-chief of ten thousand warriors, Deborah mobilized Hebrew guerrilla fighters from the tribes of Issachar, Manasseh, and Naphtali out of the highlands into the plains. Still outnumbered and out-armed, the massed force undertook a five-day march to the plain of Esdraelon on Wadi Kishon in upper Galilee (modern Lebanon). The Zebulon infantry led the attack at Mount Tabor in northern Israel, an ascent too steep for Canaanite chariots. The massacre resulted in deadly hand-to-hand combat for overconfident Canaanites who fled west along the creek to Mount Carmel.

After Deborah and Barak advanced on the superbly trained Canaanites in the Jezreel Valley, Yahweh intervened. She hyperbolized the divine miracle as turning night to day and dispatching the stars to aid the Hebrews. Because of heavy rains during the dry season, a flash flood engulfed the nine hundred Canaanite iron chariots and bogged them in marshy ground. Ironically, Canaanites revered Baal, a weather god of gales and thunder. Amid chaos, the warlord Sisera's soldiers fled thirty kilometers (18.6 miles) into a swamp and washed away in the rising Kishon River. Rather than reward male soldiers, Deborah blessed Yahweh for His intervention in a holy war.

Sisera's escape from Kedesh southeast across the Jezreel Valley involved an aggressive biblical amazon, **Jael (also Yael, 1070 BCE)**, a Kenite nomad and sympathizer with the Hebrew flight from Egypt's Pharaoh Ramses II. Deborah's war poem calls Jael "most blessed of women" (Judges 5:24). Plunging on foot through the Zaanaim swamp, the Canaanite chief reached the tent of Heber, Jael's husband, a tinsmith who repaired weaponry for armies. Sisera received hospitality in Jael's tent. According to Judges 4, Deborah foresaw that Jael would earn praise for stymying the Canaanite army with a single murder. She lured the commander with a blanket and drink of curds or cream and goat's milk served in a guest bowl. Sisera ordered her to watch for pursuers and to conceal his whereabouts with lies. While he slept, she assassinated him by crushing his head with a hammer and by piercing his temple with a tent peg into the ground. In Judges 4:21–22, she invited Barak to inspect the enemy general's corpse, a proof that Israelite females exercised judgment and artifice in aiding the Israelite cause. The psalmist added a touch of humor to the fertilizer derived from Sisera's remains, which "became as dung for the earth" (Psalm 83:10).

In the aftermath at Kedesh, Jabin's confederacy of city-states failed when Israelite forces rifled and set fire to the royal capital and seized profitable land. Receipt of nationalist glory set Deborah above other females in the Torah as the only female combat chief. She composed a winner's paean reverenced as the bible's oldest document that retained its original form. Bible scholars lauded her writing for spontaneity, passion, patriotism, and motifs set with belligerent images, symmetry, parallelism, and prosody (Pfeiffer, 1948, 326). She pictured the Israelites summoning her to recite battlefield chants to toughen Barak and to celebrate Canaan's demolition. The lyrics that resounded on the killing grounds stated her humility before God: "I will sing to Yahweh" (Judges 5:3). The overthrow of Canaan recurred in Psalm 83:16, which shamed Jabin's forces and urged them to convert to Judaism. Israel held the balance of power for four decades and proved Deborah's title of "the Mother in Israel."

Tradition states that the two heroines lie buried at a Kedesh spring.

See also May 8, 1429; 1637; June 22, 1809.

ca. 1062 BCE

A Philistine seductress and saboteur, **Delilah (fl. 1070s–1060s)** from Sorek Valley, Judaea (modern Israel) accepted a mission around 1062 BCE to overthrow Samson. In the fifth book of the Torah, Judges 16, the Nazirite military commander possessed superhuman strength that stymied Israel's enemies. Five Philistine lords bribed Delilah with offers of eleven hundred silver coins each to betray her lover. After four false answers to her question of his power source, he divulged that his brawn came from his long hair. As a result of her report to the enemy, they blinded Samson and forced him to turn a grist mill in Gaza (modern Palestine). When his hair grew long again, he pulled down Dagon's temple, crushing himself and his tormenters. The dramatic betrayal influenced mosaic, dance, engraving, and painting.

1000 BCE

At Argos on the Peloponnesus during the Greek dark ages that began the Iron Age, **Messene (fl. 1000 BCE)** assembled Argive and Laconian men in 1000 BCE to help her conquer part of the southern peninsula to increase the prestige of her husband Polycaon. West of Mount Taygetus in the southwest Peloponnese, she invaded new territory and named it Messenia after her own name. As reported in the Greek geographer Pausanias's *Descriptions of Greece*, at her palace at Andania (modern Oichalia) she erected a shrine at Mount Ithome of marble and gold, where residents worshipped her after death. She and Polycaon, the country's first king, introduced the Eleusinian cult of Demeter and Persephone. Because of her strong beginning, the Messenian line survived for five generations.

841 BCE

During 841 BCE, an era of bloodbaths in Israel, the only female monarch in Judah, **Athaliah (872–835 BCE)** of Shechem, Samaria, schemed for the throne at Jerusalem by massacring claimants, including her own grandchildren. The daughter of Ahab and Jezebel, Athaliah was suspect for her foreign, non–Davidic blood line. She built a reputation on wickedness and greed after usurping primacy in 842 BCE. According to Old Testament passages in II Kings 9:2, 11:1–3 and Chronicles 22:10–23:21, she wielded military control for six years and installed the worship of Baal and Melqart, a Herculean deity from Tyre. In 835 BCE, Jehoiada, a Hebrew high priest of Yahweh, launched a mutiny, elevated her seven-year-old grandson Joash to king, and executed Athaliah for treason at the Horse Gate of the Temple. French dramatist Jean Racine and German composer Felix Mendelssohn featured her in the stage tragedy *Athalie*.

815 BCE

A Welsh princess from Ewyas (modern Monmouthshire, Wales), **Cordelia of Britain (850–805)**, as depicted in Welsh cleric Geoffrey of Monmouth's *History Regum Britanniae* (History of the Kings of Britain), raised a Frankish army in Gaul in 815 BCE to restore Britain to her deposed father, King Leir. She resided at Karitia, where Leir petitioned for her help. She presented him a complement of forty knights and joined the retinue in reinstalling Leir as king of Britain. His death three years later enabled Cordelia, the widow of King Aganippus of Gaul, to regain her crown as ruler of Britain. When her sisters' sons attempted a coup, she engaged the enemy personally in battle. At her imprisonment, she killed herself around age forty-four, leaving her nephews Cunedagius and Marganus in a state of civil war.

811 BCE

At the beginning of the Iron Age in 811 BCE, the Assyrian warrior-queen **Shammuramat (845–783 BCE)** of Assur, Assyria (modern Shirqat, Iraq), administered and defended the empire of her deceased husband, King Shamshi-Adad V. During their twelve-year marriage, she accompanied him to foreign battlefields. By ending a six-year power struggle launched in Babylon by Shalmaneser III, she initiated a program of territorial recovery and the replacement of chariot warfare with cavalry. To strengthen Assur on the western bank of the Tigris River, she established a precedent for the building and maintenance of roads, water systems, and canals.

Over a five-year reign, Shammuramat completed defensive walls on the Euphrates River and subsequent military campaigns against the Medes and Armenians. For a sortie in India, she tricked the enemy with fake elephants. She ruled Anatolia (modern Turkey) and Mesopotamia (modern Iraq and Kuwait) until her son Adad Nirari III came of age in 806 BCE. Commemorated in Greek legend as Semiramis, she evolved into a version of Astarte, a divinity reverenced from Ascalon (modern Ashkelon, Israel) to Persia.

732 BCE

At the rise of Queen **Samsi (fl. 730s–720s BCE)**, an Arab consolidator of the Qedar (confederated tribes) in

732 BCE, domesticated nomads roaming from Syria to Egypt. Her alliance with Rakhianu, the last king of Damascus, preceded a revolt against Assyria on the Tigris River. The pair rebelled against the monarch Tiglath Pileser III, creator of Assyria's first standing army. Her intent was avoidance of a tribute owed by the warrior-queen **Zabibi (fl. 740s)**, her Arab predecessor. Assyrian cavalry equipped with javelins and bows overwhelmed Samsi's army below Mount Saquuri (unknown location). She sought refuge to the east at Bazu in the Syrian Desert and surrendered to King Tiglath Pileser III of Assyria. According to their accord, she maintained control of the Qedar for four years by paying tribute in gold and silver, camels, and spices that secured the incense trade.

703 BCE

The successor of Samsi, Queen **Yatie (fl. 720s–700s BCE)** of the Arab Qedar (consolidated nomads) allied with Aramaeans, Chaldeans, and Elamites to challenge Sennacherib of Nimrud (modern Iraq), the second Sargonid king of Assyria and Babylonia. The confrontation of Assyrians in 703 BCE against a coalition from Damascus, Israel, and Tyre near Kish in northwestern Sumer yielded a captive, Yatie's brother Baasquanu. In the aftermath, Sennacherib pacified desert Qedarites until 681 BCE.

600 BCE

Geoffrey of Monmouth's *History Regum Britanniae* (History of the Kings of Britain) depicted **Judon (fl. 600 BCE)** as the ruler who quelled Iron Age chaos in 600 BCE and ended an ancient dynasty at Cornwall. The wife of Gorbudoc, an aged king sinking into dementia, she grieved over the civil strife he had launched between their twin sons, Ferrex and Porrex over the splitting of the realm. After Ferrex retreated over the English Channel and introduced King Suhard's Gallic mercenaries into the mix, Porrex slew him in combat and annihilated the Gauls. Overwhelmed by the climate of revolt and family dissolution, she had her ladies-in-waiting help her knife Porrex in his bed and hack him to pieces for murdering her favorite son. The execution ended a doomed dynasty and opened the region to two centuries of rebellion which nobles initiated by murdering Judon. The drama reached the stage in Thomas Norton and Thomas Sackville's blank verse drama *The Tragedy of Ferrex and Porrex,* a foretaste of succession issues during the reign of Elizabeth I.

560 BCE

A Scythian (modern Iranian) warrior's wife, **Sparethra (fl. 550s)** assaulted the empire builder Cyrus II the Great in 560 BCE in retaliation for imprisoning her husband, King Amorges. By enlisting some five hundred thousand soldiers, she seized three of Cyrus's kinsmen as hostages to be ransomed for Amorges. As revealed in the Greek chronicler Herodotus's *Histories,* a congenial relationship with the Persians inspired Sparetha to lead troops against Croesus, Cyrus's enemy, whom he crushed at the battle of Thymbra near Sardis, capital of Lydia (modern

Turkey) in December 547 BCE. The coalition's success survives in stage drama, short fiction, and opera.

550 BCE

As introduced in Greek historian Ctesias's *Persica,* an intrepid Scythian (modern Iranian) warrior-queen, **Zarinaia (600–550 BCE)** fought against the Medes at Ecbatana (modern Iran) for the dynasty of her aged husband Astyages. From her residence north of the Black Sea, she rode horseback to battlefields, armed herself with bow and arrows, and excelled at quelling revolts of neighboring nomads. According to Diodorus Siculus's commentary, after General Stryangaios unseated her from her mount in combat and spared her life, she returned the deed by assassinating her second husband, Mermerus, and yielding Parthia (modern northeastern Iran) to the Medes. Before committing suicide in 550 BCE, Stryangaios composed a touching farewell letter. The Scythians acclaimed her courage with a funereal pyramid topped with the queen's likeness in gold.

September 539 BCE

A Persian troop commander, **Pantea Arteshbod (559–529 BCE)** aided Cyrus II the Great in impeding Babylon's King Nabonidus and his son, Prince Belshazzar, at the battle of Opis in September 539 BCE on the Tigris River in Mesopotamia (modern Iraq). Because the city of Sippar on the fork of the Euphrates River ceded to Cyrus after his conquest of Lydia and Elam, he annexed Babylonia and made a champion's entry as head of the expanded Achaemenid Empire. Pantea joined her husband, General Aryasb, in assembling the ten thousand Persian Immortals, an elite palace guard and infantry shock force skilled with javelin, dagger, and bow and equipped with iron breastplates and wicker shields. Contributing to the female presence at Opis was another Persian officer, Lieutenant Command **Artunis (540–500 BCE)**, daughter of General Artebaz, an officer in Darius's army.

December 530 BCE

As relayed in Greek chronicler Herodotus's *Histories,* **Tomyris (fl. 530 BCE)**, the Scythian queen of the Massagetae on the river Araxes east of the Caspian Sea (modern Iran), affirmed a place in women's military history for killing Cyrus II the Great of Persia. In widowhood, she had rejected a diplomatic union with Cyrus, who tricked her army with wine at Jaxartes (modern Syr Darya, Kazakhstan). The drunkenness and military whipping humiliated her son, General Spargapises, who killed himself with a dagger. Leading her troop of Huns and mercenary archers across the Eurasian steppes, in December 530 BCE, she crushed the Persians and killed Cyrus. To compound his degradation, she had his body decapitated, the skull soaked in blood, and his torso crucified. Peter Paul Rubens commemorated her vengeance with a painted scenario of Cyrus's abasement; an opera in London brought the story to the English stage.

525 BCE

On the North African coast, **Pheretima (ca. 570–515 BCE)** of the Greek colony of Cyrene (modern north Libya) sought help in 525 BCE to restore her son, Arcesilaus III, to power by seeking an army from Evelthon, the Greco-Phoenician king and first coin minter of Salamis, Cyprus. Instead of granting her a fighting force, he honored her gender with a gold distaff and spindle. After Arcesilaus's assassination, in 515 BCE, she plotted vengeance through Aryandes, the Persian satrap of Egypt, and headed a Persian fleet of troops to Cyrene, Libya. Herodotus's *Histories* describe how she launched a nine-month siege that involved mining the walls. As characterized by the anonymous collection *Tractatus de Mulieribus Claris in Bello* (On Famous Women in War), she punished her son's killers with crucifixion and had their wives' breasts sliced off and nailed to city walls. The survivors she sold into slavery. She died in 515 BCE during a journey east, where flesh-eating worms overwhelmed her body. A genus of earthworms bears her name.

February 509 BCE

Following the truce that Rome negotiated with Clusium (modern Chiusi, Italy) after the cavalry battle of Silva Arsia in February 509 BCE, the captive **Cloelia (fl. 509–508 BCE)** eluded prison guards and led noble girls in retreat from the enemy. According to northern Italian historian Titus Livy's *Ab Urbe Condita* (From the City's Founding), she was a Roman hostage pledged to the Etruscan general Lars Porsena, a traitor to Rome. She deceived guards by demanding privacy while she and her nineteen fellow prisoners bathed in the Tiber River. On fleeing the camp, she took horse to the Tiber and led her female escapees to safety by swimming three hundred feet despite a flurry of lances.

Porsena demanded Cloelia's return. Both Roman authorities and Porsena excoriated her for violating the truce, yet extolled her example above those of Roman heroes Horatius "One-Eye" Cocles and Mucius "Lefty" Scaevola. Because of her courageous example, Porsena extended an award: her choice of half the hostages. She selected young males who could return as soldiers and strengthen the army. At Rome, her likeness on an equestrian statue adorned the Via Sacra, the city's main thoroughfare.

495 BCE

A Celtic prophet and expert at martial arts and warcraft, **Scathach of Skye (also Sgàthach, 520 BCE–490 BCE)** operated a for-profit warrior training center in 495 BCE at her castle, Dún Scáith (Castle of Shadows) near Tarskavaig. With the aid of her amazon daughter, the security guard **Uathach (fl. 490s)**, Scathach demonstrated underwater hand-to-hand combat, vaulting over parapets, and use of her personal weapon, the *gae bolg* (barbed spear), which she designed. One of her warriors, Cu Chulainn, killed her younger virago sister, **Aife of Alba (510 BCE–480 BCE)**, for breaching Scathach's territory.

494 BCE

A helmeted Argive poet and wordsmith, **Telesilla (fl. 494 BCE)** defended her native city by stirring the women warriors of Argos in 494 BCE with abusive combat lyrics. On the advice of the seer Pythia at Delphi, Telesilla treated a spiritual depression by taking up verse, choreography, and hymns for girls' choirs honoring twin gods Apollo and Artemis, patrons of verse and chastity. Because Cleomenes I directed the Spartan army to slaughter survivors of the battle of Sepeia at Tiryns southwest of Corinth and to burn Apollo's sacred grove to kill hoplites in hiding, the population of Argos dropped to seven thousand, half its previous number. Bearing the armaments that Telesilla scavenged from home arsenals and shrines, a phalanx of slaves, females, noncombatant citizens, and outlanders from Tiryns mounted the blockaded hills and hurled stones and tiles from their roofs. The helter-skelter battery repelled the Spartans.

Cleomenes, in retribution for defiling a sacred precinct, slashed himself to death. Argive women raised a temple to the war god Enyalius; some propertyless farmers elevated their station by marrying Argive widows. Telesilla's courage survived on a carving at Aphrodite's temple and a state at the Theatre of Pompey and in the female devotion of the war god Ares. The annual *Hybristika* (Impudence Festival), a summer celebration, featured women in men's uniforms and males in veiled chitons (tunics).

490 BCE

A female ruler of the Sacae or Scythians (modern Iranians), **Zarinaea (fl. 490 BCE)** joined the Parthians in 490 BCE in a war against the Medes. A nomad from the Eurasian steppes, she trained for battle from girlhood. She gained the monarchy after the death of her husband King Cydraeus. Variants of her biography describe Median challenger Stryngaeus wounding her and knocking her from her warhorse. Because of her requests for mercy, he let her live. After proposing marriage, he threatened to abandon his wife and children for her sake. After Zarinaea refused to be a war prize, Stryngaeus killed himself.

ca. 485 BCE

A teenaged mounted warrior in an elite corps of female virgins, around 485 BCE, the **Pazyryk Amazon (fl. 480s BCE)** of Ak-Alakha, Kazakhstan, won respect for prowess in battle. Of Iron Age Scythian ancestry, according to a report in the *Siberian Times,* by age sixteen, she had mastered archery and hurling the javelin from a galloping mount. Her remains, located in the Altai Republic, lay interred with horses, beads, and objects wrapped in gold foil.

482 BCE

During the last decades of China's Spring and Autumn Era, while plotting to overthrow his old enemy King Fuchai of Wu on the Yangtze River, in 482 BCE King Goujian of Yue learned of the bow and blade skills of **Yuenu (fl. 482 BCE)**, a commoner from Yue's southern forests (modern Zhejiang at center of the East China Sea shore). Because she had followed her father from girlhood and learned archery and expertise with a bronze sword, she developed a psychological martial strategy that generated

China's first great sword culture. In hand-to-hand engagement, according to Han chronicler Sima Tan's *Records of the Grand Historian,* she maintained outward calm while scuttling in and out of range, applying a balance of yin (understated) and yang (blatant) energies. After Yuenu impressed Goujian with military acumen, he hired her to train the army in the world's first displays of martial arts. Artisans at Wu and Yue developed forges famed for shaping her battle gear. To be worthy of her loyalty, Goujian toughened himself by sleeping on a straw bed with a sword at his head.

See also 473 BCE.

Early September 480 BCE

Before the battle of Cape Artemisium in Euboea in early September 480 BCE, rescue diver and saboteur **Hydna (fl. 480 BCE)**, a native of Scione on the Chalcidian peninsula, cut ropes and anchor ties to the eight hundred warships of Persian king Xerxes I the Great. After three years of preparation, Xerxes approached eastern Greece from Sardis in spring 480 BCE with three hundred sixty thousand soldiers. In a night foray, Hydna armed herself with a knife and swam seven miles in the Aegean Sea with her father Scyllis, a swim coach and possible double agent.

Father and daughter infiltrated the enemy fleet at the hook-shaped shore at Mount Pelion in Magnesia and then returned to the Greek army on Euboeia (modern Evia Island). When a storm hit, gale winds banged the unmoored triremes together and destroyed the Persian armada, forcing Xerxes to rebuild his navy and revamp his approach to Artemisium. A tribal league raised statues at Delphi to father and daughter. A swim marathon on September 7, 2020, reenacted the deep sea feat.

September 26, 480 BCE

At the three-day naval battle of the Aegean cape of Artemisium and the battle of Salamis west of Piraeus, Greece, the widowed warrior-queen **Artemisia I of Caria (520–460)** joined Persian commander Xerxes I the Great in attacking the city states of Hellas (modern Greece). A cagy archer and admiral of five of Persia's twelve hundred and seven ships, she bore a reputation for capturing the Aegean island of Cos in 490 BCE. She fought under a Greek offer for her capture of ten thousand drachmas—enough to pay a laborer for three years. She warned Xerxes not to engage the three hundred eighty Athenian ships in a tight space and urged him to hug the shoreline and venture south and west toward the Peloponnesus (southern Greece). As tactician, she doubted adequate backup from his allies, Cilicia, Cyprus, Egypt, and Pamphylia in southern Anatolia (modern Turkey).

On September 26, 480 BCE, Artemisia I commanded Dorian troops from the city of Calyndos (modern Kas, Turkey), the islands of Cos and Nisyros, and her own state of Halicarnassus in southwestern Anatolia. While the sea fight turned against Persia, she bluffed an Athenian pursuer by raising a Greek banner on her flagship and ramming a Calyndian ship, which sank with all its crew while she sailed for Caria. Xerxes awarded her valor with captured Greek armor and an alabaster vase. On her advice, he left the invasion of the Peloponnesus to his staff, returned home in glory, and posted Artemisia at Ephesus, the port city of Ionia, to guard his family.

475 BCE

At the imperial capital of Persepolis (modern Marvdasht, Iran) **Atusa (also Atossa, 550–424 BCE)** developed military acumen from her illustrious family. The daughter of Cyrus the Great and sister of Cambyses II, she wed Darius I and influenced his conquests for the Achaemenid dynasty, the First Persian Empire, the largest expanse on the globe. In addition to controlling court business, she led a personal army in 475 BCE and dispatched warriors to war zones. She lived to see her son, Xerxes I, succeed Darius and, in 480 BCE, invade Greece.

Azusa's role in Persian politics found expression in a crowned bust and portraits. At her death at age seventy-five, her daughter-in-law, **Amestris (510–460 BCE)**, Xerxes's wife and the mother of Artaxerxes I, commanded the Persian military. The Greek historian Herodotus reported that she developed a reputation for merciless battles. Her history colored anime and an opera by George Frederic Handel.

473 BCE

During preparations for war, King Goujian of Yue raised his chance of overthrowing King Fuchai of Wu by distracting him with the sexual skills of an elegant Yue laundress, **Xi Shi (fl. 473 BCE)** of Zhuji south of Shanghai. As described in Zhao Ye's *Spring and Autumn Annals of Wu and Yue,* her inside information about Wu state gave Goujian the edge. Applying Yuenu's tactics, in 473 BCE, Goujian's army invaded the capital city of Chu (modern Xuzhou) and killed all but five thousand Yue soldiers. Fuchai committed suicide. Goujian trampled the state of Wu and annexed it to Yue, which he ruled for eight years until 465 BCE. Warriors carried his martial culture into southern China. The recovery of Goujian's bronze sword in 1965 outside the capital of Chu offered an example of the era's sharp, tarnish-resistant metalwork, which combined 80.3 percent copper with 18.8 percent tin and small amounts of iron and lead.

401 BCE

The widowed tyrant of Dardanus northeast of Troy, **Manya (also Mania, 440 BCE–399 BCE)** of Skepsis courted Pharnabazus II by advising him on warcraft and supporting his battles with her mercenary troops. She gained the admiration of Greek historians Polyaenus and Xenophon for vigorous leadership of armies, governing Aeolis (modern northwestern Turkey), and remaining candid and loyal to Pharnabazus. In addition to driving her chariot or carriage to overwhelm Hamaxitos, Kolonai, and Larisa on the southern Troad, in 401 BCE, she personally formed battle lines and immediately rewarded the best Greek warriors. In Pharnabazus's campaign against the Mysians, Manya accompanied him and advised on the mission. Strangulation in her rooms by her ambitious son-in-law Meidias left

Pharnabazus intent on avenging her death. Her realm, left in a weakened position, struggled to ward off Spartan general Dercylidas, who seized the property as war salary for his troops.

400 BCE

A little-know Galatian warrior female at an historic impasse, **Onomaris (fl. 400 BCE)** appeared at the end of the anonymous collection *Tractatus de Mulieribus Claris in Bello* (On Famous Women in War) as a leader and defender of a Celto-Turkic people in central Anatolia (modern Turkey). To improve living conditions in the highlands, in 400 BCE, she headed a diaspora southeast over the Ister River (modern Danube) and secured the shore east of the Black Sea by vanquishing its inhabitants. She became the only exemplary female fighter/ruler in Greek literature who had no male name linked to her lineage.

389 BCE

In a narrative by Greek military tactician Polyaenus, author of *Strategemata* (Battle Plans), **Tirgatao (fl. 390s–380s BCE)**, a native princess at Lake Maeotis on the Sea of Azov, led forces across the steppes during the Bosporan Wars. Among the Sindi (modern European Russia), she fled incarceration in a tower by her husband Hecataeus, king of Sinda (modern Taman Peninsula, Russia), and escaped back to her home. By forming a tribal alliance with the Ixomatae, in 389 BCE, she waged war over the Bosporus realm of the tyrant Satyrus. Infiltrating her confederacy, his two agents attempted to murder her with a sword. Tirgatao retaliated by seizing and torturing the assassins and devastating the Bosporus kingdom by siege and arson. Because Satyrus' heir, crown prince Gorgippus, defied his father's conspirators and begged for peace, Tirgatao ended the war upon his payment of a tribute.

379 BCE

During the ninth month of pregnancy, **Timycha (fl. 370s–360s)** of the Spartan colony of Taranto, Italy, remained faithful to her oath of sacred silence, a demonstration of fealty described by Syrian philosopher Iamblichus's *Life of Pythagoras*. On an annual pilgrimage that attracted devout women, Timycha traveled southwest with nine companions in 379 BCE across southern Magna Graecia (modern Italy) toward the Pythagorean colony at Kroton (modern Crotone), the home of her husband Myllias. Near Phalae, on the Gulf of Tarentum, the travelers faced a thirty-man Sicilian patrol under command of Eurymenes. The Pythagoreans refused to violate an interdiction against trampling a flowering field of fava beans (*Fabia vulgaris*).

Anticipating the religious persecution of Jews, Hindus, Muslims, and Christians, the troop killed all but Timycha and Myllias. Dionysius the Elder, tyrant of Syracusa (modern Syracusa, Sicily), sought inside knowledge of Pythagoreanism and demanded the source of the superstition that the beans harbored dead souls. Under torture, Timycha refused interrogation and chewed off her tongue. To defy Dionysius, she spat the maimed organ at his feet rather than betray an injunction of the philosopher Pythagoras.

351 BCE

A naval commander and tactician, **Artemisia II (395–344 BCE),** queen of Caria, a Persian satrap on the southwestern coast of Anatolia (modern Turkey), succeeded her brother/husband Mausolus in patrolling the islands of the Aegean Sea that threatened to join the Second Delian League. After his death in 353 BCE, she tricked the pro-Delian residents of Latmus (modern Heraclea, Turkey) with religious spectacle and usurped their marble quarry, which she plundered for her husband's grand mausoleum at the capital of Halicarnassus (modern Bodrum, Turkey). In combat against Rhodes during a rebellion in 351 BCE, she directed her one hundred-ship fleet from the city's concealed harbor to seize enemy vessels and kill their crews in the capital plaza. Disguised on Rhodian ships, Carian sailors captured the island and assassinated its leaders.

335 BCE

An audacious woman from Boeotia, **Timocleia of Thebes (fl. 330s)** won feminist acclaim for murdering the soldier who raped her. During the Balkan campaign of Alexander III the Great in 335 BCE, a Thracian captain took advantage of the custom of havoc, which allowed individual soldiers to profit freely from winning. To requite the offense to her womanhood, she informed the captain of valuables hidden in a well. When he leaned in for a look, she slew him by shoving him to the bottom and pelting him with stones. Alexander listened to her version of the crime and ordered his men to release her and her children. Plutarch honored her by including her story in his collection on strong women; Italian artist Tiepolo captured the murder scene in a painting.

Spring 334 BCE

Under direction of Macedonian conqueror Alexander III the Great, Queen **Ada (fl. 370s–326 BCE),** sister of Artemisia II, led the spring 334 BCE siege of Halicarnassus, Caria (modern Bodrum, Turkey). Ada won the conqueror's favor by surrendering Fort Alinda in southwestern Anatolia to his thirty thousand infantry and five thousand cavalry. Alexander drove out King Orontobates by water, leaving prize coastal territory overlooking the Mediterranean Sea. Ada's camaraderie with Alexander resulted in his ceding Caria to her; she adopted him as a son. Because of her loyalty, Ionian and Lycian cities fell to Alexander.

January 20, 330 BCE

In the Greco-Persian wars alongside her brother Ariobarzanes, satrap of Achaemenid Persia, **Youtab Aryobarzan (ca. 360–330 BCE)** fought Alexander III the Great outside Persepolis on January 20, 330 BCE at the battle of the Persian Gate. In a final ambush against the seventeen-thousand-man Macedonian army, she and a regiment of foreign women navigated snowy defiles through the Zagros Mountains to Cheshmeh Chenar (modern Iran). At the Persian camp north of the Persian Gulf, soldiers blocked the Macedonian route over an icy brook with a heap of rocks.

Among forty thousand foot soldiers and seven hundred cavalry, Youtab witnessed boulders crashing downhill on the enemy while the Persians waited for forty days the arrival of Darius III from the Median capital of Ecbatana. Because of the treachery of Tiridates, keeper of the Persian treasury, the garrisoned gates of Persepolis halted Ariobarzanes's army in the path of the Macedonians. Alexander's massacre of the Persians enabled him to pillage and rape, haul the treasury from Persepolis on dromedaries, and finance the rest of his conquest of the East.

See also May 330 BCE.

May 330 BCE

In repayment for Xerxes I's burning of Athena's temple and the sacking of the Acropolis in Athens in 480 BCE, **Thais (fl. 330 BCE)**, the Athenian courtesan of Macedonian invader Alexander III the Great, goaded him to set fire to Persepolis, the capital of Achaemenid Persia (modern Iran). As described in the *Deipnosophistae* (The Diners) of Roman historian Curtius Rufus, Alexander, under the influence of intoxication, agreed to her scorched earth policy. In honor of Dionysus, the Greek god of wine, the Macedonian entourage and a female marching band proceeded down the Royal Road from Sardis through Mesopotamia (modern Iraq and Kuwait) to the Persian Gates, a rocky pass in the Zagros Mountains.

Thais led a martial contingent to the Hadish Palace, named for the queen of Darius I, and hurled the first lighted torch against vulnerable cedar woods that formed four stairways, a balcony, courtyard, sentinel tower, and harem. Flames leaped from the ancestral living quarters to barricaded walls at the city center. Arson and vandalism destroyed copies of the Avesta and Zend, the bulk of Zoroastrian scripture. Her audacious retaliation against the Persians figures in literary works by Cicero, Ovid, Terence, Athenaeus, Dante, Christopher Marlowe, and Mary Renault and an engraving by French artist Gustave Doré.

Summer 328 BCE

Before the legendary clash between Greeks and Persians, **Roxana of Bactria (modern Afghanistan, 340–spring 310 BCE)** took an aversive position at the Sogdian Rock during the siege of Alexander III the Great of Macedon. While the defenders observed the outside walls, three hundred Macedonians began scaling the heights, losing thirty climbers to falls. As reported in the *Anabasis* (Uphill Journey) of Greek historian Arrian of Nicomedia, Anatolia (modern İzmit, Turkey), Roxana's company surrendered. She had secured her place as Persian princess by exterminating Alexander's war prize, **Parysatis (440–385 BCE)**, daughter of Artaxerxes II of Assyria, an intelligence networker and vicious assassin who recruited Syrian troops to aid her son Cyrus. Roxana also conspired against more war trophies—the wife of Darius II, Queen **Stateira I (370–early 332 BCE)**, a combat treasure after the abasement of Darius at the battle of Issus, Anatolia, on November 5, 333 BCE, and their two daughters, **Drypetis (350–323 BCE)** and

Stateira II (350–323 BCE), who had accompanied the unlucky Persian general in the field. Roxana murdered the sisters and had their corpses ejected into a well. At Susa, Roxana married Alexander while he plotted a foray into the Hindu-Kush Himalayan range. **Sisygambis (?–323 BCE)**, Darius's mother, survived years of battles and invasions and died of starvation in grief at Alexander's death.

Winter 326 BCE

Upon the invasion of Assacanus (modern Swat Valley, Pakistan) west of the Indus River in winter 326 BCE, **Cleophis (also Cleophylis, fl. 326 BCE)**, queen of Beira, seized command of the Assacenian army, defended the Katgala Pass, and mediated a truce with Alexander III the Great of Macedonia. Bereaved by her son Assacanus's martyrdom as war chief at the end of a five-day battle at Massaga (modern Chakdara, Pakistan), she mustered women to defend their homeland. The female unit faced thirty thousand massed infantry, twenty thousand cavalry, and thirty elephants.

In a hopeless face-off, Cleophis surrendered and coaxed Alexander with gifts and drinks poured by her ladies-in-waiting. She wrote a letter promising fealty to the pact with the famous Macedonian, who had been wounded on the battlefield when an arrow pierced his left lung near the heart. In a show of perfidy, he slew her army divisions and seven thousand Kambojan mercenaries, male and female, as they exited the bastion. He rustled two hundred thirty thousand bulls to send to Macedonia and torched Massaga, but allowed Cleophis to return to the throne. Romanticized versions of her biography state that she bore the general a son and named him Alexander.

324 BCE

The nomadic virago **Thalestris (fl. 320s BCE)** of Scythia (modern Iran) attempted to conceive a daughter by Alexander III the Great of Macedonia to inject brilliance and military might into her Amazon regiment. The presentation of one hundred female horse soldiers at Ecbatana in the Zagreb Mountains of Media (modern Hamadan, Iran) in 324 BCE pictured them wielding battle axes and bearing lightweight pelta (elliptical) shields. Whether readied for combat or garbed as bodyguards, the women annoyed the Macedonian general, who rejected female autonomy and soldiery. Queen Thalestris appears in opera and the writings of Alexander Pope, Marie Antonia of Saxony, and Mary Renault.

317 BCE

The start of the Hellenistic period brought Mediterranean women to the fore. The widowed mother of Alexander III the Great of Macedonia, **Olympias Stratonice of Epirus (375–316 BCE)** invaded Macedonia in 317 BCE to stave off usurpers and reclaimed rule by challenging a female commander. A member of the family line of Achilles and a priestess of the wine god Dionysus's snake cult, she was born at Molossia, Epirus (modern Albania), on the Ionian Sea, and wed Philip II of Macedon at age eighteen. Her forces faced those of Alexander's niece, **Adea**

Eurydice II of Macedon (?–317 BCE), the granddaughter of Philip II. Adea learned martial arts from her Illyrian mother **Cynane (357–323 BCE)**, Alexander's older half-sister, who had studied under Adea's grandmother **Audata (?–336 BCE)**, also a warrior trained from girlhood.

Cynane followed her father's army and headed her own forces. She fought on the front lines at Illyria (modern southeastern Italy) and, at age fourteen, killed warrior-queen **Caeria (?–343 BCE)** in hand-to-hand grappling, the only two-woman matchup in ancient history. Cynane died in combat at the Hellespont (modern Gallipoli, Turkey). Because Macedonians revered Alexander's sixty-eight-year-old mother, they abandoned Adea Eurydice and Cynane's militia and protected the royal person of Olympias's grandson, Alexander IV, by condemning Adea Eurydice. In October 317 BCE, she chose death by hanging rather than poison or sword. Olympias held on to the throne for a few months until seizure by Cassander, a general in Alexander's high command. He allowed her enemies to stone her to death in 316 BCE and desecrated her remains by banning funeral rites. Her biography permeates the Alexander Trilogy by Mary Renault.

314 BCE

On the Gulf of Corinth separating the Peloponnesus from mainland Achaea in 314 BCE, **Cratesipolis (fl. 310s–300s)**, the widowed Macedonian ruler of the city states of Corinth and Sicyon, replaced her assassinated husband Alexander as military commander. A mutiny at Sicyon northwest of Corinth vented citizen demand for independence. Cratesipolis, a patron of the military, regained control and set the example of punishment of disloyalty by crucifying thirty traitors. Six years later, she relinquished the cities and Corinth's citadel, Acrocorinth, to Ptolemy I Soter, a former general under Alexander III the Great who became Egypt's first pharaoh. To prevent a military backlash of mercenaries, Cratesipolis directed Egyptian forces into Corinth and departed west with her own forces to Patrae, a Peloponnesian trading hub. In 307 BCE, she returned east to Megara for a private tryst with Demetrius I the Besieger. When his enemies approached, he donned a ragged cloak and fled, leaving Cratesipolis behind.

299 BCE

The last Achaemenid princess, **Amastris (340–284 BCE)**, the Persian niece of Darius III, made her own history in coastal Bithynia in 299 BCE by seizing four towns—Croma, Cyrus, Tim, and Seamus. On the southern shore of the Black Sea on the River Lycus, she conquered four settlements and formed them into a city bearing her name. Crowned three times as a royal wife, she ruled as the first Hellenistic *basilissa* (queen) in Heraclea Pontica (modern Karadeniz Eregli, Turkey), and the first woman to issue portrait coins. Her sons Clearchus and Oxyathres rebelled against their mother's control and, in 284 BCE, drowned her in the sea. Lysimachus, Amastris's third husband and the successor of Alexander III the Great, executed the sons around 281 BCE.

Late 295 BCE

In the post–Alexandrian era, **Phila of Macedonia (ca. 348–287 BCE)**, the first basilissa of Greece, confronted Ptolemy I at Salamis, Cyprus. Over a difficult life of wars and widowhood, she served her third husband, Demetrius I, the liberator of Athens, as adviser and peacemaker in 301 BCE after the battle of Ipsus, Phrygia, against the successors of Alexander III the Great. Dispatched to Macedonia to ease tensions, she retired to Cyprus. In late 295 BCE, she and Demetrius defended Salamis against Ptolemy I, who had long coveted the island as well as Rhodes, Syria, and Peloponnesian cities (modern southern Greece). At her surrender to the Ptolemaic Nile River Fleet in early winter 294 BCE, Ptolemy annexed Cyprus as a major shipyard and naval base. Phila and her adult children, Stratonice and Antigonus II, resettled in Macedonia. Phila killed herself in 287 BCE at Cassandreia (modern Chalkidiki, Greece) on the Aegean Sea.

280 BCE

A choice city founded on the isthmus at Potideia, Macedonia, Cassandreia owed its liberty to **Eurydice of Egypt (340–ca. 280 BCE)**, who may have valued the thin strip of land for a future naval base. Her brother, Cassander of Macedon, rebuilt the city from ruins and named it after himself. Wed to Ptolemy I Soter of Egypt in 322 BCE, Eurydice lost her husband to a lady-in-waiting, Berenice I, six years later. As a rejected wife, Eurydice retained royal savvy about the preferment of her children after Cassander's death from enlarged heart in 297 B.C. She pledged her daughter Ptolemais to Demetrius near Miletus in 287 BCE and established her son Ptolemy Ceraunus as ruler of Cassandreia. At age forty, he died in battle with Gallic invaders in January 279 BCE, curtailing her plans for him.

Spring 272 BCE

A recruiter of Spartan women, **Archidamia (340–241 BCE)** defied ruling males during a siege of Laconia in spring 272 BCE in southern Greece. Because the elders herded all females to safety on Crete with King Areus I and the two thousand-man Spartan military, she brandished a sword and harangued women to adopt the aggressive stance of their realm. Her fellow princess **Chilonis (also Chelidonis, fl. 272 BCE)** tied a noose around her throat and chose execution over capture by the invader, Pyrrhus of Epirus, the great commander of his age.

To stop Pyrrhus from building a base of operations in the southern Peloponnese, Archidamia led women in the hand-digging of a trench and commanded a female battalion against Pyrrhus. The battle line defense involved rescuing the wounded and supplying swords, javelins, and food at the height of the invasion, in which Pyrrhus led twenty thousand men and five thousand elephants. On his escape to Argos, a loose roof tile felled Pyrrhus, whom the Argives beheaded. Thirty years later, enemies lured Archidamia out of sanctuary at a temple and executed the old lady along with her daughter Agesistrata and grandson Agis.

260 BCE

A cult deity in Pharaonic Egypt, "the benefactor" **Berenice II Euergetes (273–early 221 BCE)** of Cyrenaica (modern Libya) confronted invaders by leading the home guard. A skilled cavalry officer, she learned horsemanship in girlhood from her Greek father and predecessor, King Magas of Cyrene. During a rout of the royal cavalry by desert nomads, according to Greek fabulist Hyginus, she took her father's place and led the royal security guard on a roundup of the enemies. Mythic verse by Greek poet Callimachus and Roman author Catullus describes the offering of her hair to keep her husband, Ptolemy III, safe during the Third Syrian War. From a temple at Alexandria, the tresses flew upward metamorphosed into the heavenly constellation Coma Berenices.

246 BCE

The Syrian defender of the doomed Seleucid empire during the 246 BCE war of succession, **Laodice I (285–236 BCE)** maintained troops at Sardis (modern Sart, Turkey) and her home base at Ephesus, the former port city of Ionia. Because of the attacks of Ptolemy III on her son Seleucus II Callinicus in Syria and Anatolia (modern Turkey) during the Laodicean War, she strategized a sharing of power between Seleucus and his thirteen-year-old brother Antiochus Hierax, the king of Syria. At the battle of Ancyra (modern Ankara) in 239 BCE, Seleucus lost twenty thousand men and his Anatolian conquests to his envious brother.

245 BCE

For Qin Shi Huang, first emperor of a unified China and founder of the Qin dynasty, **Huang Guigu (?–221 BCE)**, a female general, archer, and army strategist, directed military expeditions in 245 BCE against mountain bandits and the northwestern nomads of China's frontier. In the two hundred fifty-year period of Warring States that began in 476 BCE, she was Lady Sima of three divisions that opposed the Xianbei and Xiongnu in barbarous combat. During peacetime, she devoted herself to responsibilities and war trials. At the beginning of the Qin dynasty in 221 BCE, she received retirement pay in jade and gold.

229 BCE

A robber of one thousand ships, **Teuta (fl. 230s–227 BCE),** the widowed Illyrian queen of the Balkan realm, blockaded the island of Issa (modern Vis, Croatia) and demanded annual tribute. She extended piracy against the Roman Republic on the Adriatic Sea by capturing Phoenice in Chaeonia (modern Phoenike, Albania). Following the death of her husband, King Agron, from pleurisy and overindulgence in winter 231 BCE, she put down a revolt and led eight hundred Gallic mercenaries on a raid on the Peloponnesus that killed Roman shopkeepers. During international negotiations involving liberation of maritime routes from privateers, she arranged the assassination of a Roman legate, Lucius Coruncanius, and Issaean emissary Cleemporus on their way home.

Teuta's expertise extended Illyrian

control south along the Adriatic to the Gulf of Corinth and along sea lanes to Italy and Sicily. In 229 BCE, Rome declared the First Illyrian War, which waylaid Teuta's convoy of galleys on the way over the Ionian Sea to invade Korkyra (modern Corfu). She strategized the capture of four triremes by commander Demetrius of Pharos and scuttled a quinquereme (four-deck ship), a source of missiles and boarding by marines. An ambitious admiral, Demetrius proved false to his oath to Teuta and yielded Korkyra to Rome. A year later, the Roman army, led by the consul Gnaeus Fulvius Centumalus, directed two hundred warships to the combat zone and filled twenty holds with booty, which supplied Roman coffers with gold and silver.

Teuta capitulated and retreated to her royal palace at the hill stronghold of Gradina at Rhizon (modern Risan, Montenegro). The ramparts defended the Bay of Kotor north of Dalmatia (modern Croatia). She ceded the southern region of her lands, promising to limit her seaborne brigandage to the area north of the Drin River at Lissus (modern Lezhë, Albania). She lost the seaports of Apollonia, Korkyra, Epidamnos, and Pharos and pledged to pay reparations. The peace treaty, which remained firm for four years, called for light, unarmed Illyrian ships only and limited their access to Epirus and Macedonia. Legend describes Teuta's death as a leap into the sea or an underground lake to prevent capture by Romans.

May 219 BCE

A Numidian charioteer, **Asbyte** (?–219 BCE) of Marmarica died in May 219 BCE during the eight-month Carthaginian assault on Saguntum (modern Valencia, Spain). During the third year of Hannibal's command of Iberia, as characterized in Roman poet Silius Italicus's epic verse *Punica* (The Phoenicians), the Saguntines begged Rome in vain to intervene. Asbyte, wielding a javelin and battleaxe with her shield, bared one breast to unfetter her shoulder for an attack on Rome. With horses she had selected, she chased and killed Eurydamas, crushing his bones under her wheels. Asbyte eluded Cretan mercenary Mopsus, who martyred her female Berber security guard **Harpe** (?–219 BCE) with an arrow through neck and mouth. Theron, a priest of Hercules, succeeded in clubbing Asbyte in the head, decapitating her remains, exhibiting her skull on a pike, and pillaging her chariot. Hannibal avenged his comrade by killing Theron, thus beginning the Second Punic War.

June 22, 217 BCE

A queen at a climactic point in the Ptolemaic dynasty, **Arsinoë III Philopator (the father-loving, 246–204 BCE)** collaborated with her younger brother/husband Ptolemy IV, Egypt's fourth pharaoh, on June 22, 217 BCE, at the battle of Raphia (modern Rafah), a Mediterranean port in northwestern Sinai Peninsula. In ongoing conflict at Palestine (modern Gaza Strip) during the Fourth Syrian War, Antiochus III the Great, a Macedonian monarch of the Seleucid Empire, led sixty-eight thousand infantry, cavalry, and elephants against Egypt. In view of her troops, Arsinoë bolstered spirits with a pre-battle harangue and promise to each victor two gold minas (approximately $485). The Seleucid army routed before the Egyptian force of seventy-five thousand, which inflicted fourteen thousand three hundred enemy casualties. In November 217, BCE, a memorial column at Memphis offered thanks for the Egyptian victory. A bronze of Arsinoë's head survives in Mantua, Italy.

205 BCE

A strategist in 205 BCE during the Second Punic War, **Sophonisba (225–203 BCE)**, the patriotic daughter of Carthaginian general Hasdrubal Gisgonis, persuaded her first husband Syphax to remain true to Carthage (modern Tunisia). Although some four thousand Iberian mercenaries backed Syphax and Hasdrubal's ninety-three thousand soldiers, at the Bagbrades (modern Medjerda) River, they lost the battle of Bagbrades in 203 BCE to Scipio Africanus and the Numidian king Masinissa, who led a smaller army. The sacking of the capital city of Cirta (modern Constantine, Algeria) cost Carthage thirty thousand dead, fifty percent more than the Roman allies lost.

The capture of Syphax enabled Masinissa to wed Sophonisba. As described in Roman historian Titus Livy's *Ab Urbe Condita* (From the City's Founding), Masinissa convinced her that death offered the only reprieve from humiliation. A model of the stoic ideal, she drank the poison he sent rather than be paraded in a Roman procession. The tragedy inspired verse, drama, manga, and cinema.

189 BCE

When Orgiagon, a Tectosagi chief of the Galatian Gauls, fled combat in 189 BCE during the Galatian War, his wife **Chiomara (fl. 180s BCE)**, a noble Galatian (modern Turkey), was thrust among prisoners of war after Rome trounced the enemy on battlefields at Mount Olympus and near Ancyra (modern Ankara). Among the females given to the legionaries as battle trophies, a centurion under the command of the consul Gnaeus Manlius Vulso attempted to seduce her. When she spurned the officer, he resorted to rape. To clear his reputation, he ransomed her to her Galatian family and met her kin at a river crossing.

Chiomara got her revenge. While he counted the hush money, she spoke an order in her native language that her security guards cut his throat with his own weapon. As described by Florentine writer Giovanni Boccaccio in *De Mulieribus Claris* (On Famous Women), she demanded the villain's head, which she concealed in a fold of her dress. She offered his head to her husband as proof of a rejected adultery. Plutarch extolled her gumption in his collection *De Mulierum Virtutibus* (On the Bravery of Women).

170 BCE

Bas reliefs of *Candace* (queen) **Shanakdakheto (fl. 170–150 BCE)**, the first known independent female ruler of Meroë (modern Sudan) in 170 BCE, depicted her in body armor raising a spear toward her enemies. She broadened Meroë's boundaries and strengthened the economy with the addition of the treasury left by her husband, King Tanyidamani, who ruled for forty years. An image of Shanakdakheto stands in the Cairo Museum dramatizing her rule as a lone monarch of the Kushite kingdom, Lord of the Two Lands, sheltered by Isis, the cult figure of Mediterranean females, and by Ma'at, the goddess of order and justice. A wall from her pyramid chapel survives in red sandstone relief.

165 BCE

According to *Strategemata* (Battle Plans), the writings of Greek military tactician Polyaenus, Queen **Amage (fl. 165 BCE)** of Sarmatia (modern Iran) defended her protectorate, the Chersonese of Crimea (modern Ukraine) on the Euxine Sea (modern Black Sea), in 165 BCE. She wrote a letter to the Scythian (modern Iranian) king in central Eurasia urging him to stop raids of nomads over the steppes from what is now southeastern Russia. For evidence of intent, she usurps the authority of her drunken, luxury-loving husband Medosacus and recruited horsemen for an army to man garrisons and repulse invaders. Because the Scythian ruler ignored her directive, she dressed in men's uniform and armed herself with bow and sword to conduct a cavalry blitzkrieg on Scythia. Heading one hundred twenty men, she gave each one horses to hasten their nonstop passage over 184.81 kilometers (114.8 miles) in twenty-four hours. In the royal palace, she executed the Scythian king and all of his family but one. According to the Greek chronicler Herodotus's *Histories*, she advanced the royal prince to rule the Chersonese peacefully with Greeks.

131 BCE

An independent Ptolemaic queen of Egypt, **Cleopatra II (185–115 BCE)** secured her throne in 131 BCE by leading an uprising against Ptolemy VIII Euergetes, her younger brother/former husband. For four years, she kept him and his niece/wife **Cleopatra III** immured in southern Egypt and Cyprus with the support of Greeks and Jews at Alexandria, her headquarters on the Nile delta. At the time, the port had developed into a commercial giant from trade with India, Arabia, and Europe. The civil war resulted in arson at the royal palace and a riot favoring Cleopatra II, who became the realm's first female pharaoh.

After Cleopatra's brother seized Thebes in November 131 BCE and assassinated her seventeen-year-old son, Ptolemy Memphites, she maintained power in October 130 BCE by militarizing redoubts outside Thebes, extending the army's reach eight hundred miles south of the Mediterranean Sea. When Ptolemy VIII regained Alexandria in 126 B.C.E, he slew Cleopatra's Greek and Jewish supporters, banished intellectuals to Athens or Rhodes, and forced her to flee for succor to son-in-law Demetrius II Nicator in Syria. The rescue was short-lived in 125 BCE, when assassins killed Demetrius at Tyre. A settlement the next year reconciled Cleopatra II with siblings Ptolemy VIII and Cleopatra III: the amnesty of April 118 BCE enabled Cleopatra II to pay the land grants promised to her soldiers during the civil war.

Winter 130–129 BCE

As described in the anonymous collection *Tractatus de Mulieribus Claris in Bello* (On Famous Women in War), Queen **Rhodogune of Parthia (fl. 130–120s BCE)**, daughter of Parthian king Mithridates I, was residing at Hyrcania (northern Iran) on the Caspian Sea when she learned of rebel action by Antiochus VII Sidetes, the last Seleucid king. She vowed to stop bathing or brushing her hair until she neutralized the revolt. Backed by her brother Phraates II, in winter 130–129 BCE, she rode in the vanguard of Parthian forces and trampled the Seleucid faction, killing Antiochus and exterminating his bodyguards. French dramatist Pierre Corneille commemorated her courage in the five-act stage play *Rhodogune*.

116 BCE

In the first century BCE Ptolemaic mayhem and conflict in the Seleucid dynasty, the dynamic controller **Cleopatra III (ca. 160–September 101 BCE)** returned the commercial center of Alexandria to Greek control. She survived her uncle/husband Ptolemy VIII and, after his death in 116 BCE, devoted much of her adulthood to manipulating her siblings and children in alliances and marriages, including her daughter **Cleopatra V Selene** of Syria. She ousted her son/grandson Ptolemy IX Soter to Cyprus in 107 BCE to make way for his younger brother, Ptolemy X Alexander, as Egyptian pharaoh. The mother and second son shared power until he assassinated Cleopatra III at age sixty-one before she could execute him.

See 96 BCE.

96 BCE

A political pawn of her mother, **Cleopatra V Selene (135–69 BCE)**, a Ptolemaic Egyptian by birth, assembled an army in 96 BCE to fight in the civil war between Antiochus IX and Antiochus X. She passed from her brother/husband Ptolemy IX Soter in April 115 BCE to brother Ptolemy X (107 BCE) and entered serial marriages with three Seleucid kings: Antiochus VIII Grypus (102 BCE), Antiochus IX Cyzenus (summer 96 BCE), and Antiochus X Eusebes (summer 94 BCE). In widowhood after 88 BCE, she ruled Syria from her residence in the Seleucid realm at Antioch (modern Antakya) in south central Anatolia.

In 80 BCE, Cleopatra V secured the Egyptian throne for her son Antiochus XIII and commanded a military garrison at Damascus. The Roman senate denied her ethnic claims on Egypt, but agreed that her Seleucid sons should control Syria. After Tigranes II the Great of Armenia conquered Antioch in 73 BCE and Damascus the following year, Cleopatra V managed parts of Cilicia and Phoenicia. Tigranes imprisoned her at Ptolemais (Acre, an Israeli port city) and executed her at age sixty-six.

Winter 66 BCE

A Scythian (modern Iranian) sixth wife, **Hypsicratea (ca. 101–63 BCE)** accompanied eight hundred soldiers and her husband, Mithridates VI the Great of Pontus, Anatolia (modern Turkey), into exile in winter 66 BCE to the Crimea north of the Black Sea. A tireless raider and bodyguard fighting on horseback, she honed warlike expertise in the Caucasus Mountains and steppes. From the palace at Sinope (modern Sinop, Turkey), she co-ruled Mithridates's confederacy of Pontus and fought with his men as far away as Armenia, where he lost to the Roman general Lucius Licinius Lucullus. Uniformed and armed with bow, lance, sword, and ax, Hypsicratea risked all in battle against the Roman Republic to protect her lord, who shielded her from capture and rape by giving her a vial of poison, possibly arsenic.

At the end of the Third Mithridatic War, the Roman general Gnaeus Pompey the Great overthrew the Pontine army by night attack at the Lycus River, Ionia, in 63 BCE. Mithridates swallowed lethal poison after his combined force of thirty-three thousand suffered more than ten thousand casualties. Pompey executed the former king's royal families. Hypsicratea appears to have survived to serve Julius Caesar as chronicler of the Bosporus. An underwater gravestone discovered at Phanagoria (modern Sennoy, Russia) in 2010 bears her name.

Summer 48 BCE

In the internecine skirmishes that followed the death of Ptolemy XII Auletes on February 51 BCE, his youngest daughter **Arsinoë IV (ca. 68–41 BCE)** adopted martial tactics to secure her inheritance. Left to share rule of Cyprus with her eleven-year-old brother/husband Ptolemy XIII Theos Philopator, she fled the palace at Alexandria at age seventeen. By building alliances with royal guardian Achillas and regional powers, in summer 48 BCE she placed herself at the head of twenty thousand infantry and two thousand cavalry to launch the siege of Alexandria in late summer against her older sister **Cleopatra VII (69–August 10, 30 BCE)**, the last Ptolemaic ruler of Egypt. In 47 BCE, Arsinoë executed Achillas, the commander and assistant in the murder of Pompey the Great, and replaced Achillas with Ganymedes, her tutor. Ganymedes's two-pronged tactics killed eight hundred Romans and stymied Julius Caesar, who abandoned the *pharos* (lighthouse) at Alexandria until arrival of backup from Mithridates of Pontus.

At the request of citizens, Julius Caesar deposed Arsinoë in favor of her brother, who drowned in the Nile River. During her jailing at Rome, in 46 BCE, Caesar had her chained and paraded in a thanksgiving procession before dispatching her to the Greek colony of Ephesus, Anatolia (modern Turkey), as a priestess. Because Cleopatra feared her sister's growing appeal, Mark Antony had the former Egyptian queen strangled at the Artemisium, the imposing temple of Artemis in northeastern Greece. Ephesus honored the young queen with a handsome marble mausoleum.

See also 31 BCE

Winter 41–40 BCE

In the two-month Perusine War, **Fulvia Flacca Bambula (83–40 BCE)**, a noted aristocrat and activist near the end of the Roman Republic, promoted the career of her third husband, Mark Antony, in winter 41–40 BCE by raising eight legions to suppress Octavian, a member of the Second Triumvirate. In her twenties, she had supported her notorious first husband, Publius Clodius

Pulcher, by co-managing a guild of street gangs. For Mark Antony, she boosted his popularity with the army by accompanying him in 44 BCE to an encampment at Brundisium (modern Brindisi, Italy). She and her five children toured veteran settlements to secure their loyalty. After the orator Cicero's proscription and assassination on December 7, 43 BCE, she delighted in maiming Antony's old enemy by sticking hairpins into his tongue.

During Antony's affair with Cleopatra VII in Alexandria, Egypt, begun in November 41 BCE, Fulvia and her brother-in-law, Lucius Antonius, marched on Rome with forty-eight thousand troops the next month to end the triumvirate and expel Lepidus, its weakest member. Against Octavian's one hundred twenty-five thousand soldiers, Lucius retreated to Praeneste (modern Palestrina, Italy), where Fulvia dispatched another army to his aid. She faced Octavian's siege at Perusia (modern Perugia, Italy), where slingers peppered her with lead bullets and set the city aflame. Lacking rations and reinforcements, in February 40 BCE, she ceded to enemy forces and withdrew to Sicyon, Achaea (modern Velo, Greece). After a hostile meeting with Antony at Athens, she died at age forty-two. Betrayed by Mark Antony, who mended the clash by marrying Octavian's sister Octavia Minor, Fulvia achieved fame by being Octavian's mother-in-law and the first live female engraved on a Roman coin.

See also summer 48 BCE.

35 BCE

Following Mark Antony's loss of thirty thousand men to Parthia (modern Iran) in 35 BCE, his fourth wife, **Octavia Minor (69–11 BCE)**, older sister of the future Emperor Augustus, delivered cash, rations, and reinforcements to Antony's mansion in Athens. After his marriage to Octavia in 40 BCE, he initiated a war in Carana, Anatolia (modern Turkey), with an unprecedented mass of sixty thousand soldiers—ten legions and ten thousand cavalry. At Caucasia Albania, after Armenian allies deserted Rome, the Parthians destroyed Antony's troops, thirty-two thousand of whom died in large numbers from hunger and infection. Octavia mediated hostilities between brother and husband.

In 37 BCE Octavia brokered an arms deal at Tarentum (modern Taranto, Italy). When she arrived in Athens with necessities for his army, he refused to see her. He deserted Octavia for Queen Cleopatra VII and dispatched his ex-wife back to Rome. Out of pity for Antony's desultory treatment—divorce of Octavia and ouster from his Roman house—Augustus freed his sister of paternalistic control. He ennobled her example of Roman wife and mother with marble likenesses, coins, the Gate of Octavia, and portraits. In films, Kerry Condon, Jean Marsh, Alexandra Moloney, Claire Forlani, and Angela Morant have played her part.

See also summer 48 BCE.

March 32 BCE

During Republican Rome's last civil war, in March 32 BCE, **Aba of Tencer (fl. 40s–30s BCE)**, a priestess-queen in Cilicia (modern Turkey), abetted the fight of **Cleopatra VII** and her husband Mark

Antony against Octavian, the heir of Julius Caesar and future Emperor Augustus. A well-trained daughter of Zenophanes, tyrant of Olba, Tencer (modern Ugura, Turkey), on the south central coast of Anatolia (modern Turkey), Aba succeeded her father in 41 BCE under the aegis of Cleopatra VII and Antony. During a three-year bi-continental struggle on land and sea, Aba served as ally and mediator for Egypt. Because her Ptolemaic and Roman backers lost the war in 30 BCE, she ceded the throne, but her descendants continued to rule Olba.

September 2, 31 BCE

Cleopatra VII Philopator (69– August 10, 30 BCE), the final Ptolemaic ruler of Egypt, fought Octavian's Roman forces by sending her armada to the aid of her lover, Mark Antony, a triumvir of Rome. After welcoming him to Alexandria in November 41 BCE, she received restored control of Cilicia and Cyprus. In exchange, she loaned him two hundred ships and bore him twins, Cleopatra Selene II and Alexander Helios. Her spy network followed Antony's campaigns for four years, during which he rewarded her with more territories— Akko (modern Acre, Israel), Ayla (Gulf of Aqaba, Jordan), Cyrene (Shahhat, Libya), Phoenicia (Lebanon), and much of Crete and Syria. In December 36 BCE, she accompanied Antony's forces in Parthia (modern Iran) along the Euphrates River and, at Berytus (Beirut, Lebanon), gave cash and uniforms to his surviving troops. She continued to bolster his armada at Ephesus, Anatolia (Turkey), in 32 BCE by donating one quarter of his eight hundred-ship fleet as a defense for Egypt against Octavian's advance.

The official declaration of war against Cleopatra VII in spring 31 BCE motivated her to muster forces at Actium in the Ionian Sea in northwestern Greece for a sea battle against Rome's Praetorian galleys. She personally directed the *Antonias*, her flagship, and a complement of sixty warships on September 2, 31 BCE. After Antony's defection, the couple fled to Paraitonion (modern Mersa Matruh, Egypt) west of Alexandria, ostensibly to recruit more men. At his surrender on August 1, 30 BCE, and suicide by a stab of his sword to the gut, she failed to negotiate their children's future with Octavian. Her death by poison—either a lethal salve or asp bite— southwest of Alexandria preceded the assassination of her seventeen-year-old son Caesarion by nineteen days. Coins, paintings, murals, temple reliefs, and statues preserve her likeness and that of her son, Ptolemy XV. Her legend grew from stage plays, opera, film, and television series.

See also summer 48 BCE; winter 41–40 BCE; 35 BCE; March 32 BCE.

24 BCE

The Kush infantry and archers, led by **Amanirenas (60s–10 BCE)**, a Kushite *candace* (queen), fought the Imperial Roman army of Augustus Caesar. To open the Red Sea to Roman traffic, Gaius Aelius Gallus, prefect of Egypt, led an expedition east from Alexandria. Amid crocodiles, rhinoceroses, and hippopotami, the Romans advanced through treacherous waters to the two small commercial islands of Philae and Elephantine on the upper Nile River and to the south at the town of Syene, Meroë (modern Sudan), on the Nubian frontier. Amanirenas engaged the Praetorian garrison of thirty thousand at the Premnis bastion. Although impeded by enemy troops and the capital city of Napata razed, she marched on Qasr Ibrim two years later and sued for peace. With Gaius Petronius, prefect of Egypt, she mediated an increase in trade with Rome. To remind her people of the successful negotiation, she buried a statue of Caesar in the sand for the Kushites to walk over.

14 BCE

During the early years of the Roman Empire, Queen **Dynamis of Bosporus (67 BCE–7 CE)** on the northern rim of the Black Sea led an army in 14 BCE against Polemon I of Pontus, a vassal king appointed by Roman emperor Augustus Caesar. While the Bosporan military battled for independence, prejudiced citizens favored Polemon over their female monarch. At war's end, he married Dynamis with the blessing of the emperor. She took the name Philoromaios (Lover of Rome).

1 CE

The fourth of Nubia's *candaces* (queens), after the decade-long reign of her mother, Amanishakheto, **Amanitore (fl. 1–25 CE)** served Meroë (modern Sudan) as a warrior monarch for a quarter century. A city planner and reclaimer of ruined temples between the Atbara and Nile rivers, she ruled alone at the Jebel Barkal palace after the death of King Natakamani, who was either her son or husband. Her deeds include leading the army, building two hundred pyramids, and raising profits on farming, irrigation, construction, and industry. East of the Nile River, her martial prowess appears in relief at the Naqa temple to the god Amun. The New Testament refers to her in Acts 8:26–40 as an Iron Age Ethiopian queen and possessor of treasure.

Late August 14 CE

During a Roman legionary mutiny to attain higher pay and reduce years of service, **Agrippina the Elder (14 BCE–33 CE)**, the Emperor Augustus's granddaughter, accompanied her husband Germanicus among riotous soldiers in Belgian Gaul on the Lower Rhine. As a treat for the army, she paraded her two-year-old, Gaius Caligula, whom she outfitted in soldier's uniform, armor, and boots. The boots supplied his nickname, Caligula (little boots).

See also summer 15 CE.

15 CE

On the Gulf of Aden on Africa's Horn, the Harla queen **Arawelo (fl. 10s)** of Murihi in the Sanaag region empowered Somali females. Before her rise to power, she joined tribal women in hauling water and hunting for food. By establishing a matriarchy, she curtailed the feudal state of women as housekeepers, child caretakers, and servants and encouraged women to educate themselves and take up leadership roles in society. Folklore claims that she established an androcidal policy as well as female genital mutilation for women via infibulation and castration for male rapists. Her intent was to end war through the dominance of more efficient peacekeepers.

Summer 15 CE

Three months before the birth of Agrippina the Younger in early November, **Agrippina the Elder** put down a military action to dismantle a bridge over the Rhine River. The intervention of a pregnant woman settled a tactical squabble that would have marooned her husband Germanicus and his forces in enemy territory. By standing at the bridge over the River Ems at Vetera (modern Xanten, Germany), she struck a belligerent pose in a decisive move to save lives. With praise for the army and gifts of food and clothing, she lifted legionary spirits. The Emperor Tiberius, out of jealousy, had her condemned to Pandateria Island (modern Ventotene) and starved to death.

17 CE

Outraged that a county magistrate executed her son Lu Yu for lax punishment of tax evaders, **Lu Mu (?–18 CE)**, a widowed wine merchant of Haiqu County, Shandong (modern Rizhao, China), became China's first female rebel captain. Behind the front of tavern keeping, she plotted a peasant revolt against the Xin dynasty. With personal funding, she amassed uniforms and munitions, bought horses, and hired several hundred mercenaries. Her person-to-person campaign targeted Emperor Wang Mang, the fomenter of conscription laws, skimming on salaries, and taxation on minting, iron, lumber, fish, liquor, and salt. Anger erupted with her sacrifice ritual at Mount Kui and a siege at Haiqu on the coast of the East China Sea. The guerrilla attack drew thousands of volunteers, who took control of the county, killed officials, decapitated the supervisor, and sacrificed his head on Lu Mu's grave. From a maritime location on Taigong Island, the movement grew to some ten thousand pirates and knights. Under the sobriquet Red Eyebrows, they continued protesting governmental injustice after Lu Mu sickened and died in 18 CE.

March 40 CE

A widowed combat strategist, **Trưng Trắc (ca. 12–43 CE)** of Jiaozhi in northern Vietnam took the role of her rebel husband, General Thi Sach, to oust the conservative Confucianism of the Han dynasty from control of Vietnam. With the assistance of aristocrats and her younger sister, martial arts expert **Trưng Nhị (ca. 14–43 CE)**, in March 40 CE, Trưng Trắc mobilized elephants and eighty thousand Lac Viet dissidents from the Red River Delta in liberating sixty-five citadels, Chinese bastions, and the kingdom of Nanyue (modern North Vietnam). Among the rebel officers were thirty-six females and **Man Thiện (fl. 40 CE)**, the sisters' widowed mother.

The Trung sisters announced an independent state reaching from Hue to south China and, at Me-linh (outside modern Hanoi) on the Hong River, elevated themselves to the only female monarchs in Vietnamese history. In the defensive line, commander **Phùng Thị**

Chính (fl. 40s CE) gave birth during the assault and balanced her infant on a backpack and a sword in her hands while continuing the fray. After losing to Ma Yuan's twenty thousand Chinese soldiers at Land Bar (modern Hanoi), in February 43 CE, they gave up at Hát Môn (modern Son Tay), where Ma Yuan decapitated them and banished three hundred rebels. The women's valor and sacrifice survive in the Hai Bà Trưng Temple Festival every January 6, a Saigon street celebration of verse, legend, and music. Their names survive on schools, postage stamps, portraits, parades, and pagodas at Hanoi and Hát Môn.

49 CE

The Empress **Agrippina the Younger (November 6, 15 CE–March 23, 59 CE)** from Ubiorum on the Rhine River (modern Cologne, Germany), seized military power in Rome and appeared on coins alongside her second husband, the Emperor Claudius. The Emperor Augustus and Empress Livia's great granddaughter and niece of the Emperor Tiberius, she gained appeal among Romans because of her birth to Agrippina the Elder and Germanicus, a victorious general whom citizens idolized. As sister of the Emperor Caligula, she strategized political success for the Julio-Claudian dynasty, herself, and her ruthless son Nero. Dressed in a military cloak in her own two-wheeled coach, she led Roman legions in training. In 50 CE, she attained the rank of *Augusta* (empress) and commander of the Praetorian Guard.

See also 51 CE.

51 CE

After the setback of the anti–Roman traitor Caratacus, the Celtic chief of the Catuvellauni tribe, he fled to Iron Age queen **Cartimandua (also Cartismandua, ?–69 CE)** of the Brigantes (highlanders) in northern England. As recorded by Roman historian Tacitus, she displayed loyalty to Rome by taking hostages and apprehending the Celtic rebel and delivering him to commander Publius Ostorius Scapula, the governor of Roman Britain. At his trial, Caratacus, his wife, and brothers in chains venerated the Roman empress **Agrippina the Younger** as army commander. She extended her military control in widowhood, when she claimed equal status with her son Nero until he murdered her on March 23, 59 CE, at age forty-three. The Romans maintained Cartimandua's reign until 69 CE.

61 CE

An East Anglian widow, **Boudicca (?–61 CE)**, the merciless queen of the Iceni tribe (modern Norfolk, England), allied four southeastern tribes—Celtic Britanni, Cornovii to the Midwest, Durotriges in the southwest, and Trinovantes, an aggressive eastern shore people—in revolting against Roman colonizers. With the command "win or die," she harangued a coalition of one hundred twenty thousand to avenge the outrage of Romans raping two royal daughters and lashing the queen. She released a rabbit, a source of prophecy from the goddess Andraste, and interpreted its direction as auspicious for her people. A week later, Boudicca and the allied Celts overran the ninth legion and a Roman temple at Camulodunum colony (modern Colchester, Essex). In addition to beheading the Emperor Nero's statue, the Celts slew two thousand infantrymen and put to flight Commander Petillius Cerialis.

Boudicca's troops torched Londinium (modern London) and Verulamium (modern St. Albans), punishing with pike or noose the impious Romans who had violated sacred ground. At the end of a sixteen-day rebellion, commander Gaius Suetonius Paulinus, the governor of Roman Britain, suppressed the rebels at Watling Street, a Saxon highway, and massacred eighty thousand Celts and their dray animals with lance and sword. The occupation troops lost only four hundred. Boudicca died under suspicious circumstances, possibly self-poisoning. A bronze statue at Cardiff, Wales, depicts her with sword in hand in defense of two small weeping girls.

Summer 68 CE

During Rome's infamous Year of Four Emperors, the second wife of a Roman senator, Lucius Vitellius, **Triaria Vitellia (fl. 60s CE)**, brandished a sword in the name of her husband, at Titus Flavius Sabinus, the city prefect of Tarracina (modern Terracina, Italy), a port city ruled by the Volsci. On the Appian Way to the resort city of Capua on the Gulf of Salerno, the fleet from Misenum had abandoned Lucius's brother, the Emperor Aulus Vitellius. Because Capuans had remained faithful to him, Lucius retaliated only against the citizens of Tarracina with a massacre. Not much of Triaria's militant stance survives in history except a theatrical scene in the Roman historian Tacitus's *De Mulieribus Claris* (On Famous Women). Fighting amid a cluster of soldiers sacking the city, she shouted warning that Sabinus not make a show of mercy by endangering the former Emperor Nero, whom the Roman senate had declared a public enemy.

August 1, 69 CE

A Bructerian leader-prophet, **Veleda (fl. 60s–70s CE)** of the Claudia Ara Agrippinensium colony (modern Cologne, Germany) guided Batavian turncoat Gaius Julius Civilis to glory. Throughout an anti–Roman insurrection along the Rhenus-Mosa (modern Rhine-Meuse delta), Veleda occupied a tower on the River Lupia (modern Lippe River), which Roman colonists valued for a supply route and bivouac location. To her isolated upper story, Civilis directed gifts and hostages to win her favor. An intermediary relayed Veleda's clairvoyant auguries to suppliants below, some of whom worshipped her as a divinity.

Veleda's prediction of the expulsion of Vespasian's ten thousand-man garrison of the Fifth and Fifteenth legions from the headquarters at Vetera (modern Xanten, Germany) in March 70 CE and the capture of a Roman flagship from the fleet base preceded the burning of winter cavalry and infantry camps at Fectio on the River Vecht and Traiectum (modern Utrecht, Holland). After the deployment of the Tenth Legion to police the region from its camp at the modern city of Nijmegen, Holland, Veleda mediated Civilis's hostilities with the Tencteri on the lower Rhine. Seizure by the Roman general Quintus Petillius Cerialis in 77 CE and detainment at Ardea south of Rome initiated Veleda's arbitration of the empire's conflicts with other German tribes. Statues and paintings of the Bructerian seer depict her with stern and pensive countenance.

Early 70 CE

An independent Kushite *candace* (queen) **Amanikhatashan (fl. 62–85 CE)** dispatched cavalry and archers from Meroë (modern Sudan) in early 70 CE to the aid of Roman general Titus in Judea during the Great Jewish Revolt. In seven months, his six legions of eighty-six thousand put down a sectarian rebellion against taxation and imperialism by seizing the capital city of Jerusalem on September 8, 70 CE, and destroying the temple that Cyrus the Great began in 538 BCE. Among her contributions until war's end in 71 CE, Amanikhatashan may have mediated culturally diverse embassies from southern tribes. A pyramid acknowledges her twenty-three-year reign.

100

In his *Strategemata* (War Strategies), the Greek historian Polyaenus admired a little known widowed Illyrian queen, **Tania of Dardania (fl. first century CE)**, who took over her husband's throne in the central Balkans. During wars with Macedonia when Dardania (modern Kosovo) came under Roman protection, she rode battlegrounds in a chariot and maintained a cycle of conquests. As commanding officer headquartered at the capital of Scupi (modern Skopje), she remained undefeated. A year after her daughter wed a soldier in Tania's army, he ordered the queen assassinated in her bed.

170

In her forties, **Faustina the Younger (September 21, 130–winter 175/176 CE)**, an emperor's daughter and cousin/wife of the beloved Roman emperor Marcus Aurelius, began accompanying his military command, the *Praetentura Italiae et Alpium* (Defense of Italy and the Alps). Faustina followed the example of **Munatia Plancina (10 BCE–33 CE)**, a Roman aristocrat who had accompanied her husband Gnaeus Calpurnius Piso to the governorship of Syria. From 17 to 20 CE, Faustina appeared on the field during parades of his four legions consisting of twenty thousand men. A patron of lowly warriors and sailors, Faustina became the first Roman woman in the past century to occupy military headquarters during a period of heavy warfare in Parthia (modern Iran), Syria, Mesopotamia (modern Iraq and Kuwait), Armenia, and Germania (north central Europe).

Faustina's domestic life consisted of sixteen children, three sets of twins, and eleven babies dead in early childhood. After her last childbirth with Vibia Aurelia Sabina, she accompanied the Roman army to camps in Pannonia (modern territory bounded by the Danube River) and its capitals—Sirmium, an expeditionary departure point, and the reinforced headquarters of the 14th Legion across the Alps at Carnuntum (modern Austria), site of a disastrous battle against the Germans in spring 170 CE After Marcus initiated the I and II Italica legions to defend Bavaria, she was in the field in 171 CE when the emperor made peace with four Germanic tribes and named them allies.

During the emperor's tour along the Danube River in 174 CE, soldiers acclaimed Faustina *mater castrorum* (camp mother) for her uplift to morale. In her last months, she appears to have falsely reported the emperor's death because of his failing health. When she succumbed that winter, reputedly to heart disease or accident, in Halala, Cappadocia (modern Toraman, Turkey), Aurelius renamed the city "Faustinopolis" and honored her with burial in Hadrian's tomb in Rome alongside her deceased children. Other commemorations include marble statuary, coins, schools for orphan girls, and public baths in Miletus (modern Söke, Turkey), a port on the southern Aegean Sea.

195

A familiar sight to Roman legionaries from Aswan, Egypt, and Epidaurus, Greece, to York, **Julia Domna (160–217 CE)** of Emesa (modern Homs, Syria), the beloved Arabo-Syrian wife of Roman emperor Septimius Severus, accompanied his campaigns to unify the Roman Empire. They set out in 195 CE to quell potential rivals in Mesopotamia (modern Iraq and Kuwait), but failed in the siege at Hatra (modern al Jazirah, Iraq) in 197. She earned the titles of "Camp Mother," "Diva Julia," and "Mother Vesta" for her support of Severus at Carnuntum, Pannonia (modern Austria) on the Danube River and his seventy-five thousand troops on February 19, 197, at the battle of Lugdunum (modern Lyon, France).

Additional threats sent Severus and Julia Domna to Syria and Nisibis (modern Nesbin, Turkey), to Egypt in 199, and to the construction of defenses in the Arabian Desert at Basie (eastern Jordan) and Dumatha in northwestern Arabia. Late in 202, the imperial couple carried Roman combat to North Africa near Leptis Magna (modern Lebda, Libya). Within the year, Severus enlarged the presence of the Roman military across the African frontier. His foray into Caledonia (modern Scotland) in 208 required outposts built with materials transported by the imperial navy. His feverish battle career ended with his death on February 4, 211.

According to biographical data in the anonymous *Historia Augusta* (Augustine History), during the fraternal competition of sons Caracalla and Geta, Julia Domna, in widowhood, arbitrated their hostilities. After Caracalla had Geta executed in December 211, she made visits to her home in Syria and followed Caracalla to war against the Germanic Alamanni on the Upper Rhine River in late 212. For renewed combat at Parthia (modern Iran), in winter 213–214, she crossed into Asia Minor at the Caspian Sea in Nicomedia, Bithynia (modern Turkey). In her final months, she followed Roman legions to war in Antioch (modern Antakya) in south central Anatolia. Two burdens motivated her self-starvation at age fifty-seven—Caracalla's assassination on April 8, 217, and her pain from breast cancer. Coins, cameos, public buildings, and statuary commemorated her loyalty to imperial duties.

200

At the battlefield death of Emperor Chaui by a rebel's arrow wound in 200 CE in Kii Province, the Empress **Jingu Kogo of Japan (also Jingo, 169–269 CE)** of the Yamato clan let her anger erupt into a war in southern Korea that established Japanese domination. While aiding her husband as a shaman, she accompanied him in combat with the Kumaso of Kyūshū, whom her Yamato troops forced into submission. After a divine spirit directed her to wage a three-year campaign, she hired her own troops. She returned home in uniform and announced ascendancy to her people, whom she urged to seek mercy and fairness with tribes that surrendered. She accorded the foiling of Baekche and Silla, a region rich in gemstones and precious metals, to divination through two jewels that controlled the tides and summoned favorable breezes and sea creatures.

From the Baeke realm, at age fifty-three, as attested in the anonymous compendium *Kojiki* (Ancient Records) and Prince Toneri's *Nihon Shoki* (Japanese Chronicles), Jingu received a branched iron sword lined with three extensions on a side. The Silla paid her annually in warhorses, farmers, and metallurgists. Her son Homutawake replaced her on the Chrysanthemum Throne as the Emperor Ojin. At her death at age one hundred and burial at Nara, she was revered at the Sumiyoshi-ku Shinto shrine, a popular tourist draw in Osaka. Artists pictured her as a confident swordswoman and wielder of the spear and battle axe. The Japanese selected her as the first female portrait on one-yen paper currency and the first woman commemorated with a postage stamp.

235

At the end of the Arsacid dynasty, **Sura (213–235 CE)** served Parthia's military in 235 CE as a general. Following the example of her father, King Artabanus V, she applied a delaying strategy to sap the enemy's strength and supplies. Her father relied on her tactics at the incursion in Media (modern Iran) and for invasions of Roman provinces. After Artabanus' murder by his son-in-law Aradashir on the battlefield in 224, Sura devoted her warcraft to vengeance. Befriended by her troops, she lived a short life as a fellow soldier rather than princess.

248

To rid Vietnam of the Wu, the southeastern-most of three Chinese states, Lady **Triệu Thị Chinh (225–248 CE)** led an insurrection in 248 CE by fifty thousand residents of Jiuzhen, a district claimed by the Han dynasty. Orphaned in childhood, she grew up in Nong Cong on the Gulf of Tonkin at the house of an older brother, tribal headman Triệu Quốc Đạt. After murdering his vicious wife, Trieu retreated to a cave in Mount Nua. In 244, she gathered chieftains and trained one thousand guerrilla fighters to raid and pillage the Mandarins. Mounted on a white war elephant's head, she rode from Cu Phong District to thirty battles spreading from

Curu Chan southeast of Haiphong. At Giao Chau, she killed the governor. Her brother joined her troops, but died on the battlefield.

As chronicled in the encyclopedia *Taiping Yulan* (Imperial Reader), the enemy dispatched General Lu Yin and eight thousand soldiers to batter walled cities and end the uprising. A thwarting of Trieu's small force enabled him to pacify Vietnam and pursue the twenty-three-year-old freedom fighter, who drowned herself in a pool on Trưng Mountain at Thanh Hoa rather than be taken alive. The struggle continued until the suppression of Wu China in 280 CE. Folk traditions revered her for long breasts, skill with sword and lance, and tenacity. The Vietnamese honor her memory with drama, opera, verse, statuary, a temple, and street names in Hanoi and Hue.

Spring 270

One of the opportunistic widowed queens of antiquity, **Zenobia Septimia (240–274 CE)**, possibly from Iraq, Lebanon, Syria, or Turkey, established the Palmyrene empire. Ruling in the name of her ten-year-old son Vaballathus after the assassination of his father, Aramean-Arabic king Septimius Oedaenathus I in August 267 CE, she came to power under a cloud of rumors that she had slain her husband. Of unknown ethnicity, she acquired a classical education from the Syrian philosopher Cassius Longinus, who counseled her to rid the realm of Roman control. While posing as a loyal client monarch to the Roman Empire, she consolidated Rome East on the Mediterranean shore. Her broad annexation and heavily armed cavalry formed a bulwark against the Sassanids of Persia. The new empress wielded power over Imperial Rome by stemming the export of grain and forcing the city into rationing bread.

Following the death from plague of Roman Emperor Claudius II Gothicus in January 270 CE, Zenobia built a capital at Palmyra in Syria Phoenice (modern Lebanon) and administered the newly freed empire from her capital at Antioch (modern Antakya) in south central Anatolia. Her holdings extended from Syria, Judea, and Palestine to Arabia Petraea, where she sacked Bostra (modern Bosra, Syria) in spring 270 CE and killed the governor. After crossing the Jordan Valley and assaulting the commercial center at Petra with seventy thousand Palmyrene soldiers, she heightened tensions with Rome by invading Roman Egypt in October and elevating her son to Augustus. Her Syrian commander Zabdas led mercenaries from Dalmatia, Mauritania, and Numidia and inflicted heavy losses on the Emperor Aurelian's fifty thousand troops and his *equites Dalmatae* (Dalmatian cavalry) from the western Balkans. Zabdas posted five thousand men to garrison the port city of Alexandria. At the battle of Immae (modern Reyhanli, Turkey), fought in May 272 CE on the Syrian border near Antioch, the Palmyrene force of cataphracts (armored cavalry) fell from desert heat and Aurelian's trap.

Unbeaten, Zenobia re-equipped her cavalry and marched with them southeast by night to Emesa, where she assembled local allies. Aurelian's forces, aided by Palestinians, crushed the Palmyrenes. The six-month Roman assault reached Palmyra before Zenobia and Vaballathus could escape with the treasury on a fast dromedary across the Euphrates River. Her downfall restored Rome's grain supply and enabled Aurelian to parade her and Vaballathus in chains while Roman legionaries distributed free loaves. In 273, Aurelian returned to Zenobia's capital, executed General Zabdas and Longinus, and leveled Zenobia's royal compound. After she disappeared from history, her likeness survived on modern sculpture, painting, opera, cinema, and television.

303

The death of Yunnan military strategist and governor Li Yi left in charge of the provincial army his daughter, **Li Xiu (285–?)**, to withstand a five-front rebel siege at Ningzhou in 303 CE on the South China Sea. The onslaught in central south China continued until a local coup over dissidents in 310. Her training in riding, martial arts, marksmanship, and archery proved essential to her win, as did her defiance of chaos. During the lengthy revolt, her father sickened and died, perhaps from famine, epidemic, and the exertion caused by a lack of imperial reinforcements.

Li Xiu dressed daily in armor and tiger amulet. She upgraded peasant life to heighten morale; to feed her soldiers, she promoted meals of rats and grass. The Emperor Hui of Jin appointed her the inspector of thirty-seven tribes and awarded her the name "Lady Who Suppresses and Pacifies the Enemy." Another title, "Lady of Brightness and Wisdom," lauded her brilliant battle tactics. Her armed likeness drew memorial gifts to the Goddess Temple in Lijiang.

316

Chinese amazon and martial arts pro **Xun Guan (303–?)** led reinforcements in 316 CE to Xiangyang to circumvent an assault by Jin supporter Du Zeng. As reported in the group compilation *Book of Jin,* a history of the Jin dynasty, the thirteen-year-old crept through enemy defenses by night and hurried to Pingnan in two days to request backup and rations. On return with two brigades through the Luoyang mountains in Henan, she armed herself with sword and longbow to attack Du's forces from the rear, quelling the siege. Du retreated from Xiangyang. Her selfless deed survives as an opera.

350

On the eastern banks of the Nile River, **Mujaji (mid–300s)**, the fabled Kushite queen of Meroë in Nubia (modern Sudan), fought against the Imperial Roman army. Ultimately, Meroë lost to King Ezana, ruler of the expansive Roman proxy kingdom of Axum (modern Ethiopia), a marine trading capital on the Horn of Africa. In the novel *She,* serialized in *Graphic* magazine, romance writer H. Rider Haggard filled in details of Mujaji's failing military command northeast of Khartoum. The film version cast Ursula Andress as the queen.

368

A queen widowed by assassins in August 359, **Pharantzem of Armenia (also**

Paranjem, Parantzem, P'arhanjem, or Pharandsem; ca. 320–winter 369–370) of Syunik Province east of the Black Sea defended Fort Artogerassa (modern Kagizman, Turkey) against a Persian siege. At the command of the vicious land grabber Shapur II the Great of Iran, Armenian traitors led an army northwest against the queen and her fifteen-year-old son Papas until she persuaded them to abandon loyalty to the Persian usurper. In 367, Shapur retaliated by battling for two years against Armenia and the queen's regiment of nobles. After sending Papas to safety in Roman Cappadocia, she manned the watchtowers every night at Artogerassa in the Caucasus Mountains on the Aras River and brandished torches to show her resolve.

The clash ended in 368 CE in epidemic and hunger that wiped out most of Queen Pharantzem's eleven thousand-man army and forced her surrender. Shapur seized Armenia's treasure and Pharantzem and destroyed the commercial center at Artaxata (modern Artashat, Armenia). He orchestrated the fall of Fort Artogerassa in autumn 369 along with her imprisonment and gang-rape by Persian troops, who killed her. With the aid of Roman emperor Valens to the west, in 371, Papas avenged his parents and others of the dynasty whom Shapur had tortured and murdered. Art elevated the warrior queen with images of her on horseback and armed with sword and shield.

Spring 378

A warrior-queen of semi-nomadic Saracens (modern Bedouin), **Mavia (also Mania or Mauia, ?–425)**, an invincible commander from Pharan in spring 378 CE in western Arabia, unnerved the Roman army of the Emperor Valens in Phoenicia and Palestine across Asia's Mediterranean shore and southwest to Egypt's frontier. In widowhood, she resisted imperial demands for Saracen men to reinforce Roman legions and withdrew Arab tribes into the barbarian Sinai. Leading her troops, she may have destroyed the Yotvata bulwark in the Arabah Valley. She prepared for a religious conflict by ceding Aleppo, Syria, and regrouped her mobile lancers in the desert for crafty guerrilla raids, for which she trained men and horses.

Mavia's boldness was evident in the breaching of the Bosporus Strait and breakthrough into Byzantium. Because she thrived across the Levant, Valens settled with her and relied on her cavalry to stave off Goths on August 9, 378, at the battle of Adrianople (modern Edirne, Turkey). Probably a proto–Christian, she stipulated the ordination of the orthodox monk Moses, a Saracen wilderness preacher and peacekeeper. To seal the bargain, Mavia pledged her daughter Chasidat to Victor, the Roman cavalry commander. She posted Saracen lancers to defend Constantinople and behead Goth casualties. Modern historians compare Mavia's prowess to that of Zenobia.

See also August 9, 378.

August 9, 378

Widowed on August 9, 378, at the battle of Adrianople, **Albia Dominica (337–ca. 380 CE)** of Rome headed

Byzantine forces combatting Chief Fritigern's twenty-five thousand Thracian cavalry and infantry. At Edirne, Turkey, the Goths sped onto the European side of Constantinople and burned to death her husband, the Emperor Valens, who was receiving treatment in a wood hut for an arrow wound to the face. As *de facto* empress, Albia launched forty-two thousand infantry, archers, and cavalry as counter measures and financed them with funds from the imperial treasury. The Romans incurred a devastating rebuff by Germanic barbarians, forerunners of medieval knights. On November 24, 380, the Byzantine emperor Theodosius I relieved Albia of war against the pagan Goths, who retreated north of the Danube River.

Middle Ages,
400–1400

The medieval period followed the fall of Rome. The Dark Ages, six centuries of violence and lack of intellectual advance, preceded the rise of Byzantium and the Renaissance. Threats to power and widespread emigration provided royal and aristocratic females the opportunities that had awaited them in the Iron Age. Key to female landholdings, the Crusades siphoned off males to the Holy Lands, leaving chatelaines to guard their property.

400

Foretokening the Viking era, Norse princess **Sela (fl. 400–420)** became the first known woman warrior to initiate a career in piracy. The sister of the spiteful Norwegian king Koller, she chose sea plunder along the trade routes of the Ionian Sea as a way to elude his dominance. She honed battlefield tactics and seamanship and dressed in chain mail to ward off spear, arrow, and sword. As described in Danish historian Saxo Grammaticus's *Gesta Danorum* (Deeds of the Danes), a cycle of brigandage in the North Atlantic Ocean earned Sela a fortune and an enviable reputation. Jutland's envious king Horwendill stalked her fleet to a small Norwegian island and hacked apart her brother's shield with a sword. He killed Koller by amputating his foot, and murdered Sela in 420.

400s

A semi-historical shield maiden, **Alfhild of Geatland (also Alvilv or Alwilda, fl. 400s)**, the daughter of the Gothic King Siward, abandoned life as a princess and adopted men's clothing to operate a fleet of female pirate longships on the Baltic Sea. She happened upon a ship with no captain and, along with her maidservant **Groa (fl. 400s)**, took command according to the Danish law allowing sea-raiders to claim abandoned boat and tackle. Her story of sea roving and skulking over frozen waves appeared in the *Gesta Danorum* (Deeds of the Danes), a saga cycle written in the 1100s by historian Saxo Grammaticus of Zealand, and in Olaus Magnus's *Historia de Gentibus Septentrionalibus* (History of Northern Peoples). A suitor, Prince Alf of Scania, Denmark, the son of King Sigar, traced Alfhild to southern Finland, where his companion revealed her gender by striking off her helmet. She gave up privateering and soldierly equipment to marry Alf. Literary experts debate how much of her story is factual.

450

A Moche queen and soldier, **Señora de Cao (also Lady of Cao, 420–450 CE)** wielded a killing force northwest of Lima on Peru's pre-Incan Pacific coast. The discovery of a burial site at Cao near Trujillo depicted her remains topped with a gold bowl, wrapped in white cotton fabric, coated with red, and arms tattooed with mythic patterns. The tomb yielded costly grave goods—sewing and weaving supplies, gold, decorative stones, twenty-eight atlatls (throwing sticks), and two ritual war clubs, suitable weapons for the first indigenous monarch.

ca. 490s

A beloved peasant warrior of northern China, **Hua Mulan (fl. 460s–490s)** of coastal Yingkuo on the Bohai Sea appears to have served the cavalry as a mounted recruit for the Wei dynasty. Educated in warfare by a veteran of the Xianbei tribe of Mongolia, she mastered horse training and martial arts and took his place on the battle line. Over a twelve-year career during the Warring State period, she concealed her femininity by removing her foot bindings while fighting in battles between the Han and the Rouran Khaganate of Mongolia on China's northern frontier. The versions of her biography and name suggest that varying clans claimed the exciting stories for their own people. Her dedication to the army survives in ballads, novels, film, drama, a temple, and a portrait statue in Yingkuo, Henan.

See also 1361.

ca. 500

A folk-historical defender of the Geats (Scandinavians), **Blenda (fl. 500)** of Varend mobilized an army of farm women at Småland, Sweden, to ward off Danish insurgents. Left without Viking protection while King Aelle fought in Norway, the sixteen-year-old rallied hundreds of shield maidens to Bravellir Plain in the southeast. By seducing the Danes with a feast of meat, bread, wine, and mead, like the biblical Jael, the farm women lulled them to sleep and battered them to death with axes, clubs, and pikes. Blenda's reward was a battlefield and village named for her, a royal coat of arms, and an epic poem.

515

A successor to the weak king of Northern Wei, **Honchi (fl. 510s)** led her realm's army against the Chinese Emperor Wu of Liang. After capturing Hefei in eastern China, a centrally located district between northern and southern Wei, the Wei army yielded to Liang opposition at Zhongli's presidio in the Huai River Valley. A resounding win, the battle satisfied Wu's ambition. For the next nine years, hostilities receded into minor border skirmishes until agrarian unrest revived Wu's military career.

520

In the Anglo-Saxon literature of the early Middle Ages, Germanic virago **Modthryth (also Modthrith, fl. 520)** earned a shameful reputation as a violent, vengeful female fighter in a hyper-masculine society. After becoming the wife of King Offa of Mercia (southern England) in *Beowulf* in 520 CE, she bore the traits of the Valkyrie, both menacing and merciful as the court's peace-weaver. By modifying her combat behavior, she earned love for just treatment of Offa's subjects.

522

The virtuous Ostrogoth Queen **Amalasuintha (also Amalasuntha, 495–April 30, 535)** quelled a conspiracy in 522 CE in Italy by exiling and executing three plotters. The youngest daughter of Theodoric the Great and niece of Frankish king Clovis I, she brought experience and learning to the throne at her accession in August 526. After her husband Eutharic's death, according to Roman scholar Cassiodorus's letters, *Variae* (Diverse Things), she ousted graft and greed from her realms through ineluctable death sentences. The demise of son and heir Athalric in 534 from diabetes and alcoholism forced her to co-rule with Theodahad, her conniving cousin, who schemed to end her reign with exile in December 534 to Martana island in Lake Bolsena, Tuscany. A faction of vengeful nobles throttled her in the bath at age forty, motivating her Byzantine ally, Emperor Justinian I, to invade Italy in 535 with seven thousand five hundred troops.

523

Ostrogoth (East German) princess **Amalafrida (455–525)** of Libya, queen of the Vandals and sister of Theodoric the Great, commanded one thousand Goths and five thousand armed mercenaries. In a rebellion against the Vandal king Hilderic, she summoned Iberian Moors for backup. In combat at Capsa (modern Gafsa, Tunisia) south of Carthage in 523, she lost to Hilderic's loyalists. After her troops died in battle, she was imprisoned and murdered in her cell two years later at age seventy.

January 13, 532

The Greek wife and co-regent of Byzantine emperor Justinian I, **Theodora (497–June 28, 548)** strengthened her co-ruler during the urban riot of January 13, 532. Her advice included the acceptance of female advisers, liberalized property laws, and the freeing of enslaved women from prostitution. When the emperor's appearance in the hippodrome caused Blues and the Greens, competitive racing factions, to arouse the week-long Nika riots begun on January 13, 532, Theodora defended the Palace of Constantinople from arsonists and her husband from terror. With royal hauteur, she offered the household staff ships for escaping, but chose to remain and die.

Backed by Theodora, the army put down the rebellion and slew some thirty thousand disloyal citizens, who had burned the Hagia Sophia Grand Mosque and senate building. The empress executed Hypatius, Justinian's chief rival. She died of breast cancer at age fifty-one. The Greek historian Procopius of Caesarea Maritima lauded her rise from lowly origins and her courage in *The Wars of Justinian* and *Buildings of Justinian*. The empress's royal demeanor impacted biography, stage, cinema, and the gilded murals of San Vitale church at Ravenna, Italy.

See also September 13, 533.

September 13, 533

As the wife of Belisarius, general of Rome's eastern army, **Antonina (484–after 565)** followed his fifteen thousand men to battle in North Africa. According to the Byzantine historian Procopius, while sailing aboard Belisarius's flagship, she earned recognition in Sicily for burying glass water jars in sand to prevent algae growth. Beginning in September 13, 533, during the Vandalic War, she rode with the cavalry to Carthage. Subsequent combat on December 15 brought the Vandal kingdom to its end.

As the secret agent of the Byzantine empress Theodora, Antonina continued her service to Belisarius during the Gothic and Cappadocian wars. From Rome to Naples, she hired five hundred reinforcements at Ostia, recruited a grain transport, and positioned sailors and bowmen around supply barges to ward off the Goths. While aiding Belisarius during the Gothic War at Hydruntum (modern Otranto, Italy) in 548, she pressed the case for more reinforcements.

Summer 548

A peacemaker and impartial leader of the coastal Li people, Lady **Xian (512–602)** from Guangdong in southern China, set a firm hand over the military and insisted on honorable conduct. As wife of General Feng Bio and adviser to their son and heir Feng Pu, she issued ultimata and followed up with harsh penalties for such crimes as human trafficking and smuggling. By avoiding entanglements with the Chen dynasty and fighting battles for the people, she instructed her son in right thinking about backing the Hou Jing Rebellion in summer 548 and disloyalty to the state. Subsequent emperors rewarded her with gifts and honors and posthumous titles. Two hundred temples and sculpture in China, Malaysia, and Vietnam commemorate her ethics.

June 554

A pre–Islamic Arab warrior in the ongoing contention between Persia and Byzantium, the Ghassanid Princess **Halima (fl. 554)** aided forces in June 554 to overrun the Sassanid client King Al-Mundhir III ibn al-Nu'man of the Lakhmid realm, a Yemenite region. Before deployment from the military pavilion on behalf of the Byzantines, she fastened coats of mail on one hundred commandos. Along with Princess Hind, Halima applied saffron fragrance, served pre-battle food platters, and recited short verse in the complex *rajaz* meter as an incentive to achievement. The two-day battle occurred at Chalcis (modern Qinnasrin), a stockaded installation southwest of Aleppo that defended coastal Syria.

Halima joined the battle line as a family member alongside her father, King Arethas, and brothers Mundir and Jabalah. Her duties included recovery and first-aid to the wounded. The soldier Labid won Halima's love by fighting well. The Ghassanid troops not only won, but also killed the famed Lakhmid raider Al-Mundhir. Unfortunately, the advance cost Arethas his heir, Jabalah. Halima's name survives in poetry and a state pasture, valley, and basalt monument to her martyred brother near the battle site. Her example set a romantic example influencing the concept of chivalry.

December 23, 582

A rebel Mayan queen and the first female to defend Palenque (Chiapas, Mexico), **Yohl Ik'nal (fl. 580s–November 7, 604)** of B'aakal maintained a twenty-one year rule from December 23, 582, during two assaults by the belligerent Calakmul kingdom (modern Campeche, Mexico). Hieroglyphs credit her with surviving a military raid on April 21, 599, that despoiled Mayan shrines. Commemorated in funereal inscriptions as "Lady Heart of the Wind Place," she preceded her daughter Sak K'uk', Palenque's second queen.

February 589

A woman-to-woman battle in February 589 at St. Radegund's nunnery, the Abbey of St. Croix at Poitiers in west central France, pitted Abbess **Leubevere of Cheribert (fl. 580–590)** against a rival, **Chrodielde (fl. 580–590)**, a warrior-nun and daughter of Charibert, King of the Parisi, who sought control of the abbey's profitable agriculture. Forced out of the Benedictine cloister, in March 589, Chrodielde sought sanctuary at the Great Church of St. Hilary. She recruited peasant and outlaw support for a phalanx of forty nuns, including a cousin, the Frankish princess **Basina (fl. 580–590)** of Soissons, Austrasia, daughter of Chilperic I. Chrodielde's forces attacked the governing bishops, forcing their flight. In 590, usurpers overran the monastery and looted its treasures. The Merovingian king Childebert II of Austrasia deployed troops to scatter Chrodielde's military base and punish wrongdoers by chopping off noses and hands. Excommunicated for heresy in 593, Clotilda and Basina jettisoned the campaign. Leubevere incurred imprisonment from the king for forming an army of nuns.

593

The widowed Merovingian queen of Chilperic I, **Fredegund (also Fredegonde, ?–December 8, 597)** strategized combat with enemies of Neustria (northern France). A kitchen slave, she abetted Chilperic's strangulation of Galswintha, his second wife. On her behalf, in 575, two assassins murdered Austrasia's King Sigebert I, Chilperic's brother, with poisoned swords. In September 584, she arranged Chilperic's murder. While ruling the Franks at Rouen in the name of her infant son Chlothar II, she led the Neustrian military in subjugating Austrasia and Burgundy.

According to the anonymous *Liber Historiae Francorum* (The History Book of the Franks), in 593, Fredegund rode with the troops who routed the forces of her Spanish sister-in-law **Brunhilda (543–613)** of Toledo, Sigebert's widow. At Berny-Rivière villa outside Droizy, capital of Soissons, Fredegund proposed deceptive tactics—concealing Neustrian fighters with tree branches during a night foray and disguising their steeds with the bells of a grazing herd. After the Austrasian massacre, she pressed on to Reims, killed and looted, and burned much of Champagne. The warring queens inspired verse, opera, fiction, and portraits.

September 617

The first general of T'ang China, Princess **Zhao Pingyang (598–623)** of Taiyuan, third of the nineteen daughters of Emperor Gaozu, conspired with her father in September 617 to besiege and uproot the feudal Sui faction, which faced the dual challenges of eastern Turks and rebels. As outlined in editor Liu Xu's *Jiu T'ang Shu* (Old History of the T'ang), she bribed rebels to fill a female army, acquired rations from a Taoist monastery, and persuaded a bandit coterie from Zhongnan Mountain to join them at Sizhuyuan (modern Beijing). To the sound of her signal gongs and drums, the seventy thousand-member "Army of the Lady" overran small villages, forbade rape and looting, and fed starving peasants. With ten thousand hand-picked fighters, she crossed the Weihe River in the southwest and, at the battle of Chang'an (modern Xian, China), quelled forces at the Sui capital, where she resided.

In Shanxi Province southwest of Beijing, Pingyang defended a strategic part of Pingding County. At Fort Niangziguan, which locals named the "Lady's Pass," she ennobled herself as an exemplary female liberator by demanding justice and compassion for peasants. As evidence of independence, she selected her own husband, Cai Shao, head of the palace security staff, and liberalized divorce laws and education for women. In 618, during the T'ang dynasty's golden age, Han Emperor Gaozu promoted her to marshal for organizing soldiers, dubbed her *zhao* (wise), and gave her a military headquarters and staff. He commemorated her passing in 623 with an armored military procession, honor guard, ritual flag, and drum and trumpet band.

March 13, 624

The Quraysh battle queen and priestess, **Hind bint 'Utbah (also Hind al-Hunnud of Kindah, fl. 620s)** outside Mecca, Arabia, fought the prophet Muhammad for control of a caravan trade route. At the battle of Badr on March 13, 624, early Muslim defenders overran one thousand ethnic Quraysh and slew her father, son, brother, and uncle. As reported in Ibn Ishaq's biography of Muhammad, at the cavalry victory the next year on March 23 outside the Islamic stronghold of Medina at Mount Uhud, her Quraysh soldiers bested Muhammad's fifty bowmen. With fifteen females, she raised victory songs and danced before her troops. She gloried in the death of Hamza, her father's killer, ate his liver, sang vengeful hymns, and shaped his nails and skin into anklets and necklaces. She led three thousand guerrilla warriors until Muslims forced her conversion to Islam in 630. Her challenge to Muhammad survives in film and television.

See also March 23, 625; August 15, 634.

March 23, 625

Adept sword fighter **Nusaybah bint Ka'ab (also Umm 'Umara, fl. 620s–634)** of the Banu Najjar tribe at Medina, Arabia, defended Muhammad at the battle of Uhud on March 23, 625.

At the first clash at which Muslims defended their stronghold at Medina against three thousand Quraysh Meccans, women were prominent combatants. When the prophet was abandoned after his archers fell to the Meccan enemy, the women sang rhymes warning that the enemy would claim Muslim wives as loot. Nusaybah equipped herself with sword, shield, and bow and arrows to kill the mount of a horseman who had wounded her older son Abdullah. In slicing off her attacker's leg, she incurred thirteen arrow wounds, a serious one to the neck and shoulder that crippled her for a year. Overwhelmed by a battleax, Muhammad lost four teeth from his lower right jaw and survived a shoulder injury.

Nusaybah's devotion to Islam led her to aid at the battle of Yamamah, Arabia, in December 632, when thirteen thousand Muslims overcame forty thousand rebels. She had proved her mettle at the Khaybar oasis on the Red Sea in June 628, when Muhammad's sixteen hundred suppressed fourteen thousand Jews, and in finishing Bedouins at the battle of Hunayn at At-Ta'if in January 630. A Jewish Yemenite hitman, **Zaynab bint al-Harith (?–629)**, attempted to assassinate the prophet north of Medina at Khaybar. She roasted a lamb shoulder and fed it to Muhammad, who spat it out and called for cupping to remove ill effects. He granted her mercy. Despite the combat death of younger son Habib, Nusaybah and Abdullah remained in the Muslim army into their sixties, when Nusaybah lost an arm to an attacker. The prophet petitioned Allah to make her family his companions in heaven.

July 2, 626

At the Xuanwuman revolt, Empress **Zhangsun (March 15, 601–July 28, 636)** confronted two rivals of her father-in-law, Emperor Gaozu, at the palace gate at Chang'an, China, and cheered the imperial army to supremacy. A strategist and adviser from China's central plains, she was born to an old military clan of the Sui dynasty well seasoned in war on July 2, 626, and acceded to the imperial throne in August 626. She aided the reigns of her husband, Emperor Taizong, and son, Emperor Gaozong of the T'ang dynasty, by interceding in clan jealousies and treachery. After her death at age thirty-five and burial with honors, she left the thirty-volume *Nuze* (Examples for Women), a compendium of instruction for female courtiers.

December 29, 626

While treating casualties and providing water, **Sulaym bint Milhan (also Salaym bint Milhan, ?–c. 650)**, a pregnant warrior from Yathrib (modern Medina, Saudi Arabia) concealed daggers and swords in her robe on her abdomen to protect the prophet Muhammad from attackers. A veteran of the siege at Mount Uhud the previous year, she returned to frontline service on the Arabian peninsula on December 29, 626, at the month-long battle of Khandaq. A lopsided confrontation, it proved Muhammad's small army more clever and audacious than the Quraysh tribe from Mecca in the use of trench warfare. Sulaym punished slackers who deserted the prophet. She commanded a Berber enclave until she fell in battle in 650.

July 30, 634

Khawla bint al-Azwar (also Kawleh bent Al Azwar al-Kindiyyah, fl. 634–639 CE), a slender Syrian brunette and woman warrior, rallied female resisters—captains **Alfra' Bint al-Humayriah, Oserrah**, and **Wafeira**—on July 30, 634, by quoting spirited war verse while advancing on the Roman enemy in Byzantine Syria. The daughter of Malik (or Tareq) Bin Awse, she was named for "female deer" and "champion." She gained respect as a member of the patrilineal Bani Assad tribe and a companion of Muhammad. From her brother Diraar (also Dhiraar, Dirar, Derar, Zarrar, or Zirrar), the commander and scout of thirteen thousand Rashidun Caliphate troops, she learned martial arts, swordsmanship, and Arab field strategy. The force flourished for twenty-four years in Byzantium, Mesopotamia (modern Iraq and Kuwait), Egypt, Yemen, Persia, and Ethiopia and made its name by impeding the Byzantine emperor Heraclius in southern Syria.

By emulating Diraar, Khawla mastered the *karr wa farr* (hit and run) tactic of soldiery, a stratagem that advanced the army and Islam across the Middle East. Central to its troop placement, a wall of 2.5 meter spears tipped in horn or iron closed ranks to protect infantry. Simultaneously, mounted archers and sharpshooters loosed flurries of arrows at the enemy. The corralling of infantry by camel- and horse-mounted cavalry concluded the field maneuvers with decisive flanking. Bearing leather and wood shields, soldiers in chain mail tunics and hardened leather armor wielded iron or steel swords, sabers, and maces in a final bloodbath.

Under forty-two-year-old veteran general Khalid bin Walid, an officer of Muhammad lauded as God's Drawn Sword, Khawla eschewed the female rear guard in late July 634, two years after Muhammad's death. Outside Jerusalem, she joined her father's twenty thousand Muslim troops, which had marched from Medina in late 633. As a rescuer and medic for the wounded, in the midst of combat, she distributed bandages and drinking water to a field hospital. In the first major assault of Arab Muslims against Byzantine Christians advancing from lower Mesopotamia (modern Iraq and Kuwait) northwest to Emesa, Syria, the Rashidun army charged at the battle of Ajnadin (or Ajnadayn, "the armies"), Israel, against some sixty thousand Eastern Romans. Ninth-century historian al-Waqidi of Medina, Arabia, flaunted exaggerated losses—fifty thousand enemy dead and only five hundred seventy-five of the Rashidun Caliphate. The disaster forced the enemy to regroup at Damascus, leaving Palestine for the taking and Syria free of Romans.

See also September 19, 634 CE; August 20, 636 CE.

August 15, 634

To surmount the Byzantines, **Asma bint Abī Bakr (594–692)** improvised strategy on August 15, 634, before the decisive battle of Yarmuk, Syria. Led by veteran Arab fighter **Hind bint 'Utbah (fl. 630s)** of Mecca, the female squad hurled themselves into combat to prevent capture and rape by the eastern Romans. To stir courage in male fighters, **Umm Ḥakim Bint al-Ḥarith (fl. 630s)** beat drums to set a march rhythm for Quraysh females from Mecca. Muslim women repeated the shaming ditties they had sung in March 625 at the battle of Mount Uhud. When Hind's husband, Abu Sufyan, tried to flee a deluge of arrows, she smacked his horse's face with a tent peg and charged Abu with disloyalty to Muhammad. Abu Sufyan survived blinded in one eye by an arrow. Asma lived to age one hundred and died blind.

September 19, 634

During protracted Muslim combat with Roman legionaries of the Byzantine emperor Heraclius, on September 19, 634, **Khawla bint al-Azwar** fought in the battle of Sanita-a-Uqab (Eagle Pass) in Syria's Qalamoun Mountains. To delay Roman reinforcements along the Damascus road, she strapped on a knight's leather scale armor and leather shield, belted on a curved scimitar, and wielded an eight-foot lance. Respecting female modesty, she swathed her face in a black cloth and her small waist and breasts in a green shawl wound around the black attire. General Khalid bin Walid found her bleeding heavily and commanded that she unwrap her head.

Forced to claim identity as female, Khawla followed orders to pursue the routed enemy and liberate Muslim captives, particularly her brother Diraar, who had lost his spear and fell to the enemy during the siege of Damascus. According to tenth-century Iranian historian al-Tabari, she equipped herself with Diraar's bloody armor and headed alone into the Roman *muqaddimah* (vanguard). Her method began with flight on her mare and a quick turn to engage the closest follower. Impressed by her valor against squads of pursuers, Syrian warrior Rafe 'Bin Omeirah Al Taei imitated her resolve without recognizing her gender. Others believed her to be Khalid himself, who cheered the tough warrior when he approached with additional knights. Her example shamed lesser men and rallied them to emulate the women's squad. The Romans, at a loss, fled the battleground, abandoning dead and wounded.

See also July 30, 634.

August 20, 636

The Syrian woman warrior **Khawla bint al-Azwar** continued to support the Rashidun Caliphate force and fight alongside her brother Diraar in Jordan and Palestine. On August 15, 636, she joined the six-day skirmish at Syria's Yarmuk River, a Jordan River tributary. After a regrouping of Muslim forces and reinforcements at their stronghold near Najd, the army camped on the Yarmuk gorge. On horseback, Khawla's brother commanded the mobile guard, which dogged Roman legionaries fleeing toward Damascus. The decisive pursuit on Israel's border killed one hundred twenty thousand Romans with a loss of only one thousand Arabs.

Because of a tumble from a wounded mount and a broken spear, on August 20, 636, the end of the battle of Yarmuk, Khawla fell into enemy hands. At a female prisoner of war compound, she refused to join the Roman general

Theodore Trithyrius in his bed at Antioch (modern Antakya) in south central Anatolia. Inciting **Afra 'Bint Ghifar al-Humayriah (fl. 630s)** and other captive veterans with epic verse about honor and freedom, she distributed tent poles and dashed at Byzantine sentries. When the general offered her marriage and prestige in Damascus, she belittled him by choosing a cameleer over the pompous Byzantine Roman and vowed to decapitate him.

Khawla led a female phalanx that felled thirty enemy guards. She killed five knights, including General Trithyrius. Her reputation grew in Jordan and Palestine, where Khalid's army massacred some three thousand Byzantine knights. During a nine-month drought and famine in Syria, she died in 639 at an Arab troop camp during the bubonic plague of Emmaus, which killed her brother as well. In 1912, Egyptian sculptor Mahmoud Mukhtar created her likeness with a spear in hand on a rearing steed. Her example survives in Jordan's Khawla Bent Al-Azwar Society for Women's Empowerment.

647

A monarch of pre-unification Korea, Queen **Jindeok of Silla (also Chindok, ?–654)** suppressed revolts against her pro–China policies toward replicating the T'ang military. A proponent of the Chinese emperor Gaozong and of T'ang culture and law, she derived from a royal lineage and valued the composition of music and poetry. She promoted a stronger defense in 647 based on the Chinese army structure and the unification of Korean states, upgraded tax collection, and enhanced relationships with China. Her biography impacted the carving of a statue and the television series *The King's Dream* and *Chronicles of Korea,* in which Son Yeo-eun and Na Mi Hee played the roles of the monarch.

651

A Persian army commander like her father, General Piran, in 651, **Apranik (632–fl. 651 CE)** led the Sassanid cavalry of Yazdegerd III, the last Sassanid emperor. Her battalion countered an attack from Medina, Arabia, on the southern border by Abdullah ibn Aamir of the Muslim Rashidun caliphate, which extended from North Africa to central Asia. At the battle of the Oxus River in 651, riding her famous white horse, she survived alongside Yazdegerd, who fled to Transoxiana in Central Asia and died on the Silk Road at Merv at the hands of a common thief. The setback and the annexation of the northeastern province of Khorasan (modern Iran) ended the Persian empire and its resistance to Islam. Because Apranik's forces failed to whip the lightly armed enemy at the Amu Darya River (modern Turkmenistan), she refused to surrender or retreat like the people of Balkh and Herat. She chose to inflict maximum damage with ongoing commando raids on desert fighters who tended to hide from engagement.

September 653

During the transitional Middle Ages in the coastal province of Zhejiang, a commercial center during the T'ang dynasty, martial arts expert **Chen Shuozhen (ca. 620s–November 653)** of Muzhou championed the needs of the Chinese underclass. By robbing nobles to feed the poor at Tonglu and Muzhou (modern Tongling and Chun'an), she defied a feudal system that encouraged famine, child selling, and slavery by overtaxing residents of the Qingxi Mountains. Captured and beaten for dispensing food stolen from a private granary, she escaped to Fuchuan Mountain and became a taoist apostle.

To inflate a denunciation of Emperor Gaozong, Chen broadcast claims of supernatural powers to return to earth as a male magician capable of saving humankind by subduing fire and water. Early in 653, she named herself Emperor Wenjia and mustered an untrained fighting force of fourteen thousand. Her crusade, propagandized in October 653 by incense burning and bell ringing, continued at Yuqian west of Hangzhou.

At Wuzhou to the south, Chen spied on the enemy blockade on the Xi River. Her followers seized Zhenzhou in Sichuan and pressed south down the coast to Zhangzhou in Fujian province. The makeshift military failed after the celestial sign of a falling meteor heightened forebodings of disaster. The three-month uprising dwindled in November 653 with ten thousand surrenders and the arrest and dismembering of China's first female emperor.

December 8, 656

Twenty-four years after Muhammad's death at the battle of the Camel, his third wife, **Ā'ishah bint Abī Bakr (613–July 16, 678)** of Mecca, Arabia, led the prophet's companions Talha and Zubayr in Islam's first civil war. At the Grand Mosque of Basra, Iraq, she had six hundred and forty suspects executed for Caliph Ali's assassination of Caliph Uthman. Throughout the one hundred-ten-day clash of archers, she rode the red camel al-Askar (meaning "the military") topped with an armored howdah and directed men leading the reins into the fray. The only female at the conflict, at Hawab, she hesitated to interpret a prophecy about barking dogs. While Captain Malik ibn Ashter amputated the arms of her honor guard and killed her camel, she showered her followers with promises of glory.

Lacking the iconic camel al-Askar as guide, Aisha's troops routed. The result of combat between equal Muslim armies of some ten thousand was the widow's capture, the deaths of her co-leaders, and an Islamic schism. She lost one-quarter of her forces while Caliph Ali's warriors incurred only five hundred casualties. Ali adopted a merciful attitude toward Basra's rebels and dispatched the "mother of believers" to Medina. To the end of her life at age sixty-seven, she led women on religious pilgrimages from Medina to Mecca.

661

An admiral of a Japanese armada in 661, two-term empress **Kogyoku Tenno (also Saimei Tenno, August 7, 594-before July 24, 661)** gained a reputation for strength by personally overseeing an expeditionary force to Baekje on the southwestern shore of Korea. Revered as the "Great Queen of Yamato," in 658, she put down the ethnic Emishi of Ezo, a tribal uprising in Honshu, by sending out one hundred eighty warships to Aguta (modern Akita) and Watarishima (modern Hokkaidō). She imitated the pre-war anticipation in a *waka* (short verse) rhyming 5-7-7 about embarking by moonlight from Hakata Bay, Fukuoka. During a rescue of Koma and Kudara kingdoms from Chinese invasion in 661, she died at the age of sixty-seven in Tsukushi (modern Kyūshū), before her fleet reached the battle zone.

On August 27–28, 663, the imperial navy, composed of soldiers whom Kogyoku recruited from Honshu, Kyūshū, and Shikoku, faced Silla regiments at the battle of Baekje, Korea. Fought on the lower Geum River against well trained, well armed, unified Chinese auxiliaries, the engagement was Japan's greatest embarrassment. The Japanese lost ten thousand soldiers, one thousand horses, and four hundred ships. Actor Kim Min-Kyung played the empress's part in the TV series *Dream of the Emperor*.

672

A member of the Kan (Snake) clan and the *kaloomte* (supreme warlord) of the Maya Waka, Queen **K'abel (fl 670s–711)**, a princess from the capital of Calakmul, entered a political marriage during Guatemala's classical period. She achieved a higher status than her native born husband, King K'inich Bahlam II of El Peru-Waka to the south. Throughout a twenty-year reign, she commanded forces in 672 against the power mongers of Tikal southwest of Chichen Itza, Guatemala. The army of "Lady Snake Lord" guarded the trade route along the San Pedro River and unified powers in Calakmul, Tikal, and Teotihuacan. By 743, Tikal completed the total overthrow of El Peru and the Jaguar Throne. Archeologists discovered the queen's tomb in 2012 under a stairway in a pyramid called the Royal Couple's Building alongside ceramic dishes, stone figurines, jade, and seashells. A shield and battle headdress substantiated her role as a warrior-monarch.

674

In Keling kingdom (also Ho-ling or Kalingga, modern Indonesia) on East Java's central coast on the Java Sea, Queen **Sima (also Dewi Shima or Ratu Shima, fl. 674–732 CE)** of southern Sumatra governed twenty-eight small realms through the backing of a skilled female army. She ruled an Indian diaspora of Brahmins who emigrated from India. About the time that Islam reached the islands from western Sumatra, she faced threats in 674 of an invasion by Umayyad caliph Muawiyah bin Abu Sufyan. During China's T'ang dynasty described in the anonymous *Book of Kings in the Archipelago* and *The Books of T'ang*, she favored equitable laws governing theft and elevated earnings from farming, trade, and small scale sculpted wood furniture produced by women. She bore the founders of the Sanjaya, a short-lived Shivaist clan ruling much of Java.

677

Arab warrior **Ghazāla al-Haruriyya of Mosul (?–696 CE)** joined her raider husband Shabib ibn Yazid in 677 in insurrection against the Umayyad Caliphate in central Iraq. The couple supported the minority opinion that women were capable of leading worship in a mosque. She issued a jeering poem ridiculing her Syrian enemy, Ḥajjāj ibn-Yūsuf, governor of the eastern Muslim territories, for hiding in his residence at Kufa south of Baghdad. After a day's advance, she prayed with male soldiers and recited two suras of the Koran. The rebels continued their uprising at Nejd, Arabia, and in Iran. At her death on the battlefield in 696, an enemy rider bore her head as a trophy until Ghazal's husband Shabib killed him and buried his wife.

679

A Saxon ruler from Northumbria, England, **Osthryth (also Ostrith, ca. 660–697)** of Mercia (southern England) became a warrior queen. As the English monk Venerable Bede described in the *Ecclesiastical History of the English People,* she came of age during the "great strife." She fought the Saxons of her homeland, including her older brothers Aelfwine and Ecgfrith, both killed in combat at the River Trent on the North Sea in 679 at the time of her marriage. Wed to Ethelred, a devout Christian king of Mercia east of the island's center, she brought as dowry the village of Fladbury southeast of Worcester in central England. While negotiating a cease-fire, Osthryth had no choice about defending Fladbury. Her loyalties antagonized aristocrats, who assassinated her in 697. At her grave at Bardney Abbey in Lincolnshire, Saxons venerated her as a saint.

Spring 696

On the north Chinese plain, the indomitable **Wu Zetian (February 17, 624–December 16, 705)**, China's only female emperor, launched an invasion in spring 696 against the Tibetan Empire to the west. At the death of the T'ang emperor Gaozong from a blinding stroke in 683, Wu Zetian maintained power as the empress dowager during a golden age of Chinese politics. She served as regent for her third son, twenty-seven-year-old Li Zhe, whom she exiled to house arrest. In 690, she ousted her fourth son Ruizong and, at the capital of Shendu (modern Luoyang), proclaimed herself head of the Zhou dynasty. To quell complaints about a female ruler, she hired informers and spies to aid secret police, who maintained militaristic control through torture.

The Tibetan War focused Wu Zetian's initial military aims on the Silk Road, the overland source of central Asian wealth and influence, and the influx of Turks. The invasion ended near Kokonor Lake in a crushing loss for the empress and a stunning celebration for Tibetan generals Gar Tsenba and Gar Trinring, leaders of a regiment of armored knights. Until a coup in 705 deposed the empress from the throne, she devoted the remainder of her reign to agrarian, Buddhist, and cultural projects. She elevated exemplary women and, defying Confucian principles, promoted military leaders and skilled foreigners through public service exams rather than class or status. Her soldiers spread her sovereignty across

T'ang territory and her dominance in Japan and Korea. At the Qianling Mausoleum on Mount Liang, he ordered her grave monument left blank for citizens to form their own opinions of her expertise.

See also 705.

698

A Berber freedom fighter, sovereign, and seer, **Kahina Dihya of Numidia (also Damya, ?–705 CE)** of the Zenata tribe battered the army and ego of Arab general al-Hasan ibn al-Numan in 698 via the scorched earth policy. Applying precognition to his North African upset at Carthage and his retreat to Cyrenaica (modern Libya), she turned a smaller force into an advantage. Pretending to withdraw, she left the battlefield in robe and sandals and gambled on mass destruction by having her troops set fire to the terrain. While dispossessing her people from their land, the loss denied the Umayyad enemy the wealth of agriculture, earthworks, and businesses as well as possible conversions of Numidians to Islam. Her final clash against al-Hasan in 705 at Bir al-Kahina, Aurès (modern Algeria), resulted in her death and beheading. Some sixty thousand Numidians left the country in chains. Her three sons remained with al-Hasan as members of his army. A bronze statue in Khenchela, Algeria, pictures her resolute and stoic, her right hand raised to the people.

705

A female premier, author, and stalwart fighter of court intrigues, **Shangguan Wan'er (664–July 21, 710)**, born a slave in Shan County, China, commanded the palace security force during an attempted coup. The personal secretary and scribe of the Empress Dowager Wu Zetian and second imperial concubine of Wu's son, Emperor Zhongzong, Shangguan superintended the imperial harem in Chang'an from the end of the T'ang dynasty to the beginning of the Zhou era. A facial tattoo marked her for misdeeds. A coup attempt in 707 warned Shangguan of her perilous status for owning a residence outside the court and for sexual corruption and avarice. An uprising of three conspirators against Empress Dowager Wei on July 21, 710, incorporated thirty executions of chancellors and the blockading of capital gates and exits. Eighteen days after Princess Taiping and her nephew Li Longji launched a coup and Empress Wei assassinated the Emperor Zhongzong with poisoned cake, rebels also decapitated Shangguan. She received a dignified interment in Hubei, China, and the issuance of her richly ornate poems and occasional verse in twenty volumes.

See also spring 696.

722

Queen **Aethelburg of Wessex (673–740 CE)** recruited an army in 722 to burn the earthen enclosure of Taunton, England, a city founded by her husband and joint monarch, King Ine. A seasoned warrior, she intended to deprive the rebel Prince Ealdbert of its capture. After Ealdbert fled to Sussex, Ine exiled him to Surrey and assassinated him in 725. Described in the *Anglo Saxon Chronicles,* the king abdicated and, in

726, arranged a pilgrimage with Aethelburg to Rome. The couple died in Rome in 740 at ages sixty-seven and seventy, leaving as heir his cousin Aethelheard. One report of the widowed Aethelburg in her last days viewed her in a convent. Sculptor Judy Chicago recognized Aethelburg's prowess at the art display *The Dinner Party*.

730

The hawkish monarch of pre–Christian Poland, **Wanda of Poland (fl. 730 CE)** of Kraków fought a constant war against aggressors. The daughter of Krakus, king of the Lechites, she dedicated her rule to upgrading the army and, in 730, to heading troops in battle. Her methods were effective against the armed Alemanni, a Germanic confederacy living east of the Rhine River. To escape a forced marriage to the usurper king Rytygier, she drowned herself in the Vistula River. Her name survives in Bishop Wincenty Kadlubek's *Chronicles of the Kings and Princes of Poland* and in the naming of the Vandalus River and the Vandals, raiders of Iberia, North Africa, and the Mediterranean. Her legend inspired an eagle statue over her burial mound, verse, stories, drama, and opera.

December 7, 730

During the Second Arabo-Khazar War, **Parsbit of Khazaria (also Prisbit, 705–737 CE)**, the daughter of commander Tar'mach of the nomadic Khagan Beks, led thirty thousand armored Turkic forces against the Muslim advance into central Asia. On the Caspian-Pontic steppe separating the Dnieper and Don rivers, conflict with raiders of the Umayyad Caliphate dated to the 720s. On December 7, 730, her invasion route crossed the narrow Alan Gates (modern Dariel Gorge) and preceded the army's plunder of Armenia and Azerbaijan. A three-day war worsened by mechanical slingers cost the Armenians the lives of Governor Djarrah bin Abdallah and Parsbit's husband, General Barjik, who died in 731. The rout enabled Khazars to sack and occupy Ardabil (Iran) for a year until twenty-five thousand mercenary Syrians drove them north of the Caucasus to the Volga delta, where they founded Atil, a center of newly converted Jews. The dowager queen ruled Khazaria as adviser to her grandson. Some sources misidentify Parsbit as male.

738

A Czech amazon, **Libuše (also Libussa, ?–738 CE)**, a prophet from Bohemia, set standards for females by training girls in weaponry and leading them in conflicts. As Latin king Aeneas Silvius explained in *Historia Boëmii* (History of the Bohemians), **Valasca (also Dlasta, Velasca, or Vlasta, ?–745 CE)** of Dívčí Hrad, a follower of Libuše, rose to general and royal aide. Valasca succeeded Libuše and sparked a women's uprising, the Maidens' War. While heading the government for seven years, she promoted women to top offices. Girls' schools encouraged army skills. Boys underwent amputation of the right eye and right thumb to reduce their effectiveness. Valasca posted her lieutenant **Šárka (fl. 745 CE)** with drugged mead to seduce and overpower the enemy. Valasca's tyranny ended when Přemysl, Libuše's husband, slew Valasca in battle at Vysehrad in 745. At Bratislava, Přemysl burned Devin Castle and restored male authority. The Maiden's War survives in verse, opera, drama, and film.

751

Along the Caspian Sea, commando **Azad Deylami (fl. 750s CE)** of Daylam (modern Guilan, Iran) resisted forced conversion to Islam by the extremist Muslim caliphate. After the assassination of Umayyad leader Marwan II on August 6, 750, she mustered rebels in 751 on the southwestern shore of the Caspian Sea against the rise of the Abbasid dynasty. Favoring Persian culture and the Zoroastrian religion, her guerrilla warriors fought suppression of ethnic equality and replacement of the Persian language with Arabic.

769

A Turkic martyr to the Abbasids, **Gülnar Hatun (also Büyük Ece, 731–769 CE)** of Merv, Khurasan (modern Mersin, Turkmenistan), resisted the Islamic caliphate led by Al Mansur. Her hometown came under the power of Arab converters in 715. During her teens, General Nasr ibn Sayyar murdered her father and her fiancé as part of the Abbasid Revolution of 747. Gülnar allied with partisans who sought safety at Al 'Awasim, a frontier zone in southeastern Asia Minor. Lying between Cappadocia and Syria, the peaceful strip separated the Abbasids from the Byzantine Empire. She joined underground forces and died in combat in 769 at Gulek Pass, Anatolia (modern Cilician Gates, Turkey). Her example remains famous in myth, a town and school names, paintings and posters, children's literature, and a life-size sculpture at Gülnar holding a basket of pomegranates, the source of her name.

Viking Age,
770–1066

A significant shift in dominance in the Middle Ages, the conquests of Norsemen raised the Scandinavian presence in raids, European commerce, and colonizing as far west as North America and south to the Dnieper and Volga rivers. Their runic writings and folklore revealed powerful females who partnered with men to spread Norse colonies to Iceland and Greenland.

ca. 770

The semi-historical Viking sea captain **Veborg (also Webiorg, fl. 770 CE)** fought in the battle of Bravalla, where King Harald Wartooth of Jutland challenged Swedish monarch Sigurd Hringr's plan to unite parts of Scandinavia. Amid bowmen, swordsmen, and spear hurlers hired from England, Germany, Ireland, and Russia, Harald drafted female generals: Swedish pirate Veborg, the sailor **Visna of the Slavs (also Wisna, Wixna, or Ursina, fl. 770 CE)**, and Jutland princess **Hedborg (also He'd Heid, Heidr, Heith, or Hetha, fl. 770 CE)** a sea captain and his daughter. Veborg felled first comer Soti. In an attack in southeastern Sweden by Starkad, leader of Geats and Swedes, Veborg chopped off his chin, which he held in place by biting his beard. Starkad wrestled free and amputated the hand of banner bearer Visna. A lengthy one-on-one against Thorkell the Stubborn ended in Veborg's death. Sigurd smashed thirty thousand soldiers and struck his enemy Harald from his chariot. Hedborg became Zealand's monarch. The epic battle recurs in legend, stage drama, epic, a music festival, and film.

783

In combat against Frankish king Charlemagne during his spread of Christianity into Austrasia (north central France), **Fastrada (764–August 10, 794 CE)** of East Francia fought bare-chested alongside Saxon rebels. During the Saxon Wars, as reported in the *Annales Qui Dicuntur Einhardi* (Annals Dictated by Einhard), Charlemagne outraged the enemy in October 782 by ordering the massacre of the Saxon town of Verden, calling for the decapitation of four thousand five hundred Germanic prisoners. A year later, on October 6, 783, he eased anti–Frank animosity by appointing Saxon counts and by marrying Fastrada, daughter of Count Radolf of Aeda and Franconia, at the Burgundian capital at Worms (modern Germany). The couple wintered at Minden, Westphalia, a Franconian headquarters, and toured Saxony in 785. Questionable sources link the queen to conspiracies in 785 and 792.

816

The widow of the prophet Javidhan, Azerbaijanian freedom fighter **Banu Khoramdin (ca. 800–January 7, 838 CE)** battered the Abbasid caliphate for over two decades. In northwestern Iran, she became the wife and comrade of rebel cult leader Babak Khoramdin, a former herder at Badhdh between Ardabil and Tabriz, and joined the Khurramite drive in 816 to restore Persian culture and the Zoroastrian faith. As an archer, she occupied an ancient Parthian stronghold and helped to oust a half million Muslims from Azerbaijan. Amid warlords and highwaymen, the couple's tactics involved ambush of troop columns and outright slaughter of government officials. They celebrated victories with orgiastic singing and drunkenness.

In winter 837, the invasive Arabs used siege machines and naphtha throwers to drive the couple and their army of "Red-Clothed Ones" out of Babak palisades, a rocky tor in the Caucasus Mountains outside Ahar on the Aras River. The standoff ended after Afshin, a Persian officer, betrayed the rebels, leaving them to the Armenian Prince Sahl ibn Sunbat, who raped Banu and Babak's mother and sister. At Samarra, Sunbat executed Babak by lopping off his hands and feet.

820s

The legendary Norwegian shield maiden **Lagertha (also Ladgertha or Ladgerda, fl. 820s CE)** fought alongside the army of Ragnar Lodbrok in the 820s to liberate women from the shame of immurement in a brothel. After Swedish king Frø killed Siward, Ragnar's grandfather, the hero marveled at militant women led by Lagertha, a warrior known for flowing hair. According to Danish chronicler Saxo Grammaticus, author of *Gesta Danorum* (Deeds of Danes), she agreed to wed Ragnar after testing his mettle against a bear and guard dog. The marriage failed, but Lagertha remained true to him during a Danish civil war, to which she despatched one hundred twenty ships. Her raid on the enemy from the rear won the day for Ragnar. Lagertha's example inspired ballet, drama, and a television series.

August 880

A Carolingian princess, **Ermengard of Provence (also Ermengardis, 852–June 2, 897 CE)** from Italy protected the holdings of her Frankish husband, Boson of Vienne on the Rhone River south of Lyon, France. Besieged from August to November 880 by Carloman II, Charles III the Fat, and Louis III, the region came under assault a second time in August 881 with Ermengard defending it. It fell to Boson's brother, Richard of Burgundy and burned in summer 882. Ermengard surrendered in September and shielded her children at Autun with their paternal uncle Richard of Burgundy. In widowhood in January 887, she succeeded Boson as queen of Vienne and regent for her three-year-old son Louis.

892

A Norwegian Viking commander and explorer, Queen **Auð Ketilsdatter the Deep-minded (also Audr, 834–900 CE)**, the widow of Olaf the White, founder of a dynasty in Dublin, ordered a merchant vessel secretly built. On her search for Iceland, she left Gills Bay in Caithness, Scotland, about 890 and crossed the Pentland Firth to Orkney, and recruited her grandson Olaf Thorsteinsson and twenty crewmen. The company ventured past Foula Island and captured the volcanic Faroe Islands. After a winter shipwreck of her navy at Veikarskeid, she sailed on to Broadfirth, Orkney, to reside with her brother, Björn Ketilsson, until spring.

Along Aud's route to settle Breidalfjord, Iceland, in 892, she named landfalls and raised crucifixes attesting to her devotion to Christianity. Residing at Hvamm (modern Hvammur) on the Char River in southwestern Iceland, she rewarded her sailors with plots of land that became permanent settlements. At her death, mourners buried their warrior queen between high and low watermark. Her younger sister, Thorun Hyrna Ketilsdatter, began a diaspora of Irish and Hibridean frontiersmen. By 1100, the Scandinavian immigrants numbered fifty thousand and settled three-quarters of the land.

Summer 893

At age forty, **Aethelflaed (870–June 12, 918 CE)**, the Mercian warrior queen, repelled a Danish Viking onslaught against England's West Midlands. Growing up in the thick of Norse assaults on England during the 870s, she developed insight and vigor from her parents, Ealhswith and Alfred the Great, to become the only Anglo-Saxon military commander. After marrying King Aethelred in 886 and producing daughter Aelfwynn, Aethelflaed renounced motherhood to take up soldiery and piracy. Constant clashes with Norsemen kept her in the field for five years with the allied forces of Mercia (southern England) and Wales. The Mercians won the battle of Buttington in autumn 893 by capturing Danish Viking supplies at Chester and chasing the enemy west into Wales. A coastal approach in 894 resulted in a Viking rout at the battle of South Benfleet, costing the Danes men and longships.

See also 905 CE; 909 CE; August 5, 910 CE; 912 CE; 913 CE; 916 CE; August 1, 917 CE

900s

A martyred virgin from Arcadia in the central Peloponnesus, **Theodora of Vasta (fl. 900s)** defended villagers by warring against bandit raids in the 900s. To protect her father from the military draft, she dressed in male uniform and assumed the name Theodore. Her spirit energized villagers. She died either by beheading for a sexual crime against a nun or in the fighting against Peloponnesian crime. Because the tenth-century Chapel of Agia Theodora was built in a wooded copse above a river and sprouted seventeen holly and maple trees from its roof, devotees of her cult declare prophetic her dying pronouncement: "Let my body become a church, my hair a forest of trees, and my blood a spring to water them." Followers honor her feast day, September 11, by processing from Megalopolis (modern Megalopoli, Greece) to her shrine.

905

Aethelflaed replaced her ailing husband as chief strategist and unified Mercians against Viking warlord Ingimundr and the massive Irish army of Dublin and Scandinavians. According to the composite *Annals of Ireland*, in 905, she shielded the towns of Worcester and Chester with defensive *burns* (hill strongholds). Her attacks thwarted Ingimundr's attempts to capture Chester, a trading port that the Vikings coveted throughout the Dark Ages as a possible Scandinavian colony.

After quartering her army in Chester opposite the River Dee and reclaiming Roman battlements, the Mercian commander **Aethelflaed** overwhelmed Irish, Dane, and Norwegian Viking invaders at the battle of Chester. By locking Ingimundr's force within city gates, her cavalry showered them with flaming beams, boulders, boiling mead and ale, and beehives. Despite the enemy massacre, Ingimundr began undermining the city walls. The queen stirred enmity between the Irish and Norsemen, who abandoned the attack after Irish warriors took up the defense.

See also summer 893 CE; 909 CE; August 5, 910 CE; 912 CE; 913 CE; 916 CE; August 1, 917 CE.

909

In alliance with her younger brother Edward the Elder of Wessex, in 909 CE, **Aethelflaed** conducted a five-week campaign against the kingdom of Lindsey in East Anglia on the North Sea. At the time, the Vikings had resumed their raids from the Danish Midlands. The Anglo-Saxon army confronted Northumbrian Norsemen and battled the stronghold at York. In early August 910, the Danish army directed an armada to the River Severn. Before they could retreat with their loot, the Mercians and West Saxons cut off their return to the fleet at the battle of Tettenhall (modern Wolverhampton, England). Dane and Irish losses included Ingimundr, three York monarchs, and thousands of soldiers as well as hopes for additional raids on eastern England. Aethelflaed continued supporting her husband Aethelred in combat until he died in 911.

See also summer 893 CE; 907 CE; August 5, 910 CE; 912 CE; 913 CE; 916 CE; August 1, 917 CE.

910

A nationalist and defender of Jutland, **Thyra Danebod (Help of the Danes, 854–935)** of Vejle on the Vejle Fjord warded off southern insurgents by entrenching the Dannevirke (Danework) stronghold in Schleswig-Holstein. The granddaughter of Alfred I the Great, daughter of Edward I and Edgina, and wife of southern Denmark's king Gorm the Old, she commanded Danish soldiers against the Saxons. As military strategist, she personally supervised defensive construction with a three-meter palisade, stockade, and moat. The earthworks in current Schleswig-Holstein, Germany, extended Iron Age timber barriers and trenches nineteen miles (thirty kilometers) from the Baltic Sea to house the entire army. On the north-south thoroughfare through Jutland, Thyra and Gorm's son and heir, unifier Harald Bluetooth Gormsson, erected the Jelling rune stones in his parents' memory. Inscriptions laud Queen Thyra as Denmark's savior and national ornament. Harald's older daughter bears her grandmother's name.

912

Rather than remarry and lose control of Mercia (southern England), **Aethelflaed** led her forces in the capture of Scargeat (modern Shrewsbury) and Bridgnorth, Shropshire, and barricaded them against Danish plunder along the River Severn. Within a year, her campaigns continued to secure waterways and roads at Stafford and Tamworth, the Mercian capital, against Viking insurgents. In addition to strengthening alliances with the Scots and Welsh, she buttressed Eddisbury and Warwick before moving on to Chirbury, Shrewsbury, and Hereford on the Welsh border. A plaque at Warwick designates the location of the keep in 914 overlooking the River Avon.

See also summer 893 CE; 909 CE; August 5, 910 CE; 913 CE; 916 CE; August 1, 917 CE.

April 914

A widowed Hindu claimant of the throne during the Kashmiri Golden Age, **Sugandha (855–914 CE)** fought the Tantrin military, which had deposed her in 906. She was returning from combat at Urusha (modern Hazard, Pakistan) in 902 when her husband, King Sankaravarman, died of an arrow wound. She hid the loss by activating his head like a puppet on strings until the royal army could retreat into Kashmir's frontier. As chronicler Kalhana described in the *Rajatarangini* (River of Kings), the murders of her son Gopalavarman and his younger brother Samkata plunged the nation into chaos. Anarchy forced her into exile at the ancient city of Huskapura (modern Ushkur). In April 914, supporters convinced her to muster an army of Ekanga police and challenge Tantrin opportunists at the battle of Srinagar, Kashmir's capital. Her downfall and capture enabled the enemy to execute her at Nispalaka Vihara, a Buddhist monastery.

916

A Toltec empress for nearly three decades, **Xóchitl (ca. 825–916)** from the capital city of Tula (modern Hidalgo, Mexico) formed a female battalion to end civil strife at Tultitlan (modern Mexico). The daughter of Papantzin, the inventor of agave sugar, in 843, she became the enslaved prisoner of Emperor Tecpancaltzin of Tula, who tricked her parents into sending her to the palace with pulque, an agave drink. According to *Historia Chichimeca* by Fernando de Alva Ixtlilxochitl, in 846, Xóchitl conspired to leave the empire. At the king's death in 911, she ruled alone until she died on the battlefield in 916. Her son Maeconetzin succeeded her. Her story survives in ballet and literature.

Sculptor Judy Chicago honored Xóchitl in *The Dinner Party*.

June 19, 916

The Mercian Register credits **Aethelflaed** with additional mayhem in Wales in summer 916. She destroyed King Hwgan Tewdwr of Brycheiniog and his queen and court in southern Wales on June 19, 916, in retaliation for the murder of Mercian abbot Ecbryht and his followers. On Llangorse Lake, Aethelflaed burned the royal *crannog* (royal quarters) and captured the queen and thirty-three Welsh courtiers. Despite Hwgan's plea for help from the Danes, the victory enabled Aethelflaed to control three Welsh realms. The Mercians forced Hwgan's son Dryffn to pay tribute.

See also summer 893 CE; 909 CE; August 5, 910 CE; 912 CE; 913 CE; August 1, 917 CE.

August 1, 917

With her younger brother Edward's aid, **Aethelflaed** appeared in person on the Anglo-Saxon battleground and overwhelmed the Danes at Derby, a borough northeast of Birmingham. Combat on August 1, 917, cost her four thanes, but added to her lands in Mercia (southern England). The enemy lost men to an epidemic, with two hundred forty-five buried in a common grave. The reconquering of Danelaw Viking land gave Aethelflaed control of York and Leicester. In summer 918, her reputation forced the Leicester Vikings to yield without a fight.

At Aethelflaed's death at the battle of Tamworth on June 12, 918, at age forty-eight, the Mercian queen was interred by her husband in Gloucester at St. Oswald's Priory. After she left the realm to daughter Alfwynn, the throne passed within days to her twenty-four-year-old nephew Aethelstan, whom Aethelflaed mentored. A statue at Tamworth Castle depicts her, sword in hand, with Aethelstan. At Runcorn, a portrait of the queen carved in stone stands at Brindley Theatre. An eighteen-foot martial likeness of Aethelflaed in armor pictures her with the broadsword and lance that contributed to England's founding.

See also summer 893 CE; 909 CE; August 5, 910 CE; 912 CE; 913 CE; 916 CE; June 19, 916 CE.

933

To secure the rule of her husband, Rudolph of Burgundy, **Emma of France (also Emma Capet, Emma of Burgundy, or Emma of Neustria, ca. 894–November 2, 934 CE)** commanded the royal army and beset her grandfather, Herbert II. Like her father, Robert I of West Francia, she did not shirk battle on behalf of the Robertian dynasty. In July 923, she promoted the monarchy of Rudolph and insisted on being crowned at Reims, making her the only official Frankish queen. Her rise to power coincided with an era of raids by Vikings and Magyars.

In addition to defending Laon, her military headquarters in north central France in 927, Emma held the bastion while Rudolph retreated south to Burgundy. Four years afterward, Emma seized Avalon Castle in Isère. In 933 on the Marne River, she and Rudolph besieged Château Thierry in Aisne, which surrendered to her control. She died at age forty on November 2, 934, while suppressing a peasant revolt.

Early 945

A vengeful widowed queen, **Olga of Kiev (890–July 11, 969)**, daughter of Oleg the Wise from Pleskov (modern Pskov, Russia), retaliated against the Drevlian tribe for dismembering her Moravian brother/husband Igor Rurikovich, Prince of Kiev. First viewed in male dress during courtship, in early 945, she led Igor's army on a campaign of reprisal. Her barbaric punishments at the state of Kievan Rus' ranged from burning Slavic assassins in a bathhouse, slaying five thousand at Igor's funeral feast, scalding enemies, and, in 946, torching their towns and burying Drevlian suitors alive in a sea trench.

Because Igor died while collecting tribute, Olga of Kiev became the first legal reformer of Eastern Europe by restructuring quit-rents and state tax collection. The historian Theophanes of Constantinople credits her with aiding Byzantine defender Nikephoros II Phokas over 960–961 in the reconquest of Crete from Muslims. She became the first Eastern Slavic ruler baptized into Russian Orthodoxy and the first Russian saint because of the incorruptibility of her remains and their mystic healing of the sick. Her example survives in medals, monuments, biography, fiction, and film.

957

At the start of the Song dynasty, seventeen-year-old cavalry rider and martial arts pro **Liu Jinding (941–1010)** of Xiaojian, Anhui Province, in east central China resolved to rescue thirty-year-old Emperor Taizu, the first Song monarch, from Shouzhou on the Fen River in northern Shanxi. As recorded in the *Mengcheng County Chronicle*, Liu headquartered at Shuangshuo Hill and drilled her men daily. She advertised her finesse with banners, a red steed, and polished saber, which she wielded against bandits and pirates. Amid Southern T'ang troops, she dispersed units attempting to blockade Shoutang Pass, an arched blue brick tunnel built between two slopes in 957 CE. Her rise to marshal of soldiers and horses enlivens operas, storytelling, and fiction.

960

In northern Ethiopia, **Gudit of Bani al-Hamusa (also Judith or Yodit, fl. 960s–1003)**, the Kushite monarch of Damot for four decades, subjugated the Aksumite kingdom. The dominant empire from 100 to the late 900s CE, Aksum had extended its feudal society from Eritrea across the Red Sea to Yemen. In a fertile terrain, Muslim marauders began displacing the Damoti inland in 646 CE and seized trade routes that extended from the Mediterranean to the Indian oceans and South China Sea. From Lake Hayq in central Ethiopia in 960 CE, Gudit led her army on an invasion of Aksumite territory, which was deteriorating from soil erosion.

Gudit's methods were intended to obliterate Aksum. She dethroned King Dil Na'od, murdered the imperial family at Debre Damo in the north at Tigray, and mounted an incendiary campaign that forced indigenous tribes south. To limit Arab and Christian influence, she burned Islamic monuments, destroyed stelae and writings, set hay aflame in worship centers, and crucified Christians. Historians name her as the first secular persecutor of the Ethiopian church.

975

Adelaide Blanche of Anjou (940–May 29, 1026), dowager ruler of Aquitaine, France, led a peace-keeping force in 975 to Le Puy, a popular Christian shrine and pilgrimage site. The daughter of Gerberge of Maine and Fulk II of Anjou, she represented her fifteen-year-old son Bertrand in support of her older brother, Bishop Guido II (Guy of Anjou), newly appointed by King Lothaire to the archdiocese of Clermont. Under the Catholic Peace of God movement that Guido initiated, she intended to stanch royal feuds in the fragmented Carolingian Empire and secure the vulnerable, hostages, and lands southeast of Bordeaux. At her death at age eighty-six in 1026 at Avignon, she was interred outside Arles at a Benedictine monastery at Montmajour Abbey, a UNESCO World Heritage Site.

June 984

As the first princess-abbess of Quedlinburg from age eleven, **Matilda (also Mechtild, December 955–February 7, 999),** a Saxon daughter of Otto I, applied military might to reforming the church against paganism and establishing an academic center in north central Germany. After her investiture as canoness at Easter in April 966, she headed royal courts at Ditfurt, Duderstadt, and Nienburg and recruited an army to man boundary redoubts. In June 984, a crisis year after the Great Slav Rising and invasion of northern Saxony by non–Christians, her army pushed the barbarians east of the Elbe River. To repulse their raids, she served her nephew, three-year-old Otto III, as regent. During the absence of the boy-king on an Italian campaign, she managed Saxony as *matricia* (governor) and *metropolitana* (overseer of bishops). In 2022, UNESCO declared the Quedlinburg environs a world heritage center.

June 986

A triumphant commander in chief and Chinese regent, **Xiao Yanyan (953–December 23, 1009)** from the nomadic Khitan tribe of northeast Asia served as empress and military strategist. As protector of her son Yelu Longxu, she led ten thousand Liao cavalry to the capital at Beijing against Northern Song dynasty invaders dispatched by Chinese emperor Taizu. At the battle of Qigou Pass in June 986, she chose to lengthen the conflict with retaliatory skirmishes into the next year. The period of ongoing war involved the conquest of Jeongan-guk in 986, and assault on the nomadic Jurchens on the Yalu River in 991, when they pledged vassalage. Her attack on Goryeo yielded annual tribute and a promise of loyalty. Her army launched a counter-invasion in 1005 on the capital of Kaifeng. Her biography remains popular in historical fiction and movies.

High Middle Ages, 1000–1300

In a period of architectural expansion and the spread of cities following barbarian raids, the High Middle Ages stimulated thought, learning, and pride in statehood over bloodbaths and massacres. Women took notable interest in exploration, defense of property, and ethnic colonialism.

ca. 1000

At Eriksfirth, Greenland, Norse explorer **Freydís Eiríksdóttir (also Frydis, 970–1004)** demonstrated military prowess to *Skraelings* (aborigines) by beating her naked chest with a sword. An aggressive Icelander named for a war goddess in the epic *Saga of Erik the Red,* she acquired fighting strength from her father Erik and brother, Leif Eriksson, the first European builders of longhouses and explorers of Straumfjord in southwest Greenland. When the Viking expeditioners reached Vinland (modern Newfoundland), Beothuk tribesmen raided their camp by night and slung projectiles. Only one month from giving birth to a child, Freydís berated Norsemen for cowardice and predicted that they could slaughter the Indians. As proof, she bared her breasts and slapped the sword of a fallen Norseman against her flesh. Her vainglory scared off the attackers, who lost four men in the fray compared to the Norsemen's two. She then proposed an expedition of one hundred men.

Accompanying the family, Erik's daughter-in-law, **Gudrid Thorbjarnardóttir (980–?)** from Laugarbrekka, Iceland, not only explored and colonized Greenland and Newfoundland, but gave birth to Snorri Thorfinnsson, the first white child in North America. The anonymous history *Saga of the Greenlanders* depicts Gudrid as the far-traveler, security guard, and leader of sixty-five settlers and herds of livestock. The venture ended after 1013 because of continued onslaughts by Beothuk natives. Armed with harpoons, deer and seal spears, and bows and arrows, they confronted European newcomers with faces and limbs painted with red ochre, the source of the term "red man." After the death of her third husband, Thorfinn Karlsefni, in an Indian raid, Gudrid returned to Iceland to farm and continued roving in eight ocean voyages. By 1829, the Beothuk died out from rampant tuberculosis carried by Europeans.

February 13, 1021

An astute Fatimid conspirator and

diplomat, **Sitt al-Mulk (September-October 970–February 5, 1023)** of al-Manṣūriyya (modern Kairouan, Tunisia), ended the corrupt regime of her unstable half-brother al-Hakim, the Mad Caliph, on February 13, 1021, by masterminding his assassination. A spoiled darling, she grew up coddled by her father, who awarded her a private palace and personal militia. Her mother provided in-house spying on family and staff. In the aftermath of al-Hakim's murder in the Mokattam hills near the royal city of Cairo, she reversed his nepotism, murderous plots, delusions of godhood, and persecutions of women and Egyptian Christians, which earned him comparisons to Nero.

Because her brother destroyed Jerusalem's Church of the Holy Sepulchre and monasteries, Sitt al-Mulk made reparations to Byzantine emperor Basil II. As commander of an elite battalion, she restored order in Aleppo, Syria, and negotiated with the Byzantine Romans the possession of the Mediterranean trade nexus revered as the "Gate of Iraq." On February 3, 1017, without threat or violence the Fatimid caliphate claimed the city for Sunni Muslims. During a two-year reign, she ensured the army's loyalty by distributing cash to commanders and extended a spy operation among officials. She died of dysentery at age fifty-three. The chaotic caliphate generated by her half-brother yielded plots for novels and short fiction.

1047

During the golden era of Karnataka in southwestern India, **Akkadevi (also Akka Mahadevi 1010–1068)**, a Chalukya princess and governor of Kishukadu, defended her clan from the imperialist Cholas, a Tamil realm dating to 200 BCE. Her major battle, the siege of the Gokak redoubt on a natural stone crest in 1022 suppressed a revolt in west central India. She earned regard from male generals by defeating a rebel chief. Under her four-decade rule, the province grew with the addition of Toragale, Masiyavadi, and Bagadage, and developed Brahmin education with grants and cultivated Hindu and Jain worship sites and ritual ceremonies. She ended her long life as a naked hermit in the Srisailam Mountains and was revered as a saint.

1050

A Norwegian rebel, **Bergljot Håkonsdatter (972–1055)** of Hlade, the daughter of the hardhanded ruler Haakon Jarl, shared her father's spirit by leading a retaliation against the Viking king Harald Hardrada. A greedy and ambitious coast raider, Harald coveted the thrones of Denmark and England. At the royal estate at Nidaros (modern Trondheim), he murdered his opposition, Einar Thambarskelfir, Bergljot's husband, and their son Eindride. She recruited Trøndish fighters in 1050 and rallied highlanders to avenge the assassinations, but Harald escaped, rowed to safety, and ruled for sixteen more years. Edvard Grieg extolled her border war in an epic musical.

October 1052

In an attack by a Vietnamese force on the Chinese border, **A-Nong (1005–1055)**, a Zhuang shaman, dowager empress, and soldier, escaped with her fourteen-year-old son Zhigao. In collaboration with Zhigao and Thai rebels against the Song dynasty, she plotted a siege of Hengzhou and Wuzhou in southern China. In October 1052, she fled a death warrant and accompanied her son to Yunnan to mobilize an army. After their capture by Song troops three years later, she died at age fifty of execution along with Zhigao. Annual festivals at Hunan and Gizhou celebrate their heroism.

1070

Thrice widowed countess **Adelaide of Turin and Susa (1014–December 19, 1091)**, at age fifty-six, put down revolts at Lodi and Asti in northwestern Italy. After her last husband Otto's death, she took charge of the inherited lands of ten-year-old son Peter and two-year-old Amadeus II, earning from her subjects a comparison to the biblical judge and warrior Deborah. Wearing armor and carrying her personal weapons, she seized Asti by burning the trade and wine center to restore the deposed Bishop Ingo of Asti, a young, ambitious landlord during the Carolingian era.

See also June 1083; March 1091.

February 22, 1071

In the far north of France, **Richilde of Hainault (1018–March 15, 1086)**, widow of Baldwin VI of Flanders, married William FitzOsbern and fought for sixteen-year-old son Arnulf's inheritance and succession. She secured funds from the bishop of Liege to hire mercenaries. Her forces, surging northward, faced the usurper Robert I the Frisian at the two-day battle of Cassel on the Franco-Belgian border, where historian Lambert of Ardes charged her with hurling magic powder in violation of gender roles. A double loss—Richilde to the Flemish and Robert to the forces of Philip I of France—concluded with an equitable prisoner exchange. After Arnulf and William died in battle, Philip settled the confrontation by naming Robert the Count of Flanders. Banished from her homeland, Richilde continued to vie for Flanders until her death at age sixty-eight at the Abbey of Messines.

The Crusades, 1096–1291

Overlapping the High Middle Ages, an eight-part series of expeditions between European Christians and Middle Eastern Muslim cost vast sums of money for supplies and travel. The idealistic campaign lost lives and property of male and female contenders.

1075

One of the early casualties of the Crusades, Norman strategist **Emma de Guader (1059–1096)** of Breteuil defended Norwich Castle while it was under a three-month siege by William I the Conqueror. She was the first daughter of William FitzOsbern of Hereford, an army tactician at the battle of Hastings in 1066. Her husband, Ralph de Gaël, fled William's ire by escaping to Montfort and Wader castles in Brittany and hastened to Denmark to hire Cnut and Håkon and their two hundred ships.

Emma at age sixteen protected citizens by planning a revolt during her wedding reception at the Suffolk village of Exning, Cambridgeshire. After stymying William with her retreat, she bartered for safe travel for herself and her forces in return for the castle. While she, Ralph, and their sixteen-year-old son Alain galloped toward Palestine to retrieve the Holy Land from Muslims during the First Crusade, she died at Outremer at age thirty-seven.

December 13, 1076

Sichelgaita "Gaita" (also Sikelgaita or Sigelgaita, 1040–April 16, 1090), Countess of Salerno, Italy, a tall, muscular Lombard amazon and princess, advised the military on riding, field medicine, and sword tactics. Born at Monte Cassino, Italy, and named for the German "victory spear," she was the first daughter of Catholic supporter Gemma di Capua and Guaimar IV, Prince of Salerno and Capua. While studying medicine at Salerno's famed university, Europe's first, she came of age in a time of lethal maneuverings for power, religious dominance, and territory.

Following a political marriage in 1058 at age eighteen to Norman warlord Robert Guiscard de Hauteville, Count of Salerno, Sichelgaita promoted Catholicism and backed the religious wars that preceded the First Crusade. During the conquest of southern Italy and Sicily, she commanded fourteen thousand seven hundred infantry and thirteen hundred knights. She rode in the vanguard on Robert's right flank during sieges, notably, the seven-month recapture of Salerno in southwestern Italy by starvation on December 13, 1076.

See also April 1080; October 18, 1081; May 28, 1084; July 17, 1085.

April 1080

With reinforcements from Bari on the Adriatic Sea, Italian warrior **Sichelgaita** launched the siege of Trani while her husband, Norman soldier of fortune Robert Guiscard, pressed southwest. He beset Byzantine garrisons at the gulf port of Taranto on the Ionian Sea. The husband-and-wife assaults ended with the cities' capture in April 1080. Annexed to Salerno, the coastal properties boosted the couple's wealth and power.

See also December 13, 1076; October 18, 1081; May 28, 1084; July 17, 1085.

June 25, 1080

A reformer and the first woman buried in Castel Sant'Angelo (now called Hadrian's tomb) in Rome, **Matilda of Tuscany (1046–July 24, 1115)** supported the election of the reformer pope Gregory VII by halting the army of Holy Roman Emperor Henry IV before it could cross the Apennine Mountains. Born in Lucca or Mantua, she came of age in a martial environment that taught her riding, weaponry, command, fortification, and field strategy. At her headquarters at Canossa Castle on June 25, 1080, the confrontation between secular and Catholic powers enhanced the value of her military might and of financial backing from inherited properties in Lombardy, Romagna, Tuscany, and Emilia.

See also July 2, 1084; October 1092.

October 18, 1081

At age forty, Countess **Sichelgaita** of Salerno advised her husband Robert Guiscard that conflict against Byzantine Turks on the Adriatic Sea was uncertain. Simultaneously, she reared sons Guy, Ruggero, and Robert and daughters Matilda, Sybille, Mabel, Heria, and Olympias, but still served as a military strategist. She compared the situation to the siege of Trani in April 1080. On the Adriatic shore at the battle of Dyrrhachium (also Durazzo, modern Durres, Albania), she equipped herself with full armor and chain mail to withstand an arrow storm. Byzantine historian Anna Comnena, author of the *Alexiad*, compared her to Pallas Athena and the Valkyries.

Acting as combat commander, according to Anna Comnena, on October 18, 1081, Sichelgaita wielded a spear to rally sixteen thousand Normans and Lombards against twenty-five thousand Byzantine Turks and Bogomils. During the assault, the Emperor Alexios I Comnenos incurred a forehead gash during his retreat. Sichelgaita suffered an arrow wound, but did not halt berating recalcitrant soldiers. Because of the loss of twelve thousand men, Alexios contended with five thousand corpses and some seven thousand who routed and fled the field. Sichelgaita's contingent celebrated seizure of Byzantine supplies and gold from the royal treasury and the control of Dyrrhachium (also Durazzo, modern Durres, Albania), the chief departure point from Italy to Greece and Constantinople.

See also December 13, 1076; April 1080; May 28, 1084; July 17, 1085.

June 1083

Countess **Adelaide of Turin and Susa** mediated hostilities with her son-in-law, Holy Roman Emperor Henry IV, the disgruntled husband of Bertha of Savoy. In exchange for part of Burgundy, Adelaide, son Amadeus, and daughter Bertha facilitated Henry during an attack on Rome's Castel Sant'Angelo, residence of Pope Gregory VII (now called Hadrian's tomb). She joined combat in Canossa, east of Asti, and Pavia, east of Turin. As a result of the successful Italian campaign, on April 1, 1084, Pope Clement III appointed Henry Rome's emperor.

See also 1070; March 1091.

May 28, 1084

The battlefield partnership of Duke Robert Guiscard of Cotenetin, Normandy, and his warrior-wife, Duchess **Sichelgaita** of Salerno, continued in 1083 with the hiring of Arab mercenaries for the march of thirty-six thousand troops to the liberation of Castel Sant'Angelo in Rome. On May 28, 1084, the force sacked and burned the city. She released her septuagenarian friend Pope Gregory VII from house arrest under Holy Roman Emperor Henry IV. Henry wisely retreated from the approaching army.

See also December 13, 1076; April 1080; October 18, 1081; July 17, 1085.

July 2, 1084

Northeast of Modena on the enemy camp at the plain of Sorbara on July 2, 1084, **Matilda of Tuscany** acquired a reputation as a medieval amazon. In a dawn raid on Holy Roman Emperor Henry IV on July 2, 1084, she wore armor while she slaughtered infantry, captured one hundred knights, and seized five hundred steeds. The sortie, begun with gifts of Tuscan wine to inebriate the emperor's men, gained temporary sway over Henry, who had charged her with treason and pillaged Rome. He retaliated by attacking her lands in northern Italy and capturing Mantua and Verona.

See also July 25, 1080; October 1092.

July 17, 1085

West of Albania and the Peloponnesus during the conquest of Corfu and Cephalonia in 1085, Duchess **Sichelgaita** of Salerno and her sixteen thousand men faced an allied fleet of Turks and Venetians. On July 17, 1085, at age seventy, her husband Robert died of malaria by her side in the Greek isles at Atheras, Cephalonia, in the Ionian Sea, thus ending the siege. In widowhood, she allied with her eldest son, twenty-five-year-old Roger Borsa, who inherited his father's duchy. Retired from the military, the dowager duchess withdrew to a sisterhood at the Abbey of Montecassino between Naples and Rome. After her death at age fifty on April 16, 1090, at Montecassino, her remains lay interred at the abbey.

See also December 13, 1076; April 1080; October 18, 1081; May 28, 1084.

October 23, 1086

Zaynab an-Nafzāwiyyah (1049–1075), a wealthy widow and Sunni Muslim from Aghmat, Morocco, helped to enlarge the Almoravid empire from al-Andalus, Spain, to Ghana and eastern Senegal. On the advice of his canny wife Zaynab, Yusuf ibn Tashfin, a Berber viceroy and commander of Muslims, advanced over Gibraltar to the port of Algeciras and won the battle of Sagrajas for the Almoravids in Badajoz, Spain. Although his forces incurred heavy loss, on October 23, 1086, they stanched Aragon, reduced Castile's forces by half, and wounded the leg of Alfonso VI so severely that the king gave up riding. By accepting Zaynab's strategy, Yusuf conquered Algeria, the Balearic Islands, Mauritania, Morocco, Spain, and the Western Sahara. He chose her to arbitrate settlements for unification and the rule of the Maghreb. The city of Marrakech accredited her regal grace and wisdom.

1088

The highest ranking Muslim female of her time, **Arwa Al-Sulayhi (1045–May 5, 1138)** of Haraz, Yemen, requited the vendetta causing the murder of her father-in-law, Sulayhid 'Ali ibn Muhammad. Because war injuries paralyzed her husband Ahmad al-Mukarram, Arwa ruled from a new palace at her capital of Jibla for fifty-two years. In addition to foreign affairs, she derived military craft by watching her enemies in Zabid on Yemen's western coast. When her commander in chief betrayed her, she had him jailed in Egypt. She rendered payback on Ethiopia for kidnapping her mother-in-law in 1066 during a pilgrimage to Mecca. To punish Shams al-Ma'ālī, the son-in-law who insulted her daughter, the queen dressed as a man and joined an army rescue team. In 1088, she besieged Shams's residence and exiled him.

1091

A Norman amazon, **Isabel of Conches (1047–April 24, 1102)** from Montfort in the western Pyrenees clasped herself in full armor to fight a Norman aristocrat, William of Evreux. In northern France, she bore the courtly traits of a chivalric knight. The 1091 battle involved other knights to settle a squabble between Helewise, William's wife, and Isabel, daughter of Simon de Montfort and wife of Raoul III de Tosny, governor of Conches. In the chronicle of English historian Orderic Vitalis, the combat details compared her to Camilla, the amazon in Virgil's *Aeneid*. Isabel's vigorous commitment to revenge resulted in a truce. She lived to age fifty-four and died in Flamsted, England.

March 18, 1091

Nine months before her death and burial in Canischio in the Italian Piedmont, at age seventy-seven, Countess **Adelaide of Turin and Susa** raided and burned Asti a second time for attempting to rid the diocese of Bishop Girlemo, whom Pope Nicholas II rejected. Her troops defied prelates and nobles who suspected her of overreaching against the papal party. Lost in the fire on March 18, 1091, was the eighth-century crypt and the abbey of Saint Anastasio, a cloister of Benedictine nuns. A niche in Susa's Cathedral of San Giusto honors the piety of "Adelheida Taurinensis comitissa" (Countess Adelaide of Turin).

See also 1070; June 1083.

October 1092

The accession of Pope Victor III and **Matilda of Tuscany** stanched a greedy clutch of Italian lands by besting Holy Roman Emperor Henry IV in October 1092 during his assault on Castle Canossa. She continued influencing dynastic marriages and controversies and restored her rule of Emilia, Lombardy, Romagna, and Tuscany. At her death after five years' reign as Italian viceroy, the Canossa dynasty ended from lack of heirs. Admirers revered her as "la Gran Contessa" (the Great Countess). Her memory survives in literature, music, and church architecture and art.

See also July 25, 1080; July 2, 1084.

August 1096

A dutiful Flemish crusader **Hadvide of Chiny (also Hadwida, Hedwig, or Halide, fl. 1096)**, wife of Dodo, a Walloon knight from Cons la Grandville, joined the campaigners of Godfrey of Bouillon, commander of the First Crusade. At the call of Pope Urban II in March 1095 to aid the Byzantines in Anatolia (modern Turkey), Godfrey led forty thousand soldiers from Lorraine. They marched from Flanders in August 1096 through Hungary, arriving in Constantinople in November. The regiment fought at Antioch, Dorylaeum, and Nicaea and at the capture of Jerusalem from Muslims. In thanks for the retrieval of the Holy Sepulcher and a safe return, in July 1099, she commemorated eighth-century saint Hubert en Ardenne with lavish vestments and a jeweled chalice.

Late August 1096

Anglo-Norman wife and campaigner **Edith de Warenne (also Ediva, 1075–1125)** of Oxfordshire, daughter of William I, earl of Surrey, accompanied her spouse Gerard of Gournay-en-Bray to the First Crusade to recover the Holy Lands from Muslims. The couple joined the armies of Hugh the Great, which departed in late August 1096 through the Alps to Rome and Bari in southeastern Italy. The company became the first to reach Constantinople. After Hugh was remanded to Constantinople in 1098, Edith and Gerard joined Robert Curthose of Normandy and his army along with one hundred knights repatriated from Hugh's assemblage. After giving birth to Hugues IV in 1098 on her return from Palestine, Edith was widowed near Yarmouth, Norfolk, at age fifty.

July 1, 1097

During the First Crusade, fourteen-year-old French princess **Florina of Bourgogne (1083–1097)** earned martyrdom at the battle of Philomelion in modern Akşehir, Turkey. A comrade of her husband, Danish prince Sweyn the Crusader Svendsen, she armed herself with battle axe and bow on July 1, 1097, and targeted Seljuk Turks on the road to Jerusalem. Guarded by fifteen hundred Danish knights, the couple incurred an ambush at Cappadocia, Anatolia (modern Nikea, Turkey) and pressed on to the mountains through all-day combat. Like their soldiers, husband and wife died of arrow wounds on the battlefield. Florina's persistence survives in art and fiction.

October 1097

A martyred Anglo-Norman crusader **Godehilde de Tosny (also Godehaut, 1081–October 1097)** of Conches, Seine-et-Marne, accompanied her husband Baldwin I of Lorraine to the First Crusade and contributed rents from her property to military upkeep. A scion of noteworthy warriors, she was the granddaughter of citadel builder Simon I de Montfort and the daughter of Raoul III, a veteran of the battle of Hastings. The company left for the Holy Lands in 1096 and reached Heraclaeon on the Black Sea. On the route to Germanicea, Cilicia, on the southeastern coast, in October 1097, at age sixteen, she died of illness at Maraş in central Turkey.

May 20, 1098

French campaigner **Humberge of Le Puiset (1065–1099)** joined her husband Guion de Chaumont (Walo II), viscount of Beaumont-sur-Oise, and brother Everard III, viscount of Chartres, France, in marching to the First Crusade with the army of Hugh the Great. Named for her paternal grandmother, she pledged Christian service in 1095 and accompanied Guion to the successful siege of Nicaea on May 14, 1097. At age thirty-three, on May 20, 1098, she was widowed at the siege of Antioch, Turkey, by the troops of Kerbogha, ruler of Mosul. According to Robert the Monk's history of the First Crusade, because Muslims and their dogs dismembered Guion, she grieved in the extreme and fell dead. On August 21, 1099, her brother Everard died after the capture of Jerusalem from Muslims.

June 28, 1098

On the route from the Pyrenees in southwestern France to the Holy Lands, **Emeline of Bouillon (fl. late 1090s)**, the wife of Fulbert (or Fulcher) of Bouillon, accompanied her husband among the twenty thousand Norman, Flemish, and French troops of Godfrey of Bouillon, commander of the First Crusade. The company left Lorraine in August 1096 and, at Constantinople, formed an army of five thousand five hundred foot soldiers and eight thousand cavalry. At the battle of Antioch on June 28, 1098, Seljuk Turk archers on horseback under command of Kerbogha of Mosul pelted the Frankish regiments with arrows. Both Emeline and Fulbert died by decapitation in Muslim custody at the strategic city of A'zaz, Syria.

ca. 1100

Because Nedega, king of the Mossi, reared the legendary princess **Yennenga (also Yennega, fl. 1100)** among warriors, she formed a cavalry battalion that joined his forces to defend Dagamba (modern Burkina Faso). A skilled rider in the Volta River basin in northwestern Africa, she excelled with bow, javelin, and spear and at pillaging enemy grain. Nedega jailed her for complaining about celibacy, but his security guard aided her escape by outfitting her with men's clothes. In the forest during the night, she overwhelmed the Malinke Muslims from Mali and became her nation's warrior queen. The Mossi declared Yennenga mother of the people for founding a royal dynasty. Her name survives in street names, statues, and a cinema award.

June 22, 1101

Italian countess and first female monarch of Sicily after the death of her first husband, Roger I, on June 22, 1101, **Adelaide del Vasto (1074–April 16, 1118)** put down revolts in Sicily and Calabria. Norman author Orderic Vitalis and Italian historian Alexander of Telese described her militance as severe and backed by military force. In her final rule, she wed Baldwin of Jerusalem and became queen consort of Jerusalem. To the First Crusade, she donated cash, Muslim bowmen, and one thousand Sicilian troops. Because Baldwin dishonored and mistreated her through bigamy, her son, Roger II, withdrew his assistance to the Second Crusade.

September 17, 1101

To redeem the Holy Lands from the Muslims, French campaigner **Corba of Thorigne (fl. 1101)**, from western France participated in the First Crusade before vanishing from history. Twice widowed, she married Geoffrey Burel of Amboise. In May 1101, the couple journeyed to Constantinople with the army of William IX of Aquitaine. After Geoffrey's death on September 17, 1101, at the battle of Heraclea, Cappadocia (modern Turkey), Turkish Sultan Kilij Arslan I of Rum ambushed and massacred Christian troops. The enemy enslaved or executed one hundred thousand European knights and abducted Corba. A fellow crusader, **Ida of Austria (1055–September 1101)**, leader of her own troops toward Jerusalem, died in the battle near Iconium (modern Konya, Turkey) possibly after being pushed from her litter and trampled.

1102

A parturient crusader, **Elvira of Leon-Castile (1082–1151)** of Toledo, Spain, daughter of Alfonso VI of León and Castile and countess of Toulouse, observed preparations to besiege the Seljuk Turks at Tripoli in 1102. In October 1096 during the First Crusade, she traveled to Dyrrhachium (also Durazzo, modern Durres, Albania) east of Constantinople with her husband Raymond IV of St. Gilles and his three hundred men. To stymy the enemy from seeking inland reinforcements, Raymond erected a citadel at Mount Peregrinus (modern Lebanon). At Mount Pèlerin, Tripoli, in the second year of the assault in 1103, she produced their son Alfonso Jordan, named for his baptism in the River Jordan. In widowhood after Raymond died at the siege of Tripoli, Palestine, on February 18, 1105, she returned to Castile, where she married Fernando Fernandez of Toledo.

July 12, 1109

Holy Lands crusader **Helie of Burgundy (also Ala, Alix, or Haelie de Bourgogne, 1080–February 28, 1141)**, a native of Dijon, France, joined the seven-year siege of Tripoli, a valuable Lebanese port on the Mediterranean. At age fifteen, she wed Bertrand of Toulouse, who mortgaged his property to fund a campaign led by William IX of Aquitaine. Their expedition departed France for Outremer in 1108. An armada from Genoa, Pisa, and Provençal assisted in snatching the city from Fakhr al-Mulk Radwan, Seljuk sultan of Aleppo on July 12, 1109. Bertrand's nephew, William II Jordan, died of an arrow to the heart, leaving control of Tripoli, the fourth crusader state, to Helie's husband. Bertrand ruled until his death three years later, when fourteen-year-old Pons, their only child, succeeded him. Pons died in combat at Tripoli in 1137. Helie remarried and bore twelve more children.

October 26, 1111

Europe's first queen regnant, **Urraca of Zamore (1079–March 8, 1126)**, the empress of Spain and ruler of León, Castile and Galicia, inflicted armed combat against an abusive husband, her second cousin Alfonso I of Aragon. Her father, Alfonso VI, arranged the political marriage without her consent. The groom intimidated her by humiliating and kicking her in public and by garrisoning towns in Castile and León with Aragonese forces. Pitting the Leonese-Castillians against the Aragonese on October 26, 1111, the battle of Candespina near Sepulveda in north central Spain resulted in the death of Urraca's lover, military tactician Gomez Gonzalez. The truce of 1112 ended civil war and the royal relationship with annulment declared by Pope Paschal II. Hostilities continued until her death in childbirth at age forty-seven with a child sired by a subsequent lover.

1116

Welsh warrior princess **Gwenllian ferch Gruffydd (1100–1136)** abetted her husband's lightning raids against Norman invaders. After eloping and marrying Prince Gruffydd ap Rhys of Deheubarth in 1116, at age sixteen, she joined him in mountain strongholds during attacks on Carmarthen, Cydweli (modern Kidwelly), and Swansea castles. The couple distributed loot in the Welsh back country to peasants who lost land to Norman colonists. During his 1136 revolt against Norman insurgents, Gwenllian commanded a few hundred forces against Maurice de Londres at Cydweli, where Chief Gruffydd ap Llewelyn betrayed her hiding place.

At her arrest, Gwenllian and twenty-year-old son Morgan died of decapitation, leaving motherless two infants, Rhys and Sion, ages four and two. The Normans also executed seventeen-year-old Maelgwn ap Gruffydd. In vengeance for his family, her husband inflicted crop and herd damage and, in October 1136, routed the enemy at Crug Mawr outside Cardigan, killing three thousand Normans. The Welsh respected Gwenllian's boldness and compared it to that of Boudicca. Legends report her ghost haunting the battlefield.

See also 61 CE.

Mid–February 1119

In a bitter fight with her father, Henry I of England, in mid–February 1119, **Juliane de Fontevrault (also Julianna FitzRoy of Breteuil, 1090—after 1136)**, one of his eighteen illegitimate children, declared war on him for blinding her two daughters and cropping their noses. A noble by birth at Westminster, she led knights to Breteuil in northern central France to secure its heavily reinforced citadel and attacked Henry from the battlements with a bolt from her crossbow. Local citizens sided with Henry and unlocked the gates for him. His immurement of Juliane in the castle caused her to maneuver down from one of the five towers, swim the freezing moat, and escape to her husband's stronghold at Pacy west of Paris. The father-daughter fracture forced her to plead for mercy, surrender Breteuil, and shelter at Fontevrault Abbey.

June 28, 1119

A Norman adviser following the First Crusade, **Cecilia of Le Bourcq (?–after 1126)**, possessor of Cilician lands, outlined tactics to save Antioch (modern Antakya, Turkey). To aid her husband, Roger of Salerno, she strategized defenses, which he reclaimed after the earthquake of November 29, 1114, in the Dead Sea fault. Seljuk Turkish Commander Ilghazi of Mardin staged an assault on Ager Sanguinis (the Field of Blood) near Sarmada Pass, Syria, on June 28, 1119. The conflict pitted twenty thousand Muslims against four thousand two hundred Christians.

Ilghazi dragged his European conquests in chains through Aleppo and tortured them in the streets. Roger was killed along with most of his three thousand infantry, seven hundred knights, and five hundred Armenian cavalry. Cecilia's brother, Baldwin II of Jerusalem, assumed the regency of Antioch and retaliated against Ilghazi on August 14, 1119, at the battle of Hab, Syria.

July 17, 1119

The disgruntled regent of Flanders, **Clementia of Burgundy (also Clemence de Bourgogne-Comté, 1078–1133)** from Champagne-Ardenne, France, led forces against King Charles the Good of Denmark, who replaced her son Baldwin VII as ruler. After 1096, she dedicated herself to stemming attacks on the devout at Bapaume in northern France on pilgrimages over the Lombard Way between Canterbury and Rome. After the death of her husband Robert II in combat at Meaux on October 5, 1111, and Count Baldwin's lethal wounding in September 1118 at the Norman battle of Bures-en-Bray, Charles succeeded to the county. Clementia's aggressive repudiation of Charles derived from her preference for a nephew, William of Ypres. She gathered fighters to combat Charles's seizure of four of her twelve inherited towns stretching from Bapaume and Douai to Lille. For the next fourteen years, she continued ruling the remaining eight towns and protesting the four losses.

New Year's Eve, 1129

A Chinese archer and general during the Jin-Song wars, **Liang Hongyu (1102–1135)** commanded Song soldiers alongside her husband, General Han Shizhong of the Song army. Her father instructed her in martial arts and soldiery. Han, a thirty-seven-year career soldier, engineered improved chain mail, bows, and training courses for archery and horse jumping. During Hun insurgencies, she commanded eight thousand troops against one hundred thousand enemy. Her meticulous use of flags and drums enabled a Song coup.

Emperor Gaozong rewarded Liang a noble rank for eluding captors and aiding General Han in overwhelming rebels. Renewed warfare at Hangzhou on New Year's Eve 1129 motivated her to signal with drum beats at the battle of

Huangtiandang northeast of Nanking. Betrayal cost the Song a win and, on April 8, 1130, possession of Hangzhou, but the enemy suffered heavy casualties.

Late June 1139

A defender of a west country home and family in Devizes, England, in the anarchic years following the death of King Henry I, **Matilda of Ramsbury (1085–?)** shielded the Bishop's Castle from capture. The Wiltshire property northwest of Salisbury was the residence of her lover, Roger, the Norman Bishop of Salisbury, King Henry's former lord chancellor. Under attack by King Stephen's army in late June 1139, she held the wood stronghold and palisades with concentric ditches for three days before yielding. Stephen blackmailed her by plotting to hang the bishop and their son, Lord Chancellor Roger le Poer, and nephew, Bishop Nigel of Ely, both of whom Stephen displayed in chains before the gallows. At the bishop's release, Roger le Poer entered exile in June. The bishop died on December 11, 1139.

September 30, 1139

For eighteen years, the Empress **Matilda (also Maud, February 7, 1102–September 10, 1167)** of Winchester warred against her usurper cousin Stephen of Blois for the English throne. The Anglo-Scots widow of Holy Roman Emperor Henry V and heir of Henry I of England, she invaded England at Arundel on September 30, 1139, with the aid of her son, fourteen-year-old Henry II. Stephen trapped her at Arundel Castle and pursued a southwestern campaign at Wallingford and Trowbridge castles. After imprisoning Stephen at Bristol Castle in February 1141, Matilda lost popularity with Londoners for her haughty demeanor. In defeat, she departed Oxford Castle at Christmas 1142 and retreated to Normandy, home of her second husband, Geoffrey V of Anjou. Her succession quandary filled historical fiction, chronicles, film, and drama.

December 24, 1144

A cradle crusader, Jerusalem's Queen **Melisende of Edessa (1105–September 11, 1161)** posted troops to the besieged state of Edessa northeast of Antioch, Syria. After four weeks, on December 24, 1144, the entrenched region fell to Seljuk commander Imad al-Din Zengi of Mosul. He slew thousands and sold women and children as slaves. Melisende begged the newly crowned pope Eugene III to promote the Second Crusade, advocated by evangelist Bernard of Clairvaux and led by Louis VII of France. She advised the capture of Aleppo as a beginning of retrieving Edessa (modern Urfa, Turkey). After mediating hostilities with her son, Baldwin III, she died of a stroke at age fifty-six. English historian William II of Tyre praised her wisdom and control of state affairs.

March 1147

An Almoravid defender of Marrakesh during a religious war, the Muslim princess **Fannu (?–April 1147)**, a Sanhaja Berber, risked all in challenging a force that plunged down from the Atlas Mountains of Morocco. Her enemy, Abd-al Mumin, an Almohad conqueror, had already succeeded at Fez, Oran, Seville, and Tlemcen in his plan to control southern Iberia and North Africa. Part of his strategy was the smearing of Almoravid morality, particularly the unveiled faces of aggressive Berber women. Dressed in men's clothing and armor, Fannu, still a virgin, extended personal endangerment in March 1147 in the line of fire at the Almoravid palace walls for days until her death in combat. The loss ended the Almoravid dynasty in favor of the Almohad caliphate, which dominated the culture, faith, and commerce of the Maghreb.

January 6, 1148

With her first husband, King Louis VII of France, **Eleanor of Aquitaine (also Aliénor, 1122–April 1, 1204)** of Poitiers accompanied his troops on the Second Crusade to retake Edessa, Jerusalem, and Aleppo from the Muslims. Urged by her uncle, Raymond of Antioch, and the popular evangelist Bernard of Clairvaux, at the Cité Palace in Paris, she recruited female campaigners: **Faydide of Toulouse (1110–1154)** and **Sibylla of Anjou (1112–1165)**, the pillager of Hainaut. Departing Vezelay, France, in June 1147, the three crusaders traveled by horseback and boat to fight the Saracens for two years.

On Christmas Eve, Eleanor and the vanguard camped near Ephesus and took a treacherous route to the Christian city of Laodicea (modern Denizli, Turkey) and up Mount Cadmus in Phrygia to Antioch. On the way, on January 6, 1148, the French battled Turk raiders commanded by Sultan Mesud I, whose men slaughtered seven thousand crusaders in the rear guard and killed the king's horse. On January 20, Eleanor and Louis booked a sea passage from Antalia to Antioch near the Syro-Turkish border. Ired by a royal quarrel, he ordered her arrest and transfer to Jerusalem. After they returned to France in 1149, she secured an annulment of their marriage in March 1152 on the grounds of consanguinity.

August 25, 1170

After marriage to Robert "Strongbow" de Clare of Pembroke, **Eva of Leinster (also Aolfe MacMurrough, 1145–1189)**, an Irish aristocrat, devoted her adult life to protecting the Leinster realm. As stated in the anonymous *La Geste des Engleis en Yrlande* (The Deeds of the English in Ireland), Dermot MacMurrough treasured her as his daughter and arranged a stable financial future for Strongbow, who imported Norman strength into a failing district. His properties included English manors in Essex and Hertfordshire, Welsh estates, and Kilkenny Castle on the River Nore, which he built to celebrate their union. Her inheritance centered on Ferns, her father's patrimony at Wexford on Ireland's southeastern coast.

Preceding her wedding on August 25, 1170, Normans overwhelmed Waterford and slaughtered two Viking strongmen. Henry II canceled Strongbow's possession of Pembroke and Norman properties. Strongbow retaliated by pressing armies to Dublin, where she joined him in the fray. More campaigns took the couple across Ireland and to France. She was left with small daughter Isabella and toddler Gilbert at Strongbow's death from a foot injury on April 20, 1176, but she refused to remarry. By commanding her own regiment, Eva claimed as "swordland" (contested territory) the districts she conquered, notably Strigoil Castle in Chepstow, Wales, in 1183. Her belligerence kept Henry II from stripping Strigoil of assets and forced him to pay her a commander's portion. She ruled Leinster until her death at age forty-four.

1171

As a wife of the energetic Hoysalan emperor Veera Ballala II, General **Umadevi (1149–1220)** from Mysore (modern Mysura, India) enabled her husband to attain the throne. In her early twenties, she fought feudal revolts and led his armies against the Chalukyas while the emperor campaigned to the north. Territorial contentions kept the empire in constant campaigns. She achieved victory in 1171 over Kavadeva, the ruler of Goa. As a result, the emperor annexed Hangal, a city passed back and forth between the Hoysala and Chalky.

In 1190, the imperial military humiliated Chalukya king Someshvara VI at Kalyani (modern Bidar in south central India), increasing conquests to the Krishna River in the north. To the south, Umadevi administered imperial business from Halebidu, Karnataka. More glory in 1196 preceded loss of war trophies in 1212 and a military resurgence in 2016. At the emperor's death in 1220, Umadevi chose the widow's custom of *sati* (self-immolation).

August 1172

To support French king Louis VII, **Ermengarde of Narbonne (1120– October 12, 1197)** commanded Provençal forces against England's Henry II. During the Second Crusade, she had served as a mediator of feudal disputes and began her military actions on July 1, 1148. Against the Count Alphonse Jordan of Toulouse, who attempted to seize her holdings, she backed Raymond Berengar IV of Barcelona at the seven-month siege of Tortosa.

More field combat ensued at peasant revolts and at Les Baux in early August 1172. The five-year clash between Henry II and Louis VII ended at Ivry on September 13, 1177, with a nonaggression pact. In 1183, Ermengarde led her garrison at the siege of Puy-Saint-Front with Henry and his Plantagenet heir, Henry the Young King. The youth died of dysentery during a campaign against his brother, Richard the Lionheart.

March 1173

At the siege of Aucona (or Ancona), an Adriatic port in east central Italy, fifty-four-year-old General **Alrude Frangipane (1120–1185),** countess of Bertinoro, backed the troops of Pope Alexander III with military action. In her thirties, she managed the inheritance of her young sons Cavalcaconte and Rainerio, named for her husband, Rainerio di Cavalcaconte. Her charge in March 1173 at age fifty-three ended the seven-month assault on Aucona. According to the writings of Byzantine emperor Manuel Komnenos and Italian historian Boncompagno da Signa, she and her co-commander, Guglielmo

Marchesella, put to flight thirteen hundred Brabantines and Germans, the imperial forces of Holy Roman Emperor Frederick I Barbarossa, led by Mainz archbishop and ambassador Christian I. Barbarossa's fifth Italian campaign ended disastrously in 1176, when he made peace with Alexander.

April 1173

The aristocratic Norman wife of Robert de Beaumont, the earl of Leicester, **Petronilla of Leicester (1123–April 1, 1212)** assisted him in an eighteen-month uprising against Henry II. In support of Queen Eleanor of Aquitaine and her eighteen-year-old son Young Henry, the disgruntled heir apparent and hobby tournament knight, in April 1173, Petronilla backed Robert's hiring of three thousand Flemish mercenaries for the invasion of Normandy. In the Anglo-Norman verse history of Jordan Fantosme, the campaign halted at Fornham when siege plans collapsed at the River Lark in Suffolk.

Robert resumed the fight at Walton on October 17, 1173, when Henry's troops burned the town and besieged Leicester Castle, a motte-and-bailey complex. Royal pursuers, led by Richard de Lucy, dispersed horsemen and hirelings from the River Lark to the marshlands. Petronilla protected herself in combat by wearing mail tunic and armor and carrying sword and shield, but she had to flee captors by crouching in an irrigation ditch. While Robert remained in a cell until January 1174, she managed family financial affairs for her five children until his demise in 1190 during the Third Crusade. She continued leading the household at the fortified castle of Breteuil in Yvelines, Normandy, until her death at age eighty-nine.

February 21, 1184

At the start of the Samurai era, horse breaker, scout, and crossbow and sword expert **Tomoe Gozen (1157–fl. 1180s)** of Heida backed her lover, late Heian general Minamoto no Yoshinaka, in his fatal battle at Awazu, Japan. Part of clan conflict during the Genpei civil war of 1180, the assault, as recorded in the anonymous epic *Heike Monogatari* (Tale of the Heike), began with a pivotal approach to the front gate of the Taira garrison at Ichinotani, Suma Ward, in south central Japan. For battle with two thousand enemy on February 21, 1184, the widowed paladin wore medieval armor and bore man-sized weapons.

Tomoe's slaying of Samurai Uchida Ieyoshi and flight from seizure by Samurai Hatakeyama no Shigetada of the Taira clan resulted in an amazing decapitation of Hatakeyama by hand on horseback and the belittling of the era's strongmen. Although wounded in the ankle, she commanded three hundred samurai who subjugated the Tairo clan and captured Kyoto. Episodes became high points of Japanese history on stage and in novels, manga, anime, storytelling, art, monuments, festivals, and video games. Wonder tales depicted her crushing a pine trunk into splinters.

1185

A warrior-wife during the five-year Genpei civil war, **Hojo Masako (1156–August 16, 1225)** of Izu Province in western Japan aided her husband in successful battles between the Taira and Minamoto clans. She trained in horse management like her younger brothers Munetoki and Hojo Yoshitoki and chose to eat at the men's table. In 1177, she wed shogun Minamoto no Yoritomo of Kamakura in south central Japan. As the victor over the Taira clan at the battle of Dan-no-Ura in 1185 in the straits of Shimonoseki between Honshu and Kyūshū, Minamoto welcomed his wife to an estate in Okura Valley.

The clan elevated Masako to second rank in the warrior class in 1192 and named Yoritomo feudal shogun. At his death at Kamakura on February 9, 1199, Masako acted as regent for their two surviving sons. She joined a Buddhist convent and received the honorific of nun-shogun. The war authorized the Taira and Minamoto colors on Japan's red and white standards. Eiko Kooke played the role of Masako in the 2022 historical television drama *The 13 Lords of the Shogun*.

September 9, 1187

A cross-bearing Cistercian nun from Palestine who took part in the Third Crusade, **Margaret of Beverley (1150–1215)**, a nun at the French abbey of Montreuil-sous-Laon east of Paris, campaigned for reclamation of the Holy Lands at the fifteen-day siege of Jerusalem. Preceding the Sunni sultan Saladin's invasions after his attainment of Hattin in the Levant (modern Israel) on July 4, 1187, while defending Jerusalem's walls, she endured battle wounds from a fragmented stone mill wheel on Michaelmas, September 9, 1187. Armed with a breastplate and a cookpot on her head for a helmet, she hurled projectiles and eased the thirst and hunger of soldiers.

Margaret's resilience expressed her Christian faith. Capture by victorious Muslims resulted in fifteen months of prison hauling rocks and hewing wood until her ransom on February 2, 1189. The fight to recover Christian territory from Saladin continued on July 29, 1188, at Antioch (modern Antakya) on the Turkish-Syrian border, where she looted a knife from the enemy dead. Following another incarceration at Tripoli, she ended her volunteer soldiery at Acre in mid-1191. In August 1192, Saladin acknowledged the Christian dominance of Palestine from Jaffa to Tyre and the access of pilgrims to Jerusalem.

Summer 1189

Following the Genpei clan war in the Heian period, the wife of samurai Kajiwara Genda Kagesue, **Fujinoye (also Fujinoe, fl. 1180s)** protected Takadachi Castle at Hiraizumi during a siege of Mutsu Province in northern Japan by Lord Minamoto no Yoritama. In her husband's absence, in summer 1189, Fujinoye armed herself with *naginata* (halberd) and samurai sword and fought enemy archers ascending stairs one by one. Her combat poem records her slaying of two warriors, Yemoto Juro and Nagasawa Uyemon-taro. The series *One Hundred and Eight Heroes* by Japanese author Kuniyoshi pictures the woman warrior with hair flying at the stairway clash. A seventeenth-century ballad drama and a nineteenth-century painting exalted Minamoto's three battalions, which seized the castle and its domain.

1198

A fierce Welsh chatelaine at Elfael of Pain's Castle at Hay-on-Wye, Wales, **Maud de Braose (also Lady of Hay and Matilda de St. Valery, 1150–August 9, 1210)** protected her property against Welsh prince Gwenwynwyn, ruler of Powys. While her husband, William III de Braose, campaigned in Normandy, Maud's verbal slur incited enmity with Gwenwynwyn. Hostility ended in 1198 when Yorkshire sheriff Geoffrey fitz Peter's army overwhelmed Gwenwynwyn and rescued Maud. During the revolt of England's barons, to ensure her loyalty, in April 1208, King John demanded her sons William and Giles as hostages. She retorted that John was not reliable at guarding relatives in view of his murder of his nephew Arthur of Brittany.

After capturing the de Braose properties, King John pursued Maud and her sons William IV de Braose and Bishop Giles de Braose to Trim Castle in County Meath, Ireland. In a twenty-one day siege at Meath, the English attackers lost three thousand troops. After Giles escaped to France in May 1208, Maud took her eldest son William and fled by ship to the Isle of Man and Scotland. The pair were captured at Galloway in southwestern Scotland and returned in shackles to England. Overwhelmed by loss of heir and wife, William III, disguised as a beggar, exiled himself in France and died in Paris of grief.

In July 1210, King John jailed Maud and son William IV at Carrickfergus Castle at Antrim on the Belfast Lough. He moved the pair to Windsor Castle, then to Corfe Castle in Dorset overlooking the English Channel. After eleven days in a bricked-up cell, Maud and Willam died of starvation at the Corfe dungeon. Outrage at the atrocity on June 15, 1215, forced the king to pledge in the Magna Carta that no citizen should suffer outlawry, exile, or prison without a trial. For chewing her son's face to ease hunger, Maud retains interest in fiction and legend for cannibalism.

1199

According to the *Chronicle of Guillaume de Puylaurens*, **Joan of England and Sicily (also Joanna, October 1165–September 4, 1199)** from Anjou sought revenge on the maligners of her husband by besieging Les Cassés in southern France. The Plantagenet daughter of Eleanor of Aquitaine and Henry II and sister of Richard I the Lion-Heart, she descended from William I the Conqueror. Joan survived house arrest in Palermo in 1189 and shipwreck and residence on Cyprus and Acre during the Third Crusade in 1199, and attacked the lords of Saint-Felix southwest of Geneva at Les Casses to redeem the reputation of her second husband, Raymond VI of Toulouse. After traitors burned her encampment, she died at Rouen before the caesarian birth of her stillborn son Richard.

1199

At the conclusion of the Heian period, samurai commander **Hangaku Gozen (also Itagaki, fl. 1190s–1200s)** of the Taira clan in Echigo in northern Japan led three thousand fighters from the Torizakayama Castle. She developed a reputation as an archer and swordswoman and armed herself with the *naginata* (halberd), an effective weapon against cavalry since the early 700s. A warrior's daughter, in 1199, she headed regiments during a three-month siege by the Kamakura shogunate army. She faced ten thousand Hojo backers and killed many by sweeping the blade against horse legs.

During the Kennin Revolt against a feudal government in February 1201, the female samurai and archer defended Torisaka Castle south of Takada Plain. Her accuracy with a bow tended to transfix attackers with arrows to head or torso. Her soldiers held the moated, clay-walled castle measuring fifty by twenty meters (1000 square meters or 3281 square feet) and camped on internal terraces. In men's attire, she chose a defensive post on the turret storehouse roof, setting an example of courage for three thousand men against ten thousand enemy. At her wounding by an arrow to the thigh, she came under the power of Shogun Minamoto, who forced her to continue surviving rather than give in to ceremonial suicide. At Kamakura, she wed Asari Yoshito, the Genji warrior who saved her life.

July 27, 1202

In a marital power struggle, Queen **Tamara of Georgia (also Tamar, 1160–January 18, 1213)** mastered and exiled her avaricious husband, Prince Yuri Bogolyubskoi. The daughter of King George III, she grew up in the Caucasus east of the Black Sea and shared her father's rule at age eighteen. After quelling two attempts at usurpation, she became Tamar the Great for securing a profitable trade zone and wine distribution center between the Caspian and Black seas. Her armies controlled earthworks in the Ararat Plain after she rallied sixty-five thousand troops to fight the battle of Basiani on July 27, 1202, against ninety-five thousand Muslims. Her martial plans advanced toward Trebizond, which she seized as a bulwark against southern Turks.

1211

After the death of her husband, Alaqush Digit Quri, the chief son of Alaqush Tegin, in 1211, military strategist **Alakhai Bekhi (1191–1247)**, daughter of Borte Ujin, the first wife of Mongol conqueror Genghis Khan, suppressed a revolt among in-laws of the Turkic Ongud, a semi-nomadic tribe. Because the rebels tried to assassinate her as well as her husband, she supplied the khan's forces with rations and horses. After escaping the Ongud, a Mongol people in the Gobi Desert, with her two stepsons, the widowed princess intervened in the execution of tribe members and legitimized the killing of only Alaqush's assassins.

Alakhai remarried to Alaqush's nephew Jingue and in 1221 to her husband's son Boyache. As regent for several young princes, until 1246, she governed her father's Chinese territories. Her grandfather, Genghis Khan, gave her the name "the princess who rules the state." Her example influenced her nephew, Kublai Khan, founder of the Yuan dynasty.

May 3, 1211

At the death of Guilhem Pierre de Lavaur during the Albigensian Crusade, his widow, **Guiraude de Lavaur (also Gerauda or Giralda de Laurac, ?–May 3, 1211),** defended her lands east of Toulouse from the onslaught of three bishops of Bayeux, Lisieux, and Toulouse and Simon IV de Montfort, a crusader and besieger of the Carcassonne in 1209. Charged with Cathar heresy for believing in dual gods of good and evil, Guiraude and her brother, Aimeric de Montreal, with four hundred townsmen and eighty knights held their ground from late March for four weeks by tunneling under the castle walls. According to Provençal writer William of Tudela, she surrendered Lavaur Castle on May 3, 2011, after a breach weakened the rampart. Simon burned Aimery and four hundred Cathars, hanged the knights, and crushed Guiraude's remains with stones after jettisoning her into a well.

1214

Amid the border clashes among the Chinese, Jurchen of Manchuria, and Genghis Khan's Mongols between Shandong and the Yangzi River, **Yang Miaozhen (1193–1250),** an adept archer, dueler, and rider from Yidu's peasant class, succeeded her deceased older brother Yang An'er in 1214 and commanded his ten thousand bandits to conflicts in the south. While her husband, smuggler and rebel Li Quan, campaigned against a series of rebels and Mongol raiders, Yang Miaozhen kept peace at her headquarters in Huai'an (modern Huaiyin) near the East China Sea and aided his skirmishes. Widowed by a Song assault at Yangzhou in early 1231, she consolidated an army from her bandits and his troops. To quell the Song, according to the Chinese chronicle *Song Shi* (History of Song), she united her warriors with the Mongols, governed Shandong, and passed her power to her son, Li Tan. A dramatist commemorated Yang Miaozhen with a spear and double swords in the play *Shui hu Zhuan* (The Water Margin), one of China's four great classical novels.

October 18, 1216

In widowhood during the Barons' War against King John, hereditary Constable **Nicola de la Haye (also Nicholaa de la Haie, 1150–November 20, 1230)** from Swaton in Lincolnshire fought English rebels and their French allies on October 18, 1216, when besieged Lincoln Castle, a royalist stronghold. During a forty-day assault, her regiment grappled with three hundred soldiers, thirty knights, and twenty cavalry. Meanwhile, forty sappers worked at destabilizing the castle walls. On May 20, 2017, William Marshal, the king's guardian, and his six hundred fifty infantry and archers ended a subsequent siege by taking the castle gate and routing the enemy.

Nicola's garrison seized half the rebels without excess loss of life. When King John approached Lincoln Castle, she humbly offered him the keys. As his reward for loyalty, he appointed Nicola sheriff of Lincolnshire on October 18, 1216. Throughout further attempts to capture Lincoln Castle, for the next decade, she held the post of sheriff until her retirement at age seventy-six.

May 20, 1217

To claim the English monarchy for her husband, Louis VIII of France, during the First Barons' War, **Blanche of Castile (March 4, 1188–November 27, 1252)** raised an army and two armadas at the French port of Calais. The death of King John of England unsettled the English barons, who had gained strength over monarchy at the signing of the Magna Carta on June 15, 1215. Despite the deaths of a daughter and twin sons, Blanche received no help from her father-in-law, Philip II Augustus. With the aid of pirate mercenary Eustace the Monk, she battled for her three-year-old son Louis's inheritance. At her army's rout at Lincoln Castle, on May 20, 1217, destruction of Mountsorrel Castle on the Soar River, and the collapse of her navy at Dover on the English Channel on August 24, 1217, her husband Louis ceded his right to England's crown.

To ensure the succession of their son as Louis IX, Blanche made concessions of land, but came under attack from the barons while journeying outside Paris. She hid the boy at Montlhéry Castle in north central France. During battles, she collected wood for camp fires. On three occasions, she mustered more troops and, in January 1229, compelled the barons to recognize Louis IX as king. For her determination, the French named her "Dame Hersent," the wolf in Renard the fox stories.

While Louis fought Muslims in the Seventh Crusade in Africa, Egypt, and the Middle East, Blanche led raids on French prisons and freed poor men. Her deeds appear in the *Miroir de l'âme* (The Soul's Reflection), written by a Cistercian nun, and *Chronica Majora* (Major History) by Matthew Paris. Poet François Villon listed her in *Ballade des Dames du Temps Jadis* (Ballad of Ladies in Past Times); William Shakespeare featured her in the drama *King John*.

Fall 1226

In Mongol conqueror Genghis Khan's last campaign, his Tatar wife **Yesui Khatun (fl. 1220s)** rode with him on a vengeful expedition southward to Tangut in central China. Progressing over the Helan Range bordering Mongolia in fall 1226, the northern army crushed Emperor Mo's three hundred thousand troops, devastated the capital of Ning Hia, and pillaged Lingzhou in November 1226. The six-month Mongol offensive continued until the Khan's lethal fall from a horse at age seventy-two and infection with bubonic plague, which Yesui treated. During his fevered last days, she concealed her control of the military and government of the Tangut empire. He rewarded her with the Tuul River, a sacred link of central Mongolia to the north. The campaign continued with Mo's surrender, murder of his dynasty, and the Mongol genocide in Western Xia.

November 1236

Delhi's only female Mamluk ruler, **Razia Sultana (?–October 15, 1240)** relied on military control to secure a pre-modern Islamic throne in India for less than four years. She acquired administrative expertise in 1231 when her father, Sultan Shamsuddin Iltutmish, left his eldest daughter to rule while he besieged Gwalior in north central India for eleven months on behalf of an Islamic theocracy. Because of her manly spirit, on October 10, 1236, he named her as his successor at Lahore. The choice generated hatred in her stepmother, Shah Turkan, who plotted to murder Razia and replace her with Turkan's sybaritic son Raknuddin Firoz Shah. Delhi subjects rejected Raknuddin because he doted on his elephant corps and their servant-class keepers.

Following a dynastic bloodbath, in November 1236, Razia led the Delhi army in seizing conspirators at prayer and jailing them. Travel writer Ibn Battuta described her at Delhi, dressed in male cap, tunic, and robe. She abandoned female veil and purdah, strapped on a sword and bow and quiver, and commanded an army that put down rebels. On April 3, 1240, a new faction imprisoned and executed her on October 15 at Kaithal. Her biographic 1983 film preserved a unique woman sultan, played by Hema Malini.

August 25, 1248

Magistra Hersend (fl. 1249–1299), a French surgeon, served Louis IX of France as royal physician and army medical adviser from departure on August 25, 1248, throughout the Seventh Crusade. Until 1254, the cavalcade journeyed to Sardinia and Limassol and Nicosia, Cyprus, where Beatrice of Provence gave birth. During the eight-month layover, disease killed five crucial knights from November 1248 to January 1249. With fifteen thousand infantry, three thousand knights, and five thousand archers, the party moved on in summer 1249 to Acre in the Jerusalem kingdom and through Syria to the port of Damietta, Egypt.

From March 16, 1250, the treatment of malnutrition, typhoid, tuberculosis, and dysentery slowed the campaign. With the aide of the royal apothecary, Hersend tended women in the entourage, including Queen Margaret of Provence, who was pregnant with son John. Both Margaret and her sister Beatrice recuperated from parturition at Acre. In August 1250, Hersend received a sizable pension of 84¢ a week. Artist Judy Chicago honored Hersend with a place at *The Dinner Party*.

See also June 6, 1249.

June 6, 1249

The only women to lead a crusade, **Margaret of Provence (1221–December 20, 1295)** from Forcalquier in the French Alps was pregnant with her sixth child, John Tristan of Valois, during the June 6, 1249, siege of Damietta, Egypt, against North African Muslims. Her companion, her younger sister **Beatrice of Provence (1229–September 23, 1267)**, also bore a short-lived son on the march at Nicosia, Cyprus, and a second child, Blanche, at Damietta. Margaret boosted the army's morale after the loss of al-Mansurah on February 8, 1250, and mediated a settlement. Because of the capture of Margaret's husband, Louis IX, on February 8, 1250, she negotiated for his release at Acre, capital of the kingdom of Jerusalem. According to noted French historian Jean de Joinville, she raised a ransom of rations and 400,000 silver *livres* and surrendered Damietta. Beatrice maintained martial control of Rome after her crowning as queen of Sicily and Naples on January 6, 1266. In widowhood in 1270, Margaret maintained dependence on a personal militia.

February 8–11, 1250

At the physical decline of her husband, As-Salih Ayyub, on February 8, 1250, Sultana **Shajar al-Durr** (?–April 28, 1257), a former Armenian slave and concubine, took charge on February 8–11, 1250, of defending Egypt against the crusaders of Louis IX of France and Pope Innocent IV. Proceeding from Cyprus to Damietta, Egypt, on the Nile Delta east of Alexandria, the Frankish invaders met with her guerrilla tactics and fell into her trap at al-Mansurah. To maintain soldier morale, she concealed the sultan's death. At the capture of Louis and the death of his brother, Robert I d'Artois, and all but five of the two hundred ninety Knights Templar, a plague epidemic further reduced crusader strength.

Another obstacle to Christian warriors, a canal separated the Franks from their crossbowmen. The battle of Fariskur on April 16, 1250, further demoralized the crusaders and ended their hopes of seizing Cairo and recapturing Jerusalem. At a low point for Christians, Shajar al-Durr had Louis expelled from Damietta and encouraged the assassination of her stepson Turanshah because of his alcoholism and violence against women. At his death, on May 2, 1250, the Egyptian army named her sultana. Her heroism survives on coins, literature, and film.

February 10, 1258

A Mongol princess and Nestorian Christian of the Turkic Kereit tribe, **Doquz Khatun (ca. 1200–June 16, 1265)** advised her husband/son, the conqueror Hülegü Khan, the Persian viceroy, and accompanied his massive army on military campaigns. For three years, she traveled in the vanguard and camped in the prioritized section of tents near a mobile bell tower. To enlarge Mongolia's southwestern region into the Mongol Ilkhanate, Hülegü overwhelmed the Abbasid Caliphate in Persia at Alamut (modern Iran) and advanced over Transcaucasia to the Middle East.

Doquz's husband besieged Baghdad from January 29 to February 10, 1258, with deft use of sappers and flooding. To his order of mass slaughter, she appended safe passage for Shiite Muslims and Christians. As he moved on toward Damascus, she urged him to erect churches in new territories. King Hetum of Cilicia admired her influence on Hülegü's mercy toward Christians. Compared in importance to the Roman emperor Constantine's mother Helena, Doquz set an example at the Al-khanid court that maintained women's rights into the fourteenth century.

1262

During a perilous time in monarchy on the Decca plains, **Rudrama (also Rudhrama, ca. 1210–November 17, 1289)**, the first Hindu queen of Kakatiya in southeastern India, expelled Mahadeva, a Yadava insurgent from Devagiri in the west. Attempting a coup in 1262 while she skirmished with quarreling states, Mahadeva seized Rudrama's battle elephants. For a recruitment incentive, she offered volunteers portions of realty tax revenue. As stated in Ekamranatha's sixteenth-century commentary *Pratapa-charita* (Commentary on

Charity), Rudrama overcame Mahadeva by the end of the next decade. Her army chased his forces west beyond the Godavari River to the spiked and moated Yadava citadel at Devagiri.

Rudrama's heightening of an earthen security wall and the addition of an inner ring impressed Italian explorer Marco Polo, who admired her style. At the end of a twenty-seven-year reign, she lost territory to Chief Ambadeva, an envious outlander. On November 27, 1289, despite advanced age, she fought at the battle of Chandupatla in Telangana state, where she died. Indian art pictured her brandishing a shield and dagger while she rode a lion; a statue shows her chest covered in mail armor. Her prowess influenced a successor, her grandson Prataparudra. In the biopic *Rudhramadevi,* Anushka Shetty played the queen.

May 14, 1264

The primary object of dissension in England, **Eleanor of Provence (1223–June 24, 1291)** from Aix hired French mercenaries to secure the throne of her husband, Henry III, against rebels during the Second Barons' War. For two decades, she outraged English barons by inviting her relatives from Provence and Savoy to take court jobs as councilors, stewards, and advisers. On February 1, 1241, she appointed her uncle, Boniface of Savoy, to Archbishop of Canterbury; on April 8, 1242, she granted Bertram de Criol, Henry's steward, possession of Dover Castle. Henry pleased her with exorbitant spending on her wardrobe and, in 1245, the construction of Westminster Abbey. When he left the throne in her charge on August 6, 1253, during his ouster of Simon V de Montfort from the English stronghold at Gascony, she collected new levies. On October 2, she ordered the Rye and Winchelsea dockyards to equip two galleys and man them with crossbowmen to protect the king.

On May 14, 1264, Simon de Montfort and the barons seized the king and his son Edward I and imprisoned them in the Tower of London. Upon her release from house arrest, Eleanor represented royal authority in Gascony and plotted an invasion of continental knights that foundered at Sluis, Flanders. With Edward's escape from Montfort on May 28, 1265, and the six-month siege on Kenilworth Castle in Warwickshire, the rebellion waned. Eleanor's twelve hundred troops added the corpses of Montfort and his son Henry on August 4 to a total of fifteen thousand casualties. The army was successful on December 13, 1266, after rebels perished from hunger and disease. Those holding out against the king surrendered in summer 1267 at Ely with the signing of the Dictum of Kenilworth, which renewed royal authority.

November 10, 1270

A Spanish warrior-wife, **Eleanor of Castile (November 20, 1241–November 28, 1290)** of Burgos followed her husband Edward I "Longshanks" to the Eighth Crusade to recover the Holy Lands. She took a personal interest in military archery and imported French bowmen. After giving birth to a first child, Eleanor lost both Katherine and Joan at age one and John at age four.

During the Second Barons' War in the late 1260s, she managed baronial prisoners at Windsor Castle while safely rearing surviving children—John, Eleanor Plantagenet, and Joan Plantagenet. For security during ongoing political strife and negotiations, Eleanor requisitioned reinforcements from Castile.

In a fertile period of marriage, Eleanor traveled the Middle East for four years of intermittent pregnancy. On August 20, 1270, the Royal armada's arrival from Dover, England, to Tunis coincided with a truce ending conflict. On return to western Sicily on November 10, 1270, the ships incurred storm damage off Trapani, a fishing port in the northwest. Eleanor, in her seventh month of pregnancy with daughter Joan of Acre, reached Acre on May 9, 1271, days before conflict with Egyptian Baibars at Cyprus and Tripoli. In late 1271, she lost another infant, Juliana.

Repatriating to England, Eleanor lay in a prison cell at Westminster Palace during a year-long civil war, in which Edward recovered from an assassin's dagger plunge at Haifa. In September 1272, she left Palestine and awaited crowning as queen at Westminster Abbey. She lost son Henry in 1274 and daughters Berengaria in 1276 and Isabella in 1279, but bore more children—Alphonso, Margaret, Mary, Isabel, Alice, and Elizabeth. In a makeshift dwelling at Caernarvon Castle in 1284 during the king's military campaign in Wales, Eleanor bore Edward II. In 1287, she suffered a bout of malaria. The fifteenth and sixteenth babes, Beatrice and Blanche, were born and died in 1290, the year of Eleanor's demise at Harby, Nottinghamshire, from fever at age forty-nine.

ca. 1280

A great granddaughter of Genghis Khan, the Mongol warrior and champion wrestler **Khutulun (1260–1306)** made a reputation for daring at the peak of the Mongol empire. A muscular female admired by Italian traveler Marco Polo, she excelled at archery, self-defense, sword fighting, and horsemanship. During her father's anger at the Chinese influence on Kublai Khan's realm, she accompanied Kaidu Khan in 1280 in battle against the Yuan dynasty. In peace times, she offered political and military advice rather than her fourteen brothers. Although Kaidu chose her as his heir at his death in 1301, custom prevailed in the precedence of sons over daughters. For five years, she remained unmarried and protected his monument until her death at age forty-five. Drama and opera revive her biography in *Turandot*. Claudia Kim acted Khutulun's part in the television series *Marco Polo*.

March 30, 1282

A haughty Guelph intriguer and sexual libertine, **Macalda di Scaletta (also Machalda, 1240–after October 14, 1308)** of Scaletta, Sicily, contested an Easter uprising on March 30, 1282, and the twenty-year war of the Ghibellines against the Angevin rule of Charles I. As described in *History Sicula* (Sicilian History) by the chronicler Bartholomaeus of Neocastro, she had a poisonous effect on her enemies. A Catalan historian Bernat Desclot described her military skills as equal to those of a knight. During her husband Alaimo's absence to fight at Messina, she governed Catania and repossessed lands of the French. Upon meeting Peter III of Aragon, she attired herself in military parade dress and wielded a silver mace. Her exhibitionism survives in art, opera, history, monograph, and stage drama.

1285

As revealed in mercenary Ramon Muntaner's *Cronica Catalana* (Catalonian History), during the Aragonese Crusade, a Catalonian ribbon and veil maker and gardener, **Mercadera (1245–1300)** of Peralada, evaded French besiegers while gardening at her plot outside city walls. The 1285 attack resulted from King Peter III of Aragon's expulsion of Anjou royalists from Sicily. To escape rape by the invaders, she wore men's clothes to cultivate cabbages and harvest them for her table. For protection, she carried sword, shield, and spear. Finding a French trooper fallen into an irrigation channel, she pierced him in the thigh. Despite her own wounds, she removed the spear and remanded him to jailers at the royal headquarters. As a reward, Peter III gave her the victim's horse, armor, and lance and the ransom paid for his release. An annual craft fair reenacts the medieval feat by the "heroine of Peralada."

1296

In the twelve-month assault on IJesselstein Castle, **Bertha van Heukelom (also Bertrada or Lady Beert, ca. 1260–February 25, 1322)** protected the manse during the 1296 jailing of her husband, Gijsbrecht van Ijesselstein, at Culemborg. Violence derived from feuding between the Utrecht bishops and Dutch counts and the struggle for the castle as a handhold on local power. Hubrecht van Vianen, lord of Culemborg, launched the siege in reprisal for the kidnap and murder of Count Floris V of Holland. To protect her nine-year-old son Arnoud and eight-year-old Willem, Bertha bartered with a boy hostage before altering her strategy within weeks to pledging half her castle security force of sixteen sick, feeble men. Hubrecht violated the deal by seizing eight men and slaying the other half. In the opinion of fourteenth-century compiler Melis Stoke's *Rijmkroniek* (Rhyme Chronicle), she deserved a hero's homage. Her legend survives in children's lore.

1297

In 1297, the year that **Jeanne of Navarre (also Joan I, 1271–1304)** of Bar-sur-Seine gave birth to Robert, her seventh child, she assembled royal troops in northeastern France to counter the invasion of Champagne by Henry III of Bar. During an expansionist era, her husband, Philip IV the Fair, left the combat to her while he battled the English for possession of Gascony. She jailed Henry before the clash with England ended in 1301 with the Treaty of Bruges. The loss cost Henry the county of Bar, which became Philip's property. Joan's arrest of Henry survives in a painting by Jean Baptiste Morret.

Late Middle Ages, 1300–1500

A two-century decline in medieval arts and productivity, the late middle ages initiated struggles against wars of succession, shortfalls in crops, hunger, and plague. The Black Death reduced the population by half, causing crises in law, government, religion, and agriculture. The introduction of printing promoted transition to the Renaissance.

ca. 1300

A late medieval spy from Yorubaland, around 1300, **Moremi Ajasoro (fl. 1300s)** from Offa (modern Nigeria) protected the realm of Ile-Ife from Ibo-Igbo raiders and enslavers. After consulting a river deity for guidance, she allowed the plunderers to capture her. As a resident of Ibo-Igbo forest culture and wife of the king, she learned their military methods. After escaping to Yorubaland, she explained how Yoruban forces could set fire to Igbo mantles, which they wove from dry grass, bamboo fiber, and raffia palm fronds. Market women followed the advice by tossing torches on the flammable uniforms. The river god demanded payment in the form of her son Ela Oluorogá whom she sacrificed. An annual festival, stage musical, and statue in Nigeria exalt the queen.

July 20, 1304

In the fourth year of Anglo-Scots border wars, begun in 1296, a Scots widow, **Evota of Stirling (also Eve of Stirling, 1250–1310)** risked reputation and land by aiding the garrison of Edward I at the siege of Stirling Castle. Historians surmise that decades of warfare left her penniless. Scouring the region and her own farmland for rations and supplies, on July 20, 1304, she came under judgment for aiding the English bowmen from April 22 until the Scots surrender on July 30, 1304. Among the military needs, Edward specified crossbows, iron-headed arrows, meat, oats, beans, timber, coal, medicine, lead, cotton thread, sulfur, and saltpeter, the makings of Greek fire for shooting from a trebuchet (siege catapult) shipped from Newcastle. He commanded local earls to halt Evota's provisioning of the twenty-five Scots guarding the castle. After ten weeks in prison, she lost her Scots citizenship and entered exile. She petitioned Walter de Amersham, the chancellor of Scotland, to lessen the punishment and restore ownership of a three-acre plot.

March 25, 1306

During the Wars of Scottish Independence, **Isabella MacDuff, Countess** of Buchan (1270–1314), a northeastern Scots proponent of outlaw king Robert the Bruce, held off an English siege at Berwick Castle in Northumberland. In defiance of her husband, John Comyn, she risked her life by crowning Robert, her nephew, at Scone on March 25, 1306. On the run with no safe residence, she first fled northeast to Kildrummy Castle with the Bruce women and fell into enemy hands at St. Duthac's Church in Tain. When the grounds fell to Edward I of England, he transported Isabella to a cell in Berwick Castle on the Tweed River. She survived four years in a wood and iron cage suspended from a turret. When Bruce gained supporters, in 1310, Edward released her from the cage and immured her in Berwick at a Carmelite monastery.

See also November 30, 1335.

1320

Against the loyalties of her son Malise, **Agnes Comyn of Strathearn (1260–1325)** from Buchan in northeastern Scotland conspired with her nephew, William II de Soulis Butler, to assassinate Robert the Bruce. For the 1320 de Soulis conspiracy, she colluded with Richard Brown and Gilbert de Malerb and employed three soldiers. The cabal failed after betrayal by Murdoch III de Menteith, an English informer. The plotters came before the Black Parliament. On August 4, 1320, a judgment of guilty at Scone ordered Agnes imprisoned for life in the stone tower at Dumbarton Castle on the River Clyde along with William, who escaped to England. A second nephew, David de Brechin, was executed for treason along with John Logie, Agnes's tenant and fellow plotter. By the mercy of Edward II, the other conspirators escaped hanging, drawing and quartering by horses, and decapitation.

September 1326

The pampered child of royalty, **Isabella of France (after April 1295–August 22, 1358)** of Paris ousted from England her homosexual mate, Edward II, during the Dispenser War. A prefatory clash at Leeds Castle drawbridge in Kent with Irish baroness Margaret de Badlesmere (also Lady Badlesmere, **Margaret de Clare, April 1, 1287–January 3, 1334)** in October 1321 pitted the Irish garrison against Isabella's personal guard. While Margaret's husband, Bartholomew de Badlesmere, attended to business at Oxford in September 1321, she controlled Leeds Castle and guarded the family treasury. At the drawbridge, she refused entrance to Queen Isabella, who deliberately incensed residents while pretending to go on pilgrimage to St. Thomas a Becket's shrine at Canterbury.

Margaret ordered castle bowmen to fire on the royal party, killing six of the queen's men. With an army of thirty thousand, King Edward II took the castle on October 31, 1321, by a fifteen-day siege of bolt-loaded ballistas. He seized the property and hanged the castle seneschal (manager) and twelve of Margaret's soldiers from the parapet. On the family's arrest in November 1321, Margaret and her son and four daughters, ages twelve to six, spent a year imprisoned in the Tower of London. For the next year, Margaret paid for attacking a queen by spending her remaining years in St. Clare convent, Aldgate.

With the aid of her lover, Roger de Mortimer, Isabella hired eight men-of-war and imported mercenaries from Brabant and Hainaut, Holland, to raise civil war. Her forces, accompanied by thirteen-year-old Prince Edward III, marched west from Suffolk and Cambridge in September 1326 through Dunstable on October 7 to Gloucester on October 16. Against the king's Flemish mercenaries, a rapid military deployment to the River Avon gained her Bristol Castle on October 26. Victims of the Despensers clustered around the queen and joined her army.

After deposing and arresting Edward II on November 16, 1326, and hanging, drawing, and quartering his traitorous cohort, Hugh le Dispenser the Younger, Isabella immured Hugh's wife Eleanor de Clare in the Tower of London. In south Wales, the queen's four hundred twenty-five troops battered Caerphilly Castle until March 1327, when the Dispensers capitulated. With Edward's unexplained death on September 21, 1327, she seated herself as regent for four years in the name of her fifteen-year-old son Edward III. For her egregious acts, in 1330, he had Isabella arrested and her lover executed at Tyburn Prison. He immured her at Castle Rising but allowed her frivolities and lavish expenditures until her death at age sixty-three.

May 1328

The widowed ruler of Sponheim-Starkenburg County between Koblenz and Trier, **Loretta of Sponheim (1300–1346)** trapped Archbishop Baldwin of Luxembourg for menacing Starkenburg Castle on the Moselle River. A tyrant and political meddler in the Moselle Valley, he violated the March 1325 treaty ending the War of Metz, a feudal property dispute that roiled the Rhineland-Palatinate. By stretching a chain over the river, in May 1328, she halted his one-masted trading cog and dispatched troop boats to curtail his highhanded violations of territory that she managed for her thirteen-year-old son, John III.

By imprisoning, fining, and cowing Baldwin with demands that he cede his claims to her lands, Loretta incurred temporary excommunication by Pope John XXII and defied Baldwin's brother, Henry VII, Holy Roman Emperor. Nonetheless, she restored her Starkenberg residence to safety. With the ransom money, in 1330, she built the dual-towered castle of Frauenberg on the Nahe River, a tributary of the Rhine.

1331

A warrior queen of the Rajasa dynasty, **Dyah Gitarja (also Tribhuwana, 1309–1350s)** commanded forces against central Javanese uprisings in Keta and Sadeng in 1331, thus ending egotistic strife between generals. At the behest of her mother, dowager queen Gayatri, Gitarja came to the throne of the Majapahit Empire in 1328, married Cakradhara, and bore son and heir Hayam Wuruk in 1334. With the aid of Prime Minister Bajah Mada, in 1343, she expanded her territory to include Bali and part of Sumatra and dispatched naval units to patrol Southeast Asian waters. Her reign spread Indian culture across ancient Indonesia. In retirement in 1350, she relinquished the throne to her son. Her fame survives in a Hindu temple, puppetry, statuary, and a video game.

November 30, 1335

Born and reared during perilous times, **Christina Bruce (also Christina de Brus or Christian Bruce, 1278–1357)** of Carrick, Scotland, held off Edward de Balliol, contender for the throne of eleven-year-old King David II, from his siege at Kildrummy Castle. Having survived eight years in a Gilbertine convent in Lincolnshire, at age thirty-six, Christina was ransomed in a prisoner exchange. In 1335, during the Second War of Scottish Succession, she led security forces at Kildrummy in Strathdon, Aberdeenshire, in stemming the attacks of Anglo-Scots schemer David III of Strathbogie. On November 30, 1335, Christina's husband, Andrew Murray, Guardian of Scotland, slew Strathbogie at the war's turning point—the battle of Culblean, which pitted eleven hundred loyalists successfully against three thousand enemy.

January 13–June 10, 1338

In East Lothian overlooking the North Sea, during the Second War of Scots Independence, **Agnes Randolph of Dunbar (1312–1369)** resisted a five-month English siege on Dunbar Castle. Born at Stranith in 1312 to Isabel Stewart and Thomas Randolph of Moray, she was the grand-niece of Robert the Bruce. At age twenty-six, "Black Agnes" faced twenty thousand English soldiers of Edward III attacking her husband Patrick's castle with catapult and battering rams from January 13 to June 10, 1338. With lead shot and rocks catapulted against the ramparts, she smashed the siege tower of William Montague of Salisbury by returning one of his own projectiles. She trapped a marauder in the portcullis, jeered at Salisbury, and rebuffed Salisbury's forty-man vanguard at the seaside gate before they could land supplies and reinforcements from Genoese galleys. Salisbury dubbed her a "brawling, boisterous, Scottish wench." Because of the cost of a five-month siege, he halted the blockade in the fifth month. She spent her last twenty-two years as earl of Dunbar and died in 1369 at age fifty-eight.

See also 1395.

Winter 1341

Near Berwick, Northumberland, on the Scottish border in winter 1341, the countess of Salisbury, **Katharine Grandison (1304–April 23, 1349)** of Bisham, England, repulsed Scots besieging Wark-on-Tweed Castle, a hexagonal hilltop redoubt. Upon return from banishment to Boulogne, France, on June 2, 1341, seventeen-year-old David II the Bruce, king of Scotland, initiated the three-week attack on her residence. Katherine's garrison—some knights, forty bowmen, and staff—killed David's standard bearer. After the castle governor, Edward Montagu, escaped the grounds during a night storm and sought aid from the king of England, Edward III ended the assault by sending one thousand royal troops to drive David out of Northumberland. In the disputed chronicle of Belgian compiler

Jean le Bel of Liege, Edward allegedly capped the military payoff by raping Katherine, leaving her badly injured.

March 2, 1342

A Bulgarian-Byzantine commander with three teenage lieutenants, **Irene Asanina (also Eileen of Asanes, ca. 1300–1379)** managed forces beginning March 2, 1342, throughout twelve years of conflict during the medieval empire's decline. A six-year civil war from September 1341 to February 2, 1347, required her leadership of the Didymoteicho (modern Demotika) garrison in Thrace on the eastern edge of Greece, where she was crowned empress. Her husband, Emperor John VI Kantakouzenos, left her controlling the border position until winter 1343 with the aid of eighteen-year-old daughter **Maria Kantakouzene (1328–1379)**, seventeen-year-old **Theodora Kantakouzene (1330–1381)**, and thirteen-year-old **Helena Kantakouzene (1333–December 10, 1396)**. By 1345, combat began to favor John VI and his Turkish allies after the enemy routed. On July 7 at the battle of Peritheorion, Greece, he led twenty thousand troops against five thousand three hundred of his foe.

On February 2, 1347, John VI entered Constantinople, where his thirteen-year-old son Andronikos died of bubonic plague. During the year-long Byzantine-Genoese War begun in 1348 over guardianship of sixteen-year-old John V Palaeologos by his mother, Anna of Savoy, John VI sought to increase custom duties from shipping through Galata (modern Istanbul) on the Bosporus to the Black Sea. Irene defended Constantinople from invasion by Doge Giovanni I di Murta of Genoa. Five years later, the Black Death killed one-third of Italy's population. Genoese sailors passing through the Black Sea carried contagion to Constantinople, which experienced eleven cyclical outbreaks.

In March 1353, Irene again shielded the capital against a civil war ignited on the Golden Horn. John VI's failure to stop Bulgarian forces at the gate in November 1354 preceded his abdication on December 4. He, Irene, Maria, at age twenty-six, and Helena, at age twenty-one, retired to monasteries. Irene lived to age seventy-nine at Hagia Martha convent under the name Sister Eugenia. Helena served Hagia Martha until 1396 under the name Hypomone (Patience). Andronikos IV Palaiologus imprisoned Theodora at Galata (modern Karakoy, Istanbul).

April 26, 1342

A determined Flemish mother and feminist exemplar, **Joanna of Flanders (also Jeanne de Montfort, ca. 1295–September 1374)** armed herself to defend the inheritance of her infant son John IV, the Conqueror of Brittany. To stop his cousins from claiming the Montfort succession, she mustered an army that captured Redon in northwestern France. She chose nearby Hannebont Castle as a redoubt in November 1341 and reinforced it for war. Dressed in armor, she defended the castle on April 26, 1342, against Charles of Blois, her son's rival for the dukedom.

Despite hunger, Joanna refused

advice to cede the castle to Charles. Admirers viewed her mounted on a charger alongside her baby boy and cheered her men-at-arms as they fired volleys of arrows and smashed Charles's siege engine. After rallying townswomen to fight like men and hurl lime and stones from the ramparts, she led three hundred knights on a raid. Her commandos set fire to the enemy camp, earning her the sobriquet "Jeanne la Flamme (Fiery Joan)."

By leading reinforcements from Brest and welcoming ships from Edward III, she forced Charles's retreat. An assault on her vessel motivated a hand-to-hand naval battle with a glaive, a bladed pike. In a greedy move to claim Brittany for himself, Edward III imprisoned Charles and confined Joanna to Tickhill Castle, south Yorkshire, on October 3, 1343, on a pretense of her mental incompetence. In 1347, support failed in the citizen attempt to rescue her from political imprisonment. Her three-decade incarceration and death in 1374 launched romances, Breton folklore, and the ballad "Jean o' Flame," and set a pattern of the "madwoman in the attic," a Victorian literary motif found in Charlotte Brontë's *Jane Eyre*.

January 19, 1343

During the defense of the city of Vannes, Brittany, **Jeanne de Clisson (1300–1359)** of Poitou, France, lost her husband, Olivier IV de Clisson, on January 19, 1343, to beheading at Les Halles on charges of treason. After the crown posted Olivier's head for public view and seized Jeanne's inherited properties at Blain, Clisson, and Nantes, the widow raised a force of four hundred to demand retribution from King Philip VI. As a privateer with a fleet of three warships, on August 2, 1343, she challenged French loyalists at Touffou castle at Vienne, where she killed an entire garrison. She attacked a second outpost at Château-Thébaut near Nantes.

Jeanne's campaign raged along the Breton shores in a red-sailed, black-hulled cargo vessel appropriately named My Revenge. From the Bay of Biscay to the English Channel to coastal islets, French merchant marine captains feared her reputation for slaying all on board with sword, bow, and dagger. By 1346, she was transferring stolen goods to the English at Crecy in northern France. Her flagship scuttled in 1356, she lost her eighteen-year-old son Guillaume to exposure, but remained a freebooter until bubonic plague threatened her crew. The sobriquet "Lioness of Brittany" and the Nantes street Rue Jeanne le Corsaire commemorate her bold vengeance against royalty.

1345

An Ibaloi warrior living in the mountains overlooking the Lingayen Gulf and the China Sea, **Urduja (also Deboxah, ca. 1330–1400)** of Pinga, Tawalisi (modern Pangasinan east of Luzon, Philippines), fostered a reputation for mastering navigation, horses, archery, kampilans (single-edged swords), and duels. Because of a dearth of male soldiers after a series of wars and rebellions, in 1345, she led a battalion of Filipina viragos. In the last years of the Shri-Visayan Empire, Muslim traveler Ibn Battuta met her on his sail by junk from Kakula Island in the Coral Sea to Canton. He learned of her military expertise, fluency in Turkish and Arabic, and intent to explore precolonial India. Her bearing on a matriarchal dynasty survived in Chinese texts, music, film, and animated cartoon.

October 17, 1346

A royal wife, mother, and commander, **Philippa of Hainault (June 24, 1310–August 15, 1369)** of black Moorish lineage at Valenciennes, Flanders, aided husband Edward III on October 17, 1346, at the battle of Neville's Cross in Durham, England. At an early campaign of the Hundred Years' War, she and the king departed Sandwich in July 1338 with a five-hundred ship armada to challenge the French king Philippe VI and his claim on Aquitaine and Ponthieu. In November, during the last weeks of pregnancy with son Lionel of Antwerp, Philippa bolstered alliances with the low countries at Antwerp, Ghent, and Coblentz, her contribution to Edward's international support. Edward secured his family with eight thousand archers and two thousand knights.

Prefacing a Scots insurgency in mid–October 1346, Philippa summoned northern regiments to York and rode a white horse to rally twelve thousand foot soldiers and longbowmen. Paintings and woodcuts depict her at Newcastle on Tyne, lance in hand galloping over the battlefield within months of giving birth to Princess Margaret of England. West of Durham, England's seven thousand knights vanquished Scots king David II Bruce and killed some three thousand or twenty percent of his fifteen thousand troops in hand-to-hand combat. Among one hundred prisoners of war, David remained captive in Hampshire at Odiham Castle for over a decade.

Queen Philippa was pregnant with Prince William of Windsor during her aid to England at the siege of Calais in 1346–1347, when camp life exposed her to epidemic disease. Despite losing fifteen-year-old daughter Joan and infant sons Thomas and William in late summer 1348 to the Black Death, the queen continued supporting Edward in Scots and Flemish war zones. At her death from enlarged heart at age fifty-nine, the naming of Queen's College, Oxford, commemorated her dutiful reign.

September 5, 1350

The outbreak of the Hook and Cod Wars pitted **Margaret II of Hainaut (also Margaret II of Avesnes or Margaretha, 1311–June 23, 1356)** against her son, William I of Bavaria, future heir of Hainaut, Holland, and Zeeland. He gave proof of aggression on July 28, 1348, by burning the village of Jutphaas in Utrecht. Warfare spawned more aggression in Delft and the Hague and muddled attempts at ceasefires. To retain rule of Holland from her grasping son, shortly after the death of her tenth child, one-year-old Louis Ludwig, on September 5, 1350, she fought a civil war over control of Hainaut.

In 1351, Margaret lost centers of power—Medemblik, Brederode, and Polanen castles—and a marine conflict off Veere a crucial trade center in Middelburg in southwestern Holland. She imprisoned William in Ath at Burbant Castle, from which he escaped. Edward III, husband of her sister Philippa, dispatched an armada in her name to Veere, which she won on May 30, 1351. The enthusiasm of her military allies ebbed within weeks. On the Meuse River at Zwartewaal, Holland, on July 3, 1351, she combined forces and seized ships, but lost to William. In December, she settled for control of Hainaut by giving her son Holland and Zeeland. Tuberculosis ended her life at age forty-four in northern France at Le Quesnoy Castle.

April 29, 1357

At age forty, **Marzia "Cia" Ordelaffi (also Marzia degli Ubaldini, June 21, 1317–1381)**, an Italian noble from Romagna, defended Cesena from papal troops who rustled local cattle. While protecting her four children, she followed her husband, Francesco II Ordelaffi of Forli, into Romagna's Ghibelline war zones or remained behind to defend Rocca Malatestiana, Cesena's fort and citadel north of San Marino. In May 1351, she rescued their five-year-old son Lodovico from the sixteen-day siege on the Montone River. At Rocca di Dovadola, the citadel of Forli, she routed Count Carlo de Guidi, a captain of the church.

In an adversarial relationship with Pope Innocent VI, on April 29, 1357, Marzia confronted enemy cavalry at Cesena backed up by eight hundred mercenary Hungarian bowmen. She dressed in armor and rode her horse among the region's four hundred knights, who won the skirmish. By June 21, 1357, she had to surrender the battlements and serve two years in prison. Widowed in 1374, she died in Venice at age sixty-three.

1358

During King Valdemar IV Atterdag's reunification of Denmark, **Richardis of Schwerin (also Rixa or Richardis of Lauenburg, 1320–April 23, 1377)**, the Duchess of Schleswig, protected Sønderborg Castle in 1358 during a protracted military attack and threat of seizure. Left in siege conditions on Alsen island in the Baltic Sea by her rebellious husband, Duke Valdemar II of Denmark, she maintained military control until her inevitable surrender to royal force. Her plea for mercy involved a dramatic procession through open gates with every female under her jurisdiction. The king agreed to vengeful terms—banning her fractious husband from the environs—and made her queen of Denmark and chatelaine *hors de combat*.

Summer 1361

A native of east central China on the Jialing River, **Han E (1345–fl. 1370s)** of Baoning, Shu, (modern Langzhong, Sichuan) posed as a man and enrolled in the government army to stop a Mongol revolt begun in Yangzhou in May 1351. Orphaned in 1352 near the end of the brutal Yuan Dynasty, she learned sword skills from her uncle Han Li, who fostered her. Because Emperor Yuan Shun ordered spear and bow raids by the Red Scarf Army, Han Li and his wife Han Du dressed the fifteen-year-old Han E as a boy to escape sexual assault. In summer 1361, conflict southwest at Chendu motivated the Yuan army to draft her as a stable laborer.

As reported in Han historian Zhang Tingyu's *The History of Ming*, Red guerrilla fighters enticed Han E to join the rebellion and serve as a spy in Chengdu. Called Han Guanbao until 1373, she fought in anti–Mongol battles with some four hundred thousand forces that claimed Sichuan and, in 1363, Yunnan. Among soldiers, she protected her secret by never bathing naked or joining drunken revelry. She revealed her gender to Commander Luo Jia, who chose her for a future son-in-law and forced her into an illicit girl-to-girl marriage. At age twenty-six, she married a fellow soldier, Ma Fuzong from Tongxing Village, which became a tourist attraction for a festival and two shrines to her military prowess. Folklore, biography, and verse called the heroine the "Hua Mulan of Shu."

Late 1370

In the first quarter of the Hundred Years' War, a seasoned, self-reliant nun, **Julienne du Guesclin (also Julianna of Guesdin, 1322–1405)** of Brittany stymied two hundred English raiders of a Breton convent at Pontorson overlooking the English Channel. Aided by her sister-in-law, Breton astrologer and prophet **Tiphaine Raguenel (1335–1373)**, Julienne recruited other postulants to stop the insurgents of Sir John Felton, sheriff of Northumberland, before they could climb ladders and breach the walled cloister. Clad in mail and armed with the sword of her brother Bertrand du Guesclin, Marshal of France, in late 1370, Julienne held her ground, flipped the ladders to the ground, and humiliated Felton. In the aftermath, two complicit novices drowned after being tied in a sack and tossed into the river. Tiphaine settled at Mont Saint-Michel, a Norman island stronghold. Julienne later governed Saint-Georges nunnery at Rennes as abbess.

May 1377

A commoner in the French cavalry during a tenuous point in the Hundred Years' War, **Janine Marie de Foix (fl. 1377–1380)** served for three years in the nation's first permanent army. A supporter of Charles V the Wise, she fought during the king's intervention in a contested election of Pope Urban VI and the removal of the papacy from Avignon to Rome. Rioting in Italy in May 1377 caused a short-term revival of the Avignon papacy. Charles's choice of antipope Clement VII on September 20, 1378, precipitated the Western Schism, which alienated Catholics for four decades. Threats from the English cost Charles the governance of Brittany. To support his army and pay war debts, he raised a hearth levy that alarmed and outraged peasants. Before his death on September 16, 1380, he rescinded the tax.

March 3, 1383

Independent judge and lawgiver **Eleanor of Arborea (1347–1404)** from Molins de Rei, Catalonia, combatted Aragon's annexation of Sardinia and salvaged individual freedoms by rejecting feudalism. A noted falconer, she passed laws shielding bird nests and falcons from damage by hunters. A four-year war against Spanish incursion began on March 3, 1383, with civil revolt and the assassination of her brother Ugone (Hugh) III and his daughter and heir Benedetta. Eleanor's husband Brancaleone and their four-year-old son Frederick lay captive in the tower of Pancrazio while she armed herself and trained forces to defend Arborea against Peter IV of Aragon. Frederick died in jail in 1387 at age ten.

With the aid of a Genoese alliance, Eleanor quelled citizen discontent and extended rule over two-thirds of Sardinia. Her successful negotiation of a treaty with Aragon in 1387 enabled islanders to enjoy two decades of sound government. Her codification of the *Carta de Logu* (Charter of the Land) liberalized punishments, inheritance rights, property ownership, and protection of orphans from abuse and of women from forced marriage to their rapists. Sardinia's last local judge, during the Black Death, she died of plague in capital city of Oristano at age fifty-seven, leaving the island nation to Brancaleone's military defense. Her modern laws governed Sardinia until 1827; her statue adorns Oristano's Piazza Eleanora.

August 14, 1385

In the epoch of the Hundred Years' War and the bubonic plague, Portuguese virago **Brites de Almeida (1349–after 1385)** of Aljubarotta earned renown at the hour-long conflict in her hometown on August 14, 1385, against Castilians endorsing Beatrice of Portugal as queen. While commanding a local regiment, she aided sixty-six hundred men, including one thousand archers. Brandishing a peal (baker's shovel), she slew seven enemy soldiers hiding in her bakery oven. By assembling a female militia, she helped her homeland to clobber thirty-one thousand troops of the Franco-Castilian alliance with Aragon that involved eight thousand bowmen and two thousand knights. Because of a decisive loss to its oversized army, Castile incurred five thousand casualties and the death of the standard bearer. John I of Castile fled the battlefield, leaving Portugal independent. At the end of the crisis of monarchy, John I of Portugal retained his throne.

April 1387

A stern ruler during the Polish succession, **Jadwiga (also Hedwig, 1373–July 17, 1399)** of Buda, Hungary, marched to Slavonia to free her sister Mary, Queen of Hungary, and their mother, Elizabeth of Bosnia, from a Croatian rebel faction favoring a male monarch. A series of Hungarian uprisings protesting Elizabeth's murder of the usurper Charles III of Naples resulted in rebel leader John Horvat's kidnap of Mary and Elizabeth on July 25, 1386, at Gorjani and imprisonment at Gomnec, the castle of the bishop of Zagreb. Before Jadwiga and her brother-in-law, Sigismund of Luxembourg, could complete the release, Horvat transferred the two women to Novigrad Castle in Croatia on the Adriatic Sea. In mid–January 1387, guards strangled Elizabeth before Jadwiga's forces could arrive. Jadwiga won in Ruthenia in April 1387 by leading forces to reclaim Halych, a Ukrainian city on the Dniester River. The army rescued Mary on June 4, 1387. Jadwiga and Sigismund executed Horvat in Pecs in Baranya County on August 15, 1394.

August 7, 1389

A widowed Frisian virago, **Foelke Kampana (also Fokeldis Kampana, Fokelt tom Broke, or Quade Folk, 1355–ca. August 4, 1419)** from Hinte, Saxony, responded to the murder of her husband, the knight Ocko I tom Brok, by raising an army. During hostilities with Frisians west of the Ems to unite east Frisia, Ocko died on August 7, 1389, at the command of Folkmar Allena, chief of Osterhusen, during the siege of Aurich Castle. Foelke fought on the Dutch side in the capture of Aurich, Saxony, and the ouster of Folkmar. At battle's end, as attested in the East Frisian historian Eggerik Beninga's *Chronica der Fresen* (History of the Frisians), she decapitated two hundred captives on the spot. The stern demeanor of "Foelke the Cruel" survives in a portrait and statue.

1390

To save the honor of Sir Robert de Hotot of Clapton, England, his daughter, seventeen-year-old **Agnes Joane Hotot (1378–1460)**, took his place in a duel over property claims. Because of an attack of gout, in 1390, Sir Robert allowed Agnes to dress in male armor, ride a war steed, and compete in a jousting match. According to a Clapton monk, she faced the challenger Ringsdale at Northamptonshire. After unseating him, she removed her helmet and breastplate to reveal her gender as the bel cavalier and reclaim the land in contention. At her marriage to Richard Dudley in 1395, the clan redesigned their crest to show a bare-breasted woman dueler. Her motto read *Galea Spes Salutis* (Hope Is the Helmet of Salvation), a pun on her disguise.

1395

A Scots castle keeper south of Aberdeen on the North Sea, **Margaret Keith de Lindsay (1337–after June 20, 1397)** from Stonehaven in Kincardineshire defended her family at Fyvie Castle in Aberdeenshire from attacks by her greedy nephew, Robert de Keith. In the absence of her husband, Lord James de Lindsay, the sheriff of Lanarkshire, to serve as an ambassador to England, in 1395, she outwitted Robert's blockade by transporting rations and water for her staff over the Ythan River. In addition to treating casualties among her security force, she advised on tactics and smuggled messages to her supporters. Robert yielded to James, who arrived from the court of Robert III with four hundred soldiers. The clash at Bourty Kirk cost Robert fifty casualties. Historians compared Margaret's courage to that of Black Agnes Randolph of Dunbar.

ca. 1400

A visionary queen and military tactician from the late fourteenth century to the early fifteenth, **Furra (fl. 1400–1510s)** of Sidama in south central Ethiopia killed her husband, Chief Dingama Koyya, and their son to rid tribes of patriarchal coercion. As monarch of a matriarchy, around 1400, she drafted a women's army and subjugated males to domestic tasks as punishment for their cowardice in battle. At the end of a seven-year reign, she ordered a war steed faster than a horse. Men presented her a wild giraffe that tore her limbs from her torso. Women wept, offered milk on her grave as a thanks for her sympathy, and compared her greatness to that of Arawelo, a first-century CE Somali liberator of women.

See also 15 CE.

1400

An Irish virago aided by Thomas FitzGerald, the 5th Earl of Desmond and lord deputy from Munster, **Maire O'Ciaragain (also Maire Ni Ciaragain or Maria Kerrigan, fl. 1400s)** of Fermanagh fomented a clan rebellion to expel the Anglo-Normans. After the Normans invaded in 1169 and established the Plantagenet rule in the Pale on the east coast, they forced the Irish to give up their culture. English tyranny required abandonment of heritage dress and customs and replacement of the Irish language with English. The English military presence dwindled after 1371 during the Hundred Years' War. Acting as warlord combating the earls of Leinster and Ulster, in 1400, Maire earned a reputation for merciless killing of Anglo-Norman captives.

August 6, 1414

Because of the conspiracies following the death of Ladislaus of Naples, at Matera in southern Italy, **Margaret of Attenduli (also Margherita Sforza, 1375–?)** from Cotignola west of Ravenna defended Tricarico Castle during a siege on August 6, 1414. She learned warcraft in girlhood. After marching with the troops of her husband, Michael de Catignola, she easily took charge of Tricarico and commanded its army. To free her older brother, Giacomuzio Attendolo Sforza, from kidnappers, she negotiated with Neapolitan envoys of Count Jacques de la Marche. Local protesters besieged his castle, causing him to threaten Margaret. When diplomacy failed, she armed herself like a knight and took the nobles prisoner. Her audacity ended the standoff and gained her brother's release from a death sentence as well as reinstatement of his position as constable of Naples.

1419

During her regency at Burgundy after the assassination of her husband John the Fearless on September 10, 1419, **Margaret of Bavaria (July 1363–January 23, 1424)** of the Hague defended her territory from attacks by the ambitious Louis de Chalon and John IV of Armagnac, a notorious intriguer. During the Hundred Years' War while her husband was in Paris, she successfully ruled Burgundy and Low Country territories of Artois, Salins, Compiegne, Tonnerre, Chatillon-sur-Seine, Montreal, Montbard, and Malines for fifteen years. Her immediate challenge involved raising cash to elevate defense, dispatching spies on enemy armies, and securing gunpowder. The assaults came simultaneously from north and south. After she stopped John of Armagnac, her husband's enemy, her regency continued in 1419 in the name of their son, Philip III of Burgundy. Her courage throughout the Armagnac–Burgundian Civil War survives in histories, portraits, and grave effigies.

1420

A widowed Chinese prophet and recruiter of the poor, **T'ang Sai'er (1399–fl. 1420s)** joined the White Lotus as a rebel soldier and martial arts specialist fighting to legitimize the reincarnation of Buddha. By enlisting five hundred cultists and aiding insurrectionists in capturing Anzhou, Chanzhou, Jimo, Ju, and Shouzhou, she helped to silence and disempower officials of the early Ming imperial court. Her following grew to tens of thousands protesting obligatory peasant labor. The uprising at Xie Shi Peng in Qingzhou resulted in a massacre of local authorities. At her loss at Anqiu, Shandong, in 1420, she melted into a crowd of temple nuns to elude arrest by the soldiers of the Emperor Chengzu. The legend of the "Godmother of the White Lotus" inspired a series of novels, histories, film, and a statue in her hometown of Putai.

April 6, 1428

During the nine-year Danish-Holstein-Hanseatic War, **Philippa of England (May 4, 1394–January 7, 1430)** from Cambridgeshire managed strategies in Copenhagen to defend the Danish-Swedish armada from bombardment. Her husband Eric of Pomerania's absence on a pilgrimage to the Middle East placed decision-making on Philippa. By swelling nationalism to fight the Hanseatic League, for two months, she positioned citizens with carbines at the battlements and tended casualties. She fought a new form of naval warship, which aimed artillery far inland. At Easter, April 6, 1428, the initial attack pitted twelve thousand enemy against Philippa's three thousand soldiers. The wise use of floating batteries crimped the Hanseatic blockade and forced a withdrawal. Fortunately, a Scandinavian spying system gave warning of the next foray.

On June 15, 1428, the enemy tried a primitive harbor closure by dumping lime, ballast, and stones from forty ships to bottle up Philippa's navy. Artillery extended fire into the marina, killing thirty men and disabling the flotilla. The onslaught damaged ninety percent of Copenhagen's fleet. The Danes expedited repairs, ravaged Bornholm Island, and obstructed Germanic privateers. The queen gained aid from Sweden to revitalize her navy with seventy ships crewed by fourteen hundred marines. By May 5, 1429, she returned the threat by assaulting Stralsund, Pomerania. A ceasefire and Sweden's alliance with Denmark in September 1430 coincided with Eric's assault on the queen for failing to take Stralsund. Her sudden death followed a stillbirth. Folklorist Hans Christian Andersen saluted Philippa's level-headedness in his anthology *Godfather's Picture Book*.

May 1428

Hungarian rescuer **Cecilia Rozgonyi (1398–1436)** thwarted an Ottoman Turk attack on King Sigismund of Luxembourg. At Fort Golubac on the Serbian bank of the Danube River, she captained a ship that joined twenty-five thousand soldiers, six thousand bowmen, and two hundred Italian gunners and Polish cavalry to oust Sultan Murad II from the redoubt. At the battle of Golubac in May 1428, Cecilia shelled the castle and commanded the river crossing. Her strategy did not save the Lithuanian contingent, but she prevented Turkish Muslims from capturing the king. When the combatants made peace in June, Sigismund posted the Teutonic Knights as security guards for Christians.

May 8, 1429

A teenage martyr, clairvoyant, and saint during the falling action of the Hundred Years' War, **Joan of Arc (1412–May 30, 1431)**, the Maid of Orléans from Domremy, Lorraine, on France's Meuse River, applied mystic foreknowledge to restore French military vigor against the English. At age seventeen before the temporary court at Chinon, she pressed her support for Charles VII on February 28, 1429, based on divine messages. Simultaneous with the unforeseen promotion, Charles received advice and money for troops and armaments from his foster mother, Yolande of Aragon (August 11, 1384–November 14, 1442). On April 29, 1429, armored, astride a war steed, and waving a banner, Joan commanded the French convoy to smash the seven-month contretemps at Orléans, where she fought alongside her brothers Jean and Pierre.

On the southern border of English-held territory, the enemy ridiculed Joan as a witch. On May 4, 1429, she welcomed two hundred reinforcements and supplies and badgered French commanders to attack the English. A message tied to an arrow threatened English siege generals with retribution. Although bruised by a stone to the head and wounded by an arrow in the neck, within nine days, she ended a tenuous stage of French fortunes by forcing the enemy retreat from Orléans on May 8, 1429. The gain enabled Charles to receive the French crown on July 17 at Reims.

On the military march to Paris in September 1429, Joan survived a third wound, a crossbow strike in the leg. Her presence strengthened troops into the winter. In spring 1430, her four hundred escort troops reached Compiegne, where she was captured on May 23. Female outrage inflamed **Pieronne of Brittany (fl. 1420–March 1430)**, a peasant who sided with her at Christmas for communion and whose death at the stake in March 1430 foreshadowed Joan's merciless end.

The English ransomed Joan and tried her for heresy at Rouen on January 9, 1431. Chained and excommunicated by church authority, on May 30, she burned to death in the old market square. As she predicted, the English could not recover from cyclical losses. A church retrial at Notre Dame in Paris in 1455 nullified the secular trial that condemned her. A treasury of verse, hymns, sketches, art, and drama drew comparisons of Joan to biblical viragos Judith and Deborah.

See also September 3, 1430; 1438.

February 16, 1430

Upon the overnight advance of armed men on the Castle Rialp south of Pamplona, **Aldonça de Bellera (1370–**

1435), a sixty-year-old widowed baroness, on February 16, 1430, organized Catalonian peasants against the pillagers. Twenty-two-year-old Arnau Roger, Count of Pallars Sobira, declared her a prisoner and seized her munitions. In the fort south of the Pyrenees, she escaped to a locked tower and resisted without violence. By sending word to peacemaker Queen Maria of Castile, Aldonca overcame Arnau within two weeks. Without exiting the refuge, she retained the dower barony along with reparations from Arnau.

September 3, 1430

A peasant visionary and imitator of Joan of Arc during the Hundred Years' War, **Pieronne of Brittany (also Pieronne la Bretonne or Perrinaïc, fl. 1420s–September 3, 1430)** promoted the Armagnac movement to rid Brittany of English occupation forces. With her predecessor, Pieronne supported Joan and mystic Catherine de La Rochelle on December 25, 1429, in violating strictures for women by taking communion at Jargeau from a Dominican friar, Brother Helie Bouffant. Pieronne experienced divine visions directing her toward military service for the French dauphin, Charles IX.

A follower of the Franciscan evangelist Brother Richard, Pieronne and another female volunteer believed in his predictions of a savior of France. She performed well as a soldier, but gained ill repute for sorcery. In company with the army at Melun, at Easter on April 16, 1430, English authorities at Corbeil arrested her and her companion. The grand inquisitor Jean Graverent tried Pieronne for blasphemy at the Sorbonne in Paris and, on September 3, 1430, burned her at the stake as a witch.

July 2, 1431

A doughty protector of her family at Bulgnéville west of the Rhine River, **Isabella of Lorraine (1400–February 28, 1453)** combatted Count Antoine de Vaudémont and his Burgundian army, which captured her husband, René I the Good of Anjou, in the first hour. The source of contention, inheritance of the duchies of Bar and Lorraine, aroused the rivalry of cousins. Within months of the death of Isabella's one year old, Count Charles of Guise, her regiment pressed for a treaty and release of René from Philip III of Burgundy. At the battle on July 2, 1431, her ten thousand men faced nine thousand troops from Burgundy, Picardy, and England, who weakened René by a scorched earth attack. Burgundian cannon and archers routed Isabella's forces, killing one thousand.

Isabella achieved a truce on April 24, 1432, hastened by a pledging of her daughter Yolande to Antoine's son Frederick. She negotiated René's one-year parole, leaving as hostages their oldest sons, John II and Louis of Anjou. After her acquisition of the throne of Naples on February 2, 1435, she maintained the government with help from Pope Eugene IV's military, who warded off Alfonso V of Aragon. René remained incarcerated for six years until he paid a sizable ransom in cash and property. He resumed ruling Naples in May 1438. Aided by a son, thirteen-year-old Louis, Isabella revived her battle against

Antoine in August 1440 and outfought him on March 27, 1441. He withdrew the claim on Lorraine.

July 1434

A widowed fief protector, **Ida Henningsdotter Königsmarck (1380–1450)** of Grensholmen, Ostergotland, secured Kastelholm Castle during the Engelbrekt uprising against Eric of Pomerania. At the death of her husband, Benedikt Wolfs Pogwisch in 1432, she maintained the property at Sund, Aland, Finland, and defended her two-year-old daughter Anna against peasant rebels, who laid siege early in July 1434. The island location overlooking a commercial marine route in the Northern Baltic Sea sparked political greed. The revolt, led by Swedish councilor Erik Nilsson Puke, forced Ida's knight, Otto Pogwisch, to quit his post as bailiff. The uprising spread for two years over Gotland and Svealand, causing the ouster of Danish soldiers from Sweden and destabilizing the Kalmar Union that joined Denmark, Norway, and Sweden into a single entity.

May 20, 1436

A commoner warrior from Metz in the Pope Eugene IV's army, Captain **Jeanne des Armoises (also Claude, Jehanne, or Joan, 1407–May 4, 1449)** received church censure for claiming to be a martyred soldier. In the two years following the horrific execution of Joan of Arc, Jeanne cut her hair, dressed in helmet and armor from 1431 to 1433, and served in the infantry alongside Joan's brothers, Jean and Pierre. She risked execution by her claims to be Joan at Metz on May 20, 1436, and subsequent appearances at Orléans, Marieulles, and Arlon.

During the Hundred Years' War after the French recaptured Dieppe and Paris, Jeanne led a mercenary regiment to Cologne on August 2, 1436, to support the choice of bishop for Trier. She achieved the rank of captain and, in 1437, battled the British at the harbor town of La Rochelle. Catholic inquisitors accused Jeanne of being a copycat version of Joan the martyr, a charge that applied to two other impersonators. Jeanne confessed the fraud to Charles VII in 1439 and retired from the military.

1439

In the absence of her husband, Jean I Grimaldi, for two years, **Pomellina Fregoso (also Pomelline, 1390–1462)** of Genoa fought off Savoyard besiegers of Monaco's stronghold. During Jean's incarceration by Louis I, the Duke of Savoy in 1439, she refused to cede Monaco to the usurpers. While protecting their eighteen-year-old daughter Bartolomea and fourteen-year-old son Catalan, she hung on to their realm and forced Louis to release Jean in 1441. In retirement to Menton, she continued to conspire against usurpers and secure Monegasque independence her until her death at age sixty-two.

1445

A Zaydiyyah fighter in north Yemen's high country, **Sharifa Fatima (fl. 1461)** added to her conquest of the cities of Saada (modern Sadah) and Najran, which lie opposite each other on the Arabo-Yemen border. A Shia Muslim in the lineage of the prophet Muhammad, she established the two cities as headquarters. She entered captivity after her husband, Imam al-Mahdi Salad al-Din, was imprisoned in Kawkaban northwest of Sana'a in 1445. After the imam's death, she fled her cell and ruled as Zaydi chief at Dhofar in the coastal mountains of Oman and Saada, Yemen.

Sharifa's reign over a Zaydi faction required a truce with her enemy, al-Mansur al-Nasir, who accepted after wedding her daughter Badr. To terminate further conspiracies, in 1453, Sharifa killed Sheikh Saad Hassan bin Muhammad for plotting her assassination. Al-Mansur's brother attacked Saad and, in 1461, held her at Sana'a. Political rivalries kept her in enemy hands until her death.

July 15, 1445

A Scots queen in lawless times, **Joan Beaufort (1404–July 15, 1445)** of Westminster, and her household lived through assassinations, imprisonment, captivity by pirates, hostage-taking, and a siege at Dunbar Castle. The daughter of John Beaufort, Constable of England, she was sixteen when she met her husband, Scotland's James I, during his jailing by Henry IV alternately at the Tower of London, Nottingham Castle, and Windsor Castle. James lauded Joan in a poem, *The King's Quair*. He was ransomed on March 28, 1424, but received death threats from rivals. He died on February 21, 1437, at the hands of his uncle, Walter Stewart, and nephew, Robert Stewart. The turncoats attacked the queen and stabbed the king while he hid in a drain at the Dominican Blackfriars priory in Perth.

Joan recovered from a stabbing to her shoulder and took charge of six-year-old James II and his annuity of four thousand marks. To strike awe in lesser rivals, she managed the seizure, torture, and execution of the king's killers. She wed James Stewart and entered prison with him on September 4, 1439, on a flimsy charge of endangering the child king. She dashed to Edinburgh Castle, buckled her nine-year-old son in her luggage, and spirited him to the north at the Dunbar artillery blockhouse overlooking the North Sea.

Joan's regency over James II ended in August 1439 in civil war. Over ten months, her enemies, Alexander Livingston of Callendar, keeper of Stirling Castle, and William Crichton, Earl of Douglas, attacked Dunbar Castle. Without weapons, lady-in-waiting Katherine Douglas attempted to ward off the intruders by barring the door with her arm. On July 15, 1445, Joan died of stab wounds while shielding the king with her body and defending her home and title.

February 17, 1448

During the Wars of the Roses, **Margaret Mautby Paston (1423–1484)** from Norfolk, England, shared home responsibilities with her husband, landowner John Paston, and defended their land from lawbreakers while he was away. Through her one hundred four letters, she narrated conflicts, beginning on February 17, 1448, with forcible eviction and damage to Gresham Manor, a moated castle outside Holt, by the covetous Robert Hungerford, Lord Moleyns. Because Robert also stole rents from tenants, Margaret urged John to reclaim his house with crossbows, iron shot, grappling hooks, poleaxes, and armor. While she waited for him to send payment to requite Moleyns, she reported barring her doors and preparing loopholes for pistol and bow shooting.

Under the lax monarchy of Henry VI, Margaret gained no redress. On January 28, 1450, Moleyns and his one thousand troops accosted her in her room, carried her out forcibly, and stole property worth two hundred pounds. More destruction to Hellesdon and Caister Castle in August 1469 resulted from a five-week artillery siege raised by the Duke of Norfolk. In widowhood, she remained firm over a contentious inheritance dispute.

April 1449

A countrywoman warrior from Vigevano in northwestern Italy, **Camilla Rodolfi (fl. 1449)** assembled a female regiment to counter a four-week attack by Francesco I Sforza, commander-in-chief of the Milanese army. Because he besieged Vigevano in April 1449, Camilla's Lombard viragos fought with lance and sword from the castle courtyard. Francesco's men, bribed with cash and the rights of plunder, fought the women until Camilla had to yield on June 6. Francesco enriched the area by installing a bishop. The following year, he began a sixteen-year rule as Duke of Milan. An opera and street bear Camilla's name.

1450

A vengeful rape victim in 1450 during the Hundred Years' War, **Marguerite de Bressieux (?–1450)** of Anjou, France, engaged twelve female horse soldiers to exact payback from the soldiers of Louis II de Chalon, Prince of Orange. After the soldiers besieged and plundered her father's castle at Isère north of Marseilles and murdered her parents, she led the household's women in garbing themselves in black over knight's armor, concealing their faces, and arming with lances, swords, and pikes. At the battle of Autun among the Holy Roman imperial army of Charles VII, their banner depicted a speared orange and read "Ainsi Tu Sera (Thus shall you be)." Before they slew the rapists and tossed their remains into the Rhode River, they revealed their identity. Marguerite died in the battle.

1451

Spy and forger **Brita Olovsdotter Tott (also Birgitte, 1420s–March 3, 1498)** of Denmark, maintained surveillance on Swedish forces throughout a dispute with Denmark over royal succession. At the selection of Christian I as heir of Sweden, the real king, Charles VIII, initiated the six-year Dano-Swedish War. For a year, she backed the Danes, who waged war in Vastergotland near the trade nexus at the Gota River, and joined a conspiracy with regicides. With her guidance, in 1451, Danes overran the Alvsborg bastion at the walled town of Lödöse (modern Gothenburg) overseeing Sweden's only access to the North Sea.

A Swedish captain retook the town

and discovered incriminating letters from Brita. Her arrest and trial for treason at Stockholm in 1452 combined charges of spying with forging legal seals. Although condemned to burn at the stake, Brita negotiated resentencing that required house arrest in Kalmar at St. John's Priory, a Dominican convent, until 1469. To atone for crime, she paid for artist Albertus Pictor to paint frescoes for Osmo Church at Nyashamn. In 1478, she repatriated to Denmark, but returned to Sweden in 1495.

August 20, 1452

A Lombard fresco artist turned crossdressing horse soldier, Captain **Onorata Rodiani (also Honorata Rodiana, 1403–August 20, 1452)** of Castelleone followed the command of Corrado Sforza Fogliani while shielding her hometown from attack. Reported in the 1630 chronicle of Clemente Fiammeni, *Historia di Castelleone* (The History of Castelleone), she stabbed a rapist in the throat with a palette knife at the palace of Prince Cabrino Fondulo at Cremona, where she served as lady-in-waiting to his wife Pomina. Muffled in a man's cloak, Onorata escaped judgment. She became a mercenary at age twenty in service to Marquis Oldrado II Lampugnani, the governor of Genoa.

The Cremona district came under assault in May 1448 by a Venetian army and their Neapolitan allies. A veteran Lombard contender in Francesco Sforza's three-year war of succession, **Bianca Maria Visconti (March 31, 1425–October 28, 1468),** his Milanese wife, dressed in parade armor to rally Cremonese soldiers. In May 1452, an alliance of Milan, Florence, and the army of Pope Nicholas V declared war on twenty-one thousand Venetians. At the raising of the siege of Castelleone that same year, Onorata died on August 20, 1452, of sword slashes. Her legend survives in fiction, painting, reenactments, drama, film, and sculptor Judy Chicago's *The Dinner Party*. Bianca's likeness appears on sculptures, religious paintings, and frescos. On May 14, 1933, Pope Pius XI beatified Bianca.

1455

Shortly after Ottoman sultan Mohammed II seized Constantinople, **Marulla (1435–?)** defended the isle of Lemnos from siege in the northern Aegean Sea. As the Ottoman Turks attacked the gate of Coccino, the island capital, in 1455, Demetrius, Marulla's father, slew besiegers until he died in combat. Although wounded by her father's killer, she leaped into the fray and sliced Turks with his sword. The female exemplar inflamed islanders with such vengeance that they drove the Muslim ships from their shores. The Venetian admiral Antonio Loredano, the patron of Lemnos, awarded her with freedom from taxation. Italian novelist Matteo Bandello recorded the story in fiction, *Marulla the Maiden*.

September 2, 1455

Norwegian noble and sea captain **Elise Eskilsdotter (ca. 1400–1492)** avenged the death of husband, the knight Olav Nilsson Skanke, and son Nils for pillaging German merchant vessels. Under the aegis of Christian I of Denmark, Olav, commander of Fort

Bergenhus overlooking the harbor, waylaid cargo ships of the Hanseatic League in the Baltic Sea. He and Elise continued piracy after the conclusion of the Hanseatic War in 1435. For their crime, Hansa merchants set fire to Munkeliv Abbey at Bergen and executed sixty Norwegians, including Olav and Nils, Olav's brother Peder Nilsson Skanke, and the bishop of Bergen, Leif Thor Olafsson, who had given Olav's family sanctuary.

Elise escaped the assassins by disguising herself in monk's cowl and robe. Aided by son Axel Olofsson Skanke, on September 2, 1455, she focused sea crimes against Bergen merchants. She lost fifteen-year-old son Olav to shipwreck in 1465. In 1468, Christian I confiscated her titles and property in the Ryfylke district. Two years after winning compensation from the Hanseatic League, she died at age ninety-two at Vittskovle in southern Scania (modern Sweden).

October 7, 1458

A Peloponnesian princess from Mystras on the Pelponnesus (southern Greece), **Helena Palaiologina (February 3, 1428–April 11, 1458)**, the queen of Cyprus, fought her stepson, James II, during a three-year barricading of Kyrenia's harbor on the north. From 1455, Helena secured the royal stronghold for herself, her eleven-year-old daughter, Charlotte, and her weakling husband, John II. They drew fresh water from a cistern in the courtyard and depended on curtain walls for interior security from projectiles. Within fourteen weeks of each other, the couple died without defeating James.

At age fourteen, **Charlotte of Cyprus (June 28, 1444–July 16, 1487)** of Nicosia escaped James's troops and seized the throne on October 7, 1458. James, the archbishop of Nicosia, gained support from the armada of Mamluk Sultan Sayf ad-Din Inal of Cairo in challenging the succession of his sister and her husband, Louis of Savoy. The couple survived a three-year siege before Charlotte fled to Pope Pius II to petition for aid to Cypriot troops. He pledged support in the form of grain and wine.

Spring 1461

At Norfolk, England, during the Wars of the Roses, Lady **Alice Lynne Knyvet (also Knyvett, 1418–after January 1490)** shielded Buckenham Castle, England's earliest manse, from repossession by Edward IV's ten Yorkist commissioners. Organizing fifty Lancastrian residents and loyalist soldiers inside the earthen wards, in spring 1461, she distributed bundles of wood, pavers, timbers, slings, swords, bladed poles, and bows and arrows as armaments. To protect her son William and teenaged daughters Christiana, Elizabeth, and Margery, she ordered the drawbridge raised. From a tower, she yelled that she refused to submit to government authorities until her husband, Justice of the Peace John Knyvet IV, returned home. At death at age seventy-two, she was interred at All Saints Churchyard in Ashwellthorpe.

1467

Ongud tribe member **Mandukhai Khatun (1449–1510)**, empress of the Northern Yuan dynasty, worked toward the unification of tribes and an end to civil uprisings in Mongolia. At her marriage to stepson Batmonkh Dayan Khan, a scion of Genghis Khan, in 1467, she led forces against the fractious Oirats, a forest people of Western Mongolia. In the Altai region of Siberia, her army recovered governmental control of the west. During a lengthy battle, she gave birth to twin boys, the first two of ten children.

Throughout Mongol raids to the south, in 1480, Mandukhai faced a Renaissance invention—Ming hand cannon primed with gunpowder, which replaced fire lances. In the late 1400s at the re-buttressing of the Great Ming Wall where it sliced the clay and sand Ordos steppe on the Yellow River, her sentinels guarded the Ordos department, which her imperial family reclaimed in the name of Genghis Khan. In 1483, she directed Mongol soldiers to the fertile oasis of Hami and crushed Turco-Mongols and Muslims. In 1501, she relocated to the north at the Kherlen River, leaving her husband in command. While fighting a Ming spy, she died in combat at age sixty-one.

1467

In payment of a debt to the Danes, **Ólöf Loftsdóttir (also Olafar, 1410–1479)** from Skardi, Iceland, replaced her deceased husband, Björn ríki Þorleifsson, in battles against illicit English commercial interests. The couple reared eleven children and amassed a fortune at Skard Manor opposite their harbor trading post. After their kidnap by Scots pirates in 1455 near the Orkney Islands, she aided King Christian I of Denmark by ousting English traders and seizing their funds. In a skirmish against traders from Lynn in 1467, the English decapitated Björn and seven of his men. At Rif on the Snæfellsnes Peninsula, the traders arrested their son, the herder Þorleifur Björnsson of Reykholar. Ólöf's vengeful retaliation freed her son and captured fifty Englishmen for jailing at Skardi. After the inmates served involuntary slavery, she beheaded them. In 1473, the Danish king issued a cease-and-desist order against English commercial interests.

May 4, 1471

The queen of England, **Margaret of Anjou (also Marguerite, March 23, 1430–August 25, 1482)**, of Pont-a-Mousson, France, ceded the battle of Tewkesbury, a pivotal segment of the Wars of the Roses. Because of the mental ills of her husband, Henry VI, she handily ruled in his place after his capture on July 10, 1460, at the battle of Northampton. She and their seven-year-old son, Prince Edward of Wales, escaped to Scotland, where she raised an army of mounted men and led them south. At St. Albans, she overcame the Yorkist army and rescued Henry, who had been held in the Tower of London.

A power wielder, Margaret negotiated at Chinon with Louis XI for two thousand men-at-arms, supplies, and twenty thousand crowns (approx. £55,636 or $74,575.54). In 1462, she used his largesse to seize Alnwick, Bamborough, and Dunstanburg castles for the House of Lancaster. She continued to draft support in Scotland in winter 1463 and, promising her mercenaries the right of havoc, used them the next April to raid and pillage south of Hadrian's Wall. During a retreat in May 1464 to Hexham Woods on the Tyne River, with her ten-year-old son in her arms, she fought off a band of marauders until a Lancastrian rescuer concealed her in a cave.

Following a decade of exile in France, where Margaret promoted jousting in the lists, she guided Henry once more to reign. Resolved to defend her resources, she risked decimation in the Lancaster-York clash by debarking at Weymouth on March 24, 1471, and tricking the Yorkists with indecipherable tactics. At the spa town of Bath, she halted a march toward Wales to purchase weapons and raise money at Bristol. She again confused the enemy by dodging the Lancastrian army of six thousand and taking cover at Sodbury Hill, a Saxon earthworks. While attempting to ford the Severn River on May 4, 1471, she lost Edward outside the market town of Tewkesbury, where pursuers lopped off his head.

The Yorkists attacked Margaret's three thousand troops with arrows, battle axes, and artillery and captured her at Tewkesbury. After being marched in shame Roman style through London streets on May 21, she was remanded to prison at Windsor and Wallingford castles near Oxford in 1472 and later at the Tower of London, where King Henry VI died of dagger wounds. Three years later, Louis XI ransomed Margaret after she had sworn an oath not to make war anymore. Various chronicles, operas, novels, TV series, film, and William Shakespeare's *Henry IV* and *Richard III* proposed conflicting accounts of the battles and Margaret's role as commander.

June 27, 1472

A one-woman defense, **Jeanne Hachette (also Jeanne Fourquet or Jeanne Laisné, November 14, 1454–?)** rallied the French at Beauvais by chopping down the enemy flag. The daughter of a royal security guard, she grew up fascinated by the courage of Joan of Arc. When Charles I the Bold of Burgundy and his eighty thousand men attacked the town's militia of three hundred on June 27, 1472, Jeanne gathered women armed with muskets, torches, and stones in lieu of artillery. On the Therain River, the female troops invaded the ramparts, loaded cannon, distributed arrows, and directed melted lead, hot embers, quicklime, and boiling water and oil on Charles's lancers and archers. The women set fire to the portcullis and kept it stoked to prevent a breach of the wall.

When arsonists inflamed parts of the city, the women caught and decapitated them. Jeanne knocked a Burgundian soldier off the battlements and into the moat. Still battling the Burgundians a month later, her militia drove the enemy away on July 22, 1472, and deposited the flag in a church. Louis XI honored her with a procession and artillery salvo and appointed her marshal of the French army. Her likeness survives in the poem "Jeanne Hachette," drama, film, and a bronze statue with hatchet in one hand and the offensive banner in the other. She was widowed in 1477, when her husband, Colin Pilon, died at the siege of Nancy.

March 1, 1476

Following a declaration of rights to the throne of Castile, **Juana la Beltraneja (also Joanna, February 21, 1462–April 12, 1530)** of Madrid led eight thousand troops against the forces of a rival, Isabella I. During the War of Castilian Succession, a disaster in Zamora at Toro on March 1, 1476, preceded a Catholic political coup for Isabella. After the battlefield deaths of one thousand supporters, Juana retreated to the west with the remains of her Portuguese army. Her fiancé, Alphonso V of Portugal, abandoned the cause of the Trastamara dynasty on September 4, 1479, by signing the Treaty of Tercerias. She opted for a cloistered life at Santa Clara of Santarem, where she pledged celibacy in November 1480. In 1522, she relinquished her claim to Castile.

May 1, 1480

In the last weeks of her life, on May 1, 1480, **Margareta of Celje (also Margareta von Cilly, 1411–July 22, 1480)**, a widow from Slovenia, shielded half Głogów and Ścinawa from the ambitions of Jan II the Mad of Zagan. Near the end of the Middle Ages, Jan began adding to his lands with the annexation of Zaghan, Szprotawa, and Kozuchow. Multiple battles brought him to Brandenburg in 1478 and to Głogów. Because her protector, Casimir II, abdicated his claims to the inherited territory, in the second week of March 1480, Duchess Margareta, at age sixty-nine, had to soldier on by herself. She died eleven weeks after Jan's capture of Głogów.

April 20, 1481

A widowed chatelaine at Franeker, **Swob Sjaarda (also Swob Hottinga or Swob Sjaerdema, 1435–1520)** of Oud-Sjaerdema, Frisia, lifted the family manse from anarchy. After the death of her husband Jarich Epes Hottinga in 1475, she took charge of defending Hottingastins, home of their six children. She fought warring Schieringer and Vetkoper clans, who pillaged and burned buildings, robbed markets, murdered owners, and rustled cattle. In her sixth year of protecting the manse from cannon fire, she challenged the warrior Scherne (Skinhead) Wybe Grovestins of Engelum.

In the history of Franeker chronicler Christianus Schotanus, Swob pretended to be ill. To invalidate her pledge of safe conduct, she let Scherne leave, then beckoned for his return, thus voiding her promise. Her ruse on the drawbridge left Scherne open to capture by security guards and jailing in the cellar until negotiation of a ceasefire. At Easter on April 20, 1481, she exchanged Scherne for Swob's brother Tjaard Grioesters. At Pentecost a year later, Scherne died by bullet during the storming of another castle.

1482

An adviser and organizer of revolt, **Aisha al-Hurra (also Aixa, fl. 1480s–1490s)** of Granada staked out territory in the Alhambra Palace in 1482 to support Arab culture and halt the Spanish interloper Soraya, a Christian convert to Islam. In concert with the Abencerrage clan, Aisha advocated the ousting of her disloyal husband Ali Abu al-Hasan and the crowning of her son Muhammad XII Boabdil as the last Nasrid sultan. By currying local support, while she resided at the Dar al-Horra residence, she commanded attacks on the palace. Her extreme patriotism demanded a fight to the death by Granada non-combatants against the Aragon-Castile forces of Ferdinand and Isabella. After Granada's surrender on January 2, 1492, she ordered Boabdil not to kiss the hands of their conquerors. Accompanied by depleted Moors, she fled into exile with Boabdil to Alpujarras, Spain, and his palace at Fes, Morocco.

August 12, 1484

Rioting in Rome after the death of Pope Sixtus IV caused **Caterina Sforza (1463–May 28, 1509)** of Milan to occupy the Castel Sant'Angelo or Hadrian's Tomb, the papal retreat overlooking the Tiber River. After bandits overran her home at Campo de' Fiori, the Riario Palace east of the pope's residence at the Vatican, on August 12, 1484, she defended the papacy against usurpers. For war, she shielded herself in a steel cuirass bearing an engraved likeness of Saint Catherine of Alexandria and trained her six-year-old daughter **Bianca Riario (March 1478–1523)** in self-defense as she had learned in girlhood.

Although only eight weeks from the delivery of her sixth child, Francesco Sforzino Riario, in 1487, Caterina mustered troops and artillery to guard cardinals while they voted for a replacement pope. Because Vatican authorities negotiated a settlement with her husband, Girolamo Riario, Sixtus's nephew, she heightened militance against the Sacred College. The standoff ended in the tenth week with her surrender and retreat from the city and the election of Pope Innocent VIII. In 1521, Bianca emulated Caterina by allying with brother Giovanni to protect her nine children and home from hostile relatives.

See also April 14, 1488; September 14, 1498.

1487

A widowed defender of Raseborg Castle on the southern tip of Finland, **Katarina Nipertz (1437–1487)** from Djursholm, Sweden, fought off the invasive troops of Sten Sture the Elder. For four years, she replaced her deceased husband, Laurens Axelsson Tott, as fiefholder at Western Uusimaa, Finland. When Sten attempted to repossess the cliffside castle, she held him at bay for several weeks while protecting her thirteen-year-old daughter Ingeborg. Katarina died in 1487 shortly after surrendering the property.

April 14, 1488

The rival Orsi family of Forli stabbed Girolamo Riario to death on April 14, 1488, tossed his remains out a window, and forced his widow, **Caterina Sforza** of Milan, to offer her children as hostages while she sought vengeance on the assassins. Locked in Rocca di Ravaldino, a redoubt in Forli on the northern Adriatic Sea, she wore down her enemies, captured the conspirators, seized their property, and retained control of Riario family lands west of Ravenna. As regent for Girolamo's nine-year-old heir, Lord Ottaviano Riario of Forli and Imola, she protected clan interests until his majority by recruiting a militia and training them in horsemanship and arms.

February 1489

The six-month siege of Baza during the decade-long Granada War motivated **Isabella I of Castile (December 11, 1474–November 26, 1504)** to advise King Ferdinand and to superintend the combat zone. She relocated the Spanish court northwest of Granada to Jaén and maintained a royal mail service to King Ferdinand in Cordova. To prevent mutiny, she eased army privations by allowing sutlers to trade food and goods at the military compound, composed of adobe huts and ramadas made from upright posts with branches overhead. From the Jaén gristmills, she dispatched some fourteen thousand mules daily with provisions, which she paid for with sale of her jewelry and crown treasures. Her presence raised soldier enthusiasm for the Reconquista of Al-Andalus.

Isabella appeared to end the conflict on December 4, 1489, following a year-long typhus epidemic. She marched across the mountains through Cordova to Seville with her entourage at the army's rear. Rekindled hostilities on 23, April 1491, extended the struggle seven months, causing the queen to equip and supply a grand army of sixty thousand, bolstered by Swiss reinforcements. When she camped in view of the Alhambra, an Arab assassin hurled a lance at her pavilion. She followed up with a personal investigation at the head of her cavalry and allowed a champion to slay the assassin one on one. Moorish forces harassed her forces all the way to Granada, losing two thousand to her Spaniards.

At the treaty of November 25, 1491, and the surrender of Granada's Moorish emir Muhammad XII to Isabella on January 2, 1492, the Spanish concluded seven hundred seventy years of Muslim control. For extra security, the queen's forces hid a militia in the Alhambra. On January 6, she joined the king in a formal military procession. Christian states celebrated the loss of one hundred thousand Muslims and Isabella's appointment of Tomas de Torquemada to head the Spanish Inquisition.

Late 1400s

A female warrior from the precolonial North Malabar hills, **Unniyarcha (also Archa, Attummanammel Unniyarcha, or Unnijarcha, fl. early 1500s)** of Katdathanad (modern Kerala, India) dismayed attackers by her skill at martial arts and the urumi sword, a hilt attached to sharp, flexible blades. The daughter of an expert fighter, she was educated in southwest Indian military maneuvers from age seven and attended gymnasium classes with her brother, Chief Aromal Chekavar. While traveling to Nadapuram on the Arabian Sea with her husband, she had to protect him from attacking Mappila Muslims.

By strength of spirit, Unniyarcha cowed the brigands with her whip-like blades and forced them to promise that women could walk the road without fear or peril from outlaws. After a traitorous cousin murdered Aromal during a duel, Unniyarcha's son Aromunni applied the Thiyyar family skills in avenging his uncle's death. Storytelling, ballads, and cinema preserve the heroics of brother and nephew and the female independence and valor of Unniyarcha.

See also January 25, 2017.

1490

The French abbess and reformer of Fontevrault, **Renée de Bourbon (May 1468–November 8, 1534)** entered armed conflict to rid religious houses of corruption. In an era of lapsed priories during the Hundred Years' War, the wealthy complex profited from the first of five Bourbon elections to superintend one hundred dominions, seventy-eight priories, fiefs, forests, mills, and bridges. At age twenty-two, she replaced Abbess Anne d'Orléans and reformed the double monastery, a Benedictine retreat located at Anjou south of the Loire River. To finance renovations, she liquidated gold jewelry and silver plate.

Reforms required a quarter century of work, beginning with higher walls dividing female postulants from males. In 1503, Renee borrowed the Swiss guards of Francis I and headed their discipline of recalcitrant residents. For sinful nuns and monks, she outlined severe punishments for violation of vows. In 1519, she requested papal bulls from Leo X to back up her strictures. Despite Protestant inroads against Catholicism, her household grew to one hundred fifty brothers and one hundred sixty sisters. UNESCO added the abbey to its list of World Heritage Sites.

September 15, 1494

A Frisian aristocrat, **Ats Bonninga (also Ath Bonninga, ?–1494)** of Sneek hurried to the aid of husband, Jelmer Ottes Sytsma, after his capture during the clash between the poor and wealthy landowners at Gaasterland in northern Holland. She defended Fort Warns to free him from the violent Vetkopers, fomenters of civil war. Because Douwe Galama, a Vetkoper, died in artillery fire, the enemy attacked Ats and Jelmer's stone house. A battle between Warns and the village of Harich killed Ats's father and wounded Jelmer. She refused to yield the entrenchment until priests could arrange a prisoner swap. When the Vetkopers leveled the parapet, Ats and Jelmer departed as exiles. A poet and street name commemorate her courage.

1496

The great grandmother of the Emperor Akbar and battlefield companion of her son Babur, **Qutlugh Nigar (all Kutlak Nigar, ca. 1460–June 10, 1505)** from Moghulistan (modern Uzbekistan) aided and advised Babur in the conquest of Samarkand from the Turco-Mongol conqueror Timur, founder of the Timurid Empire. The daughter of Yunus, the Moghulistan khan, she bore the title "Khanum" or princess. Mother and son claimed ancestry from Genghis Khan and joined in raids. On Babur's way to founding the Mughal Empire of India, his two thousand guerrilla warriors captured Kabul, Afghanistan, in 1504 and established it as a military base for the conquest of Hindustan. Qutlugh succumbed to fever on June 10, 1505, at age forty-five. Babur acknowledged her military assistance in his 1530 memoir, *Baburnama*.

August 1496

Despite pregnancy, Frisian hero **Bauck Poppema (also Bauck Foppesd van Popma or Bauck Hemmema, 1465–1501)** of the island of Terschelling defended Fort Hemmemastate during a local conflict between the poor and wealthy landowners. In the final years of a fifty-year civil war, Dutch insurgents from Gröningen laid siege to the earthen-walled acropolis and its garrison of twenty-five soldiers. After giving up firing cannon, the enemy hid under hay to swim cross the moat. Bauck's forces burned the subterfuge, wounding the swimmers. At the failure of her defense on September 3, the enemy executed her militia. She entered a Gröningen prison and bore twins before her release by prisoner exchange in May 1497.

September 14, 1498

At the death of her third husband, Giovanni de 'Medici, from pneumonia, **Caterina Sforza (1463–May 28, 1509)**, a member of a Milanese clan of mercenaries, mobilized her nine hundred soldiers of Rocca di Ravaldino, a garrison in Forli, against a Venetian troop of sixteen thousand. Her advance earned the admiration of military philosopher Niccolo Machiavelli and the sobriquet "The Tiger." Within the year, the Renaissance virago faced Duke Cesare Borgia and a French army, but was unable to capture him. At his bombardment of her defenses, on January 12, 1500, she took arms and dueled with him. He imprisoned her in Rome at the Castel Sant' Angelo until June 1501.

Renaissance, 1400–1600

During the Renaissance, a period of social and economic flowering, Europeans gravitated from religious fanaticism and medieval superstition to new challenges in scientific inquiry, architecture, humanistic writing, navigation, art, and colonialism. The collapse of Ottoman rule encouraged the rebirth of learning and experimentation that spread north and west to men and women.

August 1501

The queen of Scandinavia, **Christina of Saxony (December 25, 1461–December 8, 1521)** from Torgau, defended Stockholm's Kronor Castle for eight months. During her marriage to King John (also Hans) of Denmark, the couple resided primarily at Nykobing Castle. In the absence of her husband with his mistress, royal lady-in-waiting Edel Jernskjæg, in August 1501, Christina restored herself from ill health. In September, she fought off a fall-to-spring onslaught of Norwegian-Swedish rebels against Denmark, John, and the Kalmar Union of Scandinavian states. The confederacy governed most of Scandinavia, Iceland, Greenland, Shetland, Orkney, and the Faroe Islands.

Conflict began with rioting in Stockholm, where the queen awaited rescue by her profligate husband. The heavy winter assault reduced rations to salt meat, a cause of scurvy from the lack of vegetables. Famine and plague reduced Christina's garrison from one thousand to seventy men or .07 percent, endangering her four-year-old son Frans of Denmark.

Her son, Christian II of Denmark, participated in the fight, the beginning of the twelve-year Dano-Swedish War that advanced from Stockholm to Sweden's west coast. By May 9, 1502, Christina ceded to separatist leader Sten Sture the Elder on the stipulation that he allow her reentry to Denmark. Within days, John's fleet approached the shore, but he chose not to aid Christina.

Because of Sten's deception, she had to accept eighteen months of house arrest at Vadstena Abbey, a double monastery on Lake Vattern, Sweden, until her husband agreed to a peace pact in 1503. At Grey Friars Monastery, she came under the control of another warrior woman, **Ingeborg Åkesdotter Tott (?–December 1507)**, a Swede from Orebro Castle who commanded the military citadels in Finland and Sweden. On December 14, 1503, Christina repatriated to Denmark and resided at a farm near Odense. Two years later, Ingeborg had to defend her own castle, Häme in Finland, against Swedish rebels.

1502

South of the Dovre mountains, Danish amazon **Anne Jørgensdatter Rud (1474–June 1533)** from Vedby, West Zealand, defended Fort Bohus in 1502 during the rural revolt of Knut Alvsson against Hans, king of Denmark, Norway, and Sweden. While her husband, Henrik Krummedige, safeguarded Akershus bastion from Knut, Anne protected the medieval redoubt of Bohus, a source of wealth on the Göta River from timber, iron ore, grain, cattle, butter, and fish at Kungälv, Norway. Her charge included Sofie, a two-year-old daughter and her only child. In widowhood after 1530, Anne witnessed the end of the family line at Mogenstrup.

1503

A victim of Spanish colonialism, **Anacaona (1474–1504)**, a widowed Taino *cacica* (chief) from Yaguana, Hispaniola (modern Leogane, Haiti), followed the example of royal ancestors in preserving her Native American subjects from conquistadors. At Xaragua, the rape of women and enslavement of men in press gangs to work gold mines in August 1493 forced her to consider options to rid the island of Spanish oppression. At her brother's death in 1500, she succeeded to the throne and received Governor Nicolás Ovando and his three hundred followers at a welcome ceremony. The unexpected capture of Taino authority figures forced her to act the warrior queen to halt massacre and arson. In 1503, Ovando apprehended Anacaona and, a year later, ordered her hanged.

1503

An Hispano-Italian widow by her twenties, **Costanza d'Avalos (1460–1541)** of Pescara on the Adriatic Sea, defended the island of Ischia against French attackers. The raiders executed islanders and destroyed their villages. In 1503, her armed resistance in the Gulf of Naples saved the region for sixteen weeks from forty French galleys that bombarded the Aragonese Castle. For her valor, Holy Roman Emperor Charles V gave her family civil and military power on the island and an arts colony for her circle of Neapolitan intellectuals and artists. Historians believe that her name, "La Gioconda," identifies her as painter Leonardo da Vinci's Mona Lisa.

1504

To ensure her son Esigie's successful crowning as king of Benin, Queen **Idia (fl. 1500s–1550)**, a mystic healer from Edo (modern Benin City, southwest Nigeria) ended a brotherly power struggle. In 1504, she aided Esigie in mobilizing an army. On a Unuame battlefield in the tropical rainforest overlooking the Osse River (modern Ovia River), Esigie trounced his half-brother Arhuanran. Subsequent warfare yielded overthrow of the Igala king Aji-Ata and the Idah Kingdom on the Niger River. In the battle of Idah in 1515, she wore a male uniform and ceremonial sword and accompanied Esigie to the front lines. For her gallant support against assassins and advice on soldiery, he named her queen mother and gave her a palace at Uselu (modern Benin City outskirts). Her ivory portrait mask survives at the British Museum.

1510

While shipwrecked at Matanzas in western Cuba, in 1510, Conquistadora **María de Estrada (1475–1527)** of Seville, Spain, evaded a native American massacre of Europeans. In 1513, she ended her residency as a castaway. As detailed in chronicler Diego Camargo's *History of Tlaxcala*, in April 1520, she continued to Mexico and encountered Spanish adventurer Hernan Cortes in late May. Armed with sword and shield, she survived the "Night of Sorrows" on June 30, 1520, at Tenochtitlan, where Cortes lost horses, artillery, treasure, and one hundred fifty-four soldiers to a native reprisal for the murder of Montezuma. A week later at Otumba, she fought in Cortes's successful battle against Aztec pursuers. Her service continued the New World conquest with the crushing of the Nahua Indians at Hueyapan. She established a plantation in Morelos state, where she died in 1527 of cholera.

April 1511–1513

The Finnish widow of the knight Eric Bielke, **Gunilla Johansdotter Bese (1475–1553)** presided over Vyborg Castle, a medieval stronghold now located in northwestern Russia. To maintain control of a crucial inlet of the Gulf of Finland for eighteen months, in April 1511, she mediated a treaty with Russia and dispatched curt letters declining to leave her home. By refusing entry to the new owner, she held the property until 1513, when it passed to her son-in-law. Her example influenced the actions of a daughter, **Anna Eriksdotter Bielke (1490–1525),** who guarded Kalmar against Danish rebels. Anna had to yield to Denmark on September 6, 1520.

See February–September 6, 1520.

August 24, 1511

Tun Fatimah (fl. early 1500s), a hard-handed Malaccan queen, led a native army against the Europeans seeking to control Asiatic trade routes. During a vicious power struggle, she was forced to marry Sultan Mahmud Shah and fought his tyranny by aborting her pregnancies. At the intrusion of Portuguese trade galleys from the Gulf of Bengal into Malaya's Straits of Malacca, on September 11, 1509, she plotted reprisals. The Shah repositioned the military to a stronghold at Bintan. He conspired to murder intruder Diogo Lopes de Sequeira, but his attempts failed to overthrow the imperialism of Portuguese king Manuel I.

For recruits against Portugal's twelve hundred troops, the queen relied on mercenaries of questionable loyalty. Two years later, a traitor enabled the besiegers to capture the Malaccan sultanate and enforce Islam over the archipelago. After the collapse of the sultanate on August 24, 1511, Tun Fatimah reestablished the monarchy at Borneo and Sumatra and allied with regional monarchs through marriage. Following the Sultan's death in 1528, their son Alauddin rebuilt a capital at Hujung Tanah on the Johor River. Tun Fatimah's name disappeared from history, but survives in cinema and attached to a mausoleum at Sumatra, three colleges, a high school, and stadium.

September 9, 1513

At the boundary separating Scotland from England, **Isabella Hoppringle (1470–January 26, 1538)** from Giht served the English as a spy during an era of border clashes. In the eighth year as abbess of Coldstream convent on the River Tweed, she pitted army against army in a disastrous match-up between the twenty thousand men of Henry VIII and twenty-five thousand of James IV. On marshy ground, English troops with their maneuverable, rapid-fire artillery and billhooks massacred the pike-wielding Scots on September 9, 1513, at the battle of Flodden. Isabella aided casualties and dug graves for the ten thousand dead, which included the forty-year-old Scots king James.

Isabella's term of office with the Cistercians ended with her death at age sixty-eight, when she gave place to spy **Janet Pringle (1495–1565)**, the next prioress. With Janet's initiation to espionage in 1537, she harbored English spies and relied on her whole family to help the English. At the destruction of the abbey by fire in 1545, she became a double agent for Scotland.

1515

Kayambi defender and assassin **Quilago (1485–1515)** of Tabacundo (modern Ecuador) died trying to foster Cochasqui residents from expansionist Inca emperor Huayna Capac. Native resistance spread over two decades, forcing her tribe to unite with the Marango. In the last three years of her life, she rebuffed Inca insurgents from Quito, Peru, until her capture in combat on the Rio Quispe, the Kayambi southern border. Overwhelmed, at age thirty, she became Huayna Capac's war trophy and the mother of his son Atahualpa. Under house arrest, she set a trap for him in her bedroom by filling a pit with spikes. Because of a servant's treachery, in 1515, Quilago died in her own device.

January 19, 1520

A participant in the Dano-Swedish War, army commander **Christina Nilsdotter Gyllenstierna (1494–January 1559)** of Fogelvik led Sweden's military while defending the city of Stockholm. A scion of Dano-Swedish royalty and first lady of her country, as wife and widow, she lived on the edge of power and coercion. The invasion of Danish king Christian II at Bogesund in southern Sweden on January 1, 1520, caused the death of Christina's twenty-six-year-old husband, Sten Sture the Younger, on the frozen lake Asenden when a cannon ball crushed his leg. On January 19, 1520, Christina took Sten's role as anti-unionist leader defying the Kalmar Union, a Scandinavian confederacy of states led by Gustav Trolle, Archbishop of Uppsala.

Christina roused peasant support and, on April 9, 1520, crushed Danish insurgents and French, German, and Scots mercenaries at Uppsala. She committed heresy by seizing Trolle's keep at Staket on the eastern shore. After assuring the safety of seven-year-old son and heir Nils Stensson Sture at Danzig, she entered regional discussions of Danish aggression with Christian I, whom Trolle crowned king of Sweden. In tandem with another Swedish amazon, **Anna Eriksdotter Bielke (1490–April 1525)**, Christina ended a four-month onslaught at Stockholm on September 7, 1520, by accepting amnesty. Before Christina's jailing at Stockholm Castle under Trolle's orders, Christian decapitated two of her brothers and an uncle and sentenced her mother Sigrid to be sewn in a sack and drowned in the North Sea.

The king retracted the harsh penalty to Sigrid and chose to spare Christina either live burial or burning at the stake for heresy. After her transfer to the tower dungeon at Copenhagen Castle in September 1521, she and other political prisoners barely survived on starvation rations until their release three years later. Her sister Cecilia and two nieces died of malnutrition and plague. Christina's nephew ruled as King Gustav I Vasa. Her likeness survives on an altar bas relief at Vasteras basilica in Västmanland.

See also February–September 6, 1520.

February–September 6, 1520

A Swedish widow, **Anna Eriksdotter Bielke** fortified Kalmar and its castle at coastal Småland against attack by the Danish fleet of King Christian II. To aid the exiled King Gustav I Vasa, for seven months, in February 1520, she governed lands of her deceased husband, Privy Councilman Johan Mansson, in the south near the Danish border. At the same time, she secured the strategic Kalmar Strait, the gateway to Småland on the Baltic Sea. She attempted to recruit citizens to the Swedish cause, but surrendered Kalmar Castle to Denmark on September 6, 1520. In November, Christian II added Sweden to his realm of Denmark and Norway. Anna's actions appear in the three-act opera *Gustav Vasa*.

See also January 19, 1520; 1522.

May 20, 1520

During Spanish adventurer Hernan Cortes's conquest of Tenochtitlan (modern Mexico City, Mexico), **Beatriz Bermúdez de Velasco (1500–after 1520s)**, the wife of Francisco de Olmos and an armed Spanish soldier, shamed Spaniards and local Indians for retreating from the allied Mexica army of Aztec, Tlaxcala, and Totonac. In the summary composed by Francisco Cervantes de Salazar from Toledo, Spain, the author of *Crónica de la Nueva España* (History of New Spain), she took part in Pánfilo de Narváez's expedition and fought in the Extremadura contingent. "La Bermuda" threatened to execute with her sword all cowards who fled combat. At her urging, on May 20, 1520, the invaders reversed course and battered the Aztecs bloody within the hour. Tenochtitlan and the Aztec empire fell to Cortes on August 13, 1521.

April 23, 1521

An instigator of revolt and chief of anti-feudal peasant forces, **María Pacheco Padilla (1496–March 1531)** of Granada exhorted Castilians from Toledo, Tordesillas, and Valladolid to oust Spain's King Charles I, the grandson of Ferdinand and Isabella. For six months,

Maria replaced her husband in the *comunero* (commoner) war, a revolt over the Spanish succession after the death of Isabella I of Castile in 1504. Because the queen's grandson grew up in Holland and surrounded himself with Flemish retainers, his popularity flagged, particularly after his selection in 1519 as Holy Roman Emperor Charles V. Contributing to peasant suspicions, he authorized confinement of Isabella's daughter, Juana of Castile.

Beginning in April 1520, Castilian militias followed Captain-General Juan Lopez de Padilla, commander of Toledo's army, in an uprising. Juan, co-commanders Juan Bravo and Francisco Maldonado, and their seven thousand irregulars and four hundred horsemen protested unreasonable taxation and loss of sovereignty. They defied control by a Spanish emperor located in Burgundian territory and the appointment of Flemish counselor Jean de Sauvage over the treasury. Populists won at Torrelobatón and pressed on to Villalar de los Comuneros, where peasant artillery and arquebuses (proto-rifles) proved ineffective. Imperial cavalry assaults produced one thousand casualties or nearly fourteen percent of the peasant force.

The overwhelming rout on April 23, 1521, preceded Juan's beheading the next day along with execution of Bravo and Maldonado. Peasant factions abandoned support of Juana, a close friend and defender of Juan's widow, María Pacheco Padilla. Immediately, María Pacheco, a vengeful widow and zealous rebel, began rebuilding peasant strength at Toledo against the imperial army and the loss of civil liberties. Her procession through town with her orphaned son raised a crucifix as a banner. She recruited men and charged clergy for the army's support. For supplies and cash, she impounded saints' shrines and church goods from the Toledo cathedral.

Maria, a champion of republicanism and equality, led army forays against royalist encampments. Nonetheless, her revolt ended on October 25, 1521, when the *comuneros* gave in to feudal powers. Part of the failure was a peasant superstition that her African maid was a demon—a witch's familiar. Under dire repression, Maria escaped to Portugal in disguise and resided in exile at Oporto, where she taught Latin and Greek. On October 28, 1522, Charles V marched back to Spain with four thousand knights and issued amnesty to all but three hundred *comuneros* conspirators. María Pacheco's example inspired liberal females throughout the Peninsular War and into the 1800s.

1522

During the siege of Stockholm under Gustav I Vasa, King of Denmark, **Anna Rheinholdsdotter Leuhusen (ca. 1508–1554)**, the abbess of St. Clare's Abbey at Norrmalm smuggled Swedish courtiers and businessmen from the priory to safety. A zealous Dane like her father Bela and brother Martin, she took the post of convent mistress in 1508 out of dedication to Clare of Assisi and the Franciscan order known as Poor Clares. Among her goals were a new roof and financial aid to the prior's tenants. As reported in *Den Kroniske Peder Svart*

(Peder Svart's Chronicle), throughout the Swedish War of Liberation, from January 1521, she conspired to rescue Danish mutineers and betray the king. For signals of refugee presence, in 1522, she fluttered a white fabric from the convent window and lit a lantern by night.

Because of complicity with the Danes, Anna and her nuns increased the number of Swedish arrests and executions. In June 1524, a search of the convent located items that the Danes stole from Stockholm residents. Her punishment for treason caused King Christian II to dissolve the priory. In 1527, he relocated her to Grey Friar Abbey on Kungsholmen Island, a sanctuary and hospital where she nursed the sick until the institution's remodeling into King's College Stockholm, a theology school. At her death in 1554, a will set aside sixty-three coins for the Poor Clares.

April 21, 1524

A Chutia class martyr to her country, **Sati Sadhani (1493–April 21, 1524)** from Sadiya, Assam, in northeastern India faced a losing battle against the indigenous Ahom, a Tai ethnic minority. The queen, during ongoing clashes of the clannish Ahom with the Chutia, fought annexation of her realm. At the assault on her throne, she and her husband Nitipal fled threats from spears and crossbows and hid in the Chandragiri hills. At the head of a brigade of one hundred twenty women, Sati joined in hill strategies of tumbling boulders onto the attacking guerrillas. The Ahom tricked the queen by pounding victory drums, causing her to lower her guard. When an archer killed Nitipal, on April 21, 1524, Sati Sadhani rejected a proposal to wed an Ahom groom by leaping from a precipice. Her example survives in a national holiday and annual reward to a leader of the arts.

August 19–September 24, 1524

While Charles III, the Constable de Bourbon, combatted the nine thousand men of Francis I, the Valois king of France, on August 19, 1524, the forces of **Ameliane du Puget-Glandevès (fl. 1520s)** and sisters **Claire de Laval (fl. 1520s)** and **Gabrielle Laval** (fl. 1520s) lifted the thirty-two-day siege of Marseilles, France. At the head of a French female column, Ameliane organized the hurling of burning tar-soaked faggots and tar pots. At the breaches, in three days, she countermined a thousand-foot ditch from Joliette to Porte d'Aix called the *Tranchee des Dames* (Women's Trench), which the defenders filled with burning wood beams and balls of wool. The seven Spaniards who braved the ditch died on September 24, 1524, leaving six cannon and the dead and wounded as "un beau monument de gloire" (a handsome monument to glory). The trench serves as the basis of the Boulevard des Dames.

1527

Backed by approval from Pope Clement VII dated March 26, 1526, eighteen-year-old Prioress **Euphemia Leslie (also Eufeme, Euphame, or Eupheme, 1508–September 7, 1570)** of Perth, Scotland, assembled eighty armed troops to secure her office of head of rural Elcho Priory. A priest's daughter reared by Cistercians at Elcho convent on the Tay River, she relied on the backing of one hundred supporters and her brother, Norman Lesley of Cushney, to whom she repaid the favor with lands in Kinnaird. In 1527, they deposed former prioress Elizabeth Swinton and imprisoned her until she resigned. The change in spiritual and economic management led to court battles until a settlement on January 14, 1529. During her thirty-fourth year as superintendent, she instituted the Scottish Reformation by breaking ties to the Vatican. She promoted feminist rights for nuns by announcing a retirement system.

June 16, 1534

Dutch martyr **Hille Feicke (ca. 1500–June 27, 1534)** from Wirdum, Friesland, led a female fortification squad and plotted to assassinate Franz von Waldeck, the tyrant bishop of Munster. At the siege of Munster on June 16, 1534, the Anabaptist women refortified city walls in preparation for a New Jerusalem. Hille conspired to seduce Franz in the style of Judith with Holofernes. A man named Knipperdolling abetted her scriptural reenactment by providing gold rings and cash. On June 24, 1535, the prince-bishop's episcopal forces retook the city and authorized Catholicism. Hille's failure resulted in arrest and execution three days later. Supporters named her the "Judith of Munster."

September 8, 1535

During a German siege of Saint-Riquier in Picardy, **Marie Fourreé de Poix (fl. 535)** defended Peronne with an all-female corps. The wife of explorer Jean-François de La Rocque de Roberval, she displayed a patriotic spirit equal to his. To impress on the two thousand Flemish troops of the Count of Nassau that there were sufficient rations for the one hundred men of the city, she baked loaves and hurled them from the ramparts. When an enemy soldier tried to plant his standard on a battlement, on September 8, 1535, she scaled the wall and tossed him to the ground. In glory, in 1536, she marched over the city streets with a banner. Her legend survives in opera, verse, sculpture, and monuments.

1538

A widowed Lombard during the two-year Italian War of 1536, **Veronica Gambara (November 29, 1485–June 13, 1550)** of Pralboino protected the town of Correggio from attack by Count Galeotto II Pico della Mirandola, an enemy of Holy Roman Emperor Charles V. She produced verse and letters excoriating the militarism of Renaissance northern Italy, especially the sacking of Brescia in 1512. At age thirty-three, after the death of her husband, Count Giberto X, in 1518, she assumed the rule of Coreggio as well as rearing their three children.

In defiance of two treaties signed by Charles V, Count Galeotto besieged the town in 1538. By fostering the city during the two-year Italian War of 1536, commanding a security force, and importing grain from Romagna, Veronica saved her subjects from slaughter and hunger. Petitioning Charles on their behalf, in 1546, she gained a stipend for fort upgrades.

1539

An Inca queen from late 1533 to her execution 1539, **Kura Ocllo (also Cura Yupanqui, ca. 1515–1539)** of Tomebamba, Ecuador, supported her husband/brother Manco Inca, a sham emperor manipulated by Spanish invader Francisco Pizarro's conquistadors. Following the Spanish garroting of Atahualpa on July 26, 1533, in Cajamarca, Kura endured rape by explorer Gonzalo Pizarro, the cause of a forty-year revolt. In retaliation, she aided Manco in an anti-colonial uprising at Vilcabamba, Peru. Manco's flight to the forest in April 1536 from the battle of Fort Huayna restored Kura to safety. When he launched a siege at Cuzco on May 6, his one hundred thousand Inca warriors fought one hundred ninety invaders and their thirty thousand Indian mercenaries.

The ten-month engagement sanctioned the murder of Inca women and dismembering of male captives. Combat ended in early March 1537 with Manco's withdrawal with the queen to Vilcabamba in the Andean highlands. During a silent advance of thirty Spanish on Oncoy, she positioned females to pose as a party of Inca soldiers and scare off the enemy. After Pizarro decapitated the queen's two brothers in front of her, the Spaniards engineered her capture. She covered herself in excrement before submitting to torture with lashes and public stoning at the stake. The torment ended in 1539 with pelting with darts. Pizarro's troops transported her downriver by basket to Manco's holdout. Her son, Sayri Tupac, ruled for sixteen years until 1560.

1539

Chieftain and Inca unifier **Gaitana (also Gualtipan, fl. 1530s–1540s)**, an Indian widow, fought Spanish imperialism in 1539 by directing armed resistance of the indigenous Yalcón of Colombia's southwestern highlands against conqueror Sebastián de Belalcázar. As European trade routes permeated the coffee-producing Timana territory north of the Upper Magdalena River to link Lima with Quito and Cartagena, in December 1538, Castilian explorer Pedro de Añasco was appointed governor. He seized land, burned towns, and suppressed Native American languages and Carib culture in Cali, Guacayo, and Popayan. According to Franciscan priests and chroniclers Juan de Castellanos and Pedro Simón of Granada, Añasco demanded tribute from local tribes and targeted the Páez and Pijao. Because Gaitana's lieutenant, her son Buiponga, withheld tax money, Añasco had him burned alive in the town square.

The outraged Andaquies, Pijao, Pinao, and Timana allied with the Yalcón in an anti–Spanish confederacy of fifteen thousand guerrilla warriors, commanded by Chief Pigoanza. Emerging from a matriarchal tradition, archer Gaitana led the six thousand Yalcón and rallied volunteers to Colombia's first Indian alliance. Vengeful warriors captured the conquistador, massacred his soldiers, blinded him with an arrowhead, forced a rope under his tongue, and humiliated him by slowly dragging him through villagers by the knotted end. She ended his life by hacking off his limbs and genitals, cutting his throat, and beheading him to refashion his skull as a drinking vessel.

The replacement of Añasco with Juan del Rio motivated Gaitana's extension of the rebellion by leading new troops from the Avirama, Guanaca, and Páez. From 1539 to 1541, her tactics of suppressing Spanish weaponry and cavalry in Timana delayed Spanish colonization of the Andes for decades. Chief Matambo's betrayal of an Inca ambush enabled the insurgents to overwhelm natives, who persisted against Spain for sixty years. Juan de Ampudia, leader of reinforcements, died of a spear to the throat. His lieutenant, Francisco Tobar, retaliated with a merciless policy of torture and murder. Native numbers decreased by 99.5 percent to sixty-nine from infectious disease, press gangs, Catholic coercion, and slavery. Legends, storytelling, reenactments, and a monument in the capital city of Neiva commemorate Gaitana's courage.

April 16, 1539

In a colonial atmosphere of forced labor and sexual bondage, **India Juliana (fl. 1540s)** of Asunción, Paraguay, fought back by poisoning her Spanish Christian exploiter during Holy Week and launching a female revolt. A native Guarani from the Río de la Plata district, she was renamed Juliana as part of a forced conversion to Catholicism. She excelled at herbalism, a female specialty for cooking and healing. On Maundy Thursday, April 16, 1539, she used poisonous mountain plants as a weapon against her owner, Nuño de Cabrera.

Juliana's resistance incited an era of revolt. As characterized in *La Relación de Álvar Núñez Cabeza de Vaca* (The Account of Álvar Núñez Cabeza de Vaca), a Spanish explorer from Cadiz, the reduction of three hundred native women to commercial prizes or diplomacy gifts caused three uprisings between 1538 and 1546. Juliana confessed her retaliation, conspired with other enslaved women to kill their European masters, and, in 1542, suffered drawing and quartering as punishment. Her martyrdom in Asunción, Paraguay, fills chronicles, legends, historical fiction, and a graphic novel.

1540

At the fall of Muslims and Sephardic Jews in Granada in southern Spain to Christian monarchs Isabella I of Castile and Ferdinand II of Aragon, **Sayyida al-Hurra (also Lalla Aicha, 1485–July 14, 1561)** of the Rashid clan plotted revenge and the liberation of the Maghreb in northwestern Africa. Her family fled south from al-Andalus or Muslim Iberia to Chefchaouen in Morocco's Rif Mountains. After marrying al-Mandri at Fez and becoming governor at the port city of Tetouan in 1515, in the golden age of piracy, she joined forces with Ottoman admiral Oruc Reis—known as Hayreddin Barbarossa of Lesbos, the sultan of Algiers. The partners intended to deter the traffic of papal vessels and Catholic merchants in the western Mediterranean Sea. In 1540, she ran a pirating foray at Gibraltar that gained riches and hostages.

Wedded to Sultan Ahmed al-Wattasi in 1541, as a Muslim buccaneer, Sayyida al-Hurra empowered Arab cities to defend the coast and impede Portuguese shipping lanes that extended around Africa to southern India. After she amassed a fleet and force of exiled Moorish corsairs, her revenues grew from loot and the profits from ransoming captives and selling slaves across Iberia. Her valor in Morocco and a war on Portugal stopped Catholic colonists from annexing northwestern Africa to their empire. In October 1542, her son-in-law Moulay Ahmed al-Hassan intervened in the Algerian barbary raids, but she retained acclaim as a Moroccan freedom fighter.

1541

A teenaged chief priest, **Ōhōri Tsuruhime (1526–1543)** of Mishima, southeast of Hiroshima, Japan, commanded armed troops against the raiders of Honshu clan leader Ouchi Yoshitaka. After her two brothers died in the conflict, she applied martial arts expertise to repelling the enemy from the island. On a second attack four weeks later, she donned her armor and repelled the enemy samurai. In 1541, she secretly boarded the ship of General Ohara Takakoto and killed him in a duel. Her forces routed the enemy fleet with grenades. Because her fiancé, Yasunari Ochi, died in the conflict, she completed the war with an ambush, then drowned herself in grief for her lover. An annual festival commemorates her boldness.

September 11, 1541

The rare female *conquistadora*, explorer **Inés de Suarez (1507–1580)** of Placencia, Spain, created a theatrical defense of the newly founded capital Santiago, Chile. Ostensibly seeking her husband, who had died at the battle of the Salt Mines in 1540, she rode in the host of Chilean governor Pedro de Valdivia, an expedition of one hundred Spaniards from Cuzco over the Atacama Desert dispatched by conquistador Francisco Pizarro. During a mutiny affecting a garrison of fifty-five soldiers, she treated the injured and supplied them food and water. In Valdivia's venture south to seize more Indian territory, the Mapuche tribe besieged the capital, wounding warrior Francisco de Aguirre, one of the defenders who had marched south from Cuzco in December 1540.

For psychological effect, Inés dressed in chain mail to rally Spaniards. On her white horse, on September 11, 1541, she spooked the Indians who were refusing to labor in the Marga Marga gold mines at Valparaiso. As described in 1593 by Pedro Mariño de Lobera's *Crónica del Reino de Chile* (History of the Kingdom of Chile), she exacerbated the capital defense by decapitating seven hostage chiefs, plunging the heads on pikes, and tossing their remains in the midst of some twenty thousand natives following chief Michimalonco. The terrified attackers fled to the Andes valleys.

Preceding the Arauco War, Inés lived with Valdivia until he returned to Peru in 1548. The next year, she married Galician official Rodrigo de Quiroga, who twice served as Chile's governor. The story of the legendary "mother of Chile" enlivened historical fiction and a Chilean television series *Inés del Alma Mia* (Ines of My Soul), based on a novel by Isabel Allende.

July 12, 1542

An expert horsewoman and archer taught by half-brother François, Captain **Louise Labé, (1516–April 25, 1566)** of Lyon, France, captured the Renaissance spirit by dressing as a knight for jousts and besieging Perpignan, Aragon. To follow a beau, she reputedly enlisted in Dauphin Henry II's forty thousand-man army. They advanced from Roussillon on the Mediterranean Sea into the Pyrenees, where thousands died of wounds and dysentery. In combat against Castilian nobles and a garrison of Spanish veterans, on July 12, 1542, Henry lost heavy artillery before ceding to the enemy at great cost. She mustered out of the military with honors and a promotion to captain. Her elegies and Petrarchan sonnets compared the wounds of love to battle experience and noted the heaping of accolades on male soldiers.

August 6, 1543

A blend of history and titillating legend, laundress **Catherine Segurane (fl. 1540s)** of Nice, Savoy, commanded a citywide confrontation against Turkish insurgents attacking by sea with thirty thousand soldiers and one hundred fifty galleys. Her impromptu assault on a banner carrier with a laundry beater enabled her to seize the Ottoman flag in the name of Duke Charles III of Savoy and smash it. On August 6, 1543, she braved the ramparts to carry water buckets to the garrison. Scurrilous episodes of lifting her skirts to reveal naked buttocks to the ranks of Holy Roman Emperor Frederick I Barbarossa describe her act as dismaying to Muslim males, who bore stringent taboos about women and nudity. Historically, on August 15, the Savoyards lost to the Turks, who set fire to Nice and claimed five thousand prisoners of war. Statues, cartoons, paintings, a street name, a holiday, and a plaque honor the laundress as "Myrabella (Wonder Woman)."

February 27, 1545

Petite Scotswoman **Lilliard of Ancrum (1520s–February 27, 1545)** of Teviotdale southeast of Glasgow fought a Tudor king alongside her lover in the battle of Ancrum Moor. The clash culminated a border conflict in the ongoing hostilities between Henry VIII and the Scots militia of Archibald Douglas, the Earl of Angus. Aggravated by plunder and arson in Edinburgh in May 1544, a Scots ambush on boggy ground retaliated with pikes, pistols, and arquebuses. Lilliard took her lover's place in the battle line until wounds to both legs caused her collapse.

Before Lilliard's death on February 27, 1545, she reputedly targeted and killed the savage English assailants Ralph Evers and Brian Latoun. Meanwhile, some one thousand Scots lancers dispatched eight hundred German and Spanish mercenaries and took one thousand prisoners. A stone shrine, monument, verse, and tomb on Lilliard's Edge mark her courageous stand. Historians surmised that she took the name "Maid Lilliard" from the place just as Joan of Arc was called the "Maid of Orléans."

April 20, 1546

At the seven-month siege of Diu Island on the west coast of Portuguese

India, **Catarina Lopes (fl. 1540s)** formed a five-woman cadre to oust the Ottoman Turks led by Mahmud Shah III, the sultan of Gujarat. On April 20, 1546, she joined **Garcia Rodrígues (fl. 1540s)**, **Isabel Dias (fl. 1540s)**, and **Isabel Fernandes (fl. 1540s)** and followed Captain **Isabel Madeira (fl. 1540s)** in defending Fort Diu from ten thousand attackers. After an artillery barrage, Isabel Madeira superintended structural repair and aided casualties. At the death of her husband in battle, she buried his remains and returned to the fight. When Catarina fell into the grasp of a male soldier, she had only her fingers free to gouge out his eyes. A Portuguese armada ended the assault on November 7, 1546, by scattering the Muslims and seizing control of Diu island.

June 1546

In June 1546 at Berwickshire, Scotland, **Elizabeth Lamb (1500–1575)**, newly appointed prioress the Cistercian Abbey of St. Bathans on White-Ader Water, came before the court of James V for abetting insurgency by an enemy army. A spy for the English during Scots border wars of 1544–1545, perhaps under duress, she had supplied equipment and weapons to benefit an invasion of Scotland. By August 1546, she wangled a pardon for treason as a means of rescuing from the belligerent English a Lowlands monastery, fifteen acres of farmland, and the staff and tenants. Intimidation continued at the boundary, where the English burned the abbey's grain crop in 1561.

September 10, 1547

Scots home defender **Mariotta Haliburton** (also **Maryon** or **Marion Haliburton, Lady Home, April 19, 1503–February 26, 1563**) from Dirleton guarded the twelfth-century Hume Castle and its environs from a Tudor invasion of southern Scotland. A security force of seventy-eight kept her and her seven-year-old daughter Margaret safe from a naval bombardment. At the battle of Pinkie Cleugh on September 10, 1547, at Musselburgh, eight thousand Scots lowland pikemen fell to the two thousand cavalrymen of Henry VIII. Ten days later, Mariotta ceded the castle to the invaders of Edward Seymour of Somerset, who manned the site with twelve gunners. Her wartime experience survives in personal letters to Mary of Guise.

December 1548

During the three-year Burmese-Siamese War against the confederacy of Shan states, Siam's queen **Suriyothai (1511–December 1548)** and sixteen-year-old daughter **Boromdhilok (1532–December 1548)** followed King Maha Chakkraphat on war elephants in December 1548 to Lumpli Plain outside the capital of Ayutthaya. Disguised in uniforms, helmets, and breastplates, they exited the city walls riding double and faced combat in company with Boromdhilok's brothers Mahin and Ramesuan. Both queen and princess died in battle against Thado Dhamma Yaza I, viceroy of Prome (modern Pyay, Myanmar). Thado sliced through the queen's torso to the heart with a halberd as she dodged in front of King Chakkraphat to protect him. Sons Mahin and Ramesuan routed the enemy and bore the two royal corpses to Ayutthaya. A monument in the capital on the Chao Phraya River captures the queen's enthusiasm for defending her husband. Her heroism survives in storytelling and film.

1549

An expansionist warrior-*habe* (monarch) of Zazzau (also Kaduna or Zaria or Zozo), one of seven Hausa states in northwestern Nigeria, **Amina (also Amina Sukhera or Amina Sarauniya Zazzau or Aminatu, 1533–1610)** became the first female to rule an African kingdom and command its army. She bore the Islamic name meaning "honest" and a reputation for clan prestige and wealth. From age two, she trained in politics, target practice, and war games at the court of her grandparents, Marka and Sarkin Nohir in Zaria, Hausaland (modern Kaduna, Nigeria). With schooling from her grandfather and mother, Queen **Bakwa of Turunku (fl. 1540s)** in weaponry and combat strategy, she joined Zazzau horsemen in 1549. Armed with sword, bow, and a quiver of arrows, in her mid-teens, she rejected all suitors and instead led thirty thousand cavalry against enemy Borno, Fulani, and Mali.

See also 1566; April 1576; 1610.

1552

An Italian poet and leader of women, **Laudomia Forteguerri (June 3, 1515– after 1557)** from the Republic of Siena mobilized one thousand female resisters of Duke Cosimo I de' Medici of Florence to construct the Fortino Delle Donne (The Women's Fort). In 1552, the regiment, armed with picks and shovel, required workers to remove fill dirt in baskets on their heads. The two-story Tuscan redoubt northwest of Lake Trasimeno held firm during Cosimo's fifteen-month assault from January 26, 1554, to April 17, 1555.

At a peak of conflict—the battle of Scanniglio on August 2, 1554—Florentines amassed eighteen thousand five hundred Italo-Spanish fighters and Papal regiments at Marciano della Chiana. The overwhelming odds against Siena's fifteen thousand resulted in four thousand imprisoned and another four thousand killed, including the Sienese commander and his lieutenant. Laudomia's amazons failed to deflect Cosimo's starvation method, which forced a Tuscan surrender.

1555

An empress during a period of West African prosperity, **Orompoto (also Oronpoto, fl. 1554–1562)** of Oyo (modern Nigeria) rid Yoruban territory of Nupe insurgents from the northeast. Because of military losses to Tsoede of Nupe in 1550 and the exile of Oyo's royal household to Borgu (modern Benin), she took charge of the capital at Igboho. As the first female monarch of Oyo, she generated a myth that she had shapeshifted into a male, an explanation for her success as a mounted warrior. Key to her military supremacy in 1555, the cavalry tied fronds to horses' tails to sweep the trail clean of tracks. Her infantry and horsemen reveled at the battle of Illayi, which cost her three war chiefs. Until her death in battle against archers in 1562, she annexed land to the south, enlarging Yoruba conquests to their peak.

April 1555

A Zhuang tactician and martial arts specialist, **Lady Washi (also Chen Hua, 1498–1557)** of Guishun (modern Jingxi, China) served the Emperor Jiajing as commander of five thousand militiamen against Japan's *wokou* (international) pirates and smugglers. Born of Zhuang heritage, she weathered a clash between her husband Chen Meng and her father, Chen Zhang, a provincial administrator. The father-in-law murdered Chen Meng for preferring multiple wives over Lady Washi. When her stepson, Chen Bangxiang, led raids against her property, she killed him.

During the decline of centralized authority in the Ming dynasty, Lady Washi took the position of regent for her grandson Chen Zhi. When he died in 1553, Lady Washi reared her great grandson Chen Dashou. Acclaimed by Zhang Tingyu's *History of Ming*, she reached age fifty-seven before she earned respect as a virago by ending forays against China, Japan, Korea, and Philippines from a criminal base at Taiwan along the East China Sea and Sea of Japan. Previous attacks against thousands of buccaneer junks failed because of the government's out-of-date firearms and a dearth of archers. By leading the emperor's forces at Shengdong in Suzhou, in April 1555, Lady Washi gained respect. Emperor Jiajing rewarded her with silver.

1558

Three years after a first confrontation with Portuguese fleet commander Don Alvaro de Silveira, Jain freedom fighter Rani **Abbakka Chowta of Ullal (1525–1582)** in Mangalore, India, threw off the Iberian insurgents through field and naval strategy. Trained from age six by her uncle Thirumala Raya, she unleashed swift action with bow, saber, martial arts, and horsemanship to save Indian textiles, pepper, and spices from four decades of Iberian colonial exploitation. In 1558, she forged a security brigade from all castes and religions backed by Arab Moors and refused to pay tribute to the Portuguese.

See also January 1568; 1581.

1561

In a cabal of treachery and mayhem, **Mah Chuchak Begum (also Maha Chuchak Begum or Moon Flower, 1526–March 28, 1564)**, an Afghan conspirator from Arghun and the fourth female to rule the Mughal empire, maneuvered the Kabul power structure to advance her eight-year-old son, Mirza Muhammad Hakim. She married Humayun, the second Mughal emperor, and bore Mirza third among her sons. In widowhood in 1564, she banished her detractors from the city and replaced them with substandard regents, whom she murdered.

Mirza's older brother, Akbar, dispatched General Munim Khan and his troops to stop Mah from meddling in the line of succession. Mah headed her personal army and overwhelmed them at Jalalabad with artillery and grenades. She executed Munim's son, Ghanin

Khan, and allowed her soldiers to pillage his camp. The overthrow ensured that Akbar would not endanger her reign over Kabul as dowager empress. A rival, Shah Abul Maali, sought the regency over Kabul and assassinated Mah. Her plots survive in a 2013 television series.

1562

On the border of the Mughal Empire in east central India, Rani **Durgavati (also Durgawati, October 5, 1524–June 24, 1564)** the widowed Hindu queen of Gondwana, faced a major assault in 1562 by the imperial army of Akbar the Great. Born at Fort Kalinjar, she was well versed in sword fighting, archery, riflery, and horse riding and survived fifty-one wars. She vanquished a major attacker at Malwa in 1556. To halt a Mughal seizure, she positioned twenty thousand cavalry and one thousand war elephants with infantry at Narrai overlooking the Narmada River.

After a discouraging day, alongside her nine-year-old son, Veer Narayan, Durgavati mounted her elephant Sarman (Hindi for "Protection"). When arrows wounded mother and son, she recognized a hopeless battle. At Madhya Pradesh on June 24, 1564, bleeding heavily from ear and neck, she stabbed herself to death with a dagger to prevent capture. Her daring survives in a postal stamp, statues, and the naming of a train, coast guard ship, university, and holiday called "Martyrdom Day."

May 14, 1562

A resolute monarch and military leader from Navarre during the third of the French Wars of Religion, **Jeanne d'Albret (also Joana Albretekoa, November 16, 1528–June 9, 1572)** from Saint-Germain-en-Laye failed to stop Catholic pillage on May 14, 1562, of Vendôme's homes and churches. Unrelenting in her Huguenot faith, she and eight-year-old son Henry chose La Rochelle as a haven from Charles IX and his Catholic raiders. From 1569 to 1570, as Navarre's queen Joan III, she bolstered the fort at Pamplona and, with young Henry, followed cavalry commander Gaspard de Coligny and his Huguenot armies to the disastrous battle of Jarnac on March 13, 1569. Their deployment achieved a win at La Roche-l'Abeille on June 25 and a loss of fifty-five percent of their troops at Moncontour on October 3. To end conflict, she brokered a peace treaty in August 1570.

1565

Irish sea raider, mercenary, clan chief, and pirate queen of Connacht **Grace O'Malley (1530–1603)** of Westport earned the clan motto *Terra Marique Potens* (Powerful on Land and Sea). By caravel and galley, in 1565, she avenged the death of her warlike husband, Dónal an Chogaidh, killed in an ambush by the Joyce clan during a hunt. In an hour of giving birth to her last child, Tibbott Burke, at sea in 1567, she warded off Algerian corsairs by commanding attacks by her Scots sailors. For her dead lover, Hugh de Lacy of Wexford, who washed up from a wrecked ship, she assailed the herds of the killer MacMahons, claimed Castle Doona in Blacksod Bay, and pursued them from Fahy Strand farther offshore to Cahir Island.

In 1577, Sir Henry Sidney, Ireland's lord deputy, hired Grace to captain three galleys and a crew of two hundred for the English. Her belligerence sent tax collectors on the run and resulted in a dousing of melted lead roof tiles on deputies threatening Hen's Castle on Lough Corrib. In March 1579, she protected her four-story headquarters, Rockfleet Castle in Newport, where Galway sheriff William Oge Martyn directed attackers. In September 1593, she reputedly walked barefoot to the throne of Elizabeth I at Greenwich to negotiate a truce with English marauder Richard Bingham, Governor of Connacht. Grace's historic brigandage earned a bronze statue, dramas, music, films, and the historical novel *Grania: She-King of the Irish Seas*.

June 27, 1565

A noblewoman martyred in the chaotic Sengoku period, Lady **Shirai no Tsubone (ca. 1512–June 27, 1565)** fought a four-hour battle on June 27, 1565, at Kyoto, Japan, to halt feudal sieges at Honmaru and Ninomaru palaces against the Uesugi clan. After Lord Miyoshi Yoshitsugu attacked the sixty-eight-acre double castle, she defended the Ashikaga Shogunate from usurpers. With *naginata* (bladed pike) in hand, she fought to the death. Clan enmity over succession to power continued until the formation of an alliance in October 1568. UNESCO claimed the castle as a World Heritage Site.

1566

As a form of state building, **Amina**, an African queen from Yauran, Nigeria, fought in four cavalry campaigns planned by younger brother Karama, the King of Zazzau. According to Hausa praise hymns and the *Kano Chronicles* of 1000 CE, before the deaths of King Nikatau and Queen Bakwa of Turunku in 1566, the queen, in her thirtieth year on the throne, named her daughter Amina as her heir. Amina settled at Yauran sixty miles (96.6 kilometers) southwest of Kano, Nigeria, and ruled for thirty-six years. At his death a decade later, she replaced him on the throne of Zazzau city-state. For Hausa protection, she surrounded cities and camps with earthen walls. She called the palace after little sister Zaria, whose name identified the chief state of the Hausa.

See also 1549; April 1576; 1610.

1567

During the Spanish-Caribbean War, **Uricao (fl. 1560s)**, a Teque chief of Venezuela, fought alongside her husband Guaicaipuro and son Apure against European incursion into the Caracas Valley along the San Pedro River. Guaicaipuro died in 1560 while combatting seekers of gold in the Venezuela hills. In 1567, the widowed Uricao led twelve thousand allied Teque, Arawak, Carib, and Taino at the battle of Maracapana, a failed attempt to maintain free commerce amid a colonial encroachment. Historians compared her nerve to that of martyred Venezuelan amazons Apacuana and Ana Soto.

January 1568

Rani **Abbakka Chowta of Ullal** failed to stop General Joao Peixoto from robbing a temple, burning the city, and seizing her palace at Ullal in Tulu Nadu, southwestern India. By escaping to a mosque with two hundred soldiers and seeking reprisal by night at the port of Mangalore, she managed to kill seventy soldiers, assassinate Peixoto, and retake the port. She pressed on ninety miles (144.8 kilometers) up the coast and seized the Portuguese port of Kundapura, a trade nexus.

See also 1558; 1581.

December 1568

A defender of Hikuma castle west of Yokohama, **Otazu no Kata (also Otatsu no Kata, 1550–December 1568)** from coastal Mikawa in south central Japan, took the part of samurai and head of the Iio clan. Leading three hundred troops, in December 1568, she challenged Shogun Tokugawa Ieyasu, who insulted her and other women as weaklings. After several jubilant days and the deaths of two hundred enemy, Otazu exited the gate with a squad of eighteen women dressed in armor and bearing the *ko-naginata* (bladed pike). When she fell in battle at age eighteen in December 1568, Tokugawa took the castle, killed all its residents, and, in 1570, made it his stronghold. Otazu's memory survives in Japanese camellias said to have sprung from her grave.

1569

The wife of Ichikawa Tsuneyoshi, a Mori warlord, **Lady Ichikawa (?–April 5, 1585)** contributed to the rise of female Japanese warrior-chatelaines in the Sengoku period by defending the moated Konomine-jo castle at Yamaguchi. The raid of naval commander Ouchi Teruhiro west of Hiroshima in 1569 endangered the Ichikawa clan. With only herself and a female staff for defense, she equipped the woman with swords and led them from the castle walls to a frontal attack. After ten days, Ouchi routed from the mountaintop siege to Katsuyana Castle at Shimonoseki. He failed to escape by sea and killed himself at Mount Chausu. The clan lord, Mori Terumoto, congratulated her on the coup.

June 16, 1569

Widowed Finnish dragoon **Brita Olofsdotter (?–June 16, 1569)** fought in Sweden's cavalry in Livonia (modern Estonia and Latvia) for control of the Baltic Sea. After the death of her husband, Nils Simonson, on June 16, 1569, she put on a male uniform and engaged the enemy. She died twelve days before mediation of the Treaty of Lublin, by which Lithuania, Poland, and Sweden stymied a Russian land grab. John III, the prince of Finland, paid a military stipend to her family for service during the twenty-five-year Livonian War. History recognizes Brita as Sweden's first female soldier.

September 1569

Scots troop commander **Agnes Campbell (1526–1601), Lady of Kintire and Dunyvaig**, directed a Highland army against English insurgents in Ulster, Ireland. The daughter of Janet Gordon and Colin Campbell, nobles of the houses of Huntley and Argyll, she was born at Inveraray Castle at Argyll, Scotland, and learned Gaelic, French and Latin. While rearing two daughters and six sons, she negotiated an alliance of Campbells with McDonalds. At the death of husband James McDonald of Dunyvaig in July 1565, she accepted a marriage proposal from Turlough Luineach O'Neill, laird of the O'Neill clan at Ulster and northern Ireland, and tempered his bluster with calm rhetoric. Nearing Ireland the next month, she and daughter **Finola O'Donnell** directed twelve thousand Highland warriors as her dowry. The approach to her new home in September 1569 brought thirty-two ships and four thousand men to fight colonization. The Scots mercenaries enlarged Turlough's three thousand forces. On her return to Scotland, in April 1570, she engineered a firmer pact that established Scottish loyalty for Irish freedom fighters. With Finola, Agnes mediated with Spanish military to arouse a Catholic war against England.

November 19, 1569

At the Rising of the North, **Jane Howard (1533–June 30, 1593)** of Raby, Durham, assembled rebel forces to dethrone the Tudor Protestant queen Elizabeth I and replace her with Mary, the Catholic Queen of Scots. Jane's ulterior motive for the conspiracy was the marriage of Mary to Jane's brother, Duke Thomas Howard of Norfolk, and the restoration of Catholicism in England through their joint rule. She enlisted in her father's army of forty-six hundred men after they captured Durham on November 19, 1569, and rifled the romanesque cathedral at Durham Castle of altar goods, images, and banners after mass on November 20. The insurrectionists hoped for backup from French and Spanish Catholics, which never materialized.

Jane scorned her brother for cowardice in creeping over the Scots border to elude the Tudor army of seven thousand and bolstered her father's exiled rebels with pieces of jewelry. The Rising's failure resulted in Thomas Howard's execution at York on June 2, 1572, and the Howard family's loss of property and titles. The queen purged England of rebels by hanging seven hundred residents of Yorkdale and posting heads on pikes. Jane's testimonial of loyalty to Elizabeth resulted in no exculpation. Jane entered Kenninghall and its seven hundred-acre deer park in Norfolk and remained for the next twenty years. Elizabeth soothed Jane's penury with a pension of £200 (approx. $100,000).

April 1570

At a siege on Montelimar in southeastern France, **Marguerite "Margot" Catherine Ponsoye Delaye (fl. 1570s)** allied with local women reinforcing local Catholic soldiers against Huguenot attackers. The widow of a knight killed during the French religious wars, she became a laundress. In the absence of ammunition, in April 1570, she hurled stones, concrete, and pots to save her village. During efforts to establish Huguenot colonies as religious sanctuaries, Dutch cavalry commander Louis of Nassau crushed her right arm with a cauldron. In recompense to a local amputee, she received food, wine, and board. She retained feminist regard through a one-armed statue, legends, and a street named for her.

October 7, 1571

A maritime soldier in the Holy League of Pope Pius V, **María la Bailadora (fl. 1571)** was the only female embroiled in the battle of Lepanto, an effort to halt the invasion of Ali Pasha's Muslims into Europe. In men's uniform, she supported the seventy thousand Catholic warriors forming a coalition of the Knights Hospitallers and Knights of Malta with Spain, Sicily, Sardinia, Genoa, Naples, Savoy, Urbino, Tuscany, the Papacy, and Venice. She carried an arquebus, two-edged sword, and pike and followed her lover, an officer in the conflict. In the estimation of historian Giovanni Pietro Contarini, the battle involved four hundred warships in the Gulf of Patras northwest of the Peloponnesus of Greece.

On the *Real* (Royal), the flagship of John of Austria, on October 7, 1571, Maria served as a private under Lope de Figueroa and fought Turkish invaders after the crew boarded the galley *Sultana*. Maria's unit slew all Turks on the flagship, including Admiral Ali Pasha. Comrades cheered her as "Maria the Dancer." If she had been captured, she risked sexual bondage by the Muslims. Christian warriors admired her courage in hand-to-hand tussles and noted that she stabbed an Ottoman enemy to death. The Allied victory cost the Turks thirty thousand men and two hundred and fourteen ships or seventy-six percent of their armada.

December 11, 1572

In a seven-month siege initiated by Philip II of Spain, **Kenau Simonsdochter Hasselaer (1526–October 23, 1588)**, a Dutch brewer's daughter and widowed shipbuilder, and her sister **Amaron Hasselaer (fl. 1570s)** commanded Haarlem's walls and gate. To halt the enemy's tunneling under the battlements, on December 11, 1572, the women tossed flaming tar hoops over the necks of the Duke of Alba's troops, doused them in boiling tar, and fought them face-to-face with swords and pikes, jettisoning corpses into the Spaarne River. Compared to the biblical Judith, Kenau labored into the night to repair earthen ramparts with dirt carried in her apron.

The lengthy siege elevated younger female warriors **Trijn van Leemput (1530–1607)** of Utrecht and **Trijn Rembrands (1557–1638)** of Alkmaar farther north, both disguised as men. In July 1573, the Spanish starved Haarlem into surrender. Among the dead lay **Maria van Schooten (1555–1573)**, one of Kenau's recruits. Five years after Kenau's murder by pirates, the city recognized debts to her. A Batavian frigate bore her name. Her history lives on in portraiture, sculpture, and film.

July 26, 1575

At the Chateau de Miremont, Limousin, during the French civil wars, the widow **Madeleine de Saint-Nectaire (also Magdalaine, Dame d'Auvergne, 1526–April 27, 1588)** commanded sixty Huguenot horsemen who protected her home and three minor daughters from invasive Catholics who launched a cannon siege on July 29, 1574. The daughter of a general and proponent of Henry III, she fought in steel cuirass with her hair floating free to distinguish her from the men. They successfully dispersed the provincial governor Gilles de Montal's two thousand foot soldiers and five hundred horsemen. She summoned four units of arquebusiers (riflemen) from the viscount of Turenne to rid her chateau of raiders. On July 26, 1575, she personally shot Montal dead. Her gumption won the admiration of England's Henry IV.

April 1576

Three months into 1576 during annexation of central Nigeria, **Amina**, the new Queen of Zazzau (modern Zaria, Nigeria), launched a thirty-four-year crusade against the slave traders of the commercial center at Bauchi. In April 1576, she commanded a skilled army of twenty thousand infantry and one thousand horse soldiers. For armoring, she introduced chain mail and iron helmets. The army obstructed Hausa neighbors all the way to the Niger River, Bight of Benin, and the Gulf of Guinea on the Atlantic Ocean. The realm, including the Lower Sudan, profited from a lucrative market in slaves, kola nuts, salt, gold, leather, and horses.

Amina sold male slaves to Arab dealers and collected forty eunuchs and ten thousand kola nuts from tribute states Katsina and Kano, both of which she trounced in war. At each conquest, she chose a mate, but had lovers decapitated before she conceived children. She conquered northern Mali, shored up colonies with defensive earthen walls, and extended trade routes through the Sahara Desert to western Sudan and ultimately Egypt.

See also 1549; 1566; 1610.

1577

A Carib of the Venezuelan mountains, **Apacuana (?–1577)** instigated a five-hundred man assault of allied tribes in 1577 against Spanish press gang organizers. She held positions of *curandera* (mystic healer), war strategist, and chief from the coastal town of Valles del Tuy. In the province of Nueva Andalucia and Paria, she began a resistance movement in 1574 by forming a native confederation with the Charagatos, Cumanagotos, and Meregatos. Her tactics involved spiking the road with poisoned obstacles. On the march from Spanish outrage in Caracas, Sancho Garcia torched Quiriquires villages, farms, and stallions and fought survivors hand to hand.

As described in Colombian chronicler Jose de Oviedo y Baños's *Historia de la Conquista y Población de la Provincia de Venezuela,* on the word of an informer, the victors chose Apacuana as an example of anti-colonial rebel. After torture, she died in a noose. Her corpse remained on show to terrify Indians. Her people fled to the high country before agreeing to a truce. Her history survives in drama, novel, short fiction, and statue.

1577

Japanese amazon **Ueno Tsuruhime (?–1577)** commanded a female squadron to rescue Tsuneyama Castle from the Mouri samurai. In a no-win face-off against the encircling attackers east of Hiroshima, in 1577, she accepted martyrdom on a spiritual promise of Buddhist glory in the afterlife. With a platoon of thirty-four women, she dressed in her husband's armor, raised a halberd, and pressed her way out of the castle gate to the enemy warlord, Munekatsu Nomi. Because he rejected her demand for a duel, she and her followers retreated to the terraced courtyard and killed themselves. Her husband, Ueno Takatogu, honored her choice by doing the same, thus terminating the distinguished Ueno clan in the middle of the turbulent Sengoku period. A smiling statue commemorates her serenity. A double line of graves bears the doomed fighters.

August 9, 1578

Southwest of the Caucasus in the fractured state of Georgia, **Dedisimedi (1525–1595),** the granddaughter of Constantine II and widow of Kaikhosro II, commanded forces against civil unrest in eastern Samtskhe at forts Qveli and Tmogvi. As regent for her twenty-two-year-old son, Qvarqvare IV, she headquartered above Shoka at Okros, a medieval castle. After General Lala Mustafa Pasha visited her stronghold, he insisted that her sons convert from Christianity to Islam. For two years, Dedisimedi fought alongside thirty-two thousand Georgians and Persians against the Ottoman Turks. She yielded to the invaders on August 9, 1578, following the battle of Cildir near Kars. Ten thousand troops died as the Turks marched to the Caspian Sea.

In the first year of the war, combat destroyed Tmogvi and seized its redoubt as well as Kuvel Castle at Quell. In the second year, the Turks warred against Safavid Persians of Iran, with smallholders and peasants supporting Dedisimedi and her diffident son. In a calculated advance down the Kura River, the Turks seized redoubts and slaughtered security forces before slicing Samtskhe into eight divisions. Outmanned and outmaneuvered, Dedisimedi advised her son to surrender and take a post at Istanbul. At her withdrawal to Tbilisi, Kartli, her second son, Manuchar II, seized control as an Ottoman pasha.

1581

Accompanied by her two daughters, Rani **Abbakka Chowta of Ullal** fired burning arrows in a cavalry assault on Portugal's fleet. In clashing with the forces of Anthony D'Noronha, viceroy of Goa, India, she defied the pro-colonial opinions of her husband Lakkarasa of Bangadi. Because of a wound, she languished in prison, rebelled against her keepers, and, in 1582, died a martyr to the motherland. A public festival and folk stories, dance, and songs in Arabia, Persia, and India honor her as the only female victor over Portuguese imperialists. An Indian coast guard cutter, warship, and airport bear her name. A statue in Bengaluru depicts her directing cannon fire.

See also 1558; January 1568.

October 1, 1581

During the Spanish-Dutch War, Belgian hero **Christine de Lalaing of Espinoy (also Marie-Christine or Philippe Christine, 1545–June 9, 1582)** from Condé-sur-l'Escaut defended Tournai from Prince Alexander Farnese of Parma, the governor of the Spanish Netherlands. To stir unity, on October

1, 1581, she broadcast her patriotism to small battalions, which faced thirty-one thousand enemy. Wounded in the arm, she yielded to Farnese eight weeks later on November 30, 1581, and negotiated for mercy. She escaped to Oudenaarde and Antwerp. Her example survives in an armored sculpture bearing a battle ax, representation in Judy Chicago's *The Dinner Party,* and a three-act biodrama.

January 1, 1582

A greedy sea rogue in a corrupt era, **Mary Wolverston Killigrew (ca. 1525–1587)** of Cornwall in southwestern England abetted her husband, John IV Killigrew of Penryn, in robbing cargo vessels on the River Fals delta. She learned criminal tactics from her father, Philip Wolverston of Suffolk. John, a known rustler, earned royal regard for robbing Spanish shipping lanes in the English Channel. At Arwenack Castle, the couple accessed the coast through a hidden passage. They amassed wine, timber, and other goods in a storehouse and sold them and the pillaged ships for profit. Mary buried prime loot in the garden. In a space of two hours on January 1, 1582, she boarded the carrack *Santa María* of San Sebastian, Spain, murdered the crew, stole a load of cloth and barrels of coins, and sank the ship.

Later in 1582, Mary repeated the rapid turnaround at Falmouth Harbor on a German merchantman, which her raiders sailed to Ireland to sell. Mary was tried at Launceston for operating a pirate syndicate and sentenced to death along with her henchmen, Kendal and Hawkins, who were hanged on the pillory. Her son, John V Killigrew, negotiated release from prison after Queen Elizabeth I extended a pardon to her faithful privateers. Still selling stolen bounty in retirement, Mary died in 1587, leaving her family's deeds to fiction and cinema.

1584

At the battle of Kanayama Castle, at Ota in east central Japan, seventy-one-year-old warrior **Akai Teruko (November 6, 1514–December 17, 1594)** of Tatebayashi commanded three thousand troops to prevent a surprise attack of her strategic hilltop land. She mastered military arts in girlhood and married a warlord, Yura Shigeru, who sickened and died in 1578. For fifteen months at the end of the Sengoku period, she wielded the *naginata* (bladed pike) to stave off the Go-Hojo of Odawara, who armed themselves with arquebuses (proto-rifles). The powerful anti–Mongol clan dominated the region northwest of Tokyo and besieged Teruko's home at Kanayama, which featured stone walls and baileys for strength through previous assaults in 1574.

At their headquarters at Odawara Castle on Sagami Bay, at New Year's, 1584, the Go-Hojo posed as hosts to Teruko's sons, Yura Kunishige and Nagao Akinaga, but betrayed and kidnapped them. In exchange for the return of her abducted sons, she surrendered. In May 1590 at the siege of Odawara, she colluded with grandson Yura Sadashiga and two hundred twenty thousand soldiers in surrounding and attacking Matsuida Castle at Annaka. The Go-Hojo and their armored garrison of eighty-two thousand ceded after a month of assault by Daimyo (feudal lord) Toyotomi Hideyoshi, a renowned samurai experienced at undermining castle walls.

In August 1590, the enemy abandoned Kanayama Castle, which was decommissioned and collapsed in ruins. Go-Hojo rulers entered exile at Mount Koya, where the clan leader died in 1591, extinguishing the clan. Teruko's reward for valor included promotion to commandant of Ushiku Castle northeast of Tokyo, which she gave to older son Yura Kunishige. The Ota museum, a national historic site, commemorates Teruko for destabilizing the Go-Hojo.

See also May 1590.

September 17, 1584

The fall of Ghent, Flanders, in October 1583 to Prince Alexander Farnese of Parma preceded an attempted liberation under the English army, led in part by robust army captain **Mary Ambree (fl. 1580s)**, a surname meaning "female hero." To replace her lover, Sergeant John Major, who died in the year-long siege, on September 17, 1584, she commanded a mix of three hundred fifty Dutch and English volunteers in a seven-hour conflict at the gates of Ghent. During the Eighty Years' War, her guidance of the forces of Belgium, Holland, and Luxembourg enhanced recovery of Ghent, Antwerp, and Mechlin from one thousand enemy Spanish from Philip II. Ballads and plays depicted her tall and muscular, clad in helmet, mail, pistol, and sword belt, and marching to fife, trumpet, and drum. At capture after betrayal by her gunner, she slashed him to pieces and proved her gender to the enemy by exposing both breasts. To Alexander's offer to take her as mistress or wife, she spurned all enemies of England, particularly Calvinists and anti-Papists.

October 9, 1584

A Japanese virago in the Sengoku era, **Kato Tsune (also Otsune, 1540s–after 1599)** fought as a samurai to end the siege of Suemori Castle. The assault by Sassa Narimasa off the west central coast of Japan involved fifteen thousand troops. Pairing with husband Okumura Nagatomi, on October 9, 1584, Kato patrolled the battlements with a *naginata* (axe-headed pole), distributed food and water, and treated casualties. The couple held out to deep night, when the noble warrior Maeda Toshiie arrived to trounce the attackers and fell Sassa. In April 1599, Maeda rewarded Kato two gold coins for courage.

1586

Amid the Kyūshū campaign of the Shimazu clan, in 1586, **Tachibana Ginchiyo (September 23, 1569–November 30, 1602)** of Chikuzen in southern Japan defended the gates of her birthplace, Tachibana Castle at the port city of Fukuoka. By recruiting females for an army and training them in combat tactics and weaponry, at the end of the Sengoku period, she formed a military coalition with Toyotomi Hideyoshi, the conqueror of Kyūshū. A clan leader, she superintended territories, which, in 1587, included Yanagawa Castle. In May 1590, she aided the three-month siege of Odawara in Sagami Province, which gained Hideyoshi control of Hojo clan land. Rather than back Hideyoshi's failed Korean campaign, she retired to a convent.

1587

A Mapuche-Puelche defier of Spanish conquistadors, **Janequeo (also Yanequen, fl. 1587–1590)** led her southern Chilean people in 1587 as both widowed chief and warrior. At the new Fort Puchunqui, her multidirectional guerrilla style during the Arauco War in the Andean high country derived from outrage at the torture and slaughter of her husband Huepotaen, who died at Llifén, Chile. In retaliation, she dispatched some four thousand volunteers and personally speared the Spanish commander's head. The Spanish replied with arquebuses and artillery, but the Amerindian archers stymied European methods from the high ground. A Spanish backlash forced Janequeo to retreat into the jungle at Villarrica, a disappearance that novelist Isabel Allende reprised in the novel *Ines of My Soul*. Janequeo reputedly died of typhus, leaving her name and reputation to identify a lizard and an asteroid.

June 15, 1587

Two Dutch viragos at Sluis, Zeeland, during the Anglo-Spanish War, **Catharina Rose (fl. June 15, 1587)** and **Maeyken in den Hert (fl. June 15, 1587)** led a female corps against Spanish invaders. As commanders, to shield one of the last two rebel harbors, on June 15, 1587, they posted women soldiers on a hill between the Blauwe Toren (Blue Tower) on city hall and the Smedetoren (Forge Towers) overlooking the Zwin River. To protect the vulnerable, on June 20, they evacuated women and children via English troopships.

As reported in Pieter Bor's *Nederlantschen Oorloghen* (Netherlands Wars), the partners set the battalion to building two redoubts for the bombardment around the walls beginning on June 24. The Dutch-English alliance lost eleven hundred men. After Sluis surrendered to Alexander Farnese, the Duke of Parma and governor of the Spanish Netherlands, on August 5, 1587, the leaders and their commandos left unharmed. Farnese began readying Zeeland for the arrival of the Spanish Armada on July 21, 1588.

August 9, 1588

Following three decades of prosperity from command of the seas, **Elizabeth I of England (September 7, 1533–March 24, 1603)** from Greenwich decked herself in silver plumed helmet and steel cuirass to deliver a speech to her battlefleet. After Philip II of Spain dispatched one hundred thirty carracks and galleons from Lisbon, Portugal, to overthrow the English monarch and Anglicanism, Elizabeth's two hundred-ship flotilla scattered them, ending two decades of spying and cabals by Catholics. With the coordinated efforts of Vice Admiral Francis Drake and Rear Admiral John Hawkins, the English navy engaged the armada on August 8, 1588, killed two-thirds of Philip's thirty thousand soldiers, and damaged or sank five Spanish ships.

At Tilbury east of London on August 9, 1588, the queen, outfitted in ceremonial armor over white velvet, strolled among the viewers like the goddess Athena while carrying a mace representing military Protestantism. An escort bore the state sword and led her white warhorse. She rallied troops with a pledge of her life to ward off Spanish invaders from the Thames estuary. Having strategized her nation's defense, she promised to be commander in chief, judge, and rewarder of military feats at a cost that sapped the royal treasury. On November 24, 1588, she led the English in celebration. Her legend grew with global acknowledgment of her courage and stamina and the professional prowess of the Royal Navy and their military triumphs.

February 1589

A Greek Orthodox martyr, heiress, and abbess of a convent and school, **Philothey Benizelos (also St. Philothea of Athens or Philothée or Philothei Venizelou, November 21, 1522–February 19, 1589)** armed herself to stamp out a peasant tax revolt. Part of her appeal was mercy, ransom, and rescue of slaves of Muslim harems, women on the run, the infirm and poor, and uneducated children. Her training in self-protection yielded power to vulnerable inmates on her private turf in Athens and on Aegean isles of Aegina, Andros, and Salamine, where she offered protection, medical care, women's vocational and military training, and spiritual retreats.

In February 1589, Philothey faced disapproval of the ruling Ottoman government as well as a tenant revolt over her superintendency of lands by militant nuns carrying weapons. Her demise on February 19 involved jailing, torture, and murder by mercenaries who attacked her chapel at Patisia in the city's northern suburbs. A variant of her legend declares that she paid a security guard to help her pretend to be slain to give an opportunity for escape and a new career under an alias.

May 4, 1589

A Galician civilian, **María Pita (1565–1643)** of Sigras, Spain, protected Caruña from an English armada. While deployed at the town defenses, on May 4, 1589, she seized a spear from an English commander and plunged it into him. The loss of Francis Drake's brother convinced twelve thousand enemy to retreat in twenty ships. After Maria's husband's felling by the bolt from a crossbow, she led women in protecting the town.

A fellow war widow, haberdasher **Inés de Ben (fl. 1580s)**, helped refortify city walls with sandbags and stones, resupplied soldiers with ammunition, and survived arquebus wounds to thigh and head. Spain's king, Philip II, granted Maria an army pension, but did nothing to requite Ines for the looting of her store. A statue on town hall square and the naming of a rescue ship preserve Maria's example.

March 14, 1590

At considerable personal cost, during the French Wars of Religion, which began in April 1562, **Françoise de Cezelly (also Constance de Cezelli, May 22, 1558–October 16, 1615)** of Montpellier protected Huguenot region of Leucate in southern France against Spanish insurgents. In the absence of husband

Jean de Bourcier, on March 14, 1590, she mustered the local garrison to redoubts that repulsed attacks by the Court of Egmont from the Mediterranean Sea. In a defensive position over the bulwark, in the name of England's Henry IV, she guarded the boundary between France and Aragon and refused to cede to arbiters who offered to free her husband from prison. After Jean's strangulation by agents of the Catholic league, she remained adamant for months until the Spanish withdrew. Henry IV rewarded her with the governance of Leucate. A statue presents her in heroic pose.

May 1590

In a three-month onslaught in Sagami, Japan, the septuagenarian female warrior **Akai Teruko** attempted a second time to destroy the eighty-two thousand warriors of the Go-Hojo clan. At the third siege of Matsuida Castle, a total of two hundred twenty thousand crushed the four Go-Hojo commanders. Contributing strategy and resistance, her granddaughter, eighteen-year-old **Kaihime (1572–?)**, donned armor, mounted a warhorse, and led two hundred cavalry to bolster the army. As a reward, Akai Teruko claimed the Ushiku Castle, which she willed to her grandson, Yura Kunishige. Kaihime returned to battle in June 1590 by thwarting the siege on Oshi Castle with a flood. She thwarted Ishida Misunari, a samurai commander from Omi (modern Nagahama), by rupturing dikes and directing the deluge toward his twenty-three thousand troops.

See also 1584.

1595

A cross-dressing Portuguese knight, **Antònia Rodrigues (January 5, 1572–1641)** from Aveiro aided the colonial army of Mazagan (modern Jadida), Morocco, in fighting Moors of the Saadian dynasty at Marrakesh. A discontented girl at age twenty-two, she adopted male disguise, retreated to the docks of Lisbon, and shipped out as a cabin boy on the caravel *Nossa Senhora do Socorro* (Our Lady of Help). The route took her with a cargo of wheat to Mazagan, a braced port on the Atlantic shore. By enlisting as an infantryman in 1595, she earned regard for desert soldiery against the land-grabbing policies of Sultan Ahmad al-Mansur, a notorious spy master. To avoid a forced marriage, in 1600, she confessed her deception to the governor and adopted female dress. At age forty-seven she received from Spain's King Philip III a service medal for her successful campaigns.

October 18, 1595

After the death of her husband, Spanish navigator and explorer Alvaro de Mendaña, from malaria on October 18, 1595, Admiral **Isabel Barreto de Castro (1567–1622)** from Lima, Peru, completed Alvaro's voyage from Paita, Peru, to the Marquesas Islands and the Philippines. With the galleys *San Jerónimo* and *Santa Isabel*, the frigate *Santa Catalina*, and the galiot *San Felipe*, Alvaro had embarked on April 9 from Callao, Peru, with two hundred eighty soldiers bearing arquebuses. The fleet reached the Solomon Islands on September 7, making Mendaña the first European to view them. Isabel continued as crew commander on October 18, 1595, by suppressing native rebels, garnering water and rations, and hanging squabbling crew.

Aided by navigator Pedro de Quiros, Isabel arrived at Guam on January 1, 1596. Because of the loss to violence and fever, she reached Manila on February 11, 1596, with only one hundred of the original shipmates. She continued her voyages to Acapulco, Mexico, and Guanaco, Argentina, before returning to Spain to challenge Quiros's rights to the Solomon Islands, which her husband had discovered. Historians identify her as one of the world's first female admirals.

December 14, 1595

To liberate her Deccan homeland from Mughal takeover, **Chand Bibi (also Chand Bibbi, 1550–1599)**, sultana of Ahmednegar in west central India, battled a series of usurpers, traitors, and conquerors. As regent for nine-year-old nephew Ibrahim 'Adil Shah II, she mastered diplomacy with nobles and with Portuguese viceroy Francisco da Gama by learning Arabic, Persian, Telugu, and Kannada. She displayed foresight in 1580 by capturing and decapitating General Kamal Khan, a would-be usurper. According to Persian chronicler Firishta, a sultan court reporter, a second conspiracy involving possession of war elephants resulted in her temporary jailing at Fort Satara. Amid a snarl of political claims, intrigues, and assassinations, the childless widow encountered the greatest challenge—an alliance of sultanates proclaiming the primacy of Emperor Akbar.

During a three-year reign, the dowager sultana Chand Bibi strengthened her realm's autonomy by allying with forces of Bijapur and Golconda. Despite a famine, she gathered troops at the Ahmednagar citadel and rode horseback among the ranks to raise spirits in defiance of Akbar's son, Sultan Murad. During Murad's attack on December 14, 1595, she donned armor, rode astride and unveiled, and impeded the placement of mines along her battlements. After a charge exploded and pulverized one hundred fifty feet of curtain wall, she defended the squad that repaired the breach.

On February 9, 1597, Chand Bibi's army lost the battle of Supa, a two-day conflict on the Godavari River, but the pyrrhic upset weakened the Mughals from casualties. Worsening their loss was the death of Murad from delirium tremens two years later. In June 1599, Chand Bibi faced dual dangers—Akbar's on-site command of Mughals besieging the stronghold and rumor-monger Hamid Khan's false allegation that she had resolved to surrender. At her apartment, her dismayed soldiers overwhelmed and assassinated her. Irish historian Vincent Arthur Smith indicated that she poisoned herself, leaving Ahmednagar to the Mughals.

August 1597

A Swedish widow and loyalist to King Sigismund, **Ebba Gustavsdotter Stenbock (1547–March 8, 1614)** from Torpa secured Turku Castle at Åbo, Finland, from a three-week attack by Charles IX of Sweden. On April 13, 1597, she lost her husband, Admiral Klaus Eriksson Fleming, who died of natural causes in Pohja, Finland. Charles's assault on Finland began in August 1597 with the invasion and capture of Aland island on the Baltic Sea. She rejected the marauders' offer of safe exodus and calmed the female security force during artillery fire through windows.

When Ebba ceded the castle on September 30, 1597, she and daughters Hebla, Karin, and Margareta entered house arrest at Stockholm's Gripsholm Castle on Lake Malare. As reported in Finnish historian Zachris Topelius' *Boken om Vårt Land* (Book of Our Land), Charles opened Klaus's tomb to sneer at his remains. Ebba bribed her jailer, Captain Welam de Wijk, with marriage to one of the daughters to revolt against Charles. Before her family's release, in 1599, Charles murdered her son Johan. Ebba remained propertyless until her death.

1599

A respected Hmong archer and martial arts expert in the Ming dynasty, General **Qin Liangyu (1574–1648)** of Sichuan accompanied her husband, Ma Qiancheng of Shizhu, to Chinese battlefields. She learned from her father, Qin Kui, horse riding, archery, and weaponry. She retrieved his body from combat and adopted his sword for fighting criminals and traitors. To terminate Yang Yinglong's insurrection in Bozhou, Anhui, in 1599, she commanded five hundred cavalry alongside Ma's three thousand mounted soldiers and funded them with her own money. Motivated by loyalty to her husband, who died in prison in 1613, she replaced him as leader of the White Lance Army.

Northwest of the Korean peninsula at Liaodong, Qin's forces put down a Manchu uprising in part by scaling walls with a hooked pike. In late winter 1622, her army outflanked Yi rebel She Chongming by circumventing the Guizhou siege and rescuing its two hundred survivors. A battle at Beijing in spring 1630 required her troops as reinforcements after insurgents of the Later Jin Dynasty broke through the Great Wall of China.

Qin's takeover in 1634 swept Li Zicheng and his anti–Ming mutineers from Kuizhou, a center of classical Chinese culture. In 1640, subduing Luo Rucai's peasant mutiny at Shizhu south of the Yangtze River brought her success and advancement to security guard for the crown prince. At age seventy-four, she fell from her horse while reviewing troops at Chongqing and died of injuries. Her equipage survives in east central China at a Chongqing museum.

September 11, 1599

The modern world's noted female admiral, **Keumalahayati (also Malahayati, 1570–1630)** of Aceh Empire (modern Indonesia) defended Asian trade routes from European interlopers in the Malacca Strait. The daughter and granddaughter of admirals, she received a Muslim education, attended a military academy, and married a naval officer, Zeal Abidin. In retaliation for his death in the Haru Bay War, she formed an army of two thousand widows headquartered at Inong Balee Fort overlooking Lamer Krueng Raya Bay. Her personal launch was the sultan's galley, which preceded one hundred ships against Portuguese imperialists.

At Banten Harbor, Keumalahayati headed the Inong Balee Armada against Dutch invader Cornelis de Houtman, a merchant raider seeking to monopolize the spice trade in Bali, Java, and Madura. On September 11, 1599, she slew him in combat at Sumatra and arrested his brother, Frederick de Houtman. Because of piracy of pepper exports, as captain of the palace security guard, she negotiated a treaty in August 1601 against the Dutch and demanded remuneration of fifty thousand guilders (approx. $5,146,700). Her aggressive stance convinced England's Queen Elizabeth I to abandon plans to colonize Aceh and agree to a trade summit with the English on June 6, 1602. At age sixty, Keumalahayati died in a marine battle against the Portuguese in Kreung Raya Bay. Her resolute actions initiated a period of prosperity and independence and won road, port, hospital, city, ship, and university names and selection as National Hero of Indonesia.

Early Modern Era, 1600–1750

In a period of scientific theorizing, global exploration, and colonialism, the early modern thinkers and doers gained intellectual reasoning from the enlightenment philosophers. To upgrade humankind, proponents hypothesized improved systems of learning, liberty, and contentment devoid of medieval theocracy and barbaric control of nations. From enquiry and debate grew reference works, professional studies, and the pursuit of human and women's rights, including the opportunity to serve the military.

1600

During Tsugaru Tamenobu's rise to power in Mutsu Province, northern Honshu, in the Sengoku or Warring Period, he clashed repeatedly with **Fujishiro Gozen (ca. 1600)**, a war widow he craved for a concubine. After initiating the Tsugaru, a samurai clan, at Aomori, Japan, in 1590 and slaying her husband in battle, Tamenobu forced Fujishiro to defend her child in their small castle, Fujishiro-kan. For security, the castellan locked the gates and positioned herself, a sister, and servants outside to safeguard the family. Before dying in battle, in 1600, she cursed Tamenobu and his descendants.

October 21, 1600

A crucial conflict of shogunates during the Period of Warring States, the battle of Sekigahara on October 21, 1600, incorporated among its eighty-nine thousand warriors female Oda clan samurai **Ikeda Sen (1563–1640)** of Owari, concubine **Okaji no Kata (December 7, 1578–September 17, 1642)**, warrior **Yuki no Kata (fl. 1600s)**, amazon **Inahime (also Komatsuhime, 1573–March 27, 1620)**, and **Maeda Matsu (1547–1617)**, an experienced soldier, wife of warlord Maeda Toshiie, and the hero of the conflict. At the battle of Yamazaki in south central Japan on July 2, 1582, Ikeda displayed martial and weaponry skills at age nineteen. She led two hundred female musketeers armed with matchlock rifles in a phalanx of forty-thousand. At the siege of Sekigahara, her husband, feudal lord Nakamura Kazuuji, died in action. At the same time, Yuki defended Anotsu Castle from the battlements at the coastal town of Tsu in south central Japan. Her thirteen hundred-member security force could not stop arson by thirty thousand enemy. Wielding a *naginata* (bladed pike), she saved her husband, Tomita Nobutaka, and arranged for imperial aid to repair the castle walls.

Inahime earned a reputation for denying entrance to her father-in-law at Ueda Castle and for supplying rations during his exile and introducing him to his four grandchildren, ages eight, seven, two, and one. A military miracle worker, Maeda joined Nene, wife of Toyotomi Hideyori of western Japan, in outlining a truce. During Maeda's incarceration at Edo Castle as a hostage, she promoted peaceful relations to save her clan. The Sekigahara advantage inaugurated the shogunate of campaigner Tokugawa Ieyasu, who humiliated Hideyori and left thirty-two thousand or thirty-two percent of his eighty-two thousand soldiers dead. Honoraria bestowed a feudal fief on Ikeda and commemoration of Maeda in drama and video games.

In the aftermath, female warrior **Numata Jakō (1544–September 4, 1618)** of Wakasa Province joined her husband Fujitaka and son Tadaoki in defending Tanabe Castle at Maizuru, a coastal city in Kyoto. The attack in south central Japan began after the ritual sacrifice of Jako's daughter-in-law Gracia at the battle of Sekigahara. The castle security force at Tanabe consisted of five hundred soldiers facing the fifteen thousand men of the Western Army. Over a nineteen-day siege, Jako patrolled the battlements in armor and identified enemy artillery that fired high to save the castle from seizure. The family agreed to a surrender at the command of Emperor Go-Yozei. For their loyalty, Jako's family received rewards from Tokugawa Ieyasu. Tadaoki won property in Buzen.

See also November 8, 1614.

Early 1600s

The Kongo queen **Tembandumba (fl. 1610s)** of Matamba (modern Angola) on the Cunene River seized the throne of her mother, virago monarch **Mussasa (fl. 1590s–1600)**, who had tutored her daughter in war and conquest. In the early 1600s, Tembandumba plunged the Jaga tribe into an era of cannibalism, infanticide, and perpetual war conducted by a women's army. For strength to form a female state, she decreed the cannibalizing of adult males for food and the pulverizing of boy babies into a salve for covering her body. Her husband Culemba halted her reign of terror by poisoning her with tainted palm wine.

December 11, 1602

A legendary defender of Geneva, Swiss heroine **Catherine Cheynel Royaume (1542–1605)** foiled invading shock troops during a night assault launched by Savoyard duke Charles Emmanuel I on December 11, 1602. With only a pot of vegetable soup as a weapon, the sixty-year-old attacker hoisted it out a window and onto the enemies' heads as they scaled the city walls. At the call of the watchman and assembly of the home guard, **Jeanne Baud Piaget (July 1568–September 14, 1630),** a local silk merchant, and other residents hurled furniture in Catherine's aggressive style and slew fifty-four raiders. Catherine's surname identifies a street and the annual L'Escalade festival; a sculpture adorns the city's Grand Theatre.

April 8, 1603

A murderous "Second Lieutenant Nun," on April 8, 1603, Lieutenant **Catalina de Erauso (1585–1650)** of San Sebastian, Spain, contended with Dutch pirates at Punta de Araya, Venezuela. Posing as a male, she advanced from cabin boy to sailor on a Spanish galleon transporting silver to Spain. On return to the New World, she survived shipwreck off Manta, Ecuador. Two prison sentences for knife fighting preceded her military enlistment for an expedition from Lima to Conception, Peru. In 1619, her regiment invaded the Mapuche of Chile during the Arauco War, when she advanced to lieutenant and replaced her captain, a casualty at the battle of Puren. A spree of killings and dueling returned her to prison, more roving, and another army enlistment. Because of an autobiography, *Historia de la Monja Alferez* (History of Monja Alferez), her transgender history remains obscured by contradictions.

October 22, 1605

A combatant for justice and religious freedom, Queen **Ketevan of Kekheti (1560–September 13, 1624)** summoned Georgian forces to kill her brother-in-law, Constantine I Mirza, a patricide, fratricide, and conspirator with Safavid Iranians to behead her father-in-law, Alexander II. Widowed on October 21, 1602, with the death of King David I, she took charge of the army and repelled followers of Constantine, who died in the fray on October 22, 1605. She set an example of mercy by giving quarter to wounded Iranians. To protect her sixteen-year-old son Teimuraz I, she volunteered as hostage to Shah Abbas I the Great of Iran, who also jailed her grandsons Alexander and Levan.

To punish Teimuraz for seeking a non–Muslim shah, Abbas ordered the queen to convert to Islam and marry him. On her refusal, he had Ketevan tormented with hot tongs, fingernails ripped out, torso pierced with hot spears, a heated cauldron placed on her head, and a board nailed to her backbone. He murdered her on September 13, 1624, by striking her skull with a spade and tossing her remains to flesh eaters. Further thwarting the dynasty, Abbas ordered the castration of princes Levan and Alexander at Isfahan. The vicious emasculation killed Alexander; Levan went insane.

1610

After three and a half decades of continual warfare in Zazzau, a Hausa state in Nigeria, **Amina** died in battle in 1610 at age seventy-seven during a military campaign in Attaagar (also Atagara, modern Idah, Kogi) near Bida on the eastern bank of the Niger River. Although she ruled some five hundred square miles, her loss to Nigerian women left them stripped of authority and civil rights. A statue in front of the National Theater in the capital city of Lagos depicts Amina's skill at riding horseback and wielding a sword.

See also 1549; 1566; April 1576.

January 24, 1612

During the Kalmar War, Swedish cannoneer **Emerentia Kraków (1584–1648)** of Gothenburg defended

Gullberg Fort at Gothenburg against enemy Danes' approach from the Gota River delta. Motivated to action by the wounding of her husband, Warden Marten Thomasson Kraków, in a fall from his horse, on January 24, 1612, she immediately took his place in battle formation. According to a biography composed by their daughter Cecilia Kraków, Emerentia ejected the stronghold's captain, who hid in a rooftop room from combat. She summoned soldier's wives to six hours of withstanding assaults on the fort, by pouring garbage and hot lye on the attackers. The Danes who took over her kitchen received head wounds from blows of musket butts and a log wielded by Emerentia. A road bears her name.

August 26, 1612

A volunteer signaler of a Scots advance in the Kalmar War, **Prillar Guri (1595–after 1612)** from Sel in south central Norway alerted a peasant militia about enemy forces at Kringen. To save the five hundred locals, on August 26, 1612, she initiated an ambush by rural families armed with crossbows, scythes, axes, swords, and muskets. They overwhelmed Scottish mercenaries arriving from Romsdalen bearing claymores, axes, pistols, and broadswords. The column marched through a narrow pass at Gubrandsdalen to set fires to farm buildings and plunder Norwegian minerals and fishing lanes.

By sounding a long *lur* (cow horn) from a cliff over looking the river and waving an improvised flag, Prillar stopped the hirelings from aiding the Swedish army in the battle of Kringen. The clash enabled farmers to shoot, beat, drown, and loot half of the three hundred fifty invaders. Her example of daring filled stories, verse, fiction, drama, chain dance, memorials, and folk ballads and inspired sculpture in Otta show her blowing the cow horn.

November 8, 1614

A veteran Japanese warrior from the Ota clan during the Sengoku period, **Okaji no Kata (also Lady Okaji, December 7, 1578–September 17, 1642)** participated in the ten-month siege of Osaka beginning on November 8, 1614. The concubine of the feudal lord Shogun Tokugawa Ieyasu, she valued her experience of fighting alongside him in the battle of Sekigahara. At age thirty-six, she donned male uniform and fought with Ieyasu's one hundred sixty-four thousand soldiers in the winter campaign against the Tokugawa shogunate. She shared military companion alongside another of Ieyasu's concubines, **Acha no Tsubone (also Suwa, March 16, 1555–February 16, 1637)** from the Takeda clan.

After Okaji's capture, Okaji eluded the security force and galloped back to Ieyasu and their seven-year-old son Ichihime. The conflict concluded with the bombardment and undermining of Osaka Castle, a conflagration, and multiple suicides of the losing faction. Among the ritual deaths was that of **Okurakyo no Tsubane (?–1615)**, an enemy fighter and adviser who immolated herself in the burning castle. At the enemy's surrender, Acha negotiated peace in 1615 before entering the Buddhist priesthood; Okapi took vows as a Buddhist nun and continued parenting motherless children of her clan. The Tokugawa shogunate enjoyed stability for a quarter century.

See also October 21, 1600.

March 18, 1626

Because of the kidnap of the Mughal emperor Jahangir, the last of his eight wives, **Nur Jahan (also Noor Jahan, 1577–December 18, 1645)** of Hindustan, mounted a war elephant to combat rebels at Kabul (modern Afghanistan). A renowned tiger hunter in the Punjab, she excelled at shooting. Facing Mahabat Khan, a disgruntled general and would-be usurper, in March 1626, she yielded after the repulse of imperial troops and the wounding of her elephant. She escaped captivity by Rajput guards in Mahabat's camp on the Jhelum River and, on March 18, 1626, mustered two hundred men from Lahore to rescue Jahangir. Mahabat's hundred-day rule ended in late August. Two months later, Jahangir died on October 28, 1627, at age fifty-eight from respiratory infection on a trip from Kashmir to Lahore. Nur Jahan's fierce example inspired a landmark tomb, novels, cinema, stage drama, and television series.

1627

At the age of sixteen, **Barbara Pieters Adriaens (1611–after 1636)** from Brouwershaven, Zeeland, enlisted in the Dutch army in 1627 under the male name Willem Adriaens. She began crossdressing at Utrecht and served under Count Willem II's command for eleven months. She remained a soldier for eighteen months with Captain Cornelis de Graeff's unit before transferring to Alderman Pieter Hasselaer's troops. Because of her marriage to a female at Nieuwe Kirk on September 12, 1632, Barbara came under police scrutiny in Amsterdam on October 19. A count convicted her of homosexuality and exiled her for twenty-four years. She committed the same fraud in Gröningen on May 31, 1636. After a year in prison, she was permanently banished and disappeared from history.

June 1634

In the heyday of London's East End criminal class, riverboat raider **Elizabeth Patrickson (fl. 1634)** of Wapping and two accomplices seized paltry spoils from a Thames River wherry (passenger barge). With her husband, sailor William Patrickson, and Thomas Joyner of Milton Regis, Kent, in June 1634, she abetted the stealing of bacon, twelve ducks, and lace, a prized adornment for its hand stitchery. Elizabeth faced added charges of unlawful possession of Holland cloth (burlap), two handkerchiefs, and two sacks from a small sloop. At the couple's arrest, they entered Newgate Prison with fellow pirates **Joanna Harris (fl. 1630s), Jane Francis (fl. 1630s), Mary Percevall (fl. 1630s), Frances Stoddard (fl. 1630s),** and **Anna Carey (fl. 1630s)**. Additional court cases in September 1638 tried **Jane Randall (fl. 1630s)** and **Margaret Pope (fl. 1630s)** for seizing wool, goat's hair, and cotton sheets, curtains, and clothing from river vessels. A subsequent career buccaneer, **Mary Carleton (August 11, 1642–January 22, 1673)** of

Canterbury, went to the gallows at Tyburn Prison on January 22, 1673, for piracy on the way home from transportation to Port Royal, Jamaica.

1637

Highland warrior **Nora of Kelmendi (fl. 1630s)** of Malsia (modern Malesia, Albania) drafted three hundred women in 1637 to support five hundred Kelmendi tribesmen and fight off an Ottoman attack on the Albanian-Montenegrin border. Because Vutsi Pasha of Bosnia, a resident of Shkodra castle (modern Shkoder), received a turndown of his marriage proposal to Nora, he threatened to destroy her home. He besieged Malsia and set it afire. She withstood further attempts of his twelve thousand Turks to loot homes and rape women.

Similar in guile to the biblical assassin Jael, Nora followed Vutsi to his tent to discuss the offer to join his harem in exchange for a troop withdrawal from northwestern Albania. She settled the Albanian-Ottoman war with a duel, which she won, allegedly by wielding an heirloom dagger and assassinating the Ottoman general. The war concluded with seven hundred local losses and four thousand Turkish dead.

December 17, 1637

During the four-month Shimabara Rebellion in the Amakusa islands and at Hara Castle, **Miyagino (fl. 1630s)** and her sister **Shinobu (fl. 1630s)** of Shiroishi Banashi, Japan, swore to avenge the murder of their father, rice farmer Yomosaku. While fleeing the military, the drunk samurai Shiga Daishichi killed Yomosaku in a rice paddy. As described by seventeenth-century authors Inoue Tsūjo and Nakayama Suzuko, the girls began studying martial arts and swordsmanship in 1630. At Shiroishi Castle in east central Japan overlooking the Pacific Ocean, they requested from a commander permission to duel with the samurai slayer.

For the showdown on December 17, 1637, both sisters dressed in white mourning kimonos. The elder, Miyagino, bore the *naginata*, an ax-headed pole. Her sister chose a kusarigama, a sickle on a chain weighted by a lead ball. By tangling the samurai's sword in the chain, Shinobu, despite being wounded, left him helpless to Miyagino's death stroke lopping off his head. The duel survives in a puppet show and kabuki stage play, *Go Taiheiki Shiroishi Banashi* (The Tale of Shiroishi and the Taihei Chronicles).

1638

A famed commander and swordswoman, **Alberte-Barbe d'Ernécourt (also Barbara of Belmont or Dame de Saint-Baslemont, May 14, 1607–May 22, 1660)** defended the family's Neuville castle in northeastern France throughout her husband Jean-Jacques de Haraucourt's absence in 1638 with the infantry of Holy Roman Emperor Charles IV. Posing as the male "Chevalier de Saint-Baslemont (modern Belmont)," Alberte dueled in the field on horseback with Croatian, French, and Swedish adventurers. By mustering a security force of tenants and refugees, in 1644, she scattered Croat freebooters from the sanctuary of Benoîte-Vaux. At conclusion of the Thirty Years' War in 1648, she retired from the military and obeyed the governor of Lorraine by retreating to a nunnery of the Poor Clares in Bar-le-Duc. She spent the last of her fifty-three years composing motets and writing poetry and dramas. Her portrait remains on display in Nancy.

June 5, 1639

In the Bishops' Wars at the battle of Berwick south of Coventry, England, fifty-nine-year-old Scots Calvinist **Anna Cunningham Hamilton (1580–1646)** of Glencairn southwest of Glasgow commanded male and female sharpshooters to secure Leith Castle. Her armored cavalry, equipped with daggers and pistols, defended Scots Presbyterianism against England's King Charles I, a proponent of Anglicanism. The outcome secured a free parliament and free church choice. On May 1, Anna and her troop of horsemen challenged her son James Hamilton, a general in the British Army. When his ship reached the Firth of Forth, on June 5, 1639, she armed herself with a pistol to stop him from disembarking. At the failed pro–Anglican foray at Kelso, the Covenanters expelled Charles's army.

October 1641

During the Irish Rebellion of October 1641, **Elizabeth Dowdall (ca. 1600–1658)** of Devon, England, held off the Limerick County sheriff Richard Stephenson and three thousand Confederate Irish troops from Kilfinny Castle at Upper Connelloe in west central Ireland. For forty weeks, she commanded a regiment of eighty and claimed to have shot two hundred besiegers with iron bullets. The response to Eady Lacy's forces held off plots to smash the Elizabethan manor with two cannon and post ladders for climbing the walls. The uprising took the life of her son-in-law, John Southwell, as well as captured rebels whom Elizabeth hanged. She bragged about shooting Stephenson dead with a head shot before ceding to the insurgents.

Early Modern Civil Wars, 1640–1804

A period of internal unrest and resultant wars extended over Vietnam, Poland, Lithuania, Acadia, France, Ukraine, India, England, Ireland, Scotland, and the Russian, Ottoman, and Spanish empires. Female soldiery emerged on home fronts, where chatelaines and their daughters and maids improvised munitions to deliver their families and tenants from professional forces. The period of mayhem and pillage destroyed estates and agrarian investments as well as religious enclaves and dynasties.

August 22, 1642

After the outbreak of the English Civil War after August 22, 1642, **Dutch royalist Anne Vere Fairfax (1617–October 16, 1665)** accompanied her husband, Commander-in-Chief Thomas Fairfax, with Oliver Cromwell's New Model Army. At her seizure at Bradford after the battle of Adwalton Moor on July 2, 1643, she and five-year-old daughter Mary Fairfax remained in custody of Royalist Captain-General William Cavendish only two days before he sent them back by carriage. She received courteous treatment, unlike the wounding of **Ellen Askwith (September 12, 1616–after 1646)**, wife of Roundhead Captain John Askwith, and the pillage to their Ripley home.

Anne observed the Yorkshire campaign and witnessed the parliamentary cavalry capture Marston Moor in June 1644 and the three-hour Roundhead coup at Naseby on June 14, 1645. More battlegrounds at Leicester, Taunton, Bridgwater, and Bristol preceded more wins on the way west. On Anne's return to the port of Hull on the Humber River southeast of York, she cared for her husband Thomas's bullet wound to the wrist, which caused serious blood loss. Because he refused to pass judgment on condemned king Charles I, on January 20, 1649, Anne attended the High Court of Justice in his stead. By yelling royalist sentiments, she incurred questioning and ejection from the courtroom.

October 1642

A Protestant Irish widow and mother of ten, throughout the English Civil War, **Lettice Fitzgerald Digby (1580–December 1, 1658)** of Maynooth protected her home at Geashill estate village. While overseeing some thirty thousand acres in east central Ireland, during the 1641 Irish Rebellion, she arbitrated a false claim from Henry O'Dempsey, a local rebel who threatened arson and massacre to the town. Her security force recovered rustled cattle and survived sixteen days without water until rains came. Renewed aggression in late March 1642 caused her to demand return of her kidnapped son or she would behead a priest. Sir Richard Grenville joined the defenders, whom she equipped with provisions and weapons from Dublin. In October 1642, when she surrendered to O'Dempsey, Grenville escorted her east to safety in Dublin.

Late 1642

A fervid royalist from London, **Jane Ryder Whorwood (1612–September 1684)** maintained espionage for four years on behalf of King Charles I. Traveling six miles from Holton Park to the king's temporary court at Oxford, in late 1642, she crossed Wheatley Bridge to the east to connect with a secret network that extended north to Newcastle and Edinburgh, Scotland. In 1644, despite the use of her home for a parliamentary army headquarters, she smuggled £80,000 (approx. $98,400 today) in soap barrels to fund a royalist reprisal. One dangerous mission resulted in the transportation of 775 kilos (1708.58 pounds) of gold to the court to ferry Charles II, the Prince of Wales, and his mother, Henrietta Maria, to France.

In May 1647, Jane filched cash from Oliver Cromwell's Puritan treasury and dispatched more gold to Charles at Hampton Court. In December 1647, she conspired with her half-sister, **Elizabeth Ryder Maxwell (1620–September 1659)**, to free him from confinement to Carisbrooke Castle on the Isle of Wight in the English Channel. Jane acquired files and nitric acid to undermine the bars of his cell. After one failed escape attempt, on April 20, 1648, she awaited rescuers to spirit him east to the Medway River in Queenborough, where her ship awaited until May 29 the king's final dash to Holland. More attempts, intimate liaisons, coded correspondence, and a personal meeting preceded the Puritan parliament's beheading of Charles I at Whitehall on January 30, 1649. She faced imprisonment in 1651 for embezzlement.

1643

A military presence during the Ming dynasty, **Shen Yunying (also Shen Guandi, 1623–1660)**, a martial arts practitioner from Hunan, took her father Shen Zhixu's position as imperial army general. From Zhixu, she mastered archery and riding and viewed battlefields and tactics with him and soldier husband, Jia Wance. In the early 1640s, she overwhelmed peasant bandit Zhang Xianzhong in east central China. Shen's death in 1643 left her an exultant army to lead and Shen's cavalry to command in the war against outlawry.

To ease period hostilities, as deputy commander, Shen challenged the Manchurian Qing dynasty and its renowned commoner general **Gao Guiying (?–1647)** of Mizhi City, leader of a female rebel regiment. At the fall of Beijing on April 24, 1644, emperor Chongzhen committed suicide by hanging himself on a tree. Widowhood and the collapse of the Ming administration on April 25, 1644, left Shen dispirited for war. She channeled her physical prowess into defending the Southern Ming dynasty and opening a martial arts school for girls. Her name appears in children's literature, opera, and a memorial.

May 1643

Under the threat of massacre throughout a three-year siege, **Mary Hawtrey Bankes (August 8, 1603–April 11, 1661)** of Middlesex substituted for her father in defense of the family residence at Corfe Castle northwest of London. A loyalist to King Charles I during the English Civil War, in May 1643, she harbored daughters Arabella, Anne, Jane, Bridget, Joanna, Elizabeth, Mary, and Alice in the absence of sons Charles, Jerome, Ralph, and John, whom their father, Royal Attorney General John Bankes, secured elsewhere. Mother and girls defied six hundred Roundhead attackers by organizing cannon fire directed by her maidservants and security guard. A lack of ammunition during an assault by six hundred Puritans on June 28 forced her to hurl hot coals, boiling water, and stones from the ramparts, by which she felled one hundred men. When rations ran low, she raided a bull and eight cows for slaughter. A traitor directed the Parliamentarians to a sally port and forced her to cede the castle. A monument and school name commemorate her efforts.

May 2, 1643

In a similar quandary to that of Royalist Mary Hawtrey Bankes, sixty-year-old Welsh aristocrat **Blanche Arundell (1583–October 28, 1649)** protected Wardour Castle against a week-long siege by Oliver Cromwell's Puritan infantry. In the eighth month of the Civil War, while secretly practicing Roman Catholicism, she offered safe storage of valuables for neighboring Papists and monarchists in Tisbury, Wiltshire, while she and daughter-in-law **Cicely Arundell (1610–March 24, 1675)** of Sussex sheltered her son Henry's family from aggressive Anglicans. During Baron Thomas Arundell's assembly of a royal cavalry, Blanche's maids, twenty-five security guards, and fifty staff backed the fight against some thirteen hundred enemy armed with small cannon and barrels of gunpowder.

After blowing up a latrine shaft, on May 2, 1643, the Roundhead army forced the women to yield six days later, a surrender and truce reported in the Royalist newspaper *Mercurius Rusticus*. Blanche and Cicely shared cells in Shaftesbury along with three children. During a month's incarceration, Cromwell's officers removed two grandsons to Dorchester. On May 19, Blanche's husband died of gunshots to the thigh; her son Henry was lodged in the Tower of London. Enemy soldiers defaced artworks with axes, burned tenement homes, and looted Wardour Castle and its environs of cash, furnishings, lead pipes, herds, deer, fish, and timber. In March 1644, a Roundhead explosion demolished the rear section of the fourteenth-century mansion. The ruins, listened among the National Heritage sites, served as a setting for the film *Robin Hood: Prince of Thieves*.

July 25, 1643

Pro-Puritan during the English Civil War, **Brilliana Conway Harley**

(1600–October 4, 1643), a published Dutch letter writer from Brill, Holland, defended Brampton Bryan Castle for six weeks with the aid of her fifty-man militia. On July 25, 1643, seven hundred Cavaliers arrived south of River Teme, smashed walls and furnishings, rustled her herds, tunneled her gardens, and stole her church bells. During a September ceasefire, she dismantled the enemy barriers and ordered a commando raid by forty militiamen.

When seven hundred Royalist enemy returned in October, anxiety at the absence of Brilliana's husband, Lord Robert Harley, a Member of Parliament, and loss of income ruined her health, causing her death on October 4, 1643, from bronchitis and stroke. Her Herefordshire property fell to cannon fire by the army of King Charles I in early fall 1644, boosting Royalist hopes of victory over the Roundheads. She posted some four hundred coded letters to a secret coterie in Gloucester and to her husband and son Edward "Ned" Harley, a parliamentary soldier at the royal capital at Oxford. Her correspondence recorded the siege and public scorn of Puritans.

Late February 1644

For three months beginning in late February 1644, **Charlotte Stanley, Countess of Derby (December 1599–March 31, 1664)** of Poitou, France, protected Lathom House from Parliamentarian Forces and rejected surrender for herself and her ten children. When four thousand soldiers began bombarding again in Lancashire in July 1645, she, three hundred security forces, and fifty-four cannon defended the only Royalist enclave in the area. Stationing her sharpshooters in nine towers, she negated the threat of artillery until short rations forced a surrender on December 2, 1645. A song and poem reflect her determination.

June 1644

A devout Roman Catholic and mother of nine, **Henrietta Maria of France (also Henriette Marie; November 25, 1609–September 10, 1669)** joined Royalist troops in the English Civil War during a volatile period of religious fanaticism and injurious laws giving military control to Parliament. The war began on August 22, 1642. In February 1643, the queen came under Puritan fire at Bridlington Bay after returning from Holland from purchasing weapons for her husband, King Charles I. Despite ministers defiling her and rioters attacking her residence, she ate with soldiers and marched in the vanguard as *Generalissima* (Commander-in-chief).

Henrietta lived apart from Charles at Exeter and Bath while anticipating their daughter Henrietta Anne on June 16, 1644. In late June, her regiment captured Burton-on-Trent, where women aided her skirmish by making bullets. During a subsequent pregnancy, she and sons Charles and James survived on the run from Roundhead plotters of her kidnap. To escape a Parliamentary shore patrol, she booked the Dutch ship *George* from Falmouth on July 14. In the Channel Isles, the voyage drew fire from Puritan pursuers in the warships *Warwick* and *Constant Resolution*, but she demanded to sail on to Brest, France, while Charles sought a truce with Presbyterian Scots in Nottinghamshire.

After the king's beheading at Whitehall, London, on January 30, 1649, the queen struggled in penury and suspicion of harboring Papist spies. She sold jewels and pleaded with Pope Innocent X to garner funds for the Cavalier military and the monarchy of nineteen-year-old son Charles II and sixteen-year-old James II. Her retreat to Paris coincided with the French civil war of the Fronde, a revolt against raising taxes to pay for the Thirty Years' War, which nearly bankrupt Louis XIV. After recovering from plague in summer 1665, she died on September 10, 1669. Her profile ennobled a staunch royalist on oil paintings by court artist Peter Lely and Anthony van Dyck.

April 13, 1645

An Acadian amazon, **Françoise-Marie Jacquelin** (July 1621–1645) from Nogent-le-Rotrou, France, commanded the garrison of Fort la Tour, Nova Scotia, at the onset of the Acadian Civil War, a five-year territorial dispute over a trade zone rich in salt fish and pelts. She hastened around a blockade at the Bay of Fundy in 1640. In Paris, she presented to the Grand Prior details of the clash of elites against the merchant class. In the battleship *Gillyflower,* she returned to the Saint John River in disguise in late 1644 with combat supplies. In a four-day battle on April 13, 1645, the enemy attacked Fort St. John with two hundred troops. In response, she directed forty-five Acadians armed with muskets. At defeat by Governor Charles de Menou d'Aulnay, she witnessed the hanging of Acadians with her head in a noose and died in prison three weeks later. Her legend identifies her as the "Lioness of La Tour."

October 29, 1647

After attempting to make peace with Portuguese slave suppliers to Brazil, **Nzinga Mbande (also Jinga Mbandi or Llinga, 1583–1663)** a Mbundu warrior-queen in what is now Angola on the Cuanza River, allied with armed Dutch rivals in a fight for sovereignty. In 1629, she imprisoned the Motamba queen, Mongo Matamba, and turned Motamba into her headquarters in 1631. In 1635, she increased security from slave catchers by allying with the Dembos to the northwest, Kasanje mercenaries of Uganda, Motamba slave traders, and Ndongo highlanders east of Luanda, her former enemies. She also enlisted the Quissama on the Kwanza River and the trade-rich Kongo to the north.

Nzinga's aggressive actions led to merger of her territory with the Ndongo kingdom and to an outmaneuvering of thirty thousand Portuguese on October 29, 1647, at the battle of Kombi, where she led eight thousand archers. Her contemporary, **Llinga of Kongo (fl. 1640s)**, trained female soldiers and armed them with bow, sword, and battle axe for serious combat. Into her sixties, Nzinga halted Portuguese poaching on Mbundu territory by eluding pursuers and returning refugees to her tribe. Her military savvy achieved removal of the Portuguese kidnappers to their inland capital of Masangano.

May 12, 1649

A former slave and long-lived defender of the Ottoman Empire and its contention for Crete, **Kösem Sultan (1589–September 2, 1651)** of Tinos, an Aegean isle owned by Venetia (now Greece), lost a significant sea battle off Focchies, Smyrna (modern Foça, Turkey). She promoted army strength from 1645 by demanding higher salaries for the Janissaries, an elite regiment and directed her son Ibrahim to route warships to Crete. After Admiral Giacomo da Riva in the flagship *Rotta Fortuna* (Lucky Route) directed nineteen battleships against the Dardanelles, on May 12, 1649, Kösem commanded an armada of ninety-three vessels to end the blockade. Her intent was to protect her seven-year-old grandson, Mehmed IV. The legendary battle of warring Mediterranean superpowers resulted in seventeen Turkish vessels sunk, burned, or captured. Nonetheless, the Turks dragged out their anti–Venetian campaign and, in 1669, won the Cretan War. She was assassinated in Constantinople two years later at the Topkapi Palace.

1650

The vigilante daughters of Peruvian nobles, **Ana Lezama de Urinza (ca. 1630–1650)** and **Eustaquia de Sonza (ca. 1630–1650)** dueled with the criminal element in Potosí, a rowdy silver mining town in the Andes (modern Bolivia). Eustaquia's parents adopted Ana, who was orphaned in childhood, and educated her like an aristocrat. Around 1643, at age thirteen, the pair mastered armed conflict by emulating Eustaquia's brother, who was studying soldiery. Dressed in men's clothes, they became adept at pistols, horse riding, and sword fighting by night, even venturing into Chile looking for galoots to tackle. In one duel in 1650 against four males, Ana fell unconscious. After regaining her senses, she cut down one attacker and scared off the three confederates. After Ana's death at age twenty in the bull ring, Eustaquia gave up the street life and died within four months of her pal.

ca. 1651

English pirate **Charlotte de Berry (1636–?)** turned to marine combat to rid herself of an unwanted husband. When the Royal Navy drafted her sailor lover, she pretended to be his brother. In military service around 1651, they were veterans of six battles. Because a shipboard flogging killed her lover, Charlotte stabbed a potential rapist and escaped to the harbor, where a merchant captain abducted her to Africa. To escape a forced marriage, Charlotte orchestrated mutiny and wed a Spaniard, Armelio Gonzalez. Posing as a man, she died of suicide after a storm sank their vessel and left them marooned without provisions. Her story recurs in multiple fictional versions.

September 3, 1651

After the battle of Worcester on September 3, 1651, the final clash of the English Civil War, monarchist **Jane Lane (1626–September 9, 1689)** of Walsall plotted to spirit Charles II away from the triumphant army of Puritan commander Oliver Cromwell. In a plan similar to Flora MacDonald's rescue of Bonnie Prince Charlie as maid Betty

Burke, Jane dressed the king like a servant under the alias William Jackson. Riding double from Bentley in the Midlands west to Bromsgrove, on September 10, the pair stopped at a forge to replace a lost horseshoe. They reached Bristol on September 12 and continued to Shoreham to take passage on the *Surprise*, a coal transporter. Charles reached Normandy on October 16, 1651. In December, Jane visited the exiled king's court in Paris and received a letter of thanks, a gold watch, and a pension for her enthusiasm, which extended through the reigns of James II and William II.

March 3, 1652

The equipping of one hundred fifty merchant vessels for the First Anglo-Dutch War on March 3, 1652, involved recruitment of **Adriana la Noy (fl. 1652)**, **Anna Jans (fl. 1652)**, and **Johannan Pieters (fl. 1652)**, Dutch females disguised as male sailors during battle at sea. The English humiliated the Dutch by insisting that Holland acknowledge England as master of the seas. The battle of Dover on May 19, 1652, concluded with the seizure of the two-masted Dutch ship *Sint Laurens* and the three-masted *Sint Maria*. A year later, when Adriana, Anna and Johannan lost their naval posts because of gender discovery, transdressers **Anna Alders (fl. 1653)** and **Aagt de Tamboer (fl. 1653)** joined the Dutch navy before decisive combat in the North Sea at the battle of Gabbard off the Suffolk shore on June 2, 1653. Before an Amsterdam tribunal, Anna Alders declared that she wore men's clothes out of poverty.

July 2, 1652

A cannoneer and mediator of civil anarchy, **Anne Marie Louise d'Orléans (May 29, 1627–April 5, 1693)** defended her hometown of Paris at the battle of the Faubourg Saint Antoine. Her influence helped to end the two-stage Fronde, a bourgeois dispute over rising taxes to requite the debts of the Thirty Years' War. On March 27, 1652, she led occupation forces at Orléans to protect General Louis de Bourbon, the Prince of Condé. At the approach of the royal army to Paris on July 2, 1652, she ordered the gatekeeper to admit Condé. She fired the cannons of the Bastille on General Henri de Turenne and his pursuers of legitimate protesters. Out of favor with King Louis XIV, she exiled herself to Château de Saint-Fargeau in north central France for five years.

May 27, 1653

A former slave and substitute decision maker in the absence of her husband, Prince Vasile Lupu, and son Stefanita, **Ecaterina Cercheza (also Doamna Ecaterina, January 1, 1620–after March 1, 1666)** of Suceava, Circassia (modern Moldavia), backed the family's dynasty. Preceding the Moldavian Magnate Wars, a scramble for the Circassian throne north of the Black Sea, she defended Suceava, the Moldavian capital, and refused to cede to Gheorghe Ștefan, an upstart Boyar (aristocratic Russian). He captured her on May 27, 1653, and impounded her horses and jewels. She entered a Transylvanian prison at Bistrita after the battle of Finta (modern Romania), where thirty thousand Wallachian victors incarcerated and sold as slaves four thousand Cossacks, one thousand Moldavians, and one thousand Tatars. After six years, her son retrieved her in November 1659 and appointed her as royal adviser. Two years later, her exiled husband Vasile died in an Ottoman prison at Constantinople.

1657

A Swedish pirate, **Christina Anna Skytte (November 9, 1643–January 21, 1677)** of Dudenhof (modern Stockholm) collaborated in sea brigandage with her lover, Gustaf Drake, and older brother Gustav Adolph Skytte. In a leased Dutch freighter carrying wine and salt, in 1657, the trio killed the captain and crew of five and sailed about the Baltic Sea from their headquarters at Blekinge in the south. In fall 1662, she scuttled the ship between Bornholm and Öland Island in the south and escaped the authorities who arrested Gustav. The hulk washed up on Öland in August 1662. Crown soldiers executed Gustav in April 1663 at Jonkoping Castle; they confiscated Drake's property, but pardoned him. Christina Anna and her lover fled to Denmark and Prussia.

April 6, 1657

During Lord Protector Oliver Cromwell's occupation of Scotland, Lincolnshire native **Anne Dymoke (fl. 1650s)** joined the Ayre garrison in male uniform. In May 1655, she dressed as a man and followed John Evison, her lover, to London, where they enlisted together as brothers John and Stephen Evison. At John's death at sea, she signed up at Carlisle with Major Jeremiah Tolhurst as John Evison. On April 6, 1657, Colonel Roger Sawry accepted "Anne Dimack" as an infantryman in Captain-Lieutenant Shockley's garrison and complimented her modest behavior.

November 14, 1659

The wife of Vincents Steensen, who died during the Dano-Swedish War of 1658, **Anne Holck (December 7, 1602–June 5, 1660)** of Tryggevælde, Denmark, took his place as defender of Langeland Island. To halt a Swedish invasion and spare her seventeen-year-old daughter Hellebore and fifteen-year-old son Henrik enemy threats, in April 1659, she fought up to the surrender of November 14, 1659. While immured as a prisoner of war in her own doghouse, she lured insurgents to a peasant ambush in the Stensgaard wine cellar.

ca. 1665

Dubbed the "Mother of the Hotak Dynasty" and "Mother of the Afghan Nation," **Nazo Tokhi (also Nazo Ana, 1651–1717)**, a nationalist hero and lawgiver of Kandahar, claimed prominence among the Tokhi, a Pashtun tribe. The granddaughter of Emir Ismail Khan of Ghazni, she was born at Spozhmayiz Gul near Thazi. Her father, Sultan Malakhai Tokhi of Ghazni in east central Afghanistan, directed her education, Sunni Muslim faith, and development into a poet. She became a cultural icon for revering the pre–Islamic Pashtunwali code of self-respect, assertiveness, justice, hospitality, love, forgiveness, vengeance, and forbearance.

During a 1665 tribal uprising against the Safavid Persian regime, when the sultan and eight hundred of his cavalry died in the battle of Sur Ghar (Red Hills), at age fourteen, Nazo joined her brother, Haji Adil Tokhi, in arming against the six thousand troops of Aurangzeb, India's expansionist Mughal emperor. Because the Mughals attacked Ghazni village and the citadel that she commanded, she dressed in soldier's uniform and boots, mounted a white horse, and wielded a lance at full gallop toward the invaders. To unite Afghans against the Persian Safavids, she mediated tribal squabbles between the Ghilji and Sadozai. Beloved as Nazo Ana (grandmother Nazo), wife of trader Salim Khan Hotak, and the mother and mentor of ruler Mirwais Hotak, one daughter, and three younger sons, she died at age sixty-six in 1717 at Kandahar.

October 29, 1665

A stalwart anti-colonialist, **Aqualtune Ezgondidu Mahamud da Silva Santos (1635–1677)** commanded a warrior Kongo army of ten thousand. The battle of Mbwila on October 29, 1665, pitted Portuguese imperialists against Antonio I, king of Kongo, who died in the slaughter of five thousand. The capture of Aqualtune resulted in bondage, shackling with an iron collar, branding, forced baptism, and terrorizing by a middle passage insurrection on the eighth day. She was recaptured after a desperate leap into the Atlantic in Recife, Brazil, and sold as a breeder at a Puerto Calvo plantation. After escaping, she assisted her son, Ganga Zumba, and two hundred followers in burning a passage to Alagoas and forming a maroon commune, Quilombo dos Palmares, later ruled by grandson Zumbi and warrior-queen Dandara. At Aqualtune's death, the tribe revered her as a goddess.
See also 1878.

1667

The first female ruler of Kelantan (modern Malaysia), **Siti Wan Kembang (1585–1667)** from Gunung Chinta Wangsa kept her realm safe from cyclical Siamese aggression by leading a female cavalry. Although armed with a sword, for fifty-seven years, she encouraged peaceful crafts of hand looming and broadened the batik trade. While spreading Islam, she quashed raids by the Patani and Terengganu. By clever tactics, she suppressed Siamese invaders from Jelasin Fort in the capital Kota Bharu east of the Kelantan River. In 1667, Siti disappeared at age seventy-two. Four years later, Narai, the Siamese king of Ayutthaya (modern Myanmar) kidnapped Siti's adopted daughter, Puteri Saadong.

August 6, 1668

A legendary Venezuelan hero, **Ana Soto (also Anasoli, 1618–August 6, 1668)**, chief of the Gayon tribe northeast of Barquisimeto, rallied two thousand warriors to disempower Hispanic colonizers. Via a native underground, she abetted her husband, Pedro Monjes, in plotting surprise attacks and seizing weapons and supplies. Key to liberating her people, she sought to defend waterways and to halt the forced bondage of Indians in labor gangs. After her capture, the enemy impaled and dismembered her on August 6, 1668, in a grisly display of barbarity. The date of August 6 commemorates her martyrdom.

December 4, 1670

During the Peasant's Revolt, **Alena Arzamasskaia (?–1670)** of Arzamas in the Russia Empire, fought as a male Cossack. As a youthful widow, she entered a monastery on the Volga River to learn medicine. In command of six hundred horsemen at Temnikov, Mordovia, she joined the rebellion as an archer, cavalry officer, and medic. Following her capture on December 4, 1670, she surviving torture and trial for treason and heresy. She entered punitive imprisonment to be burned to death, a dramatic execution honored in folk songs.

June 25, 1672

In a ruse against six thousand French besiegers of Aardenburg, Zeeland, Dutch fighter **Margaretha Sandra (January 7, 1629–June 21, 1674)** from Middelburg, added visual strength to forty soldiers by distributing men's hats while defending city walls. To beef up armaments during the Third Dutch War, on June 25, 1672, she devised musket and rifle bullets from scrap iron while children lighted fuses and transported them to the militia. With reinforcements from Cadzand and Sluis, she and the other fighters killed hundreds of French, dispersed General Claude de Dreux and his French raiders, and ended the attack on June 26 without a Dutch casualty. A statue commemorates her ingenuity.

November 3, 1673

A Walloon veteran of the nine-day battle of Bonn, Germany, Sergeant **Elisabeth Someruell (also Lysbeth or Lys Sent Mourel, fl. 1670s–January 26, 1723)**, an army camp sutler from Den Bosch in north Brabant, Holland, served in male disguise until she was treated for a combat wound. After a stint as a domestic at a Tilburg Inn, her soldierly career began in a local restaurant, where she stabbed a rapist. Under the alias Tobias Morello, she fled arrest and, on November 3, 1673, enlisted in the infantry of the Spanish Netherlands at Dendermonde, Belgium.

Elisabeth accompanied her second husband, cavalryman Hendrick Weyerman, on battlegrounds as a regimental drummer. During the Franco-Dutch War, she witnessed the success of Dutch king William III and twenty-five thousand allied mercenaries. At the Charleroi camp in Wallonia, she gave birth to a baby boy on August 9, 1677, and named him Jacobus. For the garrison at Breda near Merk, on October 17, 1680, she opened a military trading post and wineshop at the city gate, but lost her supplies to bankruptcy.

February 18, 1674

A woman disguised as a Dutch Republican soldier bound for Batavia in the Dutch East Indies, **Francijntje van Lint (also Francine van Ling, fl. 1670s)** traveled partway to South Africa on February 18, 1674, to marry her lover. With fiance Jeronymus de Los van Gent, she left Hottentoos, Holland, on January 30, 1674, aboard the forty-gun warship *Gecroonde Vrede* (Crowned

Peace), which carried a cargo of hay and wheat. During treacherous times at sea in the last two weeks of the Third Anglo-Dutch War, she reached Cape Town on February 2 without being discovered and arranged her marriage. She chose February 18, 1674, the day before the signing of the Treaty of Westminster, which secured Dutch fishing rights, shipping, and trade.

June 20, 1675

During the three-year King Philip's War on Narragansett Bay, Rhode island, **Awashonks (fl. 1670s)**, female chief of the Saconet tribe, supported the expulsion of English insurgents from southern New England. War fomenter Metacomet, the Wampanoag chief, blackmailed her into joining an Algonquian coalition with the Nipmuck to drive out white settlers. Benjamin Church, North America's first army ranger, persuaded her and one hundred fifty natives to ally with the one thousand-man colonial militia from Connecticut, Massachusetts, and Rhode Island. Narragansett-Niantic queen **Quaiapen (fl. 1670s–summer 1676)** of Queen's Fort at North Smithfield, Rhode Island, mustered two hundred warriors to fight Metacomet's allies. Her army attacked Quantisset, Connecticut, stripped Nipmuck corn from the fields, and confiscated guns and ammunition, wampum, pigs, and kettles.

Beginning with the siege of Swansea, Massachusetts, on June 20, 1675, the Indian coalition inflicted guerrilla warfare through armed ambush, ritual torture, massacre, and raids that destroyed twelve towns and devastated area commerce. As part of the Great Swamp Fight, on March 29, 1676, arson leveled the town of Providence. At Nipsachuk, Quaiapen drowned in the Great Spruce Swamp, becoming the last native leader to die in King Philip's War. Total human loss cost the colonists six hundred members and Indians, three thousand or thirty percent. The women's contribution to the war enabled the allies to whip the Narragansett, martyr Metacomet, and sign a peace pact on April 12, 1678. A protruding rock at Little Compton, Rhode Island, marks Quaiapen's involvement in befriending whites.

Summer 1676

Following insurrectionist Nathaniel Bacon's assault on the Pamunkey, a Virginia tribe, Chief **Cockacoeske (ca. 1650–July 1, 1686)**, a descendent of Powhatan, made peace with the commonwealth burgesses at Jamestown by offering to assemble frontier natives into a militia to defend European colonists. Crowned with shells and wampum, she appeared in fringed deerskin mantle in summer 1676 and sat at the council table. She inserted comments about the one hundred native braves who had died in 1656 defending settlers, particularly her husband Totopotomoy. The negotiation resulted in a treaty on May 29, 1677, that pledged the Pamunkey's loyalty to King Charles II and an annual payment of game. In return, she united disparate tribes and secured hunting, fishing, and trapping rights, eviction of squatters, and deeds to lands around native villages.

September 1676

A chief Algonquian player in the one-month Bacon's Rebellion against corrupt English authorities, Queen **Anne of the Pamunkey (1630–1723)** of King William County, Virginia, succeeded her aunt Cockacoeske and softened tribal antipathy toward European colonies in September 1676 by dispatching warriors to aid settlements. At the attack of the Pamunkey queen's coastal village near Chesapeake Bay at the confluence of the Mattapony and Pamunkey rivers east of Richmond, in September 1676, she eluded captors and hid in the Virginia woods for two weeks. She adopted the name Queen Anne after the coronation on April 23, 1702, of England Queen Anne, the last Stuart monarch. Anne of the Pamunkey petitioned colonists in 1715 to reciprocate for her generosity by preventing violence to native Americans and ending the sale of and encroachment on heritage fishing, trapping, and hunting wetlands and illegal occupation by squatters.

1677

During General Wu Sangui's revolt against the Qing dynasty, **Kong Sizhen (1641–after 1681)** from Liaodong on China's Yellow Sea, replaced her deceased husband Sun Yanling, the military commander of Guangxi. She established military might by saving her family from the murderous Ming army, but could not intercede in her husband's imprisoning and assassination by Wu. The insurrectionists succeeded in capturing the provinces of Fujian, Gansu, Guangdong, Guangxi, Guizhou, Hunan, Jiangxi, Shanxi, Sichuan, Yunnan, and Zhejiang. When Wu declared himself emperor and founded a capital at Hangzhou, Kong Sizhen yielded to Manchu forces and settled at Beijing.

1678

A maroon warrior from Quilombo dos Palmares in coastal Brazil, **Dandara (?–February 6, 1694)** challenged the European bondage system and opposed appeaser Nganga Nzumbi, who created his own realm. With her husband, King Zumbi dos Palmares, she defended their commune of twenty thousand by performing Capoeira, a gymnastic-dance martial art imported from Kongo (modern Angola). In 1678, she recruited and headed women warriors to fight invasions and raids. Because of an assault on the Serra da Barriga hideout in January 1694, Portuguese troops arrested her. She chose to jump to her death from a mountain peak rather than return to slavery.

1678

The Kannada queen **Belawadi Mallamma Desai (also Belvadi, Mallavva, Savithri, or Savitribai, ca. 1650–1717)** of Bailhongal, north Karnataka in southwestern India, avenged her deceased husband by leading an all-woman army against Shivaji Maharaj, founder of the Maratha Confederation, challengers of the Mughal Empire. She became the first recruiter of an anti-colonial female regiment. At the slaughter of Yesaji Prabhu Desai for rebellion in 1678, Mallamma mounted her warhorse, lifted a sword, and galloped out of the front gate at Yadawada.

Her women prolonged the combat against the outsider and the British. She strengthened the Belavadi blockhouse and held out against the Maratha looters and rustlers for twenty-three days.

The stumble of Mallamma's wounded horse forced her into hand-to-hand fighting at ground level. At the shrine of Devi, a heavenly goddess, she lured Shivaji into an ambush and struck him down. Because of her courage, Shivaji restored her to the Belawadi court. To reward him for treating females with respect, she commissioned a carving at Yadwad's Hanuman temple. His daughter-in-law, Tarabai, added to songs, drama, and dance by raising hero stones to commemorate Mallamma's expertise.

October 13, 1678

Near Scone Palace west of Perth, **Anne Keith Smythe (March 20, 1629–December 1681)**, a devout Catholic from Beholm, Scotland, besieged Covenanters (Presbyterians) from Fife for holding a Sunday religious tent meeting with armed attendants outside her property. She rallied to Castle Hill all males from the estate of her husband, merchant and landowner Patrick Smythe of Methven. On October 13, 1678, she made good her pledge to expel interlopers via aggressive action. She led sixty retainers with her rapier and light cavalry carbine and routed the trespassers. To ensure obedience, on October 30, she elevated her muster roll to five hundred.

November 12, 1679

At the Stockholm city square on November 12, 1679, **Lisbetha Olsdotter (?–November 12, 1679)** of Ostuna parish, was beheaded for joining the Swedish army under the name of Mats Ersson. After fleeing an abusive husband and two children in 1674, she impersonated a male farmhand and found domestic employment in the Alby suburb of Stockholm for county manager Jon Persson. His brother Erik blackmailed her into enlisting in the infantry. Betrayed for posing as a male and marrying a woman, she faced capital charges of bigamy, homosexuality, and abandoning her family and died on November 12, 1679.

November 15, 1685

To rid Croatia of Hapsburg oppression, on November 15, 1685, the widowed hero **Ilona Zrínyi (also Helena or Jelena, 1643–February 18, 1703)** from Ozalj on the Kupa River promoted guerrilla combat in Croatia, Hungary, and Transylvania. To free Vienna of imperialists, she invested in war expense, assembled four thousand troops from Hungary, Slovakia, and Germany, and joined her nine-year-old son Ferenc II in protecting Munkacs citadel (modern Mukacevo, Ukraine). She stood on the battlements amid cannon blasts to show her resolve against three thousand Austrian troops of Emperor Leopold I. She suffered a miscarriage during the onslaught; her daughter Julianna tended casualties.

The three-year artillery siege ended with Ilona's surrender on January 17, 1688. Deprived of her children, she remained a prisoner of war at an Ursuline convent in Vienna for three years until an inmate release in 1691. Eight years later, she entered exile in Ottoman Turkey on the Sea of Marmara. Ilona's death at Nicomedia (modern İzmit, Turkey) on February 18, 1703, ended the family line. Her image survived in postal stamps and paintings.

1686

Famed French contralto and dueler **Julie D'Aubigny La Maupin (1670–1707)** drew fans to her arias for the Paris Opera Company and to fights with some ten challengers. From age sixteen, in 1686, she profited from training in Marseilles in martial arts, horse management, and rapier skills. Because of her notorious bisexual relationships, she incited arguments and sword fights, once with three drunks in the tavern where she performed. She repeated the one-against-three battling at a royal ball at Versailles, home of Louis XIV. After a sojourn in Brussels, she relocated to Paris and continued her stage career until her death at age thirty-seven. Novelist Theophile Gautier developed her scandalous life in the fiction *Mademoiselle de Maupin*.

1688

A Dutch adventurer, **Maria Jacoba de Turenne (1666–June 8, 1736)** of the Hague enlisted in the army in 1688 to follow her lover, brewer Jacob Nijpels. Discovery of her gender ended her service. She tried five more times to sign up with the infantry, but failed to convince others with her disguise. At Maastricht on November 2, 1689, she shot and stabbed Jacob for refusing to marry her. The couple wed on February 21, 1690. After giving birth to a son, she entered prison on September 2, 1690, and remained jailed until her acquittal on September 30. Her life story entered Dutch folklore.

September 27, 1688

A career soldier from Picardy, **Geneviève Prémoy (1660–1706)** of Guise fought for French king Louis XIV in two major sieges. In her memoir, *Histoire de la Dragone* (History of a Dragoon), she described enlisting under the Prince of Condé and advancing in rank. She fought in the Holy Roman Empire (modern Germany) on September 27, 1688, at Philippsburg in the thirty-three-day siege that brought her regiment supremacy. She was wounded at Mons during the twenty-six-day assault on the Spanish Netherlands (modern Belgium), where the French took some four thousand eight hundred captives. She gave up her alias, Chevalier Balthazard, after medics disclosed her gender. The king welcomed her into the Order of St. Louis.

March 25, 1689

With patience and wisdom, **Keladi Chennamma (ca. 1647–1696)**, queen of Keladi, Karnataka, fought the Mughal emperor Aurangzeb, the renowned conqueror of much of India. For a quarter century after her crowning in 1671 at Fort Bhuvanagiri (modern Bhongir, southern India) at the top of a tall monolith, she successfully repelled Bijapur troops while educating her adopted son Basappa Nayak for royal duties. She ruled alone after 1672, when her husband died, poisoned by an exotic dancer. The realm profited from commerce with the Arabs for horses and in spice, pepper, and rice with the English and Dutch. Portuguese traders named her "pepper queen."

In fear of loss from neighboring armies, Keladi Chennamma studied military tactics and defense and secreted the state treasure at Fort Bhuvanagiri. In the surrounding jungle, her Marathi ally destroyed the foes. She launched a severe purge of the enemy and their supporters, whom she beheaded. She risked the emperor's malice by giving sanctuary to his foe Rajaram, a rescuer of Hinduism in southern India.

Keladi proved to be a doughty adversary. She held back the Mughal guerrillas and their European cannoneers until Aurangzeb's muddy assault on March 25, 1689, during the annual monsoon. Their jungle combat ended in mutual negotiation. Before her death at age forty-nine, she catechized her son Basappa on the importance of honesty, impartiality, compassion, and bravery.

1690

A veteran soldier for seven years, **Marie Magdelaine Mouron (fl. 1690–1696)** of Boulogne successfully disguised herself as a French male. During the reign of French king Louis XIV, in 1690, she enlisted in the Royal Regiment of Wallonia. She marched with the soldiers of General Anne Jules de Noailles, the Marshal of France, in the War of the Grand Alliance and at the siege of Rosas in 1693 and the battle of Torroella at Girona, Catalonia, on May 27, 1694. The latter engagement routed the Spanish infantry and cavalry. After leaving the army, Marie took the name St. Michael and joined the cavalry at Avignon. Because of her injury fighting a duel, in March 1696, she was jailed for deserting the Debriere company to claim an enlistment bonus from the Du Biez Regiment under the name La Garenne.

July 29, 1690

Sailor **Anne Chamberlayne (January 20, 1667–October 30, 1691)** of London met the French at Beachy Head in the two-day battle of the Boyne, Ireland. On the fire-ship HMS *Gryphon* on July 29, 1690, she dressed in male uniform and facilitated Dutch allies in fighting under command of her older brother, Captain Peregrine Clifford Chamberlayne. The conquest of James II and the Jacobites allowed William III to establish Hanoverian influence in Austria and Holland. After marrying a naval officer, Anne died in childbirth at age twenty-four. An honorarium at Chelsea Old Church acclaimed her soldiery.

September 1690

In a war between the Maratha and Mughal empires, in September 1690, the widowed queen-regent of Madura **Mangammal (also Mangamma, ca. 1659–1705)** enabled artillerymen at the siege of Jinji Fort (modern Tamil Nadu, India). Under the command of Emperor Aurangzeb, the eight-year conflict with rebel Rajaram Bhosle I ended after the Mughal fighters blasted cannons at the walls and citadels on the hilltop stronghold. Following Rajaram's escape to Vellore on the Palar River, she campaigned successfully against Ravi Varma, king of Travancore in southern

India, in November 1697, and against Shahuji I of Thanjavur.

Despite her resolve, Mangammal's army lost to Raghunatha Kilavan at Ramnad because of the combat death of her general. She controlled the region until 1705, when the military leader arrested Mangammal for refusing to acknowledge her grandson, Vijayaranga, as the next ruler. She died of slow starvation in sight of food placed outside her cell. The Mangammal Highway commemorates her public works for the good of the realm.

1691

In search of her husband's regiment in Holland for four years, Irish adventurer **Christian "Kit" Cavanagh Davies (1667–July 7, 1739)**, a native of Dublin, wore men's clothes and, in 1691 at age twenty-six, enlisted in the British Army. After her husband's impressment into the military in Flanders, she chose the alias Christian Welch and benefited the infantry at the battle of Landen on July 29, 1693. The victorious French captured her and treated her leg wound before including her in a prisoner exchange. She mustered out after a duel with a rapist. Following the Peace of Ryswick, at age thirty, she enrolled in the dragoons, the Royal Scots Greys, a regiment mounted on gray horses.

Christian concealed a minie ball to the hip during the Bavarian conflict at Schellenberg on July 2, 1704, and at a huge loss for the French at Blenheim, Germany, on August 13. She successfully negotiated healing and pay after a shell fractured her skull at Ramillies, Holland, on May 23, 1706, another tactical disaster for the French in which the Scots Greys captured the flag of the Regiment du Roi (King's Regiment). Her gender revealed, she remained with her regiment as a sutler. Her husband's death at Malplaquet on September 11, 1709, left her mourning a notorious adulterer. She married another grenadier, who died in battle in 1710.

On retirement under the sobriquet "Mother Ross," Christian received linen fabric and a silk gown from her comrades for a female wardrobe and obtained from Queen Anne a £50 (approx. $3000) mustering out bounty and a pension of seven shillings (84¢) a week. In 1713, she wed a soldier named Davies. At her death on July 7, 1739, the military honored her gallantry with a soldier's funeral. English writer Daniel Defoe completed her biography, *The Life and Adventures of Mrs. Christian Davies, Commonly Called Mother Ross* (1740). For the weekly *All the Year Round*, journalist Charles Dickens wrote of her service in the essay "Famous British Regiments."

1691

A mediator and defender of Mantua against Spain during the War of Spanish Succession, in 1691, Duchess **Anna Isabella Gonzaga (February 12, 1655–August 11, 1703)** preserved Guastalla in north central Italy. Firstborn of aristocratic d'Este and Gonzaga blood, she grew up amid political and religious warfare. After her husband, Duke Ferdinando Carlo IV Gonzaga of Mantua, fled with his staff to Venice, she ruled the duchy and preserved Mantua by furthering an able military command.

A peacemaker, she mediated conflicts between Naples and Milan.

Northeast of Parma, Italy, Anna, in the last months of her life, returned to the role of negotiator and Mantua's defender in the second year of the War of Spanish Succession. Key to her command was protection of Luzzara and Bozzolo on the Po River. The traitorous Ferdinando faced a felony charge and lost his holdings to Holy Roman Emperor Joseph I. At Anna's death, the enemy forced the French north over the Alps. In 1708, following Ferdinando's death, the Austrian Hapsburgs achieved the overthrow of the Gonzaga family.

1692

A soldier during the Nine Years' War, **Philis de la Tour (also Philis de la Charce, January 5, 1645–June 4, 1703)** from Montmortin, Burgundy, in south central France buckled on a sword and scabbard and rode a warsteed to circumvent Viktor Amadeus II, Duke of Savoy and Sardinia, from attacking Grenoble. To protect protestants from massacre by aggressive Catholics, in 1692, she summoned the peasants of Dauphiné to a defensive force. Her army stopped the arson and plundering at Diois, Gap, and Nyons. Louis XIV conferred on Philis a pension of two thousand pounds. Her heroics survive in verse, street names, sculpture, history, portraits, film, and a mausoleum. An equestrian statue on the Isère River pictures her in martial pose dressed in cavalier hat and coat with sword hand raised.

October 22, 1692

During the French and Indian Wars, at age fourteen, sharpshooter **Marie-Madeleine Jarret (March 3, 1678–August 8, 1747)** defended the eleven families of her hometown of Fort Vercheres, New France (modern Quebec), on the Saint Lawrence Seaway from an eight-day onslaught by the Iroquois Confederacy of Cuyoga, Mohawk, Oneida, Onondaga, Seneca, and Tuscarora. She had already lost two brothers-in-law and sixteen-year-old brother François-Michel to the Iroquois. While cultivating cabbage rows outside the palisade on October 22, 1692, at 8:00 a.m., she eluded Indian kidnappers by slipping out of her scarf and leaving blankets and three bags of laundry at the riverbank. Under fire from forty-five Indian guns that killed two of eleven tenants, she alerted three residents at the rectangular stockade to arm themselves. To create the illusion of numerous defenders, she joined soldiers Galhet and Labonté. She fired muskets along the upper story to ward off Indians scaling the exterior and discharged a cannon, calling soldiers from the Saints-Ours and Montreal bastions.

Clad in a military helmet, Madeleine rescued the Pierre Fontaine family by guiding them from their canoe to the pier and into the gates. With her two younger brothers, twelve-year-old Pierre and five-year-old Jean-Baptiste Jarret, and an elderly servant, Pierre Laviolette, she herded cattle away from enemy rustlers. On October 30, she directed one hundred reinforcements arriving downriver to the Iroquois hiding places in the thickets, which concealed their twenty captives. After her father's death on February 16, 1700, the government transferred his pension of one thousand livres to Madeleine and her widowed mother. Following her death at age sixty-nine, her heroism survived in recruiting posters, bronze statuary, a park, a Red Cross chapter, storytelling, cinema, fiction, and drama as Marie-Madeleine de Verchères.

March 1693

Tortuga sea raider **Anne Dieu-le-Veut (August 28, 1661–January 11, 1710)** from Brittany challenged a murderer to a duel. From juvenile crime, she earned transportation as a *fille de roi* (king's daughter) to Tortuga, where she bore daughter Marie Marguerite to pirate Pierre Lelong. Motivated by revenge, in March 1693, she dared Dutch privateer and mercenary Laurens Corneille de Graaf to atone for a bar fight. A public brawl in June 1693 slew her second husband, Joseph Cherel, father of infant son Jean-François Cherel.

Because de Graaf opposed Anne's gun with a sword, on July 28, 1693, she became his wife and fellow seafarer. Plundering at Jamaica resulted in the English capture of Anne, daughter Marie Marguerite, and infant Marie Catherine de Graaf at Port-de-Paix, San Domingue (modern Haiti) in May 1695. At her liberation three years later, she and de Graaf resided in Louisiana. Following his death from a cannon shot in 1704, she commandeered his ship. She fell into Spanish hands and was tried and pardoned at Cartagena, Colombia. She inherited de Graaf's sugar plantation and one hundred twenty laborers.

November 18, 1693

Under the alias **John Brown, a black female teenager (ca.1673–?)** of unknown origin enlisted with the Royal African Company aboard the merchantman *Hannibal* to sail from London to Guinea (modern Ghana) in West Africa. On November 18, 1693, the voyage continued west to Barbados in the Lesser Antilles with a cargo of abductees intended for the auction block and enslavement to enrich the English plantation economy. Her gender discovery before the slaving vessel reached the Cape Coast Castle at Guinea ended three months of posing as a male soldier. She fled the ship and left no trace of name or ethnicity.

June 12, 1696

A Mongolian soldier-queen and khan's adviser, **Ana Dara (also Lady Anu or Queen Anu, 1653–1696)** led a garrison from Khobdo against the Qing Empire at the battle of Jao Modo on the Terelj River in north central China. In support of her husband, Galdan Khan, founder of the Dzungar Khanate to the west, she marched east to the Khentii Mountains. On the battle line on June 12, 1696, eighty thousand Chinese confronted the Dzungar khan's five thousand men and captured Ana's fourteen-year-old son Septen. Her combat charge deflected attention from Galdan's escape through a gap in the encircling enemy. Amid a thousand dead Mongols, her body fell to the slaughter from a Chinese arrow. Galvan died from disease on May 3, 1697, leaving Emperor Sheng-tsu free to annex Outer Mongolia. Ana Dara's combat death survives in fiction, drama, and film.

April 29, 1697

As a result of the Haverhill raid, **Hannah Emerson Duston (December 23, 1657–March 6, 1736)**, a Puritan settler of the northeast corner of Massachusetts Bay Colony, New England, joined fellow captives in executing and scalping ten Abenaki who held them hostage. She, her six-day-old infant Martha, fourteen-year-old Samuel Lennardson, and the nurse **Mary Corliss Neff (1646–October 17, 1722)** survived the initial massacre on April 29, 1697, and the burning of the Duston house. On the march to Boscawen Island in New Hampshire Colony, the Indians bashed the newborn against a tree. Armed with hatchets, a knife, and a flintlock rifle, Hannah, Mary, and Samuel led a rebellion against twelve native captors at the confluence of the Contoocook and Merrimack Rivers, leaving alive one female Abenaki with seven hatchet wounds. The captives sank the tribe's canoes and paddled down to Haverhill in the one left unharmed.

Hannah called for a return to the killing site to remove scalps as proof of their exploit. On June 16, a colonial court granted Hannah £25 (modern $5,458.29) and Mary and Samuel £12.5 each (modern $2,729.14) as bounty for the scalps. In his story version and sermon on the event, Puritan preacher Cotton Mather compared Hannah to Old Testament heroine Jael, impaler of Sisera with a tent peg. A monument in Haverhill dramatizes Hannah's grasp on a hatchet, the first U.S. statue commemorating a female warrior.

Colonial Wars and Revolutions, 1700–1850

Formal defiance of global imperialism altered internal revolts to full-scale movements against monarchy and mercantilism in Britain, France, Italy, Holland, Portugal, Spain, Austria, Scandinavia, Germany, Belgium, North America, much of central Africa, and the Ottoman Empire. Female and enslaved combatants proved efficient at organizing local rebellions and supplying guerrilla forces with rations and munitions.

1700

At age eighteen, Brazilian adventurer **María Ursula d'Abreu e Lencastro (1682–1730)** of Rio Janeiro expedited the Portuguese army's presence in colonial India. After sailing to Lisbon, under the name Balthazar do Couto Cardoso, she fought in 1700 at Ambon in the Banda Sea, at the cotton-growing center at Chaul, and against Marathan aggression at colonial Goa's islands of Corjuem and Panelem. In 1703, she advanced to captain and defender of the Madre de Deus (Mother of God) citadel, an Ayurvedic healing center in Goa. Maria's campaigns included the 1705 triumph over the pro–Marathan Bhonsle of Sawantwadi, India. In 1714, she gave up the gender switch and married a castle governor. King John V of Portugal awarded her a medal for service and granted her two palm groves.

April 1700

The Marathan queen from the Mohite clan **Tarabai Bhosale (April 1675–1761)** led military action against Mughal invasion of western India under Emperor Aurangzeb. Throughout an eight-year reign, beginning in April 1700, she protected the regency of her four-year-old son Shivaji II by insisting on the sacred thread ritual. Her cavalry pressed southeastward to Malwa over the Narmada River in central India, conquering small Mughal holdouts one by one on the way to the Gujarat shore.

Prison diminished Tarabai's hopes for Shivaji. During four days of captivity in a Mughal compound in 1706, she bribed a sentry with gifts of jewelry, escaped, and built renown for holding off potential seizure. In 1714, mother and son occupied a cell under the command of usurper Sambhaji II until her release in 1730. Because of mutiny in her army in 1750, she executed insurrectionist Anandrao Jadhav. Her power struggles survive in paintings, histories, and film drama.

August 4, 1700

During the Great Nordic War of 1700–1721, Copenhagen's defender, **Charlotte Amalie** of Hesse-Kassel **(April 27, 1650–March 27, 1714)**, braced her subjects for a compound naval attack by England, Holland, and Sweden. The widowed consort of King Christian V of Denmark and Norway, was born in the Holy Roman Empire and recognized from childhood the land greed of surrounding countries—Lithuania, Norway, Poland, Russia, and Saxony. She monitored the invasion of twenty-five hundred Swedish troops at Humlebæk and managed the posting of the Copenhagen garrison to halt the militant intent of Charles XII of Sweden. On August 4, 1700, her navy of forty ships blocked the western ports, forcing Sweden to re-plot its trajectory to the east. The treaty of August 12, 1700, ended Scandic hostilities.

December 19, 1700

Margareta von Ascheberg (July 9, 1671–October 26, 1753) of Malmo, Sweden, replaced her deceased husband, Colonel Kjell Christopher Barnekow, as regimental colonel of a Pomeranian cavalry regiment. She learned respect for the military from her father, Field Marshal Rutger von Ascheberg. For a decade, she followed her husband on campaigns and, on August 3, 1695, gave birth to son Rutger during ongoing combat in Brussels.

An unexpected career change thrust Margareta into military command. When Kjell died suddenly of fever at Kalmar on December 19, 1700, she assumed responsibility for his post. Before the Great Nordic War in June 1710, she drafted recruits, secured war mounts, and outfitted and equipped two hundred soldiers by spring 1702. For backing, she secured the support of Swedish king Charles XII. After controlling her family inheritance and raising four sons, she died at age eighty-two.

December 6, 1704

An exemplar and saint during the evolution of Sikhism, **Bibi Dalair Kaur (fl. 1700s)** outsmarted a Mughal strike force by rallying one hundred Sikh women to the two-day battle of Chamkaur, India. Fought in the Punjab in northern India on December 6, 1704, the seven-month standoff pitted spiritual master Gobind Singh, his two elder sons, and his apostles against the Emperor Aurangzeb's general, Wazir Khan. The tyrannic Muslim besieged them at their townhouse in Anandpur and slew Gobind's children, the two youngest by bricking them into a wall. Because of enemy suppression of rations and munitions, forty male Sikhs signed a letter of resignation and crept away. Their women belittled their manhood and remained with the Sikh faithful.

A leader of female resisters, **Mai Bhago (fl. 1700s)**, a martyr from Jhabal, India, altered the deserters' loyalties by sneering at them. She rallied the guru's daughters and the deserters along with some new recruits to follow Gobind Singh into the Malvan jungle. At the Khidrana oasis, the forty Sikhs spread shirts to resemble tents. Slipping away from their phony compound, they ambushed the Muslim mercenaries, forcing a retreat. Mai Bhago, the only soldier to survive, lost her husband and brother in the skirmish. While recuperating under Gobind's care, she changed to a male uniform, equipped herself with musket and lance, and joined his bodyguard. At his death on October 7, 1708, Gobind's wife, **Mata Sundari (also Sundri, 1667–1747)** of Bijvara managed his religious outreach and reunified the Khalsa army, which she commanded. Mai Bhago founded a camp at Janwada for meditation and spiritual instruction. Pilgrimages, a war tower, and her name in gilt letters at a worship site honor her loyalty and zeal.

June 19, 1707

A former Indo-Portuguese servant in the harem of Mughal emperor Aurangzeb, **Juliana Dias da Costa (1658–1734)** of Agra, Portuguese India, accompanied her protector, Shah Bahadur I, over battlefields atop a war elephant. She gained influence as go-between with the Dutch East India Company and the Italian Jesuits. As lady-in-waiting to the shah's four chief wives and tutor to Bahadur, she rode in a carriage curtained in red silk for the inspection of gift elephants. At a sudden foray by Mohammed Azim and the burning of Bahadur's tents at the battle of Jajou, on June 19, 1707, Juliana stopped a rout and encouraged Bahadur to overwhelm Azam. She prophesied gain.

The subsequent engagement at Dholpur outside Agra on June 20 threatened Bahadur with elephant and camel guns. Juliana suggested the drafting of Portuguese marksmen and artillery experts. The bloody battle annihilated twenty thousand foot soldiers and twenty thousand cavalry and killed Azam, who died in action from arrow wounds and a musket shot to the head. During the overthrow, she advised Bahadur not to ally with the French navy. For her combat wisdom, the shah gave Juliana four villages, a hereditary title, and an elephant retinue. A wayside inn in Delhi bears her name.

1710

At her home at Varmland in southwestern Sweden during the Great War of 1700–1721, **Maria Cameen Faxell (1678–1738)**, a vicar's wife, roused a militia in the Kola church parish on the southern border with Norway. Worsening conditions, an epidemic along the Baltic Sea weakened the Swedes. By arming domestics and posting them in key locations, in 1710, she gave the impression of a sizable defense. Her servants fired guns, rang church bells, and raised an outcry to scare off invading Norwegians. Sweden ended the war in victory at Helsingborg on March 10, 1710, inflicting on Denmark and Norway the loss of seven thousand six hundred and seventy seven or fifty-five percent of their allied army.

June 1710

At a nadir in the Great Nordic War in June 1710, Swedish buccaneer and tactician **Ingela Olofsdotter Gathenhielm (September 11, 1692–April 29, 1729)** of Gothenburg abetted the crimes of her husband, privateer Lars Gathenhielm. With legal and illegal plunder legitimized by Swedish king Charles XII, the couple operated out of Lilla Torget at coastal Gothenburg in southwestern Sweden. During the reign of French king Louis XIV, she sold loot in Dunkirk, France, a notorious corsair haven until the English destroyed it in 1713. Alone on April 25, 1718, after Lars died of tuberculosis at age twenty-eight, she operated on his royal piracy permit and managed a seafaring syndicate and fleet with goods made in her sail factory, forge, and ropewalk.

Before November 1710

A Dutch cavalry rider, **Aal de Dragonder (fl. 1700s–1710s)** of Rotterdam died a savage death at the hands of fellow dragoons. In a soldiers' fight before November 1710, she succumbed to multiple stab wounds. Examination of her remains proved her to be an undiscovered crossdresser. At the Rotterdam anatomical theater, her preserved corpse, along with that of a garden pilferer and a hanged man, served medical students as models. In ridicule of women in the military, her skin was inflated, armed with a sword and knife, dressed in armor, and placed astride a horse skeleton. The anonymous horsewoman wore a blue cap labeled in yellow "Aal de Dragonder." The pathetic travesty remained in the anatomical collection for one hundred and eighteen years, becoming a city landmark.

June 1712

A Mayan rebel and prophet, **María de la Candelaria (1698–February 1716)** from Cancuc in Chiapas, Mexico, led a native battalion against Spanish overlords. As a means of unifying indigenous Ch'ol, Tzeltal, and Tzotzil, in June 1712, she claimed that the Virgin Mary appeared to her and entreated that the rebels build a chapel. In front of the structure on August 8, she rallied locals to a war against Spanish and Catholic authority. To incite Mayans to victory, she placed them in the key roles of Hispanic church and Dominican hierarchy.

The challenge ended on November 21, 1712, when Spanish forces seized Cancuc. Maria eluded capture and hid in varied locations before seeking a wooded headquarters to the northeast at Chihuisbalam. She survived until February 1916, when she died giving birth. At the trial of her father, rebel Agustin Lopez, he confessed that Maria lied about seeing the Virgin Mary. The short-lived Tzeltal Revolt survives in folk stories and drama.

1713

In the Great Nordic War of 1700–1721, Corporal **Ulrika Eleonora Stålhammar (1688–1733)** of Småland paid a stiff penalty for posing as a male artillery expert in the Swedish royal army of King Charles XII. The daughter of Colonel Johan Stålhammar, she trained in riding and hunting in girlhood. After snatching a horse and leaving home, she renamed herself Vilhelm Edstedt and worked as bodyguard for Lieutenant Casper Johan Berch. In 1713, at age twenty-five, she enlisted at Kalmar in the army artillery for a relief force at Pomerania commanded by Magnus Stenbock. Swedes lost the engagement at Tonning, Holstein-Gottorp (modern Germany) in February 1714.

Before mustering out on August 25, 1726, Ulrika achieved the rank of corporal and posed as the husband of Maria

Lönnman. To avoid a criminal charge, she confessed in summer 1728 to engaging in a sexless lesbian marriage. She sought mercy on the basis of her thirteen-year military service. Her punishment began with pillorying and eight days on bread and water followed by exile.

1714

A domestic and housebreaker during the Great Nordic War of 1700–1721, **Anna Jöransdotter (fl. 1714)** of Finland was drafted in 1714 into the Swedish army under the alias Johan Haritu. During eighteen months engagement with the one hundred twenty thousand men serving King Charles XII, she witnessed the downfall of the Swedes against a coalition of Tsar Peter the Great and Britain's George I. By December 1716, Sweden lost its Baltic and German holdings after the surrender at Wismar, Germany. Anna married Maja Kijhi, who urged her to leave the failing army. She faced inquiry at military and civil courts and served sentence at hard labor.

February 1714

Press-ganged into the army during the ten-year Russian occupation of the Great Northern War, **Annika Svahn (also Swahn, 1696–after summer 1714)** of Joutseno in southern Finland survived kidnap, enslavement, and the Russian conquest of Swedish Finland. Her abduction from a sauna at the Joursenjoki River by cossacks in 1710 resulted in bondage as a prison cook in Saint Petersburg with thirty thousand other Finns. After an education in warcraft and horseback riding, she and fifty other abductees dressed like dragoons and wielded a sword. In January 1713, she fought for Russia in northeastern Finland in a period of slaughter known as the Great Wrath.

In her early teens, Annika suffered a bullet to the thigh at Pälkäne, the location of a Russian grand slam on October 17, 1713. At the eleven-day battle of Napue at Isokyro in February 1714, the cossacks went on a rampage of rape, torture, arson, and murder. Female soldiers dropped their weapons and called to the Finnish forces their intent to surrender. The Russians discovered Annika's hiding place in the snow and beat her. While aiding the army as a messenger in summer 1714, she gained a blacksmith's help. After a trial at Raahe, Finland, she passed to the care of a priest. Her legend survived in opera and television.

1716

An impromptu prophet and combatant at the battle of Oueme River in 1716, **Hangbe (also Ahangbe or Na Hangbe or Tassi Hang, fl. 1710s)** of Dahomey (modern Benin) dressed in armor and fought to avenge the death of her twin brother, King Akaba. On the major supply route of West African slaves, she took his place as ruler at Abomey and pursued a military end to a three-year struggle for succession. To aid the nation's standing army against raids by neighboring tribes, she mustered the Dahomey Amazons, a garrison of celibate female warriors and security guards, to achieve her aims. An aggressive feminist promoting women's roles as farmers and hunters, she exposed her genitals to display contempt for a council decision and warned that Dahomey risked seizure by European imperialists. Her prediction proved true in 1894, when Dahomey fell to the French.

March 1716

A Norwegian hero, **Kari Hiran (1658–after 1716)** from Krokskogen protected her country during the Swedish insurgency of the Great Nordic War of 1700–1721. She fell into enemy hands when a Swedish patrol arrested her at the town's stone bridge. To scare off the ruthless forces of King Charles XII after they occupied Christiana, in March 1716, she passed fabricated data about the location and size of Norwegian regiments at Fort Nordkleiva on the icy Oslo Fjord. Her falsehoods discouraged the Swedes from a spring invasion. She petitioned for a reward, but received only two riksdalers (currently $221.02). A stone memorial honors her surveillance.

March 29, 1716

Following the successful capture of Holand, Norway, on March 9, 1716, **Anna Colbjørnsdatter Arneberg (1667–1736)** of Romerike, distracted the six hundred dragoons of King Charles XII of Sweden at Fort Akershus, Oslo. A blizzard prevented the victors from further campaigning. While chatting with Colonel Axel Lowen, on March 29, 1716, she posted a message to two hundred Norwegian forces camped nearby. She prepared a banquet and served it with liquor. Historian Peter Andreas Munch reported in *Norwegians, Swedes, and Danes: History of Skoleburg* that the surprise attack on the encampment at the Norderhov church resulted in fifty dead and the capture of one hundred thirty prisoners of war. Nonetheless, Swedish troops overwhelmed Christiana in April 1716. Her clever ruse supplied a plot for a bio-drama.

November 9, 1716

A slave cook at St. Maria plantation in the Lesser Antilles **María of Curaçao (?–November 9, 1716)**, fomented a two-month revolt against Dutch colonists. On staff of the Dutch West India Company, which had flourished in the slave trade for forty-five years, she advised on the preparation of African abductees for sale. The uprising began on September 15, 1716, with Maria seeking retribution against overseer Christiaan Muller for killing her mate. The mob stole a gun and slew a West Indies raider. Maria urged the workers to murder whites and steal money. Betrayed by her lover Tromp, she remained on the run from the Willemstad garrison for ten days. She was tortured, chained to a stake, and burned on November 9, 1716.

October 1720

With her second husband, English pirate Calico Jack Rackham, **Anne "Toothless Annie" Bonny (March 8, 1698–April 1721)** aggressively fleeced Caribbean merchant ships and fishing vessels. A native of Kinsale, Ireland, as detailed in the unidentified author Captain Charles Johnson's *A General History of the Robberies and Murders of the Most Notorious Pyrates*, Anne grew up in South Carolina before heading for

Nassau, a Bahamian haven of sea criminals. With English privateer **Mary Read (1685–April 28, 1721)**, a former British infantryman, sailor on a man-'o-war, and cavalryman during the Nine Years' War, Anne hired crew in Jamaica for the single-masted sloop *William,* which she stole from Nassau harbor. The sloop carried a swivel gun and eight cannon. At Negril Point, thirteen buccaneers, armed with pistols and machetes, were arrested in October 1720 by Jamaica's governor, Nicholas Lawes, who hanged Rackham at Port Royal on November 18 and had his corpse tarred and hung on display. Four more crew members went to the gallows on November 19 at Kingston.

Because the male sailors refused to defend the female crossdressers, Mary shot several and killed one. On November 28, 1720, a flexible penalty by a Spanish Town court allowed both Anne and Mary to remain in prison to the end of their pregnancies before their hanging. Mary appears to have died of fever in childbirth. Anne disappeared from history. The women's stories filled pirate histories, songs, ballads, sculpture, film, television series, and video games.

1721

A sailor in service to the Dutch East India Company, **Lumke Thoole (1690–after 1725)** of Emden, Lower Saxony, traveled from Utrecht, Holland, to the Cape of Good Hope in 1721. After her husband, Thys Geerits, embarked for Batavia and Siam, she trained as carpenter's mate. Dressed as a man, she traveled Holland and enlisted for ninety-six gulden a year under the name Jan (or Johan) Theunisz. She set out on the merchantman *Barbices* on July 12, 1723. Upon traversing the Atlantic from Texel, Holland, to the Cape of Good Hope, she was cutting firewood on November 19 when men discovered her gender disguise. Before a judge in South Africa, her husband charged her with bigamy. She stood on the pillory at Cape Town with a wood rake hanging over her and received a fine and deportation.

November 10, 1721

Margareta Elisabeth Roos (1696–February 16, 1772) of Ingria, an Estonian soldier in the Swedish army during the Great Nordic War of 1700–1721, reached the rank of officer with a commendation for valor. Amid a fractious military family, she ran away from home at age seventeen and enlisted in 1713. Under Field Marshall Carl Gustaf Ducker, Margareta served eight years. At a low point for Swedish forces, Swedish troops lost to the Danish-Norwegian coalition at Tonning, Holstein-Gottorp (modern Germany) in February 1714. Ducker achieved a significant win at the siege of Stralsund, Pomerania, in December 1715. Russia curtailed its galley raids in spring 1721 until the Treaty of Nystad on November 10, 1721, ended Russian aggression against Estonia, Finland, and Lavonia. Margareta entered the staff of Ducker's wife as head butler and later married a veteran army officer.

1725

Maria ter Meetelen (June 20, 1704–fl. 1751) from the Amsterdam slums chose indoctrination as a soldier and nun. In 1725, at age twenty-one, she signed on with the Frisian dragoons at Sicktoria, Spain, and traversed France in male attire. Following service in a convent until 1728, she married sailor Claus van der Meer of Alkmaar. Despite his antipathy and taunting, she sailed for Holland with him in 1731. En route from Cadiz, Barbary pirates seized her, killed her husband, and remanded her to a harem at Meknes, Morocco.

As the possession of Sultan Moulay Abdallah of Morocco, Maria shared palace quarters with women who dressed like goddesses and entertained the sultan with singing and instrumental music. Because she refused to convert to Islam, she avoided burning alive by pleading pregnancy and married captive sailor Pieter Janszoon. After Pieter left her for another sea adventure, the Dutch ransomed her in 1743. She repatriated to Amsterdam before immigrating in 1751 to South Africa. She issued a memoir, *The Curious and Amazing Adventures of Maria ter Meetelen: Twelve Years a Slave* (1731–1743).

May 1727

In league with Irish-American brigand John Vidal from 1725 during piracy's golden age, English raider **Martha Farley (also Mary Farlee or Mary Harvey, fl. 1720s)** helped pillage the schooner *Anne and Francis* in May 1727. She had traveled to the New World as a prison inmate transported in 1725 to North Carolina. After Vidal vanished from capture, in a small pirogue from Cape Fear, she plundered provisions from small coasters and a wreck off Ocracoke inlet on one of North Carolina's Outer Banks. At a Williamsburg tribunal in Virginia, in September 1727, she became one of the few female buccaneers tried in an American court. Governor Robert Carter freed Martha on the grounds of her motherhood to two children.

Summer 1727

During the five-year Second Fox War, the Ho-chunk (or Winnebago) chief **Glory of the Morning (May 1709–1767)** of Menasha, Wisconsin Territory, backed the French against the Mesquaki, a Fox and Sac nation in LaCrosse. Named Ho-poe-kaw in the Siouan language, Glory lived on Doty Island among prairie hunters and fur traders of the Thunderbird Clan. She led her people for four decades and fostered peace and prosperity throughout a fractious era.

Beginning in summer 1727 after the revocation of a peace treaty, Glory of the Morning intended to fight the Mesquaki to extend French-Indian trade routes along the Fox River. The waterway was lucrative to the Mesquaki, who demanded tribute from travelers on their way to Mississippi. In 1728, she wed French army soldier Sabrevoir Descaris, a government negotiator and trader, who deserted her, leaving behind two sons, founders of a line of Decorah chiefs. By 1730, her army had caused the enemy severe depletion among their nine hundred warriors and the enslavement of women and children in Caribbean colonies of the French.

Glory of the Morning's later pro-French aggressions targeted the Illini of Upper Louisiana. With the onset of the French and Indian War in 1754, the Ho-chunk battled English immigrants and won in the Monongahela Valley of Pennsylvania at Braddock's Defeat on July 9, 1755, at Fort Duquesne. The Bureau of Indian Affairs removed the Ho-chunk from Lake Winnebago in eastern Wisconsin to Iowa and the Mesquaki to the grassy prairie. Glory of the Morning's deeds survived in drama, verse, and place names.

September 1728

Enslaved at Gold Coast (modern Ghana), the Ashanti tribeswoman **Nanny of the Maroons (1686–March 29, 1733)**, an Akan speaker, led former Jamaican slaves against English colonizers in the First Maroon War. During bondage in the Windward Islands, in alliance with West Indian Arawak and Taino aborigines, Nanny and her brothers Accompong, Cudjoe, Johnny, and Quaco and the Fante, Coromantee, and Congolese fostered the revival of West African warrior traditions of masking and belligerent posturing. At the war's outbreak in September 1728, on the Stony River, she led residents of Nanny Town as their queen. They rebelled against lashing, mutilation, press gangs, and chaining through *gumbe* (goat skin frame drum) throbs and cow horn communication, creole divination, herbalism, masking, and obeah folk liturgy and animal sacrifice. In 1733, the Africans routed a ragtag force of two hundred British sailors.

When starvation threatened the Hill Maroons in 1737, Nanny experienced a mystic dream of *jumbies* (her ancestors), who provided island gardens with pumpkin seeds. Stories circulated that she caught and refired bullets from her hands and that her magic cauldron drowned British stalkers. Maroon skirmishes in the Blue Mountains freed some one thousand laborers from plantations and evolved guerrilla tactics of hit and run raiding, decoying, camouflage, and arson until the British suppressors relented on April 20, 1740. The victors forced the officials to sign a blood pact in Maroon and British blood stirred in a calabash with rum. They drank from the gourd to sanctify the treaty. Legends of "Granny or Grandy Nanny" survive on a bank note and monument and in songs, imitative dance, and storytelling of a "Right Excellent" national hero.

Late 1728

An English sea raider, **Mary Critchett (also Maria, ?–1729)** joined five male pirates on a work detail during the late 1728 deportation from England to the colony of Virginia. In the Golden Age of Piracy, the six convicts hijacked the sloop *John and Elizabeth* by night on May 12, 1729. They sailed from the Piankatank River to Chesapeake Bay, Maryland, and released the two imprisoned crew. To halt marine predations, Captain Long of the HMS *Shoreham* arrested the felons before they could put out to sea. Mary received a capital sentence in August 1729 at the colonial capital of Williamsburg, where she was condemned to hang.

January 21, 1731

A Natchez matriarch, **Bras Piqué (also Tattooed Arm, fl. 1700s–after**

1731) of northeastern Louisiana alerted French settlers to a future raid by Natchez tribesmen armed with muzzle-loading muskets. A member of an aristocratic clan and mate of the Jesuit missionary Jean-François St. Cosme, during the Natchez Rebellion of 1729, she joined hundreds of bastion residents west of Ditto Lake on the Tensas River Basin. Preparing a massacre, the French began surrounding the area on January 11, 1731, and fired cannon and lobbed grenades from wood mortars.

While Bras Piqué at a tobacco shed of the India Company remained *hors de combat*, on January 21, 1731, four hundred fifty Natchez ceded to the French and Choctaw allies at Fort Valeur and traveled to New Orleans for deportation. In May, the duplicitous colonists packed the ships *Le Gironde* and *La Venus* with prisoners, including Bras Piqué, whom they sold in Havana. On *La Venus,* dealers transported two hundred ninety-one captives as slaves to cultivate sugar plantations on San Domingue (modern Haiti). Only one hundred sixty reached Cap Français alive.

November 23, 1733

Akwamu (modern Ghana) rebel **Breffu of St. John (?–May 1734)** led a slave revolt on November 23, 1733, in the Danish West Indies. At Coral Bay on the southeastern shore of St. Jan (modern St. John) island, she responded to three cannon blasts from Fort Fredericksvaerk (modern Fortsberg) by murdering planter Pieter Krøyer, his wife Mariana Thoma, and son Hans. The night signal indicated that wood cutters had killed the parapet security force with sugar knives they had hidden in logs. Partnering with Christian, another slave, Breffu dressed as a man and transported weapons and gunpowder to the next raid on the land of Gabriel and Neetje Van Stell, their three children, and livestock.

Breffu's lieutenants, the bush warrior Kong Juni and his wife **Atha (fl. 1733)**, led forty men in raping and slaughtering while liberating one hundred fifty slaves. They seized control of colonial dwellings and burned fields until the Danes and French halted the rebellion in early 1734. After unavoidable butchery at Newfound Bay, Breffu killed herself in the mass slave suicide at Brown Bay, but the insurrection continued until August 1734. The martyrdom of the "Queen of St. John" colors island festivals, parades, dance, drama, and exhibits at the Ghanaian Museum.

1740

A colonial serial killer in the Golden Age of Piracy, **Maria Lindsey Cobham (1700–1760)**, a buccaneer armed with pistol and dirk, targeted sea lanes off Sandy Point on Newfoundland's western shore. A native of Plymouth, England, she wed fisherman and smuggler Eric Cobham, who freed her from bartending and gambling. In 1740, the pair set out to ransack sea traffic off Cape Breton and Prince Edward Island. Boarding French freighters from their black sloop off the Gulf of St. Lawrence and Cabot Strait in eastern Canada, they thrived on hauls of salt fish, beaver pelts, olive oil, wine, brandy, and dried fruit.

Maria and Eric enjoyed two decades of total war on crew and ships, which they scuttled to the bottom to conceal evidence. Her methods of dispatching sailors included poison and sewing them into sailcloth and hurling them overboard. In retirement, they bartered their armada for a mansion at Le Havre, France, where she indulged in laudanum. She killed herself at age sixty by leaping from a cliff.

December 16, 1740

An English would-be dragoon during the nine-year War of Austrian Succession from 1740 to 1748, **Ann Mills (also Anne or Anna, fl. 1740)** signed on with the Royal British Navy on December 16, 1740, in male garb. She served as a common sailor aboard the three-masted frigate HMS *Maidenstone* during marine combat against a coalition of France, Prussia, and Spain. In a promising start of the war, the English celebrated their capture of the Spanish *Princesa* off Cape Finisterre, Spain, on April 18, 1740. A sketch of Ann on a pier pictures her in plain jacket, vest, slops, and buckled shoes. She bears a cutlass and a trophy—the dangling head of a pigtailed French victim. The crew cheered her daring and courage.

1741

A little-known North American marine felon near the end of the Golden Age of Piracy, English raider **Flora Burn (fl. 1740s)** specialized in robbing ships along the North Atlantic seaboard from Canada to Charleston, South Carolina, to the Florida Keys. She entered a felonious career in 1741. Crews tended to form at Newfoundland and sell their loot in New York. By the mid-1740s, the locus of buccaneering had shifted to the Leeward Islands of St. Bart's and Antigua.

1743

A crossdresser from Eichstätt, Bavaria, during the War of Austrian Succession, **Johanna Sophia Kettner (also Johanna Sophia Köttner, January 24, 1724–January 22, 1802)** served from 1743 until 1748 in the Hagenbach infantry. In the Rhineland-Palatinate, she admired galloping hussars in childhood. While living with an aunt at Ried in north central Austria, she dressed in her brother's clothes before making confession. At enlistment at a nearby inn, she became the first female private in the Imperial Hapsburg Army. For training at Kufstein's garrison, she adopted the alias Johann Kettner. Her battle record probably included the 2nd Silesian War from 1744 to 1745 and the Austrian gain over Franco-Bavarian troops.

Near the end of the War of Austrian Succession, Johanna deployed to northern Italy to fight in the battle of Piacenza on June 16, 1746, when the Austrians crushed the Bourbon army and forced a retreat over the Po River and southeast toward Genoa. A clash to the west at Rottofreddo, Italy, on August 10, 1746, cinched Austria's rout of the French. Johanna's medical care for fever and delirium near Luxembourg at the St. Eucharius Abbey in Trier disclosed her gender. Mustering out in Vienna, she left the military with honors, the rank of corporal, and a pension from the Empress Maria Theresa of eight guilders (approx. $167.90).

1745

Jacobite spy and secret supporter **Mary Hay (1678–August 19, 1758)** of Longforgan, Scotland, in complicity with her mother, **Anne Drummond (December 30, 1655–November 17, 1707)** of Perth, gambled on unseating of the Anglican Hanoverian dynasty from England's throne. To restore the Catholic Stuarts to power, at Slains Castle in Aberdeenshire in 1745, Mary mustered Scots loyalists from Buchan to the cause and transported them from the North Sea coast inland to Delgatie castle at Turriff. For an unsuspected go-between, she dispatched Jamie Fleeman, a court jester, with messages to the rebels from French agents, who promised money for the cause. During the reprisals of William, Duke of Cumberland, that followed the disastrous battle on Culloden Moor on April 16, 1746, the Act of Proscription stripped Mary's clan of land and title. The austere fiddle tune "Miss Mary Hay" conveys the fervor of her political opinions.

May 11, 1745

A famed English infantryman, **Phoebe Smith Hessel (March 1713–December 12, 1821)** of Stepney east of London followed lover Samuel Golding into the 5th Foot Regiment. In girlhood, she learned to play the drum and fife army style and joined the Royal Northumberland Fusiliers in 1728 as a man. Deployment took her to conclusion of the four-month siege at Gibraltar, to the Caribbean to intervene in Spanish shipping routes, and to Belgium during the War of Austrian Succession, which pitted the Duke of Cumberland's army against fifty thousand French. Among twelve thousand British casualties, Phoebe survived a bayonet gash in the arm on May 11, 1745, at Fontenoy near Belgium's border with France.

Phoebe's military career ended with medical treatment in 1745, when she became a roving merchant. In widowhood at Brighton Beach, she sold fish, oranges, gingerbread, toys, and pincushions from a donkey cart. Blindness and disease forced her into poverty and the workhouse. She retired in the 1800s on a pension of two guineas per month (approx. $2.08 or $24.96 per year) and lived to age one hundred eight.

August 19, 1745

On the arrival by rowboat of Bonnie Prince Charlie to Jacobite headquarters at Glenfinnan on August 19, 1745, **Jean "Jenny" Cameron (1698–1772)** from Glendessary, Scotland, presented him three hundred volunteers from Clan Cameron and a herd of cattle for rations. Armed with a rifle and dressed in red, green, and gold doublet and trews (breeches) in the prince's colors, she raised a sword to salute the Stuart pretender to the English throne. She declared her allegiance among one hundred fifty Jacobite females armed for battle. While leading two hundred fifty clan members, she allegedly cheered the troop's quick victory over General John Cope at the battle of Prestonpans on September 21, 1745, and suffered with starving men during the winter of 1745–1746.

After Jenny's capture at the Jacobite siege of Stirling Castle January 8–February 1, 1746, the English imprisoned her at Edinburgh Castle. The Duke of

Cumberland, leader of the English faction, turned the prisoner into ludicrous pro–Hanoverian propaganda by claiming she was the Bonnie Prince's lover. Nine and a half months later, she gained release on November 15, 1746, and retired to East Kilbride, South Lanarkshire, southeast of Glasgow. At age seventy-four, she died on the Cameron estate, where a fiery cross reputedly emerged from her grave. Her patriotism appears in ballads, storytelling, art, and historical fiction by English novelist Henry Fielding.

September 21, 1745

Scots Jacobite recruiter **Anne Farquharson Mackintosh (1723–March 2, 1787)** of Invercauld became the only female military leader during the fight for the Stuart pretender, Bonnie Prince Charlie, against the Hanoverian king George II. For mustering eight hundred Farquharson, MacBean, MacGillivray, and Mackintosh Highlanders to the Chattan regiment, she dressed in men's uniform and, armed with a firelock, rode the countryside for two weeks in search of volunteers. She became the first woman to hold the title "colonel." A rout for General John Cope and the British army, the battle of Prestonpans on September 21, 1745, succeeded because Jacobites attacked before dawn while the English slept. Her husband, Captain Angus Mackintosh, an officer of the Black Watch, supported the Hanoverians and, in March 1746, was jailed at Inverness. Anne's soldiers backed the Scots pretender at Bannockburn on January 5, 1746, and, on January 17, won the battle of Falkirk Muir.

In loyalty to the Stuart dynasty, Anne rallied nobles and the wealthy to the Jacobite cause. She interceded in an abduction plot while the Bonnie Prince lodged with her at Moy Hall on Moy Island. By dispatching five men to fire on fifteen hundred government raiders and shout out battle cries of the Camerons and MacDonalds, to protect the prince, she scared off the enemy with the pretense of a large army. On April 16, 1746, the Jacobite annihilation at the Culloden slaughter cost her six weeks in an Inverness prison. The French saluted her as "La Belle Rebelle (the beautiful rebel)"; the bitter loyalist General Henry Hawley demanded that she hang. On her release, she conspired with Jacobite women to release Robert Nairn from his cell. He was confined for supporting **Anne MacLeod McKay (fl. 1740s–1750s)** of Skye for sheltering wounded Jacobites from April 1746 to March 1747 in flight from British executioners.

November 23, 1745

An illiterate English widow who lost her daughter in infancy, **Hannah Snell (April 23, 1723–February 8, 1792)** of Worcester volunteered for the infantry of the Duke of Cumberland under the pseudonym James Gray. During the Scots uprising favoring Stuart pretender Bonnie Prince Charlie, while functioning as a cook and assistant steward disguised in uniform and cockaded hat, on November 23, 1745, she suffered five hundred lashes for her disguise and fled to Portsmouth. A volunteer with Fraser's Regiment of Royal Marines as a common seaman on the sloop *Swallow*, she sailed from Lisbon to India on Admiral Edward Boscawen's fleet of five thousand men in twenty-eight ships.

In southeastern India, Hannah engaged in the siege against the French East India Company at Fort Aranciopang outside Pondicherry on July 29, 1748, which deprived her of a right index finger from a sword slash. At the siege of Devikottai on June 23, 1749, typhoon winds wrecked two ships and destroyed goods and dray animals, forcing a British retreat. Musket ball wounds in Hannah's legs and lower torso obligated her to seek medical treatment from a native female. Giving up her disguise at Gravesend, where she disembarked from the man-o'-war *Eltham*, she secured a pension of £18.5 per year, performed military song and dance in vaudeville, opened a pub at Wapping called the Female Warrior, and issued her memoirs, *The Female Soldier*.

1746

The first military career of a transgender grenadier of the Dutch Republic, **Maria van Antwerpen (January 17, 1719–January 16, 1781)**, an orphan from Breda, ended after five years with her banishment from Brabant, Limburg, and other garrison towns. Her enrollment under the alias of sixteen-year-old Jan van Ant, her father's first name, and marriage to a female resulted in public jeers and litigation at a military tribunal. As a common soldier who never saw combat, in 1746, she moved about to varied camps and accustomed herself to shameless swearing and blasphemy. She had to share a bed with a male soldier, for which crime critics declared she deserved the death penalty. She adopted the name Michael van Hantwerpen and continued cross-dressing.

At age forty-three, Maria resigned from tailoring in Gouda and abandoned a second wife to re-enlist in Zwolle, far from Breda. After seven years in service as city guard in Amsterdam, she was placed in a cell on display to hordes of the curious. When an acquaintance recognized her, she went on trial for fraud. Before the judge in 1769 for five hearings, she claimed that, inside her body, she was "Maggiel van Handtwerpen," a male from birth. In exile from Gouda, at her demise in poverty at Breda, she lay interred in a pauper's cemetery.

April 16, 1746

A survivor of the battle of Culloden, Scotland, on April 16, 1746, **Mary Cameron Ralphson (January 1, 1698–June 27, 1808)** from Inverlochy took part in the slaughter of some two thousand Highlanders by the British. Known as Trooper Mary, during the War of the Austrian Succession, she accompanied her husband, Private Ralph Ralphson, and the 3rd King's Dragoons to combat the Hapsburgs at Flanders on May 21, 1741. Under George II, she abandoned the role of camp follower to fight in a dead horseman's uniform on June 15, 1743, at Dettingen, Holy Roman Empire, the last time that a British monarch commanded British forces. Outside Penrith on December 6, 1745, and at Falkirk Muir on January 17, 1746, she witnessed the diminution of Stuart pretender Bonnie Prince Charlie and his Jacobite Highlanders for failure to follow up. At Val in northern Holland, on

January 17, 1747, she was widowed. She retired from the army and lived at Liverpool in penury to age one hundred ten.

April 23, 1746

Jacobite enthusiast **Margaret Johnstone Ogilvy (October 30, 1724–1757)** suffered sacking and imprisonment. On a borrowed horse, she joined the regiment of her husband, David Ogilvy, while it bivouacked in Glasgow. After General Cumberland's brutal massacre of two thousand Scots at Culloden, on April 16, 1746, she was captured in June at Inverness. At the same time that David was incarcerated at St. Andrews Castle, she occupied a cell at Edinburgh Castle, from which she escaped five months later on November 21.

Disguised as an elderly laundress, Margaret journeyed south to Hull. When she sought passage on a Dutch ship to France, pursuers mistook her for Bonnie Prince Charlie. She returned to her husband's estate at Cortachy, Angus, to give a Scots birthplace to son David, who was born retarded. She died in France at age thirty-two from the rigors of prison.

November 11, 1746

Johanna Bennius (fl. 1740s) from Rotterdam, Holland, enlisted in the Dutch East India Company and sailed for Batavia (modern Jakarta, Indonesia) in northern Java as an employee of the world's largest trading emporium. She embarked on the three-masted merchantman *Overschie* (Overshoot), named for a village northwest of Rotterdam and the Maas River. The itinerary returned via the Cape of Good Hope in South Africa. In the edgy years following the October 9, 1740, pogrom slaughtering ten thousand Chinese sugar mill workers, Johanna was hired to guard stores of coffee, oil, pepper, quinine, and sugar. In a man's uniform, on January 11, 1746, she passed as male soldier Jan Drop for twenty-nine days. The disclosure of her gender on December 10, 1746, forced a dismissal. Remittance logs have no entry establishing her pay.

June 17, 1748

Dutch fishmonger **Marretje Arents (1708–June 28, 1748)** of Smallepad at Haarlemmerplein farmer's market in north central Amsterdam headed the Pachtersoproer (Leasehold Rebellion), a revolt against taxation and high rents. She, her husband, and their five children occupied a basement flat in Mandenmakersteeg and supported the family by selling flatfish, goats, and limes. On June 17, 1748, a week-long rumbling among working class Dutchwomen burgeoned on June 24 to a two-day looting of rental property. After the shooting death of two rebels, the followers of "Mat, the lime woman" conspired to enlarge their revolution by arming themselves with stones and seizing city hall.

Threatened with the rack at her arrest on June 27, Marretje confessed and was hanged the next day. To silence her cries for revolution, the city placed drummers around the gallows at city hall. Her four younger children were dispatched to a pauper's orphanage. Newspaper accounts proclaimed her a Dutch Marianne, the French goddess of liberty.

July 3, 1754

From the outset of the French and Indian War, **Aliquippa (1680–December 23, 1754)**, the aged head of the Mingo Seneca at Conestoga, Pennsylvania, backed the British and the Virginia Regiment. A member of the Iroquois Confederacy, she resided near McKeesport, Pennsylvania, at the juncture of the Allegheny, Monongahela, and Ohio rivers. During a period of short supplies in summer 1748, she sent wampum to Philadelphia to purchase powder and shot.

In support of the Lenni Lenape (or Delaware) and Shawnee at Great Meadows, on July 3, 1754, Aliquippa led her son Canachquasy and other Mingo warriors to Fort Necessity. The arrivals supported Colonel George Washington's five companies of three hundred Virginia soldiers from Williamsburg. After an attack by six hundred French and Canadians from Fort Duquesne, the British surrendered on July 4, 1754. Her son received promotion to colonial courier and spy, but died within months of smallpox. She secured her two hundred Mingo at Aughwick Creek in eastern Pennsylvania.

1755

A Cherokee-Delaware warrior and peace ambassador, **Nancy Ward (also Nanyehi, 1738–1822)** from Chota, Tennessee, fought the Muskogee-Creek in northwest Georgia in 1755 at the battle of Taliwa. At age seventeen, she accompanied her husband Kingfisher to the battlefield with Oconostata, a hero of the French and Indian War, and his five hundred warriors from Ballground in northern Georgia. To increase Kingfisher's kill rate, she chewed his ammunition to slash jagged wounds. After his death in the Creek's fifth charge, she moved into his place and fired his rifle while facing some fifteen hundred enemy.

The destruction pushed the Muskogee-Creek south of the Chattahoochee River. Strategy and courage earned her membership as a Cherokee councilwoman and judge of prisoner wrongs. At her death on the Ocoee River at Woman Killer Ford, Tennessee, she bore the title "War Woman of Chota." Her role in Southern history impacted histories and fiction, a Daughters of the American Revolution chapter, and Judy Chicago's sculpture *The Dinner Party*.

1759

English sailor and shipwright **Mary Lacy (1740–1801)** from Wickham fled domestic service in 1759 to sail with the British Royal Navy from Chatham. Under the alias "William Chandler," at age nineteen, she passed as a male. She took the post of assistant to a ship's carpenter on the H.M.S. *Sandwich*, a defender of sea lanes with the Western Squadron. After debarking from Plymouth, on April 7, 1761, the ship participated in the seizure of Belle Ile off Brittany.

Recovered from hospitalization for rheumatism, Mary transferred to the three-masted battleship *Royal Sovereign*, the flagship of the Portsmouth fleet during the Seven Years' War. In 1763, she advanced to apprentice ship builder in the Chatham Dockyard, completing licensing at age thirty. During training, she won a speed contest against three sailors in a rowboat. Because joint pain forced retirement, she applied for an annual pension of £20 (currently $5,774.95) and compiled the memoir *The Female Shipwright*.

April 7, 1760

A Fante native wrongly accused and deported from the British colony of Jamaica, **Cubah Cornwallis (also Akua, Akuba, or Couba, ?–June 1760)** requited colonial misjudgments by joining Tacky's Easter Monday revolt on April 7, 1760. An abductee from the Ashanti Empire (modern Ghana), she became the property of Captain William Cornwallis and served in Port Royal as housekeeper and herbalist. Chosen queen of Kingston for nursing the sick, she achieved rule in Jamaica over the Ashanti. A fearful island rebellion, the anti-slave war in St. Mary district inspired Akan natives to involve the Akyem, Ashanti, Fanti, and Nzema. The British suspected Cubah of fomenting rebellion and transported her for life to the west.

At sea, Cubah wheedled a stop on the island's west end, where she encountered a mounting uprising on May 25, 1760. The horde overran colonists at Esher, Frontier, and Trinity plantation. Angry marchers stole guns and gunpowder from Fort Haldane at Port Maria and marked their bodies with protective vodou powder. Amid widespread arson and murder of rebel leadership, a conspirator betrayed the movement. Maroons and militia decapitated Tacky. Cubah remained on the run for months until searchers seized her in Hanover parish in early June and executed her.

November 3, 1760

A victim of early modern global combat during the Seven Years' War of 1756–1763, Prussian warrior **Anna Sophia Detzliffin (1738–1776)** of Treptow incurred saber slashes to her left arm at Bamberg, the source of Prussian supplies. Dressed like a male armored cavalryman and doubly armed with a pistol, she joined the fight against a coalition of French, Saxons, Russians, and Austrians in Prince Frederick Augustus's regiment. Lethal wounds by the Austrian forces of Maximilian Ulysses Browne, a Hapsburg field marshal, forced her hospitalization at Meissen, Saxony. After rehabilitation, she returned to the military as a grenadier. At a Prussian victory costing more than thirty-two thousand lives, another serious wound on November 3, 1760, at the battle of Torgau, Saxony, left her open to enemy seizure. She fled a hospital at the repeatedly contested Saxon city of Dresden, breached Austrian lines, and registered a third time as a volunteer.

July 9, 1762

An enlightened militant, **Catherine II the Great (May 2, 1729–November 17, 1796)** of Stettin, Prussia, seized power in Russia by deposing her husband, Peter III, after six months as emperor. Her talent for training and managing the military earned applause from Napoleon. When her conspiracy collapsed, she contrasted Peter's pro–Prussianism with strong Russian nationalism. Dressed in regimental uniform, she harangued her soldiers in St. Petersburg to protect her from the former emperor. Her tactics required targeting rivals from the imperial Romanov party.

A campaign to access the Black Sea and add Belarus, the Caucasus, Crimea, Lithuania, and Ukraine to the empire created enemies among the Bourbons and Hapsburgs. In 1769 and 1770, Catherine thrived in sea battles against the Ottoman Turks. Her 1773 war against the Pugachev Uprising of cossacks, serfs, and immigrants ended the peasant revolt in January 1775.

July 15, 1762

A creole cannoneer from New Granada, **Rafaela Herrera** (August 6, 1742–1805) from Cartagena (modern Colombia) superintended defense of the stronghold at the Immaculate Conception. The granddaughter of a military engineer, she learned artillery terms and tactics from her father, Captain José Herrera. At age eleven, she joined him in Castillo, Nicaragua, on the San Juan River to defend the territory from a British landing party arriving from Jamaica to Granada, a possible trade route from the Caribbean Sea to the Pacific Ocean. Her words to her dying father pledged her life to saving the redoubt on the Costa Rican border.

During the six-day siege, on July 15, 1762, Rafaela forced cowards to lock the gates and assume sentry posts. With one canon blast, she killed a British leader. Her tactic of covering floating greenery in alcohol-soaked sheets enabled the indigenous army to imperil British boats with fire. Significant losses forced a British retreat on August 3. King Charles III of Spain rewarded her with land and a pension of 600 pesos. Her likeness survives on Nicaraguan currency, legends, and art.

February 23, 1763

In the guise of a male, rebel **Amelia of Berbice (fl. 1760s–March 10, 1764)** from Akwamu (modern Ghana), provided tactics and broadsword skills to a ten-month insurrection in Guyana's rainforest. With shipmate Coffij van Lelienburg, she arrived in the Western Hemisphere over the Middle Passage from West Africa and served slave masters at the Hollandia and Zeelandia plantation until it became a rebel headquarters. For Coffij, the leading revolutionary, she identified the most trustworthy rebels. To free blacks of Dutch colonialism and establish a West African state, slaves raided Goed Fortuin (Good Fortune) plantation on July 3, 1762. In collusion with indigenous Arawak and Carib, the Dutch rousted Maroons until their departure a month later. In toto, the resisters massacred fifty or 14.3 percent of colonists.

A subsequent slave uprising on February 23, 1763, at Magdalenenberg burned the main residence and outbuildings on the Canje River. The revolt spread along the Berbice River, destroying Fort Nassau and encouraging some three thousand rebels to drive out half the white populace. Forces from Amsterdam, Barbados, Sint Eustatius, and Surinam combed the swamp for dissidents and ended the rebellion on April 15, 1764. To avoid surrender,

Coffij committed suicide African style. At Amelia's execution, she died in agony on March 10, 1764, over a slow fire. Dutch forces evolved into the first Dutch marines. Marjoleine Kars's *Blood on the River,* winner of the Frederick Douglass Book Prize, summarized slave resistance and recorded how the spirits of murdered babies returned to haunt rebels.

May 28, 1763

A mestiza Filipina heroine, **Gabriela Silang (March 19, 1731–September 20, 1763)** of Santa, Ilocos Sur, spearheaded the demand for freedom from colonial oppression. In 1762, she promoted the Silang Revolt, named for her husband Diego Silang, who resisted the British seizure of the Philippines from Spain. After his imprisonment and assassination at Bantay on May 28, 1763, by Miguel Vicos, a gunman hired by the Catholic church, Gabriela recruited mountain warriors from Pidigan and distributed bows, blowguns, spears, swords, machetes, and firearms. In early August, she entrenched Cabugao, a district overlooking the South China Sea. From Santa to Abra to Vigan, she commanded Diego's two thousand rebels, earning the title "Generala."

Gabriela's army marched south and torched Bantay's aristocratic walled town, built by forced labor to glorify Spanish imperialism. Three hundred archers and six thousand enemy soldiers armed with muskets and cannon forced her to hide at the command post inland of Abra's jungle. During a retreat to the mountains on horseback, she was captured. In the Vigan city plaza, the enemy scourged, then hanged ninety of her wounded troops on September 20, 1763. She was the last to mount the scaffold. A statue of her on horseback marks the plaza in Manila; a mural in Quezon commemorates the first female general, resister, and martyr to liberation.

August 5, 1763

In the two-day battle of Bushy Run, Pennsylvania, on August 5, 1763, a Shawnee chieftain, **Nonhelema Hokolesqua (also Katherine, 1718–December 1786)** from the Ohio River Valley, observed a hard-fought afternoon conflict that resulted in seventy-nine British casualties. For Pontiac's Rebellion 1763–1765, Colonel Henry Bouquet made valuable use of rifle shots and bayonets to disperse a confederation of Algonquian, Iroquoian, Muskogean, and Siouan Indians from Fort Pitt (modern Pittsburgh). In summer 1777, Nonhelema alerted patriots to the desertion of Indians to the British redoubt at Fort Detroit and to potential sieges on West Virginia forts Donnally and Randolph in 1778.

Nonhelema continued to back the colonists as guide and translator and requested a thousand-acre parcel from legislators as payment for helping patriots win the American Revolution. They promised only daily rations and a yearly gift of clothing and a blanket. After the killing of her third husband, Moluntha, and her jailing at Fort Pitt, she wrote a reference source on the Shawnee language. The "Grenadier's" ingenuity inspired a film, stone, monument, and novel.

March 28, 1765

On campaigns to Gwalior and Gohad in north central India against fifty thousand Maratha Empire troops, **Ahilyabhai Holkar (May 31, 1725–August 13, 1795)**, a widowed rani in the state of Indore, India, relied on heavy artillery for her four battalions. On the opposite shore of the Chambal River on March 28, 1765, she set guards over rations and ordnance trains to ensure passage of food, ammunition, and explosives. Continuing the march northeast, she aimed a barrage of arrows and captured Fort Gohad with cannon balls and small musket balls she manufactured. As the Holkars retook Rampura to the west, she superintended field medicine and led fresh recruits into position on battlements left empty after gunners died. On her accession to the throne of Malwa on December 11, 1767, she attached bows and quivers to her howdah attesting to her competence as military leader and administrator.

See also early 1771; 1783; 1787.

Early 1771

During a period of anarchy at Indore, India, Queen **Ahilyabhai Holkar** maintained a small Western style security force and a women's regiment of five hundred famed for their discipline and peacekeeping. In early 1771, she wielded a sword alongside troops and sepoy mercenaries who put down a revolt. Resurgences of rebellion in 1783 and 1787 required her intervention. Revered for gallantry, she curtailed future uprisings by decapitating mutineers and by tying the Rajput leader to a cannon and exploding him. Under the aegis of the army, she built roads, inns, water systems, Hindu monuments, and twelve Shiva temples and willed her capital of Maheshwar to her commander-in-chief. Her name survives on a domed memorial erected by her daughter, Krishna Bai Holkar, and on a commemorative stamp, airport, parks and highways, and two universities.

June 25, 1772

A Tamil Nadu queen and warrior, **Velu Nachiyar (January 3, 1730–December 25, 1796)** of Sivaganga became the first Indian monarch to contest the East India Company, an invasive trading complex and colonizer of the subcontinent. At a time when British empire builder Warren Hastings established a Bengal governorship and chose Calcutta as the capital, she drew on skills at martial arts, horsemanship, archery, and weaponry as well as fluency in English, French, and Urdu. Two weeks after the East India Company faced bankruptcy during a credit crisis, on June 25, 1772, her husband, King Muthu Vaduganatha Periyavudaya Thevar, died in battle. As the mother of an infant daughter and successor to the rule of Sivaganga, she petitioned Mysore sultan Haider Ali for asylum and backup forces. During her seven years of exile, he offered five thousand armed troops, which local merchants supported during the recapture of Sivaganga from the British.

During the queen's 1780 attack on European imperialists, she relied on Tamil army commander **Kuyili (?–1780)**, a female bodyguard. Kuyili routed out spies and suffered injury while stopping an assassin from killing Queen Velu. Through reconnaissance, Kuyili located a British armory in a temple limited to female worshippers. She became India's first suicide bomber by covering herself in ghee (butter), setting herself on fire, and igniting explosives. The two women's example survives in ballet, song, and a portrait postage stamp of Velu Nachiyar.

April 1775

After her husband, David Wright, enlisted with the patriots of Pepperell, Massachusetts Bay Colony, in the lead-up to the American Revolution, Captain **Prudence Cummings Wright (November 26, 1740–December 2, 1823)** of Dunstable founded a forty-member female militia, the Minutewomen. Dressed in men's uniform, in April 1775, she distributed muskets and pitchforks to defenders of Jewett's Bridge against British insurgents marching from the battle of Lexington over the Nashua River. The town guard saved Pepperell from invasion. The Prudence Wright Guard intercepted details of troop movements and captured the traitor Leonard Whiting, a messenger to Boston tories. For prompt action, they earned £7 (modern $1,299.54) reward.

Mid–November 1775

Armed with her husband's long rifle, teenaged war widow **Jemima Warner (1758–December 11, 1775)** fought the British on behalf of the Continental Army. She traveled from Lancaster County with the 1st Pennsylvania Rifle Battalion. Following the siege of Boston on April 19, 1775, she marched for six weeks with General Benedict Arnold's troops from Maine to Quebec in autumn 1775. In mid–November 1775, General Richard Montgomery chose her to dress in women's attire and bear conditions of surrender through the snow to Quebec governor Guy Carleton. On her second presentation, Carleton destroyed the document and ejected her from the province. At age seventeen, she appears to have died on December 11, 1775, in combat at St. Roch from a peppering with grapeshot. Along with Pennsylvanian army wife **Susannah Grier (April 18, 1776)**, a probable victim of friendly fire, the women were the first females to give their lives for American freedom.

November 16, 1776

In Manhattan, New York, Irish-American nurse **Margaret Cochran Corbin (November 12, 1751–January 16, 1800)** of Franklin, Pennsylvania, replaced her husband, cannoneer John Corbin, in defending Fort Washington from four thousand Hessian mercenaries. After the battles of Lexington and Concord on April 19, 1775, John and Margaret served with the six hundred men under General "Light Horse" Harry Lee. Motivated by John's death in action at the last American stronghold in Manhattan, on November 16, 1776, Margaret took over the artillery post, loaded and fired the cannon, and carried water to cool the overheated bore. After silencing her gun, the British overran the stronghold and found her in critical condition. They transported her by wagon to a Philadelphia prisoner of war camp.

Upon parole, Margaret continued her service to the Continental Army until musket balls and grape shot wounds to jaw, left shoulder, and torso paralyzed her left arm and ended her mobility. The former "Captain Molly Pitcher" became the first female wounded warrior to receive a government clothing and rum allowance and the service of a caretaker to help her bathe and dress. On July 6, 1779, Pennsylvania granted her immediate financial relief of $30 (currently $2,427.63), half the rate allotted to men. At her death at age forty-eight, she was interred at West Point Cemetery under a monument and commemorated in a mural, tablet, bronze relief, and burial mound.

August 6, 1777

An Oneida native of Oriskany Creek in north central New York, **Tyonajanegen (1742–1822)**, a pro–American warrior also known as Two Kettles Together, fought with pistols against four hundred British colonials and their Mohawk and Seneca allies. Among sixty Oneida, on August 6, 1777, she rode into a bloody fray at the mouth of the Mohawk River alongside her son Cornelius and husband Han Yerry, chief of the Wolf clan. Because a musket ball shattered his wrist, Tyonajanegen loaded his gun. The pyrrhic victory for the British produced little gain except for the spiteful burning of Tyonajanegen's family farm at Oriska. At age eighty, she died blind.

October 4, 1777

The first female warrior in the American Revolution, **Anna Maria Lane (1755–June 13, 1810)** of New Hampshire accompanied her husband, John Lane, to serve under General George Washington at the battle of Germantown, Pennsylvania. After enlistment at age twenty-one, she dressed in uniform for engagements in Georgia, New Jersey, New York, and Pennsylvania. At Germantown on October 4, 1777, she survived a crippling wound, but re-enrolled in the Virginia Light Dragoons. Her military career continued with the month-long siege of Savannah on September 9, 1779, where John was numbered among the 828 patriot casualties. Her service ended in 1781. She later volunteered to treat men at the Richmond military hospital and received a veteran's pension of $100 (approx. $2,794 today).

December 2, 1777

An immigrant midwife, **Lydia Darragh (1729–December 28, 1789)** from Dublin, Ireland, hid in a closet and eavesdropped on British plans on December 2, 1777, to attack General George Washington and the Continental Army. A quaker pacifist, Lydia had previously retrieved data from military conferences at the camp across the street and coded them on paper to conceal behind the covered buttons of her son John's coat. After learning of General William Howe's intent to assault the forces at Whitemarsh, Pennsylvania, she had two days in which to convey a message to Patriot forces.

Pretending to need flour, Lydia carried an empty sack and a pass as she crossed the British occupation forces at Philadelphia to reach Frankford Mill.

Within hours of her delivery of the British plan to Colonel Elias Boudinot, Washington's regiments were ready for Howe and his five thousand men and thirteen cannon. British interrogation concerning who might have overheard the high-level strategy session elicited lies from Lydia, who declared she had nothing to report. In her honor, the Sons of the American Revolution offer the Lydia Darragh Medal.

Summer 1778

At a crucial need for Patriot espionage, **Anna Smith Strong (April 14, 1740–August 12, 1812)** from Setauket, New York, devised a signal system to direct couriers to hidden messages from the Culper Spy Ring, America's first intelligence gathering coterie. To indicate a waiting transmission, she pinned a black petticoat to her wash line. By adding from one to six handkerchiefs, she identified the cove in the Long Island Sound where a whaleboat could land and collect the data. By passing on observations of British troop strength and movement, Anna aided General George Washington and the Continental Army in campaign strategy. Although her husband, Judge Selah Strong, served a sentence on the prison hulk *Jersey* for spying, the British did not discover Anna's complicity.

June 28, 1778

An immigrant German laundress, cook, and medic for the colonial patriots, **Mary Ludwig Hays (October 13, 1754–January 22, 1832)** of New Jersey followed her husband, barber William Hays, to the battle of Monmouth. After wintering at Valley Forge, on June 28, 1778, she toted buckets of water from a spring to cannoneers on the front line and took his place in the Pennsylvania Artillery at the ramrod after his wounding. Dubbed "Sergeant Molly" and "Molly Pitcher," she acquired legendary status for a cannon shot that passed between her legs, ripping a piece of petticoat. General George Washington issued her a battlefield rank of sergeant. The state legislature awarded her a pension of $40 (approx. $1,117 today). A statue of Molly with ramrod mark her grave in Carlisle, Pennsylvania.

August 29, 1778

A Philadelphia teacher and spy for the British in colonial America, **Ann Bates (1748–1801)** carried identification as a Tory operative until her retirement on May 12, 1780. Answering to the code name "Mrs. Barnes," she trained for one day in New York City and accepted pay ranging from twenty to thirty-one dollars (currently worth $558–$866.14) per mission. She reported to majors John Andre and Duncan Drummond on illicit colonial activity and the number and placement of safe houses and cannon available to patriots. Her pass from traitor Benedict Arnold allowed her safe passage into the continental army headquarters in White Plains, New York.

Ann eavesdropped on details of brigade weaknesses and the weight of cannon balls. To cloak her observations of six hundred boats and troop movements to Long Island and Rhode Island, she dressed like a male tinker selling cookpots, knives, and sewing supplies. Her clever action at the battle of Rhode

Island on August 29, 1778, helped the British destroy American and French allies at Aquidneck Island near Newport. She repatriated to London on March 6, 1781. At age thirty-seven, she received a pension for military service.

December 29, 1778

An Afro-French cannoneer in the American Revolution, **Sally St. Clair (also Sarah St. Clare, ?–December 29, 1778)** from South Carolina died on December 29, 1778, at the battle of Savannah, Georgia, of a lance thrust through the chest. To accompany her lover, Sergeant Jasper, she cut her hair, dressed in men's buckskins, and marched with the Continental Army. A poem by George Pope Morris, "Sally St. Clair: A Song of Marion's Men" characterizes her secret service as guerrilla warrior through low country swamps under Lieutenant Colonel Francis Marion, the famed "Swamp Fox," who lost the siege of Savannah in fall 1779 to British General Augustine Prevost. Sally numbered among two hundred forty-four killed and six hundred wounded. She is revered for her role in black history as the only black female recorded in the war.

1780

A warrior-queen of northern Chile's indigenous Qulla or Kolla, **Huillac Ñusca (also Ñusta Huillac or Willaq, ?–1780)**, the daughter of native priest Huma, fought Spanish invaders of southwestern South America. Dubbed La Tirana del Tamarugal (the Tyrant of the Pampas) for inhumane treatments of prisoners, she suffered Spanish coercion in 1780. At the height of ore extraction in Huantajaya in the Atacama Desert to the far north, imperialists forced Incas into press gangs to mine silver and purify it with poisonous mercury. A legend, festival, and pageant commemorate her martyrdom after she converted to Christianity, for which Indians pierced her with arrows.

November 18, 1780

During the revolt orchestrated by Tupac Amaru II, Peruvian warrior **Tomasa Tito Condemayta (1729–May 18, 1781)**, an Inca rebel from Acos, successfully engaged the Spanish on November 18, 1780. Her intent was to restore humanity and dignity to indigenous people reduced to servitude. On the night before a planned siege, some six thousand followers surrounded nine hundred Spaniards at the Sangarara church near her home at Cuzco. As Spaniards left the chancel, the Inca peppered them with arrows, slings, spears, and slingshots, felling five hundred seventy-six or 64 percent.

Tomasa's executioners seated her on a chair in Cuzco's Plaza de Armas and tightened a garroting device to strangle her. Next, the Spanish martyred Tupac Amaru and his son Hippolito and rebel wife **Micaela Bastidas Puyucahua (1744–May 18, 1781)**, a recruiter, supplier, strategist, and security guard from Tamburco. Tomasa's name survives in verse, an avenue, and an indigenous potato.

See also May 18, 1781.

1781

American pirate **Rachel Wall (1760–October 8, 1789)** of Carlisle,

Pennsylvania, served at age sixteen as a privateer in the American Revolution. After marrying fisherman George Wall, she agreed to join five pirate couples. On their schooner *Essex* in 1781, they robbed ships at the Isle of Shoals off New Hampshire after she lured victims aboard by crying for help. Within a year, the coterie murdered two dozen sailors from twelve boats and stole $6,000 (approx. $129,780). After George died in 1782, she changed her method to pilfering from docks in Boston. On March 18, 1782, after Sheriff Joe Robinson arrested her on Long Wharf for trying to steal a bonnet and shoes, she was forced to confess on September 10, 1789, to highway robbery. A court condemned her to hanging at age twenty-nine on October 8, 1789, in Boston Common.

January 17, 1781

Spy and courier **Margaret Catherine Moore "Katy" Barry (November 29, 1752–September 29, 1823)** of Walnut Grove Plantation in Roebuck, South Carolina, collected data on the British wins at Camden and warned her neighbors that Lord Cornwallis's troops were crossing the Tyger River. Her surveillance, advice on ambush, and horsemanship boosted the patriots to victory on January 17, 1781. She continued collaboration with the militia and fought alongside her husband, Captain Andrew Barry, at the battle of Cowpens, South Carolina, a vital recovery of Southern territory from Cornwallis. The conflict preceded the Continental Army's success at Yorktown on October 19, 1781, and the awarding of a medal for Katy's bravery and knowledge of the terrain. After publication of the historical outline in the novel *Courageous Kate,* Alan Alda featured the event in the history film *Sweet Liberty.*

March 13, 1781

During the siege of La Paz and Sorata, Aymara guerrilla warrior **Bartolina Sisa Vargas (1750–September 5, 1782)** of Q'ara Qhatu (modern Caracoto, Peru) rallied and militarized native Americans to fight for South American liberty from Spain. With her husband, Tupac Katari, and sister-in-law **Gregoria Apaza (June 23, 1751–September 5, 1782)**, Bartolina promoted insurrection at Charcas, Bolivia. While she directed forty thousand troops for six months, royalists drew on additional soldiers from Buenos Aires. The failed assault on imperialists resulted in twenty thousand dead and the capture of Katari on October 17, 1781, before his dismemberment into four sections. In 2005, Bolivia's president Eduardo Veltze named Katari and Bartolina national heroes.

See also September 5, 1782.

March 16, 1781

A tax protester in Colombia, businesswoman **Manuela Beltran (1750–1781)** of Villa del Socorro headed peasant outcry against unfair levies among New Granadans in the Andes highlands. At the Rebelión De Los Comuneros (Peasant Insurrection), she ripped up posted tax schedules at the city square and initiated a strike in sixty municipalities. Resisters refused to underwrite the Barlovento navy, which the Spanish king Carlos III planned to coerce indigenous Andeans. A phony treaty discussion lured her into captivity and caused the execution of leaders among her two thousand followers.

April 27, 1781

To escape overseer Lund Washington, the superintendent of three hundred blacks on the Virginia plantation of George and Martha Washington, **Deborah Squash (1763–?)** took passage with Captain Charles Sterling on the British sloop-of-war HMS *Savage* and joined the British army. The audacious flight from Mount Vernon exposed the sixteen-year-old to hunger, cold, and smallpox along the Potomac River. She reached military headquarters in New Amsterdam (modern New York City). With her husband, Henry Squash, she awaited emancipation, protection, and compensation from the British in land and cash. After proving their loyal service, in 1783, the couple boarded the *Polly* for Port Rosey, Nova Scotia, before the Washingtons could add them to the eight slaves returned to Mount Vernon.

May 18, 1781

In partnership with her husband, libertarian Tupac Amaru II, **Micaela Bastidas Puyucahua (1744–May 18, 1781)**, an Afro-Incan freedom fighter and tactician from Peru, promoted a mutiny of natives, mestizos, and slaves to Spanish injustice. After 1780, her military role in the rearguard required constant resupply of seven thousand Aymara and Quechua forces and the distribution of cash, food, uniforms, and weapons.

The enemy captured Micaela in an uprising. On May 18, 1781, at Cuzco's Plaza de Armas, they cut out her tongue for resisting executioners. Alongside her husband and son Hipolito and compatriot Tomasa Tito Condemayta, the enemy strangled Micaela, then battered and kicked her corpse.

See also November 18, 1780.

Mid–November 1781

During the four-year Anglo-Dutch War of 1780–1784, **Maria van Spanjen (1759–after 1782)** of Zevenhuizen stole parts of a male costume to conceal her function as a sailor in the Dutch admiralty. Her childhood as a seven-year-old farm laborer engendered a desire for a sea life fighting the British Royal Navy. She got her wish by dressing in a maritime uniform for cruising pubs and inns. Five gender identifications disclosed her trickery, twice by former friends. The first occurred after eight months of marine combat in her brother's clothes. She received 75 guilders in earnest money before signing on to Captain A. Braat's warship *De Erfprins* (hereditary prince Willem I of Orange) out of Utrecht. Under the alias Claas van Vliet, she faced discovery by a possible relative, Hannes van Vliet.

Maria moved on as Jan Kleyweg for a month on the brig *De Thetis,* commanded by Willem Vosch van Avezaat. Her punishment for falsifying documents required ten days in a cell. In mid–November 1781, she kept the alias on the warship *De Maas* under Commander A.M. Brunet de Rochebrune. Two weeks after discovery, her enlistment on Vice Admiral Sebastian L.M. Pichot's 68-gun ship *Prins Frederik* failed. She explained her motivation to volunteer enlistment aboard a warship as a drive to serve Holland's fleet. At the Hague on December 16, 1781, she used the name Klaas Bly to serve under General Hartel on the Sas van Gent canal. Immediate arrest put the twenty-two-year-old in the Rotterdam town hall prison three days later. During questioning on January 5, 1782, she revealed additional aliases, for which she spent a year in the workhouse for deceiving the public.

July 3, 1782

A member of the Massachusetts light infantry, **Deborah Sampson (December 17, 1760–April 29, 1827)** concealed her gender under a male uniform during medical treatment at Tarrytown, New York, for two musket ball wounds to the thigh. From indenturing at age ten, she progressed to teaching school and woodworking. After entering the Continental Army at age twenty-two, she served in reconnaissance under the alias Robert Shurtliff until she had to self-treat one wound with a pocket knife. Illness in 1783 alerted a Philadelphia physician to her cross-dressing. On mustering out, she gained £34 (approx. $2,448.56) for service and a pension and padded her farm income with proceeds of lecturing on soldiery and demonstrating rifle drills.

September 5, 1782

An Aymara martyr to freedom, **Bartolina Sisa Vargas** from Q'ara Qhatu, Bolivia, spearheaded uprisings against Spanish conquest of Charcas. She grew up in an agrarian atmosphere and sold coca and weaving. As wife of Tupac Katari, she assisted her Bolivian sister-in-law **Gregoria Apaza** in Aymara and Quechua throngs assaulting La Paz and Sorata. Because a traitor identified Bartolina to the colonial military, she suffered public rape and beating. She and her husband were hanged and dismembered for display to villagers. Gregoria met a similar fate. The International Day of the Indigenous Woman commemorates their sacrifice.

See also March 13, 1781.

ca. 1785

The first Swedish Royal Guardswoman, **Carin du Rietz (also or Karin or Catharina, October 14, 1766–July 31, 1788)** of Sommenas, Småland, succeeded at her post as security for King Gustav III, Queen Sophia Magdalena of Denmark, and their surviving son, Gustav IV. As the daughter of an army lieutenant, Carin gained a career objective requiring loyalty and trust. After two failed tries, she ran away from home, dressed in men's attire, and, in 1785, supported the royal court regiment in Stockholm two years after the death of the couple's second son, Prince Karl. Amid flirtation by men and women, Carin confessed her ploy to the king. She married court librarian and priest Erik Johan Paulin, the vicar of Kungsbacka parish. At age twenty-two, she died in childbirth six days after her husband's demise. King Gustav inspired public hatred and a conspiracy in 1791. On March 16, 1792, assassins shot and stabbed him.

October 25, 1785

A Tongva shaman and prophet, **Toypurina (1760–May 22, 1799)** of

Jachivit, Alta California, a province of New Spain, instigated an uprising against Mission San Gabriel Arcángel. She blamed the abusive Catholic hierarchy for usurping traditional hunting lands, mistreating and sexually abusing twelve hundred baptized laborers, and banning traditional mourning dances. By recruiting unconverted Gabrieliños from Jachivit, Alijivit, and Juvit, she encouraged them to arm themselves with bow and arrows against the Franciscan security guard and their modern rifles. The night raid on October 25, 1785, ended in a Spanish ambush.

Soldiers disguised as priests seized twenty-one Indians, many of whom were lashed in public. After her trial for sorcery on January 3, 1786, at the San Diego presidio, Toypurina served three years in jail in chains and submitted to baptism in March 1787. The court exiled her to Mission San Carlos Borromeo up the coast at Carmel. She died on May 22, 1799, at Mission San Juan Bautista. Her deeds survive on a mural in East Los Angeles, two archways, a stone prayer mound and bust, legends, biography, video, and the dramatic stage at San Gabriel Mission.

December 1785

Famed southeast Asian tricksters during the Burmese-Siamese War of 1785–1786, **Thao Thepsatri (also Khun Ying Chan or Lady Jan, 1735–1792)** and **Thao Sriunthorn (also Khun Ying Muk or Lady Mook, 1738–?)**, Malaysian-Thai sister heroes from Thalang on the island of Phuket, devised a ruse to make the city appear well defended. By dressing women in military garb, arming them with wood swords, and posting them in the walls, in December 1785, they convinced Burmese invaders that their intended invasion would fail. A five-week siege ended in the enemy's retreat from potassium nitrate explosions on March 13, 1786. The sisters received the honorific *thao* (lady) and appeared on an elegant monument, annual festival events, and the state seal.

October 5, 1789

Because of the high price of bread, three months after Paris chocolatier **Pauline Léon (September 28, 1768–October 4, 1838)** wielded her own pike at the storming of the Bastille on July 14, 1789, **Louise-Renée Leduc (?–1793)**, a Paris fruitseller, and **Théroigne de Méricourt (August 13, 1762–June 8, 1817)** of Marcourt, Belgium, marshaled female shoppers in Paris to form the Women's March on Versailles. Forming ranks in the rain with revolutionary reformers and agitated workers, on October 5, 1789, along the six-hour route, the women roused sixty thousand into a snarling mob bent on assaulting the Versailles palace and assassinating Marie Antoinette, the frivolous Bourbon queen. Over twenty-four hours, *Les Dames de la Halle* (the Market Women) armed with muskets, scythes, and pikes and cannon liberated from city hall battled guards and inveighed against King Louis XVI to return to the Tuileries Palace in Paris with the queen and their daughters Marie Thérèse and Sophie and sons Louis Joseph and Louis XVII.

Mediation failed to satisfy the protesters. In an audience with King Louis, six female rebels insisted on a reduction of power amid the nobility and an end to regimentation and food shortages for the lower class. The shooting death of one marcher began a rumble of battery, killing, bayoneting, and beheading of bodyguards and the defection of the king's national guard to the marchers' side. Anti-Bourbon advocates dubbed the women "Mothers of the Nation."

Louise's arrest preceded three years' confinement at the Conciergerie prison. Théroigne, dressed in man's riding habit with a black plume, carried her revolutionary ideals to Belgium and remained in Austria's Kufstein stronghold until January 1792. She advocated for female rights to guns and to enlistment in a women's battalion that rioted on August 10, 1792, in the Faubourg Saint-Antoine. Nicknamed "Reine Audu, Queen of Les Halles," Louise and fellow rebel **Claire Lacombe (August 4, 1765–May 2, 1826)** from Pamiers north of the Pyrenees persisted in mob ferocity at the Tuileries Palace, where Louise engaged the Swiss guards in hand-to-hand combat. Despite a shot to the arm, Claire refused to abandon the fight. She and Pauline violently winnowed out monarchists. Pauline served a three-month prison sentence in April 1794 in Luxembourg. Both Louise and Théroigne succumbed to trauma and mental illness. Accounts of their deeds, clouded by libel and sexual innuendo, colored fiction, film, television, and art renderings of the French Revolution.

July 2–3, 1790

Brita Olsdotter Hagberg (1756–March 19, 1825) of Finnerödja, Sweden, enrolled in the royal army during the Russo-Swedish War of 1788–1790. Settled in Stockholm at age twenty-one, she married guardsman Anders Peter Hagberg. Because he was drafted into the army in 1788, she enrolled under the name Petter Hagberg to reunite with him. A marine veteran of the battles of Svensksund and Vyborg Bay, she crewed on the three-masted flagship *Styrbjörn* (ship's wheel). One of eight wounded at the battle of Björkösund, fought near Russia's Beryozovye Islands on July 2–3, 1790, she revealed her gender during medical examination. She earned an annual army pension of three riksdalers and dressed in her uniform for three decades while selling gingerbread cookies in Stockholm's town center. She was interred with military honors and celebrated in storytelling and verse.

July 9, 1790

Master mariner Captain **Dorothea Maria Lösch (1730–February 2, 1799)** of Stockholm rescued a floundering Swedish warship during the three-year Russo-Swedish War of 1788–1790. The loss of officers aboard the *Armida* (small armed vessel) during a Russian blockade of Vyborg Bay preceded the battle of Svensksund. On the night of July 9, 1790, she steered the *Armida* to safety from an assault by Russian naval commander Karl von Nassau's eighty-nine ships. As the Swedish flotilla gained on Russia, the enemy lost eighty ships and ten thousand casualties. She became the first female to be promoted to sea captain, a rank she shared with her husband, Mårten Johan Thesleff.

1791

To secure gun powder, express rider and storyteller **Anne Hennis Bailey (1741–November 22, 1825)**, an immigrant from Liverpool, England, made a three-day dash in 1791 one hundred miles through wilderness territory from the siege at Fort Lee, West Virginia, to Fort Union at Lewisburg. At her husband's demise on October 10, 1774, she dressed in buckskins and bore tomahawk, knife, and long rifle as protection for spying, scouting, Indian fighting, and carrying messages. Throughout the nine-year Northwest Indian War of 1786–1795, she served in the militia against the Shawnee war chief Blue Jacket until his failure at Toledo, Ohio. Her fame as "Mad Anne, the White Squaw of Kanawah" survived in a poem, elementary school, and state park watchtower.

1791

A Bulgarian mountain virago, **Sirma Voyevoda (also Vojvoda, 1776–1864)** from Tresonče, Macedonia, adopted male disguise to fight the Ottoman Turks. For twenty-two years, she aided the Christian forces rebelling against Islam in Vardar, Macedonia (modern Serbia). The tense situation in northern Macedonia involved Bulgaria, Greece, and Serbia. Turks slew Sirma at age eighty-eight. Bulgaria remained hostile after the June 1, 1913, Balkan treaty uniting Greece and Serbia in mutual de-escalation. On November 14, 1913, Greeks ended ongoing conflict with the Ottomans.

March 15, 1791

A Baltic Sea hero during the Russo-Swedish war of 1788–1790, **Anna Maria Jansdotter Engsten (January 1, 1762–1804)** accepted from Sweden's king Gustav III 50 riksdalers and the silver medal for Valour in Battle at Sea. Working as a domestic of fleet captain Gustaf Adolf Leijonancker, a war hero, on March 15, 1791, she collected sheep, forty barrels of peas, and valuables and evacuated from Vyborg Bay in a sailboat managed by five sailors. Under the Russian flotilla's barrage that killed one sheep, she remained alone in the leaky boat and steered it eight miles to Svenskund. On the day of the award, her employer received knighthood and the Royal Order of the Sword for chivalry.

August 14, 1791

At the fomenting of revolution and massacre in western Hispaniola (modern Haiti), enslaved midwife and healer **Victoria "Abdaraya Toya" Montou (1739–1805)** from Dahomey (modern Benin) joined the troops of revolutionary Jean-Jacques Dessalines, Haiti's first ruler. She gained lasting appreciation for rearing Dessalines and serving as his nanny. Armed with hoe, indigo knife, and scythe, on August 14, 1791, she commandeered fifty bondsmen and led them against island authorities. In the struggle to arrest her, one French soldier was wounded.

April 20, 1792

At the Austrian insurgency in France on April 20, 1792, **Félicité Fernig (May 17, 1770–August 4, 1841)** and her younger sister **Theophile Fernig (July 17, 1775–**

August 2, 1819) from Mortagne rode with the French national guard in male disguise. The teen cavalry soldiers, led by their father, enjoyed the conquest of thirty-six thousand soldiers from the Prussian army at Valmy on September 20 and at Jemappes in Wallonia six weeks later. Theophile gained renown for capturing a Hungarian officer. A victory a week later at Anderlecht allowed their forces to march into Brussels, Belgium, and add Walloon soldiers to their number.

The Fernigs' career soured four weeks after the guillotine execution of French King Louis XVI on January 21, 1793. The French loss to a Dutch-Hapsburg coalition at Neerwinden on March 18, 1793, cost them five thousand casualties and another thousand prisoners of war. Because of treason of General Charles Demouriez, the Fernig sisters were banished for nine years. Their volunteer service earned commemoration in history, posters, and painting and in Theophile's collected letters.

July 27, 1792

At the battle of Kiafa on Idra (modern Hydra island) on July 27, 1792, Captain **Moscho Tzavella (also Mosco, 1760–1803)** of Souli, Greece, the daughter and granddaughter of Christian guerrilla warriors, led a garrison of four hundred amazons against the Muslim Albanian army of Ali Pasha of Ioannina. While losing only seventy-four Greek combatants in a war for independence, the female Souliotes slew some two thousand enemies with sticks and stones to unseat the despotic Ottoman Turkish governor. Ali Pasha retreated to Ioannina in Epirus and ransomed one hundred fifty enslaved Greek combatants. Despite losing her son Fotos in the clash, Moscho advanced to military captain and adviser to the village. Her victory survives in painting, sculpture, history, fiction, and folk music.

November 6, 1792

After the French Revolution of May 5, 1789, Sergeant **Marie-Jeanne Schellinck (also Marie-Jeanne Shelling, July 25, 1757–September 1, 1840)** from Ghent, Belgium, survived six saber slashes at the battle of Jemappes, Hainaut. Dressed in men's clothes, at age thirty-five, she added enthusiasm to the 2nd Belgian Battalion of the French Republican Army. The clash with the Hapsburg infantry on November 6, 1792, proved the thirty-six thousand-man French Armée du Nord better armed and stronger. The Austrian surrender the next day raised confidence in the French.

On November 10, 1792, Marie received promotion to corporal and sergeant a year later. On March 3, 1797, she began fourteen months in an Austrian prison camp. At her military retirement in late 1795, she followed her husband, Lieutenant Louis-Joseph Decarmin, to the Italian campaign and remained a camp follower until January 1808, when he retired.

1793

An army commander, charioteer, and fortifier in the Punjab of northeastern India, **Bibi Sahib Kaur (1771–1801)** insulated her homeland at Patiala and, in 1793, directed Sikh soldiers against Marathi invaders to the west on the Himalayan border at Ambala. At age twenty-two, she strategized a way to retrieve her husband, local governor Jaimal Singh, from the captivity of Fateh Singh, a Sikh warrior and martyr. Her success over Marathan generals Anta Rao and Lachhman Rao in 1794 and Irish mercenary George Thomas of Haryana in 1799 repulsed land grabs on the north central frontier. She forced Thomas's retreat from Fatehgarh, the Jind keep.

March 1793

A French rebel and corsair, **Julienne David (March 21, 1773–January 28, 1843)** from Saint-Marc, Brittany, backed Bourbon royalty in March 1793 during the three-year Vendée Revolt of 1793–1796, a counter-revolutionary fostering of the French monarchy. She fled deportation by regicides, worked briefly on a farm, and, in 1796, sought a privateering license. Sailing from 1796 to 1798, on the *Jeune-Agathe* (Young Agatha) allowed her to waylay and plunder enemy ships. By headquartering at Nantes and calling herself Jacquot or Jacques David, she had access to English vessels, which she attacked with sword and rifle. From age thirty, she spent eight years in a Portsmouth prison, where she worked as a nurse.

June 13, 1793

Throughout the six-week assault by Austria, Britain, and Hanover on Valenciennes, France, sailor **Mary Anne Talbot (February 2, 1778–February 4, 1808)** of London posed as John Taylor and entered warfare as a drummer. After sailing the Mosquito coast to Port-au-Prince, Hispaniola (modern Haiti), she suffered musket wounds to torso and rib and a sword swipe on her lower back. She survived press-ganging on the French warship *Queen Charlotte* on June 13, 1793, and delighted in transfer as powder monkey on the East Indiaman H.M.S. *Brunswick* to fight the seventy-four-gun French schooner *Vengeur* (Avenger).

After only six cannon rounds, Mary Anne's demasted the French fluyt (cargo vessel) *Achille*. A more debilitating leg wound from enemy grapeshot off Ushant Island on June 1, 1794, required her treatment at Gosport's Haslar Hospital. On the sloop *Vesuvius* as midshipman, she viewed Gibraltar and the Mediterranean. Upon capture by the French, she spent a year and a half in Dunkirk at St. Clare Prison. A biography appeared in 1809 in the anthology *The Wonderful and Scientific Museum* as "The Life and Surprising Adventures of Mary Ann Talbot, in the Name of John Taylor."

July 1793

A French grenadier under the name "Liberté," **Rose Barreau (May 1773–January 24, 1843)** from Saint-Malens, followed her brother and husband to the Roussillon War against a Spanish-Portuguese coalition in the western Pyrenees. In July 1793, at Arnéguy, the last French redoubt, overlooking the Atlantic Ocean in the Basque town of Biriato, she ran out of ammunition during the battle that wounded her mate, François Leyrac, and killed her brother, Cyprien Barreau. She continued running through crossfire with empty musket and saber and returned to carry her husband to a hospital, a heroic rescue pictured in art.

On October 17, 1794, Rose cheered the rout in Navarre following the lopsided battle of Orbaizeta, at which the Spanish coalition lost fifty cannon and four thousand troops. The enemy suffered more disaster at the loss of eighteen thousand men in November at Black Mountain and a lethal winter epidemic killing three thousand. In September 1795, she left the infantry in her sixth month of pregnancy. Despite phlebitis and headaches obscuring sight and hearing, for thirteen years, she continued to follow François on the march with the 2nd Tarn Battalion. In Italy, Bonaparte retired her on September 30, 1805. As a wounded veteran and mother of five, she was widowed in 1840 and lived out old age at an Avignon military hospital.

Napoleonic Era,
1793–1815

An historical phenomenon in world military history, Napoleon Bonaparte advanced in the ranks to a major threat to European powers. By the end of his career at Waterloo on June 18, 1815, he had stabilized regions left ragged by the French Revolution of 1789. The fervor of warriors both for and against the upstart Corsican involved men and women in a debilitating series of conflicts. Simultaneously, an epoch of wars of independence sparked female coordination of resistance and defiance in Asia, Africa, and Latin America.

July 9, 1793

A medal-winning French career soldier and prisoner of war at Avignon, **Marie-Thérèse Figueur (also Thérèse Sansgene, January 17, 1774–January 4, 1861)** from Talmay, east of Dijon, first signed on with the Legion des Allobroges on July 9, 1793, as a cavalry member. After shifting loyalties from counter-revolutionary to republican, she suffered a rifle bullet to the chest at the recapture of Toulon on August 29, 1793, when some fifteen thousand French royalists relied on the British navy for rescue. The fifteen-week deployment introduced her to the up-and-coming artillery commander Napoleon. Marie-Thérèse adopted the fighter's powdered queue and refined her soldiery by learning to wield sword and gun. In combat against the Spanish with the 15th Dragoon Regiment in Castres north of the Pyrenees, she lost two mounts. On April 29, 1794, she dragged General Jean Nogues out of harm's way on the southern French border at the battle of Le Boulou, a debacle for the Spanish.

See also December 21, 1797; November 4, 1799.

August 26, 1793

A French royalist during the French Revolution, **Madame de Beauglie (fl. 1790s)**, intrepid wife of an officer in the Irish regiment, commanded cavalry on behalf of the crown. Five months after the guillotining of King Louis XVI, she stood against a rebel contingent retreating from the Atlantic shore. During the battle at La Vendée's capital at La Roche-sur-Yon, she bore sword, carbine, and pistol and marched with a squad of thirty cavaliers she had hired. She intended to stem a peasant revolt against the military draft and persecution of Catholics. The battlefield yielded a body count of two hundred thousand.

September 22, 1793

For the Catholic and Royal Army, **Céleste Bulkeley (1759–May 13, 1832)** and her older sister, **Jeanne de Sapinaud (August 17, 1736–May 1, 1820)** of Angers fought an uprising against the French Republic. With four more amazons, the Frenchwomen supported the peasant warriors of navy lieutenant François de Charette, who sought to restore the Bourbon monarchy. His troops won sieges at Tiffauges on September 19, Saint Fuldent on September 22, and, three weeks later, at Cholet, Tremblaye, and the Ile de Noirmourier off the Atlantic shore. In the agreement to a pact on February 17, 1795, the treaty guaranteed religious freedom. Jeanne wrote eyewitness accounts of the massacre at La Gaubretière on February 27, 1794, where German mercenaries aided the rebels.

December 1, 1793

A loyal Catholic monarchist and spy, **Françoise Deprés (December 1746–after 1815)** from Montreuil-Bellay dressed in a man's uniform to serve the Bourbon army at the thirty-hour siege of Angers. After the executions of her three brothers and sister at Nantes, she disguised herself as a beggar and scoured the country on foot and horse to gain revenge against revolutionaries. Although blind in her left eye, she excelled at soldiery, delivering messages, and gathering intelligence in Brittany, Anjou, and the Loire district from Bordeaux to Toulouse.

At the Brissac forest, on December 1, 1793, Françoise led the rebellion of two hundred peasants, for which the Republicans jailed and interrogated her. After two years of combat, she became a secret messenger endorsing the restoration of Louis XVIII. In 1817, her battlefield and prison experiences in Angers and Nantes over twenty-two years appeared in a memoir, *Détails Historiques sur Les Services de Françoise Deprés* (Historic Details of the Service of Françoise Deprés).

January 4, 1794

Spain's first female marine, on January 4, 1794, Sergeant **Ana María Antonia de Soto y Alhama (1777–December 5, 1833)** of Aguilar de la Frontera, Córdoba, began a five-year career in male disguise as Antonio de Soto. Embarking on the thirty-four-cannon frigate *Mercedes,* she fought in engagements in Catalonia and Girona, Spain, and in Cape St. Vincent, a headland in southwestern Portugal. In July 1798, she defended Cadiz from gunboats. At a medical discovery of her gender on the frigate *Matilde* on August 1, 1798, Spain's king Charles IV allowed her to remain in the navy battalion as a first sergeant with a pension of two silver *reals*. He granted permission for her to continue wearing the uniform.

July 1, 1794

Milanese crossdresser Lieutenant **Franziska Scanagatta (also Francesca Scanagatta, August 1, 1776–1865)** entered the Austrian military on July 1, 1794, as a cadet and fought among the 6th Warasdin Border Infantry. Graduation in 1797 and deployment during the French revolutionary conflicts took her to Troppau, Silesia (modern Poland),

and Klagenfurt, Styria in Austria, before she reached Moravia and Galicia. In February 1799, rheumatism prevented her from combat in the War of the Second Coalition. On the move once more, she marched with Hapsburg regiments from Serbia. At an advance in December 1799 at Barbagelata northeast of Genoa, a fast breakthrough by the French sliced the Austrian grenadiers in half.

By March 1800, Franziska gained a promotion from platoon commander to lieutenant. At the two-month Austrian siege of Genoa on April 6, 1800, she defended Barba northwest of Florence and incurred a lethal wound. Her father's intervention forced her out of the military on June 4, 1800, after six years of service. Kaiser Franz II admired her pluck and, in 1801, awarded her a pension.

August 10, 1794

A Breton fusilier and medalist, Lieutenant **Angélique Duchemin Brûlon (January 20, 1772–July 13, 1859)** of Dinan on the English Channel survived the forty-one-day bombardment of Fort Calvi, the last redoubt defending Corsica against the British. From the beginning siege on June 17, 1794, Angélique gained the nickname "Liberté the Fusilier" for battling with dirk and sword at Fort Gesco amid rampant dysentery and malaria. She mobilized sixty Corsican women to supply her regiment with ammunition and gunpowder. She served as a comrade in disguise with her husband in Napoleon's army when he plotted an invasion of Italy. The British victory in Corsica initiated a troubled era presaging civil turmoil.

A war widow impaired with a sword slash to both arms and left leg, at age twenty, Angelique insisted on avenging her husband's fall at Ajaccio, Corsica, as well as the battlefield deaths of her father and two brothers during the French Revolution of May 9, 1789. Five years later, she petitioned for admission to Les Invalides, a hospital that King Louis XIV envisioned for disabled and elderly soldiers in central Paris. Her request on the basis of deployment in seven campaigns went unanswered until 1804, when she advanced to second lieutenant. At age fifty-one, she retired. On August 15, 1851, she received from Napoleon III knighthood in the French Legion of Honor, the first to decorate a woman.

March 11, 1795

Urdu poet, court entertainer, and armament specialist **Mah Laqa Bai Chanda (also Madame Moon Cheek, April 7, 1768–August 1824)** of Hyderabad in Mughal India found favor with 'Ali Khan, the realm's second Nizam (ruler). In her palanquin (sedan chair) surrounded by one hundred security guards and kettle drummers, on March 11, 1795, she accompanied him in combat. She excelled at hawking, archery, and javelin throwing and dressed in men's clothes for participating in three wars. At age sixty-one, the Nizam capitulated to Maratha archers, cavalry, and field guns at Kharda after his fighters retreated to the fort. Mah Laqa Bai retained her influence and wrote a post-war commentary "Your heart is stained with grief." In 1798, she became the first woman to issue a verse anthology of ghazals. Her courage on the battlefront survives in art.

1797

A Chinese gymnast and martial arts expert during the Yuan Dynasty, **Wang Cong'er (1777–1797)** from Xianyang requited her husband Qi Lin's execution the previous year by battling Qing imperial troops with a sword in each hand. During the White Lotus Uprising against taxation in central China, in 1797, she allied with Commander **Wang Nangxian (1778–1798)**, mustered anti-Manchu forces at Sichuan, and armed them for guerrilla combat. At age twenty, the duo faced a mountain blockade near Yunxi, Hubei, that crushed one thousand dissidents. To avoid capture, Wang Cong'er leaped from the heights, killing herself. A similar fate awaited Wang Nangxian the next year. A movie features Wang Cong'er as consummate swordswoman.

February 22, 1797

Jemima Nicholas (also Jemima Fair or Jemima Niclas, 1750–July 16, 1832), a shoemaker from Llanrhian, Wales, captured Napoleon's soldiers who invaded Llanwnda with four ships. On February 22, 1797, she raised a pitchfork to command local women during the thwarting of twelve drunken marauders at the battle of Fishguard. To fool the men, the women wore red and black, appearing like uniformed soldiers. To secure the captives through the night, she locked them in St. Mary's Church. Three days later, the remaining twelve hundred insurgents under Lord Cawdor ceded to the women at the Royal Oak Pub. More than a quarter century later, at age seventy-four, she engaged in rioting at Fishguard, a northern Pembrokeshire town on the Atlantic Ocean. Her heroism survives in reenactments, a plaque and tapestry, and children's literature.

August 29, 1797

At a female uprising at Tranent, Scotland, **Jackie Crookston (also Jackie Crookstone or Joan, June 12, 1768–August 29, 1797)** of Old Kirk assembled several thousand women and children to protest the Scottish Militia Act of 1797, an oppressive draft law. The army relied on schoolmaster Robert Paisley for a list of male youths eligible for service. The organizer of draft resisters, Jackie beat her drum on August 29, 1797, and shouted anti-militia slogans. While Paisley hid from the ruckus, Jackie instigated the stoning and plunder of his house. The insurrectionists gathered stones, broken bottles, pokers, and sticks for weapons, destroyed school record books listing names and ages, and threatened horses and riders armed with swords and carbines.

The mob continued agitating at Meadowmill and Seton. Dragoons arrested thirty-six rioters, including servant **Elly Duncan (fl. 1797)**, for incarceration at the Haddington Tollbooth and rode down nineteen-year-old **Isabel Roger (?–August 29, 1797)**, shooting her dead. Jackie and ten males died in the rush of soldiers emerging from John Glen's pub. Her body lay in a field for three weeks before its discovery. A sculpture in the city square captured her vigor and intense anger.

December 21, 1797

Veteran French cavalry trooper **Marie-Thérèse Figueur**, nicknamed Sangène (unrestrained), fought alongside the 8th Hussars on December 21, 1797, at the capture of Berne during Napoleon's Swiss invasion. A massed army of eleven mounted regiments and thirty-one infantry units revolutionized the Swiss state into the Helvetic Republic, a Napoleonic government. Re-enlistment in the 15th Dragoons deployed Marie in Egypt and Milan and Lodi, Italy, before her return to Marseilles on February 19, 1799.

See also July 9, 1793; November 4, 1799.

March 3, 1798

Because of Napoleon's insurgency in Switzerland, on March 3, 1798, orator and recruiter **Martha Glar (1733–March 3, 1798)** rallied two hundred and sixty parish women to halt the French invasion of Berne. She included among the village amazons two daughters and three granddaughters, the youngest being ten years old. All armed themselves with pitchforks, scythes, and axes against a backlash to the French Revolution of 1789. Taking defensible positions among six thousand four hundred Swiss soldiers, the female regiment faced the eighteen thousand troops of General Henry Schauenbourg, commander of Helvetia's militia. The women's unit lost one hundred eighty martyrs at the battle of Frauenbrun, Bavaria, some eight miles north of the village and southwest of Berne. At the debacle, the dead numbered Martha and her five family members as well as father, husband, brother, and two sons.

June 12, 1798

A nationalist swordswoman and standard bearer, **Betsy Gray (c. 1778–June 12, 1798)** of Gransha, Ireland, died valiantly on June 12, 1798, alongside her lover Willie Boal and her brother George at the battle of Ballynahinch on the west central coast. At issue, persecution of non-conformers to Anglicanism forced the rebels out of schools, polling places, and public office. She entered battle armed and riding a white pony. An overnight disaster for the Irish Presbyterian rebels, the massacre by British soldiers armed with cannon and muskets killed four hundred Irish, ten times more than British losses. On July 13, 1798, the victorious 22nd Dragoons torched sixty-three cottages and amputated Betsy's hand and head.

August 1, 1798

English powder monkeys **Mary Ann Riley, Sarah Bates, Ann Taylor, Elizabeth Moore, Mary French,** and **Anne Hopping** fought Napoleon's invasion of Egypt at the three-day battle of the Nile. As marines in a fifteen-ship armada led by Horatio Nelson, the six women sailed aboard the battleship HMS. *Goliath*. The crew joined a campaign on August 1, 1798, to halt the French on a juggernaut Mediterranean campaign. The fleet journeyed from the Tagus River in Spain and Malta to Aboukir Bay, an Ottoman possession in the Nile delta near Alexandria. During the battle, one woman gave birth to a son, but is not identified by historians. Nelson's victory impressed the Ottoman Turks. It cost the French nine thousand five hundred casualties and convinced

European powers to ally against Napoleon. The female marines were eligible for the Naval General Service Medal, which Queen Victoria denied them.

September 9, 1798

When Napoleon's troops oppressed the citizens east of Berne, Swiss virago, **Veronika Gut (1757–1829)** aided the Nidwalden Canton against French tyranny. In central Switzerland, on September 9, 1798, she convened Catholic peasants in her home. For the next six years, she spearheaded a revolt in which four hundred Swiss died, some burned to death by arsonists. Until 1815, she incurred arrests and court interrogation. On the family's flight from the French, four of Veronika's daughters drowned in the Engelberger River. Her son died in combat. Re-enactor Karin Wirthner portrays Veronika's revolt.

July 7, 1799

Sikh commander **Sada Kaur (1762–1832)** from the Punjab (modern Pakistan) established control of Lahore on July 7, 1799, and built the Kanhaiya confederacy, a mainstay of the Sikh Empire. A political adviser and military leader of twenty-five thousand cavalrymen of mixed ethnic background, she replaced her husband Gurbaksh Singh Kanhaiya, who died in February 1785 at the battle of Batala. She joined her son-in-law, Ranjit Singh, in attacks on Attock, Multan, and Hazara. The alliance succeeded at Amritsar's brick and lime fortification in 1798, the Lahore citadel on July 7, 1799, Jammu's sandstone Bahu defense in 1800, and Muslim-controlled Kasur in 1807, the sixth year of the Sikh Empire.

Sada Kaur backed Ranjit and the Khalsa cavalry in targeting Shah Zaman of Kabul, the Afghan leader of twelve thousand soldiers who repeatedly ravaged the Punjab. Throughout guerrilla warfare, she restricted the Sikh military from havoc, the free pillaging of Lahore and rape of its women. Because Ranjit split with her over making peace with the British and favored the children of his second wife over her grandchildren, she lived a restricted existence at her Kanhaiya estates, including Batala, Mukerian, Gurdaspur, Dasuya, Kangra, and the Atalgarh citadel.

During the spat between Sada Kaur and Ranjit, she plotted to undermine his power and elevate her daughter's sons, Sher Singh and Tara Singh. In October 1820, Ranjit forced her to deed her holdings to him. He imprisoned her at Amritsar for attempting to relocate to British territory. Among her lost properties were the Nanga redoubt in the highlands and her headquarters at Atalgarh, which her slave girls defended for three weeks. Sada Kaur's military expertise and role as Ranjit's ladder to success survive in fiction and film.

September 10, 1799

During the French Revolutionary Wars in Italy, Switzerland, the Rhineland, and Holland, Prussian virago **Antoinette Berg (ca. 1783–after 1814)** dressed in men's clothes, engaged with the English army as a male, and, on September 10, 1799, deployed to Holland to battle Napoleon's army. The Army of the Danube heightened tension on March 1 by crossing the Rhine at Basel, traversing the Black Forest, and pressing on to Lake Constance in northern Italy. The Anglo-Russian onslaught of thirty thousand soldiers and twelve hundred cavalry into Holland resulted in the battle of Krabbendam and, nine days later, bloody combat at Bergen, Norway.

For perhaps good reason, Antoinette changed branches of service and became a sailor in the British navy. Her unit sailed to the West Indies, out of the way of Napoleon's conquests. In the celebration of his downfall in April 1814, she met Tsar Alexander I of Russia and King Frederick William III of Prussia. A Dutch biography outlines her adventures.

November 4, 1799

French dragoon **Marie-Thérèse Figueur** survived a snowy Alpine campaign, four saber slashes at Savigliano, and, on November 4, 1799, capture at the Stura River during the two-day battle of Genola, Italy, against Austrian Hapsburgs. Among the seven thousand six hundred French casualties, she escaped an eighteen-week typhus epidemic. In 1800, she received an honorable discharge, a 200-franc pension, and nomination for a Legion d'Honneur. Her rehabilitation required two years of treatment. She composed details of twenty-two years in the army in *Les Campagnes de Mademoiselle Thérèse Figueur* (The Campaign of Miss Therese Figueur), including assignment to Napoleon's imperial guard and deployment in Paris preceding the emperor's abdication and exile.

See also July 9, 1793; December 21, 1797.

February 1802

A Vietnamese commander and elephant trainer, **Bùi Thị Xuân (?–1802)** from Binh Khe east of Hanoi fought a three-year peasant rebellion against Emperor Nguyễn Ánh, the nation's corrupt elitist. Skilled at martial arts, she wed a fellow soldier, Trần Quang Diệu, one of the seven tiger generals. She relied on him and Chinese pirates in conflicts of the Tây Sơn Rebellion and provided the military with elephants trained for battle. In Quang Bin Province of central Vietnam, she engaged the imperial army, naval artillery, and French and Chinese mercenaries. Her five thousand soldiers excelled at guerrilla warfare, hit and run, ambush, and night raids, the elements of Tây Sơn psychological strategies.

Backed by twelve hundred vessels in a Saigon River fleet, the emperor based operations from the new bulwark at Saigon, ruptured Quy Nhon's coastal barrier in June 1801, and took Hanoi. Bùi Thị's army ceded to the enemy, which seized her and Tran to the north at Nghệ An, where they escorted Cảnh Thịnh, their eighteen-year-old king. The enemy recaptured the capital of Hue and consolidated Vietnam. In February 1802, Nguyễn executioners decapitated Tran, slowly sliced King Cảnh Thịnh, and forced Bùi Thị and her daughter to be trampled by elephants and their arms, lungs, liver, and heart eaten by Nguyễn soldiers. Her accomplishments survive in school and street names, storytelling, and novels.

March 4, 1802

Mulatto defender and medic **Marie-Jeanne Lamartiniére (fl. 1802)** of Hispaniola (modern Haiti) wore men's clothing during her fight on March 4, 1802, at the battle of Crête-à-Pierrot. Outside Saint-Marc in the Artibonite River valley, she wielded pistol, knife, and sword and backed the troops of her revolutionary husband, Louis Daure Lamartiniere, against the twelve thousand forces of General Charles Leclerc, one of Napoleon's officers. After her husband's beheading on November 2, 1802, island rebels yielded on the twentieth day of the siege after they used up munitions, water, and rations. The rebels united with native leader Jean-Jacques Dessalines's army in the Cahos mountains and witnessed the declaration on January 1, 1804, of the independent island nation.

May 21, 1802

An armed resister of Napoleon's re-enslavement of Guadeloupe, **La Mulâtresse Solitude (also Bayangumay, 1772–November 29, 1802)** fought the French on May 21, 1802, at the battle of Galion River. The child of a sailor's rape at sea of African abductee Rosalie, the legendary "Solitude, the mixed-blood woman" joined the maroons who revolted outside Point-à-Pitre. While fleeing from Fort Saint-Charles to Basse-Terre, she was wounded in an explosion and fell to captors in the fourth month of pregnancy. A judgment allowed a stay of her hanging until she gave birth on November 29, 1802. Her bravery inspired histories, fiction, stage musical, a road, a Paris garden, a UNESCO honorarium, and full-bellied statuary in Guadeloupe and France.

October 5, 1802

A free woman of color and rebel soldier, Lieutenant **Suzanne "Sanité" Bélair (1781–October 5, 1802)** of Verrettes, Hispaniola (modern Haiti), died a martyr for her service as an officer in the Indigenous Army of black natives. Dubbed the "Haitian tigress," she served in L'Artibonite district under Toussaint Louverture, a former slave demanding island liberation from French bondage. After Napoleon Bonaparte dispatched General Charles Leclerc and thirty thousand men to quell a budding revolution in 1801, yellow fever and a crushing loss reduced the attacking French to seven thousand or twenty-four percent the original combat strength.

In the scramble, Suzanne and her husband, General Charles Bélair, were captured at Corail-Mirrault, where she hid her belongings, money, and weapons. Although anticipating mercy from Leclerc, on October 5, 1802, both Bélairs were executed by firing squad behind the Cap graveyard. Suzanne refused a blindfold and used her last breath to acclaim freedom for slaves. Haitians honored her as a national heroine at the bicentennial in 2004 with her portrait on a banknote.

1803

To relieve the town of Guamote and central Ecuador of Spanish occupation, native rebel **Lorenza Avemanay Tacuri (1747–1803)** led an uprising in

Chimborazo Province during her country's twenty-year Independence Wars. Her extreme style of protest in the Andean highlands in 1803 earned the title "El Demonio Indigena" (The Native Demon). Her actions against major landholders and authorities duplicated the fervor of Ecuadorian sisters **Baltazara and Manuela Chuiza (fl. 1770s)**, who had spearheaded an Amerindian rebellion in 1778 at Guano to the north. After Lorenza, Manuela, and Baltazara suffered torture and military hanging, a biography and film honored Lorenza. A Quito bus station commemorates the Chuiza sisters.

September 23, 1803

A self-determined ruler and fighter, **Begum Samru (also Sumru, 1753–January 27, 1836)** of Kashmir, favored the Indian army in a campaign against the British East India Company. At age fifteen, she, like the Byzantine Empress Isadora, gave up a dancing career in Agra and Delhi. She married an admirer, Walter Reinhardt Sombre, an Austrian soldier of fortune, and began learning battle tactics by accompanying him on missions. She welcomed northern herders into her four thousand stout mercenaries impressively clad in red uniforms. On the march from a Sikh siege on the Red Fort in Panipat on March 11, 1783, she rescued Delhi from insurgency by tricking Sikh upstart Ghulam Qadir with false friendship. Four years later, she intervened for Mughal emperor Shah Alam against rebel Najaf Quil Khan and his thirty thousand soldiers at Gokalgarh by contributing one hundred troops and artillery. To protect the shah, she personally supervised the big guns and brokered a truce.

At the battle of Assaye in west central India on September 23, 1803, Begum Samru led her army against Arthur Wellesley, the Duke of Wellington, who crushed the indigenous Maratha force with his seventeen cannon, cavalry, and two regiments of foot soldiers. She ceded to the enemy at the Aligarh stronghold, which French allies had ringed with sword blades and poisoned wood barricades. Her ability to withstand the heat of combat resulted in rumors of sorcery with a magic veil. In reality, her strength lay in military maintenance of six infantry battalions, cavalry, bodyguards, and forty cannon. In the television series *Beecham House*, actor Lara Dutta portrayed the begum.

August 27, 1805

To strengthen the Don Cossacks while Napoleon deployed the Grande Armée at the Rhine River, **Tatiana Markina (1785–fl. 1805)** dressed in male uniform and, on August 27, 1805, served in the imperial light troops headquartered at Novocherkassk in Rostov, Russia. By November 11, 1805, the Russians and Austrians, headed by the Don Cossack infantry and horse artillery, faced eight thousand French troops, but lost to Napoleon on December 2, 1805, at Austerlitz, Moravia. Under the alias Krutochkin, Tatiana fought among four hundred twenty-five thousand men until her gender was disclosed. Forced out of the military, she achieved a pension.

October 21, 1805

At the rise of Napoleon's reputation for conquest, **Jane Townsend (also Jane Townshend, fl. 1800s)** joined the British Royal Marines aboard the three-masted HMS *Defiance* in pursuit of the French fleet. The ship, fresh from the inconclusive battle of Finisterre off Galicia, Spain, on July 22, 1805, continued to Cadiz. At Cape Trafalgar, the western tip of Spain north of Gibraltar, the thirty-five thousand British troops split the twenty-thousand Franco-Spanish armada, with Admiral Horatio Nelson's flagship HMS *Victory* leading the way. His blast at the eighty-gun *Bucentaure*, named for a mythical ox-man, hit it broadside, retiring it permanently from service.

Jane crouched in the fiery battle line before the French shot and killed Nelson from a musket ball passing from left to right through both shoulders, lung, and spine. Of her shipmates, one died and seven were wounded. A Scots veteran of the battle of Copenhagen, **Mary Buick Watson (also Mary Bewick Watson, 1777–1854)** of Dundee, a press-ganged sailor aboard the sixty-four-gun frigate HMS *Ardent* in 1799, removed Nelson's remains for embalming. The *Defiance* incurred multiple damages to all masts. Jane petitioned for a service medal, but was rejected.

April 1806

Australian felons **Charlotte Badger (July 31, 1778–1816)** of Bromsgrove near Worcester, England, and **Catherine "Kitty" Hagerty (?–April 1807)** of London shared the honors of being the island nation's first pirates. Charged with housebreaking, stealing several guineas, and picking pockets, they survived transportation via the three-deck East Indiaman *Earl Cornwallis* to the Parramatta Female Factory, a New South Wales penal colony at Fort Jackson. Aboard the chartered supply two-masted brigantine *Venus* in April 1806, they faced two years as servants to a settler. They armed themselves with pistols and swords and promoted mutiny among three crewmen. Charlotte assaulted the captain before marooning him.

From Hobart, Van Diemen's Land (modern Tasmania), on June 16, the female pirates escaped a sentence to domesticity. They piloted the stolen schooner from the River Tamar over the Tasman Sea to Bay of Islands, New Zealand, where they kidnapped native women. Indigenous Maoris seized the thirty-six-gun frigate H.M.S. *Venus* and stripped scrap metal before burning the wood hull and masts. The male mutineers were hanged in England for capital crimes.

In 1800, Catherine gained a pardon and repatriated to England, where she died of illness. Charlotte and her infant remained with a chief at the Bay of Islands or possibly boarded the Boston whaler and convict transport *Indispensable* on Norfolk Island before returning on July 13, 1807, to Sidney on the *Porpoise*. After marrying a year later, she returned to pilfering in 1843 by stealing a blanket.

July 23, 1806

María Loreto Sánchez Peón (January 3, 1777–August 10, 1870) of Salta and **Juana Gabriela Moro (May 26, 1785–December 17, 1874)** from San Salvador de Jujuy networked with Argentine children, servants, and revolutionaries as spies, saboteurs, and reconnaissance agents. After a British expedition crossed the Río de la Plata with seventeen hundred insurgents, they invaded Buenos Aires on July 23, 1806. The coterie observed troop deployment, propagandized monarchist officers to change sides, and conducted domestic espionage through social invitations, dances, and pastry sales to enemy bivouacs. At morning roll call, Maria kept a count of active duty soldiers and absent or deserting men by dropping corn kernels in separate bags.

The collaborators delivered parts, harbored fallen patriots, and communicated key data by leaving messages in hollow trees along the Arias River. Maria conveyed communiques on horseback to Jujay and Oran by stitching them into her skirt hem. The enemy seized her and jailed her at the Cabildo (city hall). Juana, who concealed her identity by dressing as a tourist, Inca, or gaucho, was arrested and laden with chains. Her bravery provided lyrics for a folk song.

The Salta-based agents relied on neighbors and a sisterhood of various backgrounds: **María Petrona Arias (1801–?)**, an experienced rider, and the grandmotherly **Juana Manuela Torino (1755–after 1824)**. Useful skills derived from conspirator **Celedonia Pachecho de Melo (fl. 1820s–1820s)** of Córdoba, uniform seamstress and "mother of the poor" **Magdalena Dámasa Güemes (December 11, 1787–June 7, 1866)**, flag designer **Martina Silva (November 3, 1790–March 19, 1874)**, and laundress **María Andrea Zenarruza (February 21, 1795–January 18, 1877)**. One collaborator, **Gertrudis Medeiros (April 9, 1780–after 1818)**, escaped prison to return to the revolt.

August 10, 1806

An Hispano-Creole emancipator of colonial Argentina, Lieutenant **Manuela Pedraza (Manuela la Tucumanesa, 1780–March 17, 1850)** from Tucuman, Río de la Plata, dressed as a man and partnered with her husband, Jose de Miranda, in aiding French troops on August 10, 1806, during the three-day retaking of the Castle of San Miguel (modern Casa Rosada), a Spanish fort in coastal Buenos Aires. On August 11, she bayonetted the invader who killed Jose and shot a British attacker with Jose's gun. She offered the captured British musket as a combat token to Commander Santiago de Liniers, who promoted "La Tucumanesa" to lieutenant. Spanish king Carlos IV granted her a military salary. Manuela's name graces a street, school, and citation to female activists.

October 14, 1806

After mediating an accord with Tsar Alexander I of Russia and Emperor Francis I of Austria, **Louise of Prussia (also Louise of Mecklenburg-Strelitz, March 10, 1776–July 19, 1810)** felt confident that her husband, King Frederick William III of Prussia, could thrash Napoleon's army. Five months after the death of their eighth child, two-year-old Prince Ferdinand, from diphtheria, the royal couple followed their troops from Charlottenburg to Thuringia. Louise wore a dragoon's uniform. On the front line, they rode side by side to observe the carnage of the battle of Jena and Auerstedt. Fought southwest of Berlin on October 14, 1806, the matchup proved the Grande Armée of France invincible against Prussia, which, within three hours, lost a total of forty-two thousand men, including the elderly General Charles Brunswick.

Louise and her husband ran from the killing field and reunited the family at Schwedt Castle on the Oder River. She sought a haven for her children at Stettin, then relocated them to Kustrin, Graudenz, and Königsberg, but could not outrun Napoleon's campaigns nor his calumnies against her virtue. After a stay at the baths of Pyrmont, she attempted to mediate favorable terms by wheedling them from Napoleon, who declined. Prussians revered her fortitude. Her example survives in films and sculpture.

February 7, 1807

Officers during the Napoleonic Wars, Captain **Aleksandra Tikhomirova (1770s–February 7, 1807)** and her comrade, **Nadezhda Durova (1783–1866)**, prospered in the Russo-Polish cavalry. Taking the identity and position of her brother, Aleksandra advanced to company commander as a male and died in the Prussian campaign of February 7, 1807. After enrolling in the Cossacks in 1806 under the name Sokolov to escape female manners and patriarchal control, Nadezhda mastered horse, lance, saber, and rifle. At St. Petersburg, she received commendation from Russian Tsar Alexander I for attention to sentry duty, night marching, foraging, and charging into French fire.

In December 1807, the tsar renamed Nadezhda for himself, Aleksandr Aleksandrov, and assigned her the rank of cornet (second lieutenant) in the Mariupol Hussars. For bravery in the rear guard at the battle of Borodino, Russia, in early 1812, she became the only female to earn the Cross of St. George. West of Moscow on September 7, 1814, she suffered a wound and, two years later, retired with the rank of captain. In *The Cavalry Maiden,* one of Russia's first autobiographies, she described female freedoms of a ten-year career on horseback.

November 16, 1807

The outlaw chief and tactician of the world's most successful pirate operation, **Zheng Yi Sao (also Ching Shih, 1775–1844)** of Guangdong, China, ruled sea raids on the South China Sea from Annam to the Yalu Sea. Her marriage to privateer Zheng Yi in 1801 ended labor in a marine bordello in Canton and introduced her to sea gang recruitment. Without a husband after November 16, 1807, she mothered two young sons while commanding the Guangdong syndicate with the aid of stepson Zhang Bao. Her eighteen hundred junks and eighty thousand sailors seized control of the river complex at Macao by destroying two navies, setting fires, and demanding protection money from merchantmen departing the Canton River Delta. While managing extensive blackmail, enslavement, ransom, and extortion, she controlled crews through stringent codes, which demanded loyalty and forbade pilfering loot and rape on pain of flogging to death.

After two years of plundering coastal wealth, attacking sea garrisons, and building an armed armada, in August 1809, Zheng Yi Sao recovered from a major setback at Dawanshan Island near Guangdong by ravaging ports in a coordinated onslaught. Until blockaded north of Lantau Island in late November 1809, she armed herself with a sword and competed with Chinese, English, and Portuguese shippers of precious metals, silk, spice, porcelain, cotton, and tea. She surrendered on April 20, 1810, with full pardon for her men. She bore a third child and opened a casino, which she operated until her death. Her empire colored fiction, graphic novels, film, television, and podcasts.

November 19, 1807

Imperial French soldier Lieutenant **Virginie Ghesquière (also Chesquière, 1768–1867)** from Delemont, Switzerland, took part in Napoleon's uncontested 1807 invasion of Portugal. Under General Jean-Andoche Junot, commander of the insurgency on November 19, 1807, the outbreak of war at Salamanca began with the crossing of the Bidasoa River in preparation for the Franco-Spanish occupation of Lisbon. Over eleven days, more than fifty thousand allied infantry and dragoons marched two hundred miles from Alcântara into the Tagus valley. At Lisbon, the fifteen hundred French troops met no challenge. They equipped the cavalry with horses stolen from local farms.

After seven years of service, Virginie received the Saint Helena Medal and a Legion of Honor.

May 2, 1808

At a two-day siege of Madrid, French gunners killed two female Spanish combatants: a married mother of a son and daughter, **Clara del Rey Calvo (August 11, 1765–May 2, 1808)**, and a seventeen-year-old embroiderer, **Manuela Malasaña Oñoro (March 10, 1791–May 2, 1808)**. Before the royal palace, Clara and her husband, street fighter Manuel Gonzalez Blanco, died while protesting Napoleon's occupation by grenadiers on May 2, 1808. Hundreds of rebels wielded kitchen cutlery, sewing scissors, and craft tools to aid artillery and died in the spontaneous uprising. Manuela ferried munitions and gunpowder to her father, who discharged his rifle from a San Andres Street balcony. Because the French executed her for wearing scissors tied to a string around her waist, she became a martyr to the laboring class resistance.

June 6, 1808

During the Peninsular War at the battle of Valdepeñas, **Juana Galán (1787–1812)** called local Spanish women to fight Napoleon's horsemen galloping through the streets. A Castilian tavern worker in south central Spain, she believed female peasants capable of stopping the French army's advance in Iberia. When her battalion wielded cook pots and poured boiling oil and water on aggressors on June 6, 1808, the French torched houses, then abandoned the la Mancha plain. A portrait and statue of the hero pictured "la Galana (the Gallant Woman)" with a long wood stick.

June 15, 1808

As a combatant in the Napoleonic Wars, Barcelona native **Agustina Raimunda of Aragon (March 4, 1786–May 29, 1857)**, the Maid of Zaragoza, learned artillery management from her husband, Corporal Juan Rosa Vilaseca. She was delivering water and apples to cannoneers defending the Carmen gate of Zaragoza, Spain, on June 15, 1808, when the gunners fell under an assault by the French Grande Armée on the city ramparts. Her intervention in loading and firing artillery left untended by a cannoneer's death repulsed a French advance. She shared fame with the Countess of Bureta, **María de la Consolación Azlor y Villavicencio (May 12, 1773–December 23, 1814)** from Girona, Spain, who rallied female peasants to ward off the French Imperial Army. She included in the battalion **Benita Portales, Juliana Larena, María Rafols, Josefa de Azlor,** and **Josefa Amar y Borbón**.

Beset by warriors, the women remained in the city and formed a corps of amazons to relay ammunition and food to Spanish soldiers. María de la Consolación welcomed stretcher bearers to the palace and defended the wounded with her rifle. The corps's valor in supplying food and manufacturing cartridges aroused courage in reinforcements and served the Santa Bàrbara Company in Girona as a model of female warcraft. At the second siege, citizens surrendered on February 21, 1809, when María de la Consolación took her family to safety in Cadiz. She received from King Fernando VII the citations of a patriot hero.

One of the corps, **Manuela Sancho y Bonafonte (June 16, 1783–April 7, 1863)** of Plenas chose the convent of San José as her defense post, for which she received the Shield of Distinction and a pension. Two comrades from Zaragoza, **Casta Álvarez Barceló (1776–April 26, 1846)** and **María Agustín Linares (April 13, 1784–November 22, 1831)** focused on repelling the Polish Uhlans mercenary cavalry by guarding the Carmen Gate with rifle and bayonet. For the wounding of her neck and paralyzed left arm, Maria Augustin received a disability pension and Shield of Distinction. A third local gatekeeper, **María Lostal (?–1810)**, retrieved holy relics from the Carmelite College and secured them at the Convalescent Hospital.

May 19, 1809

A defector during the Austro-Polish War, **Joanna Żubr (May 24, 1770–January 1, 1852)** from Volhynia, Poland, on the Western Bug River, earned the Virtuti Militari (Military Strengths) Medal for outstanding infantry performance on May 19, 1809, at the battle of Zamość. Because of multiple rebuffs of the Austrian-Bavarian coalition, on October 14, 1809, the treaty of Schönbrunn cost Austria sizable losses of territory, the cities of Kraków and Poznań, and nearly two million citizens, who populated the Duchy of Warsaw. A decorated female warrior, Joanna continued exemplary service as a sergeant in Poland's 17th Infantry throughout combat against Prussia. During Napoleon's disastrous winter retreat from Moscow, her deployment to Russia in 1812 left her in hazardous territory. By mid-1813, she slogged her way to Saxony, reunited with husband Michal, and continued the Central European fight for another year.

May 25, 1809

A Bolivian creole rebel against colonialism, General **Juana Azurduy de Padilla (July 12, 1780–May 25, 1862)** of Chuquisaca (modern Sucre) joined the anti-Spanish revolution of northern Peru. Left motherless at age seven, she idolized Joan of Arc and thrived under her father's training in riding and shooting. Among native Americans, she worked the land and spoke Quechua and Aymara. With her American husband, Manuel Ascencio Padilla, on May 25, 1809, she organized *las Amazonas,* a corps of twenty-five horsewomen, and commanded *los Leales,* a Buenos Aires squad of loyalists that saw frequent action. Miguel rescued her from enemy capture in 1811 after the battle of Huaqui on the Desaguadero River, but lost their land to royalist confiscation.

Juana excelled at drafting Indians and women to the patriot cause, for which poorly equipped natives fought with javelins and slingshots. She wielded a sword at the defense of Pintatora, La Laguna (modern Padilla), Pomabamba, and Tarabuco, a vengeful ambush of Spaniards by cannibals on March 12, 1816. For her daring, she rose to lieutenant colonel in August 1816. Grasping a flag from an enemy colonel, she directed troops to invade Cerro de la Plata. Her two sons and two older daughters succumbed to malaria. At her husband's demise from a saber wound and beheading at the Viloma conflict on September 14, 1816, the widow was wounded before giving birth to a fifth child on the battlefield. She warded off royalist assaults from Chacabuco in February 1817, giving Chile a boost toward liberty.

After commanding six thousand soldiers in 1818 in Argentina, Juana relied on a military pension for sustenance. Because the government revoked her pay, she reared her two-year-old daughter Luisa in want. Unrecognized as a military hero, she died in Salta, Argentina, at age eighty-one and was interred with the poor. She bore two medals and the posthumous rank of general in the Argentine military. Her likeness appears on a statue before the Peruvian president's office in the Plaza Colón and at Washington's Pan American complex.

June 22, 1809

At the seven-month siege of Girona, Spain, on the Pyrenees border of French, on June 22, 1809, Governor Mariano Álvarez de Castro authorized the Santa Bàrbara Company, a women's army unit of four squadrons named for the patron saint of gunners. Marked by red ribbon armbands, the two hundred recruits answered to officers **Carmen Custi (fl. 1809), Magdalena Bivern Puig (fl. 1809),** and **María Angela Bivern Puig (1787–1845).**

I. Female soldiers of the San Narciso Squad included Sergeant Rita Sala, squadron leaders Ana Detrell and María Mato, and soldiers María Gatell,

Catalina Vidal, Gerónima Amich, María Casademunt, Rosa Martorell, Teresa Comellas, María Ciurana, Franciscà Puig, Ana Turón, Rosa Masmitjà, Antònia Gelabert, Franciscà Fàbrega, Isabel Costa, Teresa Illas, Gerónima Sala, Rosa Barnat, Rita Costa, Catalina Delàs, Franciscà Xifreu, Rosa Massó, Ignacia Cantalosella, Claia Casellas, Margarita Carreras, Antònia Costa, Gertrudis Camps y Roger, and Margarita Cassà.

II. Squadron of la Concepción. Commander Raimunda de Nouvilas de Pagès; sergeants Florentina Serrats and Magdalena Molleras; squadron leaders Magdalena Teixidor and Franciscà Ball-llobera; soldiers Maria Llúcia de Puigy Quintana, Antònia Boer y Artolà, Isabel Metjà Ibanéz, María Rosa Falgueras, Serafina Vey o Vehi, Antònia Mora, Franciscà Feu, María Tomàs, Inés Alabreda, María Crus, Ana María Mallorquí, Mariana Perramón, Franciscà Cullell, María Vilanova, Rosa Rodríguez, Franciscà Marti, María Vidal, María Rosa Saló, Dominga Cortada, Franciscà Payret, María Marqués, Margarita Roig, Franciscà Eras, Valeriana Nató, Gertrudis Esclusa, Gertrudis Turón, María Vidal, Rosa Costa, Ana Butinà, and María Dalmau y Mar.

III. Squadron of Santa Dorotea. Commander María Àngela Bivern Puig; sergeants Rosa Costa and Antònia Betlem; squadron leaders Teresa Palau and Magdalena Daví; soldiers Catalina Pagès, Ana Noguera, María Tarrús, María Abras, Teresa Garriga, Rosa Planas, Paula Martínez, María Sureda, Rosa Llobera, Antònia Esparch, María Bandrell, Margarita Quintana, Tesesa Pujol, María Serra, Magdalena Serra, Atanasia Vidal, Teresa Vivetas, Antònia Camprubí, Paula Argimont, Felicísima Quintana, Catalina Junquet, María Pascual Balet, Teresa Pascual, Rosa Giralt, María Rocosa, Margarita Virosta, María Magdalena Mir, Teresa Mayol, Catalina Marimón, Rosa Forns, and Juana Bernagosi.

IV. Squadron of Santa Eulàlia. Commander Maria Custí; sergeants Rosa Mir and Vicenta Tornabells; squadron leaders Franciscà Soler and Eulàlia Vila; soldiers Teresa Ametller, Margarita Salabert, Franciscà Pacul, María Cendra, Rosa Joíre, María Riera, Rita Fàbregas, Ana Roure, María Pastells, María Àngela Tarragó, Eulàlia Colomer, Teresa Amat, María Casademunt, María Rosa Vala, Rita Banús, Càndida Jou, Franciscà Llogar, Margarita Carreras, Franciscà Barnés, Josefa Valls, Franciscà Artigas, Rosa Saura, Teresa Ferrarons, Franciscà Morell, Rosa Romani, Antònia Pelegri, Manuela Roig, María Yatón, Andrea Banderlú, María Esquero, and Rosa Bernagosi.

Alongside Hispano-Irish mercenaries, priests, and child volunteers, the women fought the French on the front line, dug victims from rubble, and ferried the injured on litters. They supplied walls and the north and south bastions with barrels of gunpowder from the cathedral cache and distributed bandages, brandy, water, and food. The enemy destroyed three hospitals and the Tower of St. Juan at the Castle of Montjuic. The city lost six thousand of its fourteen thousand citizens to combat, dysentery, and hunger; Napoleon's army incurred fifteen thousand casualties, most to bilious fever.

Of the five killed and eleven wounded, María Marfày Vila, Teresa Balaguer, Isabel Pi, Esperanza Llorens, and María Plajas suffered serious injury. Stretcher bearers Josefa Demà, Josefa Barrera, María Rosa Falgueras, Gerónima N., Franciscà Rexach, Magdalena Blanch, Maria Comadira, Ana Ferrer, and Agueda Alsina donated aprons, scarves, and skirts to cover naked patients. Commander **Lucía Jonama y Fitzgerald (?–December 1809)** composed diary entries that praised squadron leaders María Mato, Ignacia Alsina, Teresa Andry, Narcisa Bofill, and María Josefa Jonama. Lucia died beside her husband, Patrick Fitzgerald. Antònia Gelabert, Antònia Costa, Gertrudis Camps, Franciscà Cuell, María Vidal, Rosa Costa, Franciscà Barnés, and Margarita Sunyer, earned medals for distinguished service under fire. Sergeant Franciscà Artigas received compensation of six reis per day. For firing mortars and throwing cauldrons, Angela Puig received the Girona Siege Cross and a pension of 250 ducats. Historian Enrique Claudio Girball compared the dedication of the Santa Bàrbara company to biblical matrons Esther, Judith, Deborah, and the mother of the Maccabees.

August 9, 1809

A cattle rancher, lace maker, and hostess of Creole intelligentsia, **Manuela Cañizares (August 27, 1769–December 15, 1814)** of Quito, Ecuador, welcomed thirty-eight revolutionaries to her home, the House of the Tabernacle, on August 9, 1809, and contributed to the formation of an Ecuadorian junta. The next day, she rallied liberals to overthrow the president and proclaim a free Ecuador. Because royalists marked her for execution as a traitor, she went underground at Valle de los Chillos, but her influence continued to resonate in South America and Spain. Her likeness survives in a painting, histories, film, and fiction; a women's school bears her name.

August 19–20, 1809

During Finland's one-year war against three thousand Russian troops, **Elisa Bernerström Servenius (fl. 1700s–after 1810)**, became the only female commended for courage. She dressed in a male uniform to deploy in the Swedish army with her husband, Bernard Servenius, and aid the wounded. At the time of his capture among two hundred sixty-five combatants at the battles of Ratan and Sävar on August 19–20, 1809, she resupplied Swedish ordnance by seizing wagonloads of Russian ammunition. Authorities ended her charade during the march north up the Gulf of Bothnia to Piteå. In 1810, she reclaimed her marital status in Stockholm after Bernard gained release as a prisoner of war. The couple continued aiding the regiment in Stralsund, Pomerania, a Baltic port held by Napoleon.

September 13, 1809

Impromptu pirate **Margaret Croke Jordan (fl. 1800s)** of Wexford, Ireland, assisted her husband, Edward Jordan, a wife-beater and criminal, in capturing a vessel on September 13, 1809, and killing two crew members. To prevent Captain

John Stairs's seizure for debt of their fishing schooner, the *Three Daughters*, on a three-day voyage to Halifax, Nova Scotia, she aided in the murder of crew Ben Matthews and Tom Heath and the victimizing of Stairs, who bore pistols and an axe. Abetted by Irish sailor John Kelly, the couple commandeered weapons. Margaret wounded Stairs with a boat hook. After Stairs leaped into the sea off Cape Canso, the Jordans sailed toward Newfoundland to gather a crew and make for Ireland.

While fleeing seekers of a £100 reward (approx, $9,345.50) for capturing the pirates, the Jordans were arrested by the crew of the HMS *Cuttle*, a Royal Navy cutter. At trial, Margaret claimed to be an abused wife who followed Jordan's orders in snagging the vessel to protect her son and three daughters, for whom the schooner was named. She gained acquittal by confessing to striking the captain out of terror of Edward. On November 23, 1809, the court hanged Edward for piracy, robbery, and murder on Freshwater Bridge at Halifax and left his remains to rot in an iron cage at Point Pleasant.

April 19, 1810

A swordswoman, spy, and leader of Venezuelan females, **Josefa Venancia de la Encarnación Camejo (May 18, 1791–July 5, 1862)** of Paraguana plotted strategy and, on April 19, 1810, buoyed revolutionaries to engage in armed combat at New Granada. She headed an indigenous female caravan in the evacuation of Barinas across the Santo Domingo River to San Carlos, where she treated the injured. On October 18, 1811, she signed a feminist manifesto, the "Representation of the Fair Sex to the Government of Barinas." On August 7, 1819, the battle of Boyacá raged in the Andes Mountains near her Bogotá residence. The gain cost royalists eighteen hundred fifty casualties and possession of coastal colonies of Bolivia, Colombia, Ecuador, Peru, and Venezuela. In battle against Europeans, on May 3, 1821, she joined fifteen warriors in trouncing royalist chief Chepito Gonzalez at Baraived and aided in the seizure of the provincial capital of Coro. Her name survives at the National Pantheon, Falcon airport, a city square, paper currency, and a war monument at Coro.

July 6, 1810

An Afro-Amerindian-Argentine spy and guerrilla warrior in the army of independence, Captain **María Remedios Del Valle (1766–November 8, 1847)** of Buenos Aires abetted her husband and two sons in a campaign at Alto Peru. A stalwart soldier at Huaqui, Jujuy, Tucuman, Salta, Viclapugio, and Ayohuma, she advanced to captain before royalists wounded and captured her on November 14, 1813. At the Ayohuma prison, torturers afflicted her with nine days of lashing. When she fled captivity, she returned to the front to treat the wounded. At war's end, she lived alone after the deaths of her family members. Because military officials denied her pension petitions, she begged on the streets. Admirers named her a meritorious fighter and "mother of her country." November 8 celebrates her valor on "National Day of Afro-Argentines and Black Culture."

July 20, 1810

At the outbreak of the Colombian Revolution on July 20, 1810, **Juana Plazas (fl. 1810–1842)** from Sogamoso offered a tactical distraction to patriots by torching the chaparral on the Spaniard route. Other women found ways to support patriot battle lines. A valiant amazon, **Estefanía Parra (fl. 1810)** infiltrated royalists as a sutler selling food while overhearing information. Courier and smuggler **Agustina Mejía (?–September 8, 1816)** faced the rifle squad on September 8, 1816. Mestiza courier **Justina Estepa (?–January 16, 1817)** smuggled letters tied to her torso from patriot outposts at Casanare and Tenza. Royalists discovered Justina's complicity and murdered her before a fusillade of bullets at Moreno on January 16, 1817.

1811

A generous foster mother, spy, and rebel sloganeer, **María Baltazara Terán Garzon (1758–1825)** of Ibarra in northern Ecuador, funded libertarian guerrillas. After infiltrating networks at her inn in 1811, she carried messages and sheltered the insurgents who hid at Latacunga, Ecuador. A year later, Quito's president, Selva Alegre, ordered her jailed. In addition to government confiscation of her wealth, she endured scourging and exhibition in military dress on a donkey around Quito's city square.

1812

A defier of the Spanish demagogue and colonial governor Toribio Montes, **Antonia León y Velasco (1782–)** of Riobamba, Ecuador, complained of the corruption that caused his ejection from Puerto Rico. Throughout Ecuador's insurrection against colonialism in 1812, "la Bandola (the lute)" earned respect from patriots for her expertise with horses, gun, saber, and dagger. For her public conspiracy against "El Pacificador," the mayor, Rafael Maldonado, forced her confession on December 15, 1812. He confiscated her personal holdings and locked her in Santa Martha Prison for life. She suffered exile until March 8, 1813, when she repatriated to Ibarra.

Early 1812

An El Salvadoran rebel against Spanish imperialism, **María Miranda (1790–1812)** paired with her older sister, **Manuela Miranda (1780s–fl. 1812)** of San Vicente, on November 5, 1811, to defy colonialism. Demands for independence involved both women in public insurrection in the capital of San Salvador and the recruiting of revolutionaries from Santa María, La Bermuda, El Volcán, San Matias, and San Lorenzo. After capturing the parade ground and barracks in Sensuntepeque on December 20, 1811, the rioters lost to Spanish officials after reinforcements failed to arrive. The colonialists tried the sisters in the same town in north central El Salvador and transported to the convent of San Francisco.

From a cell at Fortaleza de San Fernando in Honduras, Maria and Manuela passed to domestic enslavement to a San Vicente priest. In early 1812, Maria died at age twenty-two from a one-hundred-lash scourging at San Vicente Plaza. Salvadorans proclaimed her a "Heroine of the Country" and added her name to the Monument to Liberty in San Jacinto and her portrait to five colonies banknotes.

May 27, 1812

A blind martyr to the war against colonialism, **Manuela Eras de Gandarillas (1740s–May 27, 1812)** harangued Bolivian women to halt a Spanish army headed for Cochabamba in the Andes Mountains. At La Coronilla Hill on May 27, 1812, her three hundred followers—women, children, and the elderly—aimed a variety of projectiles and kitchen knives at the enemy. The patriotic mission failed, leaving Manuela dead on a killing field. Monuments, film, and a school and rehabilitation center bear her name. May 27 became the "Day of the Bolivian Mother."

June 24, 1812

An anti–French peasant guerrilla, **Vasilisa Kozhina (1780–1840)** from Sychyovsky, Russia, mustered women and teens into a spontaneous partisan brigade during the Patriotic War of 1812 by which Napoleon threatened Russia. On June 24, 1812, he sought revenge for the murder of her husband, a village elder, and the pillage of Smolensk by locking drunken looters and foragers in her farmhouse and burning them alive. As Napoleon's forces routed from Moscow, her fighters wielded axes, bear-hunting spears, pitchforks, and scythes to waylay the twenty-seven besiegers. To one who jeered at her, she sliced him with a scythe. She earned cash, a medal, film, and portrait and the naming of villages, streets, and depots.

July 25, 1812

An Hispano-Irish conspirator and supplier, **Concepción Mariño Carige Fitzgerald (September 30, 1790–1854)** of El Valle del Espiritu Santo opened her Chacachacare ranch to Venezuelan rebels. To arm liberator Simon Bolivar's forces, she smuggled weapons with her own fleet from Jamaica and Trinidad to her island property near a West Indian leprosarium. Her home became the setting for the compilation and notarizing of the Chacachacare Act, a formal document of revolt against Spanish colonialism. A kindergarten and passenger vessel bear her name.

August 1812

In the fourth year of the Peninsular War, Spanish gunner **Marie Manuel (fl. 1810s)** was a prisoner of war of the French in Madrid in August 1812. The previous year, she had rescued her husband, French artilleryman Blaise Peuxe, from guerrillas. The fierce eight-year clash cost more than a million lives and immured thousands in crowded prisons. When Napoleon's army attacked Iberia with two hundred thirty thousand, she was captured. French jailers treated her like any uniformed soldier, man or woman. The couple entered prison in Scotland as the allies—Britain, Portugal, and Spain—overwhelmed the French invaders at Salamanca and took Madrid. At a time when Scots inmates constructed the Perth Depot and Edinburgh eased the inmate overflow by erecting Bridewell, James Neild surveyed prison conditions incurred by Marie Manuel and others in *State of the Prisons in England, Scotland and Wales*.

September 16, 1812

Passing as an Alsatian male enlisted with Napoleon's *grande armée*, **Elizabeth Hatzler (1790–January 16, 1882)** of Landau, France, witnessed the burning of Moscow on September 16, 1812. She accompanied her husband, dragoon officer George Hatzler to the Franco-Russian War and fought in major battles. By the evening of September 18, while Napoleon observed from the Kremlin, the fire had destroyed 75 percent of the city. It consumed eight hundred churches and eight thousand wood residences before rain extinguished the blaze. Snow on October 19, 1812, forced the French to abandon the ruins and seek rations and forage for horses.

Because of George's wounding at the battle of Berezina, Belarus, on November 26, 1812, Elizabeth dragged him by sled for nine weeks. After their capture by Cossack guerrilla warriors, the couple served nineteen months in jail before a prisoner exchange in 1814 restored them to their unit. George died in 1819. In 1846, Elizabeth emigrated to Philadelphia and died at age ninety-one.

November 1812

A creole rebel, spy, and guerrilla recruiter, **Policarpa Salavarrieta (January 26, 1795–November 14, 1817)** of Guaduas, Colombia, worked as a seamstress and teacher while gathering intelligence on Spanish imperialists. A revolutionary from age fifteen, she came of age when commander **María Larrain (fl. 1812)** and her armed all-woman militia and public protester **María Josefa de Lizarralde (fl. 1812–1816)** marched a female cadre in the streets on July 20, 1810. With nine-year-old brother Bibiano, Policarpa followed the libertarian precepts of their older brothers, Augustinian priests Manuel and José María de los Ángeles.

Policarpa proved a worthy spy. She also carried food and medicines to prisoners of war and passed on valuable information in hollowed-out oranges. Her fervor for intelligence gathering increased after the combat death of her brother-in-law, Domingo Garcia, in the Southern Campaign. She grieved at Bibiano's wounding in the March 28, 1811, battle of Bajo Palace at Papayan, in which the Spanish royalists lost one hundred dead.

Following the attack on Santafé on January 8, 1812, Policarpa aided female guerrilla warriors **Estefanía Neira de Eslava (?–January 18, 1820)** and **Teresa Izquierdo (fl. 1812–July 24, 1819)** in stitching uniform capes and coats. They faced prison in July 1819 for helping to outfit nationalist soldiers and helping soldiers escape northeast to Casanare. Their famous associate, **Mercedes Ábrego de Reyes (1770–October 13, 1813)**, embroidered a brigadier's uniform for liberator Simon Bolivar. All four women also participated in daily tasks—cleaning guns, distributing meals, and mending harnesses for horses.

The women's valor paralleled that of **Rosa Zaráte de la Peña (1763–July 17, 1813)**, from Quito, whose refusal to tremble at a firing squad and beheading on July 17, 1813. **María Mercedes Viteri (ca. 1787–?)** intercepted Rosa's skull to prevent its public exhibition.

On October 13, 1813, at Cúcuta, Spaniards beheaded collaborator Mercedes Ábrego in front of her two sons and flaunted the skull. The next year, **Eusebia Galviza (?–November 1816), Joaquina Aroca (?–September 5, 1816)** from Natagaima, **Rosaura Rivera (?–November 26, 1816)**, and **Agustina Peralta (?–November 1816)** joined the national military auxiliary as soldiers, for which they were executed in late 1816. **Ines Peñaranda (?–February 22, 1816)** and María Josefa de Lizarralda suffered the same demise at Salazar under the guns of vengeful royalists who lost the battle of Cachiri on February 22, 1816. Teresa died by firing squad at Sogamoso on July 24, 1819.

See also May 1816; November 10, 1817.

March 13, 1813

Disguised as a man, on March 13, 1813, **Eleonore Prochaska (March 11, 1785–October 5, 1813)** of Potsdam, Prussia, helped overrun the French coalition and push the insurgents toward Hamburg. A member of the Lützow Free Corps, nicknamed the Black Hunters, she passed as drummer August Renz before entering the infantry. From orphan to domestic servant, she freed herself from a low caste by joining the Prussian Army as drummer August Renz. In fighting with the infantry in Lower Saxony, at the battle of the Gohrde on September 16, 1813, she suffered severe wounds. She required transport southeast to a military hospital at Dannenberg, where she died at age twenty-eight. An honored contemporary, **Anna Lühring (August 3, 1796–August 25, 1866)** from Bremen followed Eleonore's example and entered the Lützow Free Corps as Eduard Kruse. In an army of twenty thousand Prussians, she survived the assault on Jülich, France, on March 7–10, 1815.

April 2, 1813

A war memorial at Lüneberg, Lower Saxony, commemorates the on-site heroism of citizen **Johanna Stegen (January 11, 1793–January 12, 1842)** by supplying Prussians with munitions to repulse Napoleon's *Grande Armée*. When ammunition ran low, on April 2, 1813, she carried more bullets in her apron to Prussian fusiliers and light infantry from an abandoned wagon in the line of fire. Fresh munitions enabled Russian and Prussian troops and armed citizens to capture twenty-three hundred enemy and their artillery. The Prussian coalition forced the French surrender and retreat beyond the Elbe River at Boizenburg, taking Johanna along as a prisoner of war. Friedrich Rückert honored her in verse; a street and reenactments bear her name.

May 25, 1813

During the thirteen-year Venezuelan struggle for freedom from colonialism, rebel commander **Juana Ramírez (January 12, 1790–1856)** of Chaguaramal led one hundred women in an artillery unit. An Afro-Hispanic slave and laundress, she defended newly liberated territory from Spanish reconquest by loading cannon and sheltering casualties, children, and old people. At the battle of Alto de los Godos on May 25, 1813, her charge against the forces of New Granada Captain General Domingo de

Monteverde in Plaza Piar de Maturin earned her the name "La Avanzadora (The Trailblazer)." The patriot achievement killed four hundred eighty royalists. Her courage survives in a dramatic sculpture in Maturin picturing her wielding a sword.

June 21, 1813

In service as captain under Arthur Wellesley, the Duke of Wellington, **Agustina Raimunda of Aragon (March 4, 1786–May 29, 1857)** commanded a battery at the battle of Vitoria, Spain, on June 21, 1813. Wellington's one hundred twenty-one thousand allied British, Portuguese, and Spanish forces quelled sixty thousand French troops at the cost of six thousand eight hundred casualties for the enemy and five thousand two hundred for the allies. The following year, King Fernando VII awarded her a medal and monthly pension of one hundred reals. Her patriotism survives in storytelling, Francisco Goya's art, Lord Byron's verse epic *Childe Harold*, and a 1950 film, *Agustina of Aragon*.

June 22, 1813

At a key advance by Americans in the Niagara Peninsula during the War of 1812, **Laura Secord (September 13, 1775–October 17, 1868)**, a Tory spy and courier from Great Barrington, Massachusetts, warned loyalists on June 22, 1813, of the planned assault by patriot warships. She walked seventeen miles from Queenston through woods to Twelve Mile Creek near Wilbrahim, Massachusetts. Her communique aided the British and Mohawk two days later to win the battle of Beaver Dams, Ontario. The battle cost Americans seventy-five casualties. A national historic trail parallels her route.

September 6, 1813

During the Napoleonic Wars, Sergeant **Friederike Krüger (also August Lübeck or Auguste Krüger, October 8, 1789–May 31, 1848)** from Friesland, Prussia, disguised herself in a man's uniform to enlist in the 9th Grenadiers. Under the alias "Auguste Lubbock," she mobilized successfully in spring 1813 with the Landwehr battalion and served until her high voice betrayed her gender. Acknowledged by Prussian king Frederick William III, she advanced to sergeant and helped weaken the French aims to seize Berlin. In men's clothes, she participated in the trouncing of Napoleon's army at Mockern, Prussia, on April 5, 1813. After the battle of Grossbeeren on August 23, she fought outside Berlin on September 6, 1813, at Dennewitz, Brandenburg.

Rehabilitated from battle fatigue, Friederike joined the Paris occupation the next year. She marched to the battle of Waterloo, Holland (modern Belgium), on June 18, 1815, when she fell to serious wounds along with English cross-dresser, **Mary Dixon (ca. 1783–June 18, 1815)**, sixteen-year veteran with the British army, who died in the conflict from a brain concussion. The historic overthrow of French marshal Michel Ney's hopes advanced Arthur Wellington, the Duke of Wellington, to international hero and ended Friederike's military career. The French lost twenty-six thousand casualties and two imperial eagle standards, a blow to national pride. Napoleon abdicated on June 22, 1815. For steadfast service to the Landwehr Corps, Friederike earned the Russian St. George Medal. Frederick William conferred on her a war commendation and the Iron Cross.

November 26, 1813

During the fourteen-month War of the Sixth Coalition, **Francina Broese Gunningh (also Frans Gunningh Sloet, October 3, 1783–August 16, 1824)** from Kampen, Holland, survived the battlefields of Kampen, northeast at Coevorden, and southwest to Deventer, where Napoleon's infantry fought Russian cossacks at the Yssel River on November 26, 1813. Francina's military career began in male dress in Paris, where French military police seized her and charged her with desertion. Shanghaied into the French army at Cherbourg, she fled and joined a Prussian regiment. Her deployment ended with a chest wound in Prussia, discovery, and discharge for concealing her gender. A third enlistment placed her among Dutch regulars at Bouches-de-l'yssel, in late 1813. Another deception in June 1814 and arrest at Zutphen brought fraud charges and a three-year prison sentence.

1814

A Sunni Bedouin warrior and tactician during the eight-year Ottoman-Wahhabi War of 1811–1818, General **Ghaliyya al-Wahhabiyya (?–1818)** of Tarba (modern Turabah), Arabia, led Muslim forces to demolish Ottoman Turks. Under the edict of Turkish sultan Mustafa IV, by arousing Muslims to arms in 1814, she stopped the threat of the foreign power of Mahmud II to retake the holy city of Mecca, the "cradle of Islam." The reversals of Muhammad Ali Pasha, the viceroy of Egypt, at the battles of Tarba and Qunfudhah contrasted Ghaliyya's military savvy and earned her the title of *amira* (generalissima). Egyptian critics, dismissive of female warriors, accounted for a woman's skill in battle as her focus of the evil eye, which made her troops invisible. The siege ended on September 15, 1818, with a peace treaty and the cession to Arabia of the Hijaz region along the Red Sea.

September 22, 1814

A mestizo volunteer and a rebel hero from La Paz, **Úrsula Goyzueta (October 20, 1787–November 4, 1854)** defended Santa Barbara in Potosí during the Bolivian War of Independence. With creole conspirators **Vicenta Equino (April 3, 1780–March 14, 1857)** of La Paz and **Simona Josefa Manzaneda (October 28, 1770–September 26, 1814)** a widowed spy from Mecapaca, Úrsula began defying colonial authority on July 16, 1809, while Simona carried messages in her skirt and supplied armaments. The three women fought royalist forces on September 22, 1814. Two years later, the capture of Úrsula and Simona on November 21, 1816, involved a court fine of four thousand pesos, jailing, and humiliation by walking naked behind a burro. Royalists lashed Simona fifty times before shooting her in the back. Vicenta received a death penalty later reduced to a fine of six thousand pesos, prison, and exile to Cuzco. On August 18, 1825, she rewarded liberator Simon Bolivar with the key to La Paz.

Wars of Independence, 1815–1825

Spawned by the defeat of Napoleon, indigenous resistance to colonialism prompted female rebellion in varied settings, encouraging insurrection of Latina warriors in South America and Native Americans in the United States as well as residents of Hawaii, Venezuela, New Granada, Molucca, Cuba, and South Africa. Women demonstrated group sensibilies by abetting neighborhood conspiracies and distributing materiel and rations. Those imprisoned executed for their boldness set examples of nationalism and womanly unity.

May 23, 1815

Under the title Seaman **William Brown (1789–1835)** of Grenada, a black West Indian woman entered the British Royal Navy and, on May 23, 1815, advanced to foretopman on the sloop HMS *Queen Charlotte,* a three-masted flagship that served the nation's premier battle fleet. She first volunteered in 1804 and posted to the channel fleet in March 1815 at the War of the Seventh Coalition after Napoleon returned to Paris from exile on Elba. At the disclosure of her disguise in June 1815, she declared her masquerade was a way to elude a quarrelsome husband. The next month, she boarded the schooner HMS *Cumberland,* an East Indiaman, and served until August between St. Helena in the southern Atlantic Ocean and at Long Reach, Kent, on the Thames River. When the media reported her adventures and return to Somerset-Place, in 1816, her husband demanded her earnings.

July 23, 1815

During the reconquest of New Granada (modern Colombia), peasant rebel **Antonia Santos Plata (April 10, 1782–June 18, 1819)** from Pinchot led the uprising of rural El Socorro in favor of liberator Simon Bolivar against Spanish royalist forces. Colonialists under King Ferdinand VII seized New Granada and advanced to Chile, where tropical fevers weakened the army. Spanish companies resupplied at Santa Marta on July 23, 1815, and began a five-month siege at Cartagena. Maria's forty patriots pushed back by forming the Chicelada and Coromoro companies at El Hatillo, her hacienda. They captured Spanish communications and fought at Pantano de Vargas on July 25 and at the massive triumph at Boyacá Bridge. After the creation of Colombia, Maria fell prey to a traitor. Her arrest and jailing in a Chicelada dungeon, trial, and charge of treason ended in death by firing squad at the Socorro plaza on June 28, 1819. The national military named a brigade for her.

September 24, 1815

A Creole patriot and mother-to-be, **María Luisa Cáceres Díaz de Arismendi (September 25, 1799–June 2, 1866)** of Caracas, Venezuela, set an example of stoic defiance of colonial Spanish humiliation and menace. In the fifth month of pregnancy on September 24, 1815, she entered internment for insurrection in a series of prisons, beginning with the Fort Santa Rosa dungeon on Margarita Island. A starvation diet caused the death of her newborn daughter on January 26, 1816. Captors continued transferring Maria to La Guaira and exiled her to Cadiz, Spain, where she refused under torture to side with either combatant in the Venezuelan Revolution. By negotiating with the enemy, she arranged a return to her husband in Caracas. Patriots celebrated her loyalty and resolve on June 2, 1866, with burial in the national pantheon, a painting and statue in La Asunción, a portrait on currency, and her name on a university and commercial aircraft.

1816

A spurned single mother and defender of her son, **Nandi Bhebhe (1760–October 10, 1827)** of Melmoth, South Africa, devoted her energies to grooming her son Shaka Zulu for military greatness. Born to the Mhlongo clan, she demanded recompense for seduction by Senzangakhona, Shaka's birth father. In rejection from location to location, she served as Shaka's security guard among the Qwabe and Mthethwa people. Her keen eye for danger thwarted enemies threatening assassination. After Shaka's rise to power in 1816, she advised him on battle tactics. She died of dysentery, leaving Shaka to fend alone against Dutch settlers and assassins until his death in September 1828 at the connivance of his two brothers.

May 1816

The Colombian revolution worsened in May 1816, when the sadistic general Pablo Morillo terrorized the native populace by executing rebel creoles, including patriot **Presentación Buenahora (?–1816)** at Pore. In December, rebel commander **Policarpa Salavarrieta** acquired a forged passport and safe conduct and conspired with the anti-monarchist underground to pose as a domestic and nanny in Bogotá in the spy ring of **Andrea Ricaurte de Lozano (November 10, 1755–November 13, 1829)** of Medellín. While sewing and altering garments for royalist women, "La Pola" eavesdropped on Spanish plans in social gatherings, churches, and bars. She reported the number of Spaniards in squadrons, identified their weapons, and stole maps and battle plans. By coaxing young men to join the uprising, she increased volunteerism to the patriot cause, a crime for which royalists shot a coterie of women rebels— **Ana Josefa Morales, María del Transito Vargas, Remigia Cuesta, Micaela Nieto, Mercedes Loayza, Antonia Moreno, Josefa Conde, María del Rosario Devis, Manuela Uscátegui,** and

Anselma Leyton. Also in 1817, royalists chained **Paula Contreras** with **Tomasa Rodríguez** and murdered them in Neiva for encouraging the desertion of Spanish soldiers.

See also July 20, 1810; November 1812; November 10, 1817.

July 1, 1816

A twenty-year veteran sutler for Napoleon's *grande armée*, **Consuelo Dubois (ca. 1776–July 1, 1816)** of Strasbourg, France, fled the downfall of the French at Waterloo, Holland. On the three-masted frigate *La Meduse,* she sailed from Rochefort, France, to Saint Louis, Senegal, on June 17, 1816. Two weeks later, a slacker captain, Hugues de Chaumareys, ignored dangerous waters at the sandbank of Arguin forty miles from West Africa (modern Mauritania). After the crew launched six lifeboats and supplied them with beef, bread, and water, Consuelo and her husband managed a place on a raft lashed together from spars and planks. She challenged the soldiers to overcome terror of high waves, hunger, and thirst. A mutiny of Spanish against French resulted in the wounding and drowning of Consuelo and her husband on July 1, 1816. Only three survived until the brig *Argus* rescued them on July 17. The harrowing story survives in history, painting, hymn, oratorio, opera, and film.

May 16, 1817

A Melanesian spearman and national hero, **Martha Christian Tijahahu (January 4, 1800–January 2, 1818)** of Nusalaut Island, followed rebel Thomas Pattimura on May 16, 1817, in the Moluccan underground war against Netherlands colonialism. She grew up in a motherless home headed by a clan captain, whom she aided in carrying weapons and performing war dances. Thomas impressed her by seizing Fort Duurstede outside Saparua, slaughtering residents, and drubbing enemy reinforcements. She participated in arson that destroyed Ulath and the blockhouse before retreating to the jungle. Her daring incited island women to join the resisters.

At the capture and hanging of Thomas and her father in October 1817, Martha fell into enemy hands, but gained release because of her youth. More guerrilla warfare and a second capture in December resulted in judgment at Fort Beverwijk and a severe sentence—slave labor on a Javanese coffee plantation. On the voyage of the three-masted Dutch warship *Evertsen*, she rejected food and medication for stroke and died on the Banda Sea two days before her eighteenth birthday. Her name identifies a women's magazine, streets and warships, and sculptures. She earned honors on a national day of spreading flower petals on the Banda Sea.

See also November 10, 1817.

October 11, 1817

A martyr to liberty in the seventh year of the Mexican War of Independence, **Gertrudis Bocanegra (April 11, 1765–October 11, 1817)** from Patzcuaro in southern Mexico abetted guerrilla warfare in her hometown. Following the death of her husband and eldest son in battle, she aided insurgents by relaying messages from one combat zone to another. After a traitor revealed her involvement, the Spanish tortured her and charged her with treason. Her fervid backing of insurrectionists continued until October 11, 1817, when a rifle squad at Plazuela de San Agustin ended her life. A film and a bronze likeness acclaim her as *La Heroine de Patzcuaro*.

October 21, 1817

A Uruguayan rebel from Montevideo, **Ana Monterroso de Lavalleja (September 3, 1791–March 28, 1858)** joined her husband in fighting for independence from Portuguese colonialism. During the four-year Banda Oriental conflict, she wed Juan Antonio Lavalleja, the army commander of Colonia. On October 21, 1817, at age twenty-six, she aided him on the Uruguayan battlefield, which extended to Argentina and southern Brazil. Around 1820, Portuguese-Brazilian general Carlos Frederico Lecor arrested the couple at Salto and jailed them in Rio de Janeiro. They gained their freedom in 1823.

November 10, 1817

Colombian martyr Policarpa Salavarrieta's collaboration with insurrectionists ended on November 10, 1817, after General Juan Samano discovered her name in papers carried by rebel brothers Ambrosio and Vicente Almeyda, who hid in the home of **Gertrudis Vanegas (fl. 1817)** and her mother, **María Gertrudis Romero (fl. 1817)**. In Policarpa's final minutes of freedom at spymaster Andrea Ricaurte de Lozano's residence, Policarpa destroyed documents naming other conspirators. Charged with prison escapes the previous September, stockpiling weapons, and encouraging desertions from the royal army, Bibiano and his twenty-two-year-old sister Policarpa entered prison at Bogotá's Colegio Mayor de Nuestra Señora del Rosario. On November 14, 1817, she, her lover Alejo Sabarain, and six male resisters faced a firing squad in Plaza Mayor. Policarpa refused to turn her back or kneel before her persecutors.

Policarpa's bravery marked currency and postal stamps, a Bogotá statue, stage drama, and a television series. The Colombian president and congress named November 8 as the commemorative "Day of the Colombian Woman." Included among female icons at Tenza, home of the Muisca Indians, locals mourned martyrs **María de los Ángeles Ávila, Salomé Buitrago,** and **Genoveva Sarmiento**, whom collaborators shot on December 7, 1817, without a trial. **Ignacia Medina** shared their death date in punishment for delivering rations and medicine to suffering prisoners. **Inés Osuna** went to the same scaffold without a trial. Policarpa's confederate in espionage, **Laurean Sierra,** continued the secret operation until her execution on August 4, 1819.

See also July 20, 1810; November 1812; May 1816; July 1819.

April 5, 1818

A conspirator and promoter of Commander Jose de San Martin, a South American liberator, **Brigida Silva de Ochoa (1767–1840)** of Lima, Peru, served an underground network as courier and intermediary. In 1807, she dedicated her anti–Spanish activism to political prisoners, especially her brother, Colonel Don Remigio Silva, and son Jose Ochoa. Her complicity enabled Father José Medina to escape from an imperialist seizure of his parish at Sica. In 1809, she conspired with her brothers to overthrow the viceroy. The following year, she collected food and clothing bundles for libertarians in the Callao Prison. According to her 1924 biography by Elvira Garcia y Garcia, Brigida's espionage backed freedom fighters' advance at Maipú, Chile, on April 5, 1818, for which she received a pension of thirty pesos. Her name attaches to a woman's college at Chorrillos, a portrait coin, the Orden del Sol (Order of the Sun), and a proclamation declaring her a "Daughter of the Homeland."

June 2, 1818

At the death of Aurangzeb and the decline of the Mughal empire, Sikh co-commander **Datar Kaur (1784–June 20, 1838)** of the Punjab (modern Pakistan) aided her son and heir, Kharak Singh, in the June 2, 1818, campaign at Multan on the Chenab River. She married Ranjit Singh, who founded the Sikh Empire, which stretched from Sindh and Kashmir to the Khyber Pass in Tibet. In 1808, when their boy was seven, she took control of the Sheikhupura citadel, a former redoubt of the Mughal emperor Jehangir. She refined the structure with cornices, carved wood doors, and thematic fresco and made it a six-story residence, where she home-schooled the future maharaja. Kharak used the location as a Khalsa cavalry power base for eliminating Afghans from the Punjab (modern Pakistan).

A decade later, Datar Kaur ventured west with Kharak for a more complicated conquest. In 1818, a three-month siege of the Multan keep in the fourth phase of Afghan-Sikh Wars required additional artillery and the fourteen-foot Zamzama, a copper and brass Mughal cannon that Banghi warrior **Mai Sukhan (1740s–1824)** of the Punjab had defended at the battle of Bhasin at Amritsar's Fort Govindgarh. The conflict occurred on January 2, 1805, before Mai's surrender to Emperor Ranjit Singh on February 21. More firepower enabled Sikh troops to enter a breach and capture a stronghold of the Durrani Empire. The collapse ended Afghan influence and the 1819 primacy over Kashmir and ensured the payment of annual tribute to the Sikh empire. Datar's heroics appeared in fiction and a television series.

July 1819

By July 1819, fifty female spies for Colombia's patriots had suffered the same death as Policarpa Salvarrieta, a revered martyr. Known victims include avid patriot **Carlota Armero (1798–May 28, 1816)** of Mariquita and **Estefanía Linares (?–May 28, 1816)** at Mariquita for no known reason; supporter **Dolores Salas (?–September 14, 1816)** at Neiva; patriot **Luisa Trilleras (?–September 18, 1817)** at Prado; recruiter and supplier **Dorotea Castro (?–November 1817)** of Natagaima at Palmira; courier **Bibiana Talero (?–November 21, 1817)** at Choconta; and auxiliary soldiers **Marta Tello (?–November 26, 1817)** at Neiva and **María Josefa Esguerra (?–November 26, 1817)** and **Candelaria Forero (?–November 26, 1817)** at Macheta and **Ascensión Ortega (?–January 1819)** of Málaga at Gameza. Women proved the backbone of the underground: supplies and horses from eleven-year-old **Matilde Anaray (fl. 1817)**, **Casilda Zafra (fl. 1817)**, and **Juana Velasco de Gallo (fl. 1817)**, a soldier riding her own mount in the army of Simon Bolivar. Essential to the insurrection were meetings and spy activities at the Bogotá residence of intelligence officer **Andrea Ricaurte de Lozano**; a supply of cattle and horses from **María Rosa Lazo de la Vega (fl. 1817)**; soldiery and spear expertise from First Sergeant **Juana Béjar (April 10, 1782–July 28, 1819)**; a riot reverencing Sapa Inca leader Tupac Amaru led by **Clara Tocarruncho (fl. 1817)**; and cash from **Gertrudis Vanegas (fl. 1817)** of Macheta. Supplier **María Agudelo de Olaya (fl. 1817)** bought guns to distribute to the militia.

The bloodbath continued at Socorro with the shooting of **Engracia Salgar (1795–December 2, 1818)** at Socorro; of soldiers **Fidela Ramos (?–December 11, 1818)** at Zapoteca and **Leonarda Carreño (?–December 11, 1818)** at Guadalupe; and of organizer **Antonia Santos Plata (April 10, 1782–July 28, 1819)**, who had sold her jewelry to finance soldiers. Along with the stalwart slave **Juana Santos (?–July 28, 1819)**, Antonia Santos was executed by a rifle squad at age thirty-seven. A veteran of multiple battles, **Evangelina Diaz (?–August 19, 1819)** went to her death at Zapoteca.

After intelligence officer Andrea Ricuarte's exile to Fusagasuga, her teenage grandchild **Dolores Vargas (1800–October 28, 1878)** from Santa Fe joined the struggle for liberation.

See also November 1812; August 17, 1819.

August 17, 1819

Banishment displaced four Colombian revolutionaries: **Josefa Baraya (1770–?)** from Girón and her sister **Dolores Nariño (fl. 1819)** and nieces **Isabel Nariño (fl. 1819)** and **Mercedes Nariño (fl. 1819)** in August 1816. On the same date, teacher **Barbara Forero (fl. 1819)**, a former inmate of Chiquito prison in 1797, entered exile at Suesca; Andrea Ricuarte and Policarpa Salvarrieta's confederate **Carmen Rodríguez de Gaitán (?–1852)** served time in a Bogotá prison. Army volunteers **Teresa Cornejo (ca. 1800–?)** of San Carlos and **Manuela Tinoco (fl. 1819)** fought at Paya in men's uniform alongside female warrior **Simona Amaya (?–July 25, 1819)**, who died in the clash at Vargas Swamp. **Evangelista Tamayo (fl. 1819)** marched alongside **Juana Rodríguez (fl. 1819)**, who suffered a leg wound on August 7, 1819, at the battle of Boyacá Bridge, an upturn in the patriot battle against Spanish overlords.

See also November 1812.

October 11, 1819

At Gameza, Colombia, on October 11, 1819, *campesino* (farm) sisters **Juana** and **Manuela Escobar** faced death for spying on royalists during the war of liberation. Juana had previously suffered a public beating for intelligence work.

Her espionage had aided the national guard and Venezuelan allies the previous July 25 in victorious bayonet and cavalry charges at the battle of Pantano de Vargas near Paipa. More executions took warriors **María del Carmen Olano (fl. 1819)** and **Dorotea Lenis (fl. 1819)** at Quilichao and **Carlota Rengifo (?–February 7, 1820)** at Toro and **Barbara Montes (?–February 7, 1820)** at Caloto. Another patriot spy, **Juana Ramírez (?–May 10, 1820)** held out longer than her fellow information gatherers and died before executioners in Bogotá. At an exultant speech, emancipator Simon Bolivar compared these Colombian women warriors to Spartan mothers. In 1821, Bogotá named its central square Plaza Bolivar after the founder of Colombia's independence.

December 1819

At a pivotal point in the modernization of Hawaii, war between cousins martyred chiefess **Manono II (1780s–December 1819)** of Maui in the battle of Kuamo'o over *kapu*—the system of law, religion, and social behaviors. In widowhood since King Kamehameha's death at age eighty-three on May 8, 1819, seven months later, she faced a barrage of clubs, spears, slingshots, and muskets. She died in December 1819 fighting modernizer Liholiho alongside her second husband Kekuaokalani, Kamehameha's nephew. As an island priest, he supported traditional idol worship. During the early part of the skirmish on the Kona shore at Lekeleke, he incurred a musket ball to the heart. After tending him all day, Manono begged for amity between sides, but risked death while spreading his feathered cape over his remains. She collapsed from a projectile above her left ear. Liholiho seized the cloak and buried her under stone cairns.

September 1820

A Mexican patriot and survivor of seven battles, Captain **Manuela Medina (also Maria Manuela Molina, 1780–March 2, 1822)**, a Native American from Texcoco, succumbed to two war wounds at age forty-two. A recruiter of rebels in the eleven-year Mexican War of Independence under Jose Maria Morelos, the strategist of twenty-two triumphs, she took part in the southern occupation of Acapulco and the overthrow of the Spanish at Cuautla, Guerrero, Michoacan, and Tixtla. The insurrectionist continued battling in spring 1812 at Citlalli, Tehuacan, Orizaba, and Oaxaca and aided a second assault on Acapulco on April 13, 1813. The juggernaut included battle on August 20 at San Diego and pressed on to Valladolid in winter 1813 until Moralos's capture at Temalaca in November 1815. Manuela distinguished herself on February 24, 1814, at the attack on Rancho de Las Animas, California. Lance jabs by loyalists to her back and gut in September 1820 left "La Capitana" paralyzed for eighteen months.

April 4, 1821

Female naval commander **Laskarina Bouboulina (May 1771–May 22, 1825)** of Constantinople (modern Istanbul) formed an armada to clinch Greek independence. Twice widowed during a war on pirates, she amassed a fortune from ship building, smuggling, and arms manufacture to support her seven children and the islanders of Spetses south of Attica. She ordered the building of the eighteen-cannon *Agamemnon,* captained by her son Yiannis, whom the Ottomans killed and decapitated. At the five-month siege and looting of Tripolitsa (modern Tripoli) on April 4, 1821, by Turkish cavalry, she rescued the family of Sultan Hurshid Pasha from the torture and massacre of twenty-five thousand Muslims and Jews.

By blockading Nafplion, the major port of the Argolid on the Peloponnese, Laskarina assailed the Ottoman Turks and raised a rebel flag announcing the First Hellenic Republic. To seize the southern port cities of Pylos and Monemvasia, she rallied Greeks by riding horseback up the eastern coast to distribute cash and weapons. During the autumn of 1821, as the Ottomans weakened, she took firm hold on the capital city of Nafplion with a fleet of eight ships. During the 1824 Greek civil war, to recruit another navy, she entered exile in Spetses, where armed thugs shot her on the balcony. Tsar Alexander I Romanov conferred a posthumous rank of admiral of the Russian navy. Her likeness appeared in sculpture, dramas, cinema, street names, and bank notes. Laskarina's example empowered her great granddaughter, **Lela Karagianni (1898–September 8, 1944)** from Limni, an underground leader during World War II who died by firing squad outside Athens at Haidari concentration camp.

See also September 8, 1944.

February 19, 1822

Joana Angélica de Jesus (December 12, 1761–February 19, 1822) of Salvador, Bahia, became the first martyred rebel in Brazil's War of Independence from Spain. She made a profession of faith as a nun at age twenty and rose in rank from scribe and counselor to vicar and abbess. During a raid on Salvador's Convent of Lapa, the sixty-year-old Joana risked the bayonets of Portuguese forces, who looted, burned, and murdered. At the cloister's south gate, she posed her unarmed body as a shield for the other convent inmates. The entrance where she died on February 19, 1822, received acclaim as a national historic heritage site.

May 11, 1822

A mestizo guerrilla spy, courier, and Quiros gang leader, **María Parado de Bellido (July 5, 1777–May 11, 1822)** of Ayacucho, Peru, aided saboteurs at a bridge over the Mantra River. In collaboration with her rebel husband and sons Tomas and Mariano, she furthered the revolutionary aims of General Jose de San Martin, a liberator in South America. The Spanish burned Maria's house, arrested her, and displayed her in custody around the village square for passing information in letters to guerrilla fighters about royalist intent to invade Quilcamachay on March 29, 1822. Because she refused under torture to reveal connections to rebels, the Spanish shot her on May 11, 1822, at Huamanga in the Plaza de Armas. Her name survives on a street in Callao, Peru.

May 24, 1822

Three Ecuadorian viragos, Sergeant **Nicolasa Jurado (fl. 1822)** of Loja and compatriots **Gertrudis Espalza (fl. 1822)** from Ambateña and **Inés Maria Jiménez (fl. 1822)** of Loja, fought for liberation from Spanish imperialism near Quito at the Pichincha volcano. Survivors of the disastrous highlands battle of Babahoyo on August 21, 1821, the trio took the masculine first name "Manuel," dressed in male uniforms, and marched with General José de Sucre's three thousand men. The three-house onslaught ended on May 24, 1822, in a Royalist retreat from the "Summit of Liberty." For killing four hundred Spanish, taking twelve hundred sixty captives, and freeing Quito, the cadre received local acclaim, decorations, and applause from liberator Simon Bolivar. Nicolasa, a wounded veteran, recuperated from a bullet to the chest at a Quito hospital. She advanced to sergeant and, on December 9, 1824, fought at the battle of Ayacucho in the Peruvian War of Independence, where the Spanish incurred twenty-five hundred casualties.

October 1822

A cross-dressing lieutenant, **Maria Quitéria (June 27, 1792–1853)** of Feira de Santana, Brazil, enlisted in the Brazilian army as a man at age thirty in October 1822. An illiterate peasant, she excelled at horse riding, rifles, and one-on-one bayonet warfare. During the struggle for independence from Portugal, she earned a medal from Emperor Pedro I for her advancement in the military for adroit assaults and ambushes across Bahia at Concepción, Itapúa, and Pituba. For her loyalty, she earned a Knight of the Imperial Order of the Star of the South. Her likeness survives in a portrait at the Paulista Museum of the University of São Paulo.

October 22, 1822

The wealthy defender of Mykonos, southeast of Athens, Greece, General **Manto Mavrogenous (also Mando or Magdalene, 1796–July 1848)** of Trieste in the Hapsburg dominion of Austria-Hungary, rid the island of Ottoman Turks on October 22, 1822. The owner and captain of two ships and the wielder of a sword, she expelled pirates from the Cycladean isles and prevented two hundred Turks from invading Mykonos. For the sake of Greek liberation, she armed soldiers to protect the island of Samos and the Peloponnese. In April 1821, she fought at the five-month siege of Tripolitsa (modern Tripoli).

At Karystos on Euboea and at Chios, Manto deployed a six-ship armada manned by eight hundred troops. The flexible fleet engaged Egypto-Turks at Tinos, Pelion, Phthiotis, and Livadeia, earning for her the rank of lieutenant general. On return to Mykonos, she composed an autobiography. The loss of her inheritance to military expenses left her poor, homeless, and alone at her death at age fifty-two from typhoid fever. The generosity of "La Bella Greca" (The Beautiful Greek) survives in portraiture, sculpture, cinema, coins, drama, television, buildings, airport, and the town plaza at Paroika, Paros.

January 7, 1823

An Afro-Brazilian whale knife expert and practitioner of capoeira martial arts, **María Felipa de Oliveira (?–July 4, 1873)** of Bahia joined the crusade on January 7, 1823, to end oppression by Portuguese colonists in South America. Born on the island of Itaparica, she advanced from fishmonger and shellfish gatherer to leader of minority and native Brazilians and supplier of inland volunteers. Armed with knives and sharp bones, guerrilla warriors from Tapuia and Tupinamba tribes terrified the enemy by posing as ghosts. Maria's followers—**Joana Soaleira (fl. 1820s), Brígida do Vale (fl. 1820s)**, and a woman known only as **Marcolina (fl. 1820s)**—mounted watch posts, burned offshore vessels, and dug trenches to prevent invasion. Seduction lured enemy soldiers into traps, where the women beat them with stinging nettles and set fire to their ships. The struggle ended on July 2, 1823, with Portuguese withdrawal from Brazil.

June 23, 1823

On June 23, 1823, during the Mfecane/Difaqane Wars, South African chief **Mmanthatisi (1781–1836)** from Harrismith built a formidable army of forty-thousand Tlokwa. In a catastrophe of enemy warfare, the tribe lost herds, belongings, and homes. In flight for her life, Mmanthatisi displaced villagers south of Johannesburg on the upper Vaal River and began threatening the Sotho on the Caledon River in the Drakensberg Mountains. Her rise to monarchy exterminated twenty-nine tribes all the way to Botswana. She padded her combat lines of male veterans with women armed with hoes. At the battle of Dithakong, South Africa, on June 23, 1823, she lost many warriors. She evaded Bechuana chief Makaba by retreating to Lesotho and turned her sovereignty over to her son Sekonyela.

November 1, 1823

Swedish freebooter **Johanna Jungberg Hard (December 3, 1798–March 12, 1851)** of Vrångö Island in the North Sea joined farm and sea laborers on November 1, 1823, in seizing a ship and slaying its crew. A widow since 1817, she had been acquitted of infanticide and had a criminal record of smuggling textiles from Copenhagen. On a route from Hartlepool, England to Nykjobing on the Baltic Sea, she plotted to lead a four-man gang on the fishing vessel *Styrsö* (pilot's wheel). The raiders intended to loot the Danish ship *Frau Mette* (Mrs. Mette), which was beached at Foto Island after abandonment in the North Sea.

The looters gained access by pretending to need fresh water and a fire for the galley. For boarding the *Frau Mette* and killing the captain, pilot, and ship's boy, three of Johanna's gang members were beheaded in 1824. One of the gang received a life sentence at forced labor in Fort Karlsten at Marstrand in western Sweden. Johanna negotiated release because of insufficient evidence and settled at Stockholm to clerk for the Royal Post Office until her death from stroke at age fifty-two.

October 21, 1824

A queen turned folk hero, **Kittur Chennamma (November 14, 1778–February 21, 1829)** of Belagavi in southwest India commanded armed troops in the first colonial battle against the East India Company. Like other aggressive females, she learned to handle bow, sword, and horse in girlhood. At age forty-six, she lost husband, son, and rule to British imperialists, who attacked on October 21, 1824. Victorious in a twelve-day conflict against twenty thousand eight hundred enemy, her bodyguard slew the British agent, St. John Thackeray, and seized two hostages.

Betrayed during deliberations by traitors who stuffed cannon with mud and cow manure, Kittur Chennamma fought a second siege on December 3, 1824. She was apprehended with nieces **Janaki Bai (fl. 1820s)** and **Veeramma (fl. 1820s)**. The British remanded the girls and the queen to Fort Bailhongal, where Kittur died five years later and lay interred on the grounds. Her resistance of imperial Britain recurs in folk music, cinema, storytelling, drama, and the naming of a train and patrol destroyer. A statue of her on horseback raises a sword over parliament at New Delhi.

1825

A Kootenai transsexual in the Canadian Rockies, **Bowdash (also Kauxuma Nupika, ca. 1790–1837)** of Washington State built a reputation as raider, seer, courier, guide, and healer. In her late teens, she joined the first North Western Company brigade in 1808. She impressed witnesses with her fluency in French and value at a Flathead trading post as an interpreter. On a mission through hostile territory in 1825, she suffered a wound while carrying a message down the Columbia River between Hudson Bay Company outposts. She died in combat at age forty-seven while mediating differences between the Blackfeet and Flathead.

September 25, 1825

An aged Javanese virago and tactician, **Nyi Ageng Serang (1752–1838)** from Serang replaced her father, Prince Natapraja, in ridding Indonesia of colonialism. She served a sentence in Jogyakarta prison in the Dutch East Indies for rebellion. After warcraft instruction, during the Java War on September 25, 1825, she commanded troops that included her grandson, whom she trained. By raising a five-year revolt against Prince Diponegoro, a collaborator with Dutch profiteers, she expanded the rebellion to Demak, Juwana, Kudus, Purwodadi, Rembang, and Semarang and instructed guerrilla fighters on disguising themselves behind taro leaves. Her national heroism survives at Wates on a mounted statue with spear.

March 1827

An interim governor of Nakhon Ratchasima (modern Korat, Siam) and national hero, **Thao Suranari (also Ya Mo, 1771–1852)** used guile to win the battle of Samrit Fields in March 1827 and expel Siamese invaders from Vientiane. After King Anouvong initiated the Lao revolt, he employed an elephant cavalry. Because his men forced Siamese victims on a march to Laos, Thao

Suranari outlined a successful plot. By offering strong drink to Lao troops and arming Siamese captives and kitchen knives and axes, she led a mutiny and routed the enemy. The followup turned a three-day battle into the loss of Vientiane, which lay in ruins. Her likeness stands in royal pose at the city gate in Korat.

1828

Libertarian Spanish conspirator **Mariana Pineda (September 1, 1804– May 26, 1831)** collaborated with Granada's liberal underground in 1828 to free her cousin, Captain Fernando Alvarez de Sotomayor, from prison before his execution date. After he slipped out of the cell disguised as a priest, he hid in her house. In 1831, police condemned her possession of a rebel flag—a green triangle on a purple background proclaiming liberty, equality, and law. Authorities imprisoned her at a convent and questioned her about fellow plotters against Spain's king Fernando VII. When she refused to answer, they secured her in a garrote, which strangled her and broke her neck. Dramatist Federico Garcia Lorca immortalized her in the stage play *Mariana Pineda*.

1828

In revolt against British imperialists, **Tarenorrerer (1800–June 5, 1831)** a Tommeginne orator of Emu Bay, Van Diemen's Land (modern Tasmania), led indigenous guerrillas in a two-year resistance of European settlers. During enslavement in her teens to seal hunters who raped and tortured her at the Bass Strait islands, she mastered English and the loading and shooting of guns. In 1828 at age twenty-eight, she united native warriors to spear the sheep and cattle of the English settlers of northern Tasmania. Captured a second time in 1830, she lived among bird and seal catchers. During incarceration at Gun Carriage Island (modern Vansittart) for plotting an assassination in December 1830, she succumbed to flu.

September 25, 1828

An Ecuadorian and pro–Bolivian collaborator and tactician, on September 25, 1828, Colonel **Manuela Sáenz (December 27, 1797–November 23, 1856)** of Quito rescued from an assassin her creole lover, Simon Bolivar, the liberator of Bolivia, Colombia, Ecuador, Peru, and Venezuela. The illegitimate daughter of a Spanish military officer, she grew up in an austere convent. She rejected ladylike constraints by dressing in masculine costume, training for the army, refusing to ride horses sidesaddle, wearing a fake mustache, and smoking cigarettes. Using social connections, she gleaned army secrets from gossip and abandoned her husband to follow Simon from Quito as his secretary.

During their eight-year romantic liaison on May 24, 1822, Manuela tended the wounded on Simon's three-hour campaign to Pichincha, where patriots took twelve hundred sixty Spaniards prisoner and killed twice as many soldiers as they lost. On the march south from "La Cima de la Libertad (the Summit of Liberty)," she led convoys through the snowy Andes and distributed cash to destitute veterans. At Junin, Peru, on August 6, 1824, she fought alongside Simon with nine squads of horse soldiers. She crashed a costume party to disrupt the mutiny of discontented officers. For bravery at the crucial cavalry charge at Ayacucho, Peru, on December 9, 1824, she advanced from lieutenant to colonel for aiding six thousand patriots in outflanking nine thousand Spaniards.

With Peruvian subversive **Rosa Campuzano (April 13, 1796–1851)** of Guayaquil, a seasoned veteran in Argentina, Chile, and Peru, Manuela began soliciting volunteers for the Lima militia in Peru and hid Spaniards deserting the royalist army. To promote anti–Spanish revolt, she wore a colonel's cavalry uniform with saber for addressing mutineers and aided Simon's flight from political rivals by lending him her boots. For directing Simon to escape from their bedroom window in Bogotá's San Carlos Palace and suffering a beating with Spanish swords, she received an Order of the Sun of Peru, an honor she shared with Rosa. From imprisonment on February 7, 1827, Manuela gained release and, in April, entered exile in Bogotá, Colombia, and Jamaica. Her respect for female rebels motivated her founding of the Society of Patriotic Ladies.

Grieved by Simon's death from tuberculosis on December 17, 1830, Manuela tried unsuccessfully to die like Cleopatra VII—from the bite of a venomous snake. On recovery, she relocated to the port city of Paita, Peru, and worked as a street vendor of candy and cigarettes and a translator of letters for illiterate sailors. After a quarter century of poverty and paraplegia, at age fifty-eight, she died on November 23, 1856, and was interred with diphtheria victims in a common grave. She bore the posthumous rank of general, for which Venezuela arranged a symbolic state funeral in Caracas on July 5, 2010. Her example survives in archived correspondence, film and television series, opera, museum exhibits, and fiction.

November 29, 1830

To end Lithuania's occupation by Russians, Captain **Emilia Plater (November 13, 1806–December 23, 1831)** of Vilnius, took part in the November 29, 1830, Insurrection against the imperial Romanov dynasty. As captain of the 25th Polish-Lithuanian Regiment, she remained at the front after the end of the eleven-month aggression in Lithuania, Poland, and Ukraine to batter patriarchal subjugators, symbolized by the Russian Imperial Army. The conspiracy, which besieged the Belweder Palace in Warsaw, forced Grand Duke Constantine Pavlovich to hide and disguise himself as a female. He escaped assassination attempts, but died of cholera in June 1831.

The capture of the Warsaw arsenal preceded Emilia's guerrilla tactics, but did not quell the bloodshed among eight thousand Poles as she crossed from Latvia in April 1831 to fight at Zarasai, Prastavoniai, Šiauliai, and Maišiagala. A painting from 1831 pictures her on horseback leading men armed with scythes, a foretaste of the 1917 peasant overthrow of the Russian Empire. At her death in hiding on a Polish estate from illness and exhaustion, her family lost property to Russian confiscation.

Her daring as Belarus, Lithuania, and Poland's national hero survived in the World War II Independent Women's Battalion and in verse, literature, sculpture, painting, drama, schools, a genus of clematis, and zloty bank notes.

January 1835

Afro-Brazilian deli owner **Luisa Mahin (fl. 1830s),** a Mahi native of Nago, Gold Coast (modern Ghana), recorded underground messages in Arabic to support an abolitionist uprising at Bahia. A West African abductee, she earned manumission in 1812. From a command post in Salvador, she communicated with runners through food platters bearing Arabic communiques to leaders. Her clever system aided the Malê Revolt of January 1835 and the five-month Sabinada insurrection of November 6, 1837, a separatist movement that resulted in the monarchist rule of the capital city of Salvador. Royalists identified several hundred Muslims wearing white *abadas* (prayer tunics) and retaliated with a cavalry charge, murder, arson, and deportation. Her capture during the Sabinada massacre at Palace Square led to persecution, flight to Rio de Janeiro, and banishment to Angola.

July 19, 1836

An Indian-Cuban anarchist and mother of five, **Caridad Mercader (March 29, 1892–1975)** from Santiago suffered a shrapnel wound on July 19, 1836, on the exodus from unrest in Barcelona to Aragon. Recovered from arrest and beating by police, she adopted the alias Louise Michel and saved the life of rebel general Manuel Goded, Barcelona's governor. In October 1936, she accepted a mission via the warship *Manuel Arnus* through Havana to Veracruz, Mexico. With U.S. volunteers to the Lincoln battalion, on January 7, 1937, she advanced on a machine gun nest in Brunete, Spain, and supplied munitions to Communist troops fighting the Spanish Civil War. On June 17, 1940, she immigrated to the Soviet Union as a Communist hero.

January 20, 1839

A Chilean from Santiago during the three-year War of the Confederation of 1836–1839, Sergeant **Candelaria Pérez (1810–March 28, 1870)** entered the military and won recognition for leading a charge at the six-hour battle of Yungay, Peru. The conflict on January 20, 1839, along the Santa River cost the Bolivia-Peru alliance three thousand casualties. By enabling the Chilean Expeditionary Force to retake Lima by April 1839, she earned a pension, honoraria, and a promotion to ensign.

June 27, 1839

To defend her son's inheritance from British theft, widowed sovereign **Jindan Kaur (1817–August 1, 1863)** of Amritsar in the Sikh Empire, fought annexation of the Punjab (modern Pakistan). She was revered as the last consort of Emperor Ranjit Singh, who died on June 27, 1839. A rebel against customs of female seclusion, veiling, and voluntary widow's death in a funeral pyre, she defied the British raj in the style of Lakshmibai of Jhansi. To terminate the downward spiral of Sikh fortunes, she settled at Jammu and took charge of governing. To secure power, she won military approval by reviewing and lecturing them. To better fund the Khalsa army's forty thousand cavalry and armored soldiers, she fought a traitor, Gulab Singh Dogra, who robbed the state treasury and colluded with the mercenaries of the British East India Company.

On the command of Governor General James Dalhousie, the British fomented war on Jindan Kaur's southern boundary in November 1845, when her soldiers moved on Jammu. She deployed the Sikh force on December 11 at the River Sutlej, crossed into Moran, and advanced on the British outpost at Ferozepur (modern Firozpur). Two clashes against heavy guns and howitzers and the collapse of a bridge cost ten thousand Sikh lives and capture of sixty-seven of their one hundred fifty guns. A weakened position in the wake of battles at Badowal and Aliwal on January 28, 1846, crushed independence in the Punjab. On March 9, the Treaty of Lahore ended the First Anglo-Sikh War, deposed the queen, and granted Kashmir to the British East India Company.

After the British abducted Jindan Kaur's eight-year-old son Duleep Singh, in August 1847, they jailed her at the Emperor Akbar's infamous Samman Tower in Lahore. She transitioned from a cell to house arrest at Fort Sheikhupura, transfer to Ferozepur, and exile south outside Varanesi to the Chunar citadel overlooking the Ganges River. Cloaked as a domestic, in May 1848, she crept from the Chunar stronghold and traversed eight hundred miles north through Nepalese woodland.

While Jindan Kaur's army surrendered, at Kathmandu on April 18, 1849, she negotiated political asylum from a condescending prime minister. Greatly reduced in dignity and respect, she resided at the Charburja Durbar palace, a sanctuary constructed for her in Nepal's capital. Blind and feeble, she reunited with her grown son in Calcutta on January 16, 1861, and retired to Kensington, England. A biopic of her son Duleep, the novel, *The Last Queen,* and the cinema *Rebel Queen* featured her resolute character, which the British compared to Messalina, scandalous wife of the Roman emperor Claudius.

September 1839

Aboard the cargo ship *Rio Pardo,* Brazilian warrior **Anita Ribeiro da Silva Garibaldi (August 30, 1821–August 4, 1949)** of Laguna, joined her lover, Italian hero Giuseppe Garibaldi, in combat. In fighting at Imbituba and Laguna on Brazil's south coastal isles in September 1839, she served as a privateer for the Republic of Santa Catarina, her introduction to soldiery. While awaiting the birth of her first child, she supplied munitions at the battle of Curitibanos in January 1840 and fled Portuguese captors. On September 16, she gave birth to Menotti, whose dented skull attested to her fall from a horse during pregnancy.

See also June 30, 1849.

May 5, 1841

Army volunteer and multilingual combat writer **Ana María Martínez de Nisser (December 6, 1812–September 18, 1872)** of Sonson, New Granada (present day Colombia), relied on sword fighting on May 5, 1841, in the mountain battle of Salamina. Her diary, *Events of the Revolution in the Province of Antioquía in the Years 1840–1841*, summarized the success of the revolution. She took pride in revenge for the torture of her Swedish husband in a Rionegro prison on the Venezuelan border. Buried in a hero's grave at Medellín, she gained renown for replacing dwindling ammunition with thousands of handmade cartridges.

1842

During battle with Blackfeet on the Northwest Plateau, Pend d'Oreilles warrior **Kuilix (Red Shirt, Mary Quille, Kuiliy, or Marie Quilax, fl. 1830s–1840s)** of Hope, Idaho, led men in charging a forested redoubt in 1842 to rescue fellow braves trapped near Lake Pend Oreille. Her people migrated south from British Columbia toward Kullyspell House, a fur trading post and Catholic mission. In 1846, she again pursued enemy Crow with a battle axe, a picturesque posture that author Nicholas Point, a Jesuit priest, featured in his memoir *Voyages aux Montagnes Rocheuse* (Journeys to the Rocky Mountains).

1842

West African slave dealers **Niara Bely Lightbourn (also Elizabeth Bailey Gomez or Niara Belly, ca. 1790–April 14, 1879)**, the widowed Luso-African queen of Farenya, Guinea, and her partner **Mary Faber de Sanger (1798–after 1857)** from Freetown, Sierra Leone, backed the Fula tribe in 1842 with an allied slave army that used cannon and arson to assault Thia, the Susu capital. On the windward coast, Niara operated a commercial outpost of six illicit barracoons that processed six thousand slaves from the Fouta Djallon high country. At a slave factory disguised as a coffee and peanut plantation near Lisso, Mary managed slave exports from Sangha to slave middleman Antonio de Freres in Havana, Cuba. After the outlawing of slave trading along the Rio Pongo, in 1855, Niara and Mary lost the War of the Mulattos to the Susu, who plundered commercial centers and burned Mary's fort.

December 30, 1842

To prevent Texas president Sam Houston's theft of territorial historic documents from Austin, the proposed capital on the Colorado River, innkeeper and taverner **Angelina Belle Peyton Eberly (July 2, 1798–August 15, 1860)** of Sumner, Tennessee, fired a load of grapeshot from a six-pound cannon. On the morning of December 30, 1842, her dramatic blast of the howitzer alerted the town to political malfeasance as twenty men loaded the papers on three ox-drawn wagons. The one-woman attack on the General Land Office building caused little harm to the structure and no personal injury. The event initiated the two-day Texas Archive War, which secured Austin as state capital. Her bold act survives in a bronze statue on Congress Avenue.

November 5, 1843

A West African abducted from Benin, **Carlota Lucumí (?–November 5, 1843)** from Mantanzas, Cuba, set a violent course of resistance in San Rafael on the island's western end at the Triunvirato sugar plantation. A Lucumí/Yoruban known as Black Carlota, she lived in bondage from age ten until she planned an uprising in 1843 with the slave **Lucumí Fermina (?–March 1844)**, a field laborer at the Arcana estate. Because of Fermina's flogging, interrogation, and chaining for threatening an overseer, Carlota alone torched a sugar mill and the master's residence and killed a guard. After the savage murder of María de Regla Pérez, her father, landowner Julian Luis Alfonso, fled the property.

By freeing workers and communicating rebellion via the talking drums beaten by Manuel Lucumí, on November 4, 1843, Carlota inspired Afro-Cubans at coffee plantations, cattle and dairy farms, and the Arcana sugar plantation to wield machetes in the cause of liberty. Shouts in the Lucumí language encouraged harvesters **Filomena Ganga (fl. 1840s)** at Acana and **Lucia Lucumí (fl. 1840s)** at the Purisima Conception mill and the creole Cubans **Carmita (fl. 1840s)** and **Juliana (fl. 1840s)** to run to the woods. As the clash grew deadlier, soldiers shot a woman. Carlota died from dragging behind horses; Lucumí Fermina and seven others died by firing squad. A military inquiry in March 1844 set off widespread vituperation and torture of all island blacks. Carlota's portrait sculpture commemorates her enslavement to the sugar industry.

February 27, 1844

Hispaniola nationalist and courier **María Trinidad Sánchez (May 16, 1794–February 27, 1846)** fought the guerrilla war of independence for the Dominican Republic. To elude control by Haiti, a francophone republic, the Hispanics on the eastern end of Santo Domingo captured the Puerta del Conde fort and engineered a Haitian surrender. María collaborated with Concepción Bona, Isobel Sosa, and María de Jesús Pina in designing a flag. The enemy executed María on February 27, 1846. Her death influenced a fourteen-year-old niece, Socorro Sánchez del Rosario, who furthered nationalism through journalism.

January 17, 1846

A Tahitian warrior queen, **Teriitaria II (also Pōmare Vahine or Ari'ipaea Vahine), (1790–1858)** from Huahine, successfully obstructed the French scheme to colonize the Leeward Islands. During the four-year Franco-Tahitian War, she promoted reconquest of the island cluster and led Christian soldiers on November 11, 1815, at the battle of Te Feipi in guerrilla warfare. Against advanced European weaponry, she dressed in fiber armor and carried both spear and musket as she marched past the king, Pōmare II. Thirty years later, she rebelled against French intrusion on Huahine Island. Armed with saber, cartridge belt, and pistol, she boarded a whaler with Raiatean troops to join their fight for liberty. Her leadership at the 1846 battle of Maeva on January 17 insulated island sovereignty from imperialism. At war's end in 1847, she signed a pact under which she ruled the islands of Huahine and Maiao without interference from France or Britain.

February 26, 1846

During the Kraków Uprising, Lieutenant **Appolonia Jagiello (1825–1866)** of Lithuania joined Polish dragoons to fight the Austro-Russian alliance. At the battle of Gdów on February 26, 1846, three hundred eighty Poles lost one hundred seventy-four fighters or forty-six percent of their army to the Austrian infantry and cavalry, which pressed on south to the Hapsburg stronghold at Wieliczka. Suppression of the revolt by overwhelming odds caused her to abandon a male disguise and travel to Hungary to continue battering Austrians and Russians at the Hungarian Revolution in March 1848. At a skirmish in Vienna, she fought at the suburb of Wieden, where she passed pro-liberation propaganda to Poles.

Following a stint of conveying rations to St. Paul, on August 15, 1848, Appolonia posed as a Hungarian peasant to escape to the Hungarian camp at Eneszey. She fought a battle that overwhelmed the Austrians, where her competence resulted in a promotion to lieutenant. She assumed management of the rebels' infirmary at Fort Komárno, Slovakia, and, in late June 1849, marched with twelve thousand to fight at the Raab River. Her job ended with Austria's takeover on August 9 at Temesvár and Hungary's surrender on October 2, 1849. By immigrating to Washington, D.C., Appolonia became a media sensation and interviewed President Zachary Taylor and Millard Fillmore.

May 3, 1846

At the siege of Fort Texas (modern Fort Brown) on May 3, 1846, cook and launderer Colonel **Sarah Borginis (also Sarah A. Bowman or Bourdette, 1813–December 22, 1866)** of Clay County, Missouri, added her musket to the Seventh Infantry's guns firing on the enemy. When Mexican general Santa Anna's troops crossed the Rio Grande from Matamoros, she cooked breakfast and ferried buckets of coffee from defense post to defense post despite bullet holes in her hat and tray. For her devotion to duty, General Zachary Taylor advanced her to colonel.

At the battle of Buena Vista outside Monterrey, Mexico, on February 22, 1847, Sarah continued to support Texans against twenty-five thousand enemy arriving from Potosí. She earned a pension as a wounded veteran. Following a career in mining, innkeeping in Texas, and rescuing Indian children, in 1866, she rated a military funeral at Fort Yuma, Arizona, for her loyal service during the Mexican-American War. Historians respect her honorarium as "hero of Fort Texas."

September 1846

A Maine soldier in the Mexican-American War, **Eliza Allen Billings (January 27, 1826–after 1851)** from Eastport enrolled under the alias George Mead with her lover, William Billings. Her 1851 autobiography *The Female Volunteer* summarized the September 1846 sweep of General Zachary Taylor at Monterey and, in March 1847, under General Winfield Scott at Veracruz, which American forces seized after a twenty-day fight. While recuperating from a sword blow to the shoulder at the battle of Cerro Gordo on April

18, 1847, she received treatment in Mexico City in the same hospital as William. In 1848, she took part in the capture of Mexico City, which cost the locals five thousand three hundred and twenty-three casualties.

September 16, 1847

Under the pseudonym "Bill Newcom," Missouri native **Elizabeth Caroline Newcom (1825–?)** signed up with the Missouri Volunteer Infantry on September 16, 1847, to fight in the Mexican-American War. To maintain a romance with Amandus V. Schnabel, she trained with the regiment assigned to prevent Apache and Comanche ambushes along the Santa Fe Trail. The unit engaged Indian parties from Franklin, Missouri, over the Osage Trace to Santa Fe, New Mexico. Deployment took her from her home state to Pueblo, Colorado, six hundred miles away. Because of pregnancy, she mustered out of service in May 1848 at Fort Mann, Kansas. On return to the volunteers, she transferred to Fort Leavenworth, Kansas, and soldiered on as a male in New Mexico until discovery of her disguise on October 1, 1848. Her request to the U.S. Congress for fair compensation won eight months' back pay and one hundred sixty acres in Platte County.

March 15, 1848

A Transylvanian widow, Captain **Júlia Bányai (1824–November 1, 1883)** from Vizakna adopted her husband's name, Gyula Sárossy, entered the 27th Battalion on March 15, 1848, and captured an Austrian spy. During a tussle with Gyula's rescuers, enemy foot soldiers plunged bayonets twice into her torso. A grenade shard in the back kept her out of combat until mid-1849, when she superintended a Hungarian retreat and dressed as a Parisian dancer to observe the Russians behind enemy lines. Following the Austro-Romanian massacre of some eight thousand five hundred citizens and subsequent repulses of the Hungarian army on June 28 and July 31, 1849, she eluded Austrian pursuers in August by fleeing to a Hungarian settlement in Turkey. Promoted to captain on her return, she joined the 1851 revolt against the Hapsburg Empire. A memorial in her hometown honors her daring.

March 15, 1848

Under the alias Karoly (Charles), Lieutenant **Marina Lebstuck (also Maria, August 12, 1830–May 30, 1892)** of Zagreb, Croatia, rode with Hussars in the Hungarian Revolution to replace feudalism and Hapsburg monarchy with democracy. After leaving her home at Zagreb to live in Vienna with an uncle, on March 15, 1848, she disguised her gender and followed his career in the Austrian imperial army. On the opposite side from him, she deployed with rebels in Austria and Hungary and contributed to the pressure on King Ferdinand I of Austria to acknowledge Hungarian rights. Her company received a welcome at Pest on April 24, 1849, from citizens newly liberated from the Hapsburg Empire.

At Buda Castle overlooking the Danube River, Marina fought during the eighteen-day siege that began May 4,

1849, and ended on May 21 in a rebel gain over the imperial cavalry. The confrontation cost the Austrians four thousand two hundred prisoners of war and the seizure of two hundred forty-eight cannon. She advanced to lieutenant for killing three enemy officers, but lost her freedom after gender identification. Wed to József Jónak in 1849, she was pregnant on August 13 when she entered jail in Budapest for espionage. After giving birth to a son, Pal Jónak, on Christmas Eve, 1849, at Arad, Romania, she entered exile in Zagreb.

March 18, 1848

A saloniere and patriot during the Lombardian Revolution, **Cristina Trivulzio di Belgiojoso (June 28, 1808–July 5, 1871)** backed Milanese rebels against Austrian insurgents in a five-day street war. In a fight for Italian sovereignty, she hired and deployed mercenaries on steeples and balconies and recruited outlying peasants and priests to man barricades against government blades and bayonets. The battle on March 18, 1848, against thirteen hundred regulars for the capture of Porta Tosa required judicious arming with swords, pikes, and six hundred fifty guns along with clubs, rocks, and bottles. A Sardinian seamstress, **Luisa Battistati (fl. 1840s)** of Stradella disarmed an Austrian dragoon and posted herself for three days at the Poppietti bridge, where she led men in shooting Croats and defending the Vettabbia orphanage.

When resistance failed, Cristina traveled to Paris to summarize the uprising for *Revue des Deux Mondes* (Review of Two Worlds). After February 9, 1849, she aided the newly formed Roman Republic by managing hospital service until the French intervened. Again on the run, with daughter Maria, she migrated to Malta, Constantinople, Syria, Lebanon, and Palestine before settling in Turkey as adviser to Camillo Cavour, Italy's unifier. A dramatic sculpture in Milan commemorates the revolt of Lombards.

March 24, 1848

A Prussian free thinker and revolutionary, **Luise Aston (November 26, 1814–December 21, 1871)** of Gröningen promoted democracy on March 24, 1848, by mobilizing with the seven thousand Freikorps or Freischar (volunteers). At the death of King Christian VIII of Denmark the previous January, questions of succession raised issues of control of the Danish straits between the Baltic Sea and the North Sea. To retain Schleswig as part of Prussia, she fought at the barricades during the three-year grassroots war against the Danish king, who conspired to retake Jutland. Fighting in Berlin preceded a struggle for Fort Rendsburg, a military nerve center. Twelve hundred Freikorps irregulars lost the battle for the Scheideck Pass on April 20, 1848, and scattered. In late summer, she left for Schleswig-Holstein to defend Prussia against Denmark.

June 23, 1848

A Balkan liberal nationalist, **Pelaghia Roşu (1800–June 10, 1870)** from Marisel, Transylvania, marshaled a female battalion on June 23, 1848, to protect her neighbors from Ottoman and Russian allies. Before the Wallachian Revolution, home schooling in warfare by her father, Ioan Dufle, prepared her for the military before she enrolled in a Budapest academy. Enlisted as a centurion from the Apuseni Mountains, she and her mother led spearmen at the second battle of Marisel. For the engagement, she mobilized women to drive out sixteen hundred Hungarian troops and served as the group's lookout and signaler on Mount Grohoiu.

A resounding upset by the Romanian cavalry forced revolutionaries into flight from seizure and jailing. The allied enemy remained in control until outbreak of the Crimean War on October 16, 1853, and the alliance of Wallachia with Moldavia in 1859 to form Romania. She received rewards of a gold cross and one hundred florins on October 9, 1850. A bronze bust, mural, and portrait depict her valor with pike and battle axe; a school and street bear her name.

September 5, 1848

During the siege of Messina, Sicily, sister heroes **Giuseppina Vadala (1824–October 7, 1914)** and **Paolina Vadala (fl. 1840s–1860)** marched through the port on September 5, 1848, on the way to occupying Don Blasco, a citadel commanding the entrance to the city's curved peninsula separating the harbor from the Messina Straits. Armed with muskets, the pair entered the surge led by **Teresa Testa di Lana (fl. 1840s)**, a goatherd who headed a cadre of criminals and armed herself with dagger, pistols, and saber. She marshaled four thousand peasants against Bourbon police being held at St. Anna's Cistercian nunnery. On February 21, 1848, the insurrectionists shot the worst of authoritarian law officers.

Another Sicilian street fighter, Corporal **Rosa Donato (1808–1867)** protested Bourbon tyranny by commanding peasant artillery for eight months against two thousand Bourbon militia. Until the fall of Palermo in May 1849, she attempted to conquer Swiss mercenaries headquartered at Messina's Pellizzeri rampart who canvassed neighborhoods and shot some two thousand residents. For maximum effect, Rosa set fire to gunpowder, slaying forty enemy, for which she suffered jailing and torture. For defending the chief cannoneer and endangering her own life while promoting Italian unification and autonomy in 1848 and 1860, Giuseppina earned a silver medal for bravery.

June 30, 1849

In the first year of the Italo-Austrian War of Independence, on June 30, 1849, **Anita Garibaldi** assisted her husband, General Giuseppe Garibaldi, in defending the Roman Republic against insurgents. The Italian Legion first engaged the French at Rome on April 27, 1849. During a fifth pregnancy, at age twenty-seven, she died of malaria outside Ravenna, Italy, in the midst of the Italian Legion's retreat. Three days later, the Roman Republic surrendered to the French troops of General Charles Oudinot. Anita's name marks Brazilian streets, a museum, a sculpture at Porto Alegre, and two biographical films, *Red Shirts* and *Anita e Garibaldi*.

A mounted statue of Anita tops Rome's Janiculum Hill.

See also September 1839.

1850

A Pawnee from Pahaku, Nebraska, **Old-Lady-Grieves-the-Enemy (fl. 1850s)** disguised herself as a medicine man and scared off the enemy with playacting and a heavy stick. On an eighty-five-acre site outside Cedar Bluffs northwest of Omaha, the virago refused to let Ponca and Sioux raiders destroy her village on a headland overlooking the Platte River. To threats of burning the villagers in their earth houses, she enacted mystic powers to terrify the enemy. Her illusion of magic restored courage in male villagers, who rescued Pahaku from harm.

Fall 1850

A Chinese idealist who promoted the fourteen-year Taiping Rebellion against the Qing dynasty, in fall 1850, **Qiu Ersao (1822-fall 1853)** of Qiaoxu, commanded a five-hundred-female regiment. From squalor, at age twenty-seven, she quit making sweets for sale, abandoned an opium-addicted husband, and joined a grassroots uprising against government graft and crime. She partnered with a younger rebel, swordswoman **Su Sanniang (also Sanmei, 1830-1854)** from Guangdong, and studied martial arts and fencing to ready for war. While Su investigated the murder of her peasant husband, the pair recruited opponents of corrupt wealth.

A war widow after fall 1850, Su guided some ten thousand followers to Nanjing in March 1853 before advancing on Yangzhou. Qiu supervised the front line at Dongxiangxu, distributed rations to the poor, and executed devious authorities at Tatangxu. While leading three thousand troops at Xupingli, she plunged to her death from a warhorse in autumn 1853. During the Opium Wars, Su's career ended in 1854 at the siege of Zhenjiang, then a British stronghold. She attacked from horseback with swords in each hand. Outlasting Qiu and Su in history, General **Hong Xuanjiao (1830–1856)**, a martial arts expert from Guangdong, set an example for thousands of amazons protesting the imperial troops of the Qing dynasty before she disappeared from history.

March 3, 1851

At a peak of native struggles against invasive French colonists, **Seh-Dong-Hong-Be (1835–after 1889)** of Dahomey (modern Benin), West Africa, advanced to lead warrior against the Egba stronghold of Abeokuta on the Ogun River in western Nigeria. At age ten, she had begun training for membership in the Dahomey Amazons. During the reign of the infamous slave-dealing king Guezo, the three-day assault on March 3, 1851, against the Egba ramparts showcased her six thousand fighters painted red and black with skulls tied to their waists. British author Frederick E. Forbes's journal *Dahomey and the Dahomans* pictured her armed with club and rifle and carrying the head of a male victim. She continued leading raids to feed the global demand for West African slaves and initially swept over the French in 1882, when she torched colonial settlements. The last historical reference named her as a combatant in the 1889 Franco-Dahomean War.

September 17, 1851

A Gros Ventres adopted by Crow, raider **Woman Chief (also Bíawachee-itchish, 1806–1854)** of Rotten Grass in the Montana foothills, led Upper Missouri clans on September 17, 1851, in settling the Fort Laramie treaty, a significant document favoring coexistence on the U.S. frontier. Known as Pine Leaf among her foster family in southern Montana, she advanced from buffalo hunter, warrior, and sharpshooter to avenger of her deceased brothers. She became spokesperson for her father's tribe in 1855. After ending a Blackfeet raid, she mustered her own squadron and attacked enemy villages to steal horses and take scalps. Admirers called her the "Absaroka Amazon." Ironically, she died in a Gros Ventres ambush at age forty-eight near the Fort Union, South Dakota, trading post on the Missouri River. Her name survives in Native American storytelling, poster art, and songs.

October 16, 1853

A legendary cavalry commander, **Aredvi Sura Anahita (fl. 1850s)**, a Kurd from Constantinople, commanded one thousand Ottoman horse soldiers on October 16, 1853, at the eruption of the thirty-month Crimean War. Named for the Irani deity Anahita, she faced European advancements in cannon design and naval explosives during the foundering of the Ottoman Empire. At a time when females withdrew from the area, she preceded her riders at Constantinople to the front of the sultan's palace. She followed Serbian field Marshal Omar Pasha's lead in Danube districts (modern Romania) in conflict against Russia, which lost £2,000,000 in military disasters at Oltenita, Silistria, Bucharest, and Yevpatoria. Legends named her the Black Virgin and compared her to Thalestris, the virago queen who wooed Alexander III the Great.

See also 324 BCE.

July 18, 1854

A prophetess and fierce Algerian resister of European colonialism, on July 18, 1854, **Lalla Fatma N'Soumer (1830–September 1863)** of Ouardja followed the Kabylia tribe's expectations for women by directing a *jihad* against the French. She aroused Berbers in the name of liberty, their heritage, and Allah and killed a saboteur with her hands. Her repeated challenges to Marshal Jacques Louis Randon, governor of Algeria, reached a height at Kabylia in the north at the battle of Tachekkirt, where she wrapped herself in a red cloak to lead seven thousand volunteers against forty-five thousand invaders. The drubbing cost the French eight hundred casualties, fifty-six of them officers.

Because of the assassination of resistance leader Cherif Boubaghla by a traitor on December 21, 1854, Lalla took his place. Marshal Randon returned in 1857 with a battery of artillery, outgunned the Kabylia, and erected Fort Napoleon at Larb'a. Fully aware of her doom, she retreated to the woods on June 23, 1857, in company with her brother, Sidi Thaieb. The French seized her in July and held her prisoner at Tablat, a camp where two hundred women and children looked to Lalla for divine protection. She died of infection and paralysis, a martyr to female militarism. She lies interred among heroes at Algiers, where Berbers and their folksongs revere her as a saint. A portrait pictures Lalla in desert dress with lance lifted; actor Laetitia Eido played her part in the biopic *Fadhma N'Soumer*.

1855

An Ojibwa warrior and prophet, **Hanging Cloud (also Ashaweia, Aswiyaa, Ah-shah-way-gee-she-go-qua', or Aazhawigiizhigokwe, 1835–1919)** of Rice Lake, Wisconsin, lived a military life and protected her clan during an ambush. As a career brave of the Prairie Rice Lake Band of the Lake Superior Ojibwa, she participated in war dancing, combat sports, and council meetings. She armed herself for battle, painted her face, and marched in plumed headdress before taking a male role in raiding the Sioux across the Mississippi to claim scalps. Following the death of her father, Chief Beautifying Bird, in 1855, her uncle Shakpi attacked her village. In the scuffle, she killed his son, her cousin.

1856

A participant in the 1856 Panthay Rebellion in Yunnan, China, **Du Fengyang (1849–1870)** fought the Mandarin enemies of Muslims. The war began in insurrectionist anger at persecution and slaughter of three thousand Yunnanese Muslims. Led by her father Du Wenxiu, it involved Du Fengyang as a soldier under his leadership. She eventually recruited her own regiment and besieged Kunming in 1869. A Qing dynasty conquest resulted in a Muslim massacre and Du Fengyang's capture, imprisonment, and execution in 1870 before she could attack Kunming a second time. Du Wenxiu advanced to sultan of Dali and ruled until 1873, when Qing authorities decapitated him.

April 11, 1856

An Afro-Indian mestizo **Pancha Carrasco (April 8, 1816–December 31, 1890)** of Cartago, Costa Rica, armed herself with a discarded rifle and bullets from her apron pockets to shoot American mercenaries at the battle of Rivas, Nicaragua. She was radicalized at age twenty-six to riot against the presidential usurper. A volunteer cook and nurse, she earned a place in women's history as Costa Rica's first female soldier. On April 11, 1856, by shaming male cowards into halting their retreat, she supported capture of river steamers, the Four Corners crossroads, and the Castle of San Juan de Ulloa overlooking Vera Cruz, Mexico. Her honoraria include an annual pension of 120 pesos, the naming of a U.S. coast guard cutter, a postage stamp, a painting of her with saber, and an excellence commendation awarded to policewomen.

May 10, 1857

A leading resister of imperialism, **Lakshmibai**, Queen of Jhansi **(also Laxmibai, November 19, 1828–June 18, 1858)** from Benares (modern Varanesi, India) battled the British Raj with the help of Indian women. She rounded out girlhood studies with gymnastics, weight training, horsemanship, fencing, and shooting. At the onset of the Indian Rebellion on May 10, 1857, she recruited fourteen thousand troops and initiated cannon manufacture to stave off the siege of Jhansi on March 23, 1858.

A soldier's wife, **Uda Devi (?–November 16, 1857)** of Lucknow mustered enough females for an armed battalion. Brandishing cavalry pistols, she served as sharpshooter of the advancing British column, but she died at the battle of Sikandar Bagh in a tree under anti-sniper fire. A combatant from Mankehadi, **Avanti Bai Lodhi (August 16, 1831–March 20, 1858),** the queen of Ramgarh, succeeded at recruiting four thousand combatants, who quashed the British at Mandla. A rebound attack on Lakshmibai's kingdom and widespread arson sent her to safety in the Devharigarh highlands, where overwhelming odds forced her to impale herself on a sword.

Queen Lakshimibai killed her mount Badal by leaping on horseback from the fort defenseworks with her stepson Damodar Rao on her back. A devoted female soldier and tactician, **Jhalkaribai (November 22, 1830–April 4, 1858)** posed as the queen during the getaway. An enemy assault on Kalpi succeeded, inspiring Lakshmibai to dress in cavalry uniform and fight British hussars. While awaiting treatment for wounds, she died from a carbine shot by a single soldier. At her request, followers cremated her remains to prevent their capture by the British. Statues, music, verse, film and television series, and poems revere her as the warrior/mother: an armed horsewoman defending her stepson against colonialism.

See also 1839.

July 5, 1857

At a high point in the Indian Rebellion on July 5, 1857, against the East India Company, commander and tactician **Hazrat Mahal (c. 1820–April 7, 1879),** the Begum of Awadh, mounted an elephant and led mutineers who seized the capital city of Lucknow. As regent for her twelve-year-old son Birjis Qadr after the banishment of her husband, King Wajid Ali Shah, to Calcutta, she defied authorities by refusing exile and remaining in Lucknow with the sixty royal wives and seventy-one children. She charged the British with destroying holy shrines and Hindu and Muslim temples that lay in the path of new roads. Freedom fighters expressed outrage that the Enfield rifle required lubrication with animal fat, a forbidden food in Islam and Hinduism.

The advance of Hazrat's thirty thousand cavalry, snipers, and artillery on Shahjahanpur failed to stop eight thousand British insurgents. After mining and looting Qaisarbagh Palace on March 19, 1858, they recaptured Awadh and Lucknow. She sought asylum at Burfbagh, Nepal, where she reorganized troops and plotted armed retaliation. After she died at age fifty-nine, monuments, a park and mosque complex, scholarships, and postage stamps saluted her courage.

September 1, 1858

A chief's daughter and the youngest wife of Kamiakin, **Colestah (1800–**

1865), a Klickatat-Yakama brave, fought in the three-year Coeur d'Alene War in Washington Territory at the battle of Four Lakes. Armed with a stone war club, on September 1, 1858, she dressed in buckskin and braids and joined combat at dawn alongside five hundred warriors from the Coeur d'Alene, Spokane, and Yakama. A loss to Colonel George Wright's seven hundred-man cavalry ended the encounter by two P.M. She retreated to her lodge on the Spokane River to tend her husband's wounds from a fall from his horse after a howitzer shell shattered a pine tree. After giving birth to son Tomomolow in 1864, Colestah died the next year at age sixty-five.

American Civil War,
April 12, 1861–April 9, 1865

The civil rebellion that threatened U.S. democracy severed the nation into warring opposites. Intense loyalties to the South and to the federal government caused women to battle on home ground. Casualties from combat and disease sapped the population and overtaxed national politics for decades to come.

April 1861

Confederate volunteer **Lucy Matilda Thompson Gauss (November 21, 1842–June 22, 1925)** from Bladenboro, North Carolina, entered the 18th North Carolina Infantry in April 1861 as sharpshooter and field medic under the name "Bill Thompson." Her war record described her as armed with a squirrel musket at the siege of Richmond and firing alongside her husband, Bryant B. Gauss. When a mortar fragment lacerated her scalp, she recuperated for two months at a military hospital. After the siege at Fredericksburg, Virginia, on December 11, 1862, she brought home Bryant's body on January 1, 1863. She lived to age 83. A bridge in Coffee County, Georgia, bears her name.

April 1861

A Union field medic and stretcher bearer from Detroit, Michigan, Sergeant **Annie Blair Etheridge (May 3, 1839–January 23, 1913)** volunteered in April 1861 and deployed with the 2nd, 3rd, and 5th Michigan volunteer infantry through thirty-two major conflicts of the American Civil War. Although her husband James fled his post, Annie won admiration and trust for riding horseback under fire to treat casualties at Bull Run, Antietam, Fredericksburg, Wilderness, and Gettysburg, a three-day clash that took fifty thousand lives. At Chancellorsville on April 30, 1863, she incurred a hand wound. She earned compliments and the rank of sergeant from General Philip Kearny for carrying medicine, hardtack, coffee, and water into war zones.

Despite bullets and shrapnel holes that endangered her life, Annie rallied Union soldiers to courage and sacrifice. In autumn 1864, she tended some four hundred casualties aboard the steamer *Knickerbocker* from the Pamunkey River north of Richmond, Virginia, to Washington, Philadelphia, and New York. She remained at work until three months after war's end. Dubbed "Gentle Annie," she received the Kearny Cross of Valor and a soldier's burial at Arlington Cemetery.

May 25, 1861

On May 25, 1861, a Canadian jack-of-all-trades for the Union army, **Sarah Emma Edmonds (December 1841–September 5, 1898)** from Moncton, New Brunswick, benefited the 2nd Michigan Infantry under the alias "Franklin Thompson." On July 21, 1861, she experienced the Union rout from the First Manassas and tended casualties and typhoid fever victims until March 1862, when she redeployed as regimental postal clerk. By April 5, she was involved in the month-long siege at Yorktown, Virginia, which boosted the reputation of Union general George B. McClellan.

Posing as an Irish vagabond, Sarah spied on the Confederates in various disguises, including as a contraband Negro coated in silver nitrate paint to darken her skin. Virginia battlefields at Williamsburg, Fair Oaks, and Malvern Hill preceded serious injuries and a broken leg while she delivered messages at the Second Manassas. Infected with malaria in spring 1863, she deserted to seek civilian medical care. In 1865, she compiled an autobiography, *Nurse and Spy in the Union Army*, with historic details of the arming of the USS *Monitor*, capturing a prisoner of war, surrender at Vicksburg, and relieving hunger and pain.

May 31, 1861

A legendary Sicilian cannoneer during formation of the kingdom of Italy, **Giuseppa Bolognara Calcagno (1826–1884)** of Barcellona Pozzo di Grotto fooled the tyrannic Bourbons at Catania on May 31, 1861, with a fake blast of gunpowder. At the Piazza del Duomo in the atrium of Palazzo Tornabene, she fired a real round crippling pro–Bourbon horsemen from Naples. She pulled the cannon four miles to Mascalucia to the pro-independence faction, where she fired on a man-o'-war shelling Catania until she used up all cartridges. She remained in service to the insurrectionists as sutler until June 3, 1861, when she adopted men's clothing and fought as a gunner to reclaim Syracusa. For her daring, she received a monument and silver medal, praise from world newspapers, a painting, and an annual pension of 108 ducats. Patriots revered her as "Peppa the Cannoneer" and kissed her hand.

July 16, 1861

A Cuban widow, **Loretta Janeta Velázquez (June 26, 1842–January 26, 1923)** from Havana, enlisted in the Confederate 7th Louisiana Regiment in male disguise and fought at Manassas, Virginia, the Union army's opening salvo against the rebellious South on July 16, 1861. According to her memoir, *The Woman in Battle*, published in 1876, she adopted a mustache, goatee, and uniform and took the name Lieutenant Harry T. Buford. With the help of her husband, John Williams, she assembled the Arkansas Grays, a company of two hundred thirty-six men who trained at Pensacola, Florida. At the same time, Southern soldier **Louisa Hoffman (fl. 1860s)**, a New Yorker, enlisted as "John Hoffman" in the 1st Virginia Confederate Cavalry and gained similar experience at Manassas.

Both women altered their careers

after the battle. Louisa signed on as a cook with the 1st Ohio Infantry until her arrest in 1864. After Loretta's introduction to combat at Manassas, she volunteered as a special agent for the South in Washington, D.C., and entered the detective corps. On October 20, 1861, she recoiled from the barbarity of Southerners at the battle of Ball's Bluff, Virginia, and, on February 11, 1862, suffered a foot wound at the six-day siege of Fort Donelson, Tennessee. By escaping to New Orleans, she aroused Union suspicion of spying. After the battle of Shiloh on April 6, 1862, she reunited with the Arkansas Grays and served the burial detail. For lacerations from an exploding mortar, she received care at a Richmond hospital by an army surgeon who discovered her true gender.

A skilled blockade runner, Loretta traveled widely on spy detail, gathered useful information, and delivered dispatches. Among Southern prisoners of war held at Johnsons Island in Marblehead, Ohio, she stirred revolts. To avoid hanging by Confederates, she changed allegiance and spied for the U.S. Secret Service in both male and female guise under assorted names, including Loretta J. Beard and Alice Williams. At war's end on April 9, 1865, she resided with Southern apologists in Caracas, Venezuela. The PBS video *Rebel* on her tenacity and energy starred Romi Dias as Loretta.

Loretta's service on January 16, 1861, coincided with that of Virginian **Mary Jane Richards Bowser (1841–?),** a member of Elizabeth Van Lew's espionage ring. An elusive legend of spying in the Confederate White House and a string of aliases leaves undocumented claims of surveillance valuable to the Union army. As reported in the *Brooklyn Eagle,* she continued to cloak her past in a series of lectures in Brooklyn and Manhattan and claimed to have eavesdropped on the Confederate Senate, plotted escapes from Libby Prison, read Southern war dispatches, and directed General Ulysses S. Grant and other military leaders to locations of enemy officers and contraband tobacco. Her story survives in fiction, drama, articles, TV series, and film.

August 1861

Newlyweds Ivory and **Mary Ann Berry Brown (June 30, 1840–March 15, 1936)** of Lewiston, Maine, fought slavery in August 1861 by signing up with the 1st Maine Volunteers. The unit answered President Abraham Lincoln's summons to seventy-five thousand civilians, who camped for three months in Washington, D.C., at Meridian Hill and guarded the capitol. Activated in the Union regiment as a field nurse and surgeon's aide, Mary Ann dressed in men's uniform, shouldered a musket, carried dirk and sword, and stuck near Ivory. In Bangor in October 1864, the couple re-upped in the 31st Maine Volunteers to serve the Army of the Potomac, which met serious losses in Virginia at the Wilderness and Spotsylvania. At the nine-month Petersburg siege, begun on June 9, 1864, her brother-in-law was shot dead next to her. When Ivory fell on the march, she treated him on the battlefield and at Harewood Hospital, a pavilion complex northeast of the city. The couple demobilized in June 1865 and farmed in Brownfield, Maine.

August 1861

In August 1861, Southern spy **Mary Jane Green (1846–?)**, a mail carrier in Sutton, West Virginia, received a sentence to four months in prison in Wheeling for carrying a skirtful of letters to the Confederate camp on the Gauley in central West Virginia. Because of her verbal attack on Union general William Rosecrans in December 1861, she again occupied a Wheeling cell, the second of seven prison terms. Along with three inmates—**Kate Brown (fl. 1860s)** from Braxton, West Virginia; Scots immigrant **Marian McKenzie (fl. 1860s),** a soldier in the 92nd Ohio Infantry; and **Nancy Hart Douglas (1846–1913)**, an arsonist and rustler from Raleigh, North Carolina—Mary Jane continued guerrilla warfare by sabotaging telegraph lines in Weston, Virginia, in May 1862, and felled a Yankee guard with a brick.

According to an article in the *Wheeling Intelligencer,* Mary Jane repeated the violations in early November 1862 and refused to take the oath of allegiance to the U.S. government and Constitution. While incarcerated in Wheeling on May 15, 1863, she shared jail time with spies **Jennie D. Hart (also Jennie DeHart, fl. 1860s)** and **Margaret O. Murphy (fl. 1860s)**, both West Virginians, and four prostitutes wearing army uniforms. On November 23, 1863, Margaret began a sentence in Fitchburg, Massachusetts, for attempting to burn a bridge.

See also April 1, 1863.

October 10, 1861

A private in the Union Army with the fifteen thousand Morton Rifles, during the fifth month of the four-year Civil War, **Mary Ellen Wise (1846–?)** of Jefferson in Huntington County, Indiana, volunteered on October 10, 1861, with the 34th Indiana Infantry. She chose the army to follow her only brother. Under the pseudonym "James Wise," the sixteen-year-old advanced to the ten-day siege of New Madrid, Missouri, on March 5, 1862, and, five days later, aided in the bombardment of an island with thirty captured Confederate guns defending the Mississippi River. After her treatment for wounds sustained at Lookout Mountain, Georgia, on November 24, 1863, and employment as a nurse in Louisville, Kentucky, her story appeared in the *Washington Daily Morning Chronicle.*

See also April 6, 1862.

October 21, 1861

An East Tennessee volunteer with the Confederate army, (**Sarah Jane Taylor, 1841–1886)** of Anderson County followed to war Company K, her stepfather's command. From Camp Dick Robinson, Kentucky, she put to use accurate pistol and Enfield musket shooting and swordsmanship. She participated in an early Union win, the battle of Camp Wildcat on October 21, 1861, in east central Kentucky. On horseback, she continued rallying soldiers of the 1st Tennessee Infantry regiment. She was captured on June 19, 1862, in Jacksonville, Georgia, and falsely imprisoned for spying for the Union.

January 19, 1862

Signed up in January 1862 at age fourteen, petite Union infantryman, cook, and field hospital medic **Lizzie Compton (1847–?)** of rural Nashville, Tennessee, stood duty with a record number of regiments during the American Civil War. Under the names "Jack" or "Johnny" she alternated service over a year and a half in the 125th Michigan Cavalry, 21st Minnesota Infantry, 79th New York Infantry, 3rd New York Cavalry, and the 8th, 17th and 28th Michigan infantries. She first experienced a day of combat at dawn on January 19, 1862, at Mills Springs, Kentucky, where the South lost five hundred twenty-nine casualties.

The war's most serious engagements at Antietam, Fredericksburg, Fort Donelson, Shiloh, and Gettysburg left Lizzie with shrapnel wounds. Similar to the fate at Antietam, Maryland, of Union amputee **Catherine E. Davidson (fl. 1860s)** with the 28th Ohio foot soldiers and sixteen-year-old **Mary Galloway (1842–1881)** of the 3rd Wisconsin, Lizzie required surgery and a physical examination. A soldiers' fight at the battle of Green River, Kentucky, revealed her gender to a surgeon who removed a minie ball from her shoulder. After arrest on February 20, 1864, in Rochester, New York, for cross-dressing, she joined the 11th Kentucky Cavalry, a heavily involved regiment that suffered a high casualty count owing to disease. On retirement, Lizzie settled in Ontario.

March 14, 1862

A wife following her husband Keith into the Confederate army, **Sarah Malinda Pritchard Blalock (March 10, 1839–March 9, 1903)** from Grandfather Mountain, North Carolina, survived removal of a bullet from the left shoulder after a night engagement on the Atlantic coast. From sign-up at Lenoir as Samuel, Keith's younger brother, on March 14, 1862, she took up a Spencer rifle and marched with the 26th North Carolina. On March 14, 1862, the regiment saw its first action in New Bern on the Neuse River and retreated west to Kinston. A Union color bearer and veteran of the First Battle of Manassas, Virginia, **Kady D. Brownell (1842–January 5, 1915)** from Kaffraria, South Africa, also paralleled her husband Robert in enthusiasm for the Civil War. Running into the midst of action, she led the 5th Rhode Island Infantry out of danger by waving the regimental flag. She ended her military involvement to care for Robert's wounds.

The Blalocks also reunited and continued deployment together in three skirmishes along the Virginia Peninsula. In April 1862, Keith located Malinda crouched in much pain, the flesh of her shoulder torn open. After CSA colonel Zebulon B. Vance appointed her as his personal orderly, she revealed her gender to the company surgeon. Upon her discharge, Keith gained a medical dispensation by rolling in poison ivy and claiming to have chronic contagious blistering.

On return to the backwoods, Malinda and Keith deserted the Confederate draft and joined the 10th Michigan Cavalry, which fought at Lexington, Kentucky, on January 25, 1864. They chose scouting in the Appalachian

Mountains, looting farms, and guerrilla raids on the Home Guard. Malinda withdrew from the military to give birth to Columbus Blalock on April 8, 1864. At Kinston in May, the couple joined the 3rd North Carolina Mounted Cavalry at the Union front line. They aided the Blowing Rock underground railroad, ambushed cavalry in narrow passes, and guided Union escapees to Tennessee. At their Watauga County home, Malinda aided Keith in adapting to a mangled left wrist and hand and a blind eye.

April 6, 1862

Private **Mary Ellen Wise** survived the battles of Corinth, Mississippi, and Shiloh, Tennessee, where fellow disguised soldier **Frances Louis Clayton (fl. 1860s)**, a barber from St. Paul, Minnesota, fought beside her husband, shoemaker John Clayton, in a Missouri regiment under the name Jack Williams. A casualty of three saber cuts at Shiloh, Frances continued in service and was arrested in Kentucky as a Confederate spy. At the battle of Stones River, Tennessee, on January 2, 1863, John died beside her. Frances caught a minie ball in the knee, which left her lame. She traveled to Nashville by ambulance train, chewing tobacco and spitting like an expert.

From the battle of Champion Hill, Mississippi, in mid–May 1863, Mary Ellen grappled hand-to-hand farther east at Jackson, Mississippi. On November 24, 1863, a musket ball pierced her side at the battle of Lookout Mountain, Tennessee. Treatment on a hospital boat to Louisville, Kentucky, revealed her gender and ended her service in September 1864. She renewed soldiery in the 65th Wisconsin until her arrest on a train. Although she rightly claimed to be a thrice wounded veteran, she had to petition in Washington, D.C., for soldier's pay, which President Abraham Lincoln granted.

See also October 10, 1861.

April 6, 1862

A widowed horse soldier, Lieutenant **Amy Clarke (1832–?)** from Iuka, Mississippi, rode with the Confederate cavalry until the death her husband Walter on April 6, 1862, at the two-day battle at Shiloh, Tennessee. According to the *Jackson Mississippian,* she buried Walter among thirty-five hundred corpses and moved on to Camp Cheatham to march as a foot soldier. Under the name "Richard Anderson," she transferred to the newly reorganized 11th Tennessee, which fought at Murfreesboro, Tennessee; Cumberland Gap in the Appalachian Mountains; Tazewell, Virginia; and Atlanta, Georgia. Shots to torso and ankle on August 29, 1862, precipitated her capture at the South's two-day achievement at Richmond, Kentucky, and imprisonment at Camp Douglas in Cairo, Illinois, for cross-dressing. She appears to have enrolled again in August 1863 and posted to Turner's Station, Tennessee, under CSA General Braxton Bragg only weeks before the three-day battle of Chickamauga, Georgia, on September 18, a grueling reb victory.

August 6, 1862

On August 6, 1862, nineteen-year-old Irish transdresser Private **Jennie**

Hodgers (December 25, 1843–October 10, 1915) from Clogherhead began a lengthy service in the 95th Illinois Infantry at Camp Fuller. She stowed away on a ship that carried her to North America. Under the alias "Albert D.J. Cashier," she engaged in forty battles at Vicksburg, Mississippi; Nashville, Tennessee; Red River, Arkansas; Guntown, Mississippi; Kennesaw Mountain, Georgia; Spanish Fort and Fort Blakely, Alabama; and Jonesborough, Tennessee. By knocking a Confederate guard unconscious, she eluded capture as a prisoner of war. She left the military on August 17, 1865, and led a normal life in Saunemin, Illinois, until November 1910, when medical care revealed her fraud. Permanently disabled, she spent the remaining years at Quincy's Soldiers and Sailors Home and was buried in uniform. History records her as the only female to fight in the entire Civil War without discovery of her gender.

August 20, 1862

During the U.S.–Dakota Indian War, **Adeline Stocking Foot (1834–October 6, 1879)** from Kandiyohi County, Minnesota, fell from wounds during mounting hostilities among plains tribes. She and husband Solomon Foot were recent homesteaders from Indiana to Willmar. Northwest of Minneapolis, fifteen Dakota Sioux attempted to recover ancestral lands at Hawk Creek in the Minnesota River Valley by massacring whites. Under fire from Little Crow's band after a dawn attack on the Lower Sioux Agency at Acton, Minnesota, on August 20, 1862, Adeline discharged rifle rounds from Gertrude and Oscar Erickson's barricaded homestead until she ran out of bullets. The Sioux raided the Foot cabin, but left it unharmed. Adeline led her two children to safety at Green Lake, but never healed from bone fractures. After the U.S. Army ended the conflict six weeks later on September 26, local Sioux remembered her as the "Woman Who Defended Her House with a Gun."

December 11, 1862

New York natives **Fanny Wilson (1842–September 15, 1864)**, a ballet dancer from Long Island, and her friend **Nellie Graves (1842–?)** took seriously their involvement in the three-day battle of Fredericksburg, Virginia. The pair concealed their enlistment from their lovers before training with the 24th New Jersey Infantry in Beverly, New Jersey. From September 30 to December 1862, they defended Washington, D.C. At age eighteen, Fanny and Nellie saw combat first at Fredericksburg on December 11, 1862, where the smaller force of generals Robert E. Lee, Stonewall Jackson, and James Longstreet inflicted more than twice the casualties than the Union.

Fanny and Nellie's next engagement on April 30, 1863, assigned them to Chancellorsville, a week-long battle on the Rappahannock River where Fanny's lover died of lethal wounds. Both friends, mourning their dead lovers, sickened from stress. Still disguised as Union soldiers, they received treatment at the brigade hospital on Jefferson Avenue in Cairo, Illinois, where staff discovered their gender. After discharge, Fanny continued her military career with the 3rd Illinois Cavalry, a regiment seasoned at Pea Ridge, Port Gibson, and Champion Hill. In May 1863, war took her to the eighteen-day siege at Vicksburg, Mississippi, a significant Northern gain where she survived a wound along with more than four thousand Union casualties. After her arrest in August 1863 in Memphis, Tennessee, on a charge of espionage, she died of infection.

December 31, 1862

Under the alias "John Williams," escort **Sarah Bradbury (fl. 1860s)** served the 2nd Kentucky Cavalry in Murfreesboro, Tennessee, at the three-day battle of Stones River, Tennessee. Following her lover into the American Civil War on September 1, 1862, Sarah chose the name "Frank Morton" for her signature with the 7th Illinois Cavalry, which headquartered at Memphis, Tennessee, after the fall of Vicksburg, Mississippi. On a foraging mission, she befriended teamster **Ella Reno (fl. 1860s)**, a scout under the alias "Frank Martin" in the 2nd East Tennessee Cavalry who also rode with the 5th Kentucky Cavalry and 8th Michigan Infantry.

Ella had a reputation for profanity and served two weeks in a cell for cursing a superior. The women got into a drunken squabble and fell into a mountain stream following the December 31, 1862, battle of Stones River, a loss for the South. General Philip Sheridan confined the rebel soldiers in Nashville for their masquerade. Union general Ambrose Burnside rescued Reno from discharge by finding employment for her at a Louisville army hospital.

January 22, 1863

Polish-Hungarian nationalist **Anna Henryka Pustowójtówna (July 26, 1838–May 2, 1881)** of Lubelskie in eastern Poland fought in the January Uprising, a paramilitary endeavor from January 22–March 18, 1863. Demanding revival of Polish independence over Lithuania, Latvia, Poland, Belarus, Russia, and Ukraine she rode horseback with rebels in Moldova as "Michal Smok," a woman dressed as a man. A Polish compatriot, **Maria Piotrowiczowa (1839–February 24, 1863)** of Kuźnicą, joined peasant volunteers armed with scythes at the battle of Dobra. While providing armaments, supplies, and rations, she ventured to the battle line, where Cossacks surrounded her. After lashing out with pistol and scythe, she killed a mount, shot an attacker, and wounded another one before the Russian cavalry hacked her remains, revealing her pregnancy with twins. Two young women also succumbed to the melee—**Antonina Wilczyńska (1843–February 24, 1863)** and **Weronika Wojciechowska (1844–February 24, 1863)**.

For four more weeks, Anna armed herself with sword and rifle as aide to Marian Langiewicz, the commander of armed guerrillas. For giving patriotic speeches and outlawry, on March 18, 1863, Austrian tsarists seized and jailed her as she crossed into Czech territory. In Paris, at age twenty-two, she taught music, made artificial flowers, and worked as a nurse before fighting in the Franco-Prussian War of 1870. Wed to a physician, she reared six children before her sudden death at age forty-two. A grand Paris monument at Montparnasse honors her combat career.

March 1863

A New Orleans creole actor and war widow, Major **Pauline Cushman (June 10, 1833–December 2, 1893)**, the renowned "spy of the Cumberlands," reported to Union officers Tennessee's Confederate position, strength, and readiness. While performing in Louisville, Kentucky, in March 1863 in the musical burlesque "The Seven Sisters," she accepted an offer from the Union Army Police to spy for the North. By posing as an exiled Southern sympathizer, she armed herself with a six-shooter, rescued Union captives from poisoning, and pretended to search for a rebel brother. Flirtation kept her popular among Confederate companies and enabled her to smuggle, identify spies, steal blueprints, and sketch supply routes, strongholds, and camps at Shelbyville and Tullahoma, Tennessee. At Pauline's arrest while passing beyond Confederate lines, a charge of sedition panicked her into an attempt to run.

CSA general Braxton Bragg order pauline tried for espionage and carrying significant documents in her boot. At the rebel retreat from Shelbyville, Tennessee, on June 27, 1863, she play-acted symptoms of typhoid fever and nervous collapse. Three days before she expected to hang, Federal forces evacuated her to Murfreesboro by ambulance and west by train to Nashville. General James A. Garfield honored her with the rank of cavalry major. In poverty and pain from arthritis, she killed herself with morphine in a San Francisco boarding house.

April 1, 1863

The *Baltimore American* reported the capture of West Virginian Sergeant **Jennie D. Hart**, a Confederate orderly in Albert Jenkins' Cavalry, a regiment of partisan horse soldiers. After a rout at Scary Creek, West Virginia, on July 18, 1861, the rangers promoted confusion in Union reconnaissance and disrupted supply routes on the Baltimore & Ohio Railroad. Pressing into Yankee territory, the rebs stole rations and supplies before the March 1863 raid on West Virginia. On April 1, 1863, Jennie began a sentence at Fort McHenry in Maryland while the cavalry scored a major win at the July 1, 1863, battle of Gettysburg, Virginia.

May 3, 1863

A Turco-French field medic for the Union Zouaves d'Afrique (Americans fighting Algerian style), **Marie Brose Tepe (August 24, 1834–May 24, 1901)** from Brest, France, survived thirteen incidents of close combat in the American Civil War. At the beginning of her service, she wore Zouave pantaloons and a Remington .44 pistol while riding a mule and toting water and whisky in a keg painted red, white, and blue. On July 21, 1861, she worked in the regimental hospital in Manassas, Virginia.

For the 114th Pennsylvania Infantry, Marie advanced to combat medic, for which she received the Kearny Cross for Valor. She endured an unrecoverable bullet in the left ankle at

Fredericksburg, Virginia, on December 11, 1862. For frontline work at Chancellorsville, Virginia, a major Confederate victory on May 3, 1863, and at Gettysburg, Pennsylvania, on July 1–3, 1863, she achieved recognition as "French Mary." After the three-day Wilderness battle at Spotsylvania, Virginia, she retired in May 1865.

June 2, 1863

A famed Underground Railroad conductor, nurse, cook, and launderer, midway through the American Civil War, **Harriet Tubman (March 1819–March 10, 1913)**, a freedwoman of Dorchester County, Maryland, applied to the Union army on June 2, 1863, to recruit military spies. The only woman masterminding a clandestine operation, to lead scouting and intelligence work for Colonel James Montgomery, she outlined Confederate troop movement, location of torpedoes, and supply lines through the swampland between Charleston, South Carolina, and Savannah, Georgia. As reported in *Harper's Weekly* on July 4, 1863, she strategized the Combahee Ferry Raid, a secret mission by three hundred soldiers among South Carolina rice plantations.

Traveling from Beaufort, South Carolina, on June 2 after 2:00 a.m. aboard the steam gunboat *John Adams*, the crew gathered runaways along the river banks. Harriet's eight scouts freed seven hundred fifty slaves, one hundred of whom enlisted in black Union regiments. The Moses of bondsmen, she led black soldiers through South Carolina low country to destroy the pontoon bridge at Green Pond, rob warehouses, and set fire to businesses, homes, mills, barns, and rice fields near Field's Point. Among the Union targets, she helped destroy the Burnett, Chisolm, Heyward, Kirkland, Lowndes, Manigault, Middleton, Nichols, and Paul plantations and transport refugees east to St. Helena Island. The Union army refused her pay for dangerous missions until artillery fire killed one escapee. She continued war work for the Massachusetts 54th Infantry, a regiment of black soldiers martyred at a rebel earthworks on Morris Island, South Carolina.

July 1–3, 1863

A North Carolina volunteer for the Confederacy, **Mollie Bean (fl. 1860s)** appears to have fought for the 47th North Carolina on July 1–3, 1863, at the cataclysmic battle of Gettysburg, Virginia. In two years' service under the male name "Melvin Bean," she survived two wounds to head and limbs. On February 17, 1865, she was captured near Richmond, Virginia, on suspicion of spying and was remanded among three thousand inmates to a jail at Castle Thunder, previously a tobacco clearing house. City newspapers declared her insane.

Mollie Bean arrived in custody after the incarceration of cross-dressing Southern cavalrymen **Molly Bell (1840–?)** and her cousin **Mary Bell (1847–?)** of Pulaski, Virginia. Under the names "Tom Baker" and "Bob Morgan," both had fought with distinction in Virginia at Chancellorsville, Gettysburg, and Spotsylvania. Molly advanced to sergeant for shooting three Union insurgents and survived an untreated shell fragment wound on her arm. Arrested on October 19, 1864, at Cedar Creek, Virginia, the Bell cousins gained respect for admirable soldiery. At their release on November 9, they returned home.

January 1864

Four months after marriage, in January 1864, **Sophronia Smith Hunt (also Satronia, October 1846–August 1, 1928),** an Illinois frontierswoman, followed her husband, James Andrew Jackson Smith, into the Union Army as both soldier and field medic. When the 29th Iowa Infantry deployed, the couple traveled south on the Mississippi River to Little Rock, Arkansas. They fought at the battle of Jenkins Ferry, Arkansas, on April 30, 1864, where James suffered a musket ball to the left thigh and leg amputation. Because the Union army left him on a rainy field and pressed on, Confederate forces captured him. In October, he died at age twenty at a prisoner of war camp in Camden, Arkansas. Sophronia's remains lay unheralded until November 11, 2016, when locals of Sioux City, Iowa, acknowledged her dual career with a headstone on Veteran's Day.

March 2, 1864

In the last year of the American Civil War, federal scout **Maria Lewis (1846–?)** of Albemarle County outside Charlottesville, Virginia, earned commendation for her use of carbine and sword at the battle of Waynesboro, Virginia. A preliterate slave who posed as Private George W. Harris, a swarthy teenager, she escaped bondage with two thousand runaways. At Rochester, New York, she entered Union ranks in October 1863 and, on March 2, 1864, fought with the 8th New York Cavalry, Union general Philip Sheridan's corps, a veteran force seasoned at Antietam, Maryland, and Gettysburg, Virginia.

As recorded in the diary of Julia Wilbur, a Quaker abolitionist at Rochester, New York, during three and a half weeks in the saddle, Maria aided the twisting of the Weldon rail lines into Maltese crosses on August 18, 1864, to halt supply trains from Richmond, Virginia, southeast to Wilmington, North Carolina. She burned bridges and sapped the Southern economy by torching mills and farmsteads. The cavalry targeted Mosby's Raiders, routed Southern troops in the Shenandoah Valley on March 2, 1864, and fought under General George Armstrong Custer in the Appomattox, Virginia, campaign. In late March 1864, she took part in an honor guard that presented Secretary of War Edwin Stanton seventeen Confederate banners and five hundred prisoners of war from CSA general Jubal Early's army. The New York Cavalry pressed General Robert E. Lee to capitulate to Union commander Ulysses S. Grant on April 9, 1865.

April 2, 1864

A challenger of European exploiters during the Tauranga campaign over land ownership, **Ahumai Te Paerata (1836–June 1, 1908)** of Hawke's Bay in northern New Zealand, led island women on April 2, 1864, in mutiny against British oppressors. A verbal aggressor of the Ngati-Te-Kohera and

Ngati-Raukawa tribes, she pledged to Major William Gilbert Mair in the Cavalry Defence Force that native women and children would risk death to defend their fortified village. For the three-day battle of Orakau at Kihikihi, one hundred females and two hundred male Maori faced fourteen hundred British soldiers. In retreat from the bastion, Ahumai survived bullets to her right shoulder and back and to arm, wrist, and hand. Seriously wounded, she trudged from the Orakau ridge through a swamp to the Puniu River and her family at Waipapa in Auckland's far north. Before she recuperated, she safeguarded a European settler from religious sacrifice. A memorial carving commemorates her humanity.

April 9, 1864

A runaway from a farm in Afton, New York, **Sarah Rosetta Wakeman (January 16, 1843–June 19, 1864)** left a detailed account of her introduction to combat at Pleasant Hill, Louisiana. Disguised as a coal transporter on the Chenango Canal from Binghamton to Utica and Canajoharie, she padded her age by four years. On August 30, 1863, she accepted a bounty of $152 (approx. $3,762 today) to sign up in Root with the 153rd New York infantry. As an infantryman, she slept in a Silbey tent and carried an Enfield rifle for picket duty. Her letters enclosed cash that she designated for the family's food and clothing.

Sarah deployed as a rations guard in Alexandria, Virginia, and at Carroll Prison in Washington, D.C. At the Red River Campaign in Arkansas, she fought alongside eleven thousand troops on April 9, 1864. Before the regiment dropped back toward Natchitoches, Louisiana, she contracted dysentery from lying all night on the battlefield among rotting human and animal carcasses. She died two months later at the Marine hospital in New Orleans and was interred on the banks of the Mississippi River at Chalmette cemetery under her alias, Lyons Wakeman. Her letters appeared in a compilation, *An Uncommon Soldier*.

April 10, 1864

The U.S. army's first female surgeon, **Mary Edwards Walker (November 26, 1832–February 21, 1919),** a writer and dress reformer from Oswego, New York, became the only female warrior Medal of Honor recipient. After attempting to volunteer for the Union army as a spy and accepting nursing as second best, she served the Cumberland Army and the 52nd Ohio Infantry in 1861 at Manassas, Virginia; in the battles at Fredericksburg, Virginia, and Chattanooga, Tennessee; and during the catastrophic burning of Atlanta, Georgia, on November 15, 1864. A feminist who warred against female finery, she dressed in practical uniform trousers and alerted the army to the honorable service of a female soldier from Illinois, **Frances Hook (1847–March 17, 1908)**, a veteran struck by shrapnel at Fredericktown, Missouri. Under the alias Frank Miller, Frances followed her brother to war and served at Vicksburg, Mississippi, and Missionary Ridge, Tennessee. Dressed as a man, she was remanded to a Confederate prison at Florence,

Alabama, where she refused to accept female inmate's clothes.

Mary served four months as a political detainee in Castle Thunder, a Richmond, Virginia, prison, on a charge of spying. On August 12, 1864, she gained her freedom in a prisoner exchange for a Confederate surgeon. The government awarded her a monthly $8.50 stipend (approx. $160.31) for muscle damage that occurred after her arrest. She published an autobiography in 1871 under the title *Hit,* a reference to verbal slurs cast on female soldiers.

For Mary's crossing into hostile encampment, Union general William T. Sherman recommended her for a military decoration for courage. President Andrew Johnson conferred posthumous honors for meritorious service in part for treating enemy casualties in hostile territory. Her example remains prominent in the issuance of a U.S. postage stamp, the naming of the liberty ship SS *Mary Walker,* and clinics and medical facilities. Her statue stands at the Oswego city hall.

September 8, 1864

Rebel sympathizers **Katie Beattie (fl. 1860s)** from Missouri and **Sarah Jane Smith (1846–?)** of Washington County, Arkansas, served cell time on September 8 1864, for sabotage of federal property. Katie faced charges of rescuing prisoners and setting fire to Union supply houses and dozens of boats. A guerrilla warrior from her mid-teens, Sarah Jane spent two years in Rolla and Springfield, Missouri, for slicing four miles of Union military telegraph poles and lines with an axe and smuggling munitions. In a St. Louis courtroom, she faced a verdict of death by hanging in November. Because of her diminished mental capacity and acceptance of rewards offered by her cousins, she received a commutation to imprisonment at Alton Military Prison in Illinois until war's end.

August 16, 1865

In the second year of the Paraguayan War, seventeen-year-old Sergeant **Jovita Feitosa (also Antonia Alves, March 8, 1848–August 16, 1869)** of Tauta, Brazil, marched with the National Army on August 16, 1865, in the guise of a man in a cowboy hat. Embarking from Teresina on a steamer loaded with volunteers to serve Emperor Pedro II, she achieved the rank of first sergeant when she reached Rio de Janeiro on September 9, 1865. Her unit faced invader Francisco Solano López, who advanced through Mato Grosso toward Dourados. She may have been stabbed by an inconstant English lover or killed at the lopsided battle of Campo Grande in Eusebio Ayala, Paraguay, a notorious slaughter of two thousand Paraguayans in a burning combat zone. At Fortaleza, a public square bears her name. Because of an alarming number of child deaths, August 16 serves as Paraguay's Children's Day, an indirect tribute to a teenage warrior.

June 24, 1866

For thirteen years, **Sylvia Mariotti (fl. 1860s–1870s)** distinguished herself as a member of the elite Italian Bersaglieri, marksmen in the Royal Italian Army. Dressed in black uniforms with wide-brimmed feathered hats, the regiment took part in the two-month Third Italian War of Independence, which attempted to unite Italians. On June 24, 1866, the skirmishers fought Austrians as shock troops at the battle of Custoza in the Veneto north of Venice. Under bombardment by forty Austrian cannon, the Italians retreated from an enemy cavalry advance, vacated the summit of Monte Torre, and crossed the Mincio River. Her prowess in combat and receipt of a medal of valor won mention in the *New York Times, Englishwoman's Review, The Oracle,* and *Young England.*

November 15, 1866

A Union private, **Cathay Williams (September 1842–1893)** from Independence, Missouri, earned national acclaim for advancing from slavery to contraband to membership in the Buffalo Soldiers, America's first black regiment. After her capture from the Johnson Plantation outside Jefferson City and transport down the Missouri River, she cooked and laundered for Union general Philip Sheridan's 38th U.S. Infantry. She traveled in Zouave (Algerian) uniform through hostile territory, possibly under the name "Finis E. Cathay." Her unit deployed at raids in Shenandoah Valley, Virginia, and the two-day battle of Pea Ridge northeast of Fayetteville, Arkansas, on March 7, 1862, where Union forces claimed control of Arkansas and Missouri. At the Red River offensive, a two-month expedition in Arkansas begun on March 10, 1864, federal troops cut off Southern links to rations, supplies, and ammunition passing from Texas through Shreveport, Louisiana.

Cathay advanced to the regular army on November 15, 1866. She survived smallpox and continued her military career in New Mexico before discharge at Fort Bayard, New Mexico, on October 14, 1868. She prolonged her disguise under the alias "William Cathay." To remain independent, she reenlisted with the Buffalo Soldiers at Fort Union, New Mexico, during the Indian Wars and escorted wagon trains, miners, and settlers along the Santa Fe Trail from Missouri to north central New Mexico. In 1876, the *St. Louis Daily Times* issued a biography of Cathay as the first black female in the Union army. Although she petitioned for a disability pension, in September 1893, the examining doctor at Trinidad, Colorado, rejected coverage for treatment of amputated toes, deafness, diabetes, and arthritis by labeling them pre-existing conditions. A bronze bust in Leavenworth, Kansas, commemorates her unprecedented career.

September 17, 1868

A widowed Cheyenne dog soldier and scout at the three-day battle of Beecher Island, Colorado, **Ehyophsta (also Yellow-Haired Woman, 1826–August 1915)** of Montana fought for liberation from reservations. Near the juncture of Nebraska and Kansas on the Arikaree River, a large alliance of Southern Cheyenne dog soldiers, Arapaho, and Oglala Sioux raiders led by Roman Nose faced a select unit of U.S. army veterans armed with Spencer rifles and camped on a sandbar. Native sharpshooters surrounded the spot on September 17, 1868, or crept through grass to pin down the fifty frontiersmen. The stench of the dead men and slaughtered horses threatened sickness and disease until rescue from Fort Wallace relieved the standoff on September 30. The native band lost Roman Nose, one of the great battle tacticians of the Plains Indian Wars.

Ehyophsta survived the bitter clash of whites with Indians, in which she rode her father's horse in repeated forays and sang victory songs with Lakota compatriot **Buffalo Wallow Woman (fl. 1868)** to encourage braves. Along with Ehyophsta's daughter and their dog, she returned to service as interrogator against the Shoshone captured in 1868 and 1869 at Powder River, Montana. Ehyophsta died at the Tongue River Reservation in Montana at age eighty-nine. Sculptor Judy Chicago honored the famed Cheyenne in the art display *The Dinner Party*.

September 23, 1868

A flag designer and prisoner of war, **Mariana Bracetti Cuevas (1825–1903)** of Añasco, Puerto Rico, fostered the island revolution against Spanish overlords. With a throng of eight hundred, on September 23, 1868, she followed insurrectionist Miguel Rojas from his El Triunfo plantation to Lares in the west central mountains. During the Grito de Lares (Lares Uprising), the armed rebels proclaimed the island a free republic under a red, white, and blue flag that Mariana knitted from yarn raveled from a skirt. On advance to San Sebastián del Pepino, she was arrested and jailed at Arecibo for four months. Admirers dubbed her "Brazo de Oro (Golden Arm)." Her devotion to liberty appears in histories, storytelling, sculpture, and the naming of roads, a museum, and schools.

October 16, 1868

A martyred samurai during the eighteen-month Boshin civil war, on October 16, 1868, **Nakano Takeko (April 1847–October 16, 1868)** of Edo in south central Japan mustered a thirty-member female battalion from Aizu Province. Inspired by the legends of twelfth-century heroine Tomoe Gozen, Nakano mastered martial arts, demonstrated the *naginata* (halberd), and taught hand-to-hand fighting to noncombatants at Aizuwakamatsu Castle. Throughout the four-week battle of Aizu against the Satcho Alliance in October 1868, she led an autonomous phalanx through freezing rain and threatened to commit suicide if denied a place on the front line defending Crane Castle.

Nakano's comrades incorporated martyred Aizu martial fighter **Jingo Yukiko (1845–October 10, 1868)** and Aizu warrior-medic and rifle expert **Yamamoto Yaeko (also Niijima Yae, December 1, 1845–June 14, 1932)**. Their female contemporary, **Yamatawa Futaba (1844–November 14, 1909)** of Aizu, defended the castle from inside. At the advance on the Japanese Imperial Army at Yanagi Bridge, Nakano slew six aggressors before dying from a rifle bullet to the torso. A statue in Fukushima depicts her in wide stance with bladed pole in hand and a sword in her belt. Hokai Temple displays her *naginata* (bladed pole). A landmark model of the seven-story castle replaced the original site, which collapsed from artillery shelling.

See also February 21, 1184.

October 20, 1868

A sixteen-year-old nationalist and color bearer during the Cuban fight for liberation from Spain, on October 20, 1868, **Candelaria Figueredo (December 11, 1852–January 19, 1914)** of Bayamo risked flight to the jungle and seizure by the Spanish. She played the piano to prevent neighbors from hearing rebels conspire at her home. During the Ten Years' War, she gathered medicines for peasants at the Las Mangas mill and sewed a Cuban flag. She brandished it in her hometown from a white horse and earned the nickname "La Abanderada (The Standard Bearer)."

During Candelaria's search for water in the mountains, Spanish trackers struck her senseless. A prisoner of war at Manzanillo from July 1871, she entered exile in Jamaica and rescued a younger sister and brother by sailing to New York on the schooner *Annie*. From a reunion with surviving family in Key West, she retreated to Nassau, Bahamas, to recuperate. At her death, she lay in state like a soldier in Havana beneath the original flag. Sculptor Judy Chicago featured Candelaria in *The Dinner Party*.

Spring 1869

A leader of a criminal gang, in spring 1869, **Sadie Farrell (fl. 1860s)**, the Irish queen of New York City's riverfront, profited from piracy of upriver merchantmen on the Hudson. Formerly a common thug in the Fourth Ward, she earned the named "Sadie the Goat" for body blows against drunks with her head. Her muscle man finished each job with a slingshot or club. On the Lower Manhattan piers of the East River in 1869, she joined the Charlton Street Gang in waylaying a sloop on the North River and conspired to seize more cargo from warehouses, villages, farms, and boats from the Harlem and Hudson Rivers to Poughkeepsie. Because Sadie advanced to kidnap and murder, within months, reciprocal attacks on the shores forced her gang back to the city.

March 1, 1870

Irish adviser and military supplier **Eliza Alice Lynch (November 19, 1833–July 27, 1886)** from Charleville, Cork, backed her ambitious lover, General Francisco López, in the Paraguayan War against Argentina, Brazil, and Uruguay, South America's most devastating conflict. An enslaved native, **Ramona Martínez (fl. 1870s)**, joined Eliza as a sword-carrying field medic on December 21, 1868, at the lopsided battle of Itá Ybate, Paraguay. López hoped that the War of the Triple Alliance would secure Río de la Plata as an outlet to the sea. The week-long conflict cost him three thousand casualties—his entire army. Eliza's last baby died in the combat zone from dysentery.

On March 1, 1870, Eliza soldiered on to the battleground at Cerro Corá, Brazil, with a female cadre, *Las Residentas* (The Local Women), composed of military wives and daughters. The combat support group sold their heirlooms and jewelry to pay for supplies and rations. At war's end, Paraguay lost seventy percent of male citizens. At the fall of López and their fifteen-year-old son Juan Francisco during a retreat, Eliza buried them with her bare hands. The provincial governor seized her inheritance and banished her and her four surviving sons to Paris, where she died in poverty. Her self-sacrifice survives in a street name and monument, novels, drama, ballet, and the film *Eliza Lynch: Queen of Paraguay*, in which Maria Doyle Kennedy plays Eliza.

July 19, 1870

A teenage sharpshooter on the front of the Franco-Prussian War, **Jane Magre Dieulafoy (July 29, 1851–May 25, 1916)** of Toulouse, France, accompanied her husband, archeologist Marcel Dieulafoy, to Nevers on the Loire River on July 19, 1870, to a lost cause. On the way to central France to fight Prussia, she eased travel perils by cropping her hair, flattening her chest with a board, and wearing men's suits and ties to conceal her femininity in camp. In action to the west defending Bourges, she witnessed the two hundred thousand French in the XV Corps challenging a Bavarian regiment and Prussian cavalry and infantry. The long winter exhausted her with malnutrition and marching along corpse-lined roads. In 1913, she repeated the selfless act in World War I by traveling with her seventy-year-old husband to Rabat, Morocco, to aid the engineering corps and lobby for female recruitment in the Austrian military.

1871

Among the women warriors of North American plains tribes, Hunkpapa Sioux battler **Moving Robe Woman (also Tashenamani and Mary Crawler, 1853–1936)** of Grand River, South Dakota, daughter of Sunflower Face and Chief Crawler, became a sturdy brave in 1871 from her first battle against the Crow at age seventeen. The tribal face-off began in summer 1870 when Sioux raiders scoured the Bighorn district for buffalo. The incursion into Montana caused Crow chief Blackfoot to protest to the U.S. army of boundary infractions on heritage lands.

On June 25, 1876, at the battle of the Little Bighorn, Moving Robe Women leveled vengeance at U.S. General George Armstrong Custer for killing her young brother Deeds or One Hawk. Readying for battle alongside the Cheyenne and Crow, she braided her hair and painted her face red before clutching Deeds's war staff and mounting a black horse that her father brought. One eyewitness stated that she stabbed Custer in the back and used a sheath knife and pistol to kill two more horse soldiers, one of them interpreter Isaiah Dorman. Lakota war chief Rain in the Face credited her with inciting male warriors to compete in combat. At the battle's end, she followed Sitting Bull to safety in Wood Mountain in the Northwest Territories (modern Saskatchewan).

March 18, 1871

For participating in the four-month siege of Paris on September 19, 1870, and aiding the two-month Paris Commune as explosives expert and medic on

March 18, 1871, **Louise Michel (May 29, 1830–January 9, 1905)**, a French educator and author from Vroncourt-la-Côte, was deported. Preceding the German war with Napoleon III, she served on the vigilance committee at Montmartre, dressed in a National Guard uniform, and carried a rifle. Joining her cadre were Russian medics **Anne Jaclard (October 18, 1844–October 12, 1887)** from St. Petersburg and **Elisabeth Dmitrieff (November 1, 1850–1918)** of Volok; **Nathalie Lemel (August 26, 1827–1921)**, a Breton from Bristol; **Eliska Vincent (1841–1914)** from Mézières; ambulance driver **Elisabeth Retiffe (January 9, 1834–February 24, 1882)** from Vézelise; laundresses **Leontine Suetens (May 4, 1846–November 1, 1891)** of Beauvais and **Joséphine Marchais (April 13, 1837–February 20, 1874)** of Blois; medic **Eulàlia Papavoine (November 11, 1846–May 24, 1875)** from Auxerre; and **Paule Mink (also Minck, November 9, 1839)**, of Clermont-Ferrand, France.

While Paule and Elisabeth Dmitrieff escaped a rebel roundup for fighting Paris police in the urban Père-Lachaise cemetery riot, Nathalie, Louise, Josephine, and Anne were arrested. Josephine, Leontine, Eulàlia, and Elisabeth Retiffe were condemned in September 1871 as armed arsonists marked by red scarves, even though the court presented no evidence. Sentenced to hard labor, they were deported to Saint-Laurent-du-Maroni, French Guiana, where Josephine and Leontine died in prison. Anne and Eliska eluded a death sentence on December 29, 1871. Anne married socialist philosopher Karl Marx, repatriated to Russia, and translated *Das Kapital* (Investment) into French. Louise and Nathalie were deported to Noumea, New Caledonia, on the prison ship *Virginia* and incarcerated in a cage for three years. On regaining freedom in 1880, Louise survived an assassin's shot to the skull at Le Havre and two weeks jailing in 1882 for rioting under a black flag. She detailed her anarchist career in a memoir carrying her nickname, *The Red Virgin*.

1872

In her mid-teens, **Gouyen (also The One Who Is Wise, 1857–1903)**, traveled four days on foot to assassinate a Comanche chief who murdered and scalped her first husband. The Chiricahua Apache daughter of Nahdoste and Nana, she was born in New Mexico in 1857. In the midst of a triumphal celebration in 1872, she found the killer bearing her husband's scalp on his belt. She posed as a local girl and lured the drunken chief to a tryst. After seizing his knife, she stabbed and scalped him and returned to her camp with his breechcloth, headband, moccasins, and a stolen horse.

At the battle of Tres Castillos on the Texas-New Mexico border in 1880, Gouyen traveled with Victorio's band of Texas warriors from Chihuahua. The company lost to a Mexican military assault, which killed her baby girl. Gouyen's deeds continued in 1883 with rescue of her second husband, Kaytennae, from a hidden white attacker. After her capture with Geronimo's rebels, she died in prison at Fort Sill, Oklahoma.

1874

Storied frontierswoman **Martha Jane Cannary (May 1, 1852–August 1, 1903)** from Princeton, Missouri, applied for military employment in 1874 at Fort Russell west of Cheyenne, Wyoming, as a scout and sharpshooter for U.S. General George Armstrong Custer. During the Indian Wars from 1872 to autumn 1873, she fought in skirmishes of the Muscle Shell Indian uprising and earned the nickname Calamity Jane. Deployed at the Big Horn River under General George Crook in 1875 against Sioux outbreaks, she rode hard and swam the Platte River to deliver dispatches to Fort Fetterman, Wyoming. She altered her work in 1876 by leading parties of settlers to Rapid City and Deadwood, South Dakota, and returned to riding with the 7th Cavalry in fall 1877 to Bear Butte Creek northeast of Deadwood. Her eventful life filled wild west scenarios, plays, music, fiction, and comic books. The screen version *Buffalo Girls* featured actor Anjelica Houston as Jane.

June 19, 1875

A Dutch East Indies saboteur and member of a guerrilla brigade, **Jeanne Merkus (October 11, 1839–February 1, 1897)** from Batavia (modern Jakarta, Indonesia) battled the Ottoman Turks in the Dinaric mountains above Dubrovnik, Croatia. With the aid of forces from Montenegro and Serbia, the Herzegovinian Serbs fought the cavalry of tax-hungry Balkan Muslims at Bosnia on June 19, 1875, by demolishing Turkish forts. Catholic rebels stockpiled munitions against the Ottoman alliance with Austria. By 1876, a quarter million peasants emigrated to Croatia, launching the Great Eastern Crisis. In March 1876, the enemy imprisoned Jeanne. She recovered from serious illness and, on July 1, 1876, repatriated to the Croatian military. Into 1878, Jeanne, a fan of Florence Nightingale, hero of the Crimean War, managed care for Serbian casualties, a career she began during the Franco-Prussian War.

June 17, 1876

At age thirty-two, **Buffalo Calf Road Woman (1844–May 1879)** impressed the Northern Cheyenne by rallying warriors at the battle of Rosebud, Montana Territory, on June 17, 1876. Throughout the Great Sioux War of 1876, she fought alongside her husband, Black Coyote. She rode all night from Ash Creek among eighteen hundred warriors, who attacked nearly one thousand U.S. troopers on June 17, 1876, at 8:30 a.m. After seeing her twenty-six-year-old brother Comes in Sight fall from his dead horse, she dashed to his aid. Riding double, she took him out of the six-hour battle, which pitted fifteen hundred Cheyenne and Sioux against the army's thirteen hundred cavalrymen and scouts.

Fought between U.S. General George R. Crook and Crazy Horse's alliance of Northern Cheyenne, Dakota, Arapaho, and Lakota Sioux, the battle involved a Crow army scout, **The Other Magpie (May 1849–after 1900)**, and her transsexual comrade Osh-Tisch. According to witness Pretty Shield, The Other Magpie raged against Indians who had killed her brother and sang a war song.

Armed with coup stick and knife and marked by yellow paint on her forehead and a stuffed woodpecker on her head, she struck and scalped Bullsnake, a Sioux warrior. While Crook left the field and regrouped outside Sheridan, Wyoming, The Other Magpie and Crow braves shared pieces of the scalp and danced to celebrate their bravery.

See also June 25, 1876.

June 25, 1876

Eight days after the battle of the Little Bighorn, **Buffalo Calf Road Woman** acquired lasting fame as the soldier who knocked U.S. General George Armstrong Custer from his horse with a club. During fighting on the Little Bighorn River, Montana, the Northern Cheyenne brave who held a reputation for keen marksmanship. She fell into army hands on April 10, 1879. While awaiting her husband's murder trial in Miles City, Montana Territory, she died in May 1879 at age thirty-five from malaria or diphtheria.

A Lakota Sioux, twenty-year-old **Minnie Hollow Wood (1856–1930s)** became the only female in the tribe to earn the right to wear a war bonnet after joining her Cheyenne husband Hollow Wood in attacking Custer at the battle of the Little Bighorn. After surrendering to the U.S. Army general Nelson A. Miles in 1877 at Fort Keogh, Montana Territory, she lived into her seventies. In 2019, an animated film depicted her as a highly esteemed Lakota female.

Accompanying Brule Lakota husband Crow Dog at the Little Bighorn catastrophe, Oglala Lakota fighter **One Who Walks with the Stars (fl. 1870s)** chanced on two soldiers crawling toward cavalry horses at the riverbank. She stabbed and clubbed them both to death with driftwood. Another Lakota wife, **Susie Shot-in-the-Eye (also Red Bird, 1838–after 1910)** of Pine Ridge, South Dakota, rode as battlefield comrade of husband Shot-in-the-Eye and sons High Wolf, Lone Hill, and Rock. Nearly a quarter century later, Chief Sitting Bull honored Susie by topping her head with his warbonnet. The Smithsonian displays the necklace she made of enemy fingers.

French-Arapaho war chief **Pretty Nose (1851–1952)** banded with the Arapaho and Cheyenne and carried a Springfield rifle to fight Custer and the Seventh Cavalry. After she survived the battle of the Little Bighorn, she initiated a women's warrior society. She lived to age 101 at the Wind River Reservation, Wyoming, and died in 1952. Other females—two of Sitting Bull's wives, Hunkpapa Lakota-Teton Sioux **Her Four Blankets (1855–)** and **Seen by Her Nation (1846–1897)**, and Brule Sioux **Mary Fine Weather** of Eagle Butte, South Dakota—joined the infamous defeat as backup for armed women and youths. Her Four Blankets was shielding two-week-old twin sons when the cavalry attacked the camp. She raced through combat to retrieve one of the boys. Her Four Blankets and Seen by Her Nation surrendered in 1881 with the extended family.

See also 1871; June 17, 1876.

November 9, 1877

A revenge seeker during the Russo-Turkish War in northeastern Erzurum province of the Ottoman Empire, **Nene Hatun (1857–May 22, 1955)** from Çeperli accompanied farmers on November 9, 1877, in recovering Fort Aziziye, Turkey, from enemy troops. Armed with hatchet and rifle, she left her son and infant daughter and joined a civilian crush that forced down iron doors. Amid the Balkan crisis and ethnic cleansing, over two days, a mob of Turks slew two thousand Russians and their Romanian allies and routed the remainder. Amid one hundred twenty thousand killed from epidemics or decapitation, she recovered from severe injuries and earned regard as the last survivor of the war. At her death at age ninety-eight, the "Mother of the Third Army" was interred at the fort. Her name survives in film, a statue, stories, and a rescue and salvage vessel.

1878

The only female leader of the Piegan Blackfeet, **Running Eagle (also Brown Weasel Woman or Pitamaka, ca. 1830–1878)**, of Southern Alberta, Canada, advanced from foster mother of four siblings to victorious rustler of horses and fighter in war parties. She gained manly skills from her father, who taught her buffalo stalking. An encounter with the Assiniboin about 1850 caused her to rescue her father from a dying steed and carry him on her horse. On a sweep of Kalispel stock across the Rocky Mountains at Flathead Lake, Montana, the fifteen-year-old warrior captured six pintos. Armed with her father's rifle while retaliating against a Crow encampment, she took eleven horses, killed two pursuers, and counted coup.

As a model of courage and stealth, Running Eagle continued poaching Crow, Kootenai, Pend d'Oreille, and Sioux horses, dodging enemy arrows, and narrating her adventures to the tribe. In her ninth foray in 1878, the Flathead targeted her for murder at Sun River east of the Rockies and bashed in the back of her skull. Two landmarks, a lake and Running Eagle Falls, retain her name in Montana's Glacier National Park.

See also 1910s.

June 29, 1878

Widowhood convinced Muslim strategist **Cut Nyak Dhien (1848–November 6, 1908)** of Lampadang, Aceh (modern North Sumatra), to retaliate against Netherlands conquests in the Aceh Empire. She was born to a military clan and, at age twelve, wed an army commander, who died alongside her father on June 29, 1878, at the battle of Sela Glee Tarun. She immediately took charge of their troops. Remarried to Teuku Umar, she joined him in 1880 in guerrilla warfare by foiling ambush and traps. She carried into jungle headquarters their baby girl, **Cut Gambang (1880–1910)**, a child freedom fighter disguised in the field to prevent abduction.

Cut Nyak Dhien continued leading the dwindling Aceh army through another widowhood on February 11, 1899, until the Dutch triumphed in 1901. A betrayer relayed her position at Beutong Le Sageu, where the enemy captured her on November 5, 1905. Ill with arthritis and limited vision, she fought back with a traditional blade. During her exile to West Java, daughter Gambang continued the underground resistance until the Dutch shot her in the stomach during combat in 1910. An airport and cinema display Cut Nyak's name.

July 31, 1878

Two Northern Paiutes—the daughter of Half Moon and Chief Shenkah, **Mattie Winnemucca (1846–1879)**, wife of Lee Winnemucca, and her sister-in-law, midwife and orator **Sarah Winnemucca (also Thocmentony or Shell Flower, 1844–October 16, 1891)** of Humboldt Lake, Nevada—scouted, delivered messages, and interpreted for the U.S. Army and treated war injuries. After Mattie's father's death, she passed to the care of Uncle Egan, who taught her to ride a pony on a long trek to Malheur, Nevada. At age twenty-eight, Sarah interpreted native languages at Camp McDermitt, Oregon, before accepting a scouting assignment with General Oliver Otis Howard to rescue Paiute captives on a gallop of two hundred twenty-three miles.

While serving as lookout on July 31, 1878, in the Bannock Indian War in Idaho and Oregon, Mattie suffered a lethal fall from a horse and died of paralysis in spring 1879 on a march to Fort Simcoe in Washington Territory. Made famous by lecture and an autobiography, *Life Among the Paiutes,* Sarah was widowed in 1887. She succumbed to tuberculosis in 1891 at age forty-seven.

October 1, 1878

During the St. Croix Fireburn on October 1, 1878, **Mary Leticia Thomas (1848–March 16, 1905)** of Antigua, led African laborers in torching and rifling fifty Danish plantations. Dubbed "Queen Mary" for her courage and crowned with the traditional tignon (head wrap), she was employed at Sprat Hall, a French colonial cotton, indigo, and sugar plantation. Mary relied on black Crucians **Axeline "Agnes" Elizabeth Salomon (1855–August 3, 1904)** of Estate Bethlehem, **Susanna Abrahamson (1831–July 20, 1906)** of St. Croix, and **Mathilda McBean (1857–October 10, 1935)** of Estate Hogensborg to sanction with ritual the two-week rebellion in the Virgin Islands. The ritual preceded the destruction of fields, sugar mills, and Frederiksted's government offices.

The four resisters eluded a death sentence by a judge's commutation to life in prison at hard labor. After sailing aboard the bark *Thea,* they served in Christianshavn, Denmark, and the Richmond Jail in Christiansted, St. Croix. Mary's name survives on an island highway and fountain, a screenplay, and a supersized sculpture in Copenhagen in front of the West Indian warehouse. The proud pose depicts her with cane bill (harvesting knife) and firebrand. At Blackbeard's Castle on St. Thomas, a group statue pictures Mary battling colonialism alongside Axeline and Matilda and lifting lanterns to show the way.

February 21, 1879

Libertarian undercover agent **Lyudmila Wolkenstein (September 30, 1855–January 23, 1906)** of Kiev, Ukraine, conspired to assassinate Dmitri Kropotkin, the Kharkov governor. Lyudmila provided the anti-tsarist headquarters from which the attack started on February 2, 1879. After a shot killed Kropotkin as he exited a theater on February 21, 1879, Lyudmila escaped in a zigzag flight across central and southern Europe and Turkey. On October 10, 1883, her execution was commuted to two decades in Schlüsselburg fortress in St. Petersburg, where she befriended assassin **Vera Figner**. Lyudmila composed an autobiography while exiled to the island of Sakhalin, Siberia.

See also March 1, 1881.

November 2, 1879

An acclaimed combatant in the War of the Pacific, Lieutenant **Filomena Valenzuela Goyenechea (1848–1924)** from Copiapó, Chile, fought in the landing operation of November 2, 1879, that secured the Port of Pisagua, Peru. Chile's amphibious attack by five thousand sailors and infantry repelled the combined one thousand one hundred forty-one troops of Bolivia and Peru. The successful sweep along the beachhead won Chile an introit to dominion in a six-year conflict over valuable mining territory rich in copper, saltpeter, and silver and control of Pacific trade routes. For her vigor, Filomena acquired the nickname *La Madrecita* (Little Mother).

Filomena continued military service on March 22, 1880, when four thousand five hundred combined artillery, infantry, and cavalry concluded combat with a surprise bayonet charge. Her exceptional performance earned promotion to second lieutenant. A fellow soldier, **Irene del Carmen Morales Galaz (October 22, 1848–August 25, 1890)** of Santiago, earned advancement to sergeant for accuracy with a rifle and for treating casualties.

July 27, 1880

A teen poet and martyr on July 27, 1880, during the decisive conflict at Maiwand, Afghanistan, **Malalai (1861–July 27, 1880)** of Khig, Kandahar, boosted passion and determination in Afghan soldiers by defying British imperialists. At the end of the Second Anglo-Afghan War, the Pashtun heroine joined the struggle for independence. She, along with her father and fiancé, aided former emir Ayub Khan in combatting British-Indian insurgents, who intended to annex the country as a colony. She joined a female auxiliary of medics and suppliers of food, water, and arms to drive out occupation forces. Grasping her veil in place of the national flag, at a lull in Afghan spirit, she rallied warriors with a familiar folksong until felled by a British bullet. Her grave drew patriots to commemorate a national folk hero. Hospitals and schools bear her name.

October 14, 1880

Lozen (1840–June 17, 1889), a Chiricahua Apache brave from Arizona Territory, joined her older brother Victorio as his lieutenant to combat the lies and persecutions of southwestern settlers against First Peoples. In girlhood, he taught her rock climbing, bareback riding, marksmanship, and hand-to-hand combat. She developed clairvoyance in her teens. On leaving a miserable situation at the San Carlos Reservation in 1877, she and some one hundred forty-five refugees hid in the desert. To sustain a life on the run, they raided ranches and military installations at Black Mountain, New Mexico, for horses and bullets.

At the end of Chiricahua ammunition and supplies, on October 14, 1880, the Tres Castillos Raid on an oasis in Chihuahua, Mexico, pitted two hundred fifty locals against Victorio and his companion **Gouyen**. The enemy slew sixty-two male Apaches and Gouyen's infant daughter and sold sixty-eight women into slavery. Mexican warriors lost two hundred to Lozen's vengeance. She committed herself to Apache self-determination by joining the guerrilla band of Geronimo and her uncle, Chief Nana, in August 1881.

See also October 1883; May 17, 1885

March 1, 1881

Russian assassin **Vera Figner (July 1852–June 15, 1942)** of Khristoforovka aided in the bombing of the royal Romanov carriage on March 1, 1881, that shattered the legs of Tsar Alexander II. She trained in medical studies at Zurich and Bern, Switzerland. In St. Petersburg, she headed the People's Will Executive Committee and stored dynamite for the February 1880 bombing of the Winter Palace. Terrorist conspirator **Sonia Perovskaya (September 1, 1853–April 15, 1881)** outlined both plots, made the bombs, and signaled the attack. She and two confederates died on the gallows in St. Petersburg on April 15, 1881. Vera remained free until arrest at Kharkov, Ukraine, on February 10, 1883. For two decades, she served a commuted sentence in isolation at Schlüsselburg fortress in St. Petersburg until her banishment in 1904. She summarized her insurrectionism in a six-volume tell-all, *Memoirs of a Revolutionist*.

See also February 21, 1879.

January 10, 1883

In the role of Ecuador's first lady, **Marieta de Veintimilla (1855–March 11, 1907)**, a widow from Guayaquil managed national defense in the absence of her uncle, President Ignacio de Veintemilla. At the onset of civil war in 1882, she took charge of the military. With raised revolver, she dashed among the battle lines and shouted encouragement to defenders of Quito's Carondelet Palace in Plaza Grande. Soldiers called her *La Generalita*. The uprising deposed Ignacio from his dictatorship on January 10, 1883, and installed a provisional government. At Ecuador's loss, she served a year in the Guayaquil city jail, during which she experienced attacks of angina. After banishment to Lima, Peru, she published *Pages of Ecuador*. She dedicated her last year to arming rebels to reinstate her uncle.

October 1883

Lozen and fellow Chiricahua Apache raider **Gouyen (1857–1903)** escaped the roundup of sixty-eight women and children and the Mexican parade through Chihuahua displaying Victorio's scalp. In October 1883, Gouyen showed her daring by rescuing her second husband, war chief Kaytennae, from an ambush. In company with Geronimo and Juh in the Sierra Madras, Gouyen helped steal two thousand horses, some of them belonging to the Mexican cavalry.

See also October 14, 1880; May 17, 1885.

May 17, 1885

Lozen, **Gouyen**, and **Dahteste (also Tah-das-te, 1860–1955)**, a Chokonen Apache and confederate of Cochise, joined Geronimo and his brother-in-law Nana in a jailbreak from San Carlos Reservation in Arizona. After guiding women from Warm Springs Reservation, New Mexico, Lozen continued raiding ranches and military supply depots. Following her arrest, the army lodged her in St. Augustine, Florida, and in Alabama at the Mount Vernon Barracks. Tuberculosis and malnutrition claimed her, unmarried and childless, in her late forties on June 17, 1889. Her remains lie in a communal grave.

On May 17, 1885, Gouyen survived the Fort Sill, Oklahoma, military prison and, in 1903, died in custody at age sixty. Dahteste partnered with outlaw husband Ahnandia and served the Apache as translator, scout, medic, and messenger. After eight years as a prisoner of war in St. Augustine, Florida, Dahteste told war stories at the Mescalero Apache Reservation in New Mexico. She lived to age ninety-five and died in 1955.

See also October 14, 1880; October 1883.

November 14, 1885

On November 14, 1885, Bulgarian rifleman **Yona Markova (1855–1923)** from Boynitsa fought in the two-week Serbo-Bulgarian War as a man. Disguised as "Ivan Markov" in a military overcoat crisscrossed in bandoliers, she enlisted in the Second Vidin Volunteers at Sofia on September 7, 1885. The one hundred twenty-five fighters contained Montenegrins and Slavs. The Bulgarian dependence on small arms failed to compare to the Serbian purchase of steel cannon from the Krupp factory at Essen, Germany.

Intervention by Austria-Hungary ended the Bulgarian invasion on November 28 with the countering of poorly led insurgents from the southeast. The truce of November 28, 1885, substantiated Bulgaria's unification. Yona achieved a silver medal and the Order of Courage for battles at Trun (modern Tran) and Slivnitsa, Bulgaria, and Tsaribrod (modern Dimitrovgrad) and Pirot, Serbia. Irish playwright George Bernard Shaw incorporated the war in the drama *Arms and the Man*. Yona extended her military career at the Ilinden-Preobrazhenie, Macedonia, revolt in 1903 and at Edirne, Turkey, on March 26, 1913, during the Balkan War.

1889

In the deterioration of the four-hundred-year-old Luba Empire, a precolonial nexus of the slave and ivory trade in the Congo of central Africa, the warrior-princess **Mukaya Luba (fl. 1880s)** fought for a peaceful solution to peasant uprisings. A civil war that rebels initiated on the Lualaba River (modern Congo River) stretched over six years, raising the value of ammunition and gunpowder. During the 1889 conflict with cap gun and flintlock rifle, Mukaya's brother, Kasongo Kalambo, died, leaving her to command the army. In the conclusion of revolution, the citizens severed the country, which extended from northern Zambia to Zaire. The empire merged with the Belgian Congo in 1908.

1893

An aggressive Ojibwa warrior-seer, **Chief Earth Woman (also Birtha Snyder or Snidow, 1878–?)** of Waterloo, Ohio, followed mystic dreams on her introduction to war. At age fifteen, she trusted clairvoyance to guide her on a man's warpath against the Sioux. After her marriage to White Owl in 1893, she advised a war party on staking out a river bank and waiting for the enemy to approach. In the clash that followed, White Owl killed a warrior whom she scalped. On her return to camp, the Ojibwa welcomed her to the victory dance and honored her first scalp with a gift of two feathers. She settled at Old Man's Cave, Ohio.

1895

A feminist and anti-colonial rebel, Korean militia head **Yun Hui-sun (1860–1935)** of Seoul began menacing the Japanese army and its Korean mercenaries in 1895 with militant songs and essays. To achieve independence for her country from Japanese colonialism, she circulated original war songs, beginning with "Women's Militia Song" and including "A Soldier's Song," "A Battle Song of Militia," "The Righteous Army Song," and "A Song of My Tough Life." In 1907, she assembled thirty aggressive housewives in Korea's first all-female battalion, which she trained in warcraft. She supported them with donations and managed the opening of an arms factory in Jusan.

After Yun's capture, interrogation by Japanese police in 1911 gained no information. She remained active for four years in rallying volunteers, raiding Japanese camps, liberating Korean prisoners of war, and housing them in caves. A memoir, *Ilsaengnok* (Record of My Life), recorded her grief at the combat deaths of her father-in-law, husband, and son. Her posthumous honors include the Order of Merit and a presidential medal.

April 9, 1895

During Ecuador's freedom fights against encroaching Spaniards, Colonel **Joaquina Galarza de Larrea (June 25, 1842–after 1912)** of Guaranda fought in sequential battles. At age twenty-two, she led a first skirmish on June 26, 1864. Before joining an armed uprising on April 9, 1895, she contributed money to the equipping of Montoneras from the Andean highlands. Her unit faced six hundred enemy at the battle of San Miguel on August 6, 1895, when she proposed strategy for some two thousand newly drafted patriots. Her valor earned a street name and field promotion to colonel. She counted among followers Colonel **Filomena Chávez de Duque (1884–September 27, 1961)** of Portoviejo, liberal recruiter **Angela Maclovia Lavayen (1828–May 9, 1897)** from Guayaquil, and midwife and author **María Gamarra de Hidalgo (April 13, 1846–May 21, 1916)** of Baba.

Female supporters garnered supplies and cash. Donor **Felicia Solano** de Vizuete (fl. 1895) of Guarandeñas, who lost a son at the battle of San Miguel, risked jail the next year with **Rosa Villafuerte de Castillo (fl. 1895),** a businesswoman of Los Rios. Rosa concealed freedom fighters in warehouses and conspired with underground warriors at her home. **Ana María Merchán Delgado (fl. 1895)** of Cuenca transported equipment to revolutionaries and shared rebel courier duties with **Transito Villagomez (fl. 1895)** of Guaranda, for whom a Quito street is named. **Sofía Moreira de Sabando (fl. 1895)** of Portoviejo hauled gun, rations, and medicine to guerrilla camps. Additional female resistance came from **Leticia Montenegro (fl. 1895)** of Durango, who was imprisoned with **Dolores Vela de Veintimilla (fl. 1895)**, a liberal conspirator who hid warriors and donated funds and ammunition.

Women risked lives and family to remain close to combat zones. **Delia Montero Maridueña (fl. 1895)** of Yaguache assisted **Delfina Torres de Concha (fl. 1895)** of Esmeralda and Brazilian fighter **Cruz Lucia Infante (fl. 1895)** from Rio de Janeiro in leading battle charges. **Dolores Usubillaga (fl. 1895), Juliana Pizarro (fl. 1895), Porfiria Aroca de la Paz (fl. 1895), Rosario Carifa (fl. 1895), Teresa Andrade (fl. 1895),** and **Carmen Grimaldo de Valverde (fl. 1895)**, all of Guayaquil, mustered liberals to the front to aid María Gamarra.

March 1, 1896

Because of the faulty translation of the Treaty of Wuchale on May 2, 1889, between Ethiopia and Italy, **Taytu Betul (also Wälättä Mikael, 1851–February 11, 1918)** from Debre Tabor in north central Ethiopia destroyed the document and rallied the emperor and his army to fight imperialists. At the battle of Adwa in the First Italo-Ethiopian War on March 1, 1896, Emperor Menelik II of Shewa and Empress Taytu directed seventy-three thousand troops and cannoneers. Her tactics involved damming water flowing to Fort Mekelle and overwhelming the poorly armed Italian army. The Ethiopian victors claimed thirteen thousand Italian casualties and seized eleven thousand rifles and artillery. In a triumph over colonialism, the royal couple elevated East African clout against European seekers of land and resources. During celebrations, Taytu appeared among nationalistic women dressed in black and topped with crowns and singing patriotic songs.

May 1896

A Shona spiritualist and healer since age forty-four, **Nehanda Charwe Nyakasikana (c. 1840–March 1898)** a Bantu oracle from Mazoe in Mashonaland, Zimbabwe, incited the First *Chimurenga* (rebellion) in May 1896 against the British South Africa Company. She blamed European land grabbers for importing locusts and rinderpest, a virus that infected some ninety percent of cattle as well as buffalo, deer and antelope, wildebeest, giraffes, and warthogs. The resulting famine allowed the tsetse fly to propagate in thorn bushes and spread trypanosomiasis or sleeping sickness.

In June 1896, Shona rebels abetted Ndebele fighting units to the southwest to halt mining, relocations, and forced labor at Salisbury and a hut tax on a land they named Rhodesia for explorer Cecil Rhodes. Nehanda predicted strike zones and directed combat tactics to halt the foreign advance until her people ran out of supplies. After a year's pursuit, the British captured Nehanda in 1897 and charged her with murdering a commissioner. On their way to the gallows at Salisbury in March 1898, she and her husband Kaguvi predicted that their spirits would return to overpower the enemy. The British sent her skull to England as proof of a colonial success. Her fame survived in a statue, maternity hospital at Harare, and subsequent consultations with her spirit.

August 1896

Soldier, revolutionary autobiographer, and archivist **Gregoria de Jesús (May 9, 1875–March 15, 1943)** of Kalookan, Philippines, preserved the papers, seal, and weapons of rebels in the Katipunan, a secret Filipino anti–Spanish society of eight hundred members. Her association with the women's auxiliary preceded the mustering in August 1896 of thirty female volunteers, including war heroes **Agueda Kahabagan (fl. 1896)** and **Teresa Magbanua (fl. 1896)**, medic and prisoner of war **Melchora Aquino (January 6, 1812–February 19, 1919)** of Caloocan, and **Patrocinio Gamboa (April 30, 1865–November 24, 1953)** of Jaro, a rebel spy, medic, and logician. Gregoria learned weaponry and coding and supported the rebel explosion of a Spanish ammunition dump.

After an insider betrayed the rebel sisterhood in August 1896, Gregoria's compatriot, **Marina Bartolome Dizon-Santiago (July 18, 1875–October 25, 1950)** of Tondo, burned lists of names and records before the Spanish could seize them. In widowhood under the name Manuela Gonzaga, Gregoria, like fellow raider, medic, and wounded veteran **Trinidad Peréz Tecson (November 18, 1848–January 28, 1928)** of Bulacan, chose to fight in the field. In 1928, she composed her life story under the title *The Katipunera*, a reference to Gregoria's membership in a secret organization that spread across the archipelago and promoted the Philippine Revolution.

See also May 1897; February 11, 1899.

Late 1896

In flight from a struggle for the Rwandan throne, spiritualist **Muhumusa (also Muhumuza or Nyabinghi, fl. 1860s–1945)** rallied followers to armed rebellion against Musinga, a false claimant. As the endangered widow of the assassinated warrior-king Kigeli IV since his death in November 1895, Muhumusa escaped to Ndorwa, Uganda, with their son Biregeya. To elevate his stature as future king, in late 1896, she enticed royalists to revere her channeling of the spirit of Nyabinghi, an eighteen-century Tanzanian cult hero from Karagwe. German colonizers backed Musinga and, in 1908, charged Muhumusa with sorcery. For three years, she remained in a Bukoba, Tanzania, prison overlooking Lake Victoria.

After eluding the guards, Muhumusa moved up the East African coast to Bakiga in southwestern Uganda, where she promoted resistance to Belgian,

British, and German imperialism and Christian missions. A subsequent military loss to the Anglo-Belgian-German Boundary Commission and capture by the British in Uganda on September 29, 1911, ended her anti-colonial campaign. Under the 1912 Witchcraft Act that the British devised, she endured thirty-four years of house arrest at Mengo prison in Kampala, Uganda. In August 1917, she plotted the ill-fated Nyakishenyi rebellion. Devotees continued to worship Nyaginghi in Rwandan caves with chants and drumming; at Kigezi, Uganda; and among Jamaican Rastafarians.

May 1897

The only Filipina general in the republican army during colonial wars, General **Agueda Kahabagan (fl. 1890s–1901)** of Santa Cruz, Laguna, wore white on the battlefield in May 1897 as a token of defiance. A freedom fighter of Batangas south of Manila, she combatted the enemy in the nation's revolution against Spanish imperialism, which began on August 24, 1896, and continued from February 4, 1899, against American colonialists. Her mounted regiment, bearing bolo knives and rifles, attended the wounded and won the three-day assault against a San Pablo garrison on October 9, 1897. A field promotion to *henerala* on April 6, 1899, and a statue at Santa Cruz elevated her importance to women's military history. The orange *Hibiscus rosa-sinensis Agueda* bears her name.

February 1898

Swordswoman and state builder **Mammy Yoko (also Madam Yoko, June 1849–August 1906)** of Gbo in the protectorate of Sierra Leone, built a power structure by allying with the Kpaa Mende Confederacy in the south. During the colonial era, the militia protected her non-military farmers and hunters against Christian missionaries and the British imperial army. After the death of Chief Gbanye, her third husband, in 1878, she seized control and, as Queen of Senehun, broadened her territory east of Freetown. In 1882, her military strategy involved unifying Mende subgroups, incorporating and training women in the secret Sande society, and, in 1887, choosing rivers as boundaries that denied access to the Yoni Temni from Sierra Leone. By mediating with the British, she quelled her northern rival, Kamanda, and his Temne troops.

Yoko met minor warfare after her people turned against her for promoting a British police force. To avoid a February 1898 resistance of the hut tax of four to five shillings per residence, she hired two thousand Mende carriers and enlarged the West India Regiment. They eased her expedition with the West African Regiment, armed with quick firing guns, from Freetown, Mabanta, Port Loko, and Wongkufu against rebel subchiefs wielding primitive machetes, clubs, and firebrands. At age fifty-seven, she drank poison, leaving her powers to her brother. Her tactics initiated the formation of the Sierra Leone Battalion and earned a silver medal from Queen Victoria. Yoko's snuff box remains on display at the University of Aberdeen; the Sierra Leone National Museum exhibits her portrait.

February 11, 1899

At age twenty-eight, **Teresa Magbanua (October 13, 1868–August 1947)**, a Visayan girls school teacher from Pototan, Philippines, supported rebels during the island revolution against Spanish colonialism. Leading bolo-wielding forces to the Visayan district at the island cluster center, she increased prestige by snatching victories in November and December 1898 at Yating and Sap-ong Hill. She continued fighting for liberty during the three-and-a-half year Philippine-American War, which began on February 4, 1899. On February 11, 1899, she enabled General Martin Delgado, an exemplary nationalist, to recapture Iloilo City on Panay Island.

Teresa was unsuccessful in early March 1899 in defending Iloilo City, but proved her valor on March 10 at the battle of Balantang, Jaro. In whipping the American army, she rejoiced at their four hundred casualties. She triumphed in style, riding a white horse at the victors' entry into town. Her defense of the motherland continued against Japanese occupation troops in 1942 during World War II. She paid for her largesse by selling personal belongings to supply food and medicines to guerrilla warriors. At her death in Mindanao at age seventy-nine, citizens acknowledged her courage with street names, an obelisk at Pototan, and awards to educators.

April 17, 1899

A Hausa chieftain of the Azna clan at Lougou, Benin, **Sarraounina Mangou (fl. 1899)** refused to give in to French colonialism. Known as "the panther queen," she flourished at defending her village from raids by Islamic Tuareg and Fulani. At the battle of Logo, she mustered an army to fight off the Voulet-Chanoine Mission, a French extermination force aided by Sudanese mercenaries. The war cost lives from arson, shooting, and dysentery. After abandoning her fort, Sarraounina stripped the area of herds and grain and, on April 17, 1899, led the area's strongest guerrilla resistance. Word of assassinations, hangings, roasting of children, and other atrocities against the vulnerable caused her to arrest Captain Paul Voulet on April 20. Polish novelist Joseph Conrad incorporated details of the massacre in the novella *Heart of Darkness,* which *Blackwood's Magazine* serialized in 1899. The story of the "panther queen" survives in film, dance, and children's literature.

October 5, 1899

A Mexican-American journalist, translator, and cross-dresser, **Beebe Beam (also Babe Bean, December 9, 1869–September 19, 1936)** of San Francisco accompanied U.S. troops on October 5, 1899, through Hawaii to the American-Philippine War. Born Elvira Virginia Mugarrieta, she concealed her gender aboard the troopship *City of Para* and fled the brig in military dress to take up residence at infantry quarters. During thirty months of guerrilla warfare with spears, arrows, and bolo knives, she wrote combat news of the twenty thousand Filipinos killed and the million civilians lost to hunger, atrocities, and cholera. As a medic, she treated casualties at Caloocan,

Camarines, Laguna de Bey, Luzon, and Santa Cuz and acquired a tattoo of army symbols and the word "Manila." After viewing the battle of San Mateo northeast of Manila on December 19, 1899, she assumed the name Jack Bee Garland and published a memoir in the October 1, 1900, issue of the *San Francisco Sunday Examiner*.

October 18, 1899

The emergence of the Boxer Rebellion against foreign missionaries and imperialists inspired acrobat and martial artist **Lin Hei'er (1871–1899)** of Tianjin on China's Bohai Bay, to recruit teenage girls to the Red Lantern militia. Along with widows in the Blue Lanterns and older women in the Black Lanterns, on October 18, 1899, she allied peasants, homeless, and outcasts to arm themselves with spears, swords, and medieval guns to kill Christians and destroy churches. When the uprising turned into urban anarchy in July 1900 in Beijing and Tianjin, she fought at the two-day battle of the walled city of Tientsin. On July 14, her arrest ended a military career and probably her life. In legend, song, and monuments, she bears the name "Yellow Lotus Holy Mother of the Yihetuan," an isolationist movement among Chinese during the Qing dynasty.

March 28, 1900

At the last of the five Anglo-Shanti Wars, Queen Mother **Yaa Asantewaa (October 17, 1840–October 17, 1921)** of Ejisu on the Gold Coast launched an Ashanti rebellion against the British called the War of the Golden Stool, a ceremonial token of sovereignty. She promised native men of the Ashanti Empire (modern Ghana) that tribeswomen would head an uprising if males failed to do their part. On March 28, 1900, combat killed one thousand English soldiers and twice as many Ashanti, who initially numbered twelve thousand. The English captured her and banished her to the Seychelle Islands, where she died at age eighty-one.

July 1900

A multi-talented Swiss transsexual, **Isabelle Wilhelmine Marie Eberhardt (February 17, 1877–October 21, 1904)** of Geneva posed as an Arab prophet, explorer of the Maghreb, diarist, translator, and short story writer while spying on French colonialists in North Africa. After wanderings in France, in July 1900, she lived with her lover at El Oued east of Algiers as "la bonne nomade (the good vagabond)" to survey colonial activities for the socialist journal *L'Aurore*. Because of her membership in a Sufi order and masquerade as a spiritualist/anarchist, French authorities blacklisted her and placed her under surveillance as a provocateur. On traveling to Qadiriyya in January 1901, she fell under the blade of an Arab assassin—possibly hired by the French to track her intelligence gathering—and recuperated for a month from a saber cut to her left arm in a military hospital.

While writing for socialist Victor Barrucand in March 1902, Isabelle's contributions to his newspaper *Al-Akhbar* enabled her to continue espionage against the French who suppressed Algerians. She joined the

French General Hubert Lyautey in 1903 to command his campaign in Oran, Morocco. She suffered ill health from syphilis, scrofula, marijuana addiction, and malaria that required more treatment at army clinics. She died from the collapse of a house beam during a flash flood at Ain Sefra. Her peripatetic lifestyle became material for biography, film, drama, musical, opera, and her posthumous overview *Notes de Route: Maroc-Algérie-Tunisie* (Notes on the Itinerary: Morocco, Algeria, Tunisia).

July 1, 1900

Filipina patriot, spy, and courier **Agueda Esteban (February 5, 1868–September 1944)** of Binondo, Philippines, supported rebel forces with raw materials smuggled southwest to Tangos, Cavite, from Manila. On lengthy mountain treks, she supplied saltpeter for gunpowder and lead and copper for bullets. Her report of rumors informed General Artemio Ricarte, a leader of the Philippines Revolution, when to expect sorties attacks by the Spanish. Her youngest child, Anastacia, died during the family's flight on foot from Maragondon to Talisay and was interred in a field. In the act of delivering secret outlines of tactics, Agueda was arrested on July 1, 1900, for hiding grenades.

Because Agueda's husband entered exile on Guam and died in 1902, during her pregnancy with son Artemio, she left her older children with the nuns at San José Hospice and sold meat in Cavite's Naic Plaza to feed the youngest. In 1904, young Artemio died during her imprisonment at Manila's Old Bilibid Prison. The British deported her and daughter Salud from Lema Island south of Hong Kong to Shanghai in 1915 and to Tokyo, Japan, in 1921. At Yokohama, she and Ricarte opened a restaurant that became a listening post for exiled Filipinos. After the Japanese captured the Philippines, she returned home in 1944 and died of infection at age seventy-six.

1903

During the Herero Wars in German South West Africa, liberator **Kaipkire (fl. 1900s–1910s)**, the queen of Bantu peoples, fought for Namibian freedom from enslavement and European colonialism. In 1903, she echoed the South African Khoikhoi in demonizing German occupiers of Namibia. The Herero allied with the Khoi, drafted women into a fighting force, and supported the African males who massacred sixty German settlers. Foreshadowing the Nazi Holocaust and the Rwandan genocide, General Lothar von Trotha and his *Schutztruppe* (protection force), backed by nineteen thousand soldiers, conspired to obliterate eighty thousand people as an introduction of racial purity.

After the battle of Waterberg on August 11, 1904, the German military imported artillery, machine guns, and rifles to suppress some fifty thousand Herero armed with *kirri* (wooden clubs). They intended to slaughter every male Herero and force women and children into prison camps for sexual bondage and sale or to die of thirst and hunger in the Omaheke Desert east of Windhoek. Until 1919, Kaipkire gained a reputation for ongoing revolt against Herero-Nama genocide and the commercial and sexual interests of British slave traders in Angola, Botswana, and Namibia.

February 8, 1904

A Lithuanian volunteer to the Don Cossacks, **Olga Jehlweiser (fl. 1904–1905)** served the Russian Northwest Army on February 8, 1904, during the Manchurian War, a five-month invasion by the Japanese. As a soldier under Baltic-German general Paul von Rennenkampf, a combatant in the Boxer Rebellion, she took part in fighting at Port Arthur, Manchuria. The unexpected Japanese invasion and destruction to naval vessels met with the alarm of Russian tsar Nicholas II, as did the enemy harbor blockade. Experience aided her during World War II. As a member of the six hundred Eurasian cavalrymen in the 6th Ural Cossacks Regiment, she knew well the battle terrain around Grodno, Belarus, on the Neman River.

1905

A widowed Chinese feminist, **T'ang Qunying (December 8, 1871–June 3, 1937)** from Hengshan, Hunan, promoted a Japanese underground in Tokyo to depose the Qing dynasty in China. Giving up on wifely training at Tokyo's Practical Woman's School, in 1905, she assembled rebels seeking revolutionary change under President Sun Yat-sen through espionage and demonstrations. For necessary warcraft, she studied explosives and weapons under Russian anarchists and formed a female bomb team. Her associates disrupted parliament to agitate for woman's suffrage and equal education for girls.

Admirers reverence her as a woman of the century.

August 18, 1906

Preceding World War I, Polish Catholic assassin and smuggler **Wanda Krahelska-Filipowicz (December 15, 1886–February 5, 1968)** hurled three dynamite bombs from an apartment balcony at the carriage of Imperial Russian general George Karl Scalon, the commander of Warsaw's military district. The regime brutally repressed Poles. As a co-former of the Zegota underground, on August 18, 1906, she joined seven hundred paramilitary agents under the code names Alinka and Alicja. The conspirators plotted twenty-five hundred rebel actions and a mail train robbery. During World War II, Wanda and co-conspirator **Zofia Kossak-Szczucka (August 10, 1889–April 9, 1968)** of Kosmin, code named Weronika, risked arrest by aiding Jews through rescues by the Zegota home guard.

Nazis seized Zofia in September 1943 at Warsaw and jailed her at the Auschwitz extermination camp in south central Poland. She survived to become an insurrectionist at the Warsaw Uprising along with a teenage daughter, freedom fighter and memoirist **Anna Szatkowska (March 15, 1928–February 27, 2015)** from Górki Wielkie, Silesia. Both women compiled memoirs of Warsaw rioting. Israel proclaimed Zofia Righteous among the Nations; Poland awarded her the Order of the White Eagle.

See also April 19, 1943.

1910s

Blackfoot raider **Hate Woman (1880s–1950)** of Alberta, Canada, accompanied her beloved husband on military campaigns hundreds of miles south into Montana. Over five of ten expeditions in the 1910s, she accompanied her mate Weasel Tail, a Blood warrior from Bow River in south central Ontario and an admirer of the hero tales about Running Eagle, a female brave from the late 1870s. Hate Woman excelled at counting coup and stealing horses and saddles from the Cheyenne, Crow, Shoshone, and Sioux.

See also 1878.

October 24, 1910

An Indonesian hero of the Dutch colonial period, **Cut Nyak Meutia (February 15, 1870–October 24, 1910)** of Pirak in the Aceh Empire led an army of forty-five soldiers against European imperialists. She came of age during the Aceh War of March 26, 1873, when ten thousand islanders blockaded three thousand Dutch soldiers. She divorced her first husband for siding with the Royal Netherlands East Indies Company, which offered jobs. Her second mate, Cut Muhammad, opposed the colonization of Aceh and, in 1899, recruited her to settle in the mountains. Despite rampant cholera, she backed Sultan Mahmud Shah of Malacca in rebellion against Netherlands profiteers. A June-to-August battle in 1902 ended local hopes of controlling Aceh.

With the aid of peasant spies and guerrilla warriors, into 1903, Cut Meutia and Cut Muhammad continued their resistance north of the territory into the Pasai jungle toward the ethnic stronghold of Gayo. In May 1905, the enemy captured Cut Muhammad and executed him by firing squad. Cut Meutia married old friend Pang Nangru, who aided her in jungle warfare until his death in a September 1910 skirmish. In widowhood, she and eleven-year-old son Raja Sabil retreated to the Paya Cicem marshes, where she battled the Dutch hand-to-hand with a ceremonial dagger. On October 24, 1910, the enemy shot her in the torso and head. Her soldiery survives in a biography, a chrysanthemum variety, banknotes, postage stamp, street, mosque, and hotel and among Indonesian heroes.

April 6, 1911

A famed guerrilla warrior from the Ottoman Empire, **Tringë Smajl (1880–November 2, 1917)** from Deçiq (modern Dusici, Montenegro) roused twenty-five hundred Albanian mountaineers in a strike on April 6, 1911, against twenty-eight thousand Turks. After her father died on the battlefield at Vranje, she took his place as leader of the Gruda clan. She responded to the Albanian insurrection in Kosovo and Macedonia in July 1908. In twelve hours, tribesmen wounded three hundred enemy, raised the Albanian flag, and forced an Ottoman retreat. She devoted the rest of her life to demanding independence from the Muslim Turks, amnesty for rebels, and a reversion to the Albanian language and script. Her exploits survive in folk songs and storytelling.

October 10, 1911

Nationalist commander **Wu Shuqing (1892–?)** from Hanyang, China, assembled an army of female revolutionaries on October 10, 1911, to rid the country of imperialism. During the Xinhai Revolution against the Qing dynasty, she fostered a Chinese republic by convincing hundreds to revolt and raise an army to battle for independence. After readying a regiment for the Chinese Women's Army, she fought at the disastrous six-week battle of Yangxia on October 18, 1911, at Wuhan, where insurrectionists lost eight hundred followers. On November 24, 1911, the united army's capture of Wulongshan, Mufushan, Yuhuatai, and Tianbao enabled mutineers to slaughter Manchus. The Manchu compromised their ethnicity by adopting Han surnames and language. The Qing dynasty collapsed at the end of two hundred sixty-seven years in power.

October 8, 1912

The outbreak of the First Balkan War on October 8, 1912, began the lengthy military career of Sergeant **Milunka Savić (August 10, 1888–October 5, 1973),** a highly decorated Serbian from a Novi Pazar farm. Throughout the triumph of four Slavic groups against the Ottoman Empire nine months later, she served in her brother's place in men's clothing as rifleman and grenadier. On June 30, 1913, she earned a first combat medal at a tenth deployment, the battle of Bregalnica against Bulgarian attackers, who lost some twenty thousand against the smaller Serbo-Montenegrin army. Courageous fighting won her a promotion to corporal. Grenade shrapnel in the chest forced her into a hospital, where doctors identified her true gender. On return to the infantry, Milunka fought in the Second Balkan War and World War I, taking twenty prisoners singlehandedly. As commander of the Iron Regiment's Assault Bomber Squad, Milunka survived shrapnel wounds to the head against Austro-Hungarians at Kolubara, Serbia, in mid–November 1914 and saw action at Crna Reka, Macedonia, in a two-month clash begun on October 14, 1916.

By war's end, Milunka had added seven wounds to her total. In addition to the Serbian Miloš Obilić Medal, Croix de Guerre with Palm, Cross of St. George, Order of St. Michael, two Legions of Honor, and the nickname "Bomber of Kolubara," she won the coveted Star of Karađorđe with Swords for capturing twenty-three Bulgarians. On return to civilian life, she served the Belgrade post office and lived in poverty with three adopted daughters. During World War II, she founded an infirmary for partisans. Defiance of insurgent Nazis cost her a savage beating and ten months in the anti-fascist concentration camp at Banjica, Yugoslavia. She remained unhonored until her appearance in the 1950s wearing combat medals.

November 1913

A lesbian anarchist against British colonialism, **Gulab Kaur (1890–1941)** from Bakshiwala in the far northern Punjab, enabled other female freedom fighters to distribute propaganda, weapons, and ammunition. She and her husband, rebel volunteer Mann Singh, planned a two-stage migration through Manila to the United States for the purpose of liberating colonial India. En route in November 1913, she aided Sikh immigrants in the Ghadar Movement, intended to destroy the British Raj. The pair separated, with Mann continuing to America and Gulab sailing with fifty fellow insurrectionists aboard the passenger steamer SS *Korea* from the Philippines.

Gulab Kaur profited from backup by female confederates. In Hoshiarpur, Jalandhar, and Kapurthala, the women mobilized an armed revolt by defending the printing press that produced propaganda and by sheltering other revolutionaries from capture. Under the guise of a newspaperwoman, Gulab picketed daily in 1930, recruited more defiant Indians, and offered them arms. British police arrested her and jailed her for two years at the Lahore citadel on a charge of sedition. Exhausted by lethal torture, isolation, and abuse, she died in prison around age fifty-one. In addition to a biographical novel published in 2014, poet Amal featured Gulab in the poem "name me rebel."

The Great War, 1914–1918

The collapse of the Ottoman, Qing, and Napoleonic empires set off a restructuring of the balance of power that generated World War I. Unlike the enfilade style of previous combat, the grim combination of mustard gas, submarines, and machine gun fire into trenches walled off by barbed wire introduced a new element—the survival of veterans afflicted with respiratory impairment, blindness, and amputations. From shattered boundaries and depleted dynasties emerged independent sovereignties in Armenia, Azerbaijan, Czechoslovakia, Georgia, Poland, Turkey, and Yugoslavia. Female warriors gravitated toward opportunities to promote nationalism and to grasp for themselves the image of the new woman.

March 24, 1914

Mexican medic and auxiliary *soldadera* **Adela Velarde Pérez (September 8, 1900–September 4, 1971)** of Juárez aided the Mexican Revolution at age thirteen. As a member of the White Cross, she armed herself with a saber and crisscrossed bandoleers. For eighteen months, she joined combat with her boyfriend, Sergeant Antonio Gil del Rio Armenta, at Zacatecas, Mexico City, Morelos, Aguascalientes, and Chihuahua. She failed to save her lover from bleeding to death at the March 24, 1914, battle of Gomez Palacio, Coahuila, led by General Francisco Villa. Awarded a legion of honor and pension, she lost a son in World War II. Following recognition as a veteran in 1962 and six years of marriage to Colonel Alfredo Villegas, Sr., she died of ovarian cancer in Del Rio, Texas, and was buried at San Felipe Cemetery. In 2014, a plaque recognized her heroism. Citizens replaced it in 2019 by a bronze figure in peasant dress with guitar.

Adela's name developed into the slang term *Adelita* for cadres of female volunteers: **Margarita Neri (1865–1920?)** of Quintana Roo, a Zapatista recruiter and raider at Chiapas and Tabasco; cavalry commander **Rosa Bobadilla (1875–1957)** at Morelos; Pancho Villa supporter **María Quinteras de Meras (fl. 1910s)**; **Petra Herrera (June 29, 1887–February 14, 1916)**, a comrade of brigade leader **Cosme Mendoza Chavira (fl. 1910s)** at the Torreon siege on May 30, 1914, when Pancho Villa received a boost in support; raiders of the Culiac mint, colonel and sharpshooter **Clara de la Rocha (1890–June 1, 1970)** and lieutenant **Valentina Ramírez Avitia**

(February 14, 1893–April 4, 1979) of Norotol at Culiacán; raider **Juana Ramona (fl. 1910)**, dubbed "The Tigress"; and courier **Carmen Parra (1885–December 18, 1941)**, a combatant of Victoriano Huerta's army at the battle of Juárez, which ended the tyranny of seven-term president Porfirio Diaz.

July 1914

At age sixteen, **Zoya Smirnow (1898–after 1916)** from Moscow left high school with eleven schoolmates to fight for the Russian Imperial Army. Dressed in male uniforms, in July 1914, they supported battles in Galicia (modern Poland-Ukraine), where Russians overwhelmed the Austro-Hungarian army. In retreat to the Carpathian Mountains in September 1914, Russians outnumbered the Austro-Hungarians two to one. After the deaths of her comrades, Zoya survived wounding. At the hospital, staff discovered her disguise.

July 28, 1914

Two Russian Imperial princess-pilots, **Eugenie Shakhovskaya (1889–1920)** and **Sophie Alexandrovna Dolgorunaya (also Dolgorukaya or Dolgorukov, December 25, 1887–December 8, 1949)**, a lady in waiting at the Russian court, completed reconnaissance flights for the military air service during World War I, which began on July 28, 1914. Eugenie trained in Germany and earned from historians the title of world's first female combat pilot. A survivor of a gas tank explosion, she completed battle missions for the First Field Air Detachment on the northwestern front and earned a Saint George Medal. Following a bout of malaria, Sophie aided the 26th Corps Air Squadron and continued flying until the October 1917 Russian Revolution. She issued a war memoir, *Vae Victis*, Roman historian Livy's dire warning "Woe to the Conquered." After eluding a death sentence for spying, Eugenie allied with the Bolsheviks until she was shot at Kiev, Ukraine, in 1920. She survived and retired to Rome.

July 28, 1914

At the onset of World War I on July 28, 1914, Russian long distance rider Colonel **Alexandra Kudasheva (1873–1921)** rode with the 6th Ural Cossacks, the cavalry regiment of her deceased husband. She joined him in combat on February 8, 1904, during the Russo-Japanese War. In 1914, as a colonel in the Imperial Russian Cavalry, she commanded six hundred cavalry who successfully counterattacked the Austrian army in May 1915 at Opatija, Croatia. Undercover in Kazakhstan in 1917, Alexandra was arrested by secret police and, in 1921, executed at age forty-eight.

Alexandra's gender-mixed regiment included **Olga Kokovtseva (late 1880s–?)**, a twice wounded veteran. As a soldier in the Imperial Russian army, she fought the Imperial German Uhlan in East Prussia. When she led troops into confrontation with mounted lancers, she suffered a head wound, the first of two. She posed for a photo in head bandage, high-necked tunic, wide riding breeches, and cavalry boots while she read to patients in a military hospital. Two medals adorn her uniform for bravery, which won her a Cross of St. George and military pension.

July 28, 1914

A soldier for three decades, **Halszka Wasilewska (also Halina, March 21, 1899–February 8, 1961)** a patriotic Pole born in London, enlisted as a male legionary medic and communications agent at the outbreak of World War I on July 28, 1914. Her participation in Pomerania, Prussia; Galicia (modern Poland-Ukraine); and Vienna, Austria, expanded during the Polish-Bolshevik War and the battle of Lvov in western Ukraine. The accomplishment of pushing the Russian Communists out in 1920 preceded her recovery from pulmonary illness and assignment as trainer of female underground soldiers at Warsaw, Poland.

World War II pressed Halszka into debilitating hardships. From April 3, 1943, to May 1945, she endured jailing and torture at Ravensbrück, a Nazi internment camp north of Berlin. She recovered in Sweden and took command of female soldiers in the armored division. Post-war, she worked as a cartographer outlining Polish war maps. Her honoraria include two Crosses of Valor and a War Medal.

See also July 27, 1943.

August 15, 1914

Antonija Javornik (1893–1974), a Serbian medic/soldier from Maribor, fought in the Balkan Wars and World War I, attaining the rank of sergeant. At the nine-day battle of Cer Mountain, Serbia, on August 15, 1914, the partisans incurred twenty thousand casualties, half as many as the enemy Austro-Hungarians. Under heavy shelling, she defended Belgrade and exited Serbia with the Great Retreat from November 15, 1915, to January 18, 1916. Through the Montenegrin mountains to Albania, the long march led through deep snow. Some two hundred forty thousand Serbs succumbed to typhus, hunger, and frostbite. Survivors sheltered on Corfu. Antonija's recovery from wounds preceded infantry service in September 1916 at Salonika (modern Thessalonica, Greece) and Kaymakchalan (modern Kaimaki, Macedonia), a pyrrhic Allied score against the Ottomans, Germans, and Bulgarians. For the recapture of Bitola from Bulgaria late in 1916, she added the Order of Karađorđe's Star to a remarkable slate of awards: Medal of St. George, Legion of Honor, Medal of the White Eagle, Albanian Medal, and two Serbian Obilić citations.

August 23, 1914

A Ukrainian volunteer to the Russian offensive, corporal **Helen Ruz (also Rus, 1895–)** from Czernowitz (modern Chernivitsi) fought against the Austro-Hungarian front in Galicia (modern Poland-Ukraine) on August 23, 1914. Deployment became a family affair after she left for duty alongside her father, a railway official, two brothers, and her fiancé. According to Francis Henry Gribble's 1916 compendium *Women in War,* shrapnel broke two of her ribs. The month-long battle cost the Hapsburgs four hundred fifty casualties and one hundred thousand prisoners of war. Prowess earned Helen a promotion within two weeks; her courage along the eastern front at age nineteen achieved two medals. Survivors of cold, hunger, and disease at the combat zone in the Carpathian Mountains during a five-month campaign extended the Russian sweep of the enemy. Total takeover resulted in an Austro-Hungarian surrender and permanent loss of stature among European forces.

September 1914

A sergeant of the Ukrainian Sich Riflemen in the 55th Austrian Infantry, **Hanna Dmyterko (also Anna or Handzia Dmiterko, 1893–1981)** from Senechiv, Austria-Hungary, defended local civilians in September 1914 from the Russians. According to her memoirs, the division suffered severe loss to arson at the Ukrainian battles of Nad Strypoyu and Lysovychi and illness from a typhus outbreak. For six years, she directed sharpshooters in Galicia (modern Poland-Ukraine) and Lodomeria and patrolled war zones to ward off Bolshevik insurgents from Kyiv, Ukraine. Among her trainees were **Olha Basarab (September 1, 1889–February 12, 1924)** from Rohatyn; rifleman **Sofia Galechko (1891–1918)**; and front line sharpshooter **Olena Stepaniv (December 7, 1892–July 11, 1963)** of Vyshnivchyk, Galicia. Olena incurred arrest and three years of imprisonment in Tashkent, where she initiated an inmate uprising in 1918. After skirmishes at Makivka, Ukraine, she and Sofia earned silver medals.

October 4, 1914

French underground operative **Louise de Bettignies (July 15, 1880– September 27, 1918)** from Saint-Amand-les-Eaux aided allied soldiers in Lille, France, on October 4, 1914, by initiating the Alice Network, a translation service and intelligence gathering agency for MI6 and the British military. Throughout 1915, Louise wrote secret data on her petticoats in lemon juice and revealed the messages by applying heat. Her recruits, notably French border spy and courier **Marie Leonie Vanhoutte (January 13, 1888–May 4, 1967)**, excelled at mapping, tracking munitions and trains, and smuggling operations.

The collaborators passed recovered information through Belgium and Holland until the Gestapo forced Marie to identify Louise. Louise's arrest in October 1915 preceded three years at hard labor in Brussels and respiratory infections that killed her in Cologne, Germany, at age thirty-eight. The conspirators earned medals from the French and British including the Legion of Honor, Croix de Guerre, and Order of the British Empire.

November 1914

A former abused daughter and wife, Lieutenant **Maria Bochkareva (July 1889–May 16, 1920)** of Nikolsko in Imperial Russia telegraphed for permission from Tsar Nicholas II in November 1914 to join the 2nd Army in combat on the Dvina River at Polotsk, Belarus. During her removal of casualties under fire, she survived arm and leg wounds. On recovery, she led eleven soldiers of the Russian Imperial Army. A second wounding and paralysis sidelined her in rehabilitation for four months. The much revered "Yashka" returned to the front as a supply officer and remained with a seventy-man platoon during the Lake Naroch Offensive until demobilizing in spring 1917.

Maria's design of a women's strike force, the 1st Russian Women's Battalion of Death, aimed at restoring male morale and discipline after the tsar's abdication. The two thousand volunteers dropped to three hundred recruits, who backed her against surly males brandishing pistols and demanding that the women disband. On June 25, 1917, they joined the 1st Siberian Corps and fought Germans at the nineteen-day Alexander Kerensky offensive on July 1 along the western front at Galicia (modern Poland-Ukraine) and Ukraine. The battalion captured two thousand Austrians, but the anti-war uprisings and mutinies left little male support for Maria. She fell in battle at Smarhon, Belarus, and returned to Petrograd, Russia, for treatment of hearing damage and shell shock that left her mute.

Amid belligerent males flirting with the fifteen hundred girls in the Moscow unit, Maria hurried to the front with two hundred sober battalion members and continued pressing for Russian army rejuvenation. In flight from Bolsheviks, she took a steamer from Vladivostok east to San Francisco in April 1918 and petitioned President Woodrow Wilson and England's George V to support the failing Russians. On return to Tomsk, Russia, she was questioned by the secret police and sentenced to die before a firing squad at age thirty. Maria's attempts to bolster the demoralized military appear in film and in her ghost-written autobiography, *Yashka: My Life as Peasant, Exile, and Soldier.*

See also early summer 1917.

1915

A skilled Parisian artist and organizer, **Madame Arnaud (also Arno, fl. 1910s)** recruited European females to fight the Germans as members of the Volunteer Corps of French and Belgian Women for the National Defense. Following the death of her husband, an army officer, she pressed the French military to open combat posting to women. In the same period, Russian volunteer **Apollovna Isoltsev (fl. 1910s)** became one of the forty-nine women soldiers on the front line by accompanying her father's regiment and rescuing his corpse from a fiery combat zone.

Two contemporaries, **Elena Chuba (fl. 1910s),** a soldier's wife, battled alongside the Kubanian Cossacks of southern Russia while **Alexandra Danilova (fl. 1910s)** of Baku, Azerbaijan, petitioned the local military office and enlisted in a Cossack regiment as a devout tsarist. From the east, sharpshooter **Valentina Petrova (fl. 1910s)** earned a St. George's Cross for service with a Siberian rifle unit. She continued her patriotic volunteerism by proposing a women's Black Hussars of Death. Another World War I amazon, **Maria Malko (fl. 1910s)** of Slovakia maintained her disguise as a man until the Germans immured her among prisoners of war.

1915

Flemish medic-waitress-double agent **Marthe Cnockaert (October 28, 1892– January 8, 1966)** of Westrozebeke,

Belgium, gathered information on German leadership for British Intelligence in London. During World War I, she destroyed a telephone cable and plotted an air attack on Kaiser Wilhelm II. Pretending to aid the German military, in 1915, she orchestrated the murder of a German spy. By setting explosives, she destroyed an Axis ammunition depot. Eluding a death sentence in November 1916, she remained in a cell at Ghent, Belgium, until war's end. Actor Madeleine Carroll portrayed the double agent in the 1933 film *I Was a Spy*.

May 1915

An Austrian artist trained in 1904 at Munich's Royal School of Applied Arts, **Stephanie Hollenstein (July 18, 1886–May 24, 1944)** from Lustenau sought membership in a rifle company at Vorarlberg in May 1915. Drawn to hypermasculinity, she joined the Nazi party. After revelation of her gender several months later, she redeployed with the war media as a combat painter of the Italian front in oils, charcoal, and watercolor. Her intense sketches depicted battlefield camaraderie and the raw faces of stressed and dying men. Because of her service at the front three times, she earned a Karl Troop Cross. Her work remains on display at a Lustenau gallery.

May 15, 1915

During occupation by Austrian insurgents, on May 15, 1915, **Olga Krasilnikov (fl. 1915)** of Moscow and fellow Russian soldier **Natalie Tychmini (fl. 1915)** fought at the three-day battle for Opatow, Poland. Olga survived nineteen battles and retired for treatment of a leg wound. As the front stretched along the Nida River into western Galicia (modern Poland-Ukraine), Natalie was less successful. The open battlefield involved one hundred thousand troops and four hundred field guns. After her wounding at Opatow, doctors disclosed her gender and remanded her to the American Red Cross Hospital in Kiev, Ukraine. Both women earned the Cross of St. George for dressing in male uniform and defending Opatow.

June 10, 1915

Sixteen-year-old **Viktoria Savs (June 27, 1899–December 31, 1979)** of Bad Reichenhall, Bavaria, signed up with the Austro-Hungarian Army in male disguise. Enrolled with her father under the name "Viktor" on June 10, 1915, Viktoria entered the Innsbruck II infantry rifle company at Lavarone as a courier on skis. She marched with the infantry to the Dolomite front before redeploying at the Italian front in December 1916. After a grenade shattered her right leg, she was unmasked at a Sillian field hospital on May 27, 1917, and left the army. For rescuing twenty Italian prisoners of war under artillery fire on April 11, 1917, she received a silver citation for courage and the Karl Troop Cross. She continued earning awards for medical aid to the Austrian Red Cross.

April 26, 1915

Sharpshooter, skier, and first female combat pilot **Marie Marvingt (February 20, 1875–December 14, 1963)** of Aurillac, France, dropped bombs over the Bavarian aerodrome in Alsace

Lorraine on April 26, 1915. She entered the Allied military in male disguise and assisted the 42nd Battalion's front line infantry. After discovery of her deception, she returned to war with the Italian army's 3rd Alpine Regiment to fight the Austro-Hungarian *Kaiserschutzen* (Kaiser's Guard) and the German *Alpenkorps* (Alps Mountain Corps). In the Dolomites in the Italian alps, she evacuated the wounded on skis and flew solo missions targeting the Italian front. For aerial attacks on the enemy at Metz-Frescaty, she earned the Croix de Guerre with Palms.

Between world wars, Marie joined the Red Cross as a surgical nurse and flight medic. She planned the *Aviation Sanitaire* (air ambulance service) and the metal ski for landing aeromedical evacuation operations on Sahara sand. At the beginning of World War II, she earned another medal for French Resistance work in the Dordogne with wounded aviators and the armed *maquis* (guerrillas), bringing her total commendations to thirty-four and making her France's most decorated female. Her promotion of air rescue appears in histories, school names, streets, postage stamps, video, and the film *The Perils of Pauline*.

Summer 1915

One of the first female pilots authorized to fly during combat, **Hélène Dutrieu (July 10, 1877–June 26, 1961)** of Tournai, Belgium, adapted from audacious stunt flier and tester of seaplanes to war volunteer in summer 1915 as an enemy plane spotter for the Paris Air Guard. The daughter of a Belgian artillery officer, she also joined the French Red Cross as ambulance driver. At the request of General Victor Février, she served along the Marne River for five months and managed casualty transport for Massimo Ospedale. She also directed Campagne à Val-de Grâce, a war casualty reconstructive surgery center in Paris throughout the wars following the French Revolution and Napoleonic Wars.

July 1915

A Canadian marksman on the Serbian front, Lieutenant **Leslie Joy Whitehead (February 26, 1895–June 5, 1964)** of Montmorency, Quebec, enrolled in July 1915 as an infantryman among British Balkan Allies at Kruševac in central Serbia. By aiding the Veterinary corps, at age twenty-two, she treated Serbian warhorses at Mladenovac and Valjevo. She aided frontline combat with the 9th Serbian Regiment Danube Division in Albania, Montenegro, and Serbia. From July 28, 1914, to November 24, 1915, four hundred five thousand—one quarter of the Serbian army—died in battle.

In an era that recorded incarceration of ten million people, Leslie gained an outsider's knowledge of war crimes. As a security guard for the Scottish Women's Hospitals, she outwitted the lawlessness that accompanied enemy occupation of Serbia and captured looters from the supply tents. Seized by Bulgarians on October 8, 1915, she served three months in the Kruševac prisoner of war camp under suspicion of espionage. Amid mass internment, hangings, and forced labor, in November 1915, she managed camp disinfection for a German physician and returned to Canada in February 1916.

October 1915

Serbian volunteer **Sofija Jovanović (1895–1979)** of Belgrade fought in October 1915 as a male recruit against Austro-Hungarian and German enemies. She began a military career with the Chetnik paramilitary during the Balkan Wars. Under the alias Sofronije Jovanovic, she severed the Hapsburg telephone communications. On September 17, 1914, she deployed to the front on the Drina River separating Serbia from Bosnia-Herzogovina and in heavy rain and snow at the Kolubara River on November 16, 1914.

In late November 1915 to January 18, 1916, Sofija retreated to Albania with Serbian troops, who crossed the Adriatic Sea to the Greek island of Corfu. Some two hundred twenty thousand evacuees died of exposure, disease, and hunger. Her unit advanced on Salonica, Macedonia (modern Thessalonica), on June 11, 1917, when King Constantine I's abdication destroyed the state. In November 1918, she helped to liberate Belgrade. Her thirteen medals honored her valor and disability from a foot wound.

November 1915

World War I cryptographer-spy **Sarah Aaronsohn (January 5, 1890–October 9, 1917)** coordinated forty operatives for the Nili network, the largest anti–Ottoman Jewish spy ring in Palestine and Lebanon. In addition to aiding survivors of the Armenian genocide, in November 1915, she reported her tracking of Ottoman military positions by carrier pigeon to avoid German U-boats through Cairo and Port Said, Egypt. As an agent of British Intelligence, she coded messages in a mix of Aramaic, English, French, and Hebrew. Her communiques aided General Edmund Allenby at the British headquarters in Egypt in taking Jerusalem and Palestine by Christmas 1917.

Sarah's arrest on October 1, 1917, preceded the threat of the burning of her hometown, Zikhron Jacob, south of Haifa, Palestine. After refusing to flee by ship, she endured days of torture. During interrogation, she claimed to be Nili's only spy. To prevent unintentional answers, she shot a pistol into her throat and damaged her spine. Before dying after four days of paralysis, she left a note demanding vengeance for Jewish suffering. Admirers regard her as Israel's first female Zionist martyr.

November 25, 1915

At the outbreak of the Balkan War, on November 25, 1915, Serbian volunteers **Sophie Jowanowitsch (fl. 1915)** and her husband from Poland, Stanislawa Ordynska of Romania, and **Milena Manditsch (1898–?)** of Belgrade volunteered for the Polish legion. During the First Serbian War of 1812, Sophie advanced from ambulance driver to infantryman. She and Milena inveighed against the Austrian invasion of July 28, 1914, and allied against the enemy with outsiders, notably Captain **Flora Sandes (January 22, 1876–November 24, 1956)** of Yorkshire, the first British woman to serve in World War I. With dispensation from King Peter I of Serbia, they adopted the rifles and uniforms of ordinary infantrymen. Twenty-four hundred female combatants formed the League of Death and entered the melee during riots in Paris, Berlin, Vienna, and Budapest.

On November 25, 1915, Sophie found herself alone after her medical unit was killed during the Great Retreat through Albania. A general incorporated her in the Serbian army before the advance on Bitola (modern Monastir, Macedonia). Traveling by horse with the Second Infantry above the Albanian valley, she had to borrow her first rifle and nearly died from typhus. After New Year's, she sailed with fifteen hundred refugees to Corsica and deployed at Durazzo, Vallona, and Corfu. In 1916 at the Allied retaking of Bitola, while embroiled in hand-to-hand combat, she sustained injury during a bombardment by a grenade blast. Healing required six months of surgeries and rehabilitation for shredded flesh on back and side from shoulder to knee and a mangled right arm.

Flora advanced to Captain and earned the Order of the Karadorde's Star. By issuing an autobiography, *An English Woman-Sergeant in the Serbian Army*, she raised funds for the Serbian partisans. She remained in service until October 1922 as manager of a military hospital. Remobilized on April 6, 1941, after Germany bombed Belgrade, she deployed briefly and entered a German internment camp after a nighttime Gestapo raid. Her contributions received memorials on a Serbian stamp, painted sculpture, and street and pub name and a second autobiography, *The Autobiography of a Woman Soldier*.

April 24, 1916

Feminist revolutionary and member of Fianna Fail (Soldiers of Destiny), **Constance Georgine Markievicz (February 4, 1868–July 15, 1927)** of London joined Irish Republicans in Dublin in the six-day Easter uprising, an assault on April 24, 1916, to rid Ireland of the British. She served a jail sentence in 1911 for endorsing the Irish Republican Brotherhood and protesting the presence of King George V in Ireland by burning a British flag and throwing stones at the royal family's pictures. She relied on the gun-running of historian **Alice Stopford Green (May 31, 1847–May 28, 1929)** of Kells and two outsiders—Bostonian **Molly Osgood Childers (December 14, 1875–January 1, 1964)** and Londoner **Mary Spring Rice (September 14, 1880–December 1, 1924)**, who diverted British attention by sailing the yacht *Asgard* from Milford Haven, Wales. The load of nine hundred German Mauser M1871 rifles and twenty-nine thousand rounds of black powder ammunition from Hamburg reached Irish volunteers at Howth pier on July 26, 1916. **Brigid Foley (April 14, 1887–June 18, 1970)** from Killeagh transported funds and helped move weapons out of storage, for which she served time in Kilmainham jail.

In uniform as a citizen soldier, Constance carried a Colt revolver for her part in a six-day skirmish at St. Stephen's Green, the headquarters of the Irish Citizen Army. She shot a sniper and was accused of killing a Dublin police officer. Under a sentence of life imprisonment, Constance remained in confinement in English jails until the 1917 amnesty. During the eleven-month Irish Civil War of June 28, 1922, she organized the seizure of Moran's Hotel on July 2. A Dublin statue, portrait, and plaque commemorate her devotion to Irish freedom.

Constance relied on a cadre of female soldiers: couriers **Rose Ann Murphy (fl. 1916)** of Liverpool and **Marie Perolz (May 7, 1874–December 12, 1950)** from Limerick summoned forces from Cork, Tipperary, and Waterford, and Dublin comrade **Helena Molony (January 15, 1883–January 19, 1966)** to form Fianna Eireann (Irish Warriors), the Irish national youth organization. Armed with a revolver, **Winifred Carney (December 4, 1887–November 21, 1943)** of County Down dispatched orders. For military strategy, Maltese soldier **Madeleine ffrench-Mullen (December 30, 1880–May 26, 1944)** volunteered as garrison lieutenant. **Effie Taafe (fl. 1916)** smuggled rifles. Scots spy and sniper **Margaret Skinnider (May 28, 1892–October 10, 1971)**, a teacher from Coatbridge, transported explosives from Scotland to Dublin under her hat, suffering three bullet wounds. **Martha Walsh (fl. 1916)** fought with the Imperial Hotel garrison. Killimor native **Mae Murray (1898–July 18, 1955)** supported the 1st Battalion of the Dublin Brigade and Citizen Army, of whom ninety died and one thousand were incarcerated.

Some stalwarts worked at special duties: Dubliner **Rosie Hackett (July 25, 1893–May 4, 1976)** stockpiled backpacks and first aid kits and raised a challenge flag over Liberty Hall. French cook **Louise Gavan Duffy (July 17, 1884–October 12, 1969)** from Cimiez and **Annie Higgins (fl. 1916)** from Carrickmacross worked throughout Easter week in a building under shelling. **Emily Elliott (1893–March 3, 1983)** and her younger sister **Eilís Elliott (June 26, 1896–March 29, 1966)** of Tonagh delivered meals on O'Connell Street under a barrage of bullets. Republican activist **Kathleen Florence Lynn (January 18, 1874–September 14, 1955)** from Killala as chief medical officer, pitched a hospital tent and issued munitions she stored at her home. Dubliner surgeon **Euphan Maxwell (1887–1964)** treated casualties at the Royal Victoria Eye and Ear Hospital adjacent to the heat of battle at St. Stephen's Green.

Females earned renown for their valor. Medic **Margaret Kehoe of Leighlinbridgen (March 17, 1867–April 24, 1916)** became the first civilian to fall in the rising when British soldiers shot her. She died in nurse's uniform. Eighteen-year-old Dubliner **Louisa Nolan (1898–after 1940)** received a military citation for helping tend the one hundred thirty-four wounded by carrying water and bandaging supplies through gunfire. Medic **Elizabeth O'Farrell (November 5, 1883–June 25, 1957)**, Red Cross volunteer **Martha Kelly (fl. 1916)**, **Mary Josephine Ryan (December 29, 1884–April 11, 1977)** from Tomcoole, and medic **Julia Grenan (1884–January 6, 1972)**, the Dubliner dispatchers and couriers, hid war dispatches, food, and munitions in their skirts. On April 30, 1916, under heavy fire along the British barricade at Moore Street, Elizabeth delivered the white flag of surrender to British general William Lowe at Athenry.

Recompense came swift and grim. Kathleen, Elizabeth, Madeleine, Brigid, and Julia were seized and jailed at Richmond Barracks along with organizer **Nell Ryan (July 5, 1881–December 8, 1959)** of Tomcoole, who hadn't even participated in the rising; Helena and Winifred remained at Aylesbury Prison until December 1916; Rosie and Martha served ten days in Kilmainham Jail; and Winifred, Brigid, Nell, Helena, and Marie received remands to Lewes Prison. Although **Kathleen Clarke (April 11, 1878–September 29, 1972)** of Limerick lost a pregnancy during the street fighting and witnessed the execution of her husband, brother, and a friend before a firing squad, she remained steadfast to the cause and became Lord Mayor of Dublin.

September 16, 1916

A Polish volunteer in the 96th regiment of the Austro-Hungarian army, Corporal **Marie von Fery-Bognar (also Mariska Fery Bognar)** of Lublin followed her husband, Lieutenant von Turnau, north to World War I. Her heroism earned public recognition for the KuK, the imperial ground forces in the Carpathian Mountains at the siege of Przemyśl, Poland, on September 16, 1915. A massive setback for the Austro-Hungarians, the six-month onslaught in Galicia (modern Poland-Ukraine) cost the two forces two hundred fifty-two thousand dead amid trenches edged in barbed wire. The 1916 Russian victory precipitated virulent pogroms against Jews. Among Germans, Hungarians, Czechs, Poles, Ukrainians, Croats, Serbs, Romanians, Slovaks, Slovenes, and Italian fighters, Marie became the only female soldier to receive an imperial medal, the Order of Franz Josef, and an initialed gold and diamond brooch.

November 13, 1916

Romanian medic/soldier **Ecaterina Teodoroiu (January 14, 1894–August 22, 1917)** of Vadeni survived the early battles of World War I before dying a hero's death. She impressed the royal family at the Bavarian siege on the Jiu River bridge and the retreat of the 9th Germany Army. Because she witnessed the death of brother Nicolae Teodoroiu on November 13, 1916, she took his place in the 18th Infantry. Her trickery of the enemy by pretending to surrender enabled her to shoot Germans while her squad fled. Wounded and captured at Oltenia, Romania, three nights later, she pulled a hidden gun and blasted her German guard. A bullet in the right leg failed to stop her from targeting two more enemy.

Ecaterina incurred more injury. By November 19, a mortar blast struck both legs, forcing her to a hospital at Iași, where two decorations marked her valor. On March 17, 1917, she received command of a platoon dispatched to western Moldavia. In August, she refused medical leave and advanced with her twenty-five men to the southwest. Machine Gun bursts to her torso and head at the battle of Mărășești stopped her counterattack on two hundred forty-five thousand enemy. At age twenty-three, she died on August 22, 1917, giving orders for her platoon to persevere. Acclaim for her fearlessness resulted in a statue, six monuments, four films, her portrait on a twenty lei note, and the naming of a girls' school.

March 17, 1917

A pioneering U.S. Navy yeoman and the first to achieve the rank of petty officer, **Loretta Walsh (April 22, 1896–August 6, 1925)** of Philadelphia was a sailor for four years that included World War I. She signed up on March 17, 1917, to aid the armed merchant marines in clearing seaways os German U-boats and served overseas. While employed as a clerk at the city's naval shipyard, she remained on active duty through the armistice that the Germans signed in Compiegne Forest, France, on November 11, 1918. In late autumn 1918, she transferred to the Philadelphia Naval Home to treat patients of the Spanish influenza epidemic. Her infection led to tuberculosis, which killed her at age twenty-nine. An annual wreath presentation at the gravesite in Olyphant, Pennsylvania, honors female sacrifice and duty.

Early Summer 1917

Russian combat commander Lieutenant **Marie Baktscharow (August 26, 1896–fl. 1910s)** led two hundred fifty female fighters in early summer 1917 against a machine gun barrage and bombs. Her outstanding recruits included warrior **Ludmilla Kornilov (fl. 1910s)** along with farm girls, students, unemployed factory workers, and teenage medics having wartime experience. On the northern front during the Russian Revolution, the warriors strapped pistols and rifles with bayonets over their blue smocks. For grueling battlefield heroics, Marie earned a promotion to lieutenant, an interview with U.S. President Woodrow Wilson, and medals for leading the nation's first women's unit.

A regiment called the Battalion of Death, commandeered by exiled industrial worker **Maria Botchkareva,** contributed a second women's division to World War I. As detailed in her 1918 memoir, *Yashka: My Life as Peasant, Exile and Soldier,* the unit traversed no man's land, where the "Frauenbataillone (women's regiment)" terrorized German aggressors. English feminist Emmeline Pankhurst proclaimed Maria Botchkareva a "woman of the century."

See also November 1914.

1918

In an era of military forays against isolated tribes, Northern Tibetan protester **Hor Lhamo (?–1918)** incited peasant nomads in 1918 at Thridug County, Kokonur (modern Qinghai Province), to negotiate a reduction of feudal taxes and an end to press gangs. She initiated the rebellion with representation of one hundred fifty households at Lhasa. To the governor's rejection of her demands, she formed a regiment of serfs that slew the county manager and captured forty-five prisoners of war. The Tibetan army, led by General Ma Qi, overwhelmed the serfs and executed their leader, but some one hundred grassroots uprisings continued for a half century.

February 1918

A teen rebel during the March 8, 1917, Russian Revolution, **Tatiana**

Grigorievna Solomakha (1892–November 7, 1918) of Lubińsk in southwestern Imperial Russia fought along the Bolshevik front against the White Army in February 1918. During the Northern Caucasus Operation, the Red military began a fall retreat to Astrahan, Russia, and Stavropol, Georgia, in the Volga delta. While the Whites captured the Northern Caucasus, White sentries seized Tatiana at Petrishchevo in northwestern Russia along with other insurgents infected with typhus. After lashing with whips and metal rods, she survived slicing of extremities before decapitation on November 7, 1918. Buildings and highways bear her name.

December 1918

A journalist turned multilingual undercover agent, **Marguerite Baker Harrison (September 30, 1879–July 16, 1967)** from Baltimore, Maryland, volunteered in December 1918 for the U.S. Military Intelligence Division as America's first female foreign spy. After diplomatic negotiations at Versailles ended World War I, in June 1919, she traveled to Berlin for three months as correspondent for the *Baltimore Sun*. A second deployment through Minsk to Moscow in November 1919 for the Associated Press yielded articles on economic needs, Bolshevik and socialist agents, Lenin's government, Americans imprisoned in Russia, and the role of women in war. Her advance through Poland's battlefront and surrender to the Red army preceded betrayal by a mole to the KGB and arrest on April 4, 1920.

To a Bolshevik offer of counter spying, Marguerite pretended to comply while informing the U.S. state department of the dilemma. She began the first of two sentences to Moscow's infamous Lubyanka prison on October 24, 1920. From solitary confinement, she was transported to Novinskaya women's prison hospital for treatment of tuberculosis. A prisoner exchange arranged by Herbert Hoover and the American Relief Administration returned her to family on July 30, 1921, and an opportunity to publish two memoirs, *Marooned in Moscow* and *Unfinished Tales from a Russian Prison*.

A deployment to Japan and Russia and arrest at the Chita depots on the Trans-Siberian rail line plunged Marguerite again into Lubyanka prison. The American Relief Administration freed her on February 20, 1923. She extended espionage to Asia and wrote a treatise contrasting China and Russia as enemies of the U.S. Retired from espionage, she became an anthropological filmmaker in Persia.

September 4, 1919

An Ottoman widow, Lieutenant **Kara Fatma (1888–July 2, 1955)** of Erzurum, Anatolia (modern Turkey), led a militia of seven hundred men and forty-three women on September 4, 1919, against enemy Greeks. After fleeing imprisonment, under rebel leader Mustafa Kemal Pasha (later known as Ataturk) during the Turkish War of Independence, she fought at İzmit-Bursa, İzmir, and Karşıyaka on the Mediterranean coast of Turkey. At age fifty-six, she issued an autobiography and appeared in army parades wearing the Medal of Independence. A fellow soldier, Sergeant **Halide**

Edib Adivar (June 11, 1884–January 9, 1964) of Constantinople (modern Istanbul), an instigator of the Armenian genocide of 1915, composed a combat memoir, *The Turkish Ordeal*. Her version of the war for independence included details of cannibalistic Senegalese mercenaries.

1920s

The queen of Macao's Pirates, **Lai Choi-san (also Loi Chai San or Honcho Lo, fl. 1920s–1939)** thrived from marauding and kidnapping in the 1920s. In the environs of Hong Kong, the Philippines, Canton and Shanghai, China, and the South China Sea, she commanded twelve junks fitted with cannon and bolstered with metalwork. She gave up feminine attire for a navy jacket, pants, and bare feet, but withdrew into solitude from male crewmen, who rifled cargo on steamers and houses on Bias Bay under her direction. Their muscular physiques intimidated merchantmen into paying protection. She communicated with victims by presenting an amputated ear or digit to the family. If they paid no ransom, she murdered or drowned the detainee. One version of her death describes her attack on a torpedo boat during the Chinese-Japanese War and death in marine combat. Her adventures appear in journalist Aleko Lilius's first-person memoir *I Sailed with Pirates*.

April 22, 1920

A transgender volunteer in the Mexican army at Xochipala, Guerrero, in southern Mexico, **Amelia Robles Àvila (November 3, 1889–December 9, 1984)** claimed male gender and fought for five years with the Zapatistas against President Porfirio Diaz. As a colonel, on April 22, 1920, Amelia led three hundred fifteen soldiers at the Agua Prieta Revolt to oust President Venustiano Carranza. Rebels killed Carranza in a shootout during his flight to Vera Cruz from Mexico City with the national treasury. After aiding Alvaro Obregon in suppressing the 1923 insurrection of Adolfo de la Huerta, Amelia recuperated from six bullet wounds. She earned the Mexican Legion of Honor and died mute at age ninety-five. Another fellow veteran, lieutenant **Angela Jiménez (1886–1990)** of Refugio, survived Amelia by six years and expired at age one hundred four. Lieutenant Colonel **María de la Luz Espinoza Barrera (1866–1958)**, an ex-con from Yautopec, joined raids on Tetecala, a wealthy city in south central Mexico. She found no contentment in receipt of a pension or return to feminine behavior. She died a cross-dressing wanderer.

July 21, 1920

General **Nazik Khatim (also Nazik Khatim al-'Abid Bayhum, January 18, 1887–1959)**, revered Syrian feminist and subversive, defied the Ottoman occupation, anti–Arabism, and the partitioning of Syria. The daughter of Mustafa al-Abid, an ambassador to Mosul, Iraq, she gained language skills in French, English, German, and Turkish at the Women's College in Istanbul. She began writing war analysis in 1908 and founded a newspaper, *Noir al-Fayha* (The Light of Damascus). She became a female exemplar on July 7,

1920, for initiating the Syrian Red Star Association, the forerunner of the Syrian Red Crescent Society and International Red Cross. Prince Faisal I promoted her as the first woman *naqib sharaf* (honorary general) of the Syrian Arab Army for marching in the streets in an army uniform and leading a mobile medic battalion in combat. Her female phalanx clashed with rebel forces along the Beirut-Damascus highway on July 21, 1920, at the four-hour battle of Maysalun in the Syrian mountains, where Faisal lost to some twelve thousand French forces advancing on Damascus under French general Mariano Goybet.

See also September 17, 1925.

August 1920

During the Polish-Soviet War, General **Maria Wittek (also Maria Wittekowna, August 16, 1899–April 19, 1997)** from Trebki in the Russian Empire, fought to repel Red Army invaders from Lviv (modern Lvov, Ukraine). In January 1920, the Bolsheviks began increasing troop strength from four divisions to twenty and began pushing into Kyiv on May 7 and into Poland on July 7. In August 1920, she survived a Bolshevik bounty of her weight in gold. For forcing the Russians into retreat, she and other citizens won the *Virtuti Militari* (Military Strengths) Cross.

At Bielany near Warsaw, Poland, Maria directed her military career toward training female nationalists for the Home Army. Into her forties, she fought the Nazi invasion of Poland on September 1, 1939, and eluded anti–Semite seizure of resisters at the Warsaw Uprising in summer 1944. Five years later, Communists imprisoned her for treason. In 1991, she became the nation's first female brigadier general. A life-sized bronze statue of her at Warsaw's Army Museum depicts her in uniform.

See also July 27, 1943.

September 9, 1921

Inupiat cook, seamstress, hunter, and furrier **Ada Delutuk Blackjack (1898–May 29, 1983)** from Spruce Creek, Alaska, survived a two-year expedition to Wrangel Island, a Russian possession in the Arctic Ocean. The lone female with one Canadian and three American males, she enlisted to earn enough money to treat son Bennett's tuberculosis. The five explorers set out by ship on September 9, 1921. Traveling west from Nome to Wrangel, Siberia, the men claimed for Canada and the British Empire the Russian island, a former home of paleo-eskimoes in the Chukchi Sea. The strategic location offered a land base for future wars.

Enduring bouts of depression, starvation, scurvy, and the men's bullying, Ada devised ways of killing bear, fox, and seal for food and stitched reindeer pelts into a parka. Scurvy weakened expeditioners, for whom Ada collected driftwood, built a skin boat, trapped foxes, and shot birds and seals. After three men deserted the camp, the fourth man died of scurvy on June 23, 1923. She and the ship's cat Victoria lived on seal meat and eggs until her rescue by the crew of the schooner *Donaldson* on August 20, 1923. A documentary film recounted her adventures and death in penury.

December 1921

A widowed supplier of military aid on the Black Sea, **Şerife Bacı (also Sister Şerife, 1900–December 1921)**, a herder and woodcutter from Seydiler, Ottoman Empire, hauled cannon balls and artillery shells in heavy snowfall and sleet in December 1921 from Inebolu west up Ilgaz Mountain. The town crier identified the destination as Ankara sixty-five miles away. During the three-and-a-half-year Greco-Turkish War, she carried toddler daughter Elif and breastfed her on a snowy track to the front lines. One of eighty ox drivers, Şerife died at age twenty-one on the way at Kastamonu Barracks from exposure to cold. A school, hospital, and monument commemorate her martyrdom to Turkish independence.

September 14, 1923

Bulgarian Communist **Tsola Nincheva Dragoycheva (August 18, 1898–May 26, 1993)** of Byala Slatina joined rebels in the September 14, 1923, uprising at Maglizh to oust a fascist regime. Two prison sentences halted her involvement in the insurrection. After the terrorist explosion of St. Nedelya Church at Sofia in 1925, she began her rise in the Moscow politburo. In 1941, she furthered armed aggression on the Axis alliance and survived four months at Asenovgrad women's concentration camp. The 1944 Bulgarian *coup d'etat* prefaced a series of political executions of fascist torturers and betrayers and of powerful posts that elevated women in the Soviet hierarchy. She detailed elements of World War II in her memoir, *Macedonia, Not a Cause of Discord but a Factor of Good Neighborliness and Cooperation*. Her biography preceded receipt of the Lenin Peace Prize and election as first woman cabinet member in Bulgaria.

September 17, 1925

Followers ranked Syrian nationalist **Nazik Khatim (January 18, 1898–1959)**, the "Joan of Arc of the Arabs," on a par with seventh-century charismatic Syrian poet-warrior Khawla bint al-Azwar. Hostilities against French colonialists increased during a September 17, 1925, Syrian insurrection at Jabal al-Durūz (Druze Mountain). For the twenty-five hundred Syrian guerrillas hiding in Damascus, at the battle of al-Musayfirah in the south, Nazik Khatim served as combat medic and smuggler of munitions, weapons, and food and medical supplies. Human costs of hand-to-hand fighting reached five hundred dead Syrians and another five hundred captured and executed. The eighty-eight hundred victorious French, who sustained forty-seven battlefield deaths, threatened Nazik with imprisonment and forced her to seek asylum in Lebanon. As the wife of Lebanese politician Muḥammad Jamīl Bayhum, she remained active until her death in free Syria in 1959 at age seventy-two.

See also July 30, 634 CE; September 19, 634 CE; August 20, 636 CE; July 21, 1920.

1926

In Shanghai, a Marxist promoter and expert at disguise, seduction, and identity change, **Kitty Harris (May 25, 1899–October 6, 1966)** from London, Ontario, signed on with the KGB in 1926 as a communist party courier. Postings for intelligence work took her to Berlin to forge passports and spy for the Soviet Union. By 1936, under the code names "Ada" or "Aida," she progressed to radio operator in Paris. At the Nazi seizure of France in 1940, she hurried to Moscow to aid foreign intelligence. A year later at Los Alamos, New Mexico, she abetted infiltrators of the Manhattan Project and the creation of the first U.S. atomic bomb and passed diagrams stolen from physicists. Her peripatetic life included postings as a messenger and facilitator in Mexico City and a safe house manager in Santa Fe, New Mexico. For the documentary *A Spy's Life,* Lauren Evans played the part of Kitty.

March 1926

Italian anti–Fascist **Lina Merlin (October 15, 1887–August 16, 1979)** of Pozzonovo on the northern Adriatic coast jeopardized a classroom job teaching French in March 1926 by refusing to pledge loyalty to Italian strongman Benito Mussolini's dictatorship. An outspoken Piemontese socialist, she served sixty percent of a five-year sentence in prison before forming small assault groups to harass German troops and destroy rail lines in the Alpine Susa Valley. During World War II, she recruited volunteers for women's defense cells to plot sabotage, conceal documents in maternity clothes, attack SS vehicles, transport packages of dynamite on the tram to crucial bridges, and arm squads against Nazis. After a Resistenza assault, she helped recover rations and ammunition for partisan stores.

July 1, 1927

An Albanian nationalist hero and liberator of Kosovo, **Shote Galica (November 10, 1895–after July 1927)** from Radosjeva in the Ottoman Empire accompanied her husband, Azem Galica, in rebellion against the Turks. In 1919, the couple promoted peasant defiance in western Kosovo. They cleared the region of Serbs, who retaliated by wounding Azem in battle. He died in a cave at Drenica (modern Kosovo) on July 25, 1924. On July 1, 1927, Shote continued armed resistance to Yugoslav insurgents in Kosovo and fought in Has and Lumë (modern Albania-Kosobo). At Çikatov, Kosovo, she captured a cadre of Serbian soldiers and their leader. Ill health forced her to withdraw from combat.

September 7, 1927

China's first female general, Major General **Li Zhen (February 1908–March 11, 1990)** from Liuyang, Hunan, recruited soldiers for the communist army. Her family sold her as a child bride in 1914. As commander of a guerrilla squadron during the September 7, 1927, Autumn Harvest Uprising at Hunan, she delivered documents, scouted for rations, and promoted support for Mao Zedong among five hundred rural peasants. At the collapse of the movement, she hid in the mountains and organized refugees into a branch party. While pregnant in 1928, she simulated machine fire with firecrackers in an oil drum and led forces on a suicide jump from a cliff. By August 1934, she deployed to the west with the Sixth Red Army. The fetal miscarriage in 1928 preceded a second child death in 1935 during the Long March to northern China and ended her ability to conceive. She led forces throughout the Korean War and progressed to major general on September 27, 1955.

1928

An ambidextrous sharpshooter and rescuer of the wounded, **Kang Keqing (September 7, 1911–April 22, 1992)** from Wanan, China, made herself valuable to the Red Army by shooting pistols and a rifle with either hand. Born in poverty during the 1911 Revolution that ended the Manchu dynasty, she entered the Communist youth movement during a mobilization of peasants. To elude a forced marriage, in 1928, she escaped near-enslavement to a foster father. She reached a guerrilla base and married General Zhu De.

At age seventeen, Kang enlisted in the Fourth Front Army and trained in Ruijin at the Red Military Academy. She began commanding female recruits in 1932 and survived a shootout with Nationalist forces. In October 1935, she accompanied Mao Zedong's six thousand-mile Long March. Living on starvation rations north of Sichuan, she reached Yanan, Shaanxi, a year later, and aided defense of the northwest. Two of Mao's companions, his third and fourth wives **He Zizhen (September 20, 1910–April 19, 1984)** from Yunshan and actor **Chiang Ch'ing (also Jiang Qing or Madame Mao, March 19, 1914–May 14, 1991)** from Zucheng completed the pilgrimage. He Zizhen sought treatment in the Soviet Union for a battle wound. While serving a life sentence, after eight years in a cell, Chiang Ch'ing hanged herself. Another combatant at hundreds of skirmishes, **Deng Yingchao (also Teng Ying-ch'ao, February 4, 1904–July 11, 1992)** of Nanning, Guangxi, wife of Chou En-Lai, survived pulmonary tuberculosis and transport by stretcher through war zones. She evolved into a leader of women's equality and survived to age eighty-eight.

1931

A specialist in Soviet subversive activity, London attorney **Milicent Bagot (March 28, 1907–May 26, 2006)** of Putney, England, advanced from Metropolitan Police registrar and secretary to Scotland Yard in 1931 to espionage for MI5. As an expert on global communism, she suspected infamous mole Kim Philby, who fled to Moscow. By 1953, she progressed to the first female operative to become assistant director of MI5. She compiled a history of international communism and reviewed foreign communist fronts. Spy novelist John le Carré created his "Moscow watcher" from her career for *Tinker Tailor Soldier Spy* and *Smiley's People*.

December 14, 1931

Militant Bengali assassins, fifteen-year-old **Santi Das Ghose (also Shanti, November 22, 1916–1989)**, a college professor from Calcutta, and fourteen-year-old **Suniti Chaudhuri (also Choudhury, 1917–January 12, 1988)** of Comilla conspired to murder District Magistrate Charles Buckland Stevens of Tippera. Both teens studied self-defense, swordsmanship, revolver accuracy, and lathi (pike) self-defense. Concealing automatic pistols under their wraps, on December 14, 1931, they drew arms and killed him from close fire in a second wave feminist defiance of authorities who molested women.

Under duress and torture, police pressed the teenagers for details. Their hopes to become martyrs crumbled because a Calcutta judge ordered life transportation sentences in February 1932 because they were juveniles. After seven years in exile, they gained freedom in 1939 at Gandhi's request. Suniti studied medicine and opened a doctor's office; Santi became a legislator.

1932

Chief Inspector **Lilian Wyles (August 31, 1885–May 13, 1975)** of Bourne, England, rose from Scotland Yard's first female patrol officer to investigator of sexual assault. Dressed for plain-clothes work, disguised, or uniformed in tall boots, skirts, belted tunic, gloves, and hat, she thrived despite ridicule from male police. She and colleagues **Dorothy Peto (December 15, 1886–February 26, 1974)** of Emery Down and **Mildred White (December 10, 1873–December 29, 1957)** from Warminster, a former constable in Bath and Salisbury and metropolitan superintendent, provided escorts for lost children and compiled statements in cases of abortion, child abuse, delinquency, or violent or indecent treatment of girls and youth. In 1920, Lilian commended agents **Annie Pomeroy (fl. 1920s)** and **Annie Matthews (fl. 1920s)** for undercover infiltration of cocaine traffickers in the West End's lavatory bunkers by posing as prostitutes.

For the safety of females, Lilian encouraged amateur seducers of southeast Asian seamen to avoid Chinatown, sordid gaming houses, and London brothels and taverns at Limehouse. She trained policewomen on how to investigate tactfully and lawfully rape and white slavery charges and female witnesses of crime. Lilian recorded her history in a memoir, *A Woman at Scotland Yard: Reflections on the Struggles and Achievements of Thirty Years in the Metropolitan Police.* Like Lilian, Dorothy issued a memoir including mention of her King's Police and Fire Services Medal and the Order of the British Empire.

February 6, 1932

Bengali freedom fighter **Bina Das (August 24, 1911–December 26, 1986)**, a scholarly Brahmin, tried to assassinate Bengali Governor Stanley Jackson to stop government-ordered assaults and murders in Chittagong, Hijli, and Midnapur. She enrolled with Calcutta revolutionaries in 1928 and began recruiting other anti–British rebels. A single agent, on February 6, 1932, she failed to kill Jackson with the pistol supplied by Bengali courier and bomber **Kamala Das Gupta (March 11, 1907–July 19, 2000)**. After nine years in a cell, Bina returned to prison in 1942 for aiding the Quit India movement. For her promotion of armed struggle with explosives that she hid in a women's hostel, Kamala entered prison in 1933 for three years and wrote two autobiographies about libertarian beliefs, *Rakter Akshare* (In Letters of Blood) and *Swadhinata Sangrame Nari* (Women in the Freedom Struggle).

February 16, 1932

For four weeks of the Hangrum War, on February 16, 1932, anti-Christian cultist and rebel **Gaidinliu Pamei (January 26, 1915–February 17, 1993)** from Nungkao fought the Assam Rifles in the northeastern highlands of British India (modern Bangladesh). She combatted oppression, an end to forced labor, limits to forest use and community fishing, and burdensome taxes. To ensure the safety of animistic Heraka disciples, in October 1932, she began erecting a wood palisade and fomenting an inter-tribal uprising with spears against the British.

Gaiginliu's arrest outside Kenoma on October 17, 1932, derived from betrayal to police. At Imphal, a ten-month inquiry found her guilty of murdering a hill tribe's sentry. She began a life sentence that took her to four jails in eighteen years. Upon release, negotiated by Prime Minister Jawaharlal Nehru, she retreated to the jungle in 1960. At age fifty-one, she continued insisting on self-rule for Herakan reformers. At her death on February 17, 1993, devout rebels wore her photos in lockets. A column of martyrs honored seven men killed in the Hangrum War.

September 23, 1932

A "most wanted" Bengali raider, **Pritilata Waddedar (May 5, 1911–September 23, 1932)**, a high school principal at Chittagong (modern Chittagram, Bangladesh), gave her life to end British encroachment on Indian liberties. At age twenty-one, she adopted the courageous stance of of eighteenth-century warrior Lakshmibai of Jhansi. Encouraged by a brother, Pritilata joined a rebel faction along with freedom fighter **Kalpana Datta (July 27, 1913–February 8, 1995)**, a guerrilla warrior from Sripur. Kalpana helped plan hit-and-run attacks until a court ordered her transportation. Dressed as a male Punjabi soldier and trained in weaponry at Kotwali, Pritilata raided police depots and telephone offices, once hid under water, and supplied explosives for a battle in Jalalabad, Afghanistan.

On September 23, 1932, a week after Kalpana's arrest, Pritilata alone led eight men in reprising instructions, kissing the earth, and praying. On the third day of attorney Mohandas Gandhi's fast, the company intended to halt rail and communications to Calcutta and capture two Chittagong armories. They intended to seize British hostages in a night arson attack near the railway depot on the racist Pahartali European Club. The assault killed one British woman and wounded eleven.

Because of a bullet wound, Pritilata chose martyrdom by cyanide rather than arrest, torture, and jailing. She left a suicide note demanding an end to British imperialism and the liberation of women. A college at Shikri, two university halls, a road, and a women's hostel bear her name. Inland from the Bay of Bengal, a bronze portrait statue stands before the Pahartali Railway School.

See also May 10, 1857.

1933

A bustling, argumentative Dutch resistance fighter and rescuer in 1933, **Geertruida Wijsmuller-Meijer (April**

21, 1896–August 30, 1978) from Alkmaar devoted herself to strategizing recovery transportation and guiding groups to freedom. Beginning with aid to German-Jewish children, she heightened reception of homeless children after *Kristallnacht* on November 10, 1938, when Nazi rioters conducted an anti–Semitic pogrom in Germany, Austria, and Czechoslovakia. Under the code name Madame Odi, she continued after September 1, 1939, into World War II arranging air, sea, and land escape routes from Bentheim to Spain, Switzerland, England, Vichy France, and the United States. Under cover of a Red Cross assignment, she organized food parcels and medicines for prisoners and smuggled falsified identification cards. At the height of World War II in 1941, she offered civilian clothes to Allied airmen and French soldiers and, with Canadian help, relocated them by threatening Nazi soldiers with post-war reprisals. Her rescue of more than one thousand at-risk children and soldiers won a knighthood, medals from the Dutch, Germans, and French, recognition by the German Red Cross, a statue in Amsterdam, naming of streets and a bridge, and listing as one of the Righteous among Nations.

1933

The first female Soviet navigator, in 1933, **Marina Mikhaylovna Raskova (March 28, 1912–January 4, 1943)** of Moscow in tsarist Russia joined Ukrainian colonel **Valentina Grizodubova (April 14, 1909–April 18, 1993)**, a pilot from Kharkiv, in flying a long range bomber nonstop to the Sea of Okhotsk in an effort to increase military range. In June 1942, Valentina, a member of the legendary 588th "Night Witches," flew supplies to Leningrad and bombed German Wehrmacht planes and airdromes. Within three months, she ferried three million pounds of radio and camera equipment, firearms, and ammunition in a total of eighteen hundred fifty missions. On return flights, she safely delivered twenty-five hundred casualties and orphans. A monument and eight medals honor her expertise and sense of duty to the four thousand female volunteers who learned to sideslip and zigzag craft out of the line of fire.

Both Russian aviators received Hero of the Soviet Union medals. Marina, who died in a crash on a training flight to Stalingrad at age thirty-one, earned the war's first state funeral and interment in the Kremlin Wall. Most of the subsequent Russian pilot heroes of World War II owed their careers to recruitment and training by Marina.

See also October 18, 1941; May 1942; May 18, 1943.

February 11, 1934

After Hitler instituted a dictatorship in Austria in January 1933, martial arts trainee **Maria Raps Emhart (May 27, 1901–October 9, 1981)** of Pyhra joined the *Schutzbund* (paramilitary) on February 11, 1934, in the Austrian Civil War, actually a street fight against Vienna's fascists. As a courier and arms supplier, she engaged women in conveying ammunition, medicine, and bandages across enemy lines in baby carriages. Following a raid on the Hotel Schiff in

Linz on February 12, she smuggled grenades to a weapons cache at Floridsdorf in northern Vienna. An artillery barrage at Karl-Marx-Hof forced the socialists to surrender. Maria's compatriot **Herma Paschinger (fl. 1930s)** infiltrated German officials and seized and burned the Resistance membership list to save others from interrogation and possible execution. On February 20, police questioned Maria for bruising an officer's thumb and charged her with rioting. After recuperating from tuberculosis in Davos, Switzerland, she rejoined resisters.

March 1934

A decorated undercover agent and communist telegrapher, Colonel **Úrsula Kuczyński (May 15, 1907–July 7, 2000)** from Schoneberg, Prussia, in the German Empire posted to Shenyang, Manchuria, for nine months in March 1934 to spy on Japanese military occupation forces. On August 1935, "Red Sonya" was reassigned to Moscow before her three-year espionage in Warsaw, Poland. For competent intelligence gathering, Soviet Russia's GRU named her to the Order of the Red Banner. Her career continued for fourteen months in Caux, Switzerland. By assisting Russian spy Klaus Fuchs under the Josef Stalin regime, she promoted work on Soviet atomic weapons. In fall 1944, she infiltrated the OSS to pass on names and locales of German exiles who parachuted into Germany. To avoid seizure, in March 1940, she escaped to East Berlin to compose children's literature and memoirs.

See also 1937.

May 1934

A Marxist recruiter for the Cambridge Spy ring, **Edith Tudor-Hart (August 28, 1908–May 12, 1973)**, an Austrian Jew from Vienna, deceived Britain's MI6 for more than three decades. In post–World War I Austria, she recorded a socialist bent in Bauhaus-style photography, a study of poverty on urban streets that she compiled in *The Eye of Conscience* and *Artists against Fascism and against War*. Following a secret Comintern mission to Paris and London in 1929, she served the Communist Party under the code name "Edith." At Trafalgar Square in 1931, British intelligence placed her under intense watch by reading her mail, bugging her residence, and tapping her phone. Her selection of potential subversives included the infamous Kim Philby, whom she brought to London in May 1934 and recruited the following month. Her contacts enabled clandestine connections with London's Soviet consulate, with the Austrian underground, and, in 1938, with operatives in London. In March 1938, a police raid connected her Leica camera with the Woolwich Arsenal surveillance syndicate, but turned up no substantial evidence for arrest for stealing details of rocketry, explosives, and munitions manufacture. Her life as a secret agent appears in the documentary *Tracking Edith*.

June 6, 1934

A short-term espionage operative for England's MI5, June 6, 1934, secretary-typist **Olga Isabel Gray (1906–1990)** from Manchester in Lancashire functioned as Miss X, a spy on British communists. Disguised as a member of the Friends of the Soviet Union, she accepted an undercover mission to Paris. From Europe she traveled to India as a courier for messages and cash to support the Communist Party. At her London apartment, she enabled British intelligence to waylay a communist agent bearing maps and documents from the arms, rocket, anti-aircraft guns, and explosives works at the Woolwich Arsenal. Among them were blueprints for a fourteen-inch navy gun that fired two rounds per minute weighing fifteen hundred ninety pounds each. She testified against the communist leaders before emigrating to Toronto, Ontario, to end living in constant fear.

July 17, 1936

A leftist aiding Spanish Republicans, Romanian Jew **Olga Bancic (May 10, 1912–May 10, 1944)** from Chișinău, Bessarabia, in the tsarist empire smuggled weapons from France to Iberia. On July 17, 1936, the supply route took her over the Pyrenees to the Resistance to support troops battling nationalists during the Spanish Civil War. During World War II, she became a saboteur to weaken the German Wehrmacht. After her arrest on November 6, 1943, for terrorism, she survived torture, but yielded no data useful to the enemy. The Nazis deported her to Stuttgart for beheading on May 10, 1944. Street names commemorate her dedication to ending fascism.

See also 1941.

July 17, 1936

Basque freedom fighter **Kattalin Aguirre (August 28, 1897–July 22, 1992)** of Sare, France, smuggled messages, falsified IDs, reconnaissance, cash, radio parts, and fugitives on the Comet Line, an escape network through Brussels to England. From the Spanish Civil War through World War II, she gathered bits of information from her job as a hotel maid at Ciboure overlooking the Atlantic Ocean. At her farmhouse, she hid American, British, and Canadian air crews on their way from Belgium and occupied France through the Pyrenees to Bilbao, Spain. A co-conspirator with Belgian agent **Andrée de Jongh (November 30, 1916–October 13, 2007)** from Schaerbeek, Kattalin stepped up getaways after the entrance of B-17 bombers to the allied war in December 1941. She witnessed the Russian liberation of Ravensbrück concentration camp and earned a Legion of Honor, Croix de Guerre, King George VI Medal, and military medal. Her residence and Comet Line route at Ciboure through the mountains remain open to tourists of Aquitaine.

See also August 1941.

September 18, 1936

Communist French author **Lise London (also Elisabeth Ricol London, February 16, 1916–March 31, 2012)** from Montceau-les-Mines joined the International Brigades on September 18, 1936, at the onset of the Spanish Civil War. In 1934, she and other females dressed in khaki and army boots and aided the Comintern siege against fascism at Moscow. Her front line experience in Spain continued to 1938. In service to the French Resistance after 1941, she rallied women in line to enter a department store. She survived malnutrition at Ravensbrück women's prison during incarceration and metal work at a forced labor factory in Leipzig, Germany. After deportation, she settled in Prague and combatted Stalinism during the purge trials, but remained a communist. She wrote of wartime privations in *Mégère de la rue Daguerre* (The Harlot of Daguerre Street).

See also late 1941.

1937

An East Chinese martial arts expert and outlaw during the Second Sino-Japanese War, **Huang Pei-mei (also Bamei or Wang Pa-mei, 1906–1982)** from Pinghu County mustered a company of fifty thousand sea bandits 1937. As a salt smuggler in childhood, she progressed to pirate gang leader, robber of Ganpu in 1931, steamship hijacker, and kidnapper and raider throughout Jiangsu and Zhejiang on the East China Sea. As reported in *Shen Bao* (Shanghai News), she gained ill repute as a pro–Japanese agent, provider of rifles to rebels, and Han traitor. In 1938, Mao Sen, an intelligence officer, recruited her as a guerrilla warrior for the Nationalist Army. Until March 1950, she networked familiar territory on Hangzhou Bay. After a Communist foray against her headquarters at Yangshan, she sheltered at the Dachen Islands, ran a beach inn at Zhapu, and retired to open an orphanage and nonprofit garment factory.

1937

KGB undercover agent **Melita Norwood (March 25, 1912–June 2, 1005)** from Bournemouth, England, managed an intelligence gathering career in 1937 from an unassuming home in Kent. For the Woolwich Spy Ring, she eluded discovery and posed as a secretary to a medals research firm. Seeking no reward for collecting secret reports on armaments and rocket manufacture, she passed to Soviets details of uranium-235 response to high heat. Under the direction of communist agent **Úrsula Kuczynski**, Melita and atomic spy Klaus Ruchs gained the documents from the British Tube Alloys research, a cover name for atomic weapons. In 1958, Soviets named her to the Order of the Red Banner of Labour.

March 20, 1937

The world's first female combat flier, **Sabiha Gökçen (March 22, 1913–March 22, 2001)** of Bursa in the Ottoman Empire got her introduction to war at the twenty-month Dersim rebellion, a Kurdish revolt against suppression and genocide. For the 1st Aircraft Regiment, she practiced in a Breguet XIX and Curtiss Hawk for maneuvers in Thrace and the Aegean shores and completed thirty-two fighter missions in eastern Anatolia. Releasing fifty kilogram (110.2 pound) firebombs on the uprising, she aimed at Kurds and their goats, a major source of army rations. For her support of Turkish ground troops, she received the Murassa Medal, a Romanian aviator's badge, and the Yugoslavian Badge of the White Eagle. After progressing to trainer, she composed *A Life along the Path of Ataturk*, the founder of modern Turkey. An airport in Istanbul bears her name.

1938

Norwegian resistance organizer and strategizer of escape to Sweden in 1938, **Sylvia Salvesen (January 15, 1890–June 19 1973)** survived arrests in January and September 1942 before transfer to Ravensbrück women's camp in eastern Prussia. She collaborated with operatives **Odette Sansom (April 28, 1912–March 13, 1995)** of Amiens, Parisian sketch artist **Violette Lecoq (1912–2003)**, and Norwegian author **Lise Børsum (September 18, 1908–August 29, 1985)**, whom Nazis arrested in April 1943 for transporting Jews from her hometown of Kristiania (modern Oslo) on the route to neutral Sweden. Sylvia testified that she witnessed Nazi doctors forcing abortions and murdering newborns as well as sterilizing gypsies and conducting experimental surgeries. After issuing a memoir, *Forgive—But Do not Forget*, she earned a king's medal for meritorious service. Odette received the legion of honor and the George Cross for her work as a secret courier and survivor of Gestapo torture and starvation; Violette earned a Crox de Guerre medal and citation for resistance espionage. Lise gained liberty on April 8, 1945. She pursued punishment for concentration camp authorities in her 1946 exposé *Prisoner in Ravensbrück*, where she survived for nearly two years. On return to Norway, she abandoned her family to comfort war-damaged people.

See also November 2, 1942; May 13, 1943; April 5, 1944.

March 13, 1938

After Hitler annexed Austria to Germany on March 13,1938, partisan ammunition supplier and messenger **Marianne Feldhammer (March 14, 1909–June 15, 1996)** of Altaussee, Austro-Hungary, concealed rebel routes through the alps to *Der Igel*, a deserted salt mine east of Salzburg on Lake Altaussee. She hid among peasants and posed as a laundress washing clothes for the upper class at the riverbank. Her clandestine efforts appeared in the documentary *Igel* (Hedgehog), the name of a mineshaft that resisters used as a hideout. Farther west, rebel leader **Resi Pesendorfer (June 21, 1902–October 31, 1989)** of Ischi recruited a network of female couriers to ferry arms, dynamite, food, and medicine to anti-fascist guerrillas. Following her arrest in May 1942, she joined **Agnes Primocic (January 30, 1905–April 14, 2007)** from Hallein in a female-led escape of resistance leader Josef Plieseis from a labor camp. Resi earned an honor citation and featured in the documentary *Igel*. Agnes received a Golden Medal of Merit and citation for promoting human rights. Her story was the focus of another documentary, *Don't Keep Still When Injustice Happens*.

See also October 23, 1943.

July 28, 1938

A seamstress and hero of Brazil, **Maria Bonita (1908–July 28, 1938)** from Jeremoabo, Bahia, died at Angicos in the heat of combat against the dictatorship of Getulio Vargas. Armed with a rifle, in 1931, she deserted her husband, cobbler José Nenem, and accompanied her lover Lampiao, a rebel rodeo cowboy, to revolutionary clashes in the northeast. With hundreds of followers, the pair sought to prevent the government from reducing farmers to debt-ridden day laborers. The bandits distributed loot to poor agrarians.

Recovered from a bullet wound and the birth of daughter Expedita, Maria sewed bandoliers, chaps, and packsacks for the troops. In 1935, state soldiers equipped with modern rifles, machine guns, artillery, and planes pressed inland from Rio de Janeiro and Sao Paulo. The couple spurned amnesty and, on July 28, 1938, fell victim to a night ambush arranged by a traitor. Military police despoiled the corpses with decapitation and rape. Their pitiable demise survives in folklore, songs, film, soap opera, and caricature.

1939

Translator, anti-fascist radical, and freelance spy **Karin Lannby (April 13, 1916–November 19, 2007)** of Stockholm served the Swedish Defense Office as an observer and reporter of naval officer, diplomat, and German-Jewish refugee activities. A poet and actor of the leisured class, she was captured during the Spanish Civl War while infiltrating dictator Francisco Franco's forces in Provence (southern France) and denounced Spanish Catholicism for exploiting the underclass. After May 1940, she joined the Swedish defense department and networked with Norwegian operatives, double agents, and Swedish intelligentsia in Stockholm.

During World War II when ten million noncombatants from the Soviet frontier to the North Sea fled Hitler's Wehrmacht, under the code name Annette, Karin engaged in risky missions intercepting phone calls and letter. She succeeded in delivering thousands of eyewitness accounts of suspicious characters hobnobbing at Stockholm's Mona Lisa Tavern and the Grand Hotel. Director Ingmar Bergman, her lover, used her experience as the basis for the 1947 film *Woman Without a Face*.

March 20, 1939

A Lithuanian librarian, **Ona Šimaitė (January 6, 1894–January 17, 1970)** of Akmene became a two-directional smuggler: carrying rations, mail, and weapons to the Vilna ghetto and returning with prized documents regarding Jewish culture. On the pretext of reclaiming overdue books, she moved in and out of closely guarded territory. She conspired with forgers to provide vital papers and recruited families to house Jewish children. Seizure by the Gestapo in April 1944 did not halt torture, but saved her from a death sentence. She transferred to Dachau, Germany, and a French concentration camp at Ludelange on the border of Luxembourg. Her example survives in a street name and listing as Righteous among the Nations.

May 1939

Previous to World War II, in May 1939, investigator and English undercover operative for MI5, the United Kingdom intelligence system, **Joan Miller (1918–June 1984)** began monitoring the Indian Nationalist Movement and anti–Semitic right-wingers in the Right Club. With the aid of co-conspirators **Hélène Louise de Munck (fl. 1930s–1940s)** from Brussels, Belgium, and **Marjorie Amor (1898–1975)**, also Belgian, Joan kept the British government abreast of fascist sentiments. Their espionage disclosed the Nazi leanings of White Russian propagandist **Anna Wolkoff (1902–August 2, 1973)**, a possible fascist intermediary in copying and sending secret data to Germany, including documents from Winston Churchill and Franklin D. Roosevelt. In addition to surveying secret cables, Joan intercepted a coded letter sent through the Italian consulate that led to Anna's arrest on May 20, 1940. Anna's imprisonment and ten-year sentence followed Joan and Hélène's graphic testimony at the trial on November 7, 1940. Joan issued an informative autobiography, *One Girl's War: Personal Exploits in MI5's Most Secret Station.*

Summer 1939

Twice arrested for smuggling, war diarist **Hélène Studler (March 1891–November 1944)** of Amiens returned to work as an escape arranger for the French Resistance. A nun with the Daughters of Mercy, she drove a truck to Nazi stalags at the Palatinate, Rhenania, and Westphalia to bring rations, clothes, medicine, documents, and supplies to prisoners at Charentes. As head of a cadre of agents, she began work in summer 1939 at the Moselle and designed escape networks through the Amanvillers, Moyeuvre-Grande, and Rosselange train stations and bus depots. On June 17, 1940, she treated a marching column of two thousand French for battered feet and enabled them to cross the Lorraine border.

Suffering from cancer after the first jailing on February 4, 1941, Hélène renewed her smuggling through northeastern France from her office in the Hospice of Saint Nicolas de Metz. In November 1942, the Gestapo again pursued her to Lyons for freeing future French president François Mitterand from Ziegenhain, Hesse, and General Henri Giraud, commander of the Free French, from Koenigstein fortress in Switzerland. Giraud awarded her the Legion of Honor and a Croix de Guerre. A film, *Network of Freedom,* depicts Assumpta Serna in Hélène's role. A memorial, city square, and statue elevated her to "Our Lady of Prisoners."

August 1939

Conscripted into the 3rd Military Aviation unit at Poznań, Poland, pilot **Janina Antonina Lewandowska (April 22, 1908–April 22, 1940)** from Kharkiv, Ukraine, served only until September 22, when Soviet troops arrested her. At the prison camp at Kozelsk, Russia, she apparently died in spring 1940 at the Katyn Forest massacre, in which Josef Stalin's terrorists executed twenty-two thousand Polish intelligentsia, scholars, artists, and military officers. Within weeks, Janina's younger sister, underground agent **Agnieszka Dowbor-Muśnicka (September 7, 1919–June 21, 1940)** from Lusowo, Poland, survived torture at Pawiak prison by the Nazi SS outside Warsaw. She died at the Palmiry Forest massacre of June 21, 1940, where the

SS dug burial trenches measuring 98' by 9'10". A monument and a commemorative coin honor the sisters' patriotism.

August 23, 1939

Alexandra Beiko (fl. 1930s–1940s) became the rare female tank driver during the Soviet-Finnish Winter War in which tanks and planes dominated combat artillery. She joined her husband Ivan in petitioning Soviet Union president Josef Stalin for permission to buy a tank. The conflict pitted some seven hundred sixty thousand Russians against three hundred forty thousand Finns. After the couple volunteered for combat on August 23, 1939, Russia lost more than half its six thousand five hundred forty-one tanks in battle. By March 1940, the Soviets annexed western Karelia, Petsamo, and Salla, Finland. Alexandra won a Soviet decoration, the Order of the Patriotic War, for partisan prowess.

August 31, 1939

An ambulance driver and fire control volunteer during the outbreak of the battle of the Atlantic, **Barbara Helen Bailey (February 8, 1905–December 3, 1995)** from Newcastle, England, survived the U-boat sinking of the steamer *Athenia,* the first British ship targeted by Germans. Fourteen hundred and eighteen passengers left Glasgow, Belfast, and Liverpool for Montreal on September 2, 1939. Off northwestern Ireland, one of two torpedoes from U-30 struck the *Athenia's* engine room, killing one hundred seventeen and damaging lifeboats. The chaos caused Barbara to apply civil defense rules about avoiding panic. The Norwegian merchantman *Knute Nelson* rescued her. On deck, she guarded embassy papers from a Scots clerk until the arrival of four hundred thirty survivors on September 5 at Galway, Scotland. Post-war investigations revealed that the Nazis lied about believing the *Athenia* to be an armed merchant cruiser.

September 1939

Russian warrior and paramedic **Lidia Lwow-Eberle (November 14, 1920–January 5, 2021)** of Plyos on the Volga River joined the Home Army Fifth Wilno (modern Vilnius) Brigade in September 1939 to fight Nazi insurgents. Gallantry against the enemy at Worziany on January 1, 1944, where she was wounded and at Radziusze and Białystok, Poland, earned her a field commission. After her arrest in 1948, she escaped transport to Siberia and remained at Mokotów Prison outside Warsaw. In 1956, she gained freedom with fellow medic and warrior **Janina Wasiłojć-Smoleńska (1926–September 9, 2010)** of Wilno, Lithuania, a veteran of the Polish home guard's week-long Operation Ostra Brama (Sharp Gate) in July 1944 to free the city of Nazis. At Lidia's death at age one hundred, an officer's funeral at Powązki Military Cemetery honored her among Allied fighters of World War II.

September 1939

In September 1939, Romanian-Jewish code analyst **Vera May Atkins (June 16, 1908–June 24, 2000)** of Galati aided the release of three Polish cryptographers from German invaders. As flight officer of the women's air corps, for four years, she coordinated security for British operatives entering occupied France and traversed Europe to gather intelligence for Prime Minister Winston Churchill. After the war, Vera searched for one hundred eighteen missing agents, finding all but one, and interrogated Nazis charged with war crimes. She received the Legion of Honor and Croix de Guerre. Actor Stephanie Cole played Vera's part in a BBC radio drama.

See also 1940.

September 1939

Missouri-born singer-erotic dancer **Josephine Baker (June 3, 1906–April 12, 1975)** from St. Louis served the French Resistance in September 1939 as anti-racism spy and courier. To nightly demand among royalty, ambassadors, military brass, and nightclub devotees, she vowed to cease performing in Paris until the overthrow of German occupation forces. In January 1941 at Casablanca, Morocco, she joined the spy network. Flirty and seductive, she teased out of Vichy French, Japanese, Portuguese, and Italian Axis ministers details of Nazi troop movements at airfields, harbors, and field installations. On daily entertainment tours to Allied front lines, she coded notes along her arms and hands and on sheet music in invisible ink and hid pages in her underwear. At Joséphine's death at age sixty-eight, Princess Grace Kelly arranged interment in the Monaco Cemetery with the highest honors bestowed by the French.

World War II,
September 1, 1939–September 2, 1945

A cataclysm involving much of the globe, the Second World War forced thirty countries to side with the fascist Axis or libertarian Allies. Advances in aerial warcraft aided women in flying missions and bombing industrial and rail centers that relayed victims by cattle car to genocidal camps. Underground resistance networks dispatched hundreds of women on errands of mercy as well as assassinations and sabotage. Within six years of destruction and death, European sovereignties took on new names and shapes as the balance of power shifted away from spite of Hitler, Mussolini, and Tojo to Churchill, Stalin, and FDR.

September 1, 1939

Polish photographer and spy **Lone Morgensen Masłocha (October 26, 1921–January 3, 1945)** of Klucze volunteered with the Danish resistance on September 1, 1939, after Hitler invaded Poland. She operated radio telegraphy and delivered documents to Sweden. After eluding the Gestapo's sweep of Polish fighters following the invasion of Denmark on April 9, 1944, she went into hiding at Gentofte north of Copenhagen, where the Gestapo machine-gunned her after midnight on January 3, 1945. She was the only female operative interred among the one hundred six graves at a World War II memorial cemetery in Ryvangen, Denmark. Posthumously, she earned the Silver Cross of Virtuti Militari (for Military Strength). The biographical film *A Danish Woman with Poland in Her Heart* acclaimed her fearlessness.

September 1, 1939

A Dutch hero of World War II, **Riet van Grunsven (also Maria Catharina van Grunsven, September 6, 1918–March 1, 2004)** from Geffen conspired with the Biesbosch Resistance on September 1, 1939, as an armed courier. Under the code name "Trouble" and "Ice Block," she worked as one of twenty-one commandos or "line crossers" in spying, supplying insulin and other medicines, and escorting Jews and downed pilots to safety. With the aid of a revolver, she liberated Dutch inmates from Mariënhof Prison and two concentration camps. Perilous ventures through mud flats, reed marshes, locks, and tides by rowboat or canoe into labyrinthine enemy territory cost her permanent damage to two fingers and spinal paralysis from a slip on ice.

By September 25, 1944, damage to rail

lines, arks, barges, and ferries at the battle of Arnhem forced Riot and fellow couriers to a new headquarters at Rotterdam. At Holland's liberation from German occupation in May 1945, the partisans had completed three hundred seventy crossings at Sliedrecht and Werkendam past machine gun nests and patrols. She received media acclaim, a bronze lion medal, and an audience with Queen Wilhelmina.

See also September 1944.

October 1939

A special ops paratrooper and courier born in the German Empire (modern Toruń, Poland), General **Elżbieta Zawacka (also Izbieta, March 19, 1909–January 10, 2009)** supported the Polish resistance to German fascism. Her job in communications required training in England and Italy as a *cichociemna* (underground agent) followed by an air drop into Poland on September 10, 1943. Code-named "Zelma" or "Zo," she functioned in Silesia as route manager and in combat as a freedom fighter at the Warsaw Uprising in summer 1944.

Hundreds of missions forced Elżbieta to adopt aliases to transport underground documents and letters to exiled Poles from Nazi-controlled Warsaw to Berlin, Stockholm, and London. Security agents imprisoned and tortured her in 1951 on charges of spying and treason. She gained her freedom in 1955. For courage under fire, she was promoted to general and received a monument and plaques, two Virtuti Militari (Military Strengths) commendations, five Crosses of Valor, and the Order of the White Eagle, Poland's top honor.

November 1939

Major **Wanda Gertz Kazik (April 13, 1896–November 10, 1958)** of Warsaw, a veteran who cross-dressed as a male soldier during World War I, contributed to special ops at the onset of World War II. A promoter of female warriors, she backed the resistance in November 1939 with experience gained in August 1915 at age nineteen as an armorer fighting with the 4th Warsaw Battalion. For the 1st Lithuanian-Belarusian Division, she fought at the siege of Vilnius from August–November 1920 during the Lithuanian Wars of Independence.

An anti–Nazi courier under the code name "Lena," Wanda was the first female underground member. Her work after April 1942 involved commanding seventy women in laying mines to sabotage bridges, railways, and airfields. Her capture in September 1944 resulted in authority over two thousand female inmates housed at prison camps in Altenburg and Muhlberg, Germany, and Lamsdorf and Ożarów, Poland. She served the last six weeks at Molsdorf, Germany, before her liberation in April 1945. Post-war duties put her in charge of displaced Poles and their rehabilitation. After her death from liver cancer at age sixty-two, she was buried at Warsaw's military cemetery, a soldier honored with nine medals.

December 21, 1939

England's first and longest active spy on the Nazis, **Krystyna Skarbek (May 1, 1908–June 15, 1952)** from Warsaw in the Russian Empire initiated British intelligence gathering on December 21, 1939, in Budapest, Hungary. Under the alias "Christine Granville," she assembled a spy network to outline highway, rail, and water travel between Germany and Romania. Her data collection emphasized disrupting oil delivery to the Nazis and their plans to attack the Soviet Union. She surveyed the Allied network into Istanbul, Palestine, and Cairo. Disguised as a nurse, she parachuted into France on July 6, 1944, to relay information to partisan guerrillas and retrieve airdrops. Her exploits included negotiating prisoner release and repatriating Poles into the Allied forces, for which she earned the George Medal, Order of the British Empire, and a Croix de Guerre.

Late 1939

A working-class member of the Edelweiss Pirates, **Gertrud Koch (June 1, 1924–June 21, 2016)** of Cologne co-formed a paramilitary club in late 1939 of five thousand teens who defied the Nazi brainwashing of *Hitlerjugent* (Hitler Youth). Risking public hanging by rejecting political conformity, they symbolized German resistance to fascism with the white alpine flower badge and sang the banned songs of Jewish writers. From pouring sugar into Nazi gas tanks and stealing dynamite to spray painting graffiti on rail cars, Gertrud, code named "Mucki," advanced to vandalizing the Cologne train depot, fist-fighting Hitler Youth, raiding Nazi supply dumps, and distributing food parcels stolen from government warehouses.

After Gertrud's arrest in 1942 and six months of incarceration at Brauweiler Abbey, a detention center for undesirables, Gestapo members beat and tortured her. She escaped and fled to Bavaria. Her rewards for daring included the Rhineland Thaler, Cross of Merit, Heine award, and representation in a 2005 film *Edelweiss Pirates*. She summarized the actions of Cologne teens in a memoir, *Edelweiss: My Youth as a Resistance Fighter*.

1940

The Gestapo's most wanted resistance courier in World War II, **Nancy Wake (August 30, 1912–August 7, 2011)** of Wellington, New Zealand, strategized flight routes for Jews, refugees, and Allied soldiers. After training by **Vera May Atkins,** in Auvergne, France, in 1940, Nancy masterminded the activities of seven thousand five hundred resisters, cached weapons drops, and assisted a raid on Montluçon Gestapo headquarters that slew thirty-eight Nazis. In a German assault, she aided volunteers in shooting fourteen hundred enemy. Her list of awards include the Resistance Medal, Legion of Honor, U.S. Medal of Freedom, Order of Australia, and George Medal. Her exploits filled a memoir, *The White Mouse,* and a film, *Nancy Wake: The White Mouse.*

See also September 1939.

January 1940

In London in January 1940, attorney and intelligence debriefer **Jane Sissmore Archer (March 11, 1898–September 1982)** from Bengal, British India, provided MI5, British domestic counterintelligence, with a thorough overview of Soviet Subversion. She earned a Member of the British Empire for advancing from clerk and typist to investigator of Soviet spying. In the questioning of defector Walter Krivitsky, she achieved a breakthrough in professional disclosure of clues to agent identities, notably, famous double agent Kim Philby, a Soviet mole. Jane progressed to Secret Intelligence officer overlooking Irish partisans and analyst of radio messages from Eastern Europe. Her identification of Klaus Fuchs uncloaked a Russian spy compromising the British manufacture of atomic weapons.

January 20, 1940

After qualifying for Red Cross nursing in Paris at age twenty, on January 20, 1940, **Andrée Borrel (November 18, 1919–July 6, 1944)** from Bécon-les-Bruyères became a parachutist, saboteur, and spy for the British under the code names "Monique" and "Denise Urbain." With the rank of lieutenant, until her flight through Portugal to England on April 24, 1942, she coordinated passage for six hundred aircrew and Jews on the southern border of France at the Pyrenees. Her route was the Pat Line, which networked escapes through Belgium, France, and Holland and accessed a safe house in the Pyrenees.

After the Gestapo seized her on June 23, 1943, Andrée smuggled messages to Paris written on cigarette papers. She was executed by phenol injection and thrust alive into the camp crematorium thirteen months later on July 6, 1944, at Natzweiler-Struthof in the Vosges Mountains. Her skill at dangerous assignments earned a posthumous resistance medal and Croix de Guerre.

April 9, 1940

Because of the German invasion of Denmark and Norway on April 9, 1940, nineteen-year-old rescuer and supplier **Wanda Hjort Heger (March 9, 1921–January 27, 2017)** of Kristiana (modern Oslo), began smuggling aid and letters to prison at Grini and Møllergata, Norway. In Germany, she networked information about Scandinavian inmates at Sachsenhausen, an SS prison north of Berlin for political dissidents and Soviet prisoners of war. Through a weekly delivery of potato salad and retrieval of the empty glass jars, she achieved access to inmates by name and number. The data connected Red Cross workers with the White Buses convoy, a Swedish humanitarian outreach that relieved from incarceration fifteen thousand three hundred forty-five inmates. Rescuers of Norwegians, Danes, Dutch, Belgians, Poles, Germans, French, and Jews transported some by ferry to Sweden. Wanda summarized her work in the memoir *Every Friday at the Gate*.

April 15, 1940

Prepared for international war by her surgeon father, medic **Anne Margrethe Bangs Strømsheim (December 4, 1913–October 6, 2008)** of Trondheim, Norway, survived the twenty-five day German siege at Hegra Fortress, a mountain redoubt near the Swedish border. From April 15, 1940, she treated casualties under heavy artillery fire. At her surrender on May 5, 1950, she alerted the Norwegian Red Cross of forty serious medical conditions among the two hundred fifty defenders, notably frostbite and tuberculosis. A nationally applauded resistance fighter, she suffered toe amputation because of deep snow and piercing cold. Because of Anne's role as the only Norwegian woman warrior of World War II, her decorations include the King's Gold Medal, Norwegian War honorarium, Defense Medal, and the naming of a street near the stronghold.

May 1940

Polish photographer **Julia Diament Pirotte (January 1, 1908–July 25, 2000)** of Końskowola aided French and Jewish resisters in May 1940 to oust Nazi insurgents from Marseilles. A courier disseminating underground newspapers, forged documents, and armaments, she used her Leica to shoot wartime pictures of homeless street urchins and guerrilla fighters near Venelles in summer 1944. As an agent of the Marseilles uprising, she sustained the acts of volunteers in liberating the French coastal city on August 28, 1944, and celebrated in photos liberation at war's end from Nazis and Vichy collaborators. She earned the French Order of Arts and Letters for priceless glimpses of World War II. One of her portraits captured her younger sister, **Mindla Maria Diament (February 13, 1911–August 24, 1944)**, who supported the French underground by stitching documents into her coat lining. For Mindla's contributions to the Resistance, the Vichy government tortured and guillotined her on August 24, 1944, at Breslau, Poland.

May 10, 1940

Dutch medic and freedom fighter **Catharina Aaltjen Boekbinder (September 15, 1915–December 12, 1987)** aided the underground with daring thievery and armament transfer. Because of the German seizure of the Netherlands, Belgium, and Luxembourg on May 10, 1940, under Operation Yellow Case, "Ina" volunteered to deliver sten guns hidden in bicycle saddlebags. After stealing bandages and supplies from the Nazi warehouse in Amsterdam, she loaded the goods in a hearse for dispersal. Early in 1945, during rations delivery out of Apeldoorn, she lost mobility from a wound to the legs. At age sixty-six, she received the Dutch Resistance Memorial Cross.

Ina's younger sister, **Freddie Nanda Dekker-Oversteegen (September 6, 1925–September 5, 2018)**, and fellow Dutch anti-fascist resisters—Freddie's older sister, sculptor and painter **Truus Menger-Oversteegen (August 29, 1923–June 18, 2016)**, underground warrior **Mirjam Ohringer (October 26, 1924–May 29, 2016)** from Amsterdam, and law student **Hannie Schaft (September 16, 1920–April 17, 1945)**—mastered surveillance of a Germany army airport and sabotage with explosives. Placing dynamite on rails and under bridges, they foiled German plans for transporting refugees, gays, and political dissidents to extermination camps. While riding their bicycles, the women shot and killed Nazi soldiers and collaborators or enticed them from pubs to enjoy a forest tryst that ended in murder.

Hannie was the only member of the coterie to die in World War II. After her arrest on June 21, 1944, for assassinating a police officer in Haarlem, she returned to resistance assignments liquidating Haarlem police and intelligence agents. At a second arrest in March, two guards shot her on April 17, 1945, by the sea at Holland's Overveen dunes. A posthumous statue, films, biography, a Medal of Freedom, and Dutch Cross rewarded Hannie's sacrifice. Truus authored a combat memoir and received a Mobilization War Cross, Order of Orange-Nassau, and listing as Righteous among the Nations. Freddie also received the Mobilization War Cross. For supporting Jews in hiding, Mirjam earned the Dachau Prize for Civil Courage.

June 1940

At the ouster of the British from Italy in June 1940, **Monica Wichfeld (July 12, 1894–February 27, 1945)**, a London-born aristocrat and guerrilla warrior, reinforced the Danes against Nazi insurgents. In southeastern Denmark, she opened Engestofte Estate to weapons drops, sheltered Jews, and recruited, trained, and armed operatives. In addition to commanding resistance cells at the Baltic islands of Falser and Lolland, in summer 1943, she plotted the sabotage of Nakskov shipyard, an element of the East Asiatic Company commandeered by the Nazis.

Betrayed in late 1943, Monica entered Vestre Fængsel prison at Copenhagen in January 1944 for four months of Gestapo interrogation. Despite resistance attempts to free her from Waldheim prison in Germany, she contracted tuberculosis and died of pneumonia on February 27, 1945, within eight weeks of liberation. A monument at Engestofte chapel and a biography, *Monica: Heroine of the Danish Resistance,* detail her daring.

Summer 1940

In Vichy France in summer 1940, wooden-legged Anglo-American master spy Lieutenant **Virginia Hall (April 6, 1906–July 8, 1982)** of Baltimore, Maryland, abetted armed rebellion, subversion, disrupting supply lines, smuggling, and sleuthing behind Nazi lines. A student trained at Radcliffe and Barnard, she accidentally discharged a shotgun into her leg and became "the woman who limps." In February 1940, she drove a French military ambulance for the Ninth Artillery relaying the wounded to Paris from outside Metz near the two-hundred-eighty-mile Maginot Line and the Haute-Loire Valley in central France. Some three hundred forty thousand French died along her route. For assistance in fighting fascism, she joined the U.S. Office of Strategic Services (OSS) and became the first female British Special Operations Executive (SOE) field agent.

Posing as a journalist for the *New York Post,* under the code name "Diane," Virginia networked with prostitutes, rural women, teachers, police, and doctors who supported underground funding and radio transmissions. Female spies like Virginia risked a high death rate and looked to her to avoid arrest by Klaus Barbie, a Gestapo torturer at Lyon. Attaining a reputation as most dangerous spy in occupied Vichy France, Virginia, aided the D-Day operation and became the first woman and first civilian to earn a Distinguished Service Cross. Back in the United States, in 1947, she became the first female serving the CIA. She died in Rockville, Maryland, at age seventy-six. A CIA training center bears her name.

See also January 1941.

June 14, 1940

At the fall of Paris on June 14, 1940, Anglo-French diarist, propagandist, and watercolorist **Agnes Dorothee Humbert (October 12, 1894–September 19, 1963)** of Dieppe joined librarians **Yvonne Suzanne Oddon (June 18, 1902–September 7, 1982)** of Gap, intelligence operative **Germaine Tillion (May 30, 1907–April 18, 2008)** from Allegre, and **Lucie Boutillier du Retail (fl. 1940s)** of the Musée de l'Homme in recruiting ten anti-fascist activists for the first French Resistance cell. The comrades aided the injured and helped prisoners, refugees, and airmen escape to safe houses with falsified papers and maps of escape routes. The Group du Musée de l'Homme (Group from the Museum of Mankind) compiled a file of four hundred underground members and their addresses and backed propagandist tracts and a four-page underground broadsheet, *Résistance,* until their betrayal and arrest on February 10, 1941. One member, **Sylvette Roussel Leleu (February 27, 1909–October 3, 1989)** of Bruay, was deported to Silesia in 1944 for passing information about troop movements and served out the rest of the war at Ravensbrück, a Prussian concentration camp. Museum secretary, propagandist, and archivist **Jacqueline Bordelet (January 24, 1912–May 22, 2007)** from Paris continued resistance work until the arrival in the city on August 25, 1944, of General Philippe Leclerc and the Free French forces. She assisted the establishment of a free administration.

The women's war tribunal at Fresnes lasted for a year. Jacqueline was acquitted. The Nazis executed seven men and deported women to labor camps, the Phrix rayon factory, and German prisons at Krefeld, Hovelhof, Schwelm, and Ravensbrück. The women engaged in factory sabotage until liberation by the Red Cross on April 14, 1945. Agnes suffered wounds to her feet and hands from working with acid. She received a Croix de Guerre for surviving one of the longest prison sentences and for freedom fighting on her return to France. Yvonne accepted a Legion of Honor. Germaine, winner of a Croix de Guerre, Legion of Honor, and Grand Cross of the German Merit, issued a war exposé, *Ravensbrück: An Eyewitness Account.*

See also January 1941.

June 14, 1940

A transporter and surveillance volunteer to the French resistance on June 14, 1940, **Delphine Aigle (February 23, 1891–March 30, 1967)** of Troyes concealed her rescues of Allied airmen as the midwife's normal comings and goings. In Aube in north central France, she risked deportation by driving some fifteen downed flyers to the pick-up point and hid a partisan from the Gestapo. Her information about the Messerschmitt Bf 109 aircraft identified the Luftwaffe's chief fighter planes raiding England after takeoff from

Romilly-sur-Seine. General Dwight Eisenhower presented her a Diploma of Recognition for concealing American soldiers in the trunk of her Peugeot. A city square bears her name.

June 17, 1940

Lithuanian academic **Magdalena Avietėnaitė (December 22, 1892–August 13, 1984)** served a resistance group during the Soviet occupation along the Baltic Sea. Throughout political wrangles over territory and loot, from June 17, 1940, she and fellow operative **Elena Barščiauskaitė (fl. 1940s)** smuggled crucial files to the state archives. Magdalena escaped to a German refugee camp and facilitated the Red Cross. She migrated through Paris to North America and died blind in Putnam, Connecticut, at age ninety-one. Her post-war honoraria include the Legion of Honor and the Order of the Lithuanian Grand Duke Gediminas, a fourteenth-century expansionist.

June 18, 1940

Chilean spy and courier **Giliana Balmaceda Gerson (also Gigliana Balmaceta Gerson or Gillian Gerson, September 29, 1910–?)** gave up the Paris stage on June 18, 1940, to enter a cadre of forty women working for British special operations. Posing as a South American tourist in Lyon, she was the first female subversive assigned to France. She aided her husband, English spy Victor Gerson, in transporting refugees and downed Allied air crew. At her arrival in France on May 23, 1941, she coordinated curfews, safe houses, and forged ration cards with transportation timetables for bus and train in Vichy France. On return to England on August 24, 1941, via the DF circuit, she passed through Spain and Gibraltar. Victor used her intelligence data in September 1941 to parachute into Nazi-occupied France. Historian Beryl Escott included Giliana in the compilation *The Heroines of SOE*.

June 22, 1940

Belgian strategist, courier, and guide **Gabrielle Weidner (August 17, 1914–February 15, 1945)** from Brussels created safe passages for Allied aircrew and Jews to Spain and Switzerland. Collaborating with her brother, Johan Weidner, on June 22, 1940, the Seventh Day Adventist sibling applied language skills to transfers of refugees from Paris through the Swiss Alps and Pyrenees Mountains into Iberia. She also founded a courier trail from Bern to Madrid. A betrayal in February 1944 by a fellow courier who kept a notebook of names and addresses led to Gabrielle's arrest on February 26 by the Gestapo. On August 15, she shipped out from Fresnes prison in Paris by cattle car northeast of Berlin to Ravensbrück, Germany. A posthumous recipient of the Dutch Cross, she died at age thirty from beatings, exhaustion, and starvation within days of Russian liberation of the death camp.

August 1940

Journalist and planner of the Combat Movement, Marseilles native **Berty Albrecht (February 15, 1893–May 31, 1943)** anticipated the liberation of southeastern France and farther north by a grassroots uprising. From August 1940, under the code name "Victoria," she coordinated documentation, cash, and shelter as well as remuneration to families of imprisoned operatives. On December 23, 1942, fellow resisters plotted her escape from a Lyon psychiatric facility. At Berty's incarceration at Fresnes Prison in Paris after arrest by the Gestapo on May 28, 1943, she was tortured. Three days later, she hanged herself in the prison vegetable garden. Posthumous awards for her martyrdom consisted of the Resistance Medal and the Croix de Guerre with Palm.

Fall 1940

In fall 1940, a Dutch biology student at Utrecht, **Hetty Voûte (June 12, 1918–January 16, 1999)** voluntarily spied on a map of German anti-aircraft guns and transmitted locations by secret radio to British intelligence. Aided by social worker and courier **Willemiena Bouwman (February 5, 1920–March 3, 2007)** of Gees, nineteen-year-old Chilean law student **Gisela Wieberdink-Soehnlein (October 3, 1921–November 16, 2021)** from Santiago, and classmate **Olga Hudig (fl. 1940s)**, also a law student from Utrecht, Hetty began concealing Jewish children in potato sacks, laundry bags, and milk cans and delivering them to rural families. While looking for her bicycle at the train depot in June 1943, she encountered suspicious Gestapo officers, who arrested her and Gisela.

Forced to manufacture gas masks at the Vught concentration camp in south central Holland, Hetty refused to identify fellow resistance couriers and spies. After starvation and exposure to cold worsened her tuberculosis at Ravensbrück, a women's concentration camp north of Berlin, Germany, Hetty and Gisela were liberated in April 1945 and published uplifting songs they had composed. The names of Hetty and Willemiena and a memorial tree in the Garden of the Righteous among the Nations praise their heroism on behalf of Jewish children.

December 1940

The Gestapo captured **Antonia Spath Bruha (also Toni Bruha, March 1, 1915–December 27, 2006)**, a pregnant Viennese beautician, for aiding a Czech resistance cell in December 1940 by smuggling explosive chemicals on her bicycle to a German military storage compound in Lobau, Austria. For her part in destroying Nazi arms, rations, and uniforms, she lost custody of infant Sonya on October 15, 1941, and entered a hellish cycle of pistol whippings and beatings in a Vienna jail that reduced her weight to forty-four pounds. At Ravensbrück, a German women's prison, the next October, she endured SS gynecological experiments and smuggled drugs from the clinic to inmates who later escaped in a Swedish Red Cross delivery. She fled during a death march to Vienna through Poland and Czechoslovakia and reclaimed Sonya. Antonia's autobiography *Ich War Keine Heldin* (I Was No Heroine), lectures, and archives preserved the acts of volunteer saboteurs.

1941

Recruited in 1941 to spy for the Gestapo, **Astrid Dollis Dahlgren (December 9, 1899–September 2, 1981)** worked as a Norwegian double agent for Sweden. Trained in dentistry, she settled in Stockholm in 1943 and maintained close contact with a Norwegian operative in Oslo. She gathered intelligence for Sweden until her attempt to cross into Norway on February 23, 1944. After arrest and conviction for carrying $17,000 in bribe money and notes to a German police chief, she served two years of forced labor at a Nazi concentration camp in Växjö, Sweden, until 1946. During questioning, she identified a *Schutzstaffel* (SS) informer who cooperated with the Swedish secret police.

1941

A London-born aristocrat, Subaltern **Mary Spencer-Churchill (September 15, 1922–May 31, 2014)** served the Auxiliary Territorial Service during the Blitz as a spotter of enemy planes. The daughter of Clementine and Winston Churchill, she deployed as junior commander from London's Hyde Park and Enfield as a fire control captain. In Belgium and Germany, she commanded an anti-aircraft battery, which shelled incoming aircraft. Called "Ack Ack girls" for the sound of guns firing flak, the volunteers died at the rate off one hundred twenty-three per month in the twelve weeks after the introduction of V1 rockets. In 1945, she served as aide to her father at the conference in Potsdam with Harry Truman and Josef Stalin and composed biographies of her parents. For her contribution to defending the Allies, she achieved the Order of the British Empire.

1941

Romanian Jew **Olga Bancic**, a communist veteran of the Spanish Civil War from Bessarabia, furthered some one hundred acts of sabotage against Nazis in France. In 1941, she commanded the transport of explosives and assembled bombs for derailing Germany troop trains and blockading supply routes. She was captured as a terrorist in November 1943. Under torture by the Gestapo on February 21, 1944, she refused to reveal names of accomplices. The Gestapo proclaimed her a terrorist and, on May 19, 1944, decapitated her in Stuttgart, Germany.

See also July 17, 1936.

January 1941

In an unusual form of biological warfare, French brothel owner **Germaine Guérin (1905–1983)** of Lyons aided the French underground and British intelligence by spreading disease and encouraging alcohol and heroin addiction among German fascists and their collaborators. By concealing venereal infections in her sex workers, in January 1941, she exposed Nazi clients to syphilis and gonorrhea. She aided her recruiter, subversive agent **Virginia Hall** of Maryland, in collecting intelligence and harboring Jews. As a member of the Gloria Network, Germaine opened safe houses, promoted a clandestine insane asylum, and distributed cash, food, fuel, forged papers, and weapons to escapees, radio operators, paratroopers, and informants. On August 13, 1942, Father Robert Alesch, Hitler's army intelligence agent, betrayed women of the network, including Germaine, founder **Gabrielle Jeanine "Gloria" Buffet-Picabia (also Gabriele, November 2, 1881–December 7, 1985)** of Fontainebleau, and American artist and linguist **Mary Reynolds (1891–September 30, 1950)** from Minneapolis, operating under the code name "Gentle Mary."

In company with anti–Nazi publisher **Geneviève de Gaulle-Anthonioz (October 25, 1920–February 14, 2002)** of Saint-Jean-de-Valériscle, agent **Germaine Tillion (May 30, 1907–April 18, 2008)** and Germaine's mother, writer **Emilie Tillion (February 20, 1876–March 2, 1945)**, boarded cattle cars on a Gestapo train to Auschwitz, Poland. Emilie was assassinated in Germany at Ravensbrück gas chamber in the women's division two months before V-E Day. Germaine Tillion escaped with the aid of the Swedish Red Cross and composed an exposé of forced labor and methodical operation of death machines. With a seriously wounded leg, Mary Reynolds fled over the Pyrenees to Madrid on December 14, 1942, and repatriated to New York; Gabrielle Picabia eluded the Gestapo in December 1942 and evacuated through Gibraltar to England. After release from Ravensbrück in April 1945, Geneviève testified against Gestapo torturer Klaus Barbie of Lyon and summarized the female camp friendship in *The Crossing of the Night*. Germaine Guerin joined the crusade to find and prosecute former Nazis.

See also June 14, 1940.

March 14, 1941

A Berlin-born smuggler and saboteur for the Israeli Palmach (strike force), **Bracha Fuld (also Barbara Fuld, December 26, 1927–March 26, 1946)** aided the underground Haganah, the Zionist paramilitary, on March 14, 1941, by assaulting the British occupation force. Her intent was to export Jewish refugees out of Nazi-held Europe to Palestine. During her last mission from Kibbutz Givat Haim to protect two hundred thirty-eight Holocaust survivors aboard the ship *Orde Wingate* (Wingate Night), shrapnel from a British tank battle wounded her. She died at Jaffa in police custody from loss of blood. Israelis placed her name on a Tel Aviv street and the SS *Bracha Fuld*, a refugee transport vessel. The song "Banu Heinah (We Came Here)" honored her as a nineteen-year-old martyr to resistance of British imperialism. Author Kurt Singer incorporated her soldiery in *The World's Thirty Greatest Women Spies*.

March 21, 1941

A forger for the French Resistance, **Elisabeth de la Bourdonnaye (October 8, 1898–January 2, 1972)** of Monnaie, suffered hard-handed torment on March 21, 1941, by the Gestapo at the Cherche-Midi prison. She concealed intelligence about munition dumps, troop deployment, anti-aircraft guns, and the launching of the first flying bombs, the V1 and V2 rockets. By refusing to identify the leader of her spy network, she stalled until receiving treatment for pulmonary disease in April 1941 at l'Hôpital de la Pitié in Paris. When the Gestapo released her in August, she used medical contacts to retrieve Jewish children from the Rothschild orphanage and provided them with phony identity cards. She was unable to rescue her twenty-three-year-old son Geoffroy from combat death in Alsace on January 13, 1945, or her nineteen-year-old son Guy from Mauthausen, where he died of pneumonia on March 10, 1945.

Spring 1941

A Greek-Jewish medic from Chalcis outside Athens in spring 1941, Captain **Sara Yehoshua Fortis (1927–)** migrated northeast to Kurturla in Euboea's mountains to conceal her religious upbringing from German insurgents. A dedicated teen rebel, she began recruiting women warriors at the Steni command post. Revered as Captain Sarika, she trained newcomers in diversion, a means of freeing resisters of Nazi surveillance. Men envied the female talent for throwing Molotov cocktails, assassinating collaborators, and burning Nazi housing. Because Nazi stalkers misidentified her cousin Medi Mishowitz, whom they raped and slaughtered, Sara eliminated the informer. On the withdrawal of Nazi forces in June 1944, she protested the country's conservative government. A brief arrest preceded liberation and migration to Israel, where she obtained a second passport.

April 6, 1941

The twelve-day Axis incursion into the Kingdom of Yugoslavia on April 6, 1941, drew into World War II Slovenian minority warrior **Ida Sabo (July 6, 1915–2016)** of Pecs, Austria; Jewish teenager **Žamila Kolonomos (June 18, 1922–June 18, 2013)** of Monastir, Macedonia; and partisan officer **Andreana Druzina (January 26, 1920–March 7, 2021)** of Trieste, Yugoslavia. A three-front combat confused issues of ethnicity and nationality. Andreana, who died at age one hundred one, achieved the homeland award of Order of the People's Hero. Ida, also a centenarian, received medals for heroism, brotherhood and unity, merit, and bravery. Žamila, who lost eighteen family members to extermination at the Treblinka concentration camp, began supplying guns and shoes for guerrillas. She commanded multiple battalions until shrapnel pierced her torso during the resisters' firefight with Axis forces at Debar, Macedonia, on August 30, 1944. After receiving a Partisan Medal, she issued *The Jews in Macedonia during the Second World War*.

Other Slavic resistance operatives did not survive the war. Undercover Jewish compatriot **Olga Alkalaj (November 23, 1907–March 15, 1942)** of Belgrade, Serbia, served the communist front with conspiracies for an uprising and rescue led by an operative from a prison hospital. Under Gestapo arrest, she survived torture at Banjica Concentration Camp in Serbia and died of poison vapors in a Nazi gas wagon. **Fana Kochovska (July 27, 1927–April 17, 2004)** of Lavci, Kingdom of Yugoslavia, joined the Yugoslav resistance at age thirteen and hid for six weeks with Partisans. She eluded Bulgarian police for sabotaging bunkers at a mine, but incurred wounds during a firefight in 1943. She emigrated over the mountains and died at age seventy-six in Skopje, Macedonia, where citizens claimed her as a national hero. A statue at Bitola honors her spunk.

April 10, 1941

Following the creation of the Croatian state from Austria-Hungary, on April 10, 1941, Bosnian-Jewish pediatrician and resistance supplier **Berta Bergman (1892–1945)** from Blažuj outside Sarajevo taught guerrilla warriors first aid, stocked their frontline hospitals, and treated casualties. The newly named sovereign state became *Ustaše* (Rise Up), a pro–Catholic, pro–Muslim fascist front that launched a racial purification genocide against Jews, Gypsies, and Serbs. After her capture on January 15, 1945, she was deported and executed at Jasenovac concentration camp, Croatia, an extermination facility known for starving and bludgeoning victims with hammers, axes, and knives. Guards tossed remains into pits, some still alive. After the German surrender on May 9, 1945, the Ustaše movement collapsed.

April 12, 1941

A Hungarian aristocrat, art maven, and Magyar beauty and wit, Countess **Klára Andrássy (also Klára Odescalchi de Szerem, January 18, 1898–April 12, 1941)** of Budapest, Austria-Hungary, took the rebel's hands-on approach to sabotage. A Czechoslovakian communist divorced in 1939 from Prince Karoly Odescalchi, she invited pro–British operatives to the Andrássy Palace on the Danube and allied with her sixteen-year-old son, Prince Paul Otto Odescalchi, an anti-fascist warrior. Klára frequented salons to meet the anti–Fascist elite. Her chief assignment for the Hungarian Resistance involved directing resisters to destroy crucial links in the Nazi rail lines and roadways. On the way through Egypt to England by submarine, on April 12, 1941, near Ragusa, Klára suffered terminal injury by an Italian, Bulgarian, German, and Hungarian air force raid over a boarding house at Dubrovnik, Croatia, on the Adriatic Sea. She required amputation of both legs and died at Ragusa during treatment. Historians puzzling over the muddled news surmised that she was conducting a secret mission for the British. A portrait of the "Red Countess" hangs in Budapest at the Kieselbach Gallery.

May 1941

Austro-Hungarian-Muslim resistance member **Vahida Maglajlić (April 17, 1907–April 1, 1943)** from Banja Luka furnished communist forces with guns, clothes, ammunition, food, radio parts, and medicines. She became a communist after the fascist invasion of Yugoslavia in April 1941 and supported International Red Aid. By gathering necessities from Jews, Muslims, and Serbs, in May 1941, she fostered ethnic unity in Banja Luka while preventing Nazis from seizing local supplies. Her arrest in October 1941 preceded torture and escape in December to partisan camps on Mount Cemernica, Serbia. On the battlefield at Mala Krupska Rujiška in Croatia's far northwestern corner, German troops shot her in the back alongside twenty-seven comrades. Yugoslavians made her the only female named a People's Hero.

May 19, 1941

Vietnam's leading woman communist and first female military commander, **Nguyễn Thị Định (March 15, 1920–August 26, 1992)** from Bến Tre led a female army against the French. In her teens, she promoted the Viet Minh by recruiting landless rebels from southern Vietnam by spreading propaganda in small hamlets and villages. At her direction, blacksmiths and builders crafted knives and machetes. She was jailed at Poulo Condore prison along with her seven-month-old son Phạm Văn Thời by the colonial government and reviled for mustering a long-haired brigade on May 19, 1941. Upon release, in August 1945, she spearheaded the Bến Tre uprising and agitated to oust nationalist politician Ngô Đình Diệm, a Catholic who challenged the Buddhist majority. Heading thousands of peasants, she carried the banner and welcomed release of political prisoners. She recorded wartime experiences in a memoir, *No Other Road to Take*.

June 22, 1941

After Romania entered World War II, on June 22, 1941, pilot **Mariana Drăgescu (September 7, 1912–March 24, 2013)** from Craiova began ferrying medical aid with the low-flying *Escadrila Albă* (White Squadron). The all-girl team included attorney **Irina Burnaia (1909–1997)** from Ciurari; squad founder **Marina Știrbei (March 19, 1912–July 15, 2001)** from Vienna; **Nadia Russo (June 17, 1901–January 22, 1988)** from Tver in the Russian Empire; Romanian parachutist **Smaranda Brăescu (May 21, 1897–February 2, 1948)** of Hănțești; and **Virginia Thomas (1910–November 10, 1996)** from Brasov, Austria-Hungary. The cadre dressed in white overalls to suit the cover of ten white air ambulances carrying doctors and evacuating fifteen hundred casualties for immediate surgery. Russian bombardments forced the women to alter their Red Cross colors to camouflage.

The White Squadron's Polish RWD 13D three-seaters followed a route from the eastern front to military hospitals in Bucharest. Their service included the ten-week siege at Odessa on August 8, 1941, which cost Romania twenty planes. From October 18, 1941, the eight-month Crimean campaign boosted war casualties to thirty thousand. Beginning on August 23, 1942, the five-month battle of Stalingrad downed seven hundred forty-four aircraft. The shift in combat required intense sorties from new headquarters at Stalingrad. In 1943, Virginia extended the frontline service by car to a Red Cross hospital. By war's end, Mariana remained the only flier still collecting the wounded. She earned a pilot's medal, a German Eagle, and Knight of the Order of the Star of Romania. Under communist authorities, Irina was found guilty of war crimes and fled to Beirut, Lebanon. She issued an autobiography in 1988. Nadia served seven years in prison for aiding the English, but retained a German Eagle, Queen Marie Cross, and an aviator's citation.

June 22, 1941

At the invasion of the Soviet Union on June 22, 1941, under Hitler's Operation Barbarossa, Ukrainian Jew **Sonia Shainwald Orbuch (also Sura or Suraleh Shainwald, May 24, 1925–**

September 30, 2018) of Luboml, at age sixteen, fled to the swampy Naliboki Forest to reinforce hidden saboteurs. Armed with two grenades, she exited the ghetto across fields and pastures to offer medical aid to casualties, an act that defied myths of non-aggressive Jews. While the family crouched in a barn in freezing temperatures and subsisted on one potato a day, typhus killed her mother. In spring 1944, the Soviets drafted Sonia's resistance cell into the Red Army. After three years among five thousand five hundred displaced refugees at the Zeilsheim camp twelve miles west of Frankfurt, she emigrated to New York. While battling Parkinson's disease, she gave post-war lectures on Jewish resistance and issued a memoir, *Here, There Are No Sarahs*.

August 1941

Andrée de Jongh, Belgian resistance organizer of the Comet Line through occupied Belgium in August 1941, aided one hundred eighteen Allied escapees and Jews and Gypsies, who fell short of Aryan racial standards. She provided Red Cross medical care, shelters, and an escort service by train and on foot some eight hundred kilometers over the Pyrenees. For the safety of air crew, she networked with eighteen-year-old Belgian Red Cross nurse **Monique de Bissy (March 13, 1923–November 17, 2009)** of Schaerbeek; **Virginia d'Albert-Lake (June 4, 1910–September 20, 1997)** of Dayton, Ohio; Brussels native **Michelle Dumon (May 20, 1921–November 16, 2017)**; and Javanese convoy operator **Mathilde Adrienne Eugénie Verspyck (July 16, 1908–February 11, 1945).** Mathilde led air crew and political prisoners southwest from Belgium and occupied France through Basque territory to Spain. She survived two arrests and confinement to St. Gilles Penitentiary in Brussels. During her third confinement to Ravensbrück, a women's concentration camp in Germany, at age thirty-six, she died of exhaustion. Her honoraria included the Dutch Cross and U.S. Medal of Freedom. Virginia, another inmate of Ravensbrück, weighed only seventy-seven pounds when the French liberated the camp on April 21, 1945.

Another Comet Line guide and smuggler **Elvire de Greef (June 29, 1897–August 20, 1991)** and her teenaged daughter, diarist **Janine de Greef (September 25, 1925–November 7, 2020)** traveled with Janine's brother by train, bicycle, and tram. The de Greefs' plotted the escape by ambulance of a male refugee guide from a Bayonne hospital. From Basque country, the group's rescues continued through Gibraltar and by ship, plane, or submarine to England until Andree's arrest at a safe house on January 15, 1943. On May 8, 1943, Elvire engineered a rapid rescue of Michelle from southwestern France to Spain.

Andree survived disease and malnutrition in Ravensbrück concentration camp in Germany and Mauthausen in upper Austria. During her post-war nursing among lepers in the Congo, Cameroon, Ethiopia, and Senegal, she received the Croix de Guerre, Order of Leopold, and Legion of Honor. Janine accepted British, French, Belgian, and American medals; for long service and unmasking a German double agent,

Michelle received a George Medal and U.S. Medal of Freedom. Monique, whom Germans arrested in 1944, endured torture at Maastricht, Holland, but revealed no Comet Line identities. After U.S. forces freed her in August 1944, she earned a Legion of Honor, resistance citation, King's Medal from England, and a U.S. Medal of Freedom.

See also July 17, 1936.

August 8, 1941

A world-class sharpshooter, Major **Lyudmila Pavlichenko (July 12, 1916– October 10, 1974)** from Bila Tserkva, Ukraine, earned global fame for total kills for the 54th Stenka Razin Rifle Regiment, named for a seventeenth-century anti-tsarist cossack rebel. She enjoyed shooting in her teens and earned a marksman's badge. In June 1941, she quit work in an arms factory and volunteered for the infantry. Beginning with Red Army service at the siege of Odessa, Ukraine, on August 8, 1941, she armed herself with a Mosin-Nagant bolt-action rifle and targeted Nazi snipers, officers, and scouts at Moldova. A mortar attack killed her husband, Alexei Kitsenko, leaving her a depressed war widow. She abused alcohol to combat post-traumatic stress.

Lyudmila continued her part in World War II at Sevastopol on the Crimea on October 20, 1941, and the Eastern Front. With three hundred nine kills to her credit, in June 1942, she ended soldiery for a month's treatment of a mortar shell blast to the face in Moscow. She was one of five hundred female sharpshooters out of two thousand to survive. Still enthusiastic about military involvement, under the nickname "Lady Death," she began teaching younger snipers. In 1945, she entered the Soviet Navy as a researcher. Eleanor and Franklin Roosevelt welcomed her to the White House before Lyudmila's propaganda tours of Canada and England. In 1943, she attained the status of Hero of the Soviet Union and Order of Lenin. Her memoir and biography influenced a film, historical fiction, and folk music.

Late August 1941

A Parisian communist Jew trained in chemistry, **France Bloch-Serazin (February 21, 1913–February 12, 1943)** set up a home laboratory after German intervention forbade her and other Jews from taking professional jobs. In a two-room apartment under the code name "Claudia," in late August 1941, she manufactured detonators, explosives, and grenades for use by young terrorists and formulated cyanide doses to save from atrocities the freedom fighters who blew up train lines. Police seizure in May 1942 led to questioning and torture.

France served a sentence at Lübeck in northern Germany with eighteen other inmates before her secret guillotining in Hamburg at age twenty-nine. Her co-conspirator, Jewish chemist **Marie Nordmann-Cohen (November 4, 1910–August 15, 1993)** from Paris, survived deportation to Auschwitz, Poland, where German staff forced her to formulate a rubber substitute for use by the Nazi military. France received a Legion of Honor, War Cross, and Resistance Medal; Marie earned a Legion of Honor and Croix de Guerre.

Fall 1941

French resister and fervid Gaullist **Marguerite Gonnet (October 13, 1898–May 27, 1996)**, the mother of nine children, superintended underground agents in fall 1941 at Isère northwest of her hometown of Grenoble. Code named "la Cousine (the cousin)," she organized the anti-fascist acts of **Léa Blain (March 22, 1922–August 1, 1944)**, a camouflage expert from Teche; **Marie Reynoard (October 28, 1897–January 1945)** from Bastia, a Corsican co-founder of the Combat terrorist movement; **Mimi Mingat-Lerme (April 6, 1918–December 17, 2017)**, a Grenoble-born Jewish supplier of resisters in the south with arms and explosives; and art historian Captain **Rose Valland (November 1, 1898–September 18, 1980)**, a spy from Isère on Nazi looting of French treasures from the Jeu de Paume Museum, which she directed. Marguerite was jailed at Lyon's St. Paul Prison on April 18, 1942, for carrying banned newspapers. During imprisonment, she suffered a miscarriage. At judgement in May 1942, she received a two-year prison sentence, which she survived. At Villard-de-Lans, Lea fell to a German rifle bullet to the head on August 1, 1944; Marie died at Ravensbrück women's prison at age forty-seven.

Post-war authority enabled Marguerite to search for missing resistance members. Mimi resolved to inform the younger generation of the French Resistance and its importance to liberation. Rose led a post-war recovery of stolen art and restitution to original owners. A city street preserves Marguerite's name; Marie's identity survives on an Auvergne school; a monument records Lea's courage at Villard-de-Lans, a refuge for Polish underground warriors. Historian Olivier Vallade recorded resistance heroism in the biography *Marguerite Gonnet: Déterminée à Sortir de l'Ombre* (Marguerite Gonnet: Determined to Exit the Shadows). Rose's book *Le Front de l'Art* (The Art Front) influenced the American films *The Train* and *The Monuments Men,* in which Cate Blanchett played her part. Her many awards included a Legion of Honor, U.S. Medal of Freedom, and Resistance Medal.

Fall 1941

Belgian-Jewish attorney and rescuer **Antoinette Gluck Feuerwerker (November 24, 1912–February 10, 2003)** of Antwerp recruited volunteers in fall 1941 for the French Resistance. With the aid of French Catholic spy **Germaine Ribière (April 13, 1917–November 20, 1999)**, who posed as an apartment house cleaning woman, Antoinette transported Jewish refugees from Nazi manhunts in Paris and Lyon. Her heroism involved saving Swiss younger sister and fellow operative **Rose Gluck Warfman (October 4, 1916–)** from execution at Auschwitz, Poland, by sending her a nurse's uniform. Rose survived a punitive surgery by Dr. Josef Mengele and forced labor at Birkenau by knitting socks for German babies and soldiers. Her method of passive resistance involved knotting yarn to make the socks lumpy.

Rose emigrated to Jerusalem and rescued other refugees by falsifying identity cards. Antoinette financed passages on the *Exodus* with a cache of gold coins and supported post-war efforts to reclaim Jewish orphans. Rose earned a French knighthood, Military Medal, and Croix de Guerre. Antoinette received academic medals for public health and a French Liberation Medal. She and Germaine accepted acclaim as Righteous among the Nations.

October 1941

A Stalinist teen saboteur from outside Tambov, Russia, **Zoya Anatolyevna Kosmodemyanskaya (September 13, 1923–November 29, 1941)** breached the Russo-German front to set fire to Nazi safe houses and destroy communication cables and roads. Behind enemy lines for the All-Union Leninist Young Communist League, in October 1941, she sliced telephone lines and mined highways. Seized at age eighteen by enemy militia at Petrishchevo, Zoya survived burns and two hundred lashes before she died on November 29, 1941, on the village gallows. Germans lopped off her breast and flayed her corpse, which remained on display for weeks. She received a posthumous statue, monument, and Hero of the Soviet Union medal. Her remains lie at the Kremlin Wall in Novodevichy Cemetery near the Russian intelligentsia and elite.

October 1, 1941

Intrigued by a BBC radio request for female fliers, on October 1, 1941, **Mary Wilkins Ellis (February 2, 1917–July 24, 2018)** from Leafield, England, signed up with the Air Transport Auxiliary as a ferry pilot of new aircraft. Over four years of World War II, she navigated one thousand planes to the front from the factory at Hamble. Her expertise extended to eighty body types, including the Harvard, Hurricane, Spitfire, Tiger Moth, and Wellington bomber. After the war, she added Britain's first fighter plane, the Gloster Meteor, to her experience with the Royal Air Force. Her heroics survive in monuments and the BBC documentary "Spitfire Sisters."

October 2, 1941

Soviet sniper **Natalya Venediktovna Kovshova (November 26, 1920–August 14, 1942)** from Ufa, Russia, paired with spotter **Mariya Semyonovna Polivanova (October 24, 1922–August 14, 1942)** of Naryshkino, to assist the 528th Rifle battalion in World War II as marksmen and instructors. The two friends entered the sniper courses in 1941 for the Osoaviakhim defense organization in Moscow. Natalya introduced sniper training to her regiment, for which she earned an Order of the Red Star. In Mariya's second month of deployment, she targeted machine gun nests and enemy observers and recovered casualties from the battle of Rutchevo. On October 2, 1941, the onset of the three-month battle of Moscow placed Mariya and Natalya in range of tanks, artillery, and aircraft fire against the capital city.

In August 1942 on the Northwestern Front, Natalya commanded their unit after the death of her commander. Wehrmacht mortar fire killed all but three snipers, one of them incapacitated by wounds. As the despised

"Fritzes" neared sniper positions at Sutoki-Byakovo on August 14, 1942, Natalya refused to yield ground. She and Mariya pulled pins in their last two grenades, killing themselves and the enemy. For scoring some three hundred kills in all, Mariya and Natalya achieved a posthumous Hero of the Soviet Union commendation and a battlefield pose on a postage stamp. A Soviet fishing trawler carried Natalya's name.

October 14, 1941

The organizer of a Soviet partisan spy unit of youths, **Liza Ivanovna Chaikina (also Yelizaveta Chaykina, August 28, 1918–November 23, 1941)** from Runo, Russia, gathered data to defeat the Axis powers throughout the Kalinin and Velikiye Luka regions. Her guerrillas overran Nazi strongholds and collected information on enemy garrisons. A month later, while observing urban Peno on the Volga River, she was betrayed and fell into German hands. After assassinating the people who offered her a residence, fascists jailed her in Peno and tortured her for details of underground activity. She faced a firing squad on November 23, 1941. Soviets declared her a national hero. Her portrait appeared on a postal stamp and envelope and her name on monuments, schools, an air force squadron, and a cargo ship. Russians revered her grave as a shrine.

October 18, 1941

During the Ukrainian battle of the Crimea on October 18, 1941, dive bomber **Nina Raspopova (December 31, 1913–July 2, 2009)** from Magdagachi in the tsarist empire avoided a crash landing into a trench and survived anti-aircraft shells. She faked a dive in a damaged Polikarpov Po-2 and completed her run, dropping two wing-mounted bombs weighing a half ton each. From a second attack on her canvas and plywood trainer biplane, she required surgery and two months of rehabilitation. Her record of eight hundred five campaigns with the "Night Witches" placed her in dusk-to-dawn action over the Caucasus, Germany, Crimea, Byelorussia, Ukraine, and Germany. She earned a Lenin award and Hero of the Soviet Union for demolishing a rail line, three ferries, three artillery sites, and an ammunition dump.

November 17, 1941

A French teacher educated at the Sorbonne, **Mathilde Lucia Carré (June 20, 1908–May 30, 2007)** from Le Creusot spied for the resistance until her arrest in Normandy by the Gestapo on November 17, 1941, and recruitment as a double agent. Under the code name "Victoire," she served the enemy until she confessed her deployment to a lover. In London in February 1942, she outlined German strategies to MI5, the UK counter-intelligence agency. Following arrest and imprisonment on July 1, 1942, at Holloway and Aylesbury northwest of London, England, she eluded a death sentence for treason in 1954 and gained her freedom at age forty-six. Her memoir, *I Was Called the Cat*, refuted false accusations about wartime experiences. Actor Françoise Arnoul played the spy in the film *La Chatte* (The Cat).

Late 1941

Armenian-French communist writer and combat recruiter **Louise Aslanian (May 5, 1904–January 30, 1945)** of Tabriz, Iran, aided anti-fascists in late 1941 in distributing weapons to the French underground. Arrested at home on July 26, 1944, she lost to the Nazis her manuscripts on the French Resistance and the fall of Paris. With combat author **Lise London (February 16, 1916–March 31, 2012)**, a French warrior in Spain for the International Brigade from 1936 to 1938, Louise transferred to Buchenwald and Ravensbrück women's prison in Germany, where she died at age forty, leaving verse about her incarceration. Lise survived and wrote about her wartime losses.

See also September 18, 1936.

Late 1941

International courier and smuggler, **Irena Adamowicz (May 10, 1910–August 12, 1973)** from Warsaw enlisted in the Polish Home Army in late 1941 and volunteered to cross borders to carry anti–Nazi information to the Jewish underground. A devout Catholic and constant traveler and liaison to occupied territories, she disguised herself as a German nun to witness systematic pogroms by Nazi *einsatzgruppen* (task forces). She bore encouragement and support to Jewish ghettos, including Kovno (modern Kaunas), Lithuania, in July 1942, when survivors in confinement compiled photos, chronicles, journals, and art recording urban incarceration. Irena collaborated with Belarusian warrior **Zivia Lubetkin (November 9, 1914–July 11, 1978)** to alert Jews to a mass deportation from Białystok, Vilno, and Warsaw, Poland, and from Kovno and Shavle (modern Šiauliai), Lithuania, to Dachau, Germany, and the camp at Stutthof (modern Sztutowò, Poland). Irena was listed as Righteous among Nations and revered as the "Pioneering Gentile."

See also January 18, 1943.

December 1941

A twenty-year-old journalist, chemistry student, and intelligence officer of the Norwegian Resistance, **Anne-Sofie Østvedt (January 2, 1920–November 16, 2009)** of Christiana (modern Oslo) outwitted Gestapo stalkers for five years. Because of natural gifts for security and espionage, in December 1941, she became a "gray woman" after recruitment into the ultra-secret XU (a designation for "unknown undercover"). From a University of Oslo sophomore, she rose quickly to vice commander of three thousand men, who assassinated Nazis, rescued Allied soldiers, sabotaged communications lines and the Rjukan deuterium (heavy water) plant for fueling nuclear reactors, retrieved supplies from drop zones, and ferried new British-trained operatives over the North Sea to Norway by boat. Through nonviolent methods, she coordinated five hundred pages of data per day, such as maps of troop movements, phony border passes, and documents from radio operator **Solveig Bergslien (January 4, 1919–November 21, 1943)**, a clerk at the police station of Stavanger, Norway. Solveig committed suicide in Gestapo custody at age twenty-four. A posthumous War Medal honored her expertise.

By fall 1942, the German police began searching for Anne and posted forty-six police officers to blockade her apartment. During the rise in anti-fascist crimes from passive resistance in fall 1944, intense reconnaissance under the new identity "Aslak" exposed her to exhaustion and starvation and to isolation from all friends and family. In September 1945, the American Association of University Women funded her emigration and study in food chemistry at the University of California, Berkeley. Her secret life remained hidden until 1988. A bronze medal features her portrait.

January 1942

German-Jewish secretary-cryptographer-translator **Erika Schwarze Wendt (September 20, 1917–April 9, 2003)** of Stralsund, Germany, issued coded messages identifying Gestapo agents and subversive activities in Sweden. In January 1942, she gained an inside view of key players while working for the German trade attaché in Stockholm, Sweden. Because she broke a new German code on encryption machines on March 1, 1943, she entered witness protection by Swedish security officers to elude execution as a German traitor. Under a new name, she resided in an Angermanland boarding house on the edge of Swedish Lapland. At age seventy-six, she completed her memoirs, *Kodnamn Onkel* (Code Name Uncle).

Spring 1942

A Polish-communist martyr, paratrooper **Małgorzata Fornalska (June 8, 1902–July 26, 1944)** from Fajsławice entered Nazi-occupied territory to bolster anti-fascist resisters. Germans holding the risky terrain had placed her in prison repeatedly in 1922 for subversion. After release from a Warsaw cell, she entered the Soviet Union in September 1939. Her dropped by parachute into occupied Poland in spring 1942 under the alias "Jasia" enabled a campaign to mobilize guerrilla fighters and print forged documents for refugees. At her arrest on November 14, 1943, the Gestapo remanded her to Serbia Prison, a Russian lockup for women in Warsaw. She died before a Nazi firing squad in the Warsaw Ghetto on July 26, 1944, at age forty-two. For contending against Hitler's regime, she earned a commemorative postage stamp and a posthumous Order of the Cross of Grünwald.

April 9, 1942

The only Filipina silver star winner during World War II **Magdalena Leones (August 19, 1921–June 16, 2016)** of Kalinga, Philippines, served the allies in Luzon as spy, medic, radio part supplier, and courier. In prison at Camp Holmes for five months after the fall of Bataan on April 9, 1942, she learned Niponggo (the Japanese language) and translated for Filipino captives of the Japanese Imperial Army until her release on December 25. After escaping three jailings, she served in the Philippine army signal corps and coordinated radio equipment and transmissions with General Douglas MacArthur to facilitate the recapture of Leyte on October 20, 1944. On March 23, 1945, she aided American intelligence sources in identifying an enemy ship approach to San Fernando, a newly liberated capital city on the South China Sea.

A fellow spy and forger, Michigan-born dancer **Claire Phillips (December 2, 1907–May 22, 1960)** performed a similar service for nine thousand prisoners of war. While working at the Tsubaki cabaret, she disclosed to American troops under the code name "High Pockets" the movements of Japanese forces. She joined **Naomi Flores (1921–2013)** of Baguio, Luzon, and **Margaret Utinsky (August 26, 1900–August 30, 1970)** of St. Louis, Missouri, in transporting by runner medicine, cash, food, clothes, and information to the eight thousand prisoners at Cabanatuan at Nueva Ecijal and to Camp O'Donnell outside Manila. Margaret witnessed executions and confinement of American prisoners to a dungeon at Fort Santiago. Claire's arrest on May 23, 1944, preceded questioning, burns, and waterboarding in Manila at Bilibid Prison until liberation on March 3, 1945. She compiled *I Was an American Spy;* Margaret released an autobiography, *Miss U.* Claire, Margaret, and Naomi, received the U.S. Presidential Medal of Freedom.

May 1942

A Ukrainian tactical bomber pilot of the Polikarpov Po-2 biplane, **Polina Gelman (October 24, 1919–November 25, 2005)** from Berdychiv flew sorties with the 588th Night Bomber regiment after the Germans invaded the Soviet Union. She entered combat under the influence and tutelage of Moscow-born navigator **Marina Mikhaylovna Raskova**, who did not survive the war. As navigator under combat pilot **Raisa Aronova (January 10, 1920–December 20, 1982)** from Saratov, Soviet Union, in May 1942, Polina directed bombs and incendiary shells at bridges, troop trains, depots, warehouses, and fuel depots. She risked low altitude precision approaches without a parachute, sidearm, or radio. In a canvas and plywood craft, she extended the regiment's deployment to restock the Soviets with ammunition and rations. Upon demobilization on October 15, 1945, both soldiers earned the Lenin medal and Hero of the Soviet Union, as did fellow night flyer **Irina Sebrova (December 25, 1914–April 5, 2000)** of Tetyakovka in tsarist Russia. The Order of Lenin also honored Azerbaijan pilot **Zuleykha Seyidmammadova (March 22, 1919–November 10, 1994)** from Baku, who flew in combat at Korsun, Kursk, and Stalingrad.

A Slovakian commander, pilot **Yevdokiya Bershanskaya (February 6, 1913–September 16, 1982)** from Dobrovolnoye, became the only female recipient of the Order of Suvorov, named for an eighteenth-century Russian general. She trained multi-medalist pilot **Khiuaz Dospanova (May 15, 1922–May 20, 2008)** from Ganyushkino, Turkestan, the only survivor of a two-plane collision on April 1, 1942, who returned to combat navigator. Another medalist, **Serafima Amosova (August 20, 1914–December 17, 1992)** of Krasnoyarsk Krai, Siberia, paired with **Larisa Rozanova (December 6, 1918–October 5, 1997)** from Kiev, Ukraine, in forays at Taman, Kerch, Crimea, and Sevastopol. Larisa earned a Lenin citation and Hero of the Soviet Union.

Major **Irina Rakobolskaya (December 22, 1919–September 22, 2016)** from Dankov in the Russian Soviet Federation flew missions as navigator and trained three Soviet air heroes: **Yevdokiya Pasko (December 30, 1919–January 27, 2017)** of Lipenko, Turkestan, a gunner-bombardier and medal winner; **Yevgeniya Rudneva (May 24, 1921–April 9, 1944)**, a head navigator from Berdyansk, Ukraine, died in action at Kerch, Crimea; and wounded veteran **Yekaterina Ryabova (July 14, 1921–September 12, 1974)** of Gus-Zhelezny, Russian Soviet Confederation, a squadron navigator who flew eighteen night bombing missions over Poland.

Luckier in tight situations, pilot **Nadezhda Popova (December 17, 1921–July 8, 2013)** from Shabanovka, Russian Soviet Federation, outflanked a Luftwaffe attack, an emergency landing, and bullets striking her map and helmet. Commissar **Yevdokiya Rachkevich (December 22, 1907–January 7, 1975)** of Nadnestrryanskoye, in the Russian Empire, flew as navigator and recovered soldiers missing in action. Raisa recorded female memories of combat in the Caucasus, Ukraine, Poland, Byelorussia, and Prussia in *Night Witches*.

See also 1933; May 1942; January 4, 1943; May 18, 1943.

May 12, 1942

A martyred Belarussian telegrapher **Yelena Stempkovskaya (October 1921–June 30, 1942)** of Minsk fought on May 12, 1942, at the battle of Volchansk, her introduction to World War II. Stationed on the Southern front, she continued heavy combat duty at Kharkov, Ukraine, for a tank unit and practiced machine gunnery. Her wireless communications kept tank commanders in touch with infantry during a hopeless battle to capture the city. In a face-to-face skirmish with Nazis, she shot enemies before her capture. German torturers tried to coerce secret information from her by amputating her hands and eventually shot her. The Red Army located her remains north of the Black Sea near Zimovenka on June 30, 1942. She received posthumous orders of the Red Banner and Lenin and Hero of the Soviet Union.

Summer 1942

A Jewish Romanian physicist, saboteur, spy, and strategist for the French Resistance, Lieutenant **Cristina Luca Boico (August 8, 1916–April 17, 2002)** from Botosani chose locations for train derailments, assassinations, Molotov cocktail bombings, kidnappings, and arson. Among underground female communists, in summer 1942, she stole chemicals from the Sorbonne and engaged in murder, fire bombing, capture of moles, military sabotage, and railway destruction. Under the code name "Monique," she formulated flaming bombs, stole dynamite, and investigated informers. Advancing to combat in northern France, she joined the liberation of Paris on August 19, 1944, and overran the Romanian consulate in readiness to oust the prime minister, Ion Antonescu, who served time at Moscow's Lubyanka Prison before his execution in 1946. In a film retrospect, Cristina Flutur played the agent's role.

June 7, 1942

A Red Army gunner and scout in World War II, Sergeant **Mariya Bayda (also Maria Baide, February 1, 1922–August 30, 2002)** of Novy Chuvash, Crimea, set a standard on June 7, 1942, for courageous females by killing sixteen Germans and capturing four more. A medic with the 514th Rifle Regiment at age nineteen, she distinguished herself in the North Caucasus by retrieving Nazis for questioning. Her seizure of enemy machine guns and rescue of nine prisoners of war through a mined battlefield earned her fame as a national hero. Wounded from grenade explosion near her head and imprisoned on July 12, 1942, she survived Ravensbrück concentration camp in Germany until liberation on May 8, 1945, by the Soviet vanguard. Her awards include the Order of Lenin, patriotic war citation, and Hero of the Soviet Union.

July 1942

Because of an increase in Gestapo raids, an acclaimed Dutch socialist and rescuer of Jews, **Tina Buchter Strobos (also Tineke Buchter, May 19, 1920–February 27, 2012)** of Amsterdam gambled her life in July 1942 by following bicycle routes to pass messages and deliver food, guns, explosives, and radios for the underground. In league with her mother, **Marie Schotte (March 4, 1893–1974)** of Ingelmunster and Amsterdam-born grandmother **Maria Abrahams (September 29, 1874–?)**, Tina profited from their experiences as couriers for Belgian refugees during World War I and operators of a safe house and transit station. The trio risked a death penalty for providing the household with potatoes, caching guns, stealing IDs and passports, and facilitating the rescue of one hundred Jews. They broke Nazi rules by listening to BBC broadcasts as the Canadian Army began liberating Holland in September 1944. Tina withstood nine arrests and physical abuse by the Gestapo that left her unconscious. In 1989, she received an Elizabeth Blackwell Medal, an impressionist portrait, and listing with the Righteous among the Nations.

July 25, 1942

A Russian Federation pilot for the famed 588th "Night Witches," **Marina Chechneva (August 15, 1922–January 12, 1984)** from Protasovo survived the battle of the Caucasus, for which she earned a Red Banner medal. A grueling land, air, and sea onslaught against the Wehrmacht on July 25, 1942, it initiated the million-man Red Army's retaking of mountain terrain and launched a German-Romanian retreat. The twenty-two-month campaign cost a total of six hundred twenty-five thousand lives. Marina's eight hundred ten sorties received eleven medals and appeared in her books *The Aircraft Take Off into the Night, The Sky Remains Ours,* and *Swallows Over the Front.*

July 30, 1942

The first British-trained Frenchwoman parachutist and operative to enter occupied France, courier **Yvonne Rudellat (January 11, 1897–April 23, 1945)** survived an air attack on a twin-engined Whitley bomber flying from Gibraltar on July 30, 1942. In a felucca (boat with lateen sails), she sailed to Cannes and hid in a train locomotive for passage to Lyon and Paris. By bicycle, she managed supplies, telegraphy machines, and agent drop zones in the Loire Valley. She distributed plastique and machine guns and sabotaged power lines and train rails, notably, the tunnel at Montrichard on August 11, 1944, where her eighty-pound body slid easily through the ventilation shaft. Pursuit by three German police cars resulted in a bullet wound to her head that confused interrogation. Transported from Ravensbrück women's prison in Germany to Bergen-Belsen concentration camp in the northwest, she died on April 23, 1945, at age forty-eight of dysentery and typhus and lay sprawled in a bone pit with five thousand corpses. The French and English honored her posthumously with a George Medal and British knighthood.

August 2, 1942

During the five-day invasion of Belarus by German infantry and panzers during the Great Patriotic War, Leninist courier and scout **Tatyana Savelyevna Marinenko (January 25, 1920–August 2, 1942)** of Sukhoi For in the Russian Empire surveyed Polotsk on August 2, 1942, for size and location of Axis forces. Betrayed by an insider to the Nazis, she was arrested along with twenty-eight villagers and questioned for three days. She was shot at Sukhoi For at age twenty-one and interred at Zharci alongside her fourteen-year-old brother. In death, she achieved a Hero of the Soviet Union medal, a portrait in a Belarussian museum, and a head and shoulder sculpture at Polotsk on the Dvina River.

August 23, 1942

A Soviet Army sniper, a New Yorker, **Tania Chernova (1920–2015)**, both ballerina and medical trainee, made a record forty-five kills before a midriff injury from mine shrapnel forced her out of combat. She had journeyed to Belarus to rescue her grandparents, whom Germans murdered. Arriving via the Volga River on August 23, 1942, during the siege of Stalingrad, Russia, she crept into a German chow line and ate soup and bread before continuing to Russian-held territory. During the five-month campaign, her sniper squadron, known as "The Hares," infiltrated the sewer system to pinpoint Germans and pick off guards at Nazi headquarters. She recuperated at a Tashkent hospital in Uzbekistan but lost her ability to bear children. For the film version of William Craig's novel *Enemy at the Gates,* Rachel Weisz played Tania.

Autumn 1942

Saxon-Jewish saboteur and courier **Sonia Olschanezky (December 15, 1923–July 6, 1944)** from Chemnitz, Germany, took dangerous assignments for British counterintelligence and the French Resistance from age seventeen until her death at age twenty. With phony ID, in May 1942, she eluded a death sentence and exited Drancy Deportation Camp. In autumn 1942, she conspired with agents of the Juggler espionage circuit who exploded a munitions train south of Paris at Melun. At her arrest in January 1944, she traveled with other female transportees to a cell in Karlsruhe, Germany. Six weeks after her brother Serge's execution at Auschwitz, on July 6, 1944, Gestapo officers from the Natzweiler-Struthof camp in France on the German border injected her with a lethal dose of phenol that they claimed was typhus antitoxin. Guards cremated her alive in the camp oven.

See also June 16, 1943.

September 1942

A decorated communist martyr from Epernay, France, in September 1942, **Thérèse Pierre (November 5, 1908–October 26, 1943)** headed a one-hundred-man division of armed fighters. Code-named "Madeleine," she strategized attacks on Nazi munitions trucks and kept all of her operatives safe. After arrest by the Gestapo on October 23, 1943, at Fougères, at age thirty-four, she entered Rennes and contacted other female inmates through the heating pipes. To the last, she divulged no information to the SS. Because of a two-day lashing, she died in prison on October 26, 1943. Germans staged her suicide hanging from a stocking tied to cell bars. Her honoraria include the Order of the Division and War Cross. A college, plaque, and Paris street bear her name; a biofilm, *Where Are Our Lovers,* explored her character and boldness.

September 1942

A Jewish photographer, raider, and warrior, **Faye Schulman (November 28, 1919–April 24, 2021)** of Sosnkowicze in south central Poland collected and smuggled food, medicines, and arms for the Molotava Brigade of partisans in the forests near the Lenin ghetto in Poland. After the extermination of eighteen hundred and fifty residents, German assassins forced her to photograph the massacre. To evade German insurgents on the Polish-Russian border, she agreed to the burning of her family home and, in September 1942, fled to the woods to join escapees from the Red Army prisoners of war.

As the camp's amateur medic, Faye employed a field operating table built from tree limbs. She practiced using automatic rifles and journeyed by canoe to a dangerous partisan mission with other guerrillas. After leaving other displaced Jews at Landsberg camp in Bavaria, in 1948, she and her husband, Morris Schulman, migrated to Toronto bearing pictorial evidence of Jewish resistance, SS atrocities, and mass burials of her extended family in three trenches. She compiled *A Partisan's Memoir: Woman of the Holocaust* and received medals from the U.S., Canada, and Belarus for photographic evidence of European resistance to the Nazis.

September 16, 1942

From November 1941 to the peace conference of September 16, 1942, Macedonian Stalinist warrior and assassin **Nexhmije Hoxha (February 8, 1921–February 26, 2020)**, an elementary school teacher from Manastir (modern Bitola), supported the Albanian National Liberation Movement as organizer of female resisters. The women's phalanx included Albanian composer **Dhora Leka (February 23, 1923–**

December 27, 2006), a captain of the movement who wrote rousing summons to partisans. Nexhmije's Muslim husband, prominent Communist Enver Hoxha, joined the contingent in Tirana. They fought fascism in clashes with Germans and the one hundred thousand Italian occupation forces that had seized Albania on April 7, 1939.

In summer 1944, two female Albanian freedom fighters, **Bule Naipi (1922–July 17, 1944)** from Gjirokastër and **Persefoni Kokedhima (March 1928–July 17, 1944)** from Qeparo fell into a German partisan sweep. Bule died on July 17, 1944, of interrogation and flogging; sixteen-year-old Persefoni survived torture to die the same day on the gallows at Gjirokastër, Albania. A statue in the Gjirokastër public square, a postage stamp, and the film *Triumph over Death* capture the stoic heroes.

In 1956, Dhora began serving a prison sentence during a Soviet purge. She left incarceration in 1963 and entered banishment in Albania to Berat, Fier, and Lushnjë. Her compositions reached the public in 1998. Nextmije promoted pure Marxism, served a four-year sentence for embezzlement, and completed a memoir exposing executions by the Albanian secret police. Mocked as the "Balkan Red Widow," she retreated into isolation at Tirana, Albania's capital.

September 25, 1942

When the British special ops made its first airdrop via Whitley bomber on September 25, 1942, over Nazi France of female agents of Operation Whitebeam, **Lise De Baissac (May 11, 1905–March 29, 2004)** of Curepipe, Mauritius, and Parisian **Andrée Raymonde Borrel**, code named "Odile" and "Denise," parachuted to Mer on the Loire River. Until her flight to England on August 16, 1943, Lise distributed arms from British air drops to agents in Poitiers, including colleague **Mary Herbert (October 1, 1903–January 23, 1983)**, an Irish spy and courier who arrived at Gibraltar by submarine. One of the network's associates, South African wireless operator **Phyllis Latour (April 8, 1921–)** of Durban knitted codes into scarves and wrote secret messages on the ribbon that tied up her hair. For her clever ruses, she earned a Croix de Guerre, English knighthood, War Medal, and Legion of Honor.

Andrée collaborated with Parisians **Germaine Tambour (October 14, 1903–March 2, 1945)** and her younger sister **Madeleine Tambour (December 18, 1908–March 4, 1945)**, who coordinated refugee movements. They managed communications to the English Channel from their Paris apartment until the conspirators' betrayal. The Gestapo jailed Madeleine on April 22, 1943, at Fresnes prison in Paris and Germaine in June. Because of the failure of intricate plots to free the sisters, the Nazis deported them to Ravensbrück women's prison in Germany on April 1, 1944. The Tambour sisters died separately in the camp gas chamber in early March 1945.

See also January 20, 1940; June 16, 1943.

September 29, 1942

A West Bengali marcher with women rebels, **Matangini Hazra (October 19,**

1870–September 29, 1942) of Tamluk on the Rupnaryan River, died a martyr to liberty on September 29, 1942, at age seventy-two from bullets fired by India's crown police. An underclass widow, she supported Mohandas Gandhi's drive for an independent nation. At age sixty, she assisted in tax resistance under the Salt Act of 1930 and fought imperialism through the Non-Cooperation Movement. The public display of defiance earned her six months incarceration at Baharampur central jail. Twelve years later, she joined a siege on a Tamuk police station by leading six thousand members of the Quit India movement. To halt unlawful assembly, officers shot her in the forehead, arm, and hand while she begged for nonviolent mediation. She died clutching the nationalist flag. A statue at the Tamuk jail dramatizes her defiant martyrdom.

September 29, 1942

In Brussels, Jewish ID forger and courier **Rita Arnould (1914–August 20, 1943)** of Frankfurt, Germany, volunteered as a cryptographer and wireless operator for the Soviet Union's Red Orchestra Group. She and Jewish-communist compatriot **Zofia Poznańska (also Sophia, Zosha, or Zosia, February 23, 1906–September 29, 1942)** of Lodz, Poland, were arrested in Brussels by the Radio Defense Corps on December 12, 1941, and their transmitter confiscated. Zofia hanged herself on September 29, 1942, at Brussels's St. Gilles Prison to protect Soviet operatives in Berlin and to conceal a checkerboard code based on the 1910 novel *Le Miracle du Professeur Wolmar* (The Miracle of Professor Wolmar). At Gestapo headquarters, Rita broke under interrogation and revealed top secret cyphers and details. On transfer to Plotzensee Prison in Berlin, she survived gang rape by the Gestapo before being dragged naked on August 20, 1943, to the site of her beheading. A resister's medal and a grove in Israel honor Zofia's bold actions.

October 1942

After the admission of females to the regular military, Sergeant **Irene Miawa Vivash (April 4, 1917–July 27, 1996)** of Peterborough, Ontario, left assembly line work for Westclox in October 1942 to join the Canadian Women's Army Corps. Trained at Goodwin House in Ottawa, she traveled to Aldershot, England, with one hundred female soldiers. Among her comrades, Private **Mary Greyeyes (November 14, 1920–March 31, 2011)** from a Cree Reservation at Marcelin, Saskatchewan, became the first Native American enrolled in the Canadian military. While Mary's older brother, Lieutenant David Greyeyes, taught recruits machine gunnery in England for ten dollars a day, she served in London as a cook and launderer for $6.70 and posed for ridiculous army propaganda shots as an "Indian princess." In more dignified deployment, Irene compiled and substantiated Canadian war dead and wounded. Deployed to Antwerp, Belgium, she witnessed the rubble on October 19, 1944, caused by the blast of a V-2 rocket, which killed four of her comrades.

October 1, 1942

Dutch spy and test pilot at Waltham airfield outside Maidenhead, England, **Ida Veldhuyzen van Zanten (June 22, 1911–October 19, 2000)** from Hillegom worked for MI5 (British intelligence) and, on October 1, 1942, aided the first eight recruits of the Women's Auxiliary Air Force. The women who flew alone and unarmed without radios or instruments ferried three hundred nine thousand planes for the Royal Air Force, for which they earned eighty percent of a male war pilot's salary. Under command of English pilot **Margaret Wyndham Gore (January 24, 1913–August 20, 1993)** of Worthing, Sussex, and London-born bomber pilot **Rosemary Rees (September 23, 1901–March 8, 1994)**, Ida delivered replacement aircraft, gliders, and parts from factory to bases in danger zones. With no experience in new and experimental Supermarine Spitfires, Short Sterlings, Hurricanes, Mosquitos, Tiger Moths, and Lancaster and Wellington bombers, she flew for the Air Transport Auxiliary (ATA) by consulting flight manuals of one hundred thirty types of aircraft. By fall 1945, she completed five hundred eighty-three flying hours and joined seven hundred men in receiving the Flying Cross along with the Pilot Badge and Defense Medal. She became the first female Dutch pilot flying for KLM. Commander Margaret Gore trained on the Halifax Bomber and became the first female to fly the Boeing B-17.

Members of the ATA scored firsts for women warriors, including the first Canadian recruit **Helen Harrison-Bristol (December 7, 1909–April 27, 1995)** of Vancouver, who delivered craft from Ontario and Quebec across the Atlantic and Irish Sea to Scotland. Polish volunteer **Jadwiga Piłsudska (February 28, 1920–November 16, 2014)**, a Warsaw native, risked missions over combat-heavy England. British flier **Mary Wilkins Ellis (February 2, 1917–July 24, 2018)** from Leafield, Oxfordshire, flew eleven hundred hours while directing some eighty plane types to front line locations, notably, over one thousand Harvards, Seafires, Gloster Meteors, and twin-engine bombers. American volunteer **Jacqueline Cochran (May 11, 1906–August 9, 1980)** from Pensacola, Florida, piloted the Lockheed Hudson V bomber over the Atlantic to British ports. Hong Kong native **Jean Bird (July 8, 1912–April 29, 1957)** added Beaufighters and Dakotas to the ferrying service. London-born flier **Helen Kerly (January 6, 1916–1992)** became one of the first transporters to earn a commendation. Others from London included flier **Mona Friedlander (June 2, 1914–December 24, 1993)**, who specialized in night flying over gun batteries. A third, **Diana Barnato Walker (January 15, 1918–April 28, 2008)** left nursing and ambulance driving during the London Blitz to solo in eighty aircraft types, including Mustangs, Tempests, Whitleys, Blenheims, and Mitchells. The first combat pilot for the French, Chilean pilot **Margot Duhalde Sotomayor (December 12, 1920–February 5, 2018)** of Rio Bueno ferried nine hundred war planes from English to war zones in Belgium, France, and Holland, earning a

Legion of Honor. Spanish recruit **Mary de Bunsen (May 29, 1910–1982)** of Madrid transferred Spitfires from Kirkbride, Scotland, to Allied airfields. English aeronautical engineer **Lettice Curtis (February 1, 1915–July 25, 2014)** of Denbury, Devon, became the first to fly the Avro Lancaster. Canadian pilot **Lois Butler (November 1897–August 17, 1970)** from Quebec mastered thirty-six types of planes and recorded one thousand flying hours. A Toronto native and member of the Order of Canada, **Marion Alice Powell Orr (June 25, 1918–April 4, 1995)** ferried fifteen plane types to England and Europe and became the first woman bush flier and helicopter instructor. Her Toronto-born colleague **Violet Milstead Warren (October 17, 1919–June 27, 2014)** earned the Amelia Earhart Medal for piloting the twin-engine De Haviland. Scots pilot **Marion Wilberforce (July 22, 1902–December 17, 1995)** from Aberdeen delivered planes to the Madagascar invasion and to an attack on Gestapo headquarters in Oslo, but rejected medals at the end of World War II. Argentine volunteer **Maureen Dunlop de Popp (October 26, 1920–May 29, 2012)** of Quilmes survived an emergency landing in her lengthy career of ferrying Barracudas, Typhoons, and the Fairchild Argus, a four-seater monoplane.

Fatalities martyred women ATA fliers. Canadian volunteer **Elsie Joy Davison (March 14, 1910–July 8, 1940)** of Montreal became the first female pilot lost in World War II after she died in training on the two-seater Miles Master monoplane from a carbon monoxide leak. **Margaret Fairweather (September 23, 1901–August 4, 1944)** of Newcastle upon Tyne, the first to pilot the Supermarine Spitfire, died at age forty-two in a return flight crash caused by a fuel tank problem. Award-winning English pilot **Amy Johnson (July 1, 1903–January 5, 1941)** from Kingston, Yorkshire, died after parachuting into the Thames Estuary from friendly fire that downed her twin-engine Airspeed Oxford in heavy snow.

Late October 1942

A Michigan native, **Nancy Harkness Love (February 14, 1914–October 22, 1976),** initiated the Women's Auxiliary Ferrying Squadron (WAFS) in late October 1942 to transport new planes from U.S. factories to Canada, England, and France. Her first hire, **Betty Gillies (January 7, 1908–October 14, 1998)** of Syosset, Long Island, New York, delivered heavy bombers to Alberta, Canada. In August 1943, the WAFS gave place to the Women Airforce Service Pilots (WASP), a program that Nancy commanded. She flew Mustangs, Thunderbolts, Lightnings, Fairchild PTs, Skymasters, and, in 1943, B-17 Flying Fortresses, a task she shared with Nancy. At war's end, President Harry S. Truman presented Nancy the Air Medal.

November 1942

A Savoyarde conspirator, courier, and forger in November 1942, **Jeanne Brousse (also Jeannette, April 12, 1921–October 19, 2017)** from Saint-Pierre-de-Curtille, France, used an Annecy civil service office of the Refugee Naturalization Service in

November 1942 as a source of documents for Jews and men ages twenty-two to twenty-four avoiding obligatory military service and forced labor. On a night pass, she violated the Gestapo's curfew to deliver alerts to recruits on the run and potential deportees and to present ration cards to families. The need increased in September 1943, when Italy allied with the U.S. Her devoted service to the vulnerable along the Swiss border earned a citation to righteous gentiles and listing as Righteous among the Nations for saving a rabbi's three daughters. Her selflessness was a feature of two television films and the play *The Rebellious Righteous*.

November 2, 1942

French reconnaissance operative and saboteur **Odette Sansom** concealed her secret work for the Spindle network with a nursing degree and the spy identity "Lise." She landed by sea at Cassis in southern France on November 2, 1942, and managed airdrops at Marseilles of sugar and tobacco, exchange items that served as currency. On arrest on April 16, 1943, after betrayal at Lake Annecy, an Italian enclave in the French Alps, she endured Gestapo interrogation at Fresnes Prison in Paris by red hot poker and extraction of toenails. Sentenced to two death penalties in July 1944, she occupied a cell at Ravensbrück women's prison in Germany among starving cellmates who cannibalized a corpse. Liberated by the Allies on May 3, 1945, she earned her likeness on a postage stamp, a George Cross, and Legion of Honor and testified in post-war trials against Ravensbrück guards. The 2019 biography *Code Name: Lise* featured her combat missions.

See also 1938; May 13, 1943.

November 10, 1942

A valued agent and recruiter for the Alliance network of the French Resistance, **Marie-Madeleine Fourcade (August 11, 1909–July 20, 1989)** of Marseilles entered long periods at large to elude the Gestapo. After enlisting as a network agent in 1939 under the code name "Herisson (Hedgehog)," she eluded capture by hiding in a mailbag on November 10, 1942, and radioed secret data to England with a hidden transmitter. During her series of safe house escapes, she gave birth to a son. While managing three thousand spies, she defied the Vichy regime and facilitated discovery of the V2 rocket tested at Peenemünde, Germany. The French ennobled her patriotism with the Legion of Honor, the George Cross, a funeral at Invalides, and burial at Père-Lachaise. Her memoir, *L'Arche de Noe* (Noah's Ark), became a touchstone of data on German strategies and troop movements.

November 12, 1942

Pharmacist, courier, and arms supplier Lieutenant **Marinette Menut (May 16, 1914–July 19, 1944)** from Leprugne, France, followed her husband, Max Menut, into resistance work on November 12, 1942, to halt Nazism. In addition to transporting documents, dressings, and medicines, while raising an infant, Christiane, Marinette deposited arms in warehouses and distributed mail to refugees. In August 1943, she colluded with the escape of eleven resistance agents from the Puy de Dome, a volcano in France's Massif Central. On Mont Mouchet in the southeast, she operated an underground field clinic as administrator and pharmacist for the Free Corps of Auvergne.

At a Wehrmacht ambush on June 22, 1944, Marinette shielded sixty wounded by machine gunning the enemy. Wounds to hand and kidneys forced her hospitalization on June 27 at the Saint-Flour clinic in Auvergne. The Gestapo tortured the pregnant agent at Chamalieres, executed her at Aulnat on July 19, 1944, and deposited her remains in a shell hole at the airfield. Her military honoraria include a Croix de Guerre and Legion of Honor.

November 28, 1942

An Albanian anti-fascist hero of the National liberation Front, **Margarita Tutulani (1925–July 6, 1943)** from Berat gained notoriety as a wily resister. A member of a freedom-fighting family, she became a wanted criminal for protesting Italian invaders. She abetted the Berat demonstration on November 28, 1942, when citizens secured Jews in sixty homes. At age eighteen, she and her older brother Kristaq suffered prison tortures from July 4, 1943, until their execution two days later by rifle squad at Gosë (modern Gosa, Albania). A cemetery monument honors her martyrdom.

December 1942

A Korean-American WAVE and first female gunnery officer, Lieutenant **Susan Ahn Cuddy (January 16, 1915–June 24, 2015)** of Los Angeles served as a World War II aerial gunnery instructor and intelligence officer. After graduating from San Diego State University, she defied her family and entered the U.S. Navy in December 1942. She trained in gunnery in November 1943 at Pensacola, Florida, and achieved expertise on the .50-caliber machine gun. She progressed to code breaker and adviser to the Library of Congress and the National Security Agency. The California legislature named her 2003 Woman of the Year. Three years later, she earned the American Courage Award, Korean National Merit citation, a Mormon Pioneer Award, and Los Angeles's "Susan Ahn Cuddy Day."

December 24, 1942

A Polish warrior with a sixth grade education and Red Cross certification, **Anna Ivanovna Maslovskaya (January 6, 1920–November 11, 1980)** from Kursevichi drove with a tank unit of the Red Army at age twenty-one on December 24, 1942, and breached German lines at Postavy in north central Belarus. In 1944, while working in a clothing factory, she sabotaged the production of SS uniforms and strategized an armed assault on the German military by the Russian Liberation Army. The partisan foray killed a general, twenty-three SS officers, and sixty-six Nazi soldiers. Anna rose in prominence as saboteur of three troop trains, a machine gun nest, and rail lines and as a raider of military units at Kamai, Lintupah, Myadel, and Zalesye on the Baltic Sea. One on-target grenade toss massacred fifty enemy soldiers. She received the honorarium

Hero of the Soviet Union, Gold Star, a display in the Myadel Museum of Glory, and Order of Lenin and lies among heroes and elite Russians interred at Moscow's Vagankovo Cemetery.

Late 1942

Dutch resister, forger, and assassin **Marion Philippina Pritchard (November 7, 1920–December 11, 2016)** from Amsterdam executed a Nazi informer in Huizen. During a lengthy service to the Netherlands underground, from age nineteen, she guided refugees to safe houses, claimed to be the mother of illegitimate babies, and provided rations and forged documents. In 1941, she entered prison for helping a student group disseminate radio broadcasts.

Marion's murder of a Dutch collaborator southeast of Amsterdam in late 1942 required spur-of-the-moment discharge of her pistol after the intruder discovered her hiding place under the floor. For concealment, fellow conspirators buried the traitor's corpse atop another dead man. For clandestine aid to one hundred fifty Jewish children, she earned a citation for valor, the Wallenberg Medal, commemoration at the U.S. holocaust museum in Washington, D.C., and naming as Righteous among the Nations.

1943

A Marxist saboteur, supplier, guide, and strategizer of prison escapes, **Lidia Brisca Menapace (April 3, 1924–December 7, 2020)** of Novara in the Italian alps allied with the Catholic resistance in 1943 at age nineteen. A pacifist who publicly rejected fascist racial discrimination in schools, she transported Jews, messages and maps, medicine, and explosives and bombs, which she secreted in the family basement and smuggled under her clothes. In addition to carrying coded notes to fellow rebels, she delivered war casualties from northern Italy to Switzerland by bicycling along courier routes. Her memoir, *Io, Partigiana: La Mia Resistenza* (I, Partisan: My Resistance), describes her determination.

January 1943

A covert propagandizer and saboteur for the Office of Strategic Services (OSS), **Elizabeth Peet McIntosh (March 1, 1915–June 8, 2015)** a journalist from Washington, D.C., accepted an invitation in January 1943 to work for the federal government as a spy. A colleague of OSS agent **Julia Child (August 15, 1912–August 13, 2004)** of Pasadena, California, Elizabeth and her fellow researchers composed misleading reports, news alerts, and documents and sent postcards to deflate Japanese fighting spirit. After reassignment from Kandy, Ceylon (modern Sri Lanka), in June 1945, Julia shared a residence with Elizabeth behind enemy lines in Kunming, China, where Elizabeth spread false rumors in Maymyo, Burma (modern Myanmar), wrote radio broadcasts, and abetted the destruction of a Japanese troop train on a bridge.

After the war, Elizabeth published the memoir *Undercover Girl* and *Sisterhood of Spies,* a survey of female espionage and psychological disinformation. For her service to the OSS and CIA, she received an Intelligence Medal of Merit and listing among Virginia Women in History. Julia, who established stardom as a television chef and author, earned a commendation for civilian service overseas and an emblem of meritorious civilian service, in part for formulating a shark repellent for use against German U-boats.

A fellow OSS spy, **Doris Bohrer (February 5, 1923–August 8, 2016)** of Basin, Wyoming, performed cartographic analysis of terrain in Germany and northern Italy as an aid to allied bombers. Because of her fluency in Japanese, she served in post-war Japan in the CIA as a writer for the Morale Operations. Armed with a .32 pistol, she accepted risky jobs tracing Axis rocket and electronics factories and tracking German trains carrying victims to death camps. While posted to Bari, Italy, she produced relief maps for the allied invasion of Sicily and pinpointed aerial reconnaissance and the placement and extermination of spies in the field.

January 1, 1943

A Tatar bomber pilot of the Polikarpov Po-2 biplane for the 588th "Night Witches," Commander **Maguba Syrtlanova (July 15, 1912–October 1, 1971)** from Belebey in the Russian Empire survived one hundred missions during the battle of the Taman peninsula between the Sea of Azov and the Black Sea. Her sortie count rose to two hundred seventy-two after the Crimean campaign, which involved six thousand one hundred forty bomb runs. The eight-month conflict ended in Sevastopol on July 4, 1942, with forty-two thousand Axis soldiers killed and genocide of the area's Jews. On January 1, 1943, she attained the rank of flight commander. At war's end, Maguba advanced to deputy squad commander. Her seven hundred eighty bomb runs destroyed three artillery sites, two trains, a fuel dump, and two searchlights. She achieved the Order of Lenin, Hero of the Soviet Union, and four additional honoraria.

January 18, 1943

Two Polish rescuers during the Warsaw Ghetto Uprising, smugglers **Tosia Altman (August 24, 1919–May 26, 1943)** of Lipno and **Vladka Meed (December 29, 1921–November 21, 2012)** of Warsaw, allocated arms and explosives to the Home Army. Before the Nazi invasion, Tosia and Vladka readied young Jews for migration to Palestine. After the walling off of the Warsaw ghetto on April 1, 1940, Tosia continued to travel by train to deliver rations and warnings of a Jewish genocide, which caused the deaths of Vladka's family at Treblinka concentration camp in northeastern Poland. Along with teen arms supplier **Hanna Stadnik (February 23, 1929–December 1, 2020)** of Warsaw and Belarusian smuggler **Frumka Płotnicka (1914–August 3, 1943)**, Tosia stepped up weapons transport in December 1942; Vladka supplied the Zydowska Organizacja Bojowa (ZOB) (Jewish Fighting Organization) with dynamite to halt Hitler's Great Action plan to exterminate Jews.

Wounded in head and leg on January 18, 1943, Tosia crept through sewers with weapons courier and Kraków-born smuggler **Hela Rufeisen Schüpper**

(June 7, 1921–May 23, 2017), who also recuperated from a bullet to the foot. Led by Belarusian warrior **Zivia Lubetkin**, Tosia hid in a celluloid factory until it caught fire on May 24, 1943. Two months later, Frumka died while guiding combatants during the Będzin Ghetto Uprising in Poland, for which she earned a posthumous Order of the Cross of Gruenwald. Hela hid in sewers until her arrest and imprisonment at Bergen-Belsen concentration campo north of Celle, Germany. After Nazi officers abandoned a train carrying her to Theresienstadt, Bohemia, American squads freed her. She emigrated to Palestine and compiled details of smuggling in *Farewell to Mila 18: A Courier's Story*.

The Gestapo imprisoned Tosia until her death from burns on May 26, 1943. She received a posthumous military silver cross and representation in the television documentary *Uprising*, which Vladka advised. On arrival in New York with the first boatload of Holocaust survivors, Vladka lectured on genocide and compiled the treatise *On Both Sides of the Wall*. Zivia fought alongside the Jewish resisters and escaped battle to a hospital. Upon arrival in Palestine, she aided Holocaust survivors in founding the Ghetto Fighters' kibbutz at Haifa, Israel, and issued a memoir, *In the Days of Destruction and Revolt*. In July 2001, her Israeli granddaughter, **Roni Zuckerman (1978–)** from Lohamei HaGeta'ot, became the first woman to fly a fighter jet for the Israeli Air Force. Hanna, the teen warrior, braved Skierniewice concentration camp on the German border until Soviet forces liberated it. For courage she won a Silver Cross, Warsaw Cross, German Order of Merit, Veteran Badge, Cross of Independence, and Partisan Cross.

See also late 1941.

January 25 and March 2, 1943

English parachutist and courier **Jacqueline Nearne (May 27, 1916–August 15, 1982)** of Brighton and younger sister **Eileen Nearne (March 16, 1921–September 2, 2010)**, a signals agent and telegrapher from London, entered central France separately on January 25 and March 2, 1943. By train, Jacqueline smuggled spare radio parts for the Spiritualist and Stationer circuits until her flight back to England in April 1944. For the Spiritualist network, Eileen continued deployment as spy and radio operator code named "Rose." After seizure by the Gestapo, Eileen underwent ice water torture in a Paris cell before transfer in August 1945 to Ravensbrück Women's Prison. She escaped a press gang at a Silesian camp to an American unit, but bore mental anguish from torture. She earned a Croix de Guerre and an Order of the British Empire as well as sisterly care from Jacqueline until Jacqueline's death from cancer on August 1, 1982.

January 27, 1943

One of two hundred thirty French resistance fighters, Jews, and communists transported in four cattle cars from Romainville east of Paris to Auschwitz-Birkenau, Germany, author **Hélène Solomon-Langevin (May 25, 1909–January 16, 1995)** of Fontenay-aux-Roses witnessed Nazi atrocities against the *Convoi des 3100*

(The Convoy of 3100). She and friend **Mai Politzer (August 15, 1905–March 6, 1943)** from Biarritz had contributed to the war effort by compiling lists of intellectuals taken hostage and executed by the Nazi occupation force. An associate, Paris-born photojournalist and saboteur **Marie-Claude Vaillant-Couturier (November 3, 1912–December 11, 1996)**, earned imprisonment at La Santé Prison for transporting explosives. A Parisian activist **Madeleine Passot (August 28, 1914–September 19, 2009)** entered the same prison for carrying cash and documents and archiving resistance records. Another activist and writer, **Charlotte Delbo, (August 10, 1913–March 1, 1985)** from Vigneux-sur-Seine, published anti–Nazi pamphlets and later wrote *Convoy to Auschwitz*.

Hélène was widowed in May 1942 after her husband, Jacques Solomon, was executed. Following her arrest by the Gestapo in July 1942, she occupied a Paris cell at Fort de Romainville. She and the other inmates sang "La Marseillaise" as the trustees ushered them from cattle cars into the concentration camp, where one thousand female prisoners died on February 10, 1943. Mai Politzer and Corsican dentist and rescuer of Jews **Danielle Casanova (January 9, 1909–May 9, 1943)** succumbed to typhus in spring 1943. Madeleine, who nursed the sick during the epidemic, survived.

Hélène transferred alone to a Bosch gas mask factory outside Berlin to work as a nurse. While laboring in the infirmary, she treated an infected lesion on her foot that had turned black. After removal to Raisko, she aided research into dandelion experiments until her infection with typhus. From Ravensbrück and Sachsenhausen extermination camps in Germany, she thrived among the twenty-one percent who survived an SS death march in late January 1945. She and Charlotte were rescued by the French Red Cross, but Hélène never regained robust health.

An Alsatian compatriot, physician **Adélaïde Haas Hautval (January 1, 1906–October 17, 1988)** from Le Hohwald, France, testified against Polish medical experimenter Wladislaw Dering and detailed her own refusal to sterilize Jewish women, for which she gained listing as Righteous among Nations. She issued a memoir-exposé of Nazi violation of the Hippocratic Oath, *Médecine et Crimes contre l'Humanité* (Medicine and Crimes against Humanity), which reported surgeries without anesthetic. Danielle received a posthumous Legion of Honor; Madeleine accepted a military citation, Croix de Guerre, and Volunteer combatant's cross. Charlotte earned renown for her Auschwitz trilogy and a drama, *Who Will Carry the Word?*

Early February 1943

Russo-Indian Muslim telegrapher and courier **Noor-un-Nisa Inayat Khan (also Nora Baker or Nora Inayat-Khan, January 1, 1914–September 13, 1944)** from Moscow landed in a Lysander liaison aircraft by night on early February 1943 in France's Loire Valley near Angers. Code-named "Madeleine," Noor traveled with London-born operatives **Cecily Gordon Lefort (April**

30, 1899–February 5, 1945) and **Diana Rowden (January 31, 1915–July 6, 1944)**. None of the three survived the war. Betrayed, arrested, and questioned at Fresnes Prison in Paris on October 13, 1943, Noor passed to a cell at Dachau in southern Germany. After a severe beating, she died of a bullet to the neck alongside three French agents—Parisian wireless agent **Yolande Beekman (January 7, 1911–September 13, 1944)**, parachutist and courier for the Bricklayer circuit **Madeleine Zoe Damerment (November 11, 1917–September 13, 1944)** of Lille, and **Éliane Sophie (December 6, 1917–September 13, 1944)** of Marseilles, who trained in combat, parachuting, and sabotage on the Monk circuit. A bronze bust of Noor-un–Nisa survives in London. Yolande, Madeleine, and Éliane received a posthumous Croix de Guerre.

See also August 13, 1943

February 16, 1943

In the first conflicts of the four-year Greek Civil War, on February 16, 1943, **Anna Dosa (1938–)** led twenty-three guerrillas against Nazi insurgents. Under German strafing, Anna stood and aimed her Bren machine gun at an enemy plane and brought it down. A communist-led uprising against widespread starvation under Axis occupation erupted in Athens on December 3, 1943. Female rebels marched on police barricades, forced their way through the city center, and stormed the apartment of Premier George Papandreou, who entered the U.S. Navy and comforted the wounded as a hospital corpsman. By year's end, the British escorted Papandreou in a military parade through the capital.

March 1943

Pregnant commando raider, tactician, diarist, and history teacher in Strasbourg and Lyon, France, **Lucie Bernard Aubrac (June 29, 1912–March 14, 2007)** of Mâcon aided the French resistance in March 1943 in sabotaging train depots at Cannes and Perpignan. During the summer of 1943, she co-founded Liberation-Sud and recruited Christian socialists to combat Nazi occupation through propaganda and sabotage. In rescuing a badly beaten husband and thirteen resistance fighters from a prison transport dispatched to Lyon by Klaus Barbie, head of the Gestapo, on October 21, 1943, Lucie killed six German guards. In her ninth month of pregnancy with daughter Lucie in February 1944, she escaped to London and became the first Frenchwoman parliamentarian. After a war career aiding Algerian independence and publishing the newspaper *Liberation*, she issued a history of the French underground and the diary *Outwitting the Gestapo*. At age eighty-four, she accepted a French Legion of Honor. Four films dramatized her commando raids.

March 27, 1943

Dutch-Jewish cellist, conductor, and composer **Frieda Belinfante (May 10, 1904–March 5, 1955)** of Amsterdam served the LGBTQ resistance movement as forger, saboteur, and shelterer of Jews and homosexuals. In addition to forging passports and ration cards for Jewish residents, on March

27, 1943, she and lesbian operative **Lau Mazirel (November 29, 1907–November 20, 1974)** from Utrecht strategized and carried out the destruction of Amsterdam's census registry. The bombed out building and burning of eight hundred thousand census cards disabled Gestapo matching of forged documents with originals. In late 1944, Lau served six weeks at Weteringschans, a Nazi prison in Amsterdam, and devoted her post-war activism to the human rights of gays, Gypsies, and other nomads. Frieda dressed in men's clothes and fled pursuers on foot across the Swiss Alps. Repatriated to Orange County, California, she regretted repercussions of her lesbian lifestyle.

Spring 1943

After recuperating from a leg break on an airdrop in spring 1943, Allied spy and saboteur **Andrée Borrel** reentered France in February 1944 under the guise of the widow Irene Brisee. Bicycling into the countryside with a Jew posing as her lover, she set twenty plastique charges and acid detonators on electric pylons. The couple pedaled for two miles (3.2 kilometers) before two of the towers exploded in flames. While three SS agents investigated the sabotage, the third pylon erupted, killing one Nazi and injuring the others. Andrée engaged in a gunfight with a German patrol, attacked enemy columns, and sabotaged tires in area roads with puncturing devices. After presentation of a Croix de Guerre and legion of honor, her war efforts appeared in the film *Les Femmes de l'Ombre* (Women in the Shadow).

See also January 20, 1940; June 16, 1943.

April 19, 1943

As co-founders of the Zegota underground in 1942, **Wanda Krahelska-Filipowicz (December 13, 1886–February 5, 1968)** from Sawiejka, Belarus, and **Zofia Kossak-Szczucka (August 10, 1889–April 9, 1968)** of Kosmin in the Russian Empire equipped the Home Army with weapons from airdrops. Wanda, a veteran bomber of General Georgi Skalon's carriage at Warsaw in August 1906, fought under the code name "Alinka." Zofia used the name "Weronika." The co-conspirators backed the Polish Council to Aid Jews in fighting Nazis during the Warsaw Ghetto Uprising of April 19, 1943. Zofia battled alongside her daughter, **Anna Szatkowska (March 15, 1928–February 27, 2015)**, a combat medic and combat writer from Gorky Wielkie, Silesia. A third supplier of the Home Army for the Zegota underground, **Irena Scheur-Sawicka (August 18, 1890–August 1, 1944)**, died from a German fusillade. Zofia survived incarceration at Auschwitz II-Birkenau death camp in south central Poland and detailed the experience two years later in *Z Otchlani* (From the Abyss). Wanda and Zofia achieved listing with the Righteous among the Nations.

See also August 18, 1906.

April 22, 1943

The first female honored as a Hero of the Soviet Union, Ukrainian bomber pilot **Yevdokiya Nosal (March 14, 1918–April 22, 1943)** from Burchak died on

April 22, 1943, over Novorossiysk, Russia, during the Luftwaffe shelling of her plane. One of the determined "Night Witches," she expired from shrapnel to the forehead. Russian Federation mechanic and multi-medaled navigator **Glafira Kashirina (1920–August 1, 1943)** from Sergievka in the Russian Soviet Federation completed the flight. A survivor of a disabled plane and typhus, Glafira and seven other pilots of the 588th Regiment succumbed to an aerial battle over Krasni, Ukraine, at the Kuban River Bridgehead on the Taman Peninsula on April 22, 1943, between the Sea of Azov and the Black Sea. She received a posthumous Patriotic War decoration.

April 29, 1943

Anti-fascist guerrilla "shotgun woman" and courier in Carinthia **Maria Olip' (March 29, 1913–April 29, 1943)** of Ebriach, Austria, aided combat to unite Slovenia with Yugoslavia. She served her younger brothers, Ivan and Miha Zupanc, as a battlefield messenger and recruiter for the Osvobodilna Fronta, the Slovenian national liberation front. Seized by the SS paramilitary on November 11, 1942, she fled their transport truck, but was arrested a second time the next day. For eight weeks at Klagenfurt Jail in Austria, severe torture wounded her entire body. On April 29, 1943, German executioners guillotined her in Vienna on the same day as the murders of her husband, Thomas Olip, and brother Miha.

May 1943

A pro–Nazi spy, realtor, and dentist from Bergen, Norway, **Dollis Dahlgren (December 9, 1899–September 27, 1981)** earned the sobriquet "the Scandinavian Mata Hari." In winter 1942, she identified corruption in Norwegian broadcasting and named Norwegian communists and refugees in Sweden traveling from Alesund to Shetland, Scotland. Allied with the Germanic Schutzstaffel (SS) Norway in May 1943, she conspired with Fritz Preiss, a Swedish Gestapo officer in Oslo, to report to the agency names of Berlin couriers and Norwegian resistance. She also pinpointed German ammunition depots, newly made ships, and airports in Norway.

At Dollis's arrest during an escape attempt through the Östervall forest on February 23, 1944, she was convicted for carrying $17,000 in bribe money and notes to a German police chief. During questioning, she identified an SS informer who cooperated with the Swedish secret police. The Swedish Secret Service revealed to the media her role in espionage. She served two years of forced labor at a Nazi concentration camp in Växjö, Sweden, and gained her freedom in 1946.

May 13, 1943

English fashion consultant Ensign **Vera Leigh (March 17, 1903–July 6, 1944)** of Leeds served a sentence at the Miranda de Ibro Spanish internment camp before volunteering as a courier, sharpshooter, and guide for Allied aircrew traveling across France to the Pyrenees. Code-named "Simone," she reached Tours by Lysander liaison aircraft on the night of May 13, 1943, with operative **Julienne Aisner (December**

30, 1899–February 15, 1947) of Anglure, a courier and forger for the Prosper circuit. Vera served the Donkeyman network as an escort for Allied airmen.

Because of betrayal, the Gestapo arrested Vera and jailed her in Paris as Fresnes Prison and forced her to do menial work at Karlsruhe Prison in Germany. Vera died alongside French agents **Éliane Plewman, Odette Sansom, Madeleine Zoe Damerment,** and **Yolande Beekman**, and Saxon operative **Sonia Olschanezky** at the Natzweiler-Struthof camp in France on the German border. A lethal phenol injection felled them before staff placed them in the camp crematory, some still alive. Following a trial for war crimes, the camp executioner and doctor were hanged. Leigh and Julienne received a posthumous commendation for bravery.

See also 1938; autumn 1942; early February 1943; June 16, 1943; August 13, 1943.

May 18, 1943

On May 18, 1943, Ukrainian fighter **Natalya Meklin (September 8, 1922–June 5, 2005)** of Lubny transferred from navigator for the 588th "Night Witches" to pilot of the Polikarpov Po-2. In a plywood and canvas biplane that delivered payloads on more than thirty thousand sorties, she dropped bombs over the Caucasus, Crimea, Poland, Ukraine, Byelorussia, and Germany in as many as ten missions per night. She survived nine hundred eighty campaigns and earned ten medals, including Lenin and Zhukov citations and a Hero of the Soviet Union. Her experiences appear in the co-authored memoir *We Were Called Night Witches.*

A comrade, Russian Soviet Federation fighter pilot **Yevdokiya Nikulina (November 8, 1917–March 23, 1993)** from Parfyonovo fought in the battle of the Caucasus. After rescuing wounded and flying reconnaissance in the flimsy Polikarpov Po-2, she became one of the 588th "Night Witches" and advanced to squadron commander. In a night raid over the Caucasus, she survived a shrapnel wound and set her limping trainer plane down in Soviet terrain. After recuperating, she returned to the night runs. She received the Order of Alexander Nevsky, a rare honor for female soldiers named for a medieval prince and saint.

June 16, 1943

In the Jura Mountains near Dijon, French spy and courier **Diana Hope Rowden (January 31, 1915–July 6, 1944)** coordinated airdrops of arms and explosives from a Halifax bomber for the Acrobat circuit. She volunteered for the French Red Cross and served an ambulance corps in 1940 before entering by Loire Valley by Lysander liaison aircraft in June 1943. On the night of June 16, 1943, she was assigned to destroy a Peugeot factory that employed sixty thousand laborers to make plane engines and tank turrets for the Nazis. After her arrest by German police in November, she transferred on May 13, 1944, with operatives **Andrée Borrel, Vera Leigh**, and **Sonia Olschanezky** to a cell at Germany's Karlsruhe prison in St. Petersburg, Russia. On July 6, 1944, the four agents were injected with deadly phenol and cremated. Andrée regained consciousness and clawed the face of her executioner before he burned her alive. Diana and Andrée received a posthumous Croix de Guerre.

July 1943

The first Native American U.S. marine, **Minnie Bendina Spotted Wolf (June 20, 1923–July 8, 1987)**, a Blackfoot from Heart Butte, Montana, signed on in July 1943 and trained at Camp Lejeune, North Carolina. The daughter of John and Maggie Aimsback Spotted Wolf, she had worked on a ranch as a bronco buster, fence builder, and truck driver. Continuing her bent for handling heavy machinery, she drove jeeps and operated military equipment in California and Hawaii. When her term ended in 1947, she completed a college degree, taught school, married in April 1953, and settled in Pondera, Montana. A state highway and a 1944 comic strip biography bear her name.

July 1943

At age sixteen, Commander **Janaky Athi Nahappan (also Janaky Devar or Janaki Thevar, February 25, 1925–May 9, 2014)** of Kuala Lumpur in British Malaya (modern Malaysia), enlisted in the Indian National Army to free her country from British control. During her service in July 1943 at Rani of Jhansi's Regimental Headquarters, an all-women brigade in Singapore, she and fellow British Malayan freedom fighter **Rasammah Bhupalan (May 1, 1927)** from Kuala Lumpur came under the command of Captain **Lakshmi Sahgal (also Lakshmi Swaminathan, October 24, 1914–July 23, 2012)**, a gynecologist and medic from Madras, British India. Janaky earned top scores and promotion to second regimental officer. She wrote a war memoir about the army's twenty-three-day retreat on a treacherous jungle walk from Rangoon to Bangkok. While Janaky and Rasammah fought on the Indo-Burma border throughout World War II, Lakshmi was locked in a British prison in Burma in May 1945 and remained until March 1946. Janaky's patriotism earned a Padma Shri medal for distinguished contribution to public affairs; Lakshmai received the Padma Vibhushan citation and a PhD from Calcutta University.

July 14, 1943

Dutch teacher, arms supplier, raider, and assassin **Sietje Gravendeel-Tammens (July 29, 1914–September 27, 2014)** of Koosterburen, Netherlands, plotted tactics for raiding Nazi ration stamp headquarters. Late in 1941, she deployed refugees, arranged assassinations, and stored stolen weapons and ration stamps. At the stamp dispersal center on Langmeer, she masterminded a raid. During winter 1943–1944, she arranged the murder of a pro–Nazi police chief and his successor. Another target survived a shooting on July 14, 1943, forcing Sietje to escape to Lleeuwarden under the false name "Martha." At her arrest on June 13, 1944, she passed through three concentration camps and received a death sentence in August. She bribed a guard and fled sexual torture in late March 1945 before a second arrest. Freed by the Canadian Army, she lived to age one hundred and donated her remains for medical study.

July 19, 1943

During the Allied bombing of the San Lorenzo area of Rome on July 19, 1943, Roman communist partisan **Carla Capponi (December 7, 1918–November 24, 2000)** took advantage of disruption in the freight yard and rail and communication lines and volunteered at Policlinico Hospital in northwestern Rome to tend some of the fifteen hundred victims. At a clandestine site facing the Foro di Traiano (Trajan's Forum), she conspired with fellow communist rebel **Adele Bei Ciufoli (May 4, 1904–October 15, 1976)** of Cantiano in central Italy to bomb central locations and assassinate prominent fascists. While walking the streets armed, Carla recovered German defense plans for Rome after murdering a Nazi officer outside the Hotel Excelsior in the Via Veneto tourist area. She received the Gold Medal of Military Valor.

July 19, 1943

Flight instructor and air ace **Yekaterina "Katya" Budanova (December 6, 1916–July 19, 1943)** from Konoplanka served the Soviet Army by gunning down Nazi Messerschmitts from her "Yak-1" fighter monoplane. She initiated her career with missions above rail yards in Saratov, Russia. Ending two years of lone wolf aviation over Stalingrad and Rostov on Don, Yekaterina lost out on July 19, 1943, while escorting bomb runs over Ukraine. After downing one Luftwaffe pursuer and scoring another, she crashed and died at Novokrasnovka, Ukraine, in a damaged plane that caught fire. Honoraria include Order of the Red Star, Hero of the Russian Federation, Order of the Red Banner, Order of the Great Patriotic War, and Gold Star hero.

A Muscovite comrade and fellow pilot trainer with the 437th Regiment, **Lydia "Lilya" Litvyak (August 18, 1941–August 1, 1943)** made her own record of sixty-six sorties. A thrice-wounded veteran of aerial combat, Lydia continued solo flying in a Yak-1 two more weeks after her comrade's death. Lydia presumably died over Orel at age twenty-one at the battle of Kursk, Russia. Revered as the "White Lily of Stalingrad," she earned the Order of the Red Star, Order of Lenin, Order of the Red Banner, Order of the Patriotic War, and Hero of the Soviet Union and gained name recognition in fiction, drama, film, songs, and anime. Controversy clouds her life story because of conflicting accounts of her death. The two pilots hold titles as the world's greatest female aces.

July 27, 1943

The Polish Home Army commander **Maria Wittek** of Trebki, a veteran of the July 27, 1943, battle of Lwów (modern Lviv, Ukraine), earned a battlefield promotion to lieutenant colonel. In 1915, she joined **Wanda Gertz Kazik** and Major **Halszka Wasilewska** from London in dressing in men's uniforms to assist the Polish artillery during World War I. In the Warsaw Ghetto Uprising of April 19, 1943, Maria eluded inclusion among German prisoners of war. For military courage, she received two silver crosses, honoraria for Valor and Independence with Swords, and a Warsaw Cross. At age ninety-one, she accepted from President Lech Wałęsa appointment to Brigadier General, the highest rank of any Polish female. A bronze standing likeness outside Warsaw's military museum underscores her soldierly posture.

See also July 28, 1914; August 1920; November 1939.

August 1943

A daring navigator during a sortie of the 588th "Night Witches" in August 1943, Lieutenant **Tatyana Sumarokova (September 16, 1922–May 28, 1997)** from Soviet Moscow climbed the wing of her canvas and plywood biplane to loosen an attached bomb. The payload remained stuck, forcing aviator **Vera Tikhomirova (September 30, 1918–October 14, 2002)** of Shuya in the Russian Federation to land with unexploded ordnance. Vera successfully avoided subsequent anti-aircraft fire, shrapnel, and collision with a burning plane hit by flak on December 31, 1943. The pair flew missions to the Baltics, Byelorussia, Crimea, and the Caucasus to drop paratroopers, ammunition, and rations. Tatyana earned eight honoraria for success in seven hundred twenty-five bomb runs; after flying nine hundred missions, Vera received five medals for completing nine hundred mission in the Polikarpov Po-2 biplane.

August 6, 1943

A posthumous Soviet hero, **Zinaida Ivanovna Mareseva (June 20, 1923–August 6, 1943)** from Cherkassy led her company and their wounded from bombardment. A Red Army medic, she entered World War II in 1942 and served the 38th Rifle Division at Stalingrad, Voronezh, and the steppes. On February 8, 1943, she was decorated for combat valor and promoted to senior sergeant. At the six-weeks battle of Kursk southwest of Moscow, the Soviets halted an armored Nazi offensive. For crawling to the aid of thirty-eight casualties, Zinaida received the Order of the Red Star.

Five days before Zinaida's death in combat on August 6, 1943, her unit began crossing the Northern Donets River south of Belgorod, Russia, under continuous shelling, mortar fire, bombs, and land mines. Serious losses depleted the 38th, whom she treated under perilous gunfire. By night, she carried casualties to trenches. As the Soviets faltered, she waved a pistol and rallied them to attack the Nazis and capture heavy artillery. Ferrying the wounded from danger the next day by boat, she spread her limbs over soldiers caught in a mortar barrage. At her death from shrapnel three days later, she received a posthumous Order of Lenin, two medals, and a Hero of the Soviet Union award. Public recognition included a postal portrait, naming of a medical school and the factory where she formerly worked, and erection of a memorial at her grave.

August 13, 1943

A resistance field agent trained in sabotage, combat, weaponry, and explosives for the Monk circuit, **Éliane Sophie Plewmen** of Marseilles, France, parachuted into the Jura Mountains on August 13, 1943, to organize spies and saboteurs, who detonated bombs dropped from British bombers in occupied France. After seven months of covert operations in communication, she was seized by the Gestapo and transferred to Dachau concentration camp northwest of Munich, Germany. On September 13, 1944, at age twenty-six, she died of a bullet to the neck fired by an SS executioner. A posthumous Croix de Guerre recognized her martyrdom.

August 16, 1943

Courier and arms smuggler **Haika Grossman (November 20, 1919–May 26, 1996)** of Białystok, Poland, aided partisans on August 16, 1943, in the one-day Białystok Ghetto Uprising. Coordinating anti-fascist guerrillas with data from attacks at Czenstokhov, Grodno, Lublin, Vilna, and Warsaw, Haika and co-conspirator **Bronia Klibanski (January 24, 1923–February 23, 2011)** and **Liza Czapnik (1922–November 7, 2016)**, both of Grodno, Poland, helped supply some five hundred Białystok resisters with twenty-five German rifles, dozens of molotov cocktails, bottles of sulfuric acid, dynamite, one machine gun, and one hundred pistols, some hidden in loaves of bread. Female partisans managed medic centers, sabotage, and incendiary plots while Haika recruited a secret squad of anti–Hitler Germans to prevent deportation of eleven thousand two hundred Jews under Operation Reinhard north to Treblinka extermination camp in occupied Poland.

The rebellion failed in its aims. After the SS detonated and set fire to the wood buildings and deployed a tank, motorbikes, and armored vehicles, ghetto leaders committed suicide. Haika's memoir, *Underground Army: Fighters of the Białystok Ghetto,* and court testimony described arming survivors from Smolna Street for escape to the Soviet Partisans Brigade in the Knyszyn Forest. Assisting the Home Army in sabotaging troop carriers and supply lines, refugees intended to emigrate from Europe to Palestine. The Polish government presented Haika the Gruenwald Cross for courage in combat and post-war aid to orphans and identification of anti–Semitic collaborators.

August 17, 1943

A member of the Druids circuit, spy **Jeannie Rousseau (April 1, 1919–August 2, 2017)** of Saint Brieuc, France, collected crucial details of V-1 and V-2 rocket manufacture at Peenemünde, Germany. Her intelligence report enabled Operation Hydra, a Royal Air Force convoy of five hundred ninety-six Lancaster, Halifax, and Stirling bombers targeting Peenmunde on August 17, 1943. Damage delayed the work of missile and rocketry wizard Wernher von Braun and his associates and killed the senior engineer.

After Gestapo seizure at La Roche-Derrien, France, on April 28, 1944, Jeannie was jailed at Rennes in eastern Brittany. Following deportation in August 1944, she contracted tuberculosis at Germany's Ravensbrück Women's Prison and Torgau, a Saxon labor camp that manufactured ammunition. Before war's end, Swedish Red Cross workers rescued her. The CIA awarded her the

Agency Seal Medal; she also received the Croix de Guerre, Resistance Medal, and Legion of Honor.

September 22, 1943

Parisian sharpshooter and courier **Pearl Witherington (June 24, 1914–February 24, 2008)** lived homeless and slept on trains on assignment as manager of two thousand guerrillas on the Wrestler circuit at Berry, France. A colleague of **Jacqueline Nearne**, Pearl parachuted into France on September 22, 1943, to aid the Stationer circuit. She operated as saboteur of communications lines and train routes under the secret names "Marie" and "Pauline." She caused mayhem on rail routes in June 1944 to obstruct and delay German reinforcements on the way to the D-Day Allied landing at Normandy.

Under attack by Germans on June 11, 1944, Pearl buried cash and crouched in a hayfield while Nazis destroyed her radio and armaments. A three-plane Allied airdrop restored the equipment on June 24. For successfully directing several million francs to the Allied cause, she earned a Legion of Honor, Croix de Guerre, and knighthood. She summarized operations in central France in the war memoir *Code Name Pauline: Memoirs of a World War II Special Agent*.

September 23, 1943

An Austro-Hungarian baker turned street warrior against fascism, **Käthe Wanek Odwody (March 6, 1901–September 23, 1943)** of Hulken, Austria, facilitated workers in the urban fray and loaded cartridge belts for machine guns. During city skirmishes, she remained in jail from February 17 to May 11, 1934. A serious communist under the cover name "Walli," she collected and distributed member dues and disseminated a newspaper, *Die Rote Fahne* (The Red Flag). On charges of treason at her arrest on April 29, 1941, she died on September 23, 1943, in Vienna on the guillotine. A memorial plaque and street name preserve her idealism.

September 23, 1943

Valeriya Osipovna Gnarovskaya (October 18, 1923—September 23, 1943), a valiant field medic and nineteen-year-old martyr from Modolitsy, exploded grenades to halt a Nazi attack on the Stalingrad Front. After evacuation with family females to Omsk, Siberia, she took a post office job. On April 10, 1942, she and other Communist League youth recruited with the 229th Infantry as medics. On July 31, 1942, she witnessed an enemy retreat from a panzer advance at the Chir River and contracted typhoid fever in the swampy terrain. While she tended casualties and taught first aid to the 907th Rifle Brigade at Vilniansk Raion in northern Ukraine, she experienced hearing damage.

At Ivanenki, senior medical officer Valeriya wielded a submachine gun and boosted her kill number to seventy-five Nazis. When a Tiger I tank rumbled toward her field hospital at regimental headquarters, on September 23, 1943, she grasped a bag of grenades and dived under the treads. The brave act repelled the enemy and spared the lives of seventy Soviet wounded. The Hero of the

Soviet Union commendation, a medal for courage, and the Order of Lenin honored her sacrifice, as did the renaming of Ivanenki village "Gnarovskoe."

September 27, 1943

A Neapolitan parachutist and secret agent for the British, **Maddalena Cerasuolo (February 2, 1920–October 23, 1999)** earned Allied regard for shootouts with German plunderers in a factory neighborhood and for skill with rifle and grenades on September 27, 1943, during the Four Days of Naples. She reconnoitered enemy forces and defended the Ponte della Sanita (Bridge of Health) at city center and its feeder aqueduct, which won her a medal of valor. Until her severance from British service on February 8, 1944, she participated in three failed attempts to penetrate enemy lines and to assault Liguria by bearing arms and explosives on a torpedo boat from Bastia, Corsica. A more successful operation situated her behind enemy lines southeast of Rome at Montecassino, where she parachuted into enemy territory to conduct surveillance. Her service medals included a bonze citation for military valor, a British certificate of merit, and a plaque from her hometown.

September 27, 1943

A Polish freedom fighter among the Gestapo's most-wanted, **Zofia Kossak-Szczucka (August 10, 1889– April 9, 1968)** defied Nazi interdictions against shielding Warsaw Jews from Gestapo persecution. Her arrest on September 7, 1943, and transport to Auschwitz-Birkenau, a Polish death camp, preceded an order of execution for co-founding Zegota, a movement to rescue Jews from genocide. Intervention by the Polish Resistance in July 1944 freed her in time to join the revolt on August 1. She fled from Poland in June 1945 and began compiling her experiences at Auschwitz in *From the Abyss*. Posthumous awards conferred the Order of the White Eagle and named her to Righteous among the Nations.

See also August 18, 1906.

October 1, 1943

Kseniya Semyonovna Konstantinova (April 18, 1925–October 1, 1943) of Łubna, Poland, suffered a barbaric maiming and execution on October 1, 1943, by Germans for trying to rescue a cartful of Soviet Russian casualties. She studied at Lipetsk Medical and Obstetric School before volunteering for the Volga infantry. At age seventeen in May 1943, Kseniya entered combat as a first aid instructor with the 730th Infantry at the six-weeks battle on the Kursk-Belgorod arc southwest of Moscow. After carrying bleeding soldiers on her back at Vitebsk, Belarus, and Voronezh, Russia, she required hospitalization at Tula, Russia, for a shrapnel wound to the head. Nonetheless, she continued service at the Kalinin Front against the Nazi 3rd Panzer Army.

A triumph on September 21, 1943, at Demidov prefaced heavy Russian losses at Uzgorki. Surrounded by enemy machine gunners, Kseniya fired an assault rifle and grenades and killed thirty-six Germans before being knocked unconscious. As a prisoner of war, she endured grilling, bayonetting, and mutilation of breasts, eyes, and ears. Her unit found her remains stabbed and staked to the ground and pursued the Germans, obliterating them. For courage, she received a medal for merit, the Order of Lenin, and a Hero of the Soviet Union designation. Her attempt to rescue casualties survives in a portrait, memorials, school and street names, stage drama, and a song, "Sister of Mercy."

October 8, 1943

A victim of the Nazi guillotine, Viennese opera singer **Marianne Golz (January 30, 1895–October 8, 1943)** died in Prague, Czechoslovakia, on October 8, 1943, for concealing refugees, organizing resistance meetings, and smuggling money and data out of occupied territory. She employed herself early in the underground after Germans occupied Prague in 1939. Her assistance included recruiting volunteers and networking with other operatives. She martyred herself after arrest on November 19, 1942, when she identified missions as a supplier and courier for the Austrian Resistance. At Pankrác Prison southeast of Prague, she continued smuggling information to contacts by writing on waste paper until her execution in the "axe room." Before her selection as Righteous among the Nations, publication of her letters in *Zaluji* (I Accuse) provided wartime details for articles, broadcasts, and drama.

October 23, 1943

Resi Pesendorfer, an Austro-Hungarian resistance leader outside Salzburg, abetted **Maria Wagner Plieseis (August 15, 1920–January 9, 2004)** and rescuer **Agnes Primocic (January 30, 1905–April 14, 2007)** of Hellein in liberating Josef Plieseis, Maria's husband, from a subcamp of Dachau, Germany. At *Der Igel* (The Hedgehog) in the warren of shafts in a deserted salt mine, Resi, aided by **Marianne Feldhammer (March 14, 1909–June 15, 1996)** from Altaussee and Catholic volunteer **Leni Egger (fl. 1940s),** sheltered some five hundred German deserters and arranged delivery of stolen SS uniforms, munitions, fuel, and rations. For remaining faithful to the underground army in the winter of 1944–1945, Resi received a Decoration of Honour.

October 23, 1943

A deportee to a Nazi prison north of Berlin, **Kiki Latry (February 18, 1918–October 9, 2008)** from Bourbon-Lancy, France, weathered a three-day journey to Ravensbrück women's camp in northern Germany and began promoting insurrection among ten thousand inmates. Born Antoinette Dubois, she entered the French Resistance as a spy and intelligence gatherer. After arrest on October 23, 1943, she was incarcerated at Romainville, Compiegne. Following transfer on January 13, 1944, to Ravensbrück, she aided internees of the concentration camp, including Gypsies, Jews, Jehovah's Witnesses, political prisoners, and felons. Among them she met **Geneviève de Gaulle-Anthonioz (October 25, 1920–February 14, 2002),** niece of General Charles de Gaulle, a collaborator with forger **Jeanne Brousse,** and author of three exposés of camp mistreatment.

To relieve overcrowding, camp

authorities began weeding out the physically and mentally disabled and killing them in gas chambers or by firing squad and with forced labor, chemical experiments, or lethal injections of phenol. After the Soviet army liberated twenty-seven thousand five hundred prisoners and departed on April 13, 1945, the women achieved freedom on May 18, 1945. For Kiki's energetic promotion of courage, she earned a street name, a military citation, Croix de Guerre, and Legion of Honor.

See also November 1942.

November 1943

An intelligence gatherer on the Dutch-Paris line, **Suzanne Hiltermann-Souloumiac (January 17, 1919–October 2, 2001)** of Amsterdam conspired to rescue some two hundred downed Allied paratroopers. Under the code name "Touty," in November 1943, she escorted escaping soldiers to Toulouse by night train. Following her arrest by the Gestapo on February 11, 1944, she endured questioning under torture for two months and imprisonment at Ravensbrück, Germany, on April 18. The Swedish Red Cross freed her a year later and transported her via "white buses" to Sweden for rehabilitation. President Harry S. Truman conferred on her the Medal of Freedom.

November 24, 1943

An Indonesian martyr on November 24, 1943, at age twenty-one, **Reina Prinsen Geerligs (October 7, 1922–November 24, 1943)** from Semarang in the Dutch East Indies aided the Dutch resistance as a courier and assassin. Because of the German occupation of Holland on May 10, 1940, her Amsterdam home became a secret meeting place for resisters. After her part in the March 1943 attack on a census registry, she and a comrade failed to execute police officer Pieter Kaay for informing to the Nazis. She apparently completed the liquidation the next day. For carrying a pistol, she confessed her secret acts on July 23, 1943.

In the detention hall, Reina smuggled messages in laundry and tapped encouragement on the cell wall to Jewish inmate **Rose Lopes Laguna-Asscher (May 31, 1872–February 11, 1944)**, a Dutch agent from London. Reina and resister couriers **Cornelia van den Brink (June 13, 1897–November 24, 1943)** of Amsterdam and **Truus van Lier (also Gertruida van Lier, April 22, 1921–November 24, 1943)**, an assassin and rescuer of Jews from Utrecht, sang as they marched before the firing squad. Nazi agents shot Reina, Cornelia, and Truus on November 24, 1943, at Sachsenhausen, a German slave labor and death camp at Oranienburg where one hundred Dutch resisters died. Rose died nine weeks later at Auschwitz, Poland. A statue depicts Truus in Utrecht, where a daffodil garden honors her courage; a library award commemorates Reina's regard for literature.

December 1943

A math whiz and U.S. Navy legend, Rear Admiral **Grace Hopper (December 9, 1906–January 1, 1992)** of New York City was a Phi Beta Kappa university professor when she supported the World War II effort in December 1943 to vanquish the Nazis. At age thirty-seven, she labored on top-secret war problems: developing the MARK II and UNIVAC computers, calibrating minesweepers, compiling range tables for anti-aircraft guns, and computing rocket arcs as an improvement on accuracy. Post-war adaptation of computer language to vernacular words yielded COBOL, a Common Business Oriented Language. At her death at age eighty-six, she was buried in Arlington National Cemetery. A Navy ship, the USS *Hopper,* commemorates her unique career.

December 1943

Conspirator and saboteur **Anna Goldsteiner (June 17, 1899–July 5, 1944)** of Vienna removed Gestapo propaganda posters in December 1943 and amassed explosives for use by *Schlurfs* (Shufflers) of the Austrian Resistance. She protested the German annexation of Austria's Alpine-Danube state. In Vienne, France, on July 5, 1944, she and thirteen others faced death sentences for plotting to destroy Nazi depots and to assassinate the Nazi mayor of Pulkau in Lower Austria. Their strategies began liberation of the Alpine district from the German Reich. She died on July 5, 1944, at the Regional Court at age forty-five, leaving behind four teen-aged sons.

December 19, 1943

In the Via Veneto, Italian journalist and explosives expert Lieutenant **Maria Teresa Regard (January 16, 1924–February 21, 2000)** and her Roman colleague, Captain **Lucia Ottobrini (October 2, 1924–September 26, 2015),** a supplier of food, clothing, and medicine to prisoners, exploded a bomb on December 19, 1943, at the Barberini theater and Flora Hotel. Lucia escaped questioning for killing eight Germans and continued on foot from Rome to Tivoli to defend a hydroelectric plant and destroy a military truck. On December 26, 1943, she succeeded in detonating another device that struck twenty-eight guards at the Regina Coeli Prison in Trastevere across the Tiber River.

Maria's placement of a bomb at Termini station on January 24, 1944, killed three Nazi officers and resulted in her arrest, questioning at Via Tasso, and release. Another of Lucia's sabotage in Piazza Monte d'Oro struck a fascist parade on March 10, 1944. A more destructive ignition of dynamite in a garbage cart overwhelmed a police regiment, killing thirty-three and leaving one hundred ten casualties. Maria and Lucia continued supporting partisans until June 1944. Maria's writing for the *Nuovo Corriere* (New Courier) took her to London, Tibet, China, and Hanoi with communist forces to Điện Biên Phủ, Vietnam. Lucia and Maria received silver medals of military valor.

1944

Child neuropsychiatrist **Marcella Balconi (February 8, 1919–February 5, 1999)** of Romagnano Sesia in the Italian alps served the armed members of the Garibaldi Brigade as medic and archivist. In the military style of partisans during the Spanish Civil War, in 1944, the volunteers carried out sabotage and assassination of Nazis. At Valtellina and Turin, Italy, on the Swiss border, she amassed photos, interviews, and other evidence of atrocities to the Piemontese, such as blinding and shooting of **Irma Bandiera (1915–August 14, 1944)**, a partisan fighter and weapons courier from Bologna to headquarters at Castel Maggiore. The SS captured Irma in combat. Nazis used her corpse as a warning to resisters. The First Garibaldi Brigade adopted Marcella's name as a salute to her valor. She received a posthumous Gold Medal of Military Valor and a portrait mural.

January 3, 1944

After a failed parachute drop the previous month, nineteen-year-old Swiss courier **Anne-Marie Walters (March 16, 1934–October 3, 1998)** of Geneva entered France to convey explosives by bicycle, bus, car, and train. Throughout combat on June 21, she passed grenades to volunteers. On return to England through Algiers in August 1944, she received a Reconnaissance Medal, Croix de Guerre, and Order of the British Empire. Her memoir, *Moondrop to Gascony,* described her military daring.

January 15, 1944

After Nazi Germany began Operation Weserubung to invade and occupy Denmark on April 9, 1940, resistance movement leader **Alma Allen (fl. 1940s)** led men and women on a dozen missions to rescue Jews from arrest by the Gestapo. A fellow patriot, **Monica Wichfeld (July 12, 1894–February 27, 1945)**, distributor of the Danish Communist Party newspaper *Free Denmark,* aided Jews hunted by the Gestapo. She supported the May 1945 bombing of the Nakskov shipyard in southern Denmark and the sinking of the MS *Java* and *Falastria.* Monica's arrest on January 15, 1944, preceded imprisonment and questioning. A death sentence required transfer to Cotbuss prisoner of war camp in Waldheim, Germany, where she died at age fifty of tuberculosis and pneumonia.

March 1, 1944

A pair of Soviet sharpshooters, **Klavdiya Kalugina (1926–?)** and **Marisa Chikhvintseva (1946–May 1944)** from Mogilev trained together to fight Axis forces at the Belorussian Front. After Klavdiya left a munitions factory job east of Moscow and entered the communist youth union, the teenagers honed their riflery at the Komsomol sniper academy under squad leader **Zinaida Andreevna Urantseva (fl. 1940s)** taught a dozen beginners. In the snowy field near Orsha at the confluence of the Arshytsa and Dnieper rivers, on March 1, 1944, they trained their eyes through PU telescopic sights of their bayonet-mounted, five-shot Mosin-Nagant rifles as distant as 1,200 meters (3,937 feet). For close combat, they clipped two grenades to their belts. Their kit included ammunition, a mess tin, first aid kit, and entrenching spade—too cumbrous for claiming trophies from the fascists.

The duo remained under cover for a day to conceal their positions and succeeded at obliterating machine gun nests and German couriers, snipers, and officers, who fled to the Dnieper River. Although wearing green overalls camouflaged from the enemy, in Poland, the female gunners crawled to no man's land, where fellow shooter

Zina Gavrilova (fl. 1940s) shot a German washing in a lake. During heavy bombing of Koenigsberg, Prussia (modern Kaliningrad, Russia), Marisa died in the last year of World War II when a glint from her lens disclosed her hiding place to a German sniper. Fellow sniper **Nadia Lugina (fl. 1940s)** was wounded at Vitebsk-Orsha, Belarus; **Klava Monakhova (1926-1944)** was killed in a trench. Klavdiya assisted the female unit in recovering the wounded before crawling to the swampy Leningrad Front, an Allied blockade, and reached the Baltic Sea. Among the twenty-five percent who survived the war, she achieved two hundred fifty-seven kills.

March 23, 1944

Under mortar barrage launched by Roman journalist **Marisa Musu (April 18, 1924-November 3, 2002)**, saboteur **Carla Capponi** planned an ambush in Rome on March 23, 1944, against the SS headquarters on the Via Rasella near Trevi Fountain. **Lucia Ottobrini** loaded a garbage cart with dynamite that killed thirty-two police officers and injured one hundred ten. Nazis retaliated by executing ten partisans for each assassinated officer. Carla received the Gold Medal of Military Valor and issued an ambiguous moral treatise, *Con Cuore di Donna* (With a Woman's Heart).

April 1944

French feminist **Éliane Brault (September 18, 1895-August 25, 1982)** carried rescue and rehabilitation to the front lines of World War II. She survived a Marseilled prison in January 1941 by escaping to Casablanca, Morocco. A captain of Free French Forces, in April 1944, she accompanied the French army on the Italian campaign, which broke through at Monte Cassino in May. She supplied medical aid to battlefield casualties and liberated civilians in Sicily. On August 15, 1944, she abetted the Allies in Operation Dragoon, an invasion of Provence at the Côte d'Azur. By November 20, 1944, she embroiled herself in the battle of Alsace in eastern France. She earned an Escapees' Medal and regard for seven reflective treatises on wartime work.

April 5, 1944

Widowed Parisian artillery specialist and paratrooper **Violette Szabo (June 26, 1921-February 5, 1945)** left her infant daughter in France to parachute into Cherbourg on April 5, 1945, to assess war damage to the Salesman circuit. She returned to England under heavy fire and accepted a new assignment to train Normandy volunteers in explosives and sabotage. On June 10, she engaged Germans in gunfire with her Sten gun at a Panzer regiment roadblock. At Fresnes prison in Paris, days of questioning under torture, hard labor, and meals of bread crusts preceded transfer in October to Ravensbrück Women's prison in East Prussia and execution by a bullet to the neck.

Violette died alongside Parisian telegraphers **Denise Bloch (January 21, 1916-February 5, 1945)**, a Jew to whom she was chained, and **Liliane Rolfe (April 26, 1914-February 5, 1945)**; and London-born saboteur **Cecily Gordon Lefort (April 30, 1899-February 5, 1945)**. All four were cremated.

A posthumous Croix de Guerre, Resistance Medal, and George Cross, the book *Young Brave and Beautiful: The Missions of Special Operations Executive Agent Lieutenant Violette Szabo*, and the film *Carve Her Name with Pride* rewarded Violette Szabo's courage. At the Hamburg trials, fellow operative and medic **Violette Lecoq** presented detailed sketches of Nazi murders of resistance agents. For her pursuit of justice, she won a Croix de Guerre.

See also 1938.

April 11, 1944

London-born paratrooper **Odette Sar Wilen (April 25, 1919–September 22, 2015)** of Franco-Czech lineage dropped into occupied France on April 11, 1944, at a tense time in World War II. Preceding D-Day, she set up wireless communication at Auvergne. She conspired with her lover to disrupt rail lines to Tours and destroyed German headquarters at a chateau. She extended missions as a courier in Paris. On the approach of the Gestapo, she fled by bicycle and, in August 1944, trudged over a Pyrenees escape route to Spain and Gibraltar. For perilous missions, she earned a Parachutist Badge.

April 15, 1944

Rebel, courier, and assassin **Teresa Mattei (February 1, 1921–March 12, 2013)** of Genoa, Italy, gained renown for abetting the murder of Sicilian fascist doctrinarian Giovanni Gentile. She joined Gruppi d'Azione Patriottica (Group for Patriotic Action, GAP) and commanded a cell named for her brother, Gianfranco Mattei, who hanged himself in a Roman SS prison. Because Gentile espoused Friedrich Nietzsche's *Ubermensch* (superman) theory while teaching philosophy in Milan and formulated the *Manifesto of the Fascist Intellectuals*, the communist cabal targeted him. The assassins shot him in Florence, where he was interred at the church of Santa Croce. Teresa received a knighthood of the Gran Croce Ordine al Merito (Great Cross Order of Merit).

May 1944

A Breton courier and supplier of the French Resistance before the liberation of Paris, **Cécile Rol-Tanguy (April 10, 1919–May 8, 2020)** from Royan conspired with her husband, Henri Rol-Tanguy, in May 1944 to relay work schedules, weapons, and grenades in her children's strollers. At an underground location at Place Denfert-Rochereau, she worked under the code names "Lucie," "Jeanne," and "Yvette" despite pregnancies in 1939, 1940, and 1943 and the death of their first child. The couple issued an urban mobilization against the Nazis on August 19, 1944. Six days later, French general Philippe Leclerc led the 2nd Armored Division into Paris. Cécile gained the Resistance Medal, a Legion of Honor, and an invitation to meet General Charles de Gaulle.

May 28, 1944

Nine days before D-Day, English Royal Air Force member and courier **Sonya Butt (May 14, 1924–December 21, 2014)** from Kent trained guerrillas in weaponry. For the Headmaster circuit, she allotted cash, conveyed messages, and aided the destruction of supply depots, rail lines, and telephone exchanges at Le Mans in northwestern France. Resisters mistook her for a Nazi collaborator and beat her severely until her rescue by guerrillas. On the liberation of Normandy, she returned to England, married war hero Guy d'Artois, and migrated to Montreal, Canada.

May 28, 1944

Ecuadorian anti-imperialist and freedom fighter **Nela Martínez Espinosa (November 24, 1912–July 30, 2004)** of Canar promoted the Glorious May Revolution of May 28, 1944, to import free elections, inclusion of Indians, and democracy. To remove Carlos Arroyo del Rio from the dictatorship, she conspired to seize the Government Palace and depose the loser of the Ecuadorian-Peruvian War. She ran the government for two days until the withdrawal of Peruvian troops. A supporter of freedom fighter Fidel Castro, she advocated the five-and-a-half year Cuban Revolution on July 26, 1953. Until her death at age fifty-two, she backed communism in Cuba.

June 1944

Danish journalist and courier **Hedda Lundh (September 29, 1921–March 2, 2012)** of Korsør, a student at Aarhus University, collaborated with saboteur **Else Marie Pade (December 2, 1924–January 18, 2016)** of Aarhus. The two volunteered for the resistance and mastered telephone networking and explosives. They ferried arms and dynamite from British drop points to rail depots and telephone cables. Betrayal in June 1944 brought incarceration for Else by the Gestapo at Frøslevlejren outside Padborg, Denmark; Hedda escaped to Sweden.

June 1, 1944

Slowing the German advance on Normandy from Beauvais in anticipation of an Allied landing on D-Day, Commander **Elaine Mordeaux (ca. 1915–June 1, 1944)**, a trilingual French Resistance sharpshooter, led an attack by two hundred male and female guerrillas on Hitler's 101st SS Heavy Panzer Battalion. Her combat experience proved useful to spies for the Office of Strategic Services (OSS) and the French underground. The assault on June 1, 1944, continued for less than an hour and yielded three hundred German casualties and the sidelining of fifty trucks and three dozen Tiger I tanks. From a cliff, she hurled dynamite onto the road, making it impassable. After her sten gun ran out of bullets, she scavenged ammunition from the dead. She continued tossing explosives until a German sniper killed her.

June 8, 1944

Albanian nurse and freedom fighter **Sofia Noti (1942–July 1944)** from Erind died a martyr to communism. A soldier in the Albanian Liberation Army, she served as battalion medic. When Nazi troops swept the southeast for partisans on June 8, 1944, the one hundred resisters incurred casualties. A bullet to the left thigh dazed Sofia, leaving her vulnerable to torture and the forced digging of a common grave. She riposted by leading prisoners in a round of "The Internationale," the communist anthem. Deported with five Albanian girls through Florina to Thessaloniki, Greece, on June 23, a week later, she placed the executioner's noose around her neck before her fall.

July 5, 1944

A legendary Russian medic and sniper, Corporal **Tatyana Baramzina (December 19, 1919–July 5, 1944)** from Glazov died in Belarus on July 5, 1944, from torture, stabbing, mutilation, and shooting by Nazi soldiers. A first combat experience on April 1944 placed her as a sharpshooter with the 252nd Rifle Regiment. The next month, she led a counterattack against advancing Germans. While repairing telephone lines at the front, she volunteered to blockade a road in Pekalin, Belarus, and chose to defend casualties by machine gun fire and grenades rather than hide from the enemy. For aiding the Red Army in surrounding the enemy, she earned a Hero of the Soviet Union citation, a biographical diorama, and the naming of streets.

July 23, 1944

A bold Allied agent and assassin, **Madeleine Riffaud (August 23, 1924–)** from Arvillers, France, gained renown for the daytime shooting of an SS officer on the Solferino Bridge over the Seine River. The previous year, she enabled the capture of eighty German troops aboard a Nazi supply train and tossed grenades at the enemy on the Place de la Republique in Paris. Her arrest, solitary confinement, and torture by water boarding and electric shock in Paris at Fresnes Prison preceded a Swedish prisoner exchange that saved her from execution.

Madeleine rejoiced during the celebration of the liberation of Paris on August 25, 1944, and De Gaulle's victory parade. Following newspaper reporting to *Ce Soir* (This Evening), she covered the Algerian War in the early 1960s and accompanied the Viet Cong for seven years to report efforts to free Vietnam from French colonialism. She recorded wartime scrapes in the autobiography *On L'appelait Rainer* (She Was Called Rainer). For her sixteen published works, she earned awards from Vietnam and France.

August 1944

Armed with an Enfield rifle, **Maria Svobod (fl. 1940s)**, a Hungarian freedom fighter on the Slovakian border, replaced her fallen husband in guerrilla warfare. At the death of Janos Halasi five months after Germany occupied Hungary on March 19, 1944, she led his resistance cell in the northern Carpathian Mountains in August 1944 against fascist Hungarians. Pro-allied strategy of resistance members and Zionist Jews fought daily transports of undesirables from Ruthenia in Belarus and Ukraine to the death camp at Auschwitz-Birkenau, Poland. Liberators, including **Ilona Kolonits (March 17, 1922–August 2, 2002)** of Budapest, trained in Palestine for aiding the resistance. Members dressed in German or Hungarian uniforms to rescue children and hide refugees from the anti-semitic Arrow Cross gangs. Daring interventions earned her state awards and a Righteous among the Nations designation.

Additional help from British paratroopers and the alliance with Russia on the Eastern Front in October 1944 enabled the defiers of Nazism to weaken German genocide. One of the parachutists into Yugoslavia, **Hannah Szenes (also Hannah Senesh, July 17, 1921–November 7, 1944)** of Budapest, Hungary's capital, immigrated to a kibbutz in 1939 and joined Palmach (Strike Force), an underground Israeli paramilitary. After agreeing to spy for the British, she trained in Egypt for secret deployment by air. To halt the deportation of Jews to the death camp at Auschwitz, she crept into Hungary. After her arrest, she endured days of prison whippings and bludgeoning, but refused to reveal secret codes. She signaled other resisters with a mirror and cut out Hebrew words to mount in windows. She died by firing squad on November 7, 1944. Her stoicism survives in a Budapest memorial, biography, drama, documentary, musical, and cinema.

August 10, 1944

An anti-fascist from age sixteen, **Sara Ginaite-Rubinson (March 17, 1924–April 2, 2018)** advanced the liberation of Vilnius and her hometown, Kaunas, Lithuania, on August 10, 1944. After the German invasion on June 22, 1941, she lost three uncles to a Nazi pogrom that slew ninety-two hundred people, half of them children. The Nazis jailed her, her sister and niece, and the rest of her family in Vilijampole at Lithuania's Kovno Ghetto, which grew to twenty-nine thousand inmates by August 1941. Within two months, German guards shot nearly all Jews. After her escape in winter 1943, she formed a fighting unit to mobilize ghetto survivors and, disguised as a nurse, returned to guide Jews to the Rudninkai Forest. At war's end, she composed *Resistance and Survival: The Jewish Community in Kaunas*.

August 23, 1944

A teen "free-shooter" of the French Resistance, Lieutenant **Simone Segouin (October 3, 1925–)** from Thivars near Chartres volunteered at the liberation of the cathedral city to carry messages and sabotage transportation and communication lines. She learned fighting tactics from three brothers and her father, a stout-hearted soldier in World War I. Armed with a German MP 40 submachine gun, she operated under the name "Nicole Minet" by bicycle stolen from a German. Her underground involvement included killing two Nazis in Paris, derailing trains, exploding supply lines and bridges, and serving as a security guard for General Charles de Gaulle. At age eighteen, she helped to arrest twenty-five prisoners of war. At the freeing of Paris on August 23, 1944, she engaged in the battle alongside the 2nd Armored Division. For acts of courage and patriotism, she earned a Croix de Guerre. *Life* magazine honored her on September 4, 1944, as "The Girl Partisan of Chartres."

August 25, 1944

Ukrainian war hero **Vera Belik (June 12, 1921–August 25, 1944)** of Ohrimovka died over Poland on August 24, 1944, after a bomb run when German Luftwaffe shot down her Polikarpov Po-2 plane. A member of the legendary

588th Night Bomber Regiment, she dug anti-tank traps before navigating for Russian Federation pilot **Tatyana Makarova (September 225, 1920–August 25–1944)**, a squadron commander from Moscow. The pair initiated bombardment of sites in East Prussia. Their missions to destroy ferries, ammunition dumps, searchlights, enemy platoons, and anti-aircraft guns continued in the Caucasus, Crimea, Ukraine, Poland, and Byelorussia. Both fliers died in burning wreckage. The recipients of Lenin medals and Hero of the Soviet Union citations survive in street and school names, monuments, sculpture, and a museum.

September 1944

Armed Dutch courier and rescuer **Riet van Grunsven (September 6, 1918–March 1, 2004)** carried out a jailbreak at Mariënhof Prison in September 1944 in Munich, Germany, to free two inmates condemned for dismantling a rail line. Disguised in a nursing uniform, she drugged a guard with doctored wine and fled with the inmates to a refugee drop at Taalstraat in Vught, Holland. From twenty-one deadly missions smuggling insulin and other medicines across the Biesbosch tidal wetlands in boats and canoes throughout winter 1944–1945, she suffered broken fingers and partial spinal paralysis. Borne on a stretcher, she received the Bronze Lion and a personal commendation from Queen Wilhelmina.

See also September 1, 1939.

September 1944

Civil engineer **Elena Haas (1913–early 1945)** aided the Czechoslovakia resistance as saboteur and guide. Armed with at Sten gun, she joined liberators after the Nazi invasion of March 15, 1938. In league with British and French agents in Germany, she contributed technical knowledge of structures and explosives in September 1944 by demolishing an Ohne River bridge at its confluence with the Elbe River. In destroying fascist munitions and supplies, she killed thirty-five Nazis. In early 1945, while directing partisans across an airfield past Luftwaffe jets at Melnik, Bohemia, on the Vltava River, she died of enemy gunfire.

September 8, 1944

A Greek rebel against Axis invaders, **Lela Karagianni (1898–September 8, 1944)** of Limni, Euboea, broadened her involvement in World War II from underground supplier and guide to smuggler, forger, and spy for the British. After the German and Italian insurgency at Athens of April 1941, she named her cell of resisters "Bouboulina" for her great grandmother, **Laskarina Bouboulina**, an admiral, rescuer, and hero during the 1821 Greek War of Independence. Lela, too, distributed food, shoes, and clothing. She hid British soldiers at a Megara monastery and saved Jews by sheltering them at her safe house.

In April 1944, Lela rescued the Solomon and Regina Cohen family and their twelve-year-old daughter Shelly, refugees from Thessaloniki. She transported them out of occupied Athens to Mount Paiku on the Bulgarian border to spare them the fate of fifty-nine thousand Greek Jews murdered by Nazis. After her arrest with her three daughters and four sons in July 1944, the SS tortured Lela in Athens for three days at the Merlin Street prison. From her cell, she continued directing partisan resistance against the Nazis until her execution by firing squad on September 8, 1944. The Allies expelled Axis forces a month later. Her example survives in a bronze sculpture, documentary, books, Athens street name, the Virtue and Self-Sacrifice Award, and listing as Righteous Among Nations.

See also April 4, 1821.

September 17, 1944

At the nine-day siege of Arnhem, Holland, **Audrey Hepburn (May 4, 1929–January 20, 1993)** from Ixelles, Belgium, began aiding the Dutch underground as a courier and rescuer. Despite being reared by Hitler apologist parents, she reacted at age thirteen to the SS murder of her uncle, Judge Otto van Limburg Stirum, and the forced labor of brother Ian van Ufford in a German camp. She made herself useful to the Dutch resistance by speaking English and Dutch, raising money by dancing in ballets, and assisting a physician. She distributed messages and rations to allied fliers and concealed a British paratrooper in the cellar. During an air raid, she hid under a tank.

Famine in winter 1944 forced Audrey's family to live on tulip bulbs. Still eager for humanitarian assignments, she allied with UNICEF as goodwill ambassador and dispenser of food and vaccines. Missions took her to dangerous territory in Honduras, Sudan, Ethiopia, Bangladesh, El Salvador, Somalia, Ecuador, Venezuela, Turkey, and Guatemala. She earned the 1989 Danny Kay Award for her charitable endeavors. Plagued by the anemia, breathing problems, and the malnutrition of girlhood, she died in Vaud, Switzerland, at age sixty-three of peritoneal cancer.

October 6, 1944

Albanian resistance agent **Liri Gero (1926–October 6, 1944)** operated with a guerrilla faction at age seventeen, but survived only one year of anti-fascist activism. During a firefight against German troops on October 6, 1944, she collapsed from pain and blood loss. Nazi soldiers tied her to a tree, soaked her in gasoline, and set her aflame. A posthumous People's Hero award acknowledges her heroism.

October 7, 1944

A Jewish conspirator and supplier of the Auschwitz underground, **Regina Safirsztajn (1915–January 5, 1945)** of Będzin in east central Poland fought Nazis on October 7, 1944, by smuggling gunpowder into the Auschwitz death camp. After her deportation in August 1943, she worked at the Weichsel-Union-Metallwerke (metal factory) making munitions until the Sonderkommando (labor unit) revolt, led by **Roza Robota (1921–January 6, 1945)** of Ciechanow in north central Poland. The plotters made incendiary bombs, a mine, and grenades from shoe polish tins and packed them with braided cotton wicks and black powder stolen at the rate of one to three teaspoons per day.

Group action involved Polish conspirator **Ala Gertner (March 12,**

1912–January 5, 1945), Czech inmate **Marta Bindiger Cigi (fl. 1940s)**, **Rose Grunapfel Meth (November 10, 1920–October 12, 2013)** of Zator, Poland, German rape victim **Inge Weidenau Frank (January 23, 1922–1944)**, and Czech analyst **Genia Fischer (1931–?)** of Kolin. The collaborators sought to obstruct the murder of one thousand Jews per day from as far away as Corfu and Rhodes. The enslaved laborers concealed the powder in knotted kerchiefs and bras or in food trays or garbage and murdered a Kapo to keep him from reporting their plan. Polish sisters **Ester Wajcblum (January 16, 1924–January 5, 1945)** and teen sibling **Anna Wajcblum Heilman (December 1, 1928–May 1, 2011)** of Warsaw gathered axes, knives, wire cutters, rope, hammers, and guns to arm rebels.

The coterie exploded Crematory IV at Birkenau, disarmed the SS, cut barbed wire, slew seventy guards, and threw an oven sentry alive into the furnace fire. Dashing into the woods, the Jewish resistance lost four hundred fifty rebels in combat with the SS. The women condemned themselves to weeks of interrogation and torture. The four leaders—Ala, Ester, Regina, and Roza—faced martyrdom on the gallows on January 5, 1945, thirteen days before Soviet troops liberated the camp. Before the inmates' death, they shouted God's scriptural encouragement to Joshua, "Be strong and of a good courage" (Joshua 1:9). A monument to the Holocaust rebels survives in Jerusalem at the Yad Vashem Holocaust Museum. A song, "Rose Meth, the Unsung Heroine," applied a march rhythm to the lurid preparations for execution. The books *They Fought Back* and *Fighting Auschwitz,* film *Unlikely Heroes,* and the Anna's memoir *Never Far Away: The Auschwitz Chronicles of Anna Heilman* disproved charges that Jews were passive and compliant in the extermination of seven hundred thousand Auschwitz inmates.

October 15, 1944

Like other wartime medical personnel, Parisian warrior **Collette Nirouet (1926–November 12, 1944)** entered the French First Army as a nurse, but died as a soldier. Wearing the uniform of the U.S. Women's Army Corps, at age eighteen, she advanced to nurse in central France at Auvergne and to machine-gunner in eastern France at Oberwald with the 152nd Infantry Regiment. During the battle of Alsace, she died of wounds on October 14, 1944, while ordering a German unit to surrender. A posthumous Croix de Guerre commemorated her heroism.

October 31, 1944

The first female recruit in the Royal Netherlands Navy, **Francien de Zeeuw (May 19, 1922–September 8, 2015)** served as telephone operator, spy, courier, and armed raider. After petitioning Queen Wilhelmina to accept female sailors, on October 31, 1944, Francien signed on with the Marine Vrouwenafdeling (Navy Women's Section or Marva) as the first woman in the armed forces. She eluded captors by penetrating front lines and fighting alongside Canadian troops. In 2020, admirers of her courage proposed naming a frigate after her.

November 1944

An orthodox Jewish spy, **Marthe Hoffnung Cohn (April 13, 1920–)** of Metz, France, reported crucial data on German activity in Alsace-Lorraine. While posing as a German nurse, under the alias "Marthe Ulrich," in November 1944, she crawled through the boundary wire between Germany and Schaffhausen, Switzerland, to conduct surveillance. Over a three-week mission by bike, she learned that stepped-up Allied bombing had forced evacuation of the Siegfried Line and that the Black Forest in southwestern Germany was unsafe for Allies because of plans for a counterattack by the retreating enemy. Her courage earned a military medal, Woman of Valor, French Legion of Honor, reconnaissance citation, and Croix de Guerre. She presented war memories in cinema and a biography, *Behind Enemy Lines: The True Story of a French Jewish Spy*.

November 1944

With illicit photos of Dutch misery under the Nazis, **Ingeborg Wallheimer Kahlenberg (March 27, 1920–October 2, 1996)**, a Jew from Bremen, Germany, requested Red Cross intervention to end slave labor, starvation, and disease. Trained at hiding cameras in handbags and coats and smuggling pictures out of Holland introduced her to a communications post for the Dutch resistance. In addition to documenting famine and German atrocities for viewing in the outside world, she ferried secret documents, forged papers, and weapons to the Allies. Her photos appeared at New York's Jewish Museum.

1945

A teenage Thai nun, **Lumchuan (1928–1985)** fled the Buddhist temple where she grew up to live as a male sailor. By enrolling in the merchant marine in 1945 and answering to the name "Lek," she discovered the seamy harbor life and incurred rowdiness in Filipino and Danish saloons. She passed as a crewman for seven years until a woman visiting on board recognized a nubile female figure. Lumchuan lost her career and respect for the captain, for whom she had been a reliable sailor.

January 20, 1945

An amoral Swedish newspaperwoman-courier and sexual adventurer, **Jane Horney (July 8, 1918–January 20, 1945)** conducted missions in Denmark for Nazi military intelligence. Her undercover work in January 1944 aided a Soviet operative. She continued spying under the code name "Eskima" by seducing other agents. In September 1944, she came under suspicion of Swedish police. She escaped an assassin code-named "Flame" by taking a train to Malmo, Sweden, and traveling on the fishing trawler *Tarnan* (Tern) from Helsingborg to the southwest. The next morning, January 20, 1945, at Oresund, the unidentified agent shot her, wrapped the corpse in chains, and dumped her in the sea. A confused investigation of her wartime loyalties linked them alternately with the British, Soviet Union, Swedish, and Gestapo. Rumors declared the murder a hoax to give her an exit to England to spy for the British.

January 29, 1945

A Russian Federation pilot for the 588th "Night Witches," **Zoya Parfyonova (June 21, 1920–April 7, 1993)** from Alatyr survived a bleeding wound while making an emergency landing. On a mission on January 29, 1945, to drop ammunition and supplies to Soviet infantry in eastern Prussia, she incurred shelling and a hip wound from shrapnel piercing her Polikarpov Po-2, a flimsy monoplane made of plywood and canvas. In snowy weather and zero visibility, she landed before slipping into unconsciousness from blood loss. On awakening, she reported Nazi anti-aircraft sites. A month later, she continued bombing Nazi infantry, warehouses, and artillery batteries. Among seven honoraria, she received a Hero of the Soviet Union and orders of Lenin and the Red Star and Red Banner.

April 16, 1945

A Russian Federation hero of the two-week battle of Berlin, **Rufina Gasheva (October 14, 1921–May 1, 2012)**, a lieutenant colonel from Permsky, survived bomb runs of the "Night Witches" preceding Adolf Hitler's suicide on April 30, 1945. She navigated eight hundred forty-eight campaigns in a Polikarpov Po-2 light plane built of canvas and plywood. She outlived her partner, Tatar captain **Olga Sanifirova (May 2, 1917–December 13, 1944)** of Samara in the Russian Empire. The pair flew campaigns in the Caucasus, Crimea, and Byelorussia. In their second incident against the Luftwaffe on December 13, 1944, they parachuted from a downed plane. Olga landed on a mine and died at the scene. Their missions replenished infantry with ammunition and rations and destroyed two Nazi platoons, turrets, ferries, and a warehouse. They each achieved a Lenin citation and Hero of the Soviet Union.

April 29, 1945

A Luftwaffe test pilot of the V-1 missile (flying bomb), **Hanna Reitsch (March 29, 1912–August 24, 1979)**, a loyal endorser of the Third Reich from Hirschberg, Silesia, piloted the last Nazi flight out of Berlin before the capitulation ending World War II. In 1943, she incurred serious wounds from crashing a Messerschmitt rocket plane. For expertise to Hitler's flying force, she received the Iron Cross. As Soviets of the 3rd Shock Army slogged their way to the Tiergarden Park, she improvised a flight path for her Arado monoplane. At her capture in American-held territory in October 1945, she served eighteen months in an Austrian prison at Salzburg.

May 1945

A Norwegian war widow, **Kitty Margarete Grande (March 22, 1919–January 26, 1999)** from Trondheim collaborated with the German Gestapo. A member of a coterie of fifty informants, she worked out of the Trondheim headquarters to provide surveillance to the SS. On December 11, 1944, at Alesund, resistance liquidators shot her husband Ivar Grande, a fellow Gestapo collaborator. Following the German surrender in May 1945, trials of Nazi sympathizers convicted forty-one Scandinavians of treason. Spared the firing squad in June

1945, Kitty faced twenty years imprisonment at hard labor in Bredtveit women's prison in Oslo, Norway. On May 26, 1951, she gained release.

May 3, 1945

Peruvian children's author and forger **Madeleine Truel (August 28, 1904–May 3, 1945)** of Lima died a martyr of the French Resistance. To fight fascism, she translated documents and falsified passports in Paris to aid Allied paratroopers and Jewish refugees. In January 1942, a collision with a Nazi military truck fractured her legs and skull, causing a permanent limp. Gestapo torture at Fresnes Prison in Paris after her June 19, 1944, arrest yielded no information. To hearten fellow captives, she told stories and shared food, earning for herself the nickname "Bird of the Isles." After transport to Sachsenhausen death camp in Germany, she died of head injuries on May 3, 1945, at Stolpe in suburban Berlin, while on a thirty-eight-day death march. Nazi surrender was by then mere hours away. In a 2012 film documentary, Silvana Anduaga played Madeleine's part.

December 21, 1945

On the fifth day of the siege of Bastogne, the high point of the battle of the Bulge, the bloodiest U.S. battle of World War II, five-foot nurse **Augusta Maria Chiwy (June 6, 1921–August 23, 2015)** of the Belgian Congo (modern Burundi), dressed in an army uniform and volunteered to retrieve the wounded. Under mortar and machine gun fire in two feet of snow, on December 21, 1945, she searched the battle front for casualties even though black medics were banned from treating white soldiers. A bomb from an air raid in the Ardennes Forest on Christmas Eve blew her through a wall at an army aid station of the U.S. 20th Armored Infantry and killed Belgian volunteer **Renée Lemaire (April 10, 1914–December 24, 1944)** from Bastogne while she evacuated six soldiers from flames.

When the battle of Bastogne ended the day after Christmas, Augusta boosted morale by treating hospitalized men suffering spinal injuries, her specialty. The documentary *Searching for Augusta: The Forgotten Angel of Bastogne* won an Emmy. Albert II of Belgium awarded her the Order of the Crown. The U.S. Army gave her an honorarium for humanitarianism and selflessness.

December 19, 1946

English ambulance driver General **Susan Travers (September 23, 1909–December 18, 2003)** from Kensington was the only female French Legionary to fight in the First Indochina War. The daughter of an admiral, in 1940, she served in Finland in sub-zero weather against the Russians and in Dakar, Senegal, and Brazzaville, Congo, as Croix Rouge (French Red Cross) medic and ambulance driver. On June 25, 1940, she bolstered the Free French by participating in the invasion of Transjordan (modern Lebanon) and Syria. At Gazala and in a dugout at the desert buttress Bir Hakeim, Libya, in May 1942, she and four thousand male comrades survived one hundred twenty degree heat and minefields, shells from Stuka dive bombers, Panzer tanks, shrapnel, and machine guns.

During the Axis thrust into North Africa, at top speed, Susan led the column toward the Allied front in a midnight flight from Erwin Rommel's Afrika Korps. Nicknamed "La Miss," she drove a gas engine anti-tank gun in Italy, Germany, and France and incurred a wound from a land mine on the Western Front. In the French Foreign Legion on December 19, 1946, she fought the Viet Minh in Haiphong, Indochina (modern Vietnam) by driving a heavy van for which she changed flat tires. She entitled a memoir *Tomorrow to Be Brave*. In addition to promotion to general, her seven medals include a Croix de Guerre and Legion of Honor.

Late 1947

West Nigerian tax resister **Funmilayo Ransome-Kuti (October 25, 1900–April 13, 1978)** led female Yoruba speakers in protests of King Oba Ademola II and his anti-woman's business policies. Inequitable laws allowed Egbaland magistrates to tax female vendors and seize rice from their market stall forced twenty-thousand victims to unionize in 1944. Late in 1947 at Abeokuta, thirty years after a gendered poll tax and levy on baskets of cassava, she allied with shopkeeper **Grace Eniola Soyinka (1908–1983)** in holding tax moratoriums, processions, and vigils outside Ademola's palace. Into the ten thousand rebels, police fired tear gas and arrested demonstrators for jailing in the Nigerian correction center at Ile-Ife.

For Funmiliayo's bold defiance, the *West African Pilot* dubbed her "Lioness of Lisabi." A palace blockage in February 1948 caused her to seize an official's steering wheel and refuse to give in. Ademola ceded to the female union in April 1948 and abdicated his throne. On February 18, 1977, Nigerian police retaliated against Funmilayo by tossing her out a window, causing lethal injuries. Police claimed that the assassins were unknown. Her death two months later on April 13, 1978, caused female vendors to close their stores to honor her passing.

February 11, 1948

Israeli author, sapper, and saboteur **Netiva Ben Yehuda (July 26, 1928–February 28, 2011)** of Tel Aviv began learning military dynamics for Palmach, the strike force of Haganah, a Zionist paramilitary. By mastering explosives, demolition, scouting, and cartography, she prepared to guard desert convoys and transport ammunition for assaulting bridges, urban structures, and rail lines. At Galilee, she advanced to the only female platoon leader of the underground, a deployment she detailed in *Between the Spheres*.

By February 11, 1948, Netiva was prepared for setting a mine at Kiryat Shmona, Israel, to destroy a bus from Safad, Galilee, filled with Palestinian Arabs. The London *Times* declared the explosion an act of terrorism for killing five civilians and injuring five. When Egypt, Iraq, Syria, and Transjordan invaded her homeland on May 15, 1948, she suffered a bullet to the arm that ended her Olympic-level discus throwing. After Israel achieved statehood on

May 14, 1948, the Israeli Defense Force ended the Arab-Israeli War with conquest of Nazareth in July 1948, an assault on Galilean farmland, a massacre of Palestinian Arabs, and the exodus of seven hundred thousand Muslims. She earned Jerusalem's award for worthy citizenship.

October 7, 1950

Ani Pachen (1933–February 2, 2002), a colonial Buddhist nun/chieftain and guerrilla warrior from Gonjo, Eastern Tibet, summarized Chinese barbarity toward Tibetan outlaws in a book, *Sorrow Mountain: The Journey of a Tibetan Warrior Nun*. In a violent anti–Buddhist era, on October 7, 1950, she conducted surveillance on the Chinese crossing of the Jinsha River to invade Kham, murder Tibetans, and dissolve monasteries. To fend off Chinese annexation, at age eighteen, she began shooting firearms supplied by India, riding a warhorse, and fighting alongside Khampas, the residents of eastern Kham.

As the sole female chief of the Lemdha clan, on horseback and poorly armed with antique rifles, Ani Pachen led six hundred guerrilla warriors west to a union with two clans assembled at Lhasa. She slept under sheepskin and avoided scenes of vultures pecking body parts. With CIA special ops, she combatted the Sino-Tibetan invasion by forty thousand fighters in the People's Liberation Army and its threat to Buddhism via slaying monks, bombing monasteries, and burning libraries of sacred texts. Her plots involved waylaying convoys and camps and impeding Chinese road building. Aid arrived for the Khampas from an American parachute drop of food, clothes, cash, grenades, rifles, pistols, and radios.

After the battle of Chamdo, Tibet, at the Jinsha River on October 7, 1950, China annexed the country and massacred four hundred fifty-six thousand citizens. The threat from Chinese Communist troops forced Ani Pachen to ferry Granny, Mama, and Aunt Rigzin south over snowy twenty-thousand-foot passes in the Himalayan Mountains toward India. To smash the monastic influence, the enemy captured all four women and marched them west in a group of one hundred captives. Along the way, Ani Pachen heard herself cheered as the Tibetan Joan of Arc.

At a Deyong Nang prison, the guerrilla warrior survived scourging, suspension upside down, shoulder dislocation, jailing in sewage, and survival on earthworms. Transfer east to a Chamdo prison on Tibet's eastern border with China inflicted leg shackles and more questioning. In 1963, she entered Silthog Thang, a maximum security prison on the Za Que River, and served nine months in an underground cell. At peaceful demonstrations in September and October 1987 and March 1988, she revived defiance of Chinese invaders. At age fifty-six, she mapped a trail over Mount Kailash to exile in Nepal and resided in India at the nearby Ganden Choeling (Residence of Devotees) Convent. A revered martyr, she died in her sleep on February 2, 2002, in India's far north at Dharamsala at age sixty-eight.

October 30, 1950

Puerto Rican Nationalist and crack shot **Bianca Canales (February 17, 1906–July 25, 1996)** promoted armed protest against U.S. colonialism. Most onerous to disgruntled islanders, a 1948 gag law prohibited publishing or exhibiting anti–U.S. propaganda. In addition to storing armaments at her home, she led the October 30, 1950, Jayuya Uprising in her hometown by swearing an oath to obtain sovereignty and independence or die in the struggle. In the vanguard of the revolt, she drove her car and led twenty men to cut telephone wires. At the Jayuya police headquarters, rebel gunshots wounded three officers and killed a fourth, but Bianca was innocent of the shootings.

From the station's surrender, Bianca marched on to arson at the post office and draft bureau. The raising of the Puerto Rican flag in the town square signified a free republic, which she proclaimed from a hotel balcony. A three-day bombardment by the national guard in U.S. military planes destroyed the town with bombs, machine guns, grenades, mortars, and artillery. A court sentenced Bianca to life plus sixty years for arson, murder, and armed assault in the failed uprising. In 1967, she gained a commutation from the island governor Roberto Sanchez Vilella. History identifies her as the only female to lead a revolt against the United States.

See also October 31, 1950.

October 31, 1950

Puerto Rican nationalist and revolutionary **Rosa Collazo (1904–May 1988)** of Mayaguez conspired with island rebels to assassinate President Harry S. Truman at his temporary residence at Blair House in Washington, D.C. A day after **Bianca Canales** led the Jayuya Uprising, on October 31, 1950, twenty FBI agents killed a collaborator, wounded her husband, Oscar Collazo, seized Rosa at the Harris Hotel in Washington, and charged her with sedition. While Oscar served a death sentence at Leavenworth Federal Prison in Kansas, she spend eight months in a Manhattan women's prison in a cell shared with Manhattan-born Soviet spy **Ethel Rosenberg (September 28, 1915–June 19, 1953)**. On Oscar's behalf, Rosa continued protests of political imprisonments in early 1954 and plotted to attack the U.S. Capitol. Ethel died in the electric chair along with her husband, Julius Rosenberg, at Sing Sing Prison in Ossining, New York.

See also October 30, 1950; March 1, 1954.

1951

Canada's first black female soldier, **Marelene Clyke (1934–)** from Nova Scotia gained a placement in 1951 in the Canadian Women's Army Corps. Her motivation was need—too few jobs for black women who rejected low-paying, low status domestic work. To afford clothes and school books, she entered the army reserves at age seventeen. With training at Camp Aldershot in Annapolis Valley, she found clerical jobs in Halifax. Her ambition to advance her career in the air force met with rejection because of the era's segregation of nonwhite races. In 2017, the Nova Scotia legislature thanked her for inspiring all Canadians.

March 10, 1952

An accomplice of insurrectionist Fidel Castro and instigator of the Cuban Revolution, **Celia Sánchez Manduley (May 9, 1920–January 11, 1980)** of Media Luna on the island's southwestern tip, organized an uprising on March 10, 1952, in Manzanillo. An arms and rations supplier, troop transporter, and warrior, she was the first woman to promote the Sierra Maestra guerrillas. In December 1956, she directed islanders to rescue rebels threatened after a doomed landing party from Mexico reached Cuba. She was the first female to fight at El Uvero on May 28, 1957, when the rebels made a major foray against dictator Fulgencio Batista. Her contributions to island liberation earned commemoration on pesos and institutions and in war histories. For managing the day-to-day necessities of lodging, clothing, and medicine, admirers named her the godmother of the Sierra Maestra campaign.

Early 1954

A covert field networker for the Central Intelligence Agency (CIA) and the first female to manage foreign agents, **Elizabeth Sudmeier (May 12, 1912–April 7, 1989)** from Timber Lake, South Dakota, met a courier from Moscow at a Baghdad cafe in early 1954 to receive blueprints for the Soviet MiG-19 jet fighter, the world's first mass-produced supersonic plane. A veteran of the Women's Army Corps during World War I, from 1947, Elizabeth built a reputation as a Middle East spy recruiter and, in August 1953, a champion of gender equity for female operatives. At age thirty-nine, she left office assignments to enter the field of counterespionage, where she thrived for nine years. Her achievements included acquiring technical manuals for military hardware and plans for the MiG-21 and the high-altitude SA2 missile, the first Soviet surface-to-air missile. On July 14, 1958, she remained in Iraq as the lone CIA agent during a sudden revolution that killed King Faisal. For courage and analysis of an anti–Western, pro-communist coup that threatened U.S. Middle Eastern relations, she achieved the Intelligence Medal of Merit.

March 1, 1954

Armed with a semi-automatic pistol, nationalist rebel **Lolita Lebrón (November 19, 1919–August 1, 2010)** of Lares, Puerto Rico, directed an attack on March 1, 1954, against the U.S. House of Representatives. At the Capitol before the 83rd Congress, she led **Rosa Collazo** and other co-conspirators in the Lord's Prayer and an outcry for freeing the island from U.S. control. At the raising of the Puerto Rican flag, rebels fired thirty shots, striking five legislators. Lolita, Rosa, and two male attackers faced charges of sedition.

Rosa remained at Alderson Prison in West Virginia until 1961 and continued promoting freedom for political prisoners, including her husband, Oscar Collazo, who served a life sentence at Leavenworth Federal Prison in Kansas. After a quarter century in jail, Lolita gained amnesty by President Jimmy Carter. Posters, paintings, a documentary, nonfiction, and the Order of Playa Girón commemorated her nationalism.

Subsequent revolts against the use of Vieques island for U.S. Navy ordnance exercises on June 26, 2001, earned Lolita two more months of cell time.

See also October 31, 1950.

November 29, 1954

A Bulgarian hero, Private **Esther Arditi (1937–February 20, 2003)** from Sofia achieved renown and praise for rescuing a pilot and navigator from a burning plane. After enlisting in the Israeli Air Force as a paramedic, she observed lightning strike a twin-engine Mosquito FB6 on November 29, 1954, as it landed at Hatzor Israeli Air Force Base in southern Israel. She tried to drive an ambulance to the crash through mud, then ran on foot to pull the two men from the wreckage away from exploding ammunition. She became the only female recipient of the Israeli Medal of Distinguished Service.

Esther's dedication to Israel's military continued as a combat medic with the 35th Paratroopers Brigade in Jerusalem. On June 5, 1967, she provided field treatment of casualties of the Six-Day War at the Golan Heights, Judea, Sinai, and Samraia, Palestine. Armed with an Uzi submachine gun, she accompanied paratroopers to the post-war retaking of the Western Wall and deployed near the Suez Canal outside Ismailia, Egypt, during the Yom Kippur War on October 6, 1973. A street name at Givat Hannaya in the Elah Valley commemorates Esther as the "Angel in White."

1955

A surgeon from Madras, British India, **Vijayalakshmi Ramanan (February 27, 1924–October 18, 2020)** joined the Indian Army Medical Corps before switching to the air force in 1955 to become its first female officer. Her expertise at gynecology and family planning aided combat casualties in the Sino-Indian border clash on September 21, 1962; the bombing of Indian civilians at Aizawl on March 5, 1966; and war with Pakistan on December 3, 1971. Throughout standbys, she remained on duty during Sundays and holidays. By August 1972, she advanced to wing commander and trained military nurses in female health until retirement on February 28, 1979. She earned the Vishisht Seva Medal for treating women and children from military families for twenty-four years.

August 1956

A counterintelligence agent and cryptanalyst, **Adelaide Mulheran Hawkins (March 6, 1914–July 10, 2008)** from Wheeling, West Virginia, revealed a buildup of air power in Israel and coded communications with Britain and France in August 1956 preceding a Zionist plan to seize the Suez Canal. She began learning secret ciphers and analyzing messages in Washington, D.C., nine days after the Japanese bombing of Pearl Harbor, Hawaii. From managing communications for the Army Signal Corps, in September 1947, she progressed to projects for the Central Intelligence Agency. While posted to London in 1956, she identified the swept wings of sixty French Dassault Mystere IV fighter-bomber jets as a violation of peace negotiations. She correctly predicted the Suez Crisis of October 29,

1956, and Israel's invasion of the Sinai Peninsula, in which the Mysteres completed one hundred forty-seven sorties. The planes remained in use on June 5, 1967, during the Six-Day War.

October 29, 1956

Piloting the lead Douglas C-47 Dakota transport plane in a sixteen-ship convoy, on October 29, 1956, Captain **Yael Rom (October 10, 1932–May 24, 2006)** of Tel Aviv, Israel, launched a parachute drop in the Sinai Desert at Mitla Pass, Egypt. As a result, Commander Ariel Sharon whipped Egypt's Second Brigade. After triggering combat in the Suez War, Yael ferried supplies and a jeep to isolated divisions and landed in wheels-deep sand to airlift wounded. Additional airdrops involved her at A-Tur on the Gulf of Suez on November 3, 1956. She retired at age thirty.

October 29, 1956

Egypt's first female military officer, Captain **Rawya Ateya (April 19, 1926–May 9, 1997)** from Giza readied the women's commando unit on October 29, 1956, during the Suez War. A wounded veteran of the Liberation Party, she participated in the 1939 anti-British protests at age seventeen. In the Liberation Army, she returned to international battles with Israel, France, and the United Kingdom during the Nine Day War, which lionized President Gamal Abdel Nasser for pledging to reconquer Palestine. Egypt's three hundred thousand troops suffered nine thousand casualties and thirty thousand prisoners of war as well as closure of the Suez Canal.

A more serious clash pressed Rawya again into service. On October 6, 1973, the combined forces of President Anwar Sadat's Egyptian army and troops from Cuba, Jordan, Morocco, Saudi Arabia, and Syria on the Golan Heights and Sinai fronts halted the Israeli invasion of the Sinai Peninsula. A halt to bombardment by France and the United Kingdom on October 24, 1973, left United Nations troops patrolling vacated territory. For her soldiery, Rawya earned a badge, medal, and medallion of the 1973 Arab-Israeli War. Post combat, she supported families of martyrs and soldiers and the Red Crescent, a Muslim relief agency.

October 9, 1957

A *moudjahida* (guerrilla saboteur) in the Algerian war for independence from French colonialism, **Hassiba Ben Bouali (also Hasibah, January 18, 1938–October 9, 1957)** from Orleansville was martyred on October 9, 1957, at the battle of the Casbah. She had allied with Algerian Muslim teens in 1954 and fought at the battle of Algiers with fellow explosive experts **Djaouher Akrour (April 23, 1939–March 8, 2018)**, a fellow Algiers native **Baya Hocine (May 20, 1940–May 1, 2000)**, **Jacqueline Guerroudj (April 27, 1919–January 18, 2015)** of Rouen France, and Tiaret native **Zoulikha Bekkadour (1934–)**. The Casbah, a hideout and explosive storage for rebels, came under attack by French paratroopers, who trounced the National Liberation Front with pinpoint bombing.

Emboldened by their success, the French oppressed surviving rebels through execution, disappearance, and torture, which saboteur **Djamila Bouhired (also Djamilah or Jamila, June 1935–)** of Algiers endured for seventeen days. Zoulikha served three years at El Harrach prison under her escape to Lausanne, Switzerland. Hassiba's heroism remains prominent in film, graphic comics, and the naming of a university and avenue in Algiers. Djamila, the focus of the cinema *The Battle of Algiers,* recruited saboteurs **Zohra Drif (December 8, 1934–)** from Tissemsilt and Berber co-conspirator **Samia Lakhdari (1934–2012)** to civilian targets in the Cafe Wars, which Zohra recorded in her memoir *Inside the Battle of Algiers.* Djamila Bouhired and fellow saboteur **Djamila Bouazza (1938–June 12, 2015)** from Blida faced the guillotine for terrorism, a sentence later commuted by the Evian Accord of March 19, 1962. Djamila Bouhired recovered from pistol wounds and four years' imprisonment in Rheims and continues resistance into old age with compatriot Zoulikka Bekkadour.

1961

Norway's first female soldier and first lieutenant colonel, **Haldis Elisabeth Arentz Sveri (October 21, 1927–January 30, 2018)** represented women warriors in 1961 at the first NATO conference on female deployment. She began a military career at age nineteen as a platoon leader and advanced to company liaison promoting officer's training for women and equality in combat. Backed by Crown Princess Sonja and by female officers from Denmark, Holland, Great Britain, and the United States, she encouraged the involvement of Belgian, German, Greek, Canadian, Latvian, Bulgarian, Romanian, and Italian women. Her awards range from a National Service honor and Defense Medal to knighthood in the Order of St. Olav and a portrait displayed at armed forces command.

Early 1960s

A member of the 44th Vietnamese Rangers in the early 1960s, Sergeant **Ho Te Que (early 1930s–mid–December 1965)** rose to a respected officer with the Biệt Động Quân (Special Action Warriors). As a former intelligence agent for the Viet Minh, she thrived as spotter of guerrilla insurgent hideouts and field medic to casualties. For fierce engagements with the Viet Cong requiring her .45 sidearm, she earned the nickname "the Tiger Lady of the Delta" and the reputation of a she-devil. Listed as a combat death, her shooting in mid–December 1965 was the work of her jealous husband, a fellow soldier who served one year in prison for murder.

February 7, 1961

Nigeria's first military officer, Captain **Josephine Okwuekeleke Tolefe (December 15, 1931–2014)** from Aniocha chose army service over professional midwifery on February 7, 1961. She modeled a military career on the intelligent, confident women of the British Army. During the six-year Congo Crisis of 1960, she was posted in Abeokuta Canton with the West African Frontier Force. With the secession of Igbo to Biafra in 1967, she rose from second lieutenant to captain in a force of eight thousand. At the end of six years and the beginning of the Nigerian Civil War, she was repulsed by the idea of countrymen fighting countrymen. On July 6, 1967, she retired from a force that had grown to one hundred fifty thousand.

1963

A Christian Assyrian leader of male Kurds for eight years during the First Iraqi-Kurdish War, medic **Margaret George Shello (also Margaret George Malik or Margrete George, January 21, 1942–December 26, 1969)** from Dura, Iraq, joined the army in 1963 at Akre in northern Iraq as the first female *peshmerga* (guerrilla fighter). After Syria donated planes and six thousand troops to the enemy in June 1963, her reputation grew from incisive command of a male regiment at the battle of Zawita Valley in the Zagros Range of northern Iraq. Recruitment posters featured her armed and in uniform. Because Margaret demanded Assyrian rights, on December 26, 1969, she was assassinated in her sleep—apparently by Mulla Mustafa Barzani—through a window in a prison cell with fifty shots. Forces honored her military funeral with rifle volleys. Her cult survives in photos, songs, verse, monuments, and myths of the "mother of Kurdistan."

January 15, 1965

Two women, **Ding Le Tunn (fl. 1960s)** and **Hui Po Yung (fl. 1960s)**, directed female recruits on January 15, 1965, at Min Top, South Vietnam, in parachuting, strategy, intelligence, and counter-insurgency tactics. A U.S. Women's Army Corps training program in Saigon led by **Anne Marie Doering (October 5, 1908–June 6, 2001)** of North Vietnam, the only WAC in the war zone; **Kathleen I. Wilkes (April 24, 1925–December 25, 1999)** of Evans, Georgia; and Bronze Star medalist **Betty L. Adams (December 3, 1932–January 20, 2012)** from Astoria, New York, expanded on the success of female combat troops in early 1962 at Hoc Mon in suburban Hanoi. Hands-on demonstrations of machine gunnery and setting bamboo and rope snakes and tree traps yielded resilient soldiers, particularly at tag team efforts to outwit ambushes. Among some three thousand fighters in the Women's Armed Forces Corps of South Vietnam, a star performer, **Dho Minde (fl. 1960s)**, outran the Vietcong over forty-five miles of jungle trails.

February 21, 1967

A volunteer to the North Vietnamese army at age twenty on February 21, 1967, **Dương Thu Hương (1947–)** from Thái Bình in the Red River Delta of northern Vietnam, endured jungle and tunnel warfare for seven years. In south coastal Vietnam, she served in Bình tại Thiên as medic and company entertainer and aided burial details for the Communist Youth Brigade. Her survival of the bombing in Quang Binh saved her from the annihilation of 92.5 percent of her comrades. In mid–February 1979, her military career took a new direction as frontline war correspondent during the four-week Sino-Vietnamese War, a costly follow-up that killed some seventy thousand Vietnamese militia and downgraded into intermittent skirmishes. An exile in Paris, she revisited war propaganda, mutilation of females, and spiritual disintegration in her fiction *Novel Without a Name* and *No Man's Land*. The Vietnamese banned her anti-war novels, which earned her a French Order of Arts and Letters.

August 31, 1967

An Argentine guerrilla warrior, translator, and spy for Argentine Marxist Che Guevara's Operation Fantasma (ghost), **Tamara Haydée Bunke Bider (November 19, 1937–August 31, 1967)** of Buenos Aires died from a shot in the arm and torso on August 31, 1967, by a Bolivian Army patrol in an ambush at a Rio Grande crossing in Villegrande. Reared in a Marxist household, she learned in girlhood how to hide arms and aid rebel escapes. In October 1964, she initiated an underground rebel network in Bolivia. Che schooled her in coding messages to Cuban revolutionary Fidel Castro and defending herself with knife, pistol, and submachine gun. Her aggressive fighting earned her the sobriquet "Tania the Guerrilla." Her heroism survived in a biography, fiction, folk song, film, stage play.

April 8, 1968

Medic **Đặng Thùy Trâm (November 26, 1942–June 22, 1970)**, a Vietnam War noncombatant from Hanoi, performed trauma surgery while observing and recording barbarities in diaries. For three months over the Troung Son Mountains along the Ho Chi Minh Trail, she aided Vietcong rebels against French colonizers. Traveling southeast through rice-growing farms along Route 1, she joined the staff of Duc Pho Hospital in Quảng Ngãi and treated guerrilla fighters damaged in the fray. At age twenty-five on April 8 during the Viet Cong January 30, 1968, Tet Offensive of surprise attacks, she enlisted with the National Liberation Front to staff a hidden hospital and a poorly equipped clinic.

Deployment varied by demand—a battlefield at Quang Binh Province and a mountain field hospital, where Đặng Thùy Trâm admitted up to eighty wounded resulting from U.S. air strikes and burn victims targeted by phosphorus explosions. After her death at age twenty-seven from an American bullet to the forehead on June 22, 1970, the rescued journal reached print in September 2007 under the title *Last Night I Dreamed of Peace*. The commentary grieved over loss of some four million Vietnamese, one-fourth of them missing in action.

July 19, 1969

On July 19, 1969, a Nicaraguan revolutionary, **Nora Astorga (December 10, 1948–February 14, 1988)** from Managua, aided liberators in providing transport and safe havens for Sandinistas, a socialist front disputing U.S. occupation forces in Nicaragua. Her underground activities reached a pinnacle on March 8, 1978, with conspiracy to overturn the Anastasia Somoza government by assassinating "El Perro (the Dog)," the vicious General Reynaldo Peréz Vega, commander of the national guard. On a run to the jungle during a national manhunt, she disguised herself in camo fatigues and carried a pistol and AK-47. "La Norita's" military career ended in pregnancy and, on July 19, 1979, with the formation of a new government and the assumption of national power on July 21.

1970

A Nicaraguan rebel and poet, **Gioconda Belli (December 9, 1948–)** from Managua aided the Sandinista National Liberation Front in 1970 to overthrow dictator Anastasio Somoza. In the same period, El Salvadoran commander **Melida Anaya Montes (May 17, 1929–April 6, 1983)** from Santiago Texacuangos established the nation's first guerrilla regiment, the beginning of the National Liberation Front. The guerrillas captured Managua's corrupt national guard and liberated Sandinistas from their cells. When the rebellion spread to Nicaragua in 1980, under the name "Ana Maria," she continued the insurrection until a betrayer assassinated her with an ice pick on April 6, 1983, on a Managua street.

As reported in a memoir, *The Country Under My Skin,* guerrilla leader Camilo Ortega recruited Gioconda to distribute arms, deliver documents and messages, transport agents, and canvass the Southern Hemisphere and Europe for funds. She sketched floor plans of embassies, opened safe houses, made speeches, and provided supplies and medical aid to mountain troops. Questioning at a military tribunal in 1975 forced her into a four-year exile in Mexico. On return, she served revolutionaries as anti–Ortega media representative and communications director and reviver of the original Sandinista movement. The National Theater medal honored her for a quarter century for service to Latin America.

March 7, 1971

A medal-winning infantryman in the Bangladesh war of independence, **Taramon Bibi (1956–December 1, 2018)** from Shankar Madhabpur, Pakistan, fought guerrilla style on March 7, 1971, in Rangpur border outposts west of the Teesta River. Her comrades relied on Enfield rifles, Italian howitzers, Czech machine guns, and Sten submachine guns as well as field artillery, grenades, and air cover from India. The women's brigade also owed success to child lookouts and to **Sitara Begum (1946–)** of Kishoreganj for operating a rebel field hospital specializing in combat wounds. Another volunteer, **Amena Sultana Bokul (1953–)** trained in explosives and photographed war zones. At Brahmanberia, she partnered with **Nazma Shaheen (1957–)**, a nutritionist at the University of Dhaka, who reported on atrocities against intellectuals that she and a sister, math teacher **Lutfa Haseen Rosy (1956–)**, witnessed in the March 25, 1971, Dhaka University massacre. Pakistani insurgents focused their gunfire, torture, arson, and rape on Hindu students, Bengali intellectuals, and staff.

Warriors aimed to turn East Pakistan into the republic of Bangladesh. Over nine months, the resistance forces, backed by Indian and West Bengali freedom fighters, battled via raids, ambush, arson, and blockades. The fighters succeeded at underwater and land-based sabotage of rail lines, harbors, arms and fuel depots, and power dynamos. By December 16, 1971, Pakistan's surrender freed Dhaka and legitimized the Bangla language. Sitara's medical treatment and Taramon's soldiery won the Bir Protik award.

January 1972

The first female and first woman U.S. Navy officer to go to sea and to serve in a Vietnam War combat zone, in January 1972, Commander **Elizabeth Merriman Barrett (1932–March 28, 2021)** from Woburn, Massachusetts, supervised four hundred fifty enlisted personnel during the Vietnamization of the battle against communism. Over fifteen months of deployment to Saigon until March 1973, she took only three personal days from operational command. After President Richard Nixon suspended warfare against North Vietnam, combatants signed the Paris Peace Accords on January 2, 1973. Over the next eight weeks, her command oversaw the withdrawal of the last U.S. military units on March 29, 1973, leaving one thousand six hundred twenty-six Americans missing in action.

1974

A two-year veteran of protests against Ferdinand Marcos, a corrupt Filipino dictator, **Nelida Cabigayan (fl. 1970s)** surrendered in 1974. Her revolt against Marcos defied his authoritarianism, which imposed suspension of *habeas corpus*, brutality, bribery, waste of the treasury on military expansion, and a nine-year rule under martial law. The rebel brigade profited from Chinese gifts of twelve hundred rifles and AK-47s. Revered as "Commander Lina" of the New People's Army, she became an example of folk heroism.

February 17, 1974

During the fifteen-year Rhodesian Bush War, Shona machine gunner **Joice Runaida Mujuru (April 15, 1955–)** of Mount Darwin, Zimbabwe, destroyed a helicopter over Murehwa on February 17, 1974. She served under the nickname Teurai Ropa (blood spiller). Within the year, she advanced to instructor of military personnel. By 1976, she superintended the Chimoio military camp in Manica, Mozambique, and a Mozambique refugee shelter. Under President Robert Mugabe, on November 23, 1977, she ducked would-be kidnappers while leading Zimbabwe African National Liberation Army guerrilla forces. Within days of bearing her first daughter, Priscilla Kumbirai, in 1978, Joice survived a camp raid by Rhodesia's security units. At war's end on December 12, 1979, she initiated a political career that led to four terms in parliament and her nation's vice presidency.

March 1974

Ship-fitter, rescuer, damage controller, and hull technician **Donna Tobias (May 22, 1952–September 21, 2010)** of Los Angeles served the U.S. Navy as its first female sea diver. As a search and salvage specialist, she wore thirty-four-pound boots and carried two hundred pounds of copper hard-hat gear. Working in varied visibilities and water conditions, she gained expertise for diving under sunken vessels.

At New London submarine base in Groton, Connecticut, she volunteered for experimental physiological research, instructed submariners on escape methods, and operated hyperbaric treatments for victims of gangrene, carbon monoxide, and embolisms. The New London base named a dive locker for Donna.

1976

Petite Sandinista rebel **Aminta Granera Sacasa (September 18, 1952–)** of Leon, Nicaragua, left a religious calling in 1976 to help overthrow the corrupt regime of dictator Anastasio Somoza. Traveling from Ecuador and then to the Sisters of the Assumption, a Guatemala City novitiate, at age twenty-four, she joined the National Liberation Front. As chief of staff to co-founder Tomas Borge, she served as courier and strategist of Sandinistas, who fought the corrupt Somozan Guard. An El Salvadoran underground comrade, **Lilian Mercedes Letona (September 24, 1954–August 1, 1983)** from Turin promoted armed aggression and the 1981 major offensive at San Salvador.

Lilian, under the popular name "Comandante Clelia," disappeared from the action on February 11, 1981, when captors forced her into the prison at Ilopango. On release in 1983, she died on August 1, 1983, in battle. Aminta left the front long enough to deliver her first child by caesarean. The successful rebellion and a free election on April 25, 1990, enabled her to aid women and children as a National Police officer fighting gangs, bribery, and drugs. From September 5, 2006, until Aminta's retirement in July 2018, she directed Nicaragua's state police.

1978

As a pioneering female station chief of the Central Intelligence Agency (CIA), in 1978, **Eloise Randolph Page (February 19, 1920–October 16, 2002)** from Richmond, Virginia, functioned in Athens, Greece, as a specialist on terrorism. She entered the spy field for the Office of Strategic Services (OSS) in May 1942 and aided General William Donovan in mapping out Operation Torch, the invasion of Algeria and French Morocco on November 8, 1942. In the final months of World War II, she developed the X-2 division to track operatives in Algeria, China, France, Sicily, and Italy. Eloise collaborated with **Betty Ann Lussier (1922–November 30, 2017)** from Medicine Hat, Alberta, a veteran Canadian pilot, journalist, decoder, and counterspy, and with master spy runner, cartographer, and X-2 case officer **Jane Wallis Burrell (1911–January 6, 1948)** from Dubuque, Iowa, the first female CIA agent to die in service. The special operations branch monitored art looters and uncovered three thousand Axis subversives.

In 1945, Eloise managed post-war projects in Brussels, Belgium. She continued as case officer for the CIA's Science & Technology Division at its establishment in 1947. Her work involved hiring agents, facilitating the microdot camera, and gathering global intelligence, including groundbreaking predictions on the launch, orbit, and size of Sputnik, the first Soviet satellite, in October 1957. In February 1959, she formulated plans for eyewitness fact gathering by ten bio-astronautics specialists touring Russia to learn of missiles and the Soviet deployment of a man in space. For her crucial analysis applying technology to covert espionage operations, the much respected "Iron Butterfly" earned a Distinguished Intelligence Medal and Trailblazer Award.

1979

Nepalese airborne soldier Lieutenant **Annapurna Kunwar (fl. 1970s)** became the nation's first female paratrooper. Over Chobar south of Kathmandu, Nepal, in 1979, she made her initial jump from Trishul air base, India's largest air force command center and home of a helicopter squadron and Sukhoi fighter jets.

November 1984

An Illinois native and twenty-three-year veteran U.S. Marine, **Juliet Beyler (1967–)** from Chicago provided coding, language, and intelligence analysis in Korea in November 1984. A age seventeen, she initiated a military career as a combat engineer on the DMZ on the 38th parable north. Her multiple skills aided combat in Iraq and commands in the Balkans, Haiti, Philippines, Russia, and Thailand. She continued her work overseeing manpower in 2022 by directing the U.S. sixth fleet in Africa and Europe in protecting thirty percent of the global population and sixty-seven percent of coastlines.

1985

A thirty-six-year veteran, Rear Admiral **Bette Bolivar (1962–)** from Honolulu, Hawaii, completed an oceanography degree from the U.S. Naval Academy in 1985 before specializing in diving, towing, explosive disposal, spacecraft recovery, and salvage. She deployed to Guam and the Marianas islands as a navy subaquatic explorer and later earned the nickname "Navy Mayor of San Diego." She became the first Filipino-American to command the southwest region of Arizona, California, Colorado, Nevada, New Mexico, and Utah. After serving on four salvage ships, in 2003, she commanded the USS *Salvor*, a Safeguard-class rescue and recovery ship based in Pearl Harbor, Hawaii. On February 9, 2009, the crew dislodged the cruiser USS *Port Royal* from a coral reef near Honolulu. On February 27, 2018, the ship excavated planes shot down in the Palau cluster at Ngerekebesang Island.

August 6, 1986

A northern Acholi warrior-spiritualist, **Alice "Mama Alice" Auma of Gulu (1956–January 17, 2007)**, waged a three-month holy war on August 6, 1986, against Ugandan President Yoweri Museveni. By channeling the spirit of Lakwena, a deceased army officer serving as divine messenger, she gave up selling flour and fish to fight until late November 1987. Her eighteen thousand Holy Spirit Mobile Forces formed the Lord's Resistance Army. Soldiers coated in shea butter conducted a healing war with sticks and stones. Chanting the mantra "James Bond! James Bond! James Bond!," they died by the thousands. Under army artillery fire, seven thousand survivors abandoned the fight in the woodlands eighty kilometers from the capital of Kampala. Fleeing on a bicycle to exile in northeastern Kenya, she appears to have died of AIDS at age fifty in the Ifo United Nations refugee camp at Garrisa. Her co-leader, Joseph Kony, faced war crime indictments at an International Criminal Court in The Hague.

1987

Warrant Officer **Michelle Thompson (1965–)** of Bridgetown, Barbados, began a thirty-three-year career in 1987 in the Barbados Defence Force that took her to the highest rank for the island's female soldier. Training assignments on security and policing for the land force posted her to India, Belize, and Edinburgh, Scotland. Answering to Commander-in-Chief Queen Elizabeth II until 2021, when the island became a republic, Michelle served the military court as a panelist. Her decorations include a Glendairy citation and a fifteen-year Service Medal.

February 1991

A medic with the U.S. army's 3rd Armored Division, Specialist **Kathy Piccollo (1961–)** from Rochester, New York, led a crew of rescuers in February 1991 to treat thirty-eight ailing Iraqi prisoners of war. In the first days of the Gulf War, she brought three and a half years of experience into combat. Key to her ministrations, feeding casualties and debriding and cleaning wounds kept the unit busy for seven hours. They comforted Arab men who were unaccustomed to seeing and being washed and treated by female soldiers. The worst of the men's hurts derived from shrapnel and foot injuries during a three-day march over one hundred ten miles, some without shoes or socks.

Spring 1991

After graduating from the U.S. Naval Academy at Annapolis, Maryland, in spring 1991, Rear Admiral **Heidi Berg (ca. 1969–)** from LaCrosse, Wisconsin, refined her skills in military cryptology with training in the Arabic and Russian languages at Oxford University and Kalimat Institute in Cairo, Egypt. She deployed aboard the destroyer USS *Kidd*, the aircraft carrier USS *Saratoga*, and the submarine USS *Key West* and in airborne signal intelligence units in Spain, Italy, England, Afghanistan, Bahrain, and Iraq. On May 18, 2021, she progressed to U.S. Cyber Command Director of Plans and Policy at Fort Mead, Maryland, and garnered multiple honoraria for service and campaign efficiency.

1992

A successful transvestite disguised as a decorated Portuguese army officer, **Teresinha Gomes (1933–July 2007)** from Funchal, Madeira, posed for eighteen years as General Tito Gomes to flee debt. With a uniform marked with ranking stars from a Lisbon tailor, she changed her identity under the name of her deceased baby brother Tito and attended a carnival as a male. The deception freed her of the social restrictions on women. Until her outing in November 1992 and arrest for identity theft, she bilked investors with a gendered ruse and pretended to be an attorney and staff member of Lisbon's U.S. embassy. Courts suspended "la generala's" three-year sentence for fraud. A TV series covered her biography in eight episodes.

1993

A pioneer Canadian navy diver, in 1993, Commander **Leanne Crowe (fl. 1980s–2010a)** of Hamilton, Ontario, became the first female to qualify for clearance diving. After the military introduced mixed-gender service in Halifax frigates, she trained for difficult underwater deployment during combat. She learned sea mine recognition and disposal, ship repair, and reconnaissance of docks and piers for hazards and booby traps. Her three decade career incorporated deck and wartime operations before she entered Toronto's experimental diving unit and advanced to commander. Service took her to the Maritime Warfare Centre in Halifax before posting in Afghanistan to counter improvised explosive devices, the most common cause of soldier deaths.

January 1, 1994

Chiapas guerrilla warrior **Comandante Ramona (1959–January 6, 2006)**, headquartered on January 1, 1994, in the Lacandon Jungle on the Guatemalan border, strategized the seizure of San Cristóbal de las Casas as well as Altamirano, Chanel, Huixtan, Las Margaritas, Ocosingo, Oxchuc, and Rancho Nuevo. A leader of the Zapatista Army of National Liberation and outlaw condemned to death, she rode into conflict on horseback with fellow officer **Major Anna Maria (1969–)** from Los Altos de Chiapas, who commanded one thousand infantry. The two women and an army of three thousand Zapatistas promoted the support and elevation of marginalized Tzotzil Maya women to political importance through nutritional and reproductive services, advancement of small business and education, and freedom from abuse.

Zapatista resistance began with the release of jailed commandos, capture of the Municipal Palace, and the theft of weapons from a military base. After a surprise counter assault by the Mexican army, Ramona and Anna Maria's fellow soldier, **Subcomandante Elisa (January 1955–)**, and sixteen other rebels faced arrest and torture in February 1995 for felonious weapons possession, criminal conspiracy, and terrorism. Ramona died at age forty-six from kidney failure. Toy sellers imitated her unique style in an armed doll in black ski mask or red mask carrying an infant and riding a knitted horse.

February 21, 1995

England's first girl jet pilot, **Joanna "Jo" Mary Salter (August 27, 1968–)** from Bournemouth protected Saudi Arabia and Turkey on February 21, 1995, by flying Iraq's no-fly zone. After mastering the Panavia Tornado and joining the 617 Squadron in ground attacks, she completed a fourteen-year career with the Royal Air Force. Throughout the dropping of eighteen hundred bombs, she deployed over the northern sector to protect Kurds and over the southern zone to shield Shiites from the antagonism of Iraqi president Saddam Hussein's forces. The combat period resulted in one hundred and forty-four civilian deaths. She earned a Member of the British Empire (MBE) and 2022 New Year Honors.

1996

A drone squadron leader in the Indian Air Force, **Varsha Kukreti (1970–)** of New Delhi spent twelve years developing aero technology and logistics. She graduated in 1996 from the Indian Air Force Academy specializing in materials and supply chain management. Her post-military career at Bagdogra and Pathankot continued personal endorsement of light surveillance planes. She trained the next generation of pilots to survey rough terrain for defense and security.

December 1996

Lieutenant Colonel **Jozette McLean (ca. 1978–)** of Port-of-Spain received promotion to the first woman commander in the Trinidad and Tobago Defence Force. Since the army's gender integration in 1980, she became the first female commandant of the Support and Service Battalion Learning Center. After enlistment in December 1996, she studied at the Royal Military Academy at Sandhurst, England, and continued training in Jamaica; Cranwell and Nottingham, England; Buenos Aires, Argentina; and Fort Leavenworth, Kansas. Her proficiency extends to logistics in budgeting, procurement, storage, and distribution of rations, especially support for humanitarian and disaster relief of such crises as the eruption of La Soufriere volcano on April 29, 2021, impacting nearby Kingstown, St. Vincent, and the Grenadines. Her awards include a citation for composition skill and the Iron Major Award for fitness.

December 24, 1996

The Indian Air Force lost to an air accident its first female to solo, Lieutenant **Harita Kaur Diol (November 10, 1971–December 24, 1996)** of Chandigarh. She answered an enlistment ad in 1992 for women to fill eight vacancies, for which there were twenty thousand applicants. With three months of training at the Air Force Academy in Hyderabad, only seven candidates passed mastery of the Indian Deepak prop trainer. Successful in the final course at Yelahanka Air Force Station in Bangalore, at age twenty-two, Harita accompanied seven other pilots as short service, non-combat transport fliers.

In a twin-engine Russian-made Antonov military plane, Harita's first flight passed an altitude of ten thousand feet. The next cadets, **Archana Kapoor**, daughter of a helicopter pilot, and **Bindu Sebastian**, a physics major, earned their wings in the same plane. The Air Force celebrated the remaining four lone flights by **Priya Nalgundwar, Pamela Rodrigues Pereira, Priya Paul**, and **Anisha Shinh**. Two years later on December 24, 1996, Harita and twenty-one passengers died outside Nellore when her British-made Hawker Siddeley turboprop airliner went down at Bukkapuram because of technical errors.

Other careers rewarded the first cadets: Archana became a squadron leader, Priya Nalgundwar a chief pilot, Pamela a wing commander, Anisha a Jet Airways captain, Priya Paul an Airasia captain, and Bindu a rescuer of Indians stranded in other countries. Three additions to the sisterhood—**Avani Chaturvedi**, **Bhawana Kanth**, and **Mohana Singh**—flew India's supersonic MiG fighter planes. **Ayesha Farooq** gained renown as a frontline pilot of the Chinese-made missile carrier Chengdu J-7. **Alka Shukla** and **M.P. Shumathi** were licensed to handle assault helicopters.

Afghan War,
October 15, 1999–September 11, 2021

In the longest U.S.-backed conflict, al-Qaeda leader Osama bin Laden advanced Middle Eastern terrorism from Pakistan and Sudan to Afghanistan. Assassinations and mass murders preceded the 9/11 attacks in 2001 on the World Trade Center in New York City and the Pentagon in Washington, D.C. With support from Australia, Canada, France, and Germany, U.S. bombings forced the Taliban surrender in Kandahar, but did not halt a substantial body count. After bin Laden's execution in Pakistan on May 1, 2011, the lengthy conflict ended with U.S. withdrawal on September 11, 2021.

June 7, 2000

East of the Black Sea during a Russian raid on Alkhan-Kala, Chechens **Luiza Magomadova (1984–June 7, 2000)** and **Khava Barayeva (also Khava Baraeva, 1983–June 7, 2000)** colluded with a Muslim cabal of anti–Russian liberators to avenge the wartime death of Arbi Barayev, Khava's warlord cousin. The pair drove a truck filled with explosives into the Alkan-Yurt paramilitary headquarters. The blast that struck officer barracks on June 7, 2000, mutilated both women, two special forces officers, and twenty-three bystanders and wounded five more. Khava's martyrdom inspired a "black widow" movement among the Wahhabist women of Chechnya to sacrifice themselves in acts of vengeance. Of the total of bombers, forty-three percent were female ages fifteen to forty-five.

December 4, 2000

Teenage Chechen terrorist **Mareta Duduyeva (1984–November 29, 2001)** from Grebenskaya Stanitsa attempted a truck bombing of the Motor Vehicle Division on December 4, 2000, at Grozny, Chechnya. One of a coterie of vengeful "black widows" in a surge of Muslim-led mass killings, she had no close connection to victims of the Chechen wars. She operated under the extremist manipulation of warlord Magomet Tsaragaev's widow. As ordered, Mareta packed the Ural vehicle with explosives and drove it through checkpoints to the front door, where it struck a concrete barrier. The failed attack resulted in her capture and shooting by Russian occupation forces, who found her slumped on the truck bench seat. In court, she blamed Chechen outlaws for forcing her into the truck and handing her a grenade. Under threats to her family, she complied with the order, which earned her ten years in prison.

August 9, 2001

Jordanian talk show host on Al-Quds TV and operative of the Jihadist Arab League **Ahlam al-Tamimi (January 20, 1980–)** of Zarqa on the West Bank, robed and veiled, planned the bombing of a Sbarro pizzeria in Jerusalem, Israel, that killed eight children and seven adults and injured one hundred forty-five. Previous to the attack, she attempted to destroy a Jerusalem grocery store in July 2001, but failed. On August 9, 2001, she interrupted the college studies of journalism to imitate a Jewish tourist and planted the bomb before exiting the scene by bus. At Secret service agents jailed her with other female supporters of Hamas, a Palestinian terrorist cell, for targeting U.S. citizens with weapons of mass destruction.

Following a tribunal at Ofer in northern Israel and imprisonment, Ahlam gained release in October 2011 from sixteen life sentences via a prisoner exchange for an Israeli soldier. After Ahlam entered exile to Jordan, on July 15, 2013, she came under a U.S. Department of Justice indictment. Pursuers sought a reward of $5 million for her capture. Her television appearances promoted more terrorism and the kidnap of Israeli soldiers.

November 9, 2001

The only female recipient of a Distinguished Flying Cross, U.S. Navy Lieutenant Commander **Sara Stires (1976–)**, an oral and maxillofacial surgeon from Billings, Montana, took aggressive action against a Taliban convoy at Kabul in north central Afghanistan. Flying an F-14B Tomcat from the USS *Theodore Roosevelt* under the call name "Goalie," she was serving as radar intercept officer during Operation Enduring Freedom when she led a reconnaissance sortie identifying an enemy retreat from Mazari Sharif northwest of Kabul. Her direct hits with laser-guided bombs blocked the trucks below and aided two other aircraft to destroy four more vehicles. The rapid destruction halted the resupply and resurgence of Al-Qaeda and Taliban troops.

November 29, 2001

In an attack on a Russian general, **Aiza "Luiza" Gazuyeva (1983–November 29, 2001)** died along with her target on November 29, 2001, in a hand grenade explosion. Born in Chechnya in Russia's northern Caucasus, she was eighteen years old when she volunteered with a fifteen-member terrorist cell to become one of twenty-three suicide bombers in Russia. Her motivation was revenge for the deaths of her husband and two brothers and the disappearance of her cousin Akhmed during the Second Chechen War of 1999.

Detonation of devices hidden in Aiza's clothing targeted Russian army commandant Gaidar Gadzhiyev for war crimes, specifically, knifing her wounded husband during questioning at a hospital and shoving her face into the slit. The street-side blast ripped out Gadzhiyev's eyes and an arm and killed two security guards and two soldiers. On December 1, Russian troops demolished her home and those of three neighbors in Urus-Martan, beat her parents, and arrested seventy-two citizens, four of whom died of explosions.

October 26, 2002

In a plot against Russian occupation troops, **Zura Barayeva (?–October 26, 2002)**, aunt of a Chechen war victim and widow of a Chechen warlord, led eighteen female and twenty male martyrs in mass murder. In retaliation for murders and rapes in Chechnya by Russian soldiers, the Islamic rebels dressed in black chadors during a three-day siege. Zura draped a bomb belt over her shoulder. On the second floor of the Dubrovka theater in Moscow, terrorists took nine hundred hostages from Russia, Australia, Armenia, Austria, Kazakhstan, Holland, Germany, Ukraine, Great Britain, and the United States and planted a bomb, mines, and grenades.

International Red Cross staff entered the building carrying a white flag; *Médecins Sans Frontières* (Doctors Without Borders) tried to negotiate a peaceful truce. As one of nineteen fundamentalist terrorists from the Shelkovskoi district of Chechnya, She and three other "black widows" clad in mourning died on October 26, 2002, in a 5 a.m. raid. The Russian commandos released poisonous gas that killed forty-one guerrillas and one hundred twenty-nine hostages, including children, sick people, and pregnant women.

December 27, 2002

In the North Caucasus, teen terrorist **Alina Tumriyeva (1985–December 27, 2002)** abetted her father Glean and seventeen-year-old brother Ilyas in a two-truck assault on a government office in the Chechen capital of Grozny. On December 27, 2002, she disguised herself in Russian army uniform and presented an official permit at the guardhouse. Suspicious sentries at the fourth checkpoint fired on the trucks. The explosion of a Kamaz eighteen-wheeler, initiated by remote control, was recorded on camera as it demolished a four-story government building and injured Deputy Prime Minister Zina Batyzheva. The force of one ton of TNT killed eighty-three, wounded two hundred ten, and avenged the death of a second brother from the Caucasus during a battle against Russian occupation. Despite claims that Alina died in the suicidal attack, in 2014, she reputedly remained at large at Sochi, Japan, during the Olympic games.

2003

An Iowa journalist and soldier in Baghdad, Iraq, Sergeant **Miyoko Hikiji (1976–)** of Cedar Rapids served a year as a five-ton truck driver of prisoners of war and American troops. To earn college tuition, she enlisted in the 2133rd Transportation Company of the Iowa Amy National Guard in 1995 and mobilized through Kuwait to Iraq in 2003. Her arrival followed the March 19, 2003, invasion by one hundred thirty thousand U.S. forces and forty-seven two hundred thousand fighters from its allies, Australia, Poland, and the United Kingdom.

In week-long supply convoy missions and raids over stark desert, Miyoko armed herself with an M-16 rifle and became familiar with dangers of roadside improvised explosives and attack. By month's end, the Iraqi coalition had experiences forty-five thousand war deaths and more than seventy-two hundred civilian losses. For commitment to the campaign, Miyoko won twelve military citations; her company earned a Valorous Unit Award. She detailed her experiences in *All I Could Be: My Story as a Woman Warrior in Iraq*.

2003

Jamaican sergeant **Samanthia Griffiths (1981–)** from Negril began a sixteen-year career in 2003 in the Jamaica Defence Force as an electrician in the Engineering Regiment. Answering to Commander-in-Chief Queen Elizabeth II, Samanthia broke barriers for women by completing induction with the brigade at Newcastle Training Depot in St. Andrew. In the sultry Blue Mountains, soldiers learned explosives demolition, military construction, logistics for ground forces, maritime safety and recovery, security and disaster relief, intelligence, and anti-smuggling offensives. She became the first female trainer of a male and a mixed platoon. As head of thirty-three recruits, in 2003, she led company competitions in flat foot, rifle, and sentry drills and marching.

March 23, 2003

The first American casualty of Operation Iraqi Freedom at Nasiriyah, Hopi native **Lori Ann Piestewa (also White Bear Girl, December 14, 1979–March 23, 2003)** of Tuba City, Arizona, died in the battle of Nasiriyah, a Fedayeen ambush on March 23, 2003, near the Euphrates River. By serving the 57th Maintenance Company of the Quartermaster Corps in the Iraq invasion, she followed the example of her paternal grandfather and father, both soldiers. Northwest of Basra, a grenade struck the Humvee she was driving and injured her head. The attack enabled the enemy to capture her until Special Operations Marines recovered the casualties. A purple heart and multiple honors acknowledged her loss. Piestewa Peak outside Phoenix bears Lori's name.

Two women on the front line survived the battle of Nasiriyah, at which body count totaled thirty-two for Americans and British and four hundred thirty-one for Iraqis. Lori's comrade, **Jessica Dawn Lynch (April 26, 1983–)** of Palestine, West Virginia, received treatment at an Iraqi hospital for a broken thigh and arm, head gash, and dislocated vertebra, right foot, and ankle. Her recovery by U.S. special ops made news as the first retrieval of an American prisoner of war since World War II. In her book *I Am a Soldier, Too*, she reported sexual assault. Sharpshooter **Shoshana Nyree Johnson (January 18, 1973–)** of Pedro Miguel, Panama, became the first black female American prisoner of war. After twenty-two days of internment, she survived a bullet wound to the ankle and returned to Kuwait City. She received a Purple Heart, Bronze Star, and Prisoner of War Medal and a contract to write *I'm Still Standing*.

June 5, 2003

At Mozdok, North Osetia, a suicidal attack on June 5, 2003, on air force pilots and maintenance laborers from Prokhladny air base aboard a crowded military shuttle bus killed Chechen religious extremist **Lida Khildehoroeva**

(1980s–June 5, 2003). For the third suicide bombing in three weeks opposing Chechnya's Kremlin-financed oligarchy and atrocities by the Russian army, the teen martyr dressed in a white medical tunic. She chased the bus northeast of town after it halted for passengers. Stopped at a railroad crossing, at 7:30 a.m., she stood outside the vehicle because the driver refused to open the door. In a planned attack during the separatist war, she detonated explosives on a belt supplied by Islamic guerrillas. The eruption killed her along with seventeen casualties and sixteen wounded by shrapnel. She chose martyrdom to avenge her brother's death.

See also July 10, 2003.

July 5, 2003

At the *Krylya* (Wings) outdoor rock concert at Tushino airfield, radical Islamic suicide bombers from Chechnya **Zulikhan Elikhadzhiyeva (1983–July 5, 2003)** and **Maryam Sharipova (1986–March 29, 2010)** of Dagestan, Russia, killed fourteen viewers and injured sixty. At the festival admission booth outside Moscow, Zulikhan armed herself with metal shards and nails in a bomb belt, which only partially detonated. The eruption on July 5, 2003, coincided with a nearby blast by Chechen martyr **Zinaida Aliyeva (1977–July 5, 2003)**, which slew eleven.

Maryam survived the dual detonations and assisted seventeen-year-old Dagestan war widow **Dzhennet Abdurakhmanova (also Janet Abdullaev, 1992–March 29, 2010)** in a coordinated assault on a Moscow metro subway at Lubyanka station at city center on March 29, 2010. The combustion of Maryam's explosive belt near the Kremlin killed thirty-nine civilians. In Moscow's southeast, the discharge at the Park Kultury station killed twenty-year-old Chechen widow **Markha Ustarkhanova (1983–July 5, 2003)** along with forty train passengers.

See also July 10, 2003.

July 9, 2003

Moscow police captured Chechen radical **Zarema Muzhikhoeva (1980–)**, a Sunni Islamic extremist, while she attempted to bomb a hotel and cafe on Tverskaya Street, a main artery northwest of the Bolshoi Theater. Identified in the Russian media as a "Black Widow," Zarema studied explosives at a Wahhabist (extremist Muslim) training camp and accepted the urban assignment for monetary reward. Terrified to complete her first suicide detonation of a Mozdok military bus, she passed the task to **Lida Khildehoroeva**, who avenged the death of a brother.

On July 9, 2003, Zarema lost her nerve before a second attack in a Moscow cafe on Tverskaya Street. She concealed her identity in a black niqab (face veil) and held a black satchel to her torso. A police explosives expert died while disabling the device. Despite extensive lies about coercion and her previous criminal record for drug dealing and theft, in April 2004, Zarema lost her case in court. At the failure of her appeal in September, she pledged to avenge a twenty-year sentence at Moscow's Lefortovo Prison for attempted assassination, premeditated murder, and terrorism.

See also June 5, 2003.

July 21, 2003

In a meeting hall in Accra, Ghana, **Leymah Gbowee (1972–)** from central Liberia led interfaith female demonstrators in blockading with their unarmed bodies the warlords meeting with President Charles Taylor. A survivor of two Liberian civil wars, in 1989 she rescued family and friends by seeking sanctuary in a Lutheran church in the coastal city of Monrovia. With the collaboration of Muslim peace reformist **Asatu Bah Kenneth (fl. 2000s)**, Leymah mobilized two thousand followers of Women of Liberia Mass Action for Peace. Some derived from displaced persons camps that had lost inmates to missile attacks. Inspired by her radio address comparing Liberian women to biblical hero Queen Esther, Ghanian rebels gathered at the fish market to confront President Taylor.

The women resisted corruption in sit-ins and a sex strike of the type energizing Aristophanes's Greek satire *Lysistrata* of 411 BCE. As recorded in the documentary *Pray the Devil Back to Hell,* Leymah led two hundred women protesters on July 21, 2003, in barricading peace talks in an Accra hotel. To threats of violence by security guard, Leymah disrobed, a serious gesture among West African males. Her revolt convinced Taylor to negotiate on guaranteeing safety for women and an end to the drugging and arming of small boys as child soldiers. The female defiance forced Taylor into exile in Nigeria and prompted a formal accord on August 18, 2003. For her determination in the face of danger as described in her autobiography, *Mighty Be Our Powers*, she earned the 2011 Nobel Peace Prize.

September 2003

Sergeant **Susan Sonnheim (1959–)** of Milwaukee, Wisconsin, became the first National Guard member to achieve a Purple Heart. While serving in Operation Iraqi Freedom in Baghdad on night patrol with military police, she armed herself with an M203 grenade launcher and tracked enemy insurgents on foot and by Humvee. At an intersection, a suspicious box proved to be an enemy explosive device that erupted, tossing her into the air. She suffered shrapnel wounds that ruptured her eardrums, struck her wrist, spine, and legs, and blinded her on the left. She was transported from a military hospital to Landstuhl, Germany, and on to Walter Reed Hospital in Washington, D.C.

October 1, 2003

After a year's service in the U.S. army, Private **Analaura Esparza-Gutiérrez (June 19, 1982–October 1, 2003)** from Monterrey, Mexico, died in an assault on a convoy near Saddam Hussein's residence in Tikrit, Iraq. Three hundred yards from the base on October 1, 2003, her Humvee met with rocket-propelled grenades and hit an improvised explosive device (IED). The double blast killed her immediately. The army awarded her a posthumous Purple Peart, Bronze Star, and retroactive U.S. citizenship.

October 26, 2003

A victim of a mortar attack west of Baghdad, Iraq, on October 26, 2003,

Specialist **Rachel Bosveld (November 7, 1983–October 26, 2003)** from Neenah, Wisconsin, died serving the 527th Military Police Company. After signing on with the army in June 2002, she deployed to Giesen, Germany, then to Middle East war zones in Kuwait and Iraq to provide security, train local police, and patrol anti–American demonstrations. After surviving a rocket-propelled grenade on September 12, 2003, at a roadside ambush that burned her Humvee and dislocated her shoulder, she transferred to day patrol. At age nineteen, she succumbed to combat in a vehicle at the Abu Ghraib police station. Her sacrifice earned two Purple Hearts and a Bronze Star, the naming of a scholarship, a plaque, and a community memory walk.

November 2, 2003

Two female soldiers, army radio and network switchboard operator **Karina S. Lau (1983–November 2, 2003)**, from Livingston, California, and mail distributor **Frances M. Vega (September 2, 1983–November 2, 2003)** from San Juan, Puerto Rico, died in combat of the Iraq War over Fallujah west of Baghdad, Iraq. After the March 13, 2003, invasion of the U.S.-headed coalition, Karina, a member of the 16th Signal Battalion, and Frances, a clerk for the 151st Adjutant General Postal Detachment, died when a CH-47 Chinook helicopter crashed while carrying sixteen troops on two weeks' leave from Iraq. The shoulder-fired ground-to-air missile strike near Amiryah also wounded twenty soldiers. Karina received a posthumous Bronze Star, Purple Heart, and letter from President George Bush. Frances earned a Purple Heart, Bronze Star, three medals, and the renaming of a post office and army base gate.

November 7, 2003

On a last mission as adviser for the Judge Advocate General Office, Chief Warrant Officer **Sharon T. Swartworth (1959–November 7, 2003)** from Warwick, Rhode Island, died over Tikrit north of Baghdad, Iraq, on November 7, 2003, when enemy fire downed her UH-60 Black Hawk helicopter. After enlistment straight out of high school, she directed legal technology operations. She had been assigned to temporary quarters on 9/11 in 2001 when terrorists targeted the Pentagon, striking her old office. After a quarter century of service to the army, she died over the Tigris River with five others. When the aircraft on its way from Mosul exploded and crashed into shore mud, high grass, and reeds, investigators blamed a shoulder-fired missile. Sharon received a posthumous Distinguished Service Medal and a memorial stained glass window. Her remains lie in Arlington Cemetery.

November 9, 2003

During the Iraq War, military police sergeant **Mary Jessie Herrera (1981–)** of Somerton, Arizona, served army Humvee convoys as a security escort until her crippling in Kuwait on November 9, 2003, by enemy attack. As a Quick Response Force gunner, she rode the front Humvee turret and carried a machine gun and grenade launcher. On a relay of prisoners of war to Fallujah,

Iraq, she anticipated enemy rifle fire and rocket-propelled grenades at a bridge. After hits with a double round from an AK-47 in the bicep and radius of her right arm, she continued firing. After twenty surgeries at Brooke Army Medical Center in San Antonio, Texas, she regained partial use of the arm. For braving hostile action, she earned a Purple Heart.

December 5, 2003

On approach to the border town of Yessentuki in southern Russia north of Chechnya, Chechen separatist and suicide bomber **Khadijat Mangerieva (?–December 5, 2003)** detonated plastic explosives on December 5, 2003, in the second car of the Stavropol electric commuter train. In the northern Caucasus on the route from Kislovodsk to Mineralnye Vody, she prepared herself for the 8:00 a.m. mission with a bag carrying twenty-two pounds of TNT. After two Muslim conspirators jumped from the car on its approach to the central depot, she killed herself and forty-three students traveling by rail to schools and universities.

The eruption burst windows, blew one car on its side, ripped open the side of a second car, and dumped victims to the ground. Others burned in the fiery wreckage. Some one hundred fifty required hospitalization. Police removed grenades strapped to a male terrorist's legs. On December 26, 2004, investigators arrested Chechen conspirator Ibrahim Israpilov at Yessentuki for possession of firearms, detonators, remote controls, grenades, and forty-four pounds of explosives, for which he received a twenty-year prison sentence.

December 14, 2003

In Iskandariyah south of Baghdad, Iraq, Staff Sergeant **Kimberly Voelz (August 24, 1976–December 14, 2003)** a career soldier from Carlisle, Pennsylvania, died while disarming a bomb for the 703d Explosive Ordnance Company. Her army assignments ranged from six to eight bomb defusing daily. Her last mission targeted an undetonated explosive suspended from a power line on December 14, 2003, when she attempted to cut it down. The detonation tore off her left arm and put her in a coma.

At the Combat Surgical Hospital near the Baghdad airport, Kimberly never regained consciousness and died in the arms of her husband, Staff Sergeant Max Voelz. Her competent soldiery earned a Purple Heart, army medals, a Bronze Star, and the renaming of a Veterans of Foreign Wars post. National Public Radio broadcast her story.

2004

An Iraq War veteran during a 2004 augmented coalition involvement, **Tulsi Gabbard (April 12, 1981–)** of Leloaloa, American Samoa, advanced to major in the Hawaii Army National Guard. At age twenty-four, she relinquished an elected seat in the Hawaii house of representatives to deploy for two tours to provide logistical support to a war zone. Over a year's involvement, she aided the 29th Support Battalion at a field medical station, a service that earned honors from the Kuwait National Guard and a combat medical badge.

Tulsi's military career continued in 2007 with distinction in the officer preparedness at Alabama Military Academy and membership on the House Armed Service Committee. In 2009, she returned to the Middle East with the military police and trained the Kuwait National Guard, a task she repeated in 2011 with the Indonesian Army. From a veteran's vantage point, she urged the United States military to avoid war in Iran, Syria, and Venezuela.

January 2, 2004

The first female pilot fatally shot down in combat, Captain **Kimberly Hampton (August 18, 1976–January 2, 2004)** from Easley, South Carolina, died over Fallujah, Iraq, a Sunni Muslim town on the Euphrates River. A commander in the ROTC and the 17th Cavalry, in South Korea and Afghanistan, she flew the OH-58D Kiowa Warrior helicopter, a craft designed for reconnaissance, observation, and cover for ground raiders recovering illegal weapons. On transfer to the 82nd Airborne in Iraq in September 2003 six months after Saddam Hussein's government collapsed, she served west of Baghdad under the nickname "Darkhorse Six" before a missile destroyed her craft on January 2, 2004, and instantly killed her. Her service in strongly anti–American territory earned a purple heart, Air Medal, and Bronze Star and the naming of a library, primary school, scholarship, and state highway. The military named a service dog "Hampton" in her honor.

January 31, 2004

Specialist **Holly J. McGeogh (August 29, 1984–January 31, 2004)**, a mechanic from Taylor, Michigan, was servicing light trucks for the 4th Forward Support Battalion on January 31, 2004, when an explosion killed her outside Kirkuk north of Baghdad, Iraq. Upon transferring to the Middle East, she drove a troop transport mounted at back with a 40mm grenade launcher, which she volunteered to fire. On one patrol, she captured an enemy in flight. Her off-duty projects included treating Iraqi children to licorice, teaching them the circle game duck-duck-goose, and supplying a village with water. As Holly's convoy traveled toward Tikrit, it tripped a roadside bomb that demolished the Humvee and killed two other soldiers. Her eight decorations included a Purple Heart, Bronze Star, plaque, memorial motorcycle torch ride, naming of a highway, and monument in her hometown.

February 16, 2004

On a convoy to Baqubah northwest of Baghdad, Iraq, Specialist **Nichole M. Frye (February 16, 2004)** of Lena, Wisconsin, died in combat on February 16, 2004, from the detonation of an improvised explosive devices (IED). A member of the 415th Civil Affairs Battalion since 2002, despite sandstorms, she drove army vehicles and delivered rations, water, and books to children as a community service to the needy. The explosion happened near the front gate at her office in a government building and wounded four soldiers. In addition to service medals and ribbons, she received a Purple Heart, Bronze Star, and the naming of a scholarship, quilt, and memorial plaque on Highway 141.

March 23, 2004

An Air Force career officer, Captain **Tamara Long-Archeleta (May 12, 1979–March 23, 2004)** from Belen south of Albuquerque, New Mexico, died on March 23, 2004, while co-piloting a Komodo II helicopter for the 41st Rescue Squad to aid two injured Afghan children. A martial arts expert, she entered service in 1999, arrived in Afghanistan late in 2002, and relished the noncombat job of medical evacuations by HH-60 Pave Hawk. The crash ten feet from the summit of a remote mountain in Panjshir Province northeast of Kabul occurred on a stormy night during refueling and killed six crew members. Her valor earned a Purple Heart and eight medals. Her unselfishness survives at a Girl Scout camp, air force base, memorial scholarship, and karate championship.

April 9, 2004

A National Guard cop in Iraq, Specialist **Michelle Witmer (February 13, 1984–April 9, 2004)** of New Berlin, Wisconsin, died of a bullet wound to the heart on April 9, 2004, while serving the 32nd Military Police Company in Baghdad. On the Tigris River, she deployed in March 2003 to a hot battleground along with her twin, medic Charity Witmer and older sister Rachel, a fellow MP. In her off hours, she volunteered at a Sisters of Charity orphanage for handicapped children in Baghdad. In a three block fire zone, Michelle died as a gunner on patrol when enemy stalkers ambushed her Humvee with small arms fire and a roadside bomb. A Purple Heart, service medal, and Bronze Star honored her dedication.

May 25, 2004

A former Illinois basketball star and a member of the 571st Military Police Company, Corporal **Danielle Greene-Byrd (1977–)** of Chicago, lost her left lower arm on May 25, 2004, to a firefight in Iraq. She was inspired to join up after 9/11 and enlisted in 2003. A rocket-propelled grenade excised the lower part of her left arm and scored a nine-inch cut in her left leg when she checked security in 2004 on the roof of a Baghdad police station. Her rescuers located the arm in seven inches of sand to remove her wedding rings, which she had worn only two weeks.

Following recovery at Walter Reed in Washington, D.C., and fitting with a prosthetic arm, Danielle returned to Notre Dame University in Indiana to finish a master's degree in counseling and began aiding veterans as readjustment counselor in South Bend, Indiana. The Wounded Warriors named a basketball tournament after her. She received a Purple Heart, the 2015 Pat Tillman Award for Service, and, in 2016, the Arthur Ashe Courage trophy.

June 19, 2004

West Point graduate Captain **Dawn Halfaker (1979–)** from San Diego, California, lost her right arm to a rocket-propelled grenade on June 19, 2004, during a military police patrol outside Baqubah northwest of Baghdad, Iraq. Her military career began in South

Korea for the 3rd Infantry. In February 2004, she transferred to Operation Iraqi Freedom as a trainer of local police in Kuwait and security officer protecting a police station from rockets and improvised explosive devices (IEDs). A pre-dawn explosion on the edge of the Sunni Triangle destroyed her right shoulder blade and arm, broke five ribs, bruised her head, and collapsed her right lung during an enemy ambush of her armored Humvee.

Medevaced in a coma by helicopter to Landstuhl, Germany, Dawn received transport for treatment at Walter Reed Hospital in Washington, D.C. As a liaison in military support for the House Armed Services Commission, she studied helmet and equipment quality and care of casualties. Her service earned a Purple Heart and Bronze Star. With a master's degree in security from Georgetown University and an Ernst & Young citation as entrepreneur of the year, she continued aiding the army through her company, Halfaker & Associates in Arlington, Virginia.

August 24, 2004

Chechen suicide bombers **Aminat Nagaev (also Amina Nagayev, 1974–August 24, 2004)** and **Satisita Dzhbirkhanova (also Satsita or Sacita Jibirkhanov, 1967–August 24, 2004)** exploded two Tupolev turbojets from Volga-Aviaxpress airlines bound from Moscow's Domodedovo Airport to Volgograd. On August 24, 2004, airport security failed to search the saboteurs. Aminat plotted the 11:00 p.m. blast in the tail section of the Tu-134 jetliner to demolish it over Kimovsky in the Tula district. She intended to avenge the murder of her brother Uvais by Russian operatives, who tormented him with electric shocks in Khattuni before exploding him. Satisita hijacked the 9:30 p.m. flight of a Tu-154 turbojet from Moscow to Sochi and placed a bomb under a wing. The crash struck amid forty trees at Rostov. The mid-air sabotage terrorized southern Russians and killed both separatist saboteurs and all on board.

See also September 3, 2004.

September 3, 2004

Martyred murderers **Mariam Tuburova (?–September 3, 2004)** and **Roza Nagaev (also Nagayev, ?–September 3, 2004)**, sisters of martyred Chechen terrorist **Aminat Nagaev**, attacked the Beslan school in North Ossetia-Alana, Russia, and the metro depot in Rizhskaya, Moscow. The three-day catastrophe in the northern Caucasus began with the kidnap of eleven hundred twenty hostages by a guerrilla force from Chechnya. On September 3, 2004, the impact and shrapnel massacred three hundred thirty-four civilians at Beslan, one hundred eighty-six of them pupils. The eruptions killed ten subway passengers at Rizhskaya in retaliation for the death of Roza's brother Uvais by Russian special ops. They also beat her son and attached him to electric currents. Counterterrorism operations resulted in more torture and executions of Islamic cell members.

See also August 24, 2004.

November 12, 2004

The downing of a UH-60 Blackhawk helicopter piloted by Lieutenant

Colonel **Tammy Duckworth (March 12, 1968–)** from Bangkok, Thailand, resulted on November 12, 2004, from the strike of a rocket-propelled grenade (RPG) north of Baghdad. She had joined the army reserve in 1992 and entered the Iraqi conflict in 2004 in the town of Balad as a battle plan captain. Daily transports of cargo and troops subjected her to machine gun bursts and, near the Kurdistan capital of Erbil, a close call with a rocket-propelled grenade (RPG). The burst under the plexiglass cockpit floor cost her the right leg at the hip and the left leg below the knee, blackened burns, painful debriding surgeries, and full articulation of her shattered right arm.

From first aid over Taji and immediate treatment at Baghdad's 31st Support Hospital requiring forty units of blood, Tammy progressed to rehabilitation at Walter Reed Hospital in Washington, D.C. The recipient of a Purple Heart, two army medals, prosthetic legs, and a statue in Mount Vernon, Illinois, she served the Department of Veterans Affairs before her election to the 2012 U.S. House of representatives and the 2016 U.S. Senate. Her 2021 memoir *Every Day Is a Gift* recounts Iraqi experiences in combat and rehabilitation.

March 20, 2005

The first U.S. woman recipient of a Silver Star, **Leigh Ann Hester (January 12, 1982–)** from Bowling Green, Kentucky, killed three attackers during a twenty-five-minute ambush of thirty trucks on the Eastern Convoy Route at Salman Park, Iraq. A four-year veteran of the Army National Guard and sharpshooter, Sergeant Hester had served in the war zone since the previous July. She and her company of ten from the 503rd Military Police Battalion, armed with an M-4 carbine, fragmentation grenades, and an M-203 grenade launcher, eliminated thirty-four enemy hidden in orchard irrigation ditches. The five-to-one assault occurred during round-the-clock patrols three miles south of Baghdad on the Tigris River, location of Saddam Hussein's germ and chemical warfare center. Leigh Ann later served in the Afghan war and earned a Bronze Star, NATO medal, and army commendation. A wax figurine at the Army Women's Museum in Fort Lee, Virginia, preserves her likeness.

October 26, 2005

A wounded army driver and turret gunner with the Virginia Army National Guard, Sergeant **Monica Beltran (1985–)** from Prince William County, Virginia, defended a sixty-man convoy from the 1173rd Transportation Company on October 26, 2005, during an enemy ambush outside Balad, Iraq. The confrontation occurred near the largest U.S. air base, fifty miles north of Baghdad. After a grenade smashed into Monica's Humvee and a bullet fractured her left thumb, she continued firing a .50 caliber machine gun to counter small arms fire. For saving fifty-four soldiers, she earned promotion to sergeant. Her commendations include a Bronze Star, Purple Heart, and Virginia Women in History citation. In service to the XVIII Airborne Corps, she fought in Afghanistan in 2013.

November 24, 2005

A double amputee, Specialist **Marissa Strock (1984–)** of Petersburg, Virginia, lost both lower legs during a search for a mass grave on Thanksgiving Day, November 24, 2005, in southern Baghdad, Iraq. A member of the 170th Military Police since November 2004, she discharged duties in security checkpoints and patrols and witnessed eight terrorist attacks. She operated the turret gun of an armored Humvee when it detonated an improvised explosive device (IED), killing three soldiers. She plunged backward, incurring brain trauma and broken arm, wrist, and clavicle. Suffering a medically induced coma from cranial edema, Marissa progressed to a year and a half recovery at Walter Reed Hospital in Washington, D.C., which *Newsweek* pictured on the cover. She earned a United Service Operations citation, competed in Ms. Veteran America, and co-featured in the 2017 documentary film *Served Like a Girl*.

January 7, 2006

Tactical support specialist during Operation Iraqi Freedom Lieutenant **Jaime L. Campbell (1985–January 7, 2006)**, a pilot from Ephrata, Washington, died in the wreckage of a Sokorsky UH-60 Black Hawk helicopter. A former rodeo queen and enlistee in the Army National Guard at Anchorage, Alaska, she served in the Middle East simultaneously with her father, Sergeant Major Jeff Krausse, and husband, Captain Sam Campbell. Her deployment began in September 2005. The plane and eleven passengers were conducting reconnaissance over Tal Afar in northern Iraq on January 7, 2006, when bad weather caused the crash.

January 21, 2006

An army tow truck mechanic and driver for the 54th Engineering Battalion deployed in Al-Ramadi, Iraq, Specialist **Crystal Davis (1984–)** of Camden, South Carolina, lost her right leg after hitting a roadside remote-controlled improvised explosive device (IED). Her last automotive job, recovering trucks and Humvees disabled by explosives, began at 2:00 a.m. January 21, 2006. Insurgents from Ramadi planted the bomb that exploded under her truck in urban traffic. Her morning ended with soldiers defending the site and her transport to a Baghdad army hospital. The impact crushed bones in her left leg, reducing her mobility and increasing rehabilitation time to a year at Walter Reed Hospital in Washington, D.C. When she returned home from Landstuhl, Germany, in June 2006, with a prosthesis, scarred leg, and walker, she intended to re-enlist as a military physical therapist. In 2015 at Hickory Motor Speedway, she drove in a NASCAR competition for America's Veterans Racing.

May 6, 2006

The death of Flight Lieutenant **Sarah-Jayne Mulvihill (June 10, 1973–May 6, 2006)**, an English Royal Air Force warrior from the cathedral city of Canterbury, aroused sorrow among the British at the first female sacrifice to war in two decades. In a nine-year career, she completed RAF training at Cranwell in Lincolnshire, served in air traffic control in Benson, Oxfordshire, and extended training in Kenya. Posting in Basra during her second Iraq tour placed her in a hazardous war zone. On May 6, 2006, she died along with a four-man flight crew after ground fire of a rocket-propelled grenade downed their Lynx helicopter over a two-story building in Basra. Shia rebels in the Mahdi army dishonored the five casualties by jeering at the crash site and tossing stones and firebombs that ignited three armored vehicles. A children's play area at Cherry Orchard commemorates Sarah's sacrifice.

May 17, 2006

A casualty to Operation Peacemaker, Captain **Nichola Goddard (May 2, 1980–May 17, 2006)** from Madang, Papua New Guinea, died in battle west of Kandahar, Afghanistan, the first female Canadian casualty of the Afghan War. Trained at the Royal Military College in Ontario, she deployed to a war zone in Panjwaii district of southeastern Afghanistan as a member of the Canadian Light Infantry. Her platoon was part of a two-day mission to seize Taliban occupants of a mosque. On May 17, 2006, a rocket-propelled grenade struck their LAV III armored personnel carrier, adding her to the forty enemy dead. Her bravery earned a sacrifice citation, Memorial Cross, campaign star, and the naming of a memorial arch, two middle schools, a trophy, coast guard patrol vessel, bagpipe dirge, biography, and scholarship.

June 11, 2006

A hero of the Iraq War, Private **Michelle Norris (1987–)**, a medic from Stourbridge, England, gained international renown on June 11, 2006, for reconnaissance against two hundred enemy on the Tigris River at Al Amarah. In Iraq's southeast, with the 1st Battalion Princess of Wales's Royal Regiment, she retrieved a wounded sergeant to the top of an armored vehicle and treated his facial injury while receiving heavy fire. She and the casualty flew to safety in a Lynx helicopter. On March 21, 2007, she received the Military Cross, Iraq medal, and Diamond Jubilee medal from Queen Elizabeth II.

August 12, 2006

Israel's first woman helicopter mechanic, Sergeant Major **Keren Tendler (September 26, 1979–August 12, 2006)** of Rehovot died over Lebanon on August 12, 2006, when enemy fire shot down her CH-53 Sea Stallion *Yas'ur*, a heavy-lift transport. She was the first female to die in the war with Lebanon, which began on July 12, 2006, with a naval blockade and enemy buildup south of the Litani River. On August 12, 2006, Hezbollah guerrillas claimed the direct hit, which also felled four male soldiers. The losses brought the total of Israeli dead to one hundred sixty-five and Lebanese casualties to thirteen hundred. Rescue operations required thirty-six hours of scouring Palestinian territory before locating Karen's remains. A memorial garden and scholarship honor her service.

August 13, 2006

A multitalented soldier, Senior Chief Mass Communication Specialist **Jackey Smith (1979–)** from Lincoln,

Nebraska, became the first woman combat photographer to earn a Bronze Star. The commendation derived from a documentation mission in Iraq on August 13, 2006, with a Nikon D2X. She defended her navy unit from terrorists with a pistol and M-4 carbine. When the soldiers re-deployed on armored vehicles, she photographed their return to duty. After surviving stage three breast cancer, on October 19, 2021, she took command of the USS *William P. Lawrence*, a guided-missile destroyer.

November 28, 2006

On a rations delivery by truck from Bagram Air Base to residents of Logar in eastern Afghanistan, Army Corporal **Sue Downes (1979–)** of Tazewell, Tennessee, a gunner in the military police, lost both legs to two anti-tank mines. She signed up for the army after 9/11 in 2001. Her daily assignments ranged from checkpoints and patrols to raids and village searches. The explosion on November 28, 2006, killed two soldiers and twisted the truck frame, forcing her under the turret shield. The impact sliced her liver and intestines. From treatment at a NATO hospital and Landstuhl in Germany she progressed to treatment and therapy at Walter Reed Hospital in Washington, D.C. She recovered with the aid of prosthetic legs and a service dog named Lyla, a yellow lab. Her medals include a combat badge, Bronze Star, and two Purple Hearts.

January 10, 2007

For the troop escalation to protect Baghdad, Iraq, on January 10, 2007, Australian Major General Simone **Wilkie (1964–)** of Ballarat, Victoria, received her first command post. A soldier since age nineteen, she completed Officer Cadet School in New South Wales and entered the 136th Signal Squad with a background in strategy and defense. From NATO deployment in telecommunications in Cambodia in 1993, she advanced to commandant of eighteen hundred staff at Camp Victory, the multi-national headquarters at Al Faw Palace, Iraq, for which she earned a U.S. Bronze Star. In September 2010, she served in Afghanistan as commander of fifteen hundred Australians and allied troops in a war zone before returning to Canberra. Her ten medals include commendations for foreign war service and a NATO citation.

February 21, 2007

Major **Christine Nyangoma (January 1, 1967–)** from Fort Portal, Uganda, began serving in African bush wars in 1982. Her deployment as commander of a women's unit took her from the Rwenzori Mountains in Uganda to Congo, Somalia, and southern Sudan. In service to the African Union Mission in Somalia on February 21, 2007, she collaborated with contingents from Burundi, Djibouti, Ethiopia, Ghana, Kenya, Nigeria, and Sierra Leone against Al-Shabaab's Islamic terrorists, who wreaked havoc throughout the Horn of Africa. Of the total twenty thousand, six hundred seventy-four fighters, more than three thousand died in the operation. Contributing to danger were suicide bombing and outbreaks of ebola and leptospirosis.

March 23, 2007

A victim of unrest in the Middle East, Seaman **Faye Turney (1983–)** of Plymouth, England, was the only female marine seized from an English frigate by an Irani sea patrol. When the HMS *Cornwall* searched a merchant dhow (small lateen-sailed boat) for contraband vehicles in Iraqi waters on March 23, 2007, Iranians arrested fifteen members of the Royal Navy and impounded two inflatable boats. Faye and fourteen males underwent interrogation in Tehran about intrusion into contested territory. She was forced to sleep in a stone cell, conceal her hair under a hijab (head scarf), and write an apology letter. After a period of psychological torment, Faye and the others returned to the north Devon marine base on April 5. Media demand for the inside scoop earned Faye £100,000 for her story.

April 27, 2007

Texas-born army medic **Monica Lin Brown (May 24, 1988)** of Lake Jackson followed Iraq hero **Leigh Ann Hester** as the second female recipient of the Silver Star. Deployed to Pasta, Afghanistan, at age nineteen, Monica was patrolling north outside Jani Khail with five vehicles on April 27, 2007, when a roadside pressure plate bomb ignited a fuel tank. Under fire from the Taliban mortars and grenades for two hours, Monica retrieved a soldier trapped under a burning Humvee. She evaluated burns and cuts, stopped bleeding, and started IVs while shielding casualties from shrapnel with her body. Moved to a distant location, she continued to work without cover to ready two soldiers for helicopter evacuation. She earned a combat medical citation, commendation of merit, and a presidential unit award for fearlessness in close combat.

June 17, 2008

A British casualty in Lashkar Gah, Afghanistan, Corporal **Sarah Feely (December 17, 1981–June 17, 2008)** of Liverpool became England's first female to die in the Afghan War. Following training at Winchester, England, she specialized in combat intelligence. Her six-year career began in Germany, Basra, and Baghdad, Iraq, where she learned to speak Pashtu, and preceded stationing in an Afghan war zone as target analyst. The explosion of an improvised roadside bomb on June 17, 2008, killed her and the other four troops riding in a Snatch Land Rover. A scholarship, citation, and memorial bear her name and example.

July 2008

Chantelle Taylor (1970–), a Scots Medical Corps sergeant with the Argyll and Sutherland Highlanders, became the first female British soldier to kill an enemy aggressor in close combat. She enlisted in the infantry in 1998 and built a career from action in Kosovo, Sierra Leone, Iraq, and Helmand Province, Afghanistan, where she patrolled Nad-e Ali, a British base at Lashkar Gah. During a midday ambush in Marjah in southern Afghanistan in July 2008 while her lightly armored convoy came under grenade and machine gun fire, she aimed an SA80 rifle at a Taliban fighter. From the Land Rover, she fired seven times, stopping him from shooting her with his AK47. The firefight ended with the landing of an Apache gunship and her help in treating a soldier hemorrhaging from a gut wound. After a grueling friendly fire accident in August 2008, she retired the following year to work in security in Baghdad and published a memoir, *Battleworn: The Memoir of a Combat Medic in Afghanistan*.

July 18, 2008

Pakistani neuroscientist and terrorist **Aafia Siddiqui (1972–)** acquired an FBI identity as the jihadist "Lady Al-Qaeda" and the only female Al Qaeda operative, facilitator, and fund raiser. She left Karachi in 1989 to study at Massachusetts Institute of Technology and Brandeis University. Pakistani intelligence arrested her as a saboteur. On July 18, 2008, American forces in Ghazni, Afghanistan, shot her in the abdomen and seized bomb-making drawings, chemicals, and maps of the Brooklyn Bridge, Empire State Building, and Statue of Liberty. On September 22, 2010, a Manhattan court handed down an eighty-six-year prison term in Fort Worth, Texas, for attempted murder after firing an M-4 rifle at FBI agents and American interrogators in Afghanistan.

March 20, 2009

The first British female in the Afghan War against the Taliban, twenty-year-old lance corporal **Amy Thomas (1989–)** of Port Talbot, South Wales, accompanied the elite Royal Marine 42 Commandos to investigate terrorism. An honor student, she earned a bachelor's degree in primary education at the University of South Wales. Carrying an SA80 rifle during her six-month engagement as a military police officer, she routinely frisked female suspects and gathered intelligence on sabotage. On secondment (detached from her original company), she dropped from a helicopter on March 20, 2009, to fire on the enemy in Marjah, Helmand province. For the all-day firefight, she carried a load of body armor and helmet, ammunition, evidence kit, and food and water for two days. She was the only female to fight alongside Marines or infantry. Officers respected women like Amy for interacting with local families and respecting Middle Eastern culture and traditions.

November 11, 2009

Among the first Chinese women to enroll in the army, on November 11, 2009, at the Military Affair Office, **Wang Yi (1988–)** from Shanghai volunteered on the sixtieth anniversary of the People's Republic of China. Exiting coursework in foreign language at East China Normal University in Shanghai, she and two hundred eight female students, including **Deng Yulan (1988–)** from Mianyang, Sichuan, and **Wang Shaowen** from Xinjiang in the far northwest, wholeheartedly embraced military life. They had to pass a physical exam that rejected anyone with two ear piercings. On October 1, the trio paraded with a female squad in Tian'anmen Square, a 53.5 acre plaza in central Beijing. After two years of service to the Women's Independent Battalion, they returned to the university in 2011, where

Wang Shaowen studied tuition free on the army subsidy of six thousand yuan (currently $826.8).

May 11, 2010

On U.S. Army military police patrol in Charkh, Afghanistan, with the 173rd Airborne Brigade Combat Team, Sergeant **Kendra Coleman (1987–)** of Jackson, Georgia, suffered a second Taliban improvised explosive device (IED) burst that mangled her left leg above the knee. At age fourteen, she gained inspiration from the surge of patriotism following 9/11 in 2001 and joined up six years later. The first incident on April 3, 2010, wrecked her vehicle and injured her brain, hearing, and torso. The last blast twenty-three days later on May 11, 2010, occurred on foot patrol near a pile of tires. Activated by remote control, detonation caused bladder, brain, and torso damage from shrapnel. Kendra remained conscious and applied arterial pressure.

Kendra airlifted to Bagram Airfield, Landstuhl Hospital in Germany, and Walter Reed Hospital in Washington, D.C., before entering Brooks military hospital in San Antonio, Texas. For service to her country as a police paratrooper, she earned two Purple Hearts, two army combat medals, and a furnished, handicap accessible home in Cinco Ranch, Texas, from Helping a Hero, a non-profit veteran's organization based in Houston. Still in recovery from mental and emotional scarring, she planned coursework in communications and prosthetics at University of Houston with help from her brother Troy Pieper and service pitbull, Smokey James.

July 29, 2010

On July 29, 2010, Vice Admiral **Nora Tyson (1957–)** from Memphis, Tennessee, became the first woman to command a U.S. naval fleet. In March 2003, she aided Operation Iraqi Freedom, followed by task force command in Singapore. While commanding a carrier strike force, she managed the USS *George H.W. Bush* flagship as part of the 6th Fleet in the Mediterranean and the 5th Fleet in the Persian Gulf. To assist hurricane Katrina victims in late August 2005, she removed debris and distributed food and water. As head of the 3rd Fleet until January 12, 2012, she built on experience navigating the nuclear-powered USS *Enterprise* and, aboard the amphibious assault vessel USS *Bataan* in the Gulf of Mexico. Before retirement in September 2017, Nora earned battle ribbons, a war on terrorism citation, and the NATO medal.

February 15, 2011

A Spanish combatant in the Libyan War, Captain **Rosa García-Malea (1981–)** of Almería earned a Medal of Andalusia for piloting the F/A-18 Hornet. The first woman in the Spanish Air Force to fly a supersonic fighter jet, she aided a revolution against dictator Muammar Gaddafi. Following protests in Benghazi on February 15, 2033, Spain joined Belgium, Britain, Canada, Denmark, France, Italy, Norway, Qatar, and the U.S. in patrolling a no-fly zone. A coalition of British, Canadian, French, and U.S. troops initiated mass attacks and a harbor blockade. NATO fighters employed a bombing campaign, which ended with Gaddafi's assassination on

October 20, 2011. She progressed to one of the seven demonstrators for the Patrulla Aquila (Eagle Patrol) of the Casa C-101, a light attack jet.

March 8, 2011

Revolt leader **Aya Virginie Touré (fl. 2010s)** of Ivory Coast mobilized some forty-five thousand Christian and Muslim women in defiance of election fraud in the ten districts of Abidjan. Facing down police harassment, Humvees, and tanks in Abobo and Koumassi, she trusted the women who followed African tradition by banging pots and marching in red or black dresses or in leaves or clay or nude to defy President Laurent Gbagbo for refuting a free election. On March 3, 2011, her forces weathered machete slashes and automatic rifle fire, which killed seven women, one of them pregnant. Aya collected bodies and summoned the Red Cross.

March 8, 2011, proved Aya capable of withstanding telephone and personal threats to her six children. While demonstrators spilled over into villages and menaced the presidential palace, men shielded Aya, female rebels, and their children from tank and rocket fire in the market by lining the highway with cars. In a BBC interview on March 23, she proposed military intervention to stop the massacre. Her tactics spread to Ghana, Liberia, Nigeria, Sierra Leone, and Togo and stymied police, tanks, and fifty thousand mercenaries. With the aid of two thousand United Nations forces, the rebels succeeded in ousting Gbagbo on March 30 and installing as president Alassane Dramane Ouattara.

March 19, 2011

A pilot with the 89th Airlift Wing and U.S. Air Force major general, **Margaret H. Woodward (February 11, 1960–)** of Andrews Air Force Base, Maryland, activated a twelve-day United Nations intervention in Libya on March 19, 2011, and superintended a no-fly zone. Her thirty-two year career began with refueling planes and at the mid–December 1989 invasion of Panama. Subsequent deployment to the Kosovo War and in Iraq against Saddam Hussein, Al Qaeda, and the Taliban preceded the assignment to Libya. As commander of actions in Africa, she oversaw B-2 Spirit stealth bombers, F-16C Fighting Falcons, and F-15E Strike Eagles and guided planes through Muammar Qaddafi's anti-aircraft fire from Tripoli. She received a distinguished service citation, Legion of Merit, and Bronze Star and renown for being the first U.S. female to command a senior combat campaign.

April 18, 2011

An ammunition technical officer during a second tour of duty, Captain **Lisa Jade Head (November 30, 1981– April 19, 2011)** of Huddersfield, England, died at Nahr-e-Saraj in south central Afghanistan's Helmand Province. After graduating from the Royal Military Academy at Sandhurst, she worked a high threat post for the 11th Explosive Ordnance Disposal Regiment in Iraq in 2006 and Afghanistan in 2007. While neutralizing a cluster of roadside bombs in an alley, she was knocked backward by a first blast before returning to defusing. She incurred wounds to both arms and both legs from the third device, a five-pound bomb that was intended to kill an explosives specialist. Wrapped in field dressing and nine tourniquets, the Yorkshire native survived helicopter evacuation to Camp Bastion at Lashkar Gah and succumbed the next day on April 18, 2011, in Birmingham at Queen Elizabeth Hospital.

May 12, 2011

Brigadier-General **Ramatoulie D.K. Sanneh (fl. 2010s)** of Serrekunda, Gambia, rose to the highest ranking female in the nation's army on May 12, 2011. At the confluence of the Gambia River with the Atlantic Ocean, she completed her education at Gambia Technical Training Institute. She focused on ending the nation's gender-based violence by counseling soldiers in their barracks on respect for girls and women. Her achievements with the Women's Initiative include a 2010 membership in the National Order of the Republic of Gambia and collaboration with the German Peace Support to educate soldiers on mounting and dismounting vehicles within range of terrorist-made improvised explosive devices (IEDs).

October 11, 2011

A hero of the Afghan War, Lieutenant **Ashley White (September 3, 1987–October 11, 2011)** from Alliance, Ohio, died in combat in Kandahar on October 11, 2011, while leading a special operations task force. A first lieutenant in the U.S. Army Medical Service Corps, she trained in Fort Benning, Georgia, with forty-pound packs over twenty miles of terrain and earned medals as a parachutist. Two years before the full use of women in combat, she was one of the first female participants in support deployment to Afghanistan. She accompanied Army Rangers and Navy Seals on raids and collected information from Afghan women as part of a program of cultural support. Among challenges in the field, she excelled at night mountain climbing. On a final mission, she entered a compound wired with improvised explosive devices, which triggered, killing her and two other soldiers. In death, she received a Purple Heart, Bronze Star, and combat badge. A biography, *Ashley's War: The Untold Story of a Team of Women Soldiers on the Special Ops Battlefield*, characterized her difficult job.

April 2012

In April 2012, an underground female squad engineered the eight-months downfall of Libyan tyrant Muammar Gaddafi. A rebel secret agent of the Warfalla clan, **Inas Fathy (1986–)** in Souq al-Juma concentrated on building consensus in Tripoli. While NATO forces pounded the official compound with bombs, she organized three tons of military meals for combatants in Miserata and the western mountains. She surveyed government buildings with photos and maps and reported troops, military vehicles, and weapons caches to rebels in Tunisia. Her comrades carried coded messages, smuggled ammunition by tugboat, formed a hospital for casualties, aided former political prisoners, and gathered cash to buy more, which rebels slipped in by sea from Benghazi.

Female support kept the underground alive. Attorney **Hweida Shibadi (1970–)** pinpointed airstrike targets for NATO. Outside Miserata, sales manager **Asma Gargoum (1982–)** spied on tank positions and troop movements by bus and car in Tripoli and directed rebels through courier. **Dalla Abbazi (1969–)** from Sidi Khalifa, enabled the February 20 uprising in Benghazi to smuggle AK-47s and Belgian FAL rifles from Tunisia, hide them, and distribute guns, bandoliers, and homemade liberation flags. She chose the second floor of her house as an explosives lab for making Molotov cocktails and pipe bombs. On a March 20 attempt at arresting her, she fought off soldiers with teeth and claws.

Female professionals contributed what they knew best. Psychologist **Aisha Gdour (1967–)** financed and secured bullets in a leather bag, delivered guns by car, and raised cash to supply families with clothing; physician **Rabia Gajun (fl. 2012)** channeled pharmaceuticals and a printer to the underground. Art teacher **Amal Bashir (fl. 2012)** catalogued munition orders in cypher. Armed with a Kalashnikov rifle, which rebels coded a "bottle of milk," hairdresser **Fatima Bredan (1983–)** of Tajura treated the injured at Metiga, a Turkish hospital, and proposed transfers of patients to better care in Tunisia. A pregnant attorney, **Nabila Abdelrahman Abu Ras (1971–)** arranged demonstrations and sped through city streets distributing leaflets.

April 27, 2012

Nigerian Air Force officer **Blessing Liman (March 13, 1984–)** of Zango Kataf, Katuna, became West Africa's first female military pilot on April 27, 2012, at the capital city of Abuja. After study at the Nigerian College of Aviation Technology at Zaria, in July 2011, she joined the national air force specialists called "knights of the air." She continued duties to the Presidential Air Fleet and flew missions to annihilate Boko Haram weapons transport.

Contemporary Nigerian female record breakers include instructor pilot **Geneviève Nwaogwugwu (fl. 2012)**, a graduate of the Nigerian Defence Academy. She worked in airlift at Katsinna and Maiduguri and co-piloted the all-female Intelligence, Surveillance, and Reconnaissance (ISR) operation. Geneviève's partner, Captain **Olubunmi Ijelu (fl. 2012)**, Nigeria's first female captain and flier, trained in surveillance and reconnaissance at Abu Dhabi, United Arab Republic, to fly the Beechcraft KingAir ISR helicopter on reconnaissance missions over Niger.

Contemporaries added expertise to the servicewomen. **Kafayat Sanni (1997–)**, the first female pilot of fighter aircraft in sub-Saharan Africa, trained at the Columbus Air Force Base in Mississippi and at South Africa's Starlite International Training Academy. Sergeant Major **Grace Garba (February 14, 1966–)**, a nurse-midwife from Garkida, became the first female Nigerian Air Warrant Officer. **Tolulope Arotile (1996–July 14, 2020)**, first woman pilot of a combat helicopter, trained at Air Force Base Kaduna to combat Boko Haram insurgents. Tolulope died in Kaduna of head injuries from an on-base car accident.

October 1, 2012

A member of the 514th Military Police Company during Operation Enduring Freedom in Afghanistan, Staff Sergeant **Donna Johnson (May 10, 1983–October 1, 2012)** from Raeford, North Carolina, succumbed on October 1, 2012, to detonation of bombs carried by a suicidal motorcyclist. She had already served a year's rotation in 2007. While on patrol in Khost, in 2012, she and two other soldiers died in the ambush. Her achievements earned a long list of citations from the army and NATO. Her sexual orientation stirred a bitter rebuke from a Raeford Baptist church that blamed gays in the military for the combat death. Donna's wife, army Staff Sergeant Tracy Dice Johnson, received insulting treatment by military officials who disdained same-sex unions.

October 24, 2012

A British marine teaching first aid for the 3rd Medical Regiment, Corporal **Channing Day (1987–October 24, 2012)** from Swindon, England, died on October 24, 2012, at Nahr-e-Saraj, Afghanistan. A bullet struck her chest during an eight-person foot patrol. Along with two fellow soldiers, she succumbed during an assault at a police checkpoint by a drug addict carrying an AK-47. A support for Royal Marine commandos, she had served seven years in the British military.

October 6, 2013

Captain **Jennifer M. Moreno (June 25, 1988–October 6, 2013)**, a decorated nurse paratrooper from San Diego, California, died in the Afghan War on October 6, 2013, while tending injured members of the Army Rangers. She enlisted in the National Guard in 2006 and served in Iraq. In the third month of special operation Enduring Freedom, a Taliban booby trap killed her and three others in Zhari, Kandahar, while she treated a military casualty and a working dog. The army honored her with a posthumous promotion to captain, NATO medal, Purple Heart, and Bronze Star commendation for foiling an enemy plot to slaughter multiple soldiers. Veterans named a VA Medical Center for Jennifer. The sergeant who incurred wounds while recovering her body received a Silver Star.

October 21, 2013

A north Caucasus terrorist **Naida Asiyalova (1983–October 21, 2013)** from Dagestan, Russia, conspired with a terrorist cell to bomb a local bus at Volgograd in southern Russia. Because of the ease of female saboteurs to infiltrate security, the successful explosion of a suicide belt on October 21, 2013, killed her and seven others and wounded thirty-six. Three of the dead were teenage students. In November, Naida's Russian husband, Dmitry Sokolov, described fitting the belt and arranging the explosion to further creation of an Islamic state. He died at a police shootout at his house.

October 25, 2013

Private **Elise Toft (1990–)**, a combat engineer from Lyngdal, Norway, became the first female Norwegian awarded a combat citation since World

War II. Trained at Rena and assigned to the war in Afghanistan for two years, she aided the United Nations International Security Assistance Force as point guard for convoys. In 2011, she assisted a unit of the Norwegian Provincial Reconstruction Team's Task Unit searching for roadside bombs. Under fire, she cleared the route of explosives to secure the axis. Two years later on October 25, 2013, she traveled to Oslo to accept the award for serenity and presence of mind in a war zone.

January 21, 2014

At large in Sochi, Japan, on January 21, 2014, the venue of the February winter Olympics, **Ruzanna "Salima" Ibragimova (1992–)** headed the list of Chechen "black widows." She and her co-conspirators were eager to annihilate Russians by smuggling explosives in hand cream. The twenty-two-year-old widow of a militant jihadist from Dagestan, Chechnya, in the northern Caucasus, she bears a scar on the left cheek, a stiff left elbow, and a limp.

May 25, 2014

As one hundred fifty thousand Russians packed the border on the day of the national election, Sergeant **Andriana Susak-Arekhta (1988–)** from Kosiv in southwestern Ukraine volunteered with a paramilitary assault force of the Ukrainian army on the Donets River to recapture the industrial center of Shchastia. While processing documents for the Luhansk district checkpoint during a national anti-terrorist operation at the airport, she arrested fourteen insurgents, some armed men wearing priestly robes and others who dubbed themselves "Don Cossacks." Equipped with an assault rifle and disguised behind a black balaclava, bullet-proof vest, and camo uniform, Andriana, during the first months of pregnancy, fought in male guise at the airport on the eastern front line on May 25, 2014, alongside paramedic **Kateryna Pryimak (1994–)**, and Lieutenant **Nadia Savchenko (May 11, 1981–)**, a helicopter gunship and supersonic aircraft pilot from Kyiv. Another cohort deployed to locate terrorists in the donetsk area, **Kateryna "Ket" Noskova (1989–August 16, 2015)** was killed by a mine explosion on August 16, 2015, when the motorized brigade tried to rescue a casualty at Horlivka in northeastern Ukraine.

On September 25, 2015, in collaboration with the Ukrainian national guard, the company's strategy shifted to trench warfare and anti-tank guided missile launchers mounted on trucks. During phosphorus attacks, mortar rounds, rockets, and shelling from hostile territory at a Metalist power plant, Andriana's husband suffered wounds to chest, shoulder, and knee. Nadia was captured and charged with terrorism in the artillery barrage that killed Russian journalists. Through intervention by the Red Cross and United Nations, she gained release on April 15, 2019, in exchange for two Russian intelligence officers, and returned to parliament.

In December 2022, Andriana redeployed in expectation of a Russian invasion. To support other female veterans and obliterate stereotypes, she and Kateryna Pryimak co-founded Women's

Veteran Motion. The society of former soldiers promoted women's rights, security for medics, female uniforms, and full financial and social benefits for chronic illness, depression, and effects of sexism, ageism, public condemnation, and the Covid pandemic. For activism and military acumen, Andriana, Nadia, and Kateryna Noskova earned United Nations respect and the titles "People's Hero of Ukraine" and "Cavalier of the Order of Courage." Andriana appeared in the 2017 documentary *Invisible Battalion*.

July 8, 2014

An Israeli fighter pilot of the F-16D Fighting Falcon during the Gaza War, Captain **Tamar Ariel (September 12, 1989–October 14, 2014)** an Orthodox Jew from Masu'ot Yitzhak near Ashkelon, flew the highest number of combat missions during Operation Protective Edge. She survived a spinal injury after her plane crashed on July 8, 2014, from mechanical malfunction. Over seven weeks, the confrontation over the Gaza Strip weakened Hamas by killing two thousand three hundred ten enemy and wounding more than ten thousand six hundred. Recognized as a fallen warrior, Tamar died in a blizzard on October 14, 2014, on Nepal's Annapurna Trail. Her heroism survives in the naming of a high school and synagogue.

August 19, 2014

A commander of heavily armed female Iraqi raiders, **Sedar Botan (fl. 2014)** led a seven-unit squadron of rescuers on August 19, 2014, among the Kurdish women of Erbil, Makhmour, and the Qandil Mountains in northern Iraq. Under United States air support with Hellfire air-to-surface missiles and aid from the Kurdistan Workers' Party, some eight hundred females tracked Islamic State (ISIS) guerrilla forces. They placed roadside bombs, captured forty-nine Turkish embassy workers in Mosul in June, and kidnapped three thousand females, including two thousand from the Yazidi religious minority. To save Kurdistan women from sex slavery and abuse, execution, suicide, or forced marriage, she promoted Jihadist fears that males killed by female soldiers would not reside in heaven.

September 2014

A Kurdish strategist at the siege of Kobani, **Rojda Felat (1977–)** of Qamishli in northern Syria, commanded eleven lightly armed women against an Islamic cult equipped with tanks, machine guns, and mortars. On Mishtanour Hill, her squad fired rifles, machine guns, and a rocket-propelled grenade launcher. She lost five warriors and suffered shrapnel wounds requiring hospitalization. Her Kurdish Muslim commander, **Arin Mirkan (1994–October 5, 2014)** from Mirkan, died in a suicide attack on a tank with hand grenades that killed ten ISIS attackers. A statue in Kobani commemorates Arin's dramatic martyrdom while the Turkish Army looked on and did nothing to help her. Rojda advanced in military command to forty-five soldiers and a promotion to lead three hundred in a first strike at Tell Hamis in northeastern Syria in May 2016. On the Tigris River, her fighters seized Raqqa in late October 2017.

October 11, 2014

A member of Peshmerga, a Kurdish women's combat regiment in Iraq, **Rengin Yusuf (c. 1980s–October 11, 2014)** died in battle while deployed as a sniper. During the assault on Daquq south of the Zagros Mountains, she observed the retreat of ISIS, a radical wing of Sunni Muslims. The AK-47 machine gun fire that felled her caused her death within the week on October 11, 2014, at a military hospital. Sandor Jászberényi, a writer for the *Wall Street Journal,* honored her spunk under the title "The Mother Who Fought ISIS to the Death."

March 24, 2015

A five-year career sailor and martyr in southwest India, Lieutenant **Kiran Shekhawat (May 1, 1988–March 24, 2015)** from Mumbai died at sea on March 24, 2015, in the line of duty as a naval officer. Posting to Goa in military intelligence put her in charge of analysis of the environment and battle strategy. When the Dornier turboprop crashed on a pre-midnight training mission, she was eyeing the coastline to track enemy ships. Divers retrieved her body from the fuselage. The example of the first female naval casualty survives in a charitable foundation, park, sculpture, and road name.

June 16, 2015

Her nation's first female merchant navy captain **Radhika Menon (fl. 1970s–2010s)** of Kodungallur in southwestern India made headlines for rescuing seven men from a sinking fishing boat in the Bay of Bengal. She advanced from radio officer to mastered of the oil tanker *Sampurna Swarajya,* traveling some six months per voyage. Her recovery of the marooned fishermen off Orissa on June 16, 2015, occurred in twenty-five-foot waves and sixty-knot winds. It began with her on-deck sighting by binoculars of the anchorless *Durgamma* and involved extending a pilot rope ladder on the starboard side and passing down life jackets. The International Maritime Organization in London conferred on her the Panna Thai citation for bravery. Lloyd's of London nominated her for 2107 Seafarer of the year.

November 24, 2015

The first Pakistani pilot killed in combat, **Marium Mukhtiar (May 19, 1992–November 24, 2015)** of Karachi, died in a Chengdu air force fighter jet that crashed at Kundian in the Punjab. A fighter pilot from a military family, she graduate from the Army Public School and College. On a training flight at low altitude, mechanical failure in the FT-7PG forced her ejection from the cockpit, but she succumbed to injuries on November 24, 2015, at a military hospital. Authorities declared her a national martyr and presented her a military citation. A film documentary featured actor Sanam Baloch in the hero's part.

2016

Major **Mariam Al Mansouri (1979–)**, a pilot of the F-16 warplane from Abu Dhabi, became the first female fighter pilot of the United Arab Emirates. After completing training at Khalifa bin Zayed Air College in Abu

Dhabi, she waited a decade for a combat assignment in a Fighting Falcon or Viper. Her deployment against terrorists began under the call name "Lady Liberty." Aerial missions in 2016 took her over Syria to lead a strike against Daesh/Isis, an extremist Iraqi-Syrian jihadist sect of Sunni Muslims. Her achievements included the Pride of the Emirates citation.

March 11, 2016

A member of the Mongolian army for a decade, Sergeant **Muncunchimeg Nyamaajav (1986–)** from Bayankhongor City mastered warrior leadership in south central Alaska at the Noncommissioned Officer Academy. With the 25th Infantry on March 11, 2016, she practiced field tactics in the rough terrain at Joint Base Elmendorf-Richardson northeast of Anchorage, Alaska, on the Knik Arm inlet. Paratroopers learned skiing behind motor vehicles in a freezing winter climate as cold and semi-arid as her hometown. She completed the course in 2017.

January 11, 2017

Zambia's first woman fighter pilot, Lieutenant **Thokozile Muwamba (1993–)** left freshman coursework at Copperbelt University in Kitwe in 2012 to join the nation's air force. Early experiences introduced her to the SAAB Safari MFI-15 trainer aircraft and the SF260TW, an Italian aerobatics plane. In preparation for flying a K-8 aircraft or the L-15 ground attack plane, on January 11, 2017, she dressed in helmet, gloves, and zip-up suit. As a feminist, on February 23, 2021, she launched a charity walk from Lusaka to Livingstone near Victoria Falls to raise consciousness of cyberbullying and social media abuse of female soldiers.

January 25, 2017

A septuagenarian practitioner of medieval Indian martial arts, **Meenakshi Amma (1941–)** of Vadakara, British India, demonstrated to the younger generation on January 25, 2017, a warrior's stance and daring with stick, cudgel, dagger, and sword. She began studying classical dance, yoga, and dueling at age six. In 1958, she became an arms master teacher in her husband's school, which charges no fee. At his death in 2007, she took over the school. Still posed behind her original shield, at age seventy-four, she armed herself with a sword, crouched to the arena floor, and twirled her weapon at an opponent in the eight animal poses.

After sixty-eight years of training and practice of Kalaripayattu, Meenakshi offers public performances sixty times annually to one hundred fifty students, both boys and girls. To prepare youth for self-defense, she advocates that parents introduce military techniques as early as possible, using fifteenth-century warrior Unniyarcha as an example. Meenakshi's fame increased with the film *Look Back* and the 2017 Padma Shri award for contribution to military arts.

See also late 1400s.

February 6, 2017

The first female victim of Ukraine's anti-terrorism campaign, **Natalia Khorunzha (June 9, 1972–February**

6, 2017), a forty-five-year-old sergeant and medic from Pershotravensk, died on February 6, 2017, from a Russian anti-tank missile aimed at an ambulance. One of the army's ten percent women, she fought to retrieve and evacuate the wounded from Svitlodarsk in a standard vehicle marked with a Red Cross. When the projectile burst, it killed her, ripped a leg from the driver, and left the hurt soldiers with concussions. The Ukrainian army awarded her a medal for heroism. She left behind a husband, daughter, parents, sister, and job in nursing education. Her comrade, Nazar Prykhodko, called Natalia a true amazon. She received a posthumous Order for Courage.

February 20, 2018

A selfless hero and senior nurse on her second deployment, Sergeant **Sabina Halytska (September 20, 1994–February 20, 2018)**, a medic and obstetrician from Bastova Rudnia, died on February 20, 2018, from an anti-tank guided missile attack at her hometown in eastern Ukraine on her armored reconnaissance car. As a member of the 10th Mountain Assault Brigade under the nickname "Sunshine," she regretted not receiving a frontline assignment. Instead of military needs, she carried medicines for the elderly civilians in liberated Katerynivka. The Ukrainian Women's Congress honored her on October 13, Defender's Day. The Ministry of Defence awarded her one of five posthumous medals to steadfast female warriors.

June 28, 2018

A strategy planner during Operation Iraqi Freedom, General **Suzanne Puanani Vares-Lum (1967–)** from Wahiawa, Hawaii, received promotion June 28, 2018, to Major General in the National Guard. As a specialist in intelligence and mobilization for the Indo-Pacific Command, during the second year of the campaign, she assisted headquarters of the 29th Brigade Combat Team from August 2004 to March 2006. Posted in Balad, Iraq, she maintained disaster management and homeland defense during clashes between Shi'ite and Sunni militias, when the death count burgeoned above two thousand. At age forty-eight, she became the first Hawaiian female promoted to general. Among her list of honoraria, she holds a Bronze Star, Legion of Merit, and service medal from the Global War on Terrorism.

2019

The first black female army ranger, paratrooper, and artillery specialist, Master Sergeant **Janina Simmons (1990–)** completed a sixty-one-day cross-country course in 2019 over Florida swamps and the Appalachian mountains. Born in Ulm, Germany, to a military family and enlisted in Colorado, she finished training at Fort Bliss in El Paso, Texas, and advanced to manager of a missile launching station. In fall 2021, she sustained leg injuries during parachute exercises.

January 16, 2019

Navy Chief Petty Officer and cryptologist **Shannon Mary Kent (May 11, 1982–January 16, 2019)** of Oswego, New York, died in northwestern Syria during the noontime bombing of an urban street in Manbij. A sixteen-year veteran, she entered the military in 2003 and attained expertise in Arabic, French, Portuguese, and Spanish. Within four years, she supported Navy Seals with intelligence, a task she continued in 2012 in Afghanistan and in November 2018 again in Afghanistan. A suicide bomber in civilian dress and wired vest detonated the explosive on January 16, 2019, in a market at the entrance to the Palace of Princes restaurant near the Turkish border. In an area liberated from an Islamic caliphate by American and Kurdish allies, the ISIS terrorist strike ignited a fireball that killed nineteen and injured three others. She received navy and marine service medals, a Bronze Star, and Purple Heart. Among the dead was a Syrian-American linguist, **Ghadir Taher (1992–January 16, 2019)**, an employee of a U.S. Department of Defense contractor living in East Point, Georgia. Nicknamed "Jasmine," Ghadir looked forward to serving her new homeland.

February 8, 2019

A veteran of bush war, on February 8, 2019, General **Proscovia Nalweyiso (June 1, 1954–)** of Mpigi, Uganda, advanced to East Africa's highest ranking female. Her volunteering as a guerrilla warrior in the Uganda People's Defense Forces emerged from anger at government soldiers persecuting and terrorizing political opponents. She fought her first outback skirmishes in 1982 for the National Resistance Army. Posting took her to command of a women's regiment attack on Mbarara military police barracks in early December 1985 southwest of Kampala. The clash enabled the National Resistance Army to seize power.

April 2019

Major **Mandisa Mfeka (1990–)** of Ntuzuma northeast of Durban became South Africa's first woman fighter pilot. To satisfy an aim to fly in combat, after training at Central Flying School in Langebaan, Western Cape, she began piloting the Hawk Mk 120 jet under the call name "Comet." On assignment in April 2019, she paired with the United Nations in defending airspace by patrolling national borders, a form of air police. She anticipated commanding a Saab JAS 39 Gripen, an advanced Swedish aeronautical weapon preferred for attack and reconnaissance in Botswana, Brazil, Canada, Colombia, Czech Republic, South Africa, Sweden, Thailand, and the United Kingdom. To relieve stress, Mandisa meditated.

October 18, 2019

At age twenty-two, **Audrey Esi Swatson (February 23, 1997–)** of Accra, Ghana, became the nation's youngest female pilot. From high school, she progressed to the Mach1 Aviation Academy in South Africa and soloed in April 2016. On October 18, 2019, she flew the De Havilland Canada Dash 8, a turboprop airliner. For young Ghanaians, she advocated a government aviator's fund to promote pilot training. Her awards include a citation from the International Women in Aviation and the Future Awards Africa Prize for Young Person of the Year.

November 16, 2019

A part of a bicultural combat experiment in the seventh year of her deployment with the Canadian army reserves, Sergeant **Meaghan Frank (fl. 2010s)** from St. Johns, Newfoundland, engaged in training Jordan's new all-woman infantry. The first female member of the Royal Newfoundland Regiment in Canada's eastern-most province to advance to infantry sergeant, she served the 1st Battalion from 2012 and deployed to Jordan September 10, 2019. To Islamic recruits, she and two comrades in the Canadian Female Engagement Team introduced weaponry and marksmanship on November 16, 2019, at a training field in Amman as part of Operation Impact. The mission, set to end instruction to the Quick Reaction Force in March 2020, spread from headquarters in Kuwait to Jordan, Iraq, Lebanon, and Qatar.

January 28, 2020

Ugandan helicopter pilot Major **Naomi Karungi (December 1, 1978–January 28, 2020)** from Akajumbura died in action while commanding a squadron of the Uganda People's Air Force. A commercial pilot and graduate of the East African Civil Aviation Academy, she served for seventeen years supporting infantry, transporting troops to hot zones, rescuing casualties, and defending national airspace. Her military flight of a three-seater Jet Ranger from Kalama to Entebbe crashed on January 28, 2020, in fog and rain outside Bulo, killing Naomi and a cadet pilot.

March 28, 2020

Uganda's first female military aircraft maintenance engineer, brigadier **Rebecca Mpagi (1956–)** of Buganda was influenced by Idi Amin's ouster during the nine-month Uganda-Tanzania War of 1978 to become a military pilot. At age thirty, she signed on with the National Resistance Army. From training at the East African Civil Aviation Academy in Soroti, she advanced on March 28, 2020, to director of women's affairs for the Uganda People's Defence Forces outside Kampala at Mbuya. Her chief role as female advocate was to prevent sexual harassment and abuse. In the field, she avoided Lakwena rebel attack while refueling a plane and fled ambush by the Lord Resistance Army. Her example influenced **Doreen Kyomuhangi (1988–)** from Rwanbu to study at the Singo Training Wing in Nakaseke to fly fighter jets for the Uganda People's Defense Air Force.

May 29, 2020

An expert at teamwork and motivation, mechanical engineer **Carla Monteiro Araújo (1969–)**, a naval commander from Rio de Janeiro, oversaw a United Nations peacekeeping mission in the Central African Republic. She replaced Lieutenant Commander **Marcia Andrade Braga (fl. 2010s)**, a fellow Brazilian who superintended the 2018–2019 campaign against wartime exploitation, intimidation, and sexual assault of women, boys, and girls. The method involved encouraging three thousand three hundred and forty-nine soldiers or thirty percent of the military personnel to shield vulnerable citizens in everyday situations, including hands-on food preparation and sharing, sanitation, female empowerment, and patrolling conflict zones, whether in Haiti, Mozambique, or the Middle East. Principles of human rights, justice, law, free speech, and disarmament preceded campaigns to demobilize and repatriate. On May 29, 2020, an International Day of Peacekeepers, both officers received from the UN secretary general Antonio Guterres the UN Military Gender Advocate of the Year, as did army signal corps Major **Suman Gawani (1987–)**, a physicist from Uttarkashi, India, and role model to the eighty-two tribes of South Sudan.

January 2, 2021

A fifteen-year Gallo-Vietnamese veteran deployed in West Africa for a second tour, Sergeant **Yvonne Huynh (1988–January 12, 2021)** from Trappes, France, died on January 2, 2021, from the explosion of a roadside bomb in Menaka, Mali. While driving an armored vehicle for the 2nd Hussards, she was collecting intelligence for Operation Barkhane on ethnic antipathies toward Muslims. Some five thousand one hundred soldiers from Burkina Faso, Chad, Mali, Mauritania, and Niger began targeting Jihadist terrorists in the Sahel in 2013. Al Qaeda, a world terrorism syndicate, accepted responsibility for the ambush, which brought the total war deaths to fifty. The enemy blamed French media for ridiculing the prophet Muhammed in cartoons.

March 19, 2021

Uruguayan paratrooper Lieutenant Colonel **Ana Lucas (1981–)** gained the command of army infantry on March 19, 2021. The first female to achieve the post, she graduated from military school in December 2002. As head of the Delta Combat Team in the Busurungi jungle, she completed a UN peacekeeping mission in the eastern Congo by leading a security force. The purpose of her mission was to halt destruction of remote villages by arsonists who burned seventy-six houses and pillaged schools and churches. The rebels raped seven thousand five hundred women and girls, some of them Rwandan Hutu refugees whom attackers carved across breasts and torso. Two years later, she deployed as a paratrooper in 2008 before returning to the Congo.

March 24, 2021

Norwegian major general **Ingrid Gjerde (July 29, 1968–)** from Bærum outside Oslo accepted command of the United Nations peacekeeping troops in Cyprus on March 24, 2021. After completion of a political science degree in Oslo and training at the Norwegian Military Academy and the U.S. Army War College, she gained respect as a leader and strategist for the Norwegian army in Afghanistan and Lebanon. Her medals include citation from NATO, Latvia, and the UN. She replaced Australian major general **Cheryl Pearce (1965–)** of Loxton, a thirty-seven-year veteran of military police training and command posts in Afghanistan and East Timor. After winning Australian of the Year, on August 30, 2021, Cheryl enforced the Australian Border Fence.

September 2, 2021

A specialist in intelligence analysis, **Allene "Ally" Somera-Zyko (1996–)** of Ewa Beach became the first Hawaiian to complete the U.S. Army Ranger School on September 2, 2021. At enlistment in 2015, she entered the World Class Athlete Program with a background in wrestling and achieved membership in the 2017 U.S. Armed Forces Military World Team Member. At four foot ten, she was shorter than the other soldiers. She added another challenge, airborne training.

November 15, 2021

A Californian serving the Israeli military, on November 15, 2021, Sergeant **Dana Colvin (fl. 2021)** operated drones that spied on Hezbollah operations on the Lebanese border and the Gaza Strip. The eleven-member all-girl unit of the 869th Shahaf Battalion trained at Tze'elim in southern Israel in 2020 to compile reconnaissance for ground troops. Beginning with surveillance on Egypt, she reported on rocket fire, which totaled six launchings over seven months, including three Palestinian missiles in August aimed at Kiryat Shmona in the Hula Valley near Lebanon.

January 4–5, 2022

A sergeant and paramedic of the Kazakhstan national guard, Sergeant **Rashida Salmeeva (fl. 2020s)** treated civilian and military injuries on November 4–5, 2022, during a night riot in Nur-Sultan at Kabanbay Batyr and Nazarbayev streets. The protest brought one thousand looters, arsonists, and anarchists to Almaty's Republic Square under assault by stun grenades and tear gas. In a late night attack on an ambulance, the twenty-two-year veteran survived broken windows, a blow to the back of the head, and flames, which she escaped. She received a commendation for bravery. Her comrade, **Dinana Kolbaeva (fl. 2020s),** a major and psychologist, counseled casualties arriving at a medical station.

February 4, 2022

A crack shot, marine sniper Lieutenant **Olena Bilozerska (1980–)**, a photojournalist from Kyiv, took aim on February 4, 2022, at pro–Russian separatists from the Ukrainian trench by thermal night vision. Until 2016, she functioned as an "irregular," a volunteer role she described in the memoir *Diary of an Illegal Soldier*. She trained as a forest-based saboteur and first experienced combat on June 28, 2014. Her sniper rifle, a Zbroyar-Z10 made in the Ukraine that she saved two years to buy, bears the name Halia (serene). After the restrictive law changed, she was grateful for the British gift of two thousand light anti-tank weapons, disposable single-shot, shoulder-launched systems.

In August 2017, after Olena's transfer to night patrol at the front, she caught three Cossacks creeping from enemy lines in the Donbas war zone toward a location she policed with her husband, Valeriy Voronov. Video footage on the Internet recorded how she dispatched them with three blasts. She suffered paralysis in her right cheek from a phosphorus burn after a machine gun tracer bullet struck her. As a reservist, in 2020, she and her husband joined the Territorial Defense Services.

August 24, 2022

Sergeant **Ariana Sánchez (1993–)** from Ecuador set standards for women in the Sapper Leader Course at Fort Leonard Wood, Missouri. Advanced from water purification specialist in the National Guard, she transferred to the regular army at Fort Bragg, North Carolina, and entered the combat engineers. Her challenges included bridge building, demolition, field defense, mine placement and clearing, boat rigging, and road and runway construction. With paratrooper training, in February 2019, she achieved an Air Assault Badge and led courses as the first female instructor for the Army Engineer Regiment. Promoted to Expert Soldier on August 24, 2022, she continued developing skills in rope insertion and extractions at Ranger School in Fort Benning, Georgia, before entering the 173rd Airborne Brigade in Vicenza, Italy.

September 4, 2022

On September 2, 2022, Lieutenant Colonel **Yarden Shukron Yifrah (also Jordan Shokron Yifrah, fl. 2020s)** took command of the Home Front 498th Shahar Battalion of the Israel Defense Forces. She joined the brigade in 2005 and led the Ram Battalion, which relied on helicopter search and rescue teams. Her post involved salvaging Israelis from disasters, earthquakes, and rocket attacks and preventing terrorist assaults. The combat-trained unit swept the West Bank roads and communities for Palestinian felons and confiscated their weapons. In 2021, the group concentrated operations in Judea and Samaria. In Operation Breaking Dawn in August 2022, the force embedded Sderot to defend residents from the criminal plots of the Palestinian Islamic Jihad in the Gaza Strip.

September 14, 2022

An Amenian medic and martyred sniper on the Armenia-Azerbaijan border, **Anush Apetyan (1986–September 14, 2022)** died from rape, blinding, and dismemberment by Azerbaijan soldiers. At an enemy raid on Jermuk in southern Armenia, Anush had fired all her bullets on September 14, 2022, before insurgents captured her along with ten other soldiers. The Azero captors mounted a video of their atrocities—stripping Anush naked, writing across her midriff and breasts, blinding her with a stone in one eye, partially beheading her, and dismembering her legs and a finger, which they shoved into her mouth. Visual evidence aroused outrage worldwide.

October 7, 2022

Israeli military police charged three Palestinian assailants with killing teen Israel Defense Force officer Sergeant **Noa Lazar (2004–October 7, 2022)** from Bat Hefer in the Old City of east Jerusalem. A retaliatory night strike at a checkpoint near the Shu'afat Crossing refugee camp on October 7, 2022, during the Sukkot holiday, the shooting death occurred amid hordes of Jewish visitors to the Temple Mount, Judaism's holiest site. Three Israeli soldiers suffered shrapnel wounds inflicted by

Gaza-based Hamas terrorists. Special forces in helicopters mounted a manhunt for the twenty-two-year-old assassin from Modi'in in central Israel, who fired seven rounds of a handgun before fleeing the scene. Palestinians celebrated the murder with fireworks.

July 26, 2023

Vermont celebrated its first female brigadier general, **Tracey Poirier (1974-)** of Barre Town. After joining the U.S. Army Reserve in 1991, she served thirty years while rearing four children with her husband, infantry commander Len Poirier. With degrees in English, anthropology, and human resources from Norwich University, the Army War College, and as a Rhodes Scholar at Oxford, she joined the Marines. She took tactical command posts in Europe, Hawaii, and Quantico, Virginia, leading army and air support staff in mountain warfare and data gathering. She deployed twice with Operation Iraqi Freedom after Vermont became the first U.S. state in 2013 to admit women to combat posts. She dedicates her activism to recruiting more women to the national guard.

Glossary

abbey a convent or monastery housing nuns or monks

aborigine the first human occupant of any territory

Aceh westernmost Indonesia on northern Sumatra deriving from a pre–Islamic kingdom

Achaemenid the first Persian Empire from 522–486 BCE

ack-ack gun a battery aimed at enemy aircraft and firing flak

al-Andalus Muslim stronghold in Iberia

Allies cooperative armies of Great Britain, the United States, and the Soviet Union against Axis aggressors

amazon a tall, muscular woman

Anatolia a western peninsula of Turkey dating to paleolithic settlers

annexation the addition of territory to another sovereignty

Aquitaine southwestern France bordering the Pyrenees Mountains

armada a fleet of warships in battle formation

arquebus forerunner of the rifle

artillery fields guns, missiles launchers, or rockets

ashram Hindu spiritual retreat

atlatl throwing stick that increases the range of a lance, dart, or javelin

augusta empress of Roman Empire or Byzantium

Austrasia kingdom of north central France from 500–800 CE

Axis collaborative armies of Germany, Italy, and Japan during World War II with the addition of Bulgaria, Croatia, Hungary, Romania, and Slovakia

basilissa queen of ancient Greece of Byzantium

Batavia eighteenth-century name for Jakarta, Indonesia

battalion a small army of some one thousand fighters

battery an emplacement of heavy artillery

Bengal northeastern India containing Bangladesh

bivouac temporary army encampment or military base

Blitz the eight-month Nazi aerial compaign against Great Britain

blockade a stoppage of people, vehicles, rations, or goods from passage

Bohemia a principality of Moravia in the Holy Roman Empire

Bourbon a European dynasty that ruled France, Italy, Spain, and Sicily from 1272 to 1527

Boyar aristocratic Russian noble

Brittany a peninsula of northwestern France on the English Channel

burgess a commissioner or council member of a town

burn fortified hillside

cabal a secret band of plotters or conspirators

cache hidden storage of weapons, coins, or artifacts

Caledonia Latin name for Scotland

campaign a large-scale military operation or course of action

castellan governor of a medieval castle or manse

Catalonia northeastern community of Spain

cataphracts armored Persian cavalry

cession a yielding of rights to property or control by treaty

chatelaine a female housekeeper of a castle

Circassian aborigines of the northwestern Caucasus Mountains

citadel a hilltop or fort guarding or policing a city

claymore a large, heavy, medieval two-handed sword

collaborator a partner or co-conspirator

colonialism possession of a country for the purpose of exploiting its wealth

Comintern Josef Stalin's political organization that controlled Russian citizens

compound land and structures fenced in for a particular use

conquistador a Spanish explorer and conqueror of Mexico, Africa, and Peru

Constantinople capital of the Roman and Ottoman empires renamed Istanbul, Turkey

contraband goods or slaves transported illegally for use or trade

cornet cavalry's second lieutenant and flag bearer

Cossack eastern Slavic militants of southern Russia and Ukraine

counting coup claiming an assault or kill to claim courage

coup d'état a sudden overthrow of governmental power

courier a transporter of documents, oral information, or goods

Crusades a medieval campaign to return the Holy Lands to Christian occupants

Cyrenaica northeastern Libya settled by Berbers

Dagamba prehistoric Burkina Faso

daimyo Japanese feudal lord from the 900s to 1850

Danework an Iron Age earth fortification from the mid-seventh century CE

deployment placement in combat position for tactical support

dirk a short thrusting dagger for use in hand-to-hand combat

dragoon cavalry rider who fought on foot

dysentery a bowel infection that dehydrates the body from lethal diarrhea

fireship a vessel that delivers explosives or burnables to spread among enemy ships

fl. flourished or thrived

flagship the lead ship or vessel of a fleet commander

flintlock a seventeenth-century rifle fired by ignition of a flint striker

flotilla a fleet of warships and boats

fluyt Dutch cargo vessel manned by a small crew

forage scour the countryside for rations, fodder, or supplies

frigate a warcraft carrying heavy armament

Frisia a coastal culture bordering Holland and northwestern Germany

gae bolg a barbed or notched spear

Galicia name for southeastern Poland and western Ukraine in Roman times

garrison the troops guarding a fort or town

Geat Scandinavian tribe occupying southern Sweden

genocide the mass murder of a race or ethnic or religious group

gentile a non-Jew or outsider from Judaism

Gestapo the Nazi secret police in German-occupied lands

Gold Coast colonial West Africa from the fifteenth–twentieth century; currently Ghana

grenadier a mid-seventeenth-century soldier who led assaults by hurling grenades

guerrilla an irregular or independent combatant or raider

Guinea ancient land bordering the Gulf of Guinea; currently Ghana

gumbe goat skin frame drum used as a signal

gunboat a small watercraft that aims one or more guns at a shore

Haganah Zionist paramilitary that defended Israel

Hamas a Palestinian terrorist organization based on Islamic extremes

Hispaniola Caribbean island that became Haiti and Dominican Republic

hors de combat sidelined or out of action

howdah a canopied seat for riding an elephant

hussar fifteenth-century European light cavalry scouts

Iberia the peninsula southwest of France containing Spain and Portugal

imperialism power extended over another country through occupation forces

insurgent violent raider or invader

jihad a religious war against unbelievers

Jutland a peninsula jutting out from Denmark and north Germany

kampilan single-edged Filipino sword with a spiked tip

kapu the Hawaiian system of law, religion, and social behavior

Khurasan ancient Persian plateau; currently Turkmenistan

Kongo seventeenth-century West African kingdom; currently Angola

kusarigama a Japanese sickle on a chain weighted by a lead ball

Levant southwestern Asia preceding formation of Syria

Livonia thirteenth-century Estonia and Latvia on the eastern Baltic shore
Lubyanka secret Russian police headquarters and prison in Moscow
Luftwaffe German air force during both world wars
machete a long, broad-bladed farm or combat knife
Maghreb Arab territory in northwestern Africa
mandarin an official of the imperial Chinese civil service
man-o'-war an armed sailing vessel
manumission an owner's voluntary liberation of a slave
marines a strike force transported by navy vessels
martial arts combative self-defense
Matamba seventeenth-eighteenth-century African kingdom; currently Angola
Media ancient Iranian kingdom dating from 678–226 BCE
mercenary a private or independent soldier hired for warfare
merchantman a commercial trading vessel
Mercia southern English kingdom from 527–918 CE
Meroë Sudanese city on the eastern bank of the Nile River from 590–700 BCE
Mesopotamia historic Fertile Crescent from 3100 BCE–270 CE; currently Iraq and Kuwait
mestizo a person of mixed races, usually Native American and European
MI5 the United Kingdom intelligence system for defending its citizens
MI6 the United Kingdom intelligence system for gathering data on foreign powers
militia a civilian regiment or committee of safety deployed in times of danger
moat a protective ditch or water defense around a castle or fort
Moghulistan ancient Uzbekistan
mole a spy or embedded special operative unsuspected of being a double agent
Molotov cocktail crude incendiary bomb made by lighting a fuse in a glass bottle of gasoline
musket a muzzle-loading rifle from the early 1500s
mystic a communicant with the spirit realm
naginata Japanese halberd or bladed or axe-headed pike
Nanyue Chinese possession from 204–111 BCE; currently North Vietnam, Macau, and Hong Kong
Nazi a fascist who promotes dictatorship, cultural prejudice, and racial purification
New France seventeenth-century name for Quebec
Nordic concerning Denmark, Finland, Greenland, Iceland, Norway, and Sweden
Northumberland northeastern territory of England on the Scots border
Northwest Territory nineteenth-century name for Saskatchewan, Canada
Nuestria northern France in pre-modern era
Nubia Lower Egyptian kingdom from 2500 to 25542 BCE; currently Sudan
Offa a city in Kwara, Nigeria
Office of Strategic Services (OSS) first U.S. spy agency until creation of the CIA
pacifist advocate of non-violence and opposer of obligatory military service or militarism
palanquin sedan chair or litter carried by servants
Palenque Mayan city state from 226 BCE–799 CE; currently Chiapas, Mexico
parapet a low wall, battlement, or edging on a roof or rampart
Parthia political entity between the Black Sea and Caspian Sea and the Persian Gulf from 700 BCE–300 CE; currently northeastern Iran
partisan a backer or devotee of a cause or political party
peal baker's shovel
Peloponnesus the southern peninsula of Greece
pharaoh the hereditary ruler of Egypt from 3150 BCE–314 CE
pharos Greek word for lighthouse
Phoenicia a maritime civilization of the eastern Mediterranean shore from 2500 to 2564 BCE; currently coastal Lebanon
pike a long infantry pole with pointed or hooked end
pogrom massacre or expulsion of an ethnic or religious group
Pomerania the Baltic Sea coast of Germany and Poland
prioress chief nun of a convent
profiteer a seeker of illegal or black market profits through illicit trade
Punjab northern Indian civilization from 3000 BCE; currently Pakistan

Puritan an English Protestant who favored simple liturgy
Qing China's last imperial dynasty lasting from 1644 to 1911
quinquereme four-deck Roman ship
raj a governmental or power structure
ramada an open-air shelter composed of thatch or branches atop upright posts
rampart a defensive wall topped with a walkway
ranger an armed soldier given leave to scout hostile territory
regent a parent or relative who rules for an underage or incompetent monarch
retainer an employee or debtor pledging loyalty to a household
Romanov Russia's last tsarist dynasty, ruling fro, 1613–1917
saber a lightweight curved sword carried by cavalry riders
Samurai noble Japanese military officer
San Domingue seventeenth-century name for the island of Hispaniola
sapper military engineer or demolitions expert
Saracen bedouin or Arabian tribesman; modern name for a Muslim
sati self-immolation of a widow on her husband's funeral pyre
Safavid concerning the Iranian dynasty ruling from 1501 to 1736
Savoy southeastern alpine region of France bordering Italy
Scania southern tip of Sweden
Schutzstaffel **(SS)** organizers of Germany's genocide of undesirables
Seleucid concerning a Greek empire in Western Asia from 312–63 BCE
seneschal castle manager, steward, or supervisor
Sengoku concerning a Japanese period of anarchy from 1467 to 1615
serf agricultural worker or indentured servant for a feudal lord
shrapnel a fragment of a bomb or explosive artillery shell
siege a prolonged military assault involving surrounding the enemy
Silbey tent a conical shelter for housing a dozen soldiers
Silesia a section of eighteenth- and nineteenth-century Poland, Germany, and Czechoslovakia
sloop a one-masted sailboat
sniper a concealed rifle specialist who targets the enemy over long distance

Song a Chinese dynasty from 960–1279
Spanish Netherlands seventeenth-century Hapsburg territory from 1556 to 1714; currently Belgium
Special Operations Executive (SOE) British secret agency commanding resistance and sabotage
standard a flag or ensign of a military regiment or army
sten machine gun used during World War II, Arab-Israeli War, and the Korean and Vietnam wars
Styria southeastern Austria occupied by Celts until Roman occupation forces changed the name to Pannonia
swivel gun a small cannon mounted on a fork or rotating stand
swordland contested territory
Tenochtitlan Central American city on Lake Texcoco built by the Mexica in 1325; currently Mexico City
Tory monarchist, conservative, or traditionalist
Transylvania central Romanian territory incorporated into the Roman Empire from 106–275 CE
trebuchet siege catapult balanced with a counterweight
tyranny control by force, repression, or intimidation
urumi a Japanese sword consisting of a hilt and sharp, flexible blades
usurper an expropriator or claimant who takes power by force
Uzi a post–World War II Israeli submachine gun
Van Diemen's Land nineteenth-century British island colony founded in 1803; currently Tasmania
vanguard leaders or forerunners of an army on the march
Vinland Viking settlement in coastal North America from 986–1600 CE; currently Newfoundland
virago a strong, spirited female warrior
waka short Japanese verse
war of succession conflict over the naming of an heir to the throne
wherry passenger barge or skiff for use on canals or rivers
white buses transport of escapees and refugees operated by the Swedish Red Cross
yin/yang understated/blatant

Appendix A:
Warriors by Birthplace and Time

Aceh
Cut Gambang June 29, 1878
Cut Nyak Dhien June 29, 1878
Cut Nyak Meutia October 24, 1910
Keumalahayati September 11, 1599

Afghanistan
Mah Chuchak Begum 1561
Malalai July 27, 1880
Nazo Tokhi ca. 1665

Akwamu
Amelia of Bernice February 23, 1763
Atha November 23, 1733
Breffu of St. John November 23, 1733

Al-Andalus
Sayyida al-Hurra 1540

Albania
Bule Naipi September 16, 1942
Dhora Leka September 16, 1942
Liri Gero October 6, 1944
Margarita Tutulani November 28, 1942
Nora of Kelmendi 1637
Persefoni Kokedhima September 16, 1942
Sovia Noti June 8, 1944

Algeria
Baya Hocine October 9, 1957
Djamila Bouazza October 9, 1957
Djamila Bouhired October 9, 1957
Djaouher Akrour October 9, 1957
Hassiba Ben Bouali October 9, 1957
Lalla Fatma N'Soumer July 18, 1854
Samia Lakhdari October 9, 1957
Zohra Drif October 9, 1957
Zoulikha Bekkadour October 9, 1957

American Samoa
Tulsi Gabbard 2004

Angola
Llinga of Kongo 1640s
Mussasa early 1600s
Nzinga Mbande October 29, 1647
Tembandumba early 1600s

Anjou
Adelaide Blanche of Anjou 975 CE
Joan of England and Sicily 1199
Marguerite de Bressieux 1450

Antigua
Mary Leticia Thomas October 1, 1878

Aquitaine
Eleanor of Aquitaine January 6, 1148

Arabia
Ā'ishah bint Abī Bakr December 8, 656 CE
Asma bint Abī Bakr August 15, 634 CE
Ghaliyya al-Wahhabiyya 1814
Hind bint 'Utbah March 13, 624; August 15, 634 CE
Mavia spring 378 CE
Nusaybah bint Ka'ab March 23, 625 CE
Sulaym bint Milhan December 29, 626 CE
Umm Ḥakīm bint al-Ḥārith August 16, 634 CE

Arcadia
Theodora of Vasta 900s CE

Argentina
Celedonia Pachecho de Melo July 23, 1806
Gertrudis Medeiros July 23, 1806
Juana Gabriela Moro July 23, 1806
Juana Manuela Torino July 23, 1806
Magdalena Dámasa Güemes July 23, 1806
Manuela Pedraza August 10, 1806
María Andrea Zenarruza July 23, 1806
María Loreto Sánchez Peón July 23, 1806
María Petrona Arias July 23, 1806

María Remedios Del Valle July 6, 1810
Martina Silva July 23, 1806
Maureen Dunlop de Popp October 1, 1942
Tamara Haydée Bunke Bider August 31, 1967

Argos
Messene 1000 BCE
Telesilla 494 BCE

Armenia
Anush Apetyan September 14, 2022
Pharantzem of Armenia 368 CE
Shajar al-Durr February 8–11, 1250

Ashanti Empire
Cubah Cornwallis April 7, 1760
Yaa Asantewaa March 28, 1900

Assacanus
Cleophis winter 326 BCE

Assyria
Drypetis summer 328 BCE
Parysatis summer 328 BCE
Samsi 732 BCE
Shammuramat 811 BCE
Sisygambis summer 328 BCE
Stateira II summer 328 BCE
Yatie 703 BCE
Zabibi 732 BCE

Athens
Philothey Benizelos February 1589
Thais May 330 BCE

Austrasia
Basina February 589 CE
Brunhilda 593 CE
Chrodielde February 589 CE
Fastrada 783 CE
Leubevere of Cheribert February 589 CE

Austria
Ida of Austria September 17, 1101
Ida Sabo April 6, 1941

Marianne Golz October 8, 1943
Maria Olip' September 1939
Marina Ştirbei June 22, 1941
Stephanie Hollenstein May 1915

Austria-Hungary
Agnes Primocic October 23, 1943
Anna Goldsteiner December 1943
Anna Szatkowska August 18, 1906
Antonia Spath Bruha December 1940
Berta Bergman April 10, 1941
Edith Tudor-Hart May 1934
Hanna Dmyterko September 1914
Hannah Szenes August 1944
Herma Paschinger February 11, 1934
Ilona Colonist August 1944
Käthe Wanek Odwody February 11, 1934
Klára Andrássy April 12, 1941
Leni Egger October 23, 1943
Manto Mavrogenous October 22, 1822
Maria Emhart February 11, 1934
Maria Svobod August 1944
Maria Wagner Plieseis October 23, 1943
Marianne Feldhammer March 13, 1938
Marie von Fery Bognar September 16, 1916
Marina Lebstuck March 15, 1848
Olena Stepaniv September 1914
Olha Basarab September 1914
Resi Pesendorfer March 13, 1938
Sofia Galechko September 1914
Vahida Maglajlić May 1941
Virginia Thomas June 22, 1941

Australia
Cheryl Pearce March 24, 2021
Simone Wilkie January 10, 2007

Azerbaijan
Alexandra Danilova 1915
Banu Khoramdin 816 CE
Zuleykha Seyidmammadova May 1942

Bactria
Roxana of Bactria summer 328 BCE

Barbados
Michelle Thompson 1987

Bavaria
Johanna Sophia Kettner 1743
Viktoria Savs June 10, 1915

Belarus
Anna Ivanovna Maslovskaya December 24, 1942
Frumka Płotnicka January 18, 1943
Tatyana Savelyevna Marinenko June 22, 1941
Zivia Lubetkin late 1941; January 18, 1943

Belgian Congo
Augusta Maria Chiwy December 21, 1945

Belgium
Andrée de Jongh August 1941
Antoinette Gluck Feuerwerker fall 1941
Audrey Hepburn September 17, 1944
Elvire de Greef August 1941
Gabrielle Weidner June 22, 1940
Hélène Dutrieu summer 1915
Hélène Louise de Munck May 1939
Janine de Greef August 1941
Marie-Jeanne Schellinck November 6, 1792
Marjorie Amor May 1939
Marthe Cnockaert 1915
Michelle Dumon August 1941

Monique de Bissy August 1941
Renée Lemaire December 21, 1945
Théroigne de Méricourt October 5, 1789

Bengal
Bina Das February 6, 1932
Kalpana Datta September 23, 1932
Kamala Das Gupta February 6, 1932
Matangini Hazra September 29, 1942
Pritilata Waddedar September 23, 1932
Santi Das Ghose December 14, 1931
Suniti Chaudhuri December 14, 1931

Benin
Carlota Lucumí November 5, 1843
Filomena Ganga November 5, 1843
Idia of Benin 1504
Lucia Lucumí November 5, 1843
Lucumí Fermina November 5, 1843
Sarraounina Mangou April 17, 1899

Bithynia
Amastris 299 BCE

Bohemia
Libuše 738 CE
Šárka 738 CE
Valasca 738 CE

Bolivia
Bartolina Sisa Vargas September 5, 1782
Gregoria Apaza September 5, 1782
Juana Azurduy de Padilla May 25, 1809
Manuela Eras de Gandarillas May 27, 1812
Simona Josefa Manzaneda September 22, 1814
Úrsula Goyzueta September 22, 1814

Vicenta Equino September 22, 1814

Bosporus
Dynamis of Bosporus 14 BCE

Brazil
Anita Garibaldi September 1839; June 30, 1849
Jovita Feitosa August 16, 1865
Brígida do Vale January 7, 1823
Carla Monteiro Araújo May 29, 2020
Cruz Lucia Infante April 9, 1895
Dandara 1678
Joana Angélica de Jesus February 19, 1822
Joana Soaleira January 7, 1823
Jovita Feitosa August 16, 1865
Marcia Andrade Braga May 29, 2020
Marcolina January 7, 1823
Maria Bonita July 28, 1938
María Felipa de Oliveira January 7, 1823
Maria Quitéria October 1822

British India
Gaidinliu Pamei February 16, 1932
Jane Sissmore Archer January 1940
Lakshmi Sahgal July 1943
Meenakshi Amma January 25, 2017
Vijayalakshmi Ramanan 1955

British Malaya
Janaky Athi Nahappan July 1943
Rasammah Bhupalan July 1943

Briton
Judon 600 BCE

Brittany
Anne Dieu-le-Veut March 1693

Julienne du Guesclin late 1370
Pieronne of Brittany September 3, 1430
Tiphaine Raguenel late 1370

Bulgaria
Esther Arditi November 29, 1954
Tsola Nincheva Dragoycheva September 14, 1923
Visna of the Slavs ca. 770 CE
Yona Markova November 14, 1885

Burgundy
Clementia of Burgundy July 17, 1119
Florina of Bourgogne July 1, 1097
Helie of Burgundy July 12, 1109
Philis de la Tour 1692

Burkina Faso
Yennenga ca. 1100

Byzantium
Antonina September 13, 533 CE
Halima June 554 CE
Helena Kantakouzene March 2, 1342
Helena Palaiologina April 11, 1458
Irene Asanina March 2, 1342
Maria Kantakouzene March 2, 1342
Theodora Kantakouzene March 2, 1342

Canada
Dorothy "Babs" Gardner October 24, 1942
Sage German October 24, 1942

Alberta
Betty Ann Lussier 1978
Hate Woman 1910s
Running Eagle 1878

British Columbia
Helen Harrison Bristol October 1, 1942

New Brunswick
Sarah Emma Edmonds May 25, 1861

Newfoundland
Meaghan Frank November 16, 2019

Nova Scotia
Marelene Clyke 1951

Ontario
Elsie Joy Davison July 8, 1940
Irene Miawa Vivash October 1942
Jean Migotti October 24, 1942
Kitty Harris 1926
Leanne Crowe 1993
Lilias Ahearn October 24, 1942
Marion Alice Powell Orr October 1, 1942
Melodie Massey October 24, 1942
Stella Tate October 24, 1942
Violet Milstead Warren October 1, 1942

Quebec
Leslie Joy Whitehead July 1915
Lois Butler October 1, 1942
Marie-Madeleine Jarret October 22, 1692

Saskatchewan
Mary Greyeyes October 1942

Caria
Ada spring 334 BCE
Artemisia I September 26, BCE
Artemisia II 351 BCE

Carthage
Sophonisba 205 BCE

Castile
Eleanor of Castile November 10, 1270
Elvira of Leon-Castile 1102

Catalonia
Aldonça de Bellera February 15, 1430
Eleanor of Arborea March 3, 1383
Mercadera 1285

Chalcis
Hydna of Scione early September, 480 BCE

Chechnya
Aiza Gazuyeva November 29, 2001
Alina Tumriyeva December 27, 2002
Aminat Nagaev August 24, 2004
Khadijat Mangerieva December 5, 2003
Khava Barayeva June 7, 2000
Lida Khildehoroeva June 5, 2003
Luiza Magomadova June 7, 2000
Mareta Duduyeva December 4, 2000
Mariam Tuburova September 2, 2004
Maryam Sharipova July 5, 2003
Markha Ustarkhanova July 5, 2003
Roza Nagaev September 4, 2004
Ruzanna "Salima" Ibragimova October 21, 2013
Satisita Dzhbirkhanova August 24, 2004
Zarema Muzhikhoeva July 10, 2003
Zinaida Aliyeva July 5, 2003
Zulikhan Elikhadzhiyeva July 5, 2003
Zura Barayeva October 26, 2002

Chile
Candelaria Pérez January 20, 1839
Filomena Valenzuela Goyenechea November 2, 1879
Giliana Balmaceda Gerson June 18, 1940
Gisela Wieberdink-Soehnlein fall 1940
Huillac Ñusca 1780
Irene del Carmen Morales Galaz November 2, 1879
Janequeo 1587
Margot Duhalde Sotomayor October 1, 1942

China
A-Nong October 1052
Chen Shuozhen September 653 CE
Chiang Ch'ing 1928
Deng Yingchao 1928
Deng Yulan November 11, 2009
Du Fengyang 1856
Fu Hao 1250 BCE
Fu Jing 1250 BCE
Han E summer 1361
He Zizhen 1928
Honchi 515 CE
Hong Xuanjiao fall 1850
Hua Mulan ca. 490s CE
Huang Guigu 245 BCE
Huang Pei-mei 1937
Kang Keqing 1928
Kong Sizhen 1677
Lady Washi April 1555
Lai Choi-san 1920s
Li Xiu 303 CE
Li Zhen September 7, 1927
Liang Hongyu New Year's Eve, 1129
Lin Hei'er October 18, 1899
Liu Jinding 957 CE
Lu Mu 17 CE
Qin Liangyu 1599
Qiu Ersao fall 1850
Shangguan Wan'er 705 CE
Shen Yunying 1643
Su Sanniang fall 1850
T'ang Qunying 1905
T'ang Sai'er 1420
Wang Cong'er 1797
Wang Nangxian 1797
Wang Shaowen November 11, 2009
Wang Yi November 11, 2009
Wu Shuqing October 10, 1911
Wu Zetian spring 696 CE, 705 CE
Xi Shi 473 BCE
Xian summer 548 CE
Xiao Yanyan June 986 CE
Xun Guan 316 CE

Yang Miaozhen 1214
Yuenyu 482 BCE
Zhangsun July 2, 626 CE
Zhao Pingyang September 617 CE
Zheng Yi Sao November 16, 1807

Cilicia
Aba of Tencer March 32 BCE

Circassia
Ecaterina Cercheza May 27, 1653

Colombia
Agustina Mejía July 20, 1810
Agustina Peralta November 1812
Ana Josefa Morales May 1816
Andrea Ricaurte de Lozano May 1816; November 10, 1817; July 1819; August 17, 1819
Anselma Leyton May 1816
Antonia Moreno May 1816
Antonia Santos Plata July 1819
Ascensión Ortega July 1819
Barbara Forero August 17, 1819
Barbara Montes October 11, 1819
Bibiana Talero July 1819
Candelaria Forero July 1819
Carlota Armero July 1819
Carlota Rengifo October 11, 1819
Carmen Rodríguez de Gaitán August 17, 1819
Casilda Zafra July 1819
Clara Tocarruncho July 1819
Dolores Nariño August 17, 1819
Dolores Salas July 1819
Dolores Vargas July 1819
Dorotea Castro July 1819
Dorotea Lenis October 11, 1819
Engracia Salgar July 1819
Estefanía Linares July 1819
Estefanía Neira de Eslava November 1812
Estefanía Parra July 20, 1810
Eusebia Galviza November 1812
Evangelina Diaz August 17, 1819
Evangelista Tamayo August 17, 1819
Fidela Ramos July 1819
Gaitana 1539
Genoveva Sarmiento November 10, 1817; December 7, 1817
Gertrudis Vanegas November 10, 1817; July 1819
Ignacia Medina November 10, 1817; December 7, 1817
Inés Osuna November 1812; December 7, 1817
Ines Peñaranda November 1812
Isabel Nariño August 17, 1819
Joaquina Aroca November 1812
Josefa Baraya August 17, 1819
Josefa Conde May 1816; 1817
Juana Béjar July 1819
Juana Escobar October 11, 1819
Juana Plazas July 20, 1810
Juana Ramírez October 11, 1819
Juana Rodríguez August 17, 1819
Juana Santos July 1819
Juana Velasco de Gallo July 1819
Justina Estepa July 20, 1810; January 16, 1816
Laurean Sierra November 10, 1817; August 4, 1819
Leonarda Carreño July 1819
Luisa Trilleras July 1819
Manuela Beltran March 16, 1781
Manuela Escobar October 11, 1819
Manuela Malasaño Oñoro May 2, 1808
Manuela Tinoco August 17, 1819
Manuela Uscátegui May 1816
María Agudelo de Olaya July 1819
María de los Ángeles Ávila November 10, 1817; December 7, 1817
María del Carmen Olano October 11, 1819
María del Rosario Devis May 1816
María del Transito Vargas May 1816
María Gertrudis Romero November 10, 1817
María Josefa de Lizarralde November 1812
María Josefa Esguerra July 1819
María Larrain November 1812
María Mercedes Viteri November 1812
María Rosa Lazo de la Vega July 1819
Marta Tello July 1819
Matilde Anaray July 1819
Mercedes Ábrego de Reyes November 1812
Mercedes Loayza May 1816
Mercedes Nariño August 17, 1819
Micaela Nieto May 1816
Paula Contreras May 1816
Policarpa Salavarrieta November 1812
Presentación Buenahora May 1816
Remigia Cuesta May 1816
Rosa Zaráte de la Peña November 1812
Rosaura Rivera November 1812
Salomé Buitrago November 10, 1817
Simona Amaya July 1819; August 17, 1819
Teresa Cornejo August 17, 1819
Teresa Izquierdo November 1812
Tomasa Rodríguez May 1816

Congo
Mukaya Luba 1889

Cornwall
Gwendolen of Cornwall 1075 BCE

Appendix A

Corsica
Danielle Casanova January 27, 1943
Marie Reynoard fall 1941

Costa Rica
Pancha Carrasco April 11, 1856

Croatia
Ilona Zrínyi November 15, 1685
Marina Lebstuck March 13, 1848

Cuba
Carmita November 5, 1843
Candelaria Figueredo October 20, 1868
Caridad Mercader July 19, 1936
Celia Sánchez Manduley March 10, 1952
Juliana November 5, 1843
Loretta Janeta Velázquez July 16, 1861

Curaçao
María of Curaçao November 9, 1716

Cyprus
Charlotte of Cyprus October 7, 1458

Cyrenaica
Berenice II Euergetes 260 BCE
Pheretima 525 BCE

Czechoslovakia
Elena Haas September 1944
Genia Fischer October 7, 1944
Marta Bindiger Cigi October 7, 1944

Dahomey
Hang 1716
Seh-Dong-Hong-Be March 3, 1851
Victoria "Toya" Montou August 14, 1791

Dardanus
Manya 401 BCE

Daylam
Azad Deylami 751 CE

Delhi Empire
Razia Sultana November 1236

Denmark
Alma Allen April 9, 1940; January 15, 1944
Anne Holck November 14, 1659
Anne Jørgensdatter Rud 1502
Anna Rheinholdsdotter Leuhusen 1522
Brita Olovsdotter Tott 1451
Else Marie Pade June 1944
Hedda Lundh June 1944
Monica Wichfeld June 1940

Dutch East Indies
Jeanne Merkus June 19, 1875
Reina Prinsen Geerligs November 24, 1943

Ecuador
Ana María Merchán Delgado April 9, 1895
Angela Maclovia Lavayen April 9, 1895
Antonia León y Velasco 1812
Ariana Sánchez August 24, 2022
Baltazara Chiuza 1803
Carmen Grimaldo de Valverde April 9, 1895
Delfina Torres de Concha April 9, 1895
Delia Montero Maridueña April 9, 1895
Dolores Usubillaga April 9, 1895
Dolores Vela de Veintimilla April 9, 1895
Felicia Solano de Vizuete April 9, 1895
Filomena Chávez de Duque April 9, 1895
Gertrudis Espalza May 24, 1822
Inés María Jiménez May 24, 1822
Joaquina Galarza de Larrea April 9, 1895
Juliana Pizarro April 9, 1895
Leticia Montenegro April 9, 1895
Lorenza Avemanay Tacuri 1803
Manuela Cañizares August 9, 1809
Manuela Chuiza 1803
Manuela Sáenz September 25, 1828
María Baltazara Teran Garzon 1811
María Gamarra de Hidalgo April 9, 1895
Marieta de Veintimilla January 10, 1883
Nela Martínez Espinosa May 28, 1944
Nicolasa Jurado May 24, 1822
Porfiria Aroca de la Paz April 9, 1895
Quilago 1515
Rosa Villafuerte de Castillo April 9, 1895
Rosario Carifa April 9, 1895
Sofía Moreira de Sabando April 9, 1895
Teresa Andrade April 9, 1895
Transito Villagomez April 9, 1895

Edessa
Melisende of Edessa December 24, 1144

Egypt
Ahhotep I ca. 1530 BCE
Arsinoë III Philopator June 22, 217 BCE
Arsinoë IV summer 48 BCE
Cleopatra II 131 BCE
Cleopatra III 116 BCE
Cleopatra V Selene 69 BCE
Cleopatra VII Philopator September 2, 31 BCE
Hatshepsut 1479 BCE
Rawya Ateya October 29, 1956

England
Aagt de Tamboer 1653
Adriana la Noy March 3, 1652
Aethelburg of Wessex 722 CE
Agnes Joane Hotot 1390
Alice Lynne Knyvet spring 1461

Amy Johnson October 1, 1942
Ann Mills December 16, 1740
Ann Taylor August 1, 1798
Anna Carey June 1634
Anna Jans March 3, 1652
Anne Chamberlayne July 29, 1690
Anne Dymoke April 6, 1657
Anne Hennis Bailey 1791
Anne Hopping August 1, 1798
Barbara Helen Bailey August 31, 1939
Blanche Arundell May 2, 1643
Boudicca 61 CE
Cartimandua 51 CE
Catherine Hagerty April 1806
Channing Day October 24, 2012
Charlotte Badger April 1806
Charlotte de Berry ca. 1651
Cicely Arundell May 2, 1643
Constance Georgine Markievicz April 24, 1916
Diana Barnato Walker October 1, 1942
Edith de Warenne late August 1096
Eileen Nearne January 25 and March 2, 1943
Elizabeth Dowdall October 1641
Elizabeth I of England August 9, 1588
Elizabeth Moore August 1, 1798
Elizabeth Patrickson June 1634
Elizabeth Ryder Maxwell late 1642
Ellen Askwith August 22, 1642
Faye Turney March 23, 2007
Flora Burn 1741
Flora Sandes November 25, 1915
Frances Stoddard June 1634
Halszka Wasilewska July 28, 1914; July 27, 1943
Hannah Snell November 23, 1745
Helen Kerly October 1, 1942
Jacqueline Nearne January 25 and March 2, 1943
Jane Francis June 1634
Jane Howard November 19, 1569
Jane Lane September 3, 1651
Jane Randall June 1634
Jane Ryder Whorwood late 1642
Jane Townsend October 21, 1805
Joan Beaufort July 15, 1445
Joan Miller May 1939
Joanna Harris June 1634
Joanna "Jo" Mary Salter February 21, 1995
Johannan Pieters March 3, 1652
John Brown November 18, 1693
Juliane de Fontevrault mid–February 1119
Julienne Aisner May 13, 1943
Katherine Grandison winter 1341
Lisa Head April 18, 2011
Lettice Curtis October 1, 1942
Lilian Wyles 1932
Margaret Fairweather October 1, 1942
Margaret Mautby Paston February 17, 1448
Margaret Pope June 1634
Margaret Wyndham Gore October 1, 1942
Maria Lindsey Cobham 1740
Martha Farley May 1727
Mary Ann Riley August 1, 1798
Mary Ann Talbot June 13, 1793
Mary Carleton June 1634
Mary Critchett late 1728
Mary Dixon September 6, 1813
Mary French August 1, 1798
Mary Hawtrey Bankes May 1643
Mary Lacy 1759
Mary Percevall June 1634
Mary Read October 1720
Mary Spenser-Churchill 1941
Mary Spring Rice April 24, 1916
Mary Wilkins Ellis October 1, 1942
Mary Wolverston Killigrew January 1, 1582
Matilda of Ramsbury late June 1139
Matilda of Winchester September 30, 1139
Melita Norwood 1937
Michelle Norris June 11, 2006
Milicent Bagot 1931
Mona Friedlander October 1, 1942
Monica Wichfeld June 1940
Nicola de la Haye October 18, 1216
Odette Sar Wilen April 11, 1944
Olga Gray June 6, 1934
Philippa of England April 6, 1428
Phoebe Smith Hessel May 11, 1745
Rose Ann Murphy April 24, 1916
Rose Lopes Laguna-Asscher November 24, 1943
Rosemary Rees October 1, 1942
Sarah Bates August 1, 1798
Sarah Feely Bryant June 17, 2008
Sarah-Jayne Mulvihill May 6, 2006
Sonya Butt May 28, 1944
Susan Travers December 19, 1946
Vera Leigh May 13, 1943

El Salvador
Lilian Mercedes Letona 1976
Manuela Miranda early 1812
María Miranda early 1812
Melida Anaya Montes 1970

Epirus
Olympias Stratonice 317 BCE

Estonia
Margareta Elisabeth Roos November 10, 1721

Ethiopia
Furra 1400
Gudit 960 CE
Taytu Betul March 1, 1896

Finland
Anna Jöransdotter 1714
Annika Svahn February 1714
Brita Olofsdotter June 16, 1569
Elisa Bernerström Servenius August 19–20, 1809
Gunilla Johansdotter Bese April 1511–1513

Flanders
Hadvide of Chiny August 1096
Joanna of Flanders April 26, 1342
Mary Ambree September 17, 1584

France
Adélaïde Haas Hautval January 27, 1943
Agnes Dorothee Humbert June 14, 1940
Alberte-Barbe d'Ernécourt 1638
Ameliane du Puget-Glandevès August 19–September 24, 1524
Andrée Borrel January 20, 1940; September 25, 1942
Angélique Duchemin Brûlon August 10, 1794
Anne Marie Louise d'Orléans July 2, 1652
Beauglie, Madame de August 26, 1793
Berty Albrecht August 1940
Cécile Rol-Tanguy May 1944
Cecily Gordon Lefort early February 1943
Céleste Bulkeley September 22, 1793
Charlotte Delbo January 27, 1943
Charlotte Stanley late February 1644
Claire de Laval August 19–September 24, 1524
Claire Lacombe October 5, 1789
Collette Nirouet October 15, 1944
Consuelo Dubois July 1, 1816
Corba of Thorigne September 17, 1101
Delphine Aigle June 14, 1940
Diana Rowden early February 1943
Elaine Mordeaux June 1, 1944
Éliane Brault April 1944
Éliane Sophie Plewmen early February 1943; August 13, 1943
Elisabeth de la Bourdonnaye March 21, 1941
Elisabeth Retiffe March 18, 1871
Eliska Vincent March 18, 1871
Elizabeth Hatzler September 16, 1812
Emeline of Bouillon June 28, 1098
Emilie Tillion January 1941
Eulàlia Papavoine March 18, 1871
Faydide of Toulouse January 6, 1148
Félicité Fernig April 20, 1792
France Bloch-Serazin late August 1941
Françoise Déprés December 1, 1793
Françoise-Marie Jacquelon April 13, 1645
Gabrielle Jeanine "Gloria" Picabia January 1941
Gabrielle Laval August 19–September 24, 1524
Geneviève de Gaulle-Anthonioz January 1941
Geneviève Prémoy September 27, 1688
Germaine Guerin January 1941
Germaine Ribière fall 1941
Germaine Tambour September 24, 1943
Germaine Tillion June 14, 1940; January 1941
Guiraude de Lavaur May 3, 1211
Hélène Solomon-Langevon January 27, 1943
Hélène Studler summer 1939
Henrietta Maria of France June 1644
Humberge of Le Puiset May 20, 1098
Isabella of France September 1326
Jacqueline Bordelet June 12, 1940
Jacqueline Guerroudj October 9, 1957
Jane Magre Dieulafoy July 19, 1870
Janine Marie de Foix May 1377
Jeanne Brousse November 1942
Jeanne de Clisson January 19, 1343
Jeanne de Sapinaud September 22, 1793
Jeanne des Armoises May 20, 1436
Jeanne Hachette June 27, 1472
Jeannie Rousseau August 17, 1943
Joan of Arc May 8, 1429
Joséphine Marchais March 18, 1871
Julie D'Aubigny La Maupin 1686
Julienne David March 1793
Kattalin Aguirre July 17, 1936
Kiki Latry October 23, 1943
Leontine Suetens March 18, 1871
Léa Blain fall 1941
Liliane Rolfe April 5, 1944
Lise London September 1936; late 1941
Louise de Bettignies October 4, 1914
Louise Gavan Duffy April 24, 1916
Louise Labé July 12, 1542
Louise Michel March 18, 1871
Louise-Renée Leduc October 5, 1789
Lucie Bernard Aubrac March 1943

Lucie Boutillier du Retail June 14, 1940
Madame Arnaud 1915
Madeleine Zoe Damerment early February 1943
Madeleine de Saint-Nectaire July 26, 1575
Madeleine Passot January 27, 1943
Madeleine Riffaud July 23, 1943
Madeleine Tambour September 25, 1942
Magistra Hersend August 25, 1248
Mai Politzer January 27, 1943
Marguerite Delaye April 1570
Marguerite Gonnet fall 1941
Marie-Claude Vaillant-Couturier January 27, 1943
Marie Leonie Vanhoutte October 4, 1914
Marie-Madeleine Fourcade November 10, 1942
Marie Magdelaine Mouron 1690
Marie Marvingt April 26, 1915
Marie Nordmann-Cohen late August 1941
Marie-Thérèse Figueur July 9, 1793; December 21, 1797; November 4, 1799
Marinette Menut November 12, 1942
Marthe Hoffnung Cohn November 1944
Mary Brose Tepe May 3, 1863
Mathilde Carré November 17, 1941
Mimi Mingat-Lerme fall 1941
Nathalie Lemel March 18, 1871
Odette Sansom 1938; November 2, 1942
Paule Mink March 18, 1871
Pauline Léon October 5, 1789
Pearl Witherington September 22, 1943
Philippa of Hainault October 17, 1346

Renée de Bourbon 1490
Richilde of Hainault February 22, 1071
Rose Barreau July 1793
Rose Valland fall 1941
Sibylla of Anjou January 6, 1148
Simone Segouon August 23, 1944
Sylvette Roussel Leleu June 14, 1940
Theophile Fernig April 20, 1792
Thérèse Pierre September 1942
Violette Lecoq 1938; April 5, 1944
Violette Szabo April 5, 1944
Yolande Beekman early February 1943
Yvonne Huynh January 2, 2021
Yvonne Suzanne Oddon June 14, 1940
Yvonne Rudellat July 30, 1942

French Indochina
Nguyễn Thị Định May 19, 1941

Frisia
Ats Bonninga September 15, 1494
Bauck Poppema August 1496
Hille Feicke June 16, 1534
Swob Sjaarda April 20, 1481

Galatia
Chiomara 189 BCE
Onomaris 400 BCE

Galilee
Deborah 1070 BCE
Jael 1070 BCE

Gambia
Ramatoulie D.K. Sanneh May 12, 2011

Geatland
Alfhild 400s CE
Blenda ca. 500 CE
Groa 400s CE

Genoa
Pomellina Fregoso 1439

Georgia
Dedisimedi August 9, 1578
Ketevan of Kekheti October 22, 1605
Tamara of Georgia July 27, 1202

Germania
Veleda August 1, 69 CE

German South West Africa
Kaipkire 1903

German Empire
Elżbieta Zawacka October 1939
Úrsula Kuczyński March 1934

Germany
Bracha Fuld March 14, 1941
Erika Wendt January 1942
Gertrud Koch late 1939
Inge Weidenau Frank October 7, 1944
Ingeborg Wallheimer Kahlenberg November 1944
Janina Simmons 2019
Rita Arnould May 10, 1940

Ghana
Audrey Esi Swatson October 18, 2019

Gold Coast
Luisa Mahin January 1835
Nanny of the Maroons September 1728
Yaa Asantewaa March 28, 1900

Greece
Anna Dosa February 16, 1943
Lela Karagianni September 8, 1944
Moscho Tzavella July 27, 1792
Philothey Benizelos 1650
Sara Yehoshua Fortis spring 1941
Theodora January 13, 532 CE

Grenada
María Pacheco Padilla April 23, 1521
William Brown May 23, 1815

Guadeloupe
La Mulâtresse Solitude May 21, 1802

Guatemala
K'abel 672 CE

Guinea
Niara Bely Lightbourn 1842

Hainaut
Margaret II of Hainaut September 5, 1350

Hawaii
Manono II December 1819

Hindustan
Nur Jahan March 18, 1626

Hispaniola
Anacaona 1503
Marie-Jeanne Lamartiniére March 4, 1802
María Trinidad Sánchez February 27, 1844
Suzanne "Sanité" Bélair October 5, 1802

Holland
Aal de Dragonder before November 1710
Amaron Hasselaer December 11, 1572
Anna Alders 1653
Anne Vere Fairfax August 22, 1642
Barbara Pieters Adriaens 1627
Bertha van Heukelom 1296
Brilliana Conway Harley July 25, 1643
Catharina Aaltjen Boekbinder May 10, 1940
Catharina Rose June 15, 1587
Cornelia van den Brink November 24, 1943
Elisabeth Someruell November 3, 1673
Francien de Zeeuw October 31, 1944
Francijntje van Lint February 18, 1674
Francina Broese Gunningh November 26, 1813
Freddie Nanda Dekker-Oversteegen May 10, 1940
Frieda Belinfante August 13, 1943
Geertruida Wijsmuller-Meijer 1933
Hannie Schaft May 10, 1940
Hetty Voûte fall 1940
Ida Veldhuyzen van Zanten October 1, 1942
Johanna Bennius November 11, 1746
Kenau Simonsdochter Hasselaer December 11, 1572
Lau Mazirel August 13, 1943
Maeyken in den Hert June 15, 1587
Margaret of Bavaria 1419
Margaretha Sandra June 25, 1672
Maria Abrahams July 1942
Maria Jacoba de Turenne 1688
Maria ter Meetelen 1725
Maria van Schooten December 11, 1572
Maria van Spanjen mid–November 1781
Maria von Antwerpen 1746
Marie Schotte July 1942
Marion Philippina Pritchard late 1942
Marretje Arents June 17, 1748
Mirjam Ohringer May 10, 1940
Olga Hudig fall 1940
Riet van Grunsven September 1944
Sietje Gravendeel-Tammens July 14, 1943
Suzanne Hiltermann-Souloumiac November 1943
Tina Buchter Strobos July 1942
Trijn Rembrands December 11, 1572
Trijn van Leemput December 11, 1572
Truus Menger-Oversteegen May 10, 1940
Truus van Lier November 24, 1943
Willemiena Bouwman fall 1940

Holy Roman Empire
Charlotte Amelie August 4, 1700
Christine de Lalaing of Espinoy October 1, 1581
Margaret of Anjou May 4, 1471
Philippa of Hainault October 17, 1346

Hong Kong
Jean Bird October 1, 1942

Hungary
Cecilia Rozgonyi May 1428
Hannah Szenes August 1944
Jadwiga April 1387

Iceland
Freydís Eiríksdóttir ca. 1000
Gudrid Thorbjarnardóttir ca. 1000
Ólöf Loftsdóttir 1467

Illyria
Audata 317 BCE
Caeria 317 BCE
Cynane 317 BCE
Tania of Dardania 100 CE
Teuta 229 BCE

Inca Empire
Kura Ocllo 1539

India
Ahilyabhai Holkar March 28, 1765; early 1771; 1783; 1787
Akkadevi 1047
Alka Shukla December 24, 1996
Anisha Shinh December 24, 1996
Archana Kapoor December 24, 1996
Avani Chaturvedi December 24, 1996
Avanti Bai Lodhi May 10, 1857
Ayesha Farooq December 24, 1996
Belawadi Mallamma Desai 1678
Bhawana Kanth December 24, 1996
Bibi Dalair Kaur December 6, 1704
Bibi Sahib Kaur 1793

Bindu Sebastian December 24, 1996
Chand Bibi December 14, 1595
Durgavati 1562
Harita Kaur Diol December 24, 1996
Hazrat Mahal July 5, 1857
Janaki Bai October 21, 1824
Jhalkaribai May 10, 1857
Keladi Chennamma March 25, 1689
Kiran Shekhawat March 24, 2015
Kittur Chennamma October 21, 1824
Lakshmibai May 10, 1857
Mah Laqa Bai Chanda March 11, 1795
Mai Bhago December 6, 1704
Mangammal September 1690
Mata Sundari December 6, 1704
Meenakshi Amma January 25, 2017
Mohana Singh December 24, 1996
M.P. Shumathi December 24, 1996
Pamela Rodrigues Pereira December 24, 1996
Priya Nalgundwar December 24, 1996
Priya Paul December 24, 1996
Radhika Menon June 16, 2015
Rudrama 1262
Sati Sadhani April 21, 1524
Suman Gawani May 29, 2020
Tarabai Bhosale April 1700
Uda Devi May 10, 1857
Umadevi 1171
Varsha Kukreti 1996
Veeramma October 21, 1824

Indus Valley
Vishpala 1900 BCE

Iran
Louise Aslanian late 1941

Iraq
Margaret George Shello 1963
Rengin Yusuf October 11, 2014
Sedar Botan August 19, 2014

Ireland
Alice Stopford Green April 24, 1916
Anne Bonny October 1720
Annie Higgins April 24, 1916
Betsy Gray June 12, 1798
Brigid Foley April 24, 1916
Christian "Kit" Cavanagh Davies 1691
Effie Taafe April 24, 1916
Eilís Elliott April 24, 1916
Eliza Alice Lynch March 1, 1870
Elizabeth O'Farrell April 24, 1916
Emily Elliott April 24, 1916
Euphan Maxwell April 24, 1916
Eva of Leinster August 25, 1170
Grace O'Malley 1565
Helena Molony April 24, 1916
Jennie Hodgers August 6, 1862
Julia Grenan April 24, 1916
Kathleen Clarke April 24, 1916
Kathleen Florence Lynn April 24, 1916
Lettice Fitzgerald Digby October 1642
Louisa Nolan April 24, 1916
Lucía Jonama y Fitzgerald June 22, 1809
Lydia Darragh December 2, 1777
Mae Murray April 24, 1916
Maire O'Ciaragain 1400
Margaret Croke Jordan September 13, 1809
Margaret de Badlesmere September 1326
Margaret Kehoe April 24, 1916
Marie Perolz April 24, 1916
Martha Kelly April 24, 1916
Martha Walsh April 24, 1916
Mary Herbert September 25, 1942
Mary Josephine Ryan April 24, 1916
Nell Ryan April 24, 1916
Rosie Hackett April 24, 1916
Sadie Farrell spring 1869

Winifred Carney April 24, 1916

Israel
Keren Tendler August 12, 2006
Noa Lazar October 7, 2022
Roni Zuckerman January 18, 1943
Tamar Ariel July 8, 2014
Yael Rom October 29, 1956
Yarden Shukron Yifrah September 4, 2022

Italy
Adele Bei Ciufoli July 19, 1943
Alrude Frangipane March 1173
Anna Isabella Gonzaga 1691
Carla Capponi July 19, 1943
Costanza d'Avalos 1503
Cristina Trivulzio di Belgiojoso March 18, 1848
Ermengard of Provence August 880 CE
Franziska Scanagatta July 1, 1794
Irma Bandiera 1944
Lidia Brisca Menapace 1943
Lina Merlin March 1926
Lucia Ottobrini December 19, 1943
Luisa Battistati March 18, 1848
Maddalena Cerasuolo September 27, 1943
Marcella Balconi 1944
Margaret of Attenduli August 6, 1414
Maria Teresa Regard December 19, 1943
Marisa Musu March 23, 1944
Matilda of Tuscany June 25, 1080; July 2, 1084, October 1092
Sichelgaita December 13, 1076; April 1080; October 18, 1081; May 28, 1084; July 17, 1085
Sylvia Mariotti June 24, 1866
Teresa Mattei April 15, 1944

Ivory Coast
Aya Virginie Touré March 8, 2011

Jamaica
Samanthia Griffiths 2003

Japan
Acha no Tsubone November 8, 1614
Akai Teruko 1584; May 1590
Fujinoye summer 1189
Fujishiro Gozen 1600
Hangaku Gozen 1199; February 1201
Hojo Masako 1185
Ikeda Sen October 21, 1600
Inahime October 21, 1600
Jingo Yukiko October 16, 1868
Jingu Kojo 200 CE
Kaihime May 1590
Kato Tsune October 9, 1584
Kogyoku Tenno 661 CE
Lady Ichikawa 1569
Maeda Matsu October 21, 1600
Miyagino December 17, 1637
Nakano Takeko October 16, 1868
Numata Jakō October 21, 1600
Ōhōri Tsuruhime 1541
Okaji no Kata November 8, 1614
Okurakyo no Tsubane November 8, 1614
Otazu no Kata December 1568
Shinobu December 17, 1637
Shirai no Tsubone June 27, 1565
Tachibana Ginchiyo 1586
Tomoe Gozen February 21, 1184
Ueno Tsuruhime 1577
Yamamoto Yaeko October 16, 1868
Yamatawa Futaba October 16, 1868
Yuki no Kata October 21, 1600

Java
Dyah Gitarja 1331
Mathilde Adrienne Eugénie Verspyck August 1941
Nyi Ageng Serang September 25, 1825

Jordan
Ahlam al-Tamimi August 9, 2001

Judaea
Delilah ca. 1062 BCE

Jutland
Hedborg ca. 770 CE
Richardis of Schwerin 1358
Thyra Danebod 910 CE

Kashmir
Begum Samru September 23, 1803
Sugandha 914 CE

Katdathanad
Unniyarcha early 1500s

Kazakhstan
Dinana Kolbaeva January 4–5, 2022
Pazyryk Amazon ca. 485 BCE
Rashida Salmeeva January 4–5, 2022

Kelantan
Siti Wan Kembang 1667

Khazaria
Parsbit December 7, 730 CE

Khurasan
Gülnar Hatun 769 CE

Kievan Rus'
Olga of Kiev early 945 CE

Kingdom of Yugoslavia
Andreana Druzina April 5, 1941
Olga Alkalaj April 5, 1941

Kongo
Aqualtune Ezgondidu Mahamud da Silva Santos October 29, 1665

Korea
Jindeok of Silla 647 CE
Yun Hui-sun 1895

Kush
Amanirenas 24 BCE

Lemnos
Marulla 1455

León
Urraca of León October 26, 1111

Liberia
Asatu Bah Kenneth July 21, 2003
Leymah Gbowee July 21, 2003

Libya
Aisha Gdour April 2012
Amal Bashir April 2012
Amalafrida 523 CE
Asma Gargoum April 2012
Dalla Abbazi April 2012
Egee ca. 1200 BCE
Fatima Bredan April 2012
Hweida Shibadi April 2012
Inas Fathy April 2012
Nabila Abdelrahman Abu Ras April 2012
Rabia Gajun April 2012

Lithuania
Appolonia Jagiello February 26, 1846
Elena Barščiauskaitė June 17, 1940
Emilia Plater November 29, 1830
Janina Wasiłojć-Smoleńska September 1939
Magdalena Aviėtėnaitė June 17, 1940
Olga Jehlweiser February 8, 1904
Ona Šimaitė March 20, 1939
Sara Ginaite-Rubinson August 10, 1944

Lombardy
Bianca Maria Visconti August 20, 1452
Camilla Rodolfi April 1449
Onorata Rodiani August 20, 1452
Veronica Gambara 1538

Lorraine
Isabella of Lorraine July 2, 1431

Lycia
Eurypyle 1760 BCE

Macedonia
Adea Eurydice II of Macedon 317 BCE
Cratesipolis 314 BCE
Eurydice of Egypt 280 BCE
Nexhmije Hoxha September 16, 1942
Phila of Macedonia late 295 BCE
Sirma Voyevoda 1791
Žamila Kolonomos April 6, 1941

Madeira
Teresinha Gomes 1992

Maeotia
Tirgatao 389 BCE

Magna Graecia
Timycha 379 BCE

Malacca
Tun Fatimah August 24, 1511

Malta
Madeleine ffrench-Mullen April 24, 1916

Mangalore
Abbakka Chowta of Ullal 1558; January 1568; 1581

Mauritius
Lise De Baissac September 25, 1942

Mercia
Aethelflaed summer 893 CE; 905 CE; 909 CE; August 5, 910 CE; 912 CE; 913 CE; 916 CE; August 1, 917 CE
Modthryth 520 CE

Meroë
Amanikhatashan early 70 CE
Amanirenas 24 BCE
Amanitore 1 CE
Mujaji 350 CE
Shanakdakheto 170 BCE

Mesopotamia
Ghazāla al-Haruriyya 677 CE

Mexico
Adela Velarde Pérez March 24, 1914
Amelia Robles Àvila April 22, 1920
Analaura Esparza-Gutiérrez October 1, 2003
Angela Jiménez April 22, 1920
Carmen Parra March 24, 1914
Clara de la Rocha March 24, 1914
Comandante Ramona January 1, 1994
Cosme Mendoza Chavira March 24, 1914
Gertrudis Bocanegra October 11, 1817
Juana Ramona March 24, 1914
Major Anna Maria January 1, 1994
Manuela Medina September 1820
Margarita Neri March 24, 1914
María de la Candelaria June 1712
María de la Luz Espinoza Barrera April 22, 1920
María Quinteras de Meras March 24, 1914
Petra Herrera March 24, 1914
Rosa Bobadilla March 24, 1914
Subcomandante Elisa January 1, 1994
Valentina Ramírez Avitia March 24, 1914
Yohl Ik'nal December 23, 582

Milan
Bianca Riario August 2, 1484
Caterina Sforza August 12, 1484; April 14, 1488; September 14, 1498

Moghulistan
Qutlugh Nigar 1496

Molucca
Martha Christian Tijahahu May 16, 1817

Mongolia
Alakhai Bekhi 1211
Ana Dara June 12, 1696
Doquz Khatun February 10, 1258
Khutulun ca. 1280
Mandukhai Khatun 1467
Muncunchimeg Nyamaajav March 11, 2016
Yesui Khatun fall 1226

Morocco
Fannu March 1147
Zaynab an-Nafzāwiyyah October 23, 1086

Navarre
Jeanne d'Albret May 14, 1562
Jeanne of Navarre 1297

Nepal
Annapurna Kunwar 1979

Neustria
Emma of France 933 CE
Fredegund 593 CE

New Granada
Ana María Martínez de Nisser May 5, 1841
María Antonia Santos Plata July 23, 1815
Rafaella Herrera July 15, 1762

New Zealand
Ahumai Te Paerata April 2, 1864
Nancy Wake 1940
Te Kooti 1870

Nicaragua
Aminta Granera Sacasa 1976
Gioconda Belli 1970
Nora Astorga July 19, 1969

Nigeria
Amina 1549; 1566; April 1576; 1610
Bakwa of Turunku 1549
Blessing Liman April 27, 2012
Funmilayo Ransome-Kuti late 1947
Geneviève Nwaogwugwu April 27, 2012
Grace Eniola Soyinka late 1947
Grace Garba April 27, 2012

Josephine Okwuekeleke Tolefe February 7, 1961
Kafayat Sanni April 27, 2012
Olubunmi Ijeli April 27, 2012
Tolulope Arotile April 27, 2012

Normandy
Cecilia of Le Bourcq June 28, 1119
Emma de Guader 1075
Godehilde de Tosny October 1097
Isabel of Conches 1091
Petronilla of Leicester April 1173

Northumbria
Osthryth of Mercia 679 CE

Norway
Anna Colbjørnsdatter Arneberg March 29, 1716
Anne Margrethe Bangs Strømsheim April 15, 1940
Anne-Sofie Østvedt December 1941
Astrid Dollis Dahlgren 1941
Auð Ketilsdatter 892 CE
Bergljot Håkonsdatter 1050
Dollis Dahlgren May 1943
Elise Eskilsdotter September 2, 1455
Elise Toft October 24, 2013
Haldis Elisabeth Arentz Sveri 1961
Ingrid Gjerde March 24, 2021
Kari Hiran March 1716
Kitty Grande May 1945
Lagertha 820s CE
Lise Børsum 1938
Prillar Guri August 16, 1612
Sela 400 CE
Solveig Bergslien December 1941
Sylvia Salvesen 1938
Wanda Hjort Heger April 9, 1940

Numidia
Asbyte May 219 BCE
Harpe May 219 BCE
Kahina Dihya of Numidia 698 CE

Ostrogoth Kingdom
Amalasuintha 522 CE

Ottoman Empire
Aredvi Sura Anahita October 16, 1853
Halide Edib Adivar September 4, 1919
Kara Fatma September 4, 1919
Laskarina Bouboulina April 4, 1821
Nene Hatun November 9, 1877
Sabiha Gökçen March 20, 1937
Şerife Bacı December 1921
Shote Galica July 1, 1927
Tringë Smajl April 6, 1911

Oyo
Orompoto 1555

Pakistan
Aafia Siddiqui July 18, 2008
Amena Sultana Bokul March 7, 1971
Lutfa Haseen Rosy March 7, 1971
Marium Mukhtiar November 24, 2015
Nazma Shaheen March 7, 1971
Sitara Begum March 7, 1971
Taramon Bibi March 7, 1971

Palestine
Margaret of Beverley September 9, 1187
Netiva Ben Yehuda February 11, 1948
Sarah Aaronsohn November 1915

Palmyra
Zenobia Septimia spring 270 CE

Panama
Shoshana Nyree Johnson March 23, 2003

Papua New Guinea
Nichola Goddard May 17, 2006

Paraguay
India Juliana April 16, 1539
Ramona Martínez March 1, 1870

Parthia
Rhodogune of Parthia winter 130–129 BCE
Sura 235 CE

Persia
Amestris 475 BCE
Apranik 651 CE
Artunis September 539 BCE
Atusa 475 BCE
Pantea Arteshbod September 539 BCE
Youtab Aryobarzan January 20, 330 BCE

Peru
Ana Lezama de Urinza 1650
Bartolina Sisa Vargas March 13, 1781; September 5, 1782
Brigida Silva de Ochoa April 5, 1818
Eustaquia de Sonza 1650
Gregoria Apaza March 13, 1781; September 5, 1782
Isabel Barreto de Castro October 18, 1595
Madeleine Truel May 3, 1945
María Parado de Bellido May 11, 1822
Micaela Bastidas Puyucahua May 18, 1781
Rosa Campuzano September 25, 1828
Señora de Cao 450 CE
Tomasa Tito Condemayta September 18, 1780

Philippines
Agueda Esteban July 1, 1900
Agueda Kahabagan May 1897
Gabriela Silang May 28, 1763
Gregoria de Jesús August 1896
Magdalena Leones April 9, 1942
Marina Bartolome Dizon-Santiago August 1896
Melchora Aquino August 1896
Naomi Flores April 9, 1942

Nelida Cabigayan 1974
Patrocinio Gamboa August 1896
Teresa Magbanua February 11, 1899
Trinidad Peréz Tecson August 1896
Urduja 1345

Picardy
Marie Fourreé de Poix September 8, 1535

Portugal
Antònia Rodrigues 1595
Brites de Almeida August 14, 1385

Portuguese Brazil
María Ursula d'Abreu e Lencastro 1700

Portuguese India
Catarina Lopes April 20, 1546
Garcia Rodrígues April 20, 1546
Isabel Dias April 20, 1546
Isabel Fernandes April 20, 1546
Isabel Madeira April 20, 1546
Juliana Dias da Costa June 19, 1707

Poland
Agnieszka Dowbor-Muśnicka August 1939
Anna Henryka Pustowójtówna January 22, 1863
Anna Wajcblum Heilman October 7, 1944
Antonina Wilczyńska January 22, 1863
Bronia Klibanski August 16, 1943
Ester Wajcblum October 7, 1944
Faye Schulman September 1942
Frumka Płotnicka August 3, 1943
Haika Grossman August 16, 1943
Hanna Stadnik January 18, 1943
Hela Rufeisen Schüpper January 18, 1943
Irena Adamowicz late 1941
Irena Scheur-Sawicka April 19, 1943
Jadwiga Piłsudska October 1, 1942
Joanna Żubr May 19, 1809
Julia Diament Pirotte May 1940
Liza Czapnik August 16, 1943
Lone Morgensen Masłocha September 1, 1939
Małgorzata Fornalska spring 1942
Maria Piotrowiczowa January 22, 1863
Mindla Maria Diament May 1940
Regina Safirsztajn October 7, 1944
Rose Gunapfel Meth October 7, 1944
Roza Robota October 7, 1944
Sofia Kossak-Szczucka August 18, 1906
Tosia Altman January 18, 1943
Vladka Meed January 18, 1943
Wanda Gertz Kazik November 1939; July 27, 1943
Wanda Krahelska-Filipowicz August 18, 1906; April 19, 1943
Wanda of Poland 730 CE
Weronika Wojciechowska January 22, 1863
Zofia Kossak-Szczucka April 19, 1943
Zofia Poznańska September 29, 1942

Provence
Beatrice of Provence June 6, 1249
Eleanor of Provence May 14, 1264
Ermengarde of Narbonne August 1172
Margaret of Provence June 6, 1249

Prussia
Anna Lühring March 13, 1813
Anna Sophia Detzliffon November 3, 1760
Antoinette Berg September 10, 1799
Catherine II the Great July 9, 1762
Eleonore Prochaska March 13, 1813
Friederike Krüger September 6, 1813
Hanna Reitsch April 29, 1945
Louise of Prussia October 14, 1806
Luise Aston March 24, 1848

Puerto Rico
Bianca Canales October 30, 1950
Frances M. Vega November 2, 2003
Lolita Lebrón March 1, 1954
Mariana Bracetti Cuevas September 23, 1868
Rosa Collazo October 31, 1950; March 1, 1954

Punjab
Bibi Amar Kaur November 1913
Bibi Joginder Kaur November 1913
Bibi Kartar Kaur November 1913
Bibi Sahib Kaur 1793
Datar Kaur June 2, 1818
Gulab Kaur November 1913
Jindan Kaur June 27, 1839
Mai Sukhan January 2, 1805
Mata Daya Kaur November 1913
Mata Sundari December 6, 1704
Sada Kaur July 7, 1799

Rhineland Palatinate
Loretta of Sponheim May 1328

Río de la Plata
Manuela Pedraza August 10, 1806

Roman Empire
Agrippina the Elder late August, 14 CE; summer, 15 CE
Agrippina the Younger 49 CE, 51 CE
Albia Dominica August 9, 378
Faustina the Younger 170 CE
Munatia Plancina 17 CE
Triaria Vitellia summer 68 CE

Roman Monarchy
Cloelia February 509 BCE

Roman Republic
Fulvia Flacca Bambula winter 41–40 BCE
Octavia Minor 35 BCE

Romagna
Marzia Ordelaffi April 29, 1357

Romania
Cristina Luca Boico summer 1942
Ecaterina Teodoroiu November 13, 1916
Irina Burnaia June 22, 1941
Mariana Drăgescu June 22, 1941
Smaranda Brăescu June 22, 1941
Stanislawa Ordynska November 25, 1915
Vera May Atkins September 1939

Russian Empire
Aleksandra Tikhomirova February 7, 1807f
Alena Arzamasskaia December 4, 1670
Alexandra Kudasheva July 28, 1914
Anna Wolkoff May 1939
Anne Jaclard March 18, 1871
Apollovna Isoltsev 1915
Elena Chuba 1915
Elisabeth Dmitrieff March 18, 1871
Eugenie Shakhovskaya July 28, 1914
Irina Sebrova May 1942
Krystyna Skarbek December 21, 1939
Lidia Lwow-Eberle September 1939
Ludmilla Kornilov early summer 1917
Lyudmila Pavlichenko August 8, 1941
Lyudmila Wolkensteon February 2, 1879
Maguba Syrtlanova January 1, 1943
Maria Botchkareva November 1914; early summer 1917
Maria Wittek August 1920; July 27, 1943
Marie Baktscharow early summer 1917
Marina Mikhaylovna Raskova 1933; May 1942; January 4, 1943
Nadezhda Durova February 7, 1807
Nadia Russo June 22, 1941
Natalie Tychmini May 15, 1915
Nina Raspopova October 18, 1941
Noor-un-Nisa Inayat Khan early February 1943
Olga Bancic July 17, 1936; 1941
Olga Kokovtseva July 28, 1914
Olga Krasilnikov May 15, 1915
Olga Sanifirova April 16, 1945
Sonia Perovskaya March 1, 1881
Sophie Alexandrovna Dolgorunaya July 28, 1914
Tatiana Grigorievna Solomakha February 1918
Tatiana Markina August 27, 1805
Valentina Petrova 1915
Vasilisa Kozhina June 24, 1812
Vera Figner February 21, 1879; March 1, 1881
Vera Tikhomirova August 1943
Yevdokiya Rachkevich May 1942
Zoya Anatolyevna Kosmodemyanskaya October 1941
Zoya Smirnow July 1914

Russian Soviet Federation
Dzhennet Abdurakhmanova July 5, 2003
Glafira Kashirina April 22, 1943
Irina Rakobolskaya May 1942
Janina Antonina Lewandowska August 1939
Kseniya Konstantinova October 1, 1943
Marina Chechneva July 25, 1942
Mariya Bayda June 7, 1942
Maryam Sharipova July 5, 2003
Nadezhda Popova May 1942
Rufina Gasheva April 16, 1945
Tatyana Baramzina July 5, 1944
Vera Belik August 25, 1944
Yekaterina Ryabova May 1942
Yelena Stempkovskaya May 12, 1942
Yevdokiya Nikulina May 18, 1943
Zoya Parfyonova January 29, 1945

Rwanda
Muhumusa late 1896

Samaria
Athaliah 841 BCE

Sardinia
Luisa Battistati March 18, 1848

Sarmatia
Amage 290 BCE

Savoy
Catherine Segurane August 6, 1543

Saxony
Christina of Saxony August 1501
Foelke Kampana August 7, 1389
Ingeborg Åkesdotter Tott August 1501
Johanna Stegen April 2, 1813
Lumke Thoole 1721
Matilda of Quedlinburg June 984 CE
Sonia Olschanezky autumn 1942

Scotland
Agnes Campbell September 1569
Agnes Comyn of Strathearn 1320
Agnes Randolph of Dunbar January 13–June 10, 1338
Anns Cunningham Hamilton June 5, 1639
Anne Drummond 1745
Anne Farquharson Mackintosh September 21, 1745
Anne Keith Smythe October 13, 1678
Anne MacLeod McKay September 21, 1745
Chantelle Taylor July 2008
Christina Bruce November 30, 1335
Elizabeth Lamb June 1546
Elly Duncan August 19, 1797
Euphemia Leslie 1527
Evota of Stirling July 20, 1304
Finola O'Donnell September 1569
Isabel Roger August 29, 1797
Isabella Hoppringle September 9, 1513
Isabella MacDuff March 25, 1306
Jackie Crookston August 29, 1797
Janet Pringle September 9, 1513
Jean "Jenny" Cameron August 19, 1745
Lilliard of Ancrum February 27, 1545
Margaret Keith de Lindsay 1395
Margaret Johnstone Ogilvy April 23, 1746
Margaret Skinnider April 24, 1916
Marian McKenzie August 1861
Marion Wilberforce October 1, 1942
Mariotta Haliburton September 10, 1547
Mary Buick Watson October 21, 1805
Mary Cameron Ralphson April 16, 1746
Mary Hay 1745

Scythia
Hypsicratea winter 66 BCE
Sparethra 560 BCE
Thalestris 324 BCE
Tomyris December 530 BCE
Zarinaia 550 BCE

Serbia
Antonija Javornik August 15, 1914
Milena Manditsch November 25, 1915
Milunka Savić October 8, 1912
Olga Alkalaj April 6, 1941
Sofija Jovanović October 1915
Sophie Jowanowitsch November 25, 1915

Siam
Boromdhilok December 1548
Suriyothai December 1548
Thao Sriunthorn December 1785
Thao Suranari March 1827
Thao Thepsatri December 1785

Siberia
Serafima Amosova May 1942

Sicily
Adelaide del Vasto June 22, 1101
Giuseppa Bolognara Calcagno May 31, 1861
Giuseppina Vadala September 5, 1848
Macalda di Scaletta March 30, 1282
Paolina Vadala September 5, 1848
Rosa Donato September 5, 1848
Teresa Testa di Lana September 5, 1848

Siena
Laudomia Forteguerri 1552

Sierra Leone
Mammy Yoko February 1898
Mary Faber de Sanger 1842

Skye
Aife of Alba 495 BCE
Scathach of Skye 495 BCE
Uathach 495 BCE

Slovakia
Maria Malko 1915
Yevdokiya Bershanskaya May 1942

Slovenia
Margareta of Celje May 1, 1480

Somalia
Arawelo 15 CE

South Africa
Kady D. Brownell March 14, 1862
Mandisa Mfeka April 2019
Mmanthatisi June 23, 1823
Nandi Bhebhe 1816
Phyllis Latour September 25, 1942

Soviet Union
Alexandra Beiko August 23, 1939
Klava Monakhova March 1, 1944
Klavdiya Kalugina March 1, 1944
Liza Ivanovna Chaikina October 14, 1941

Lydia "Lilya" Litvyak July 19, 1943
Marisa Chikhvintseva March 1, 1944
Mariya Semyonovna Polivanova October 2, 1941
Nadia Lugina March 1, 1944
Naida Asiyalova October 21, 2013
Natalya Venediktovna Kovshova October 2, 1941
Raisa Aronova May 1942
Tatyana Sumarokova August 1943
Valeriya Osipovna Gnarovskaya September 23, 1943
Yekaterina "Katya" Budanova July 19, 1943
Zina Gavrilova March 1, 1944
Zinaida Andreevna Urantseva March 1, 1944
Zinaida Ivanovna Mareseva August 6, 1943

Spain
Agueda Alsina June 22, 1809
Agustina Raimunda of Aragon June 15, 1808; June 21, 1813
Aisha al-Hurra 1482
Ana Detrell June 22, 1809
Ana Ferrer June 22, 1809
Ana María Antonia de Soto January 4, 1794
Ana María Mallorquí May 23, 1809, and December 16, 1810
Ana Turó June 22, 1809
Andrea Banderlú June 22, 1809
Antònia Betlem June 22, 1809
Ana Butinà June 22, 1809
Antònia Boer y Artolà June 22, 1809
Antònia Camprubí June 22, 1809
Antònia Costa June 22, 1809
Antònia Esparch June 22, 1809
Antònia Gelabert June 22, 1809
Antònia Mora June 22, 1809
Antònia Pelegri June 22, 1809
Atanasia Vidal June 22, 1809
Beatriz Bermúdez de Velasco May 20, 1520
Benita Portales June 15, 1808
Blanche of Castile May 20, 1217
Càndida Jou June 22, 1809
Carmen Custi June 22, 1809
Casta Álvarez Barceló June 15, 1808
Catalina de Erauso April 8, 1603
Catalina Delà June 22, 1809
Catalina Junquet June 22, 1809
Catalina Pagès June 22, 1809
Catalina Marimón June 22, 1809
Catalina Vidal June 22, 1809
Claia Casellas June 22, 1809
Clara del Rey Calvo May 2, 1808
Dominga Cortada June 22, 1809
Esperanza Llorens June 22, 1809
Eulàlia Colomer June 22, 1809
Eulàlia Vila June 22, 1809
Felicísima Quintana June 22, 1809
Florentina Serrats June 22, 1809
Franciscà Artigas June 22, 1809
Franciscà Ball-llobera June 22, 1809
Franciscà Barnés June 22, 1809
Franciscà Cullel June 22, 1809
Franciscà Eras June 22, 1809
Franciscà Fàbrega June 22, 1809
Franciscà Feu June 22, 1809
Franciscà Llogar June 22, 1809
Franciscà Marti June 22, 1809
Franciscà Morel June 22, 1809
Franciscà Pacul June 22, 1809
Franciscà Payret June 22, 1809
Franciscà Puig June 22, 1809
Franciscà Rexach June 22, 1809
Franciscà Soler June 22, 1809
Franciscà Xifreu June 22, 1809
Gerónima Amich June 22, 1809
Gerónima N. June 22, 1809
Gertrudis Camps y Roger June 22, 1809
Gertrudis Esclusa June 22, 1809
Gertrudis Turón June 22, 1809
Her Four Blankets June 25, 1876
Ignacia Alsina June 22, 1809
Ignacia Cantalosella June 22, 1809
Inés Alabreda June 22, 1809
Inés de Ben May 4, 1589
Inés de Suarez September 11, 1541
Isabel Costa June 22, 1809
Isabel Metjà Ibanéz June 22, 1809
Isabel Pi June 22, 1809
Isabella I of Castile February 1489
Josefa Amar y Borbón June 15, 1808
Josefa de Azlor June 15, 1808
Josefa Barrera June 22, 1809
Josefa Demà June 22, 1809
Josefa Valls June 22, 1809
Juana la Beltraneja March 1, 1476
Juana Galán June 6, 1808
Juliana Larena June 15, 1808
Lucía Jonama y Fitzgerald June 22, 1809
Magdalena Bivern Puig June 22, 1809
Magdalena Daví June 22, 1809
Magdalena Mollera June 22, 1809
Magdalena Serra June 22, 1809
Magdalena Teixidor June 22, 1809

Manuela Malasaña Oñoro May 2, 1808
Manuela Roig June 22, 1809
Manuela Sancho y Bonafonte June 15, 1808
Margarita Carreras June 22, 1809
Margarita Cassà June 22, 1809
Margarita Quintana June 22, 1809
Margarita Roig June 22, 1809
Margarita Salabert June 22, 1809
Margarita Sunyer June 22, 1809
Margarita Virosta June 22, 1809
María Abras June 22, 1809
María Agustín Linares June 15, 1808
María Angela Bivern Puig June 22, 1809
María Àngela Tarragó June 22, 1809
María Bandrell June 22, 1809
María Casademunt June 22, 1809
María Cendra June 22, 1809
María Ciurana June 22, 1809
María Crus June 22, 1809
Maria Curti June 22, 1809
María de Estrada 1510
María de la Consolación Azlor y Villavicencio June 15, 1808
María Esquero June 22, 1809
María Gatell June 22, 1809
María Josefa Jonama June 22, 1809
María la Bailadora October 7, 1571
Maria Llúcia de Puig y Quintana June 22, 1809
María Lostal June 15, 1808
María Magdalena Mir June 22, 1809
María Marfày Vila June 22, 1809
María Marqués June 22, 1809
María Mato June 22, 1809
Maria Pita May 4, 1589
María Plajas June 22, 1809
María Rafols June 15, 1808
María Vidal June 22, 1809
María Pascual Balet June 22, 1809
María Pastells June 22, 1809
María Riera June 22, 1809
María Rocosa June 22, 1809
María Rosa Falgueras June 22, 1809
María Rosa Saló June 22, 1809
María Rosa Vala June 22, 1809
María Serra June 22, 1809
María Sureda June 22, 1809
María Tarrús June 22, 1809
María Tomàs June 22, 1809
María Vidal June 22, 1809
María Vilanova June 22, 1809
María Yatón June 22, 1809
Mariana Perramón June 22, 1809
Mariana Pineda 1828
Marie Manuel August 1812
Mary de Bunsen October 1, 1942
Narcisa Bofill June 22, 1809
Paula Argimont June 22, 1809
Paula Martínez June 22, 1809
Raimunda Nouvilas de Pagès June 22, 1809
Rita Banús June 22, 1809
Rita Costa June 22, 1809
Rita Fàbregas June 22, 1809
Rita Sala June 22, 1809
Rosa Barnat June 22, 1809
Rosa Bernagosi June 22, 1809
Rosa Costa June 22, 1809
Rosa Forns June 22, 1809
Rosa Garcia-Malea February 15, 2011
Rosa Giralt June 22, 1809
Rosa Joíre June 22, 1809
Rosa Llobera June 22, 1809
Rosa Martorell June 22, 1809
Rosa Masmitjà June 22, 1809
Rosa Massó June 22, 1809
Rosa Mir June 22, 1809
Serafina Vey o Vehi June 22, 1809
Teresa Amat June 22, 1809
Teresa Ametller June 22, 1809
Teresa Andry June 22, 1809
Teresa Balaguer June 22, 1809
Teresa Comella June 22, 1809
Teresa Ferrarons June 22, 1809
Teresa Garriga June 22, 1809
Teresa Illas June 22, 1809
Teresa Mayol June 22, 1809
Teresa Palau June 22, 1809
Teresa Pascual June 22, 1809
Teresa Pujol June 22, 1809
Teresa Vivetas June 22, 1809
Valeriana Nató June 22, 1809
Vicenta Tornabells June 22, 1809
Yolande of Aragon May 8, 1429

Sparta
Archidamia spring 272 BCE
Chilonis spring 272 BCE

St. Croix
Axeline "Agnes" Elizabeth Salomon October 1, 1878
Mathilda McBean October 1, 1878
Susanna Abrahamson October 1, 1878

Sumatra
Queen Sima 674 CE

Sweden
Anna Eriksdotter Bielke April 1511–1513; February–September 6, 1520
Anna Maria Jansdotter Engsten March 15, 1791
Brita Olsdotter Hagberg July 2–3, 1790
Carin du Rietz ca. 1785
Christina Anna Skytte 1657
Christina Nilsdotter Gyllenstierna January 19, 1520
Dorothea Maria Lösch July 9, 1790
Ebba Gustavsdotter Stenbock August 1597
Emerentia Kraków January 24, 1612
Ida Henningsdotter Königsmarck July 1434
Ingela Olofsdotter Gathenhielm June 1710

Jane Horney January 20, 1945
Johanna Jungberg Hard November 1, 1823
Karin Lannby 1939
Katerina Nipertz 1487
Lisbetha Olsdotter November 12, 1679
Margareta von Ascheberg December 19, 1700
Maria Cameen Faxell 1710
Ulrika Eleonora Stålhammar 1713
Veborg ca. 770 CE

Switzerland
Anne-Marie Walters January 3, 1944
Catherine Cheynel Royaume December 11, 1602
Isabelle Wilhelmine Marie Eberhardt July 1900
Jeanne Baud Piaget Decembere 11, 1602
Martha Glar March 3, 1798
Rose Gluck Warfman fall 1941
Veronika Gut September 9, 1798
Virginie Ghesquière November 19, 1807

Syria
Afra 'Bint Ghifar al-Humayriah July 30, 634 CE, August 20, 636 CE
Arin Mirkan September 2014
Ghadir Taher January 16, 2019
Julia Domna 195 CE
Khawla bint al-Azwar July 30, 634 CE; September 19, 634 CE; August 20, 636 CE
Laodice I 246 BCE
Nazik Khatim July 21, 1920; September 17, 1925
Oserrah August 20, 636 CE
Rojda Felat September 2014
Wafeira August 20, 636 CE

Tahiti
Teriitaria II January 17, 1846

Tamil Nadu
Kuyili 1780
Velu Nachiyar June 25, 1772

Thailand
Lumchuan 1945
Tammy Duckworth November 12, 2004

Thebes
Timocleia of Thebes 335 BCE

Tibet
Ani Pachen October 7, 1950
Hor Lhamo 1918

Toltec Empire
Xochitll 916 CE

Transylvania
Júlia Bányai March 15, 1848
Pelaghia Roşu June 23, 1848

Trinidad and Tobago
Jozette McLean December 1996

Tunisia
Sitt al-Mulk February 13, 1021

Turin
Adelaide of Turin and Susa 1070; May 1084; March 18, 1091

Turkestan
Khiuaz Dospanova May 1942
Yevdokiya Pasko May 1942

Uganda
Alice Auma August 6, 1986
Christine Nyangoma February 21, 2007
Doreen Kyomuhangi March 28, 2020
Naomi Karungi January 28, 2020
Proscovia Nalweyiso February 8, 2019
Rebecca Mpagi March 28, 2020

Ukraine
Andriana Susak-Arekhta May 25, 2014
Helen Ruz August 23, 1914
Kateryna Noskova May 25, 2014
Kateryna Pryimak May 25, 2014
Larisa Rozanova May 1942
Nadia Savchenko May 25, 2014
Natalia Khorunzha February 6, 2017
Natalya Meklon May 18, 1943
Olena Bilozerska February 4, 2022
Polina Gelman May 1942
Sabina Halytska February 20, 2018
Sonia Shainwald Orbuch June 22, 1941
Valentina Grizodubova 1933
Vera Belik August 25, 1944
Yevdokiya Nosal April 22, 1943
Yevgeniya Rudneva May 1942

United Arab Emirates
Mariam Al Mansouri 2016

United States

Alaska
Ada Blackjack September 9, 1921

Arizona
Dahteste May 17, 1885
Gouyen 1872; October 14, 1880; 1883; May 17, 1885
Lori Ann Piestewa March 23, 2003
Lozen October 14, 1880; October 1883; May 17, 1885
Mary Jessie Herrera November 9, 2003

Arkansas
Sarah Jane Smith September 8, 1864

California
Beebe Beam October 5, 1899
Dana Colvon November 15, 2021
Donna Tobias March 1974
Dawn Halfaker June 19, 2004
Jennifer M. Moreno October 6, 2013
Julia Child January 1943

Karina S. Lau November 2, 2003
Susan Ahn Cuddy December 1942
Toypurina October 25, 1785

Florida
Jacqueline Cochran October 1, 1942

Georgia
Kathleen I. Wilkes January 15, 1965
Kendra Coleman May 11, 2010

Hawaii
Allene "Ally" Somera-Zyko September 2, 2021
Betty Bolivar 1985
Suzanne Puanani Vares-Lum June 28, 2018

Idaho
Kuilix 1842
Mattie Winnemucca July 31, 1878

Illinois
Danielle Greene-Byrd 2004
Frances Hook April 10, 1864
Juliet Beyler November 1984
Sophronia Smith Hunt January 1864

Indiana
Mary Ellen Wise October 10, 1861; April 6, 1862

Iowa
Jane Wallis Burrell 1978
Miyoko Hikiji 2003

Kentucky
Leigh Ann Hester March 20, 2005

Louisiana
Bras Piqué January 21, 1731
Pauline Cushman March 1863

Maine
Eliza Allen Billings September 1846
Mary Ann Berry Brown August 1861

Maryland
Harriet Tubman June 2, 1863
Margaret H. Woodward March 19, 2011
Marguerite Baker Harrison December 1918
Virginia Hall summer 1940

Massachusetts
Deborah Sampson July 3, 1782
Elizabeth Merriman Barrett January 1972
Hannah Emerson Duston April 29, 1697
Laura Secord June 22, 1813
Mary Corliss Neff April 29, 1697
Molly Osgood Childers April 24, 1916
Prudence Cummings Wright April 1775

Michigan
Annie Blair Etheridge April 1861
Claire Phillips April 9, 1942
Holly J. McGeogh January 31, 2004
Nancy Harkness Love late October 1942

Minnesota
Adeline Stocking Foot August 20, 1862
Frances Louis Clayton April 6, 1862
Mary Reynolds January 1941

Mississippi
Amy Clarke April 6, 1862

Missouri
Cathay Williams November 15, 1866
Elizabeth Caroline Newcom September 16, 1847
Josephine Baker September 1939
Katie Beattie September 8, 1864
Margaret Utinsky April 9, 1942
Martha Jane Cannary 1874
Sarah Borginis May 3, 1846

Montana
Buffalo Calf Road Woman June 17, 1876; June 25, 1876
Buffalo Wallow Woman September 17, 1868
Ehyophsta September 17, 1868
Her Four Blankets June 25, 1876
Mary Fine Weather June 25, 1876
Minnie Hollow Wood June 25, 1876
Minnie Bendina Spotted Wolf July 1943
Moving Robe Woman 1871
One Who Walks with the Stars June 25, 1876
Pretty Nose June 25, 1876
Sara Stires November 9, 2001
Seen by Her Nation June 25, 1876
The Other Magpie June 17, 1876
Woman Chief September 17, 1851

Nebraska
Jackey Smith August 13, 2006
Old-Lady-Grieves-the-Enemy 1850

Nevada
Sarah Winnemucca July 31, 1878

New Hampshire
Anna Maria Lane October 4, 1777

New Jersey
Mary Ludwig Hays June 28, 1778

New Mexico
Tamara Long-Archeleta March 23, 2004

New York
Anna Smith Strong summer 1778
Betty Gillies late October 1942
Betty L. Adams January 15, 1965

Ethel Rosenberg October 31, 1950
Fanny Wilson December 11, 1862
Grace Hopper December 1943
Kathy Piccollo February 1991
Louisa Hoffman July 16, 1861
Mary Edwards Walker April 10, 1864
Nellie Graves December 11, 1862
Sarah Rosetta Wakeman April 9, 1864
Shannon Mary Kent January 16, 2019
Tanya Chernova August 23, 1942
Tyonajanegen August 6, 1777

North Carolina
Donna Johnson October 1, 2012
Lucy Matilda Thompson Gauss April 1861
Mollie Bean July 1–3, 1863
Nancy Hart Douglas August 1861
Sarah Malinda Pritchard Blalock March 14, 1862

Ohio
Ashley White October 11, 2011
Catherine E. Davidson January 19, 1862
Chief Earth Woman 1893
Virginia d'Albert-Lake August 1941

Oregon
Mattie Winnemucca July 31, 1878
Sarah Winnemucca July 31, 1878

Pennsylvania
Aliquippa July 3, 1754
Ann Bates August 29, 1778
Jemima Warner mid–November 1775
Kimberly Voelz December 14, 2003
Loretta Walsh March 17, 1917
Margaret Cochran Corbon November 16, 1776
Nonhelema Hokolesqua August 5, 1763
Rachel Wall 1781
Susannah Grier mid–November 1775

Rhode Island
Awashonks June 20, 1675
Quaiapen June 20, 1675
Sharon T. Swartworth November 7, 2003

South Carolina
Crystal Davis January 21, 2006
Kimberly Hampton January 2, 2004
Margaret Catherine Moore "Katy" Barry January 17, 1781
Sally St. Clair December 29, 1778

South Dakota
Elizabeth Sudmeier early 1954
Moving Robe Woman 1871
Susie Shot-in-the-Eye June 25, 1876

Tennessee
Angelina Belle Peyton Eberly December 30, 1842
Ella Reno December 31, 1862
Lizzie Compton January 19, 1862
Nancy Ward 1755
Nora Tyson July 29, 2010
Sarah Bradbury December 31, 1862
Sarah Jane Taylor October 21, 1861
Sue Downes November 28, 2006

Texas
Monica Lin Brown April 27, 2007

Vermont
Tracey Poirier July 26, 2023

Virginia
Anne of the Pamunkey September 1676
Cockacoeske summer 1676
Deborah Squash April 27, 1781
Eloise Randolph Page 1978
Maria Lewis March 2, 1864
Marissa Strock November 24, 2005
Mary Bell July 1–3, 1863
Mary Jane Richards Bowser July 16, 1861
Molly Bell July 1–3, 1863
Monica Beltran October 26, 2005

Washington
Bowdash 1825
Colestah September 1, 1858
Jaime L. Campbell January 7, 2006

Washington, D.C.
Elizabeth Peet McIntosh January 1943

West Virginia
Adelaide Mulheran Hawkins August 1956
Jennie D. Hart April 1, 1863
Jessica Dawn Lynch March 23, 2003
Kate Brown August 1861
Margaret O. Murphy August 1861
Mary Jane Green August 1861

Wisconsin
Glory of the Morning summer 1727
Hanging Cloud 1855
Heidi Berg spring 1991
Mary Galloway January 1862
Michelle Witmer April 9, 2004
Nichole M. Frye February 16, 2004
Rachel Bosveld October 26, 2003
Susan Sonnheim September 2003

Wyoming
Doris Bohrer January 1943

Uruguay
Ana Lucas March 19, 2021
Ana Monterroso de Lavalleja October 21, 1817

Van Diemen's Land
Tarenorrerer 1828

Venezuela
Ana Soto August 6, 1668
Apacuana 1577
Concepción Mariño Carige Fitzgerald July 25, 1812
Josefa Venancia de la Encarnación Camejo April 19, 1810
Juana Ramírez May 25, 1813
María Luisa Cáceres Díaz de Arismendi September 24, 1815
Uricao 1567

Venice
Kösem Sultan May 12, 1649

Vietnam
Anne Marie Doering January 15, 1965
Bùi Thị Xuân February 1802
Đặng Thùy Trâm April 8, 1968
Dho Minde January 15, 1965
Ding Le Tunn January 15, 1965
Dương Thu Hương February 21, 1967
Ho Te Que early 1960s
Nguyễn Thị Định May 19, 1941

Wales
Amy Thomas March 20, 2009
Jemima Nicholas February 22, 1797

Zambia
Thokozile Muwamba January 11, 2017

Zimbabwe
Joice Runaida Mujuru February 17, 1974
Nehanda Charwe Nyakasikana May 1896

Appendix B: Warriors by Role

Admiral
Artemisia I
Auð Ketilsdatter
Cleopatra VII
Empress Kogyoku Tenno
Isabel Barreto de Castro
Keumalahayati
Kogyoku Tenno
Laskarina Bouboulina
Nora Tyson

Ambulance Driver
Barbara Helen Bailey
Diana Barnato Walker
Diana Rowden
Elisabeth Retiffe
Flora Sandes
Hélène Dutrieu
Jean Migotti
Lilias Ahearn
Melodie Massey
Natalia Khorunzha
Sophie Jowanowitsch
Susan Travers
Virginia Hall

Archer
Ahilyabhai Holkar
Alena Arzamasskaia
Artemisia I
Banu Khoramdin
Durgavati
Gaitana
Hangaku Gozen
Khutulun
Li Xiu
Liang Hongyu
Louise Labé
Mah Laqa Bai Chanda
Pazyryk Amazon
Qin Liangyu
Shen Yunying
Tomoe Gozen
Urduja
Velu Nachiyar
Yang Miaozhen
Yuenyu

Armorer
Laskarina Bouboulina
Wanda Gertz Kazik

Arsonist
Adelaide of Turin and Susa
Aqualtune Ezgondidu Mahamud da Silva Santos
Axeline "Agnes" Elizabeth Salomon
Bianca Canales
Breffu of St. John
Brígida do Vale
Carlota Lucumí
Cristina Luca Boico
Elisabeth Retiffe
Eulàlia Papavoine
Gudit
Herma Paschender
Harriet Tubman
Joana Soaleira
Joséphine Marchais
Juana Plazas
Katie Beattie
Leontine Suetens
Marcolina
Margaret O. Murphy
María Felipa de Oliveira
Maria Lewis
Martha Christian Tijahahu
Mary Leticia Thomas
Mathilda McBean
Nancy Hart Douglas
Sara Yehoshua
Seh-Dong-Hong-Be
Susanna Abrahamson
Zoya Anatolyevna Kosmodemyanskaya

Artillery Specialist/ Cannoneer
Agustina Raimunda of Aragon
Angelina Belle Peyton Eberly
Anna Dosa
Anne Marie Louise d'Orléans
Begum Samru
Blanche Arundell
Cicely Arundell
Durgavati
Emerentia Kraków
Giuseppa Bolognara Calcagno
Grace Hopper
Hweida Shibadi
Janina Simmons
Joice Runaida Mujuru
Juana Ramírez (Venezuela)
Lakshmibai
Margaret Cochran Corbin
María Angela Bivern Puig
Marie-Madeleine Jarret
Marie Manuel
Marinette Menut
Marissa Strock
Mary Anne Talbot
Mary Ludwig Hays
Mary Spenser-Churchill
Monica Beltran
Rafaella Herrera

Sally St. Clair
Sonya Butt
Sue Downes
Susan Ahn Cuddy
Ulrike Eleanora Stålhammar
Valeriya Osipovna Gnarovskaya
Violette Szabo
Yevdokiya Pasko

Assassin
Aafia Siddiqui
Abbakka Chowta of Ullal
Adele Bei Ciufoli
Agnes Comyn of Strathearn
Anna Goldsteiner
Anne-Sofie Østvedt
Athaliah
Bina Das
Carla Capponi
Chiomara
Cristina Luca Boico
Freddie Nanda Dekker-Oversteegen
Fredegund
Gouyen
Grace O'Malley
Hannah Emerson Duston
Hannie Schaft
Hille Feicke
Jael
Judon
Ketevan of Kekheti
Lyudmila Wolkenstein
Madeleine Riffaud
Marion Philippina Pritchard
Marthe Cnockaert
Mary Corliss Neff
Minnie Hollow Wood
Moving Robe Woman
Nexhmije Hoxha
Nora of Kelmendi
Parysatis
Pritilata Waddedar
Quilago
Reina Prinsen Geerligs
Rosa Collazo
Roxana of Bactria
Santi Das Ghose
Sara Yehoshua Fortis
Sietje Gravendeel-Tammens
Sitt al-Mulk
Sonia Perovskaya
Suniti Chaudhuri
Tarenorrerer
Teresa Mattei
Truus Menger-Oversteegen
Truus van Lier
Vera Figner
Wanda Krahelska-Filipowicz
Zarinaia
Zaynab bint al-Harith

Betrayer
Cartimandua
Delilah
Marie Leonie Vanhoutte

Bodyguard/Security Detail
Carin du Rietz
Cathay Williams
Gudrid Thorbjarnardóttir
Harpe
Hypsicratea
Johanna Bennius
Keumalahayati
Kuyili
Leslie Joy Whitehead
Mai Bhago
Maria Lewis
Maria van Antwerpen
Mary Ann Berry Brown
Sarah Rosetta Wakeman
Shangguan Wan'er
Thalestris
Ulrika Eleonora Stålhammar

Burial Squad
Dương Thu Hương
Loretta Janeta Velázquez

Camouflagist
Léa Blain

Cartographer
Ani Pachen
Doris Bohrer
Eloise Randolph Page
Halszka Wasilewska
Inas Fathy
Jane Wallis Burrell
Louise de Bettignies
Marie Leonie Vanhoutte

Cavalry
Aal de Dragonder
Abbakka Chowta of Ullal
Agueda Kahabagan
Aleksandra Tikhomirova
Alena Arzamasskaia
Alexandra Danilova
Alexandra Kudasheva
Amage of Sarmatia
Amina
Amina Sukhera
Amy Clarke
Anna Sophia Detzliffin
Annika Svahn
Appolonia Jagiello
Apranik
Aredvi Sura Anahita
Beauglie, Madame de
Berenice II Euergetes
Bianca Maria Visconti
Christian "Kit" Cavanagh Davies
Datur Kaur
Durgavati
Elena Chuba
Elizabeth Hatzler
Fanny Wilson
Félicité Fernig
Hua Mulan
Hypsicratea
Isabella I of Castile
Janine Marie de Foix
Jennie D. Hart
Joan of Arc
Johanna Sophia Kettner
Kaihime
Lakshmibai
Liu Jinding
Louise of Prussia
Manuela Sáenz
Maria Lewis
Maria ter Meetelen
Marie Magdelaine Mouron
Marie-Thérèse Figueur
Marina Lebstuck
Mary Bell
Mary Cameron Ralphson
Mary Read
Molly Bell
Nadezhda Durova
Nazo Tokhi
Olga Jehlweiser
Olga Kokovtseva
Onorata Rodiani
Orompoto
Qin Liangyu
Rosa Bobadilla

Sarah Bradbury
Sarah Malinda Pritchard Blalock
Shen Yunying
Sichelgaita
Tatiana Markina
Thalestris
Theophile Fernig
Yennenga

Charioteer
Asbyte
Bibi Sahib Kaur
Manya
Tania of Dardania
Vishpala

Color Bearer
Betsy Gray
Candelaria Figueredo
Kady D. Brownell
Nguyễn Thị Định

Combat Engineer
Ariana Sánchez

Combat Writer
Adélaïde Haas Hautval
Agnes Dorothee Humbert
Ana María Martínez de Nisser
Ani Pachen
Anna Comnena
Anna Szatkowska
Anna Wajcblum Heilman
Antonia Spath Bruha
Beebe Beam
Betty Ann Lussier
Carla Capponi
Catalina de Erauso
Chantelle Taylor
Charlotte Delbo
Claire Phillips
Cristina Trivulzio di Belgiojoso
Đặng Thùy Trâm
Deborah
Dhora Leka
Dorothy Peto
Dương Thu Hương
Eliza Allen Billings
Elizabeth Peet McIntosh
Empress Kogyoku Tenno
Erika Schwarze Wendt
Faye Schulman
Faye Turney

Flora Sandes
Françoise Déprés
Fujinoye
Geneviève de Gaulle-Anthonioz
Geneviève Prémoy
Germaine Guérin
Germaine Tillion
Gertrud Koch
Gioconda Belli
Gregoria de Jesús
Haika Grossman
Halide Edib Adivar
Hannah Snell
Hela Rufeisen Schüpper
Hélène Solomon-Langevin
Irina Burnaia
Isabelle Wilhelmine Marie Eberhardt
Janaky Athi Nahappan
Jane Horney
Jeanne de Sapinaud
Jessica Lynch
Joan Miller
Kamala Das Gupta
Kara Fatma
Leymah Gbowee
Lidia Brisca Menapace
Lise Børsum
Lise London
Loretta Janeta Velázquez
Louise Aslanian
Louise Labé
Louise Michel
Lucía Jonama y Fitzgerald
Lucie Bernard Aubrac
Lilian Wyles
Lyudmila Pavlichenko
Lyudmila Wolkenstein
Madeleine Riffaud
Mah Laqa Bai Chanda
Manto Mavrogenous
Margaret Utinsky
Marguerite Baker Harrison
Maria Bochkareva
Maria ter Meetelen
Marianne Golz
Marie-Thérèse Figueur
Marieta de Veintimilla
Marina Chechneva
Marthe Hoffnung Cohn
Mary Lacy
Mathilde Lucia Carré
Miyoko Hikiji

Nadezhda Durova
Nancy Wake
Natalya Meklin
Nazik Khatim
Nazma Shaheen
Netiva Ben Yehuda
Nguyễn Thị Định
Pearl Witherington
Raisa Aronova
Rose Valland
Sabiha Gökçen
Sarah Emma Edmonds
Sarah Rosetta Wakeman
Shoshana Nyree Johnson
Sofia Kossak-Szczucka
Sonia Shainwald Orbuch
Sophie Alexandrovna Dolgorunaya
Susan Travers
Sylvia Salvesen
Tammy Duckworth
Telesilla
Theophile Fernig
Truus Menger-Oversteegen
Tsola Nincheva Dragoycheva
Vera Figner
Virginia d'Albert-Lake
Virginia Hall
Vladka Meed
Wanda Hjort Heger
Yun Hui-sun
Yvonne Oddon
Žamila Kolonomos
Zhangsun
Zivia Altman
Zofia Kossak-Szczucka
Zohra Drif

Commander
Ada of Caria
Adea Eurydice II of Macedon
Adelaide Blanche of Anjou
Adelaide del Vasto
Adelaide of Turin and Susa
Aethelburg of Wessex
Aethelflaed
Agnes Campbell
Agnes of Dunbar
Agrippina the Younger
Ahhotep I
Ahilyabhai Holkar
Ahumai Te Paerata

Ā'ishah bint Abī Bakr
Akai Teruko
Akkadevi
Alakhai Bekhi
Albia Dominica
Aldonça de Bellera
Alrude Frangipane
Amalafrida
Amanikhatashan
Amanirenas
Amanitore
Amastris
Amestris
Ameliane du
   Puget-Glandevès
Amina
Anne Keith Smythe
Anne of Pamunkey
Anne-Sofie Østvedt
Apranik
Aqualtune Ezgondidu
   Mahamud da Silva Santos
Arawelo
Aredvi Sura Anahita
Arsinoë III Philopator
Arsinoë IV
Artemisia II
Arwa Al-Sulayhi
Atusa
Beatriz Bermúdez de Velasco
Beauglie, Madame de
Begum Samru
Bianca Canales
Bibi Sahib Kaur
Brunhilda
Bùi Thị Xuân
Carme Custi
Caterina Sforza
Catherine II the Great
Catherine Segurane
Chand Bibi
Cheryl Pearce
Christina Nilsdotter
   Gyllenstierna
Christine Nyangoma
Cleopatra II
Cleopatra III
Cleopatra V Selene
Cleopatra VII Philopator
Cratesipolis
Cynane
Datur Kaur
Deborah
Du Fengyang

Durgavati
Dyah Gitarja
Dynamis of Bosporus
Egee
Eleanor of Arborea
Elizabeth Dowdall
Elizabeth I of England
Emilia Plater
Emma of France
Eurypyle
Finiola O'Donnell
Françoise-Marie Jacquelin
Fredegund
Frumka Płotnicka
Fu Hao
Fu Jing
Fulvia Flacca Bambula
Gaitana
Gao Guiying
Ghaliyya al-Wahhabiyya
Glory of the Morning
Gwendolen of Cornwall
Hazrat Mahal
Helena Kantakouzene
Henriette Maria of France
Hind bint 'Utbah
Ingeborg Åkesdotter Tott
Ingrid Gjerde
Irene Asanina
Isabella I of Castile
Janequeo
Jeanne of Navarre
Jindan Kaur
Joan of Arc
Joaquina Galarza de Larrea
Juana Azurduy de Padilla
K'abel
Kahina Dihya of Numidia
Kaipkire
Kang Keqing
Keladi Chennamma
Kösem Sultan
Kittur Chennamma
Kong Sizhen
Lady Washi
Lalla Fatma N'Soumer
Laodice I
Liang Hongyu
Libuše
Llucia Joana
Lucía Jonama y Fitzgerald
Madeleine de Saint-Nectaire
Magdalena Bivern Puig
Mammy Yoko

Mandukhai Khatun
Mangammal
Manya
Margaret H. Woodward
Margaret of Anjou
Margaret of Attenduli
Margaret Wyndham Gore
Margareta von Ascheberg
Marguerite de Bressieux
María Angela Bivern Puig
Maria Botchkareva
María Custi
María de la Consolación
   Azlor y Villavicencio
Maria Kantakouzene
Maria Wittek
Marie Baktscharow
Marieta de Veintimilla
Mary Ambree
Mary Faber de Sanger
Mata Sundari
Matilda of Quedlinburg
Matilda of Tuscany
Matilda of Winchester
Mavia
Melisende of Edessa
Mmanthatisi
Monica Wichfeld
Mujaji
Mussasa
Nancy Harkness Love
Nakano Takeko
Nazo Tokhi
Niara Bely Lightbourn
Nora Tyson
Nyi Ageng Serang
Nzinga Mbande
Olympias Stratonice
Parsbit
Pearl Witherington
Pheretima
Phùng Thị Chính
Princess Zhao Pingyang
Qin Liangyu
Raimunda Nouvilas de
   Pagès
Ramatoulie D.K. Sanneh
Razia Sultana
Rhodogune of Parthia
Rojda Felat
Roza Robota
Rudrama
Sada Kaur
Seh-Dong-Hong-Be

Señora de Cao
Shajar al-Durr
Shanakdakheto
Shen Yunying
Sichelgaita
Sima of Java
Simone Wilkie
Siti Wan Kembang
Sparethra
Sura
Tamar of Georgia
Tarabai Bhosale
Tarenorrerer
Taytu Betel
Tembandumba
Teuta
Thalestris
Theodora Kantakouzene
Tomyris
Triệu Thị Chinh
Ueno Tsuruhime
Umadevi
Urduja
Valasca
Velu Nachiyar
Wanda of Poland
Wang Cong'er
Wang Nangxian
Woman Chief
Wu Shuqing
Wu Zetian
Xian
Xiao Yanyan
Xóchitl
Yaa Asantewaa
Yang Miaozhen
Yarden Shukron Yifrah
Žamila Kolonomos
Zenobia Septimia

Commando
Amy Thomas
Apranik
Azad Deylami
Brilliana Conway Harley
Channing Day
Joanna of Flanders
Lucie Bernard Aubrac
Rawya Ateya
Riet van Grunsven

Conqueror
Messene

Conspirator
Ala Gertner
Anna Goldsteiner
Anna Szatkowska
Anna Wajcblum Heilman
Anne Drummond
Anne Farquharson Mackintosh
Anne MacLeod McKay
Brigida Silva de Ochoa
Brilliana Conway Harley
Brita Olovsdotter Tott
Bronia Klibanski
Chand Bibi
Clara Tocarruncho
Concepción Mariño Carige Fitzgerald
Dolores Vela de Veintimilla
Elizabeth Ryder Maxwell
Ester Wajcblum
Felicia Solano de Vizuete
Genia Fischer
Gertrudis Vanegas
Gulab Kaur
Inas Fathy
Inge Weidenau Frank
Jane Howard
Jane Ryder Whorwood
Jeanne Brousse
Liza Czapnik
Lolita Lebrón
Macalda di Scaletta
Mah Chuchak Begum
Manuela Cañizares
María Gertrudis Romero
Mariana Pineda
Marretje Arents
Marta Bindiger Cigi
Olga Alkalaj
Regina Safirsztajn
Rosa Collazo
Rose Grunapfel Meth
Rosa Villafuerte de Castillo
Roza Robota
Šárka
Sitt al-Mulk
Sofia Kossak-Szczucka
Sonia Perovskaya
Tarenorrerer
Trưng Nhị
Trưng Trắc
Tun Fatima
Vicenta Equino
Wanda Krahelska-Filipowicz

Counselor
Dinana Kolbaeva

Crusader
Adelaide del Vasto
Arawelo
Beatrice of Provence
Cecilia of Le Bourcq
Corba of Thorigne
Edith de Warenne
Eleanor of Aquitaine
Eleanor of Castile
Elvira of Leon-Castile
Emeline of Bouillon
Ermengarde of Narbonne
Faydide of Toulouse
Florina of Bourgogne
Godehilde de Tosny
Hadvide of Chiny
Helie of Burgundy
Humberge of Le Puiset
Ida of Austria
Magistra Hersend
Margaret of Beverley
Margaret of Provence
Melisende of Edessa
Sibylla of Anjou
Sichelgaita

Cryptanalyst/Cryptographer
Adelaide Mulheran Hawkins
Betty Ann Lussier
Eloise Randolph Page
Erika Schwarze Wendt
Fatima Bredan
Gregoria de Jesús
Heidi Berg
Juliet Beyler
Sarah Aaronsohn
Shannon Mary Kent
Susan Ahn Cuddy
Tamara Haydée Bunke Bider
Vera May Atkins

Defender
Adeline Stocking Foot
Agustina Raimunda of Aragon
Ahumai Te Paerata
Alice Lynne Knyvet
Aliquippa

Amaron Hasselaer
Amastris
Anacaona
Ana María Antonia de Soto
Ana Soto
Angélique Duchemin Brûlon
Anita Garibaldi
Anna Cunningham Hamilton
Anna Eriksdotter Bielke
Anna Isabella Gonzaga
Anne Holck
Anne Jørgensdatter Rud
Anne Margrethe Bangs Strømsheim
Anne Marie Louise d'Orléans
Anne of the Pamunkey
Antonija Javornik
Ats Bonninga
Bauck Poppema
Benita Portales
Bertha van Heukelom
Bibi Dalair Kaur
Blanche Arundell
Blanche of Castile
Blenda
Boromdhilok
Bras Piqué
Brilliana Conway Harley
Brites de Almeida
Camilla Rodolfi
Carla Monteiro Araújo
Casta Álvarez Barceló
Catarina Lopes
Catharina Rose
Catherine Cheynel Royaume
Cecilia Rozgonyi
Céleste Bulkeley
Charlotte Amalie
Charlotte of Cyprus
Charlotte Stanley
Christina of Saxony
Christine de Lalaing of Espinoy
Cicely Arundell
Claire de Laval
Clementia of Burgundy
Costanza d'Avalos
Ebba Gustavsdotter Stenbock
Ecaterina Cercheza
Eleanor of Provence
Elizabeth Dowdall
Emerentia Kraków
Emma de Guader
Ermengard of Provence
Eva of Leinster
Fannu
Foelke Kampana
Freydís Eiríksdóttir
Fujinoya
Fujishiro Gozen
Furra
Gabrielle Laval
Garcia Rodrígues
Guiraude de Lavaur
Gunilla Johansdotter Bese
Hangaku Gozen
Helena Palaiologina
Honchi
Huillac Ñusca
Ida Henningsdotter Königsmarck
Ilona Zrínyi
Isabel Dias
Isabel Fernandes
Isabel Madeira
Isabella MacDuff
Janaky Athi Nahappan
Jeanne Baud Piaget
Jeanne d'Albret
Jeanne Hachette
Jemima Nicholas
Jingo Yukiko
Joana Angélica de Jesus
Joan Beaufort
Joan of Arc
Joanna of Flanders
Josefa Amar y Borbón
Josefa de Azlor
Juliana Larena
Juliane de Fontevrault
Julienne du Guesclin
Kari Hiran
Katerina Nipertzf
Katherine Grandison
Kato Tsune
Kenau Simonsdochter Hasselaer
Kong Sizhen
Lady Ichikawa
Lettice Fitzgerald Digby
Li Xiu
Lilliard of Ancrum
Loretta of Sponheim
Louise of Prussia
Luisa Battistati
Maddalena Cerasuolo
Maeyken in den Hert
Mai Bhago
Manono II
Manuela Pedraza
Manuela Sancho y Bonafonte
Marcia Andrade Braga
Margaret de Badlesmere
Margaretha Sandra
Margaret II of Hainaut
Margaret Keith de Lindsay
Margaret Mautby Paston
Margaret of Attenduli
Margaret of Bavaria
Marguerite Delaye
María Agustín Linares
Maria Cameen Faxell
María de la Consolación Azlor y Villavicencio
María Lostal
María Pacheco Padilla
María Rafols
María Úrsula d'Abreu e Lencastro
Marie Fourreé de Poix
Marieta de Veintimilla
Marinette Menut
Mariotta Haliburton
Marulla
Mary Hawtrey Bankes
Marzia Ordelaffi
Maud de Braose
Mukaya Luba
Nakano Takeko
Natalie Tychmini
Nela Martínez Espinosa
Nene Hatun
Nicola de la Haye
Numata Jakō
Nzinga Mbande
Ōhōri Tsuruhime
Old-Lady-Grieves-the-Enemy
Olga Krasilnikov
Onomaris
Otazu no Kata
Petronilla of Leicester
Pharantzem of Armenia
Phila of Macedonia
Philis de la Tour
Philippa of England
Philothey Benizelos

Pieronne of Brittany
Pomellina Fregoso
Prudence Cummings Wright
Quilago
Rafaela Herrera
Richardis of Schwerin
Sarah Borginis
Sarraounina Mangou
Sati Sadhani
Señora de Cao
Shirai no Tsubone
Sima of Java
Siti Wan Kembang
Sugandha
Sulaym bint Milhan
Suman Gawani
Suriyothai
Swob Sjaarda
Tachibana Ginchiyo
Thao Sriunthorn
Thao Thepsatri
Theodora of Vasta
Thyra Danebod
Tiphaine Raguenel
Trijn Rembrands
Trijn van Leemput
Unniyarcha
Vasilisa Kozhina
Veronica Gambara
Veronika Gut
Yamamoto Yaeko
Yamatawa Futaba
Yesui Khatun
Yevgeniya Rudneva
Yohl Ik'nal
Yuki no Kata

Died in Combat/Custody

Aal de Dragonder
Adea Eurydice
Aethelflaed
Agnieszka Dowbor-Muśnicka
Agustina Peralta
Aiza Gazuyeva
Aleksandra Tikhomirova
Alina Tumriyeva
Amelia of Bernice
Amina
Aminat Nagaev
Amy Johnson
Ana Dara
Ana Josefa Morales
Ana Lezama de Urinza
Ana Soto
Analaura Esparza-Gutiérrez
Andrée Borrel
Anna Goldsteiner
Anselma Leyton
Antonia Moreno
Antonia Santos Plata
Antonina Wilczyńska
Anush Apetyan
Apranik
Archidamia
Arin Mirkan
Asbyte
Ascensión Ortega
Ashley White
Atha
Athaliah
Avanti Bai Lodhi
Baltazara Chuiza
Barbara Montes
Bartolina Sisa Vargas
Berta Bergman
Berty Albrecht
Betsy Gray
Boromdhilok
Bracha Fuld
Breffu of St. John
Brilliana Conway Harley
Bùi Thị Xuân
Bule Naipi
Candelaria Forero
Carlota Armero
Carlota Lucumí
Carlota Rengifo
Cecily Gordon Lefort
Chand Bibi
Channing Day
Charlotte de Berry
Chiang Ch'ing
Clara del Rey Calvo
Collette Nirouet
Consuelo Dubois
Corba of Thorigne
Cornelia van den Brink
Cubah Cornwallis
Cut Gambang
Cynane
Dandara
Đặng Thùy Trâm
Danielle Casanova
Diana Rowden
Dolores Salas
Donna Johnson
Dorotea Castro
Dorotea Lenis
Du Fengyang
Durgavati
Drypetis
Dzhennet Abdurakhmanova
Ecaterina Teodoroiu
Eleonore Prochaska
Éliane Plewman
Elsie Joy Davison
Emeline of Bouillon
Emilie Tillion
Empress Kogyoku Tenno
Engracia Salgar
Estefanía Linares
Ethel Rosenberg
Eugenie Shakhovskaya
Eusebia Galviza
Evangelina Diaz
Fannu
Fidela Ramos
Florina of Bourgogne
France Bloch-Serazin
Frances M. Vega
Françoise-Marie Jacquelin
Frumka Płotnicka
Fujishiro Gozen
Funmilayo Ransome-Kuti
Gabriela Silang
Gabrielle Weidner
Gaitana
Genoveva Sarmiento
Germaine Tambour
Gertrudis Bocanegra
Ghadir Taher
Glafira Kashirina
Gregoria Apaza
Guiraude de Lavaur
Gulab Kaur
Gülnar Hatun
Gwenllian ferch Gruffydd
Hannah Szenes
Hannie Schaft
Harpe
Hassiba Ben Bouali
Hille Feicke
Ho Te Que
Holly J. McGeogh
Hor Lhamo
Huillac Ñusca
Ida of Austria
Ignacia Medina
India Juliana

Inés Osuna
Ines Peñaranda
Irena Scheur-Sawicka
Irma Bandiera
Isabel Roger
Jaime L. Campbell
Jane Horney
Jane Wallis Burrell
Janina Antonina
    Lewandowska
Jemima Warner
Jennifer M. Moreno
Jhalkaribai
Joan Beaufort
Joan of Arc
Joan of England and Sicily
Joana Angélica de Jesus
Joanna of Flanders
Joaquina Aroca
Josefa Conde
Jovita Feitosa
Juana Escobar
Juana Ramírez (Colombia)
Juana Santos
Judon
Justina Estepa
Kahina Dihya
Karina S. Lau
Kateryna Noskova
Käthe Wanek Odwody
Keren Tendler
Khadijat Mangerieva
Khava Barayeva
Kimberly Hampton
Kimberly Voelz
Kiran Shekhawat
Kittur Chennamma
Klára Andrássy
Klava Monakhova
Kösem Sultan
Kseniya Semyonovna
    Konstantinova
Kura Ocllo
Kuyili
Lakshmibai
La Mulâtresse Solitude
Lai Choi-san
Laurean Sierra
Léa Blain
Lela Karagianni
Leonarda Carreño
Leontine Suetens
Lida Khildehoroeva
Lilian Mercedes Letona

Liliane Rolfe
Lilliard of Ancrum
Liri Gero
Lisa Jade Head
Lisbetha Olsdotter
Liza Ivanovna Chaikina
Lorenza Avemanay Tacuri
Lori Ann Piestewa
Louise Aslanian
Louise de Bettignies
Lucía Jonama y Fitzgerald
Lucumí Fermina
Luiza Magomadova
Lydia "Lilya" Litvyak
Madeleine Zoe Damerment
Madeleine Tambour
Madeleine Truel
Mai Politzer
Małgorzata Fornalska
Mandukhai Khatun
Mangammal
Manono II
Manuela Chuiza
Manuela Eras de Gandarillas
Manuela Escobar
Manuela Medina
Manuela Uscátegui
Mareta Duduyeva
Margaret Fairweather
Margaret George Shello
Margaret Kehoe
Margarita Tutulani
Marguerite de Bressieux
Maria Bochkareva
Maria Bonita
María de los Ángeles Ávila
María del Carmen Olano
María del Rosario Devis
María del Transito Vargas
María Josefa Esguerra
María Miranda
María of Curaçao
Maria Olip'
María Parado de Bellido
Maria Piotrowiczowa
Mariam Tuburova
Marie Reynoard
Marina Mikhaylovna
    Raskova
Marinette Menut
Marisa Chikhvintseva
Marium Mukhtiar
Mariya Semyonovna
    Polivanova

Markha Ustarkhanova
Marretje Arents
Martha Glar
Marta Tello
Mary Carleton
Mary Critchett
Mary Dixon
Mary Read
Maryam Sharipova
Matangini Hazra
Mattie Winnemucca
Maud de Braose
Melida Anaya Montes
Mercedes Loayza
Micaela Bastidas Puyucahua
Micaela Nieto
Michelle Witmer
Mindla Maria Diament
Monica Wichfeld
Movsar Barayev
Naida Asiyalova
Nakano Takeko
Naomi Karungi
Natalia Khorunzha
Natalya Venediktovna
    Kovshova
Nehanda Charwe
    Nyakasikana
Nichola Goddard
Nichole M. Frye
Noa Lazar
Noor-un–Nisa Inayat Khan
Ōhōri Tsuruhime
Olga Bancic
Olga Alkalaj
Olympias Stratonice
Onorata Rodiani
Orompoto
Otazu no Kata
Paula Contreras
Persefoni Kokedhima
Pieronne of Brittany
Presentación Buenahora
Pritilata Waddedar
Quaiapen
Quilago
Rachel Bosveld
Razia Sultana
Reina Prinsen Geerligs
Remigia Cuesta
Renée Lemaire
Rengin Yusuf
Rita Arnould
Rosa Zaráte de la Peña

Rosaura Rivera
Rose Lopes Laguna-Asscher
Rose Valland
Roxana of Bactria
Roza Nagaev
Rudrama
Sabina Halytska
Sally St. Clair
Salomé Buitrago
Sarah Aaronsohn
Sarah Feely Bryant
Sarah-Jayne Mulvihill
Satisita Dzhbirkhanova
Şerife Bacı
Shannon Mary Kent
Sharon T. Swartworth
Shirai no Tsubone
Simona Amaya
Simona Josefa Manzaneda
Sisygambis
Siti Wan Kembang
Solveig Bergslien
Sonia Perovskaya
Sonia Olschanezky
Stateira I
Stateira II
Sugandha
Sulaym bint Milhan
Suriyothai
Susannah Grier
Suzanne "Sanité" Bélair
Tamar Ariel
Tamara Haydée Bunke Bider
Tamara Long-Archeleta
Tarenorrerer
Tatiana Grigorievna Solomakha
Tatyana Baramzina
Tatyana Savelyevna Marinenko
Tembandumba
Thérèse Pierre
Tomasa Tito Condemayta
Tomasa Rodríguez
Tosia Altman
Triệu Thị Chinh
Trưng Nhi
Trưng Trắc
Truus van Lier
Uda Devi
Ueno Tsuruhime
Vahida Maglajlić
Valasca
Valeriya Osipovna Gnarovskaya
Veborg
Vera Leigh
Weronika Wojciechowska
Woman Chief
Xóchitl
Yekaterina "Katya" Budanova
Yelena Stempkovskaya
Yevdokiya Nosal
Yevgeniya Rudneva
Yolande Beekman
Yvonne Huynh
Yvonne Rudellat
Zinaida Aliyeva
Zinaida Ivanovna Mareseva
Zofia Poznańska
Zoya Anatolyevna Kosmodemyanskaya
Zulikhan Elikhadzhiyeva
Zura Barayeva

Diver
Betty Bolivar
Donna Tobias
Hydna of Scione
Leanne Crowe

Drummer
Eleonore Prochaska
Elisabeth Someruell
Jackie Crookston
Mary Anne Talbot
Phoebe Smith Hessel
Umm Ḥakīm bint al-Ḥārith

Dueler
Agnes Joane Hotot
Alberte-Barbe d'Ernécourt
Ana Lezama de Urinza
Anne Dieu-le-Veut
Catalina de Erauso
Caterina Sforza
Christian "Kit" Cavanagh Davies
Eustaquia de Sonza
Joanna of Flanders
Julie D'Aubigny La Maupin
Marie Magdelaine Mouron
Meenakshi Amma
Miyagino
Nora of Kelmendi
Ōhōri Tsuruhime
Shinobu
Urduja
Yang Miaozhen

Excommunicated
Chrodielde
Joan of Arc
Leubevere of Cheribert

Executed
Alena Arzamasskaia
Alexandra Kudasheva
France Bloch-Serazin
Joan of Arc
Manuela Malasaña Oñoro
Pieronne of Brittany
Shangguan Wan'er

Exiled/Banished
Agueda Esteban
Ahlam al-Tamimi
Aisha al-Hurra
Alice Auma
Amalasuintha
Andrea Ricuarte
Ani Pachen
Anna Rheinholdsdotter Leuhusen
Anne Marie Louise d'Orléans
Antonia León y Velasco
Ats Bonninga
Barbara Forero
Barbara Pieters Adriaens
Candelaria Figueredo
Cubah Cornwallis
Cut Nyak Dhien
Dolores Nariño
Dương Thu Hương
Evota of Stirling
Félicité Fernig
Gioconda Belli
Hypsicratea
Ilona Zrínyi
Isabel Nariño
Jindan Kaur
Josefa Baraya
Laskarina Bouboulina
Lise London
Louise Michel
Luisa Mahin
Lumke Thoole
Lyudmila Wolkenstein
Manuela Sáenza
María Luisa Cáceres Díaz de Arismendi

María Pacheco Padilla
Maria van Antwerpen
Marie Nordmann-Cohen
Marieta de Veintimilla
Marina Lebstuck
Mathilde Carré
Mercedes Nariño
Nandi Bhebhe
Nathalie Lemel
Nazik Khatim
Pritilata Waddedar
Richilde of Hainault
Shanti Das Ghose
Suniti Chaudhuri
Sylvette Roussel Leleu
Theophile Fernig
Toypurina
Ulrika Eleonora Stålhammar
Velu Nachiyar
Vera Figner
Yaa Asantewaa

Explorer
Ada Blackjack
Auð Ketilsdatter
Freydís Eiríksdóttir
Gudrid Thorbjarnardóttir
Inés de Suarez
Isabel Barreto de Castro
Isabelle Wilhelmine Marie Eberhardt
Urduja

Field Medic
Adela Velarde Pérez
Adélaïde Haas Hautval
Agnes Dorothee Humbert
Ahilyabhai Holkar
Alena Arzamasskaia
Andrée Borrel
Andrée de Jongh
Anna Szatkowska
Anne Jaclard
Anne Margrethe Bangs Strømsheim
Annie Blair Etheridge.
Antonija Javornik
Anush Apetyan
Augusta Maria Chiwy
Beebe Beam
Berta Bergman
Carla Capponi
Channing Day
Chantelle Taylor

Colestah
Đặng Thùy Trâm
Dinana Kolbaeva
Dương Thu Hương
Ecaterina Teodoroiu
Éliane Brault
Elisa Bernerström Servenius
Elisabeth Dmitrieff
Elizabeth O'Farrell
Esther Arditi
Eulalie Papavoine
Euphan Maxwell
Fatima Bredan
Faye Schulman
Gioconda Belli
Halszka Wasilewska
Ho Te Que
Irene del Carmen Morales Galaz
Janina Wasiłojć-Smoleńska
Jennifer M. Moreno
Julie Grenan
Kateryna Pryimak
Kathleen Florence Lynn
Kathy Piccollo
Kseniya Semyonovna Konstantinova
Lakshmi Sahgal
Leslie Joy Whitehead
Lidia Lwow-Eberle
Lizzie Compton
Louisa Nolan
Louise Michel
Lozen
Lucy Matilda Thompson Gauss
Madeleine Passot
Magdalena Avietėnaitė
Magdalena Leones
Magistra Hersend
Malalai
Manuela Sáenz
Marcella Balconi
Margaret George Shello
Margaret Kehoe
María Remedios Del Valle
Marie-Jeanne Lamartinere
Marie Marvingt
Marinette Menut
Mariya Bayda
Martha Kelly
Mary Ann Berry Brown
Mary Brose Tepe
Mary Edwards Walker

Mattie Winnemucca
Melchora Aquino
Michelle Norris
Monica Lin Brown
Monique de Bissy
Natalia Khorunzha
Nazik Khatim
Patrocinio Gamboa
Princess Halima
Ramona Martínez
Rashida Salmeeva
Renée Lemaire
Sabina Halytska
Sarah Emma Edmonds
Sarah Winnemucca
Sichelgaita
Sitara Begum
Sofia Noti
Sonia Shainwald Orbuch
Sophronia Smith Hunt
Susan Travers
Tatyana Baramzina
Trinidad Peréz Tecson
Valeriya Osipovna Gnarovskaya
Vijayalakshmi Ramanan
Violette Lecoq
Virginia Hall
Yesui Khan
Zinaida Ivanovna Mareseva

Forger
Anne-Sofie Østvedt
Brita Olovsdotter Tott
Claire Phillips
Elisabeth de la Bourdonnaye
Frieda Belinfante
Geneviève de Gaulle
Ingeborg Wallheimer Kahlenberg
Jeanne Brousse
Julienne Aisner
Kitty Harris
Lela Karagianni
Madeleine Truel
Małgorzata Fornalska
Marion Philippina Pritchard
Ona Šimaitė
Rita Arnould
Rose Gluck Warfman

Grenadier
Anna Sophia Detzliffin
Kseniya Semyonovna Konstantinova

Maria van Antwerpen
Milunka Savić
Rose Barreau
Valeriya Osipovna Gnarovskaya

Guerrilla Warrior
Ana Soto
Apranik
Awashonks
Baya Hocine
Bùi Thị Xuân
Celia Sánchez Manduley
Christine Nyangoma
Comandante Ramona
Cut Gambang
Cut Nyak Dhien
Cut Nyak Meutia
Djaouher Akrour
Emilia Plater
Gaitana
Hassiba Ben Bouali
Huang Pei-mei
Jacqueline Guerroudj
Jeanne Merkus
Joice Runaida Mujuru
Kate Brown
Lilian Mercedes Letona
Lutfa Haseen Rosy
Major Anna Maria
Margaret George Shello
María Remedios Del Valle
Maria Svobod
Marian McKenzie
Martha Christian Tijahahu
Mary Jane Green
Melida Anaya Montes
Nancy Hart Douglas
Nanny of the Maroons
Nazma Shaheen
Policarpa Salavarrieta
Proscovia Nalweyiso
Quaiapen
Sada Kaur
Sarraounina Mangou
Subcomandante Elisa
Tamara Haydée Bunke Bider
Taramon Bibi
Teriitaria II
Tomasa Tito Condemayta
Tringë Smajl
Zoulikha Bekkadour

Guide
Andrée de Jongh
Bowdash
Elena Haas
Elvire de Greef
Geertruida Wijsmuller-Meijer
Harriet Tubman
Janine de Greef
Josefa Venancia de la Encarnación Camejo
Kattalin Aguirre
Lidia Brisca Menapace
Manuela Sáenz
Mathilde Adrienne Eugénie Verspyck
Mattie Winnemucca
Monique de Bissy
Nonhelema Hokolesqua
Olga Bancic
Onomaris
Sara Ginaite-Rubinson
Sarah Winnemucca
Vera Leigh
Virginia d'Albert-Lake
Zivia Lubetkin

Infantry
Afra 'Bint Ghifar al-Humayriah
Ana María Martínez de Nisser
Angela Jiménez
Anne Dymoke
Collette Nirouet
Frances Louis Clayton
Hannah Snell
Lilliard of Ancrum
María de la Luz Espinoza Barrera
Mary Ellen Wise
Moving Robe Woman
Nazik Khatim
One Who Walks with the Stars
Pretty Nose

Interpreter/Translator
Beebe Beam
Bowdash
Dahteste
Dorothy "Babs" Gardner
Ghadir Taher
Heidi Berg
Juliet Beyler
Louise de Bettignies
Madeleine Truel
Mattie Winnemucca
Nonhelema Hokolesqua
Sage German
Sarah Winnemucca
Susan Ahn Cuddy
Tamara Haydée Bunke Bider

Lookout and Scout
Ann Hennis Bailey
Hélène Dutrieu
Ho Te Que
Mariya Bayda
Martha Jane Cannary
Mattie Winnemucca
Pelaghia Roşu
Prillar Guri
Sarah Malinda Pritchard Blalock
Sarah Winnemucca
Tatyana Savelyevna Marinenko

Marine
Amy Thomas
Ana María Antonia de Soto
Ann Taylor
Anne Hopping
Channing Day
Elizabeth Moore
Faye Turney
Hannah Snell
Jane Townsend
Juliet Beyler
Mary Ann Riley
Mary French
Minnie Bendina Spotted Wolf
Olena Bilozerska
Sarah Bates

Martial Arts Expert
Abbakka Chowta of Ullal
Adea Eurydice II of Macedon
Amanitore
Audata
Bùi Thị Xuân
Chen Shuozhen
Cynane
Dandara
Hong Xuanjiao
Hua Mulan
Huang Pei-mei
Jingo Yukiko
Julie D'Aubigny La Maupin

Khawla bint al-Azwar
Khutulun
Li Xiu
Liang Hongyu
Lin Hei'er
Liu Jinding
Maria Raps Emhart
Meenakshi Amma
Miyagino
Nakano Takeko
Qin Liangyu
Qiu Ersao
Scathach of Skye
Shen Yunying
Shinobu
Su Sanniang
T'ang Sai'er
Trưng Nhi
Uathach
Unniyarcha
Velu Nachiyar
Wang Cong'er
Xun Guan
Yuenu

Mechanic
Crystal Davis
Glafira Kashirina
Holly J. McGeogh
Melodie Massey
Rebecca Mpagi

Medalist
Adela Velarde Pérez
Agnes Humbert
Agnes Primocic
Agustina Raimunda of Aragon
Ahhotep
Alexandra Kudasheva
Amelia Robles Àvila
Analaura Esparza-Gutiérrez
Andreana Druzina
Andrée Borrel
Andrée de Jongh
Andriana Susak-Arekhta
Angela Puig
Angélique Duchemin Brûlon
Anna Ivanovna Maslovskaya
Anna Lühring
Anna Maria Jansdotter Engsten
Anne Margrethe Bangs Strømsheim
Anne-Marie Walters
Annie Blair Etheridge
Antoinette Gluck Feuerwerker
Antònia Costa
Antònia Gelabert
Antonija Javornik
Augusta Maria Chiwy
Berty Albrecht
Betty L. Adams
Brigida Silva de Ochoa
Carla Capponi
Carla Monteiro Araújo
Catharina Aaltjen Boekbinder
Cheryl Pearce
Claire Phillips
Danielle Greene-Byrd
Dawn Halfaker
Delphine Aigle
Diana Hope Rowden
Donna Johnson
Dorothy Peto
Dương Thu Hương
Eileen Nearne
Éliane Sophie Plewman
Elise Toft
Elizabeth Peet McIntosh
Elizabeth Sudmeier
Eloise Randolph Page
Elżbieta Zawacka
Esther Arditi
Eugenie Shakhovskaya
Flora Sandes
France Bloch-Serazin
Frances M. Vega
Francisca Barnés
Francisca Cullel
Friederike Krüger
Frumka Lubetkin
Gabrielle Weidner
Geertruida Wijsmuller-Meijer
Geneviève Prémoy
Germaine Ribière
Germaine Tillion
Gertrud Koch
Gertrudis Camps y Roger
Giuseppina Vadala
Giuseppa Bolognara Calcagno
Glafira Kashirina
Haika Grossman
Haldis Elisabeth Arentz Sveri
Halszka Wasilewska
Hanna Reitsch
Hanna Stadnik
Heidi Berg
Helen Kerly
Helen Ruz
Hetty Voûte
Holly J. McGeogh
Ida Sabo
Ida Veldhuyzen van Zanten
Ilona Kolonits
Irina Rakobolskaya
Irina Sebrova
Jackey Smith
Janaky Athi Nahappan
Janine de Greef
Jeanne Brousse
Jeannie Rousseau
Jennifer M. Moreno
Joanna Żubr
Josephine Baker
Jozette McLean
Juana Azurduy de Padilla
Julia Diament Pirotte
Julienne Aisner
Karina S. Lau
Kateryna Noskova
Kattalin Aguirre
Khiuaz Dospanova
Kiki Latry
Kimberly Hampton
Kimberly Voelz
Krystyna Skarbek
Kseniya Semyonovna Konstantinova
Lakshmi Sahgal
Larisa Rozanova
Leigh Ann Hester
Lela Karagianni
Lise de Baissa
Lolita Lebrón
Lone Morgensen Masłocha
Louisa Nolan
Louise de Bettignies
Lucia Ottobrini
Lucie Bernard Aubrac
Lyudmila Pavlichenko
Maddalena Cerasuolo
Madeleine Zoe Damerment
Madeleine Riffaud
Magdalena Avietėnaitė
Magdalena Leones
Maguba Syrtlanova
Małgorzata Fornalska

Mammy Yoko
Manuela Sáenza
Manuela Sancho y Bonafonte
Marcia Andrade Braga
Margaret Catherine Moore "Katy" Barry
Margaret H. Woodward
Margaret Utinsky
Margarita Sunyer
Margot Duhalde Sotomayor
María Agustín Linares
María de la Consolación Azlor y Villavicencio
Maria Quitéria
Maria Teresa Regard
María Vidal
Maria Wittek
Mariam Al Mansouri
Mariana Drăgescu
Marie Leonie Vanhoutte
Marie-Madeleine Fourcade
Marie Marvingt
Marie Nordmann-Cohen
Marie-Thérèse Figueur
Marie von Fery Bognar
Marina Mikhaylovna Raskova
Marion Alice Powell Orr
Marion Philippina Pritchard
Marion Wilberforce
Marium Mukhtiar
Mariya Bayda
Mariya Semyonovna Polivanova
Marthe Hoffnung Cohn
Mary Brose Tepe
Mary Edwards Walker
Mary Jessie Herrera
Mary Spenser-Churchill
Mathilde Adrienne Eugénie Verspyck
Melita Norwood
Michelle Dumon
Michelle Norris
Michelle Thompson
Michelle Witmer
Milunka Savić
Mirjam Ohringer
Miyoko Hikiji
Monica Beltran
Monica Lin Brown
Monique de Bissy
Nadezhda Durova
Nadezhda Popova
Nadia Russo
Nadia Savchenko
Nancy Harkness Love
Nancy Wake
Naomi Flores
Natalia Khorunzha
Natalie Tychmini
Natalya Meklin
Natalya Venediktovna Kovshova
Netiva Ben Yehuda
Nichola Goddard
Nichole M. Frye
Nina Raspopova
Nora Tyson
Odette Sansom
Odette Sar Wilen
Olena Stepaniv
Olga Kokovtseva
Olga Krasilnikov
Pearl Witherington
Phyllis Latour
Polina Gelman
Rachel Bosveld
Radhika Menon
Raisa Aronova
Ramatoulie D.K. Sanneh
Rashida Salmeeva
Rawya Ateya
Resi Pesendorfer
Riet van Grunsven
Rosa Campuzano
Rosa Costa
Rosa Garcia-Malea
Rose Gluck Warfman
Rose Valland
Sabiha Gökçen
Sabina Halytska
Sara Stires
Serafima Amosova
Shannon Mary Kent
Sharon T. Swartworth
Shoshana Nyree Johnson
Simone Segouin
Simone Wilkie
Sofia Galechko
Sofija Jovanović
Solveig Bergslien
Sophia Galechko
Stephanie Hollenstein
Suman Gawani
Susan Ahn Cuddy
Susan Sonnheim
Susan Travers
Suzanne Hiltermann-Souloumiac
Suzanne Puanani Vares-Lum
Sylvia Mariotti
Sylvia Salvesen
Tamara Long-Archeleta
Tatyana Baramzina
Tatyana Savelyevna Marinenko
Tatyana Sumarokova
Teresa Mattei
Tulsi Gabbard
Úrsula Kuczyński
Valentina Grizodubova
Valentina Petrova
Valeriya Osipovna Gnarovskaya
Vasilisa Kozhina
Vera Leigh
Vera May Atkins
Vera Tikhomirova
Vijayalakshmi Ramanan
Viktoria Savs
Violet Mistead Warren
Violette Lecoq
Violette Szabo
Virginia Hall
Virginie Ghesquière
Wanda Gertz Kazik
Wanda Krahelska-Filipowicz
Yekaterina "Katya" Budanova
Yekaterina Ryabova
Yelena Stempkovskaya
Yevdokiya Bershanskaya
Yevdokiya Nikulina
Yevdokiya Nosal
Yevdokiya Pasko
Yevdokiya Rachkevich
Yevgeniya Rudneva
Yolande Beekman
Yvonne Humbert
Yvonne Rudellat
Yun Hui-sun
Yvonne Rudellat
Žamila Kolonomos
Zinaida Ivanovna Mareseva
Zofia Kossak-Szczucka
Zoya Anatolyevna Kosmodemyanskaya

Zoya Parfyonova
Zuleykha Seyidmammadova

Mediator
Aba of Tencer
Adelaide of Turin and Susa
Aethelflaed
Agnes Campbell
Agrippina the Elder
Amanikhatashan
Amanirenas
Cleophis
Dahteste
Emma de Guader
Finola O'Donnell
Gunilla Johansdotter Bese
Jindeok of Silla
Julia Domna
Lozen
Margaret of Provence
Mavia
Sharifa Fatima
Sitt al-Mulk
Tirgatao
Veleda
Zhangsun

Messenger/Courier
Agustina Mejía
Aminta Granera Sacasa
Ana María Merchán Delgado
Anna Colbjørnsdatter Arneberg
Anne Hennis Bailey
Asma Gargoum
Audrey Hepburn
Bibiana Talero
Bowdash
Brigida Silva de Ochoa
Carmen Parra
Cécile Rol-Tanguy
Cornelia van den Brink
Dahteste
Diana Rowden
Elizabeth O'Farrell
Elżbieta Zawacka
Frances M. Vega
Francien de Zeeuw
Françoise Déprés
Gabrielle Weidner
Giliana Balmaceda Gerson
Gioconda Belli
Gregoria de Jesús
Haika Grossman
Hela Rufeisen Schüpper
Irena Adamowicz
Jacqueline Nearne
Jane Horney
Jeanne Brousse
Josephine Baker
Julia Diament Pirotte
Julia Grenan
Julienne Eisner
Justina Estepa
Kamala Das Gupta
Kattalin Aguirre
Kitty Harris
Laura Secord
Liang Hongyu
Lidia Brisca Menapace
Lone Morgensen Masłocha
Louise de Bettignies
Luisa Mahin
Lydia Darragh
Madeleine Damerment
Madeleine Passot
Madeleine Riffaud
Magdalena Leones
Mai Politzer
Margaret Catherine Moore "Katy" Barry
María Baltazara Teran Garzon
Maria Olip'
María Parado de Bellido
Marianne Feldhammer
Marianne Golz
Marinette Menut
Martha Jane Cannary
Martha Kelly
Mary Herbert
Mary Josephine Ryan
Mindla Maria Diament
Noor-un–Nisa Inayat Khan
Odette Sar Wilen
Olga Gray
Reina Prinsen Geerligs
Rose Ann Murphy
Rose Lopes Laguna-Asscher
Sarah Emma Edmonds
Simona Josefa Manzaneda
Simone Segouin
Sonia Olschanezky
Sonya Butt
Tamara Haydée Bunke Bider
Tatyana Savelyevna Marinenko
Teresa Mattei
Tina Buchter Strobos
Transito Villagomez
Truus van Lier
Vera Leigh
Viktoria Savs
Winifred Carney
Zivia Lubetkin

Military Police/Patrol Officers
Amy Thomas
Annie Matthews
Annie Pomeroy
Danielle Greene-Byrd
Dawn Halfaker
Donna Johnson
Dorothy Peto
Kendra Coleman
Leigh Ann Hester
Lilian Wyles
Mandisa Mfeka
Marissa Strock
Mary Jessie Herrera
Michelle Witmer
Mildred White
Noa Lazar
Rachel Bosveld
Sue Downes
Susan Sonnheim

Missile Specialist
Ayesha Farooq
Janina Simmons

Modernizer
Jindeok of Silla
Mandukhai Khatun

Munitions Maker
France Bloch-Serazin
Margaretha Sandra
Marie Nordmann-Cohen

Navigator
Glafira Kashirina
Irina Rakobolskaya
Khiuaz Dospanova
Marina Mikhaylovna Raskova
Natalya Meklin
Nora Tyson
Polina Gelman
Raisa Aronova
Rufina Gasheva
Tatyana Sumarokova

Vera Belik
Yekaterina Ryabova
Yevdokiya Rachkevich
Yevgeniya Rudneva

Ordnance Specialist
Kimberly Voelz

Painter
Stephanie Hollenstein

Paratrooper
Allene "Ally" Somera-Zyko
Amy Johnson
Ana Lucas
Andrée Borrel
Annapurna Kunwar
Anne-Marie Walters
Ariana Sánchez
Ashley White
Ding Le Tunn
Eileen Nearne
Éliane Sophie Plewman
Elżbieta Zawacka
Hannah Szenes
Hui Po Yung
Jacqueline Nearne
Janina Simmons
Jennifer M. Moreno
Krystyna Skarbek
Lise de Baissac
Maddalena Cerasuolo
Madeleine Zoe Damerment
Małgorzata Fornalska
Muncunchimeg Nyamaajav
Odette Sar Wilen
Olga Sanifirova
Pearl Witherington
Rufina Gasheva
Smaranda Brăescu
Violette Szabo
Yvonne Rudellat

Patron
Faustina the Younger
Munatia Plancina
Yolande of Aragon

Photographer
Amena Sultana Bokul
Edith Tudor-Hart
Faye Schulman
Ingeborg Wallheimer Kahlenberg
Jackey Smith
Julia Diament Pirotte
Marie-Claude Vaillant-Couturier
Nazma Shaheen

Pilot (Drone)
Dana Colvin
Varsha Kukreti

Pilot/Mechanic (Helicopter)
Alka Shukla
Jaime L. Campbell
Keren Tendler
Kimberly Hampton
M.P. Shumathi
Marion Alice Powell Orr
Nadia Savchenko
Naomi Karungi
Tamara Long-Archeleta
Tammy Duckworth
Tolulope Arotile

Pilot (Plane)
Amy Johnson
Anisha Shinh
Archana Kapoor
Audrey Esi Swatson
Avani Chaturvedi
Ayesha Farooq
Betty Gillies
Bhawana Kanth
Bindu Sebastian
Blessing Liman
Diana Barnato Walker
Doreen Kyomuhangi
Elsie Joy Davison
Eugenie Shakhovskaya
Geneviève Nwaogwugw
Glafira Kashirina
Grace Garba
Hanna Reitsch
Harita Kaur Diol
Helen Harrison-Bristol
Helen Kerly
Hélène Dutrieu
Ida Veldhuyzen van Zanten
Irina Burnaia
Irina Sebrova
Jacqueline Cochran
Jadwiga Piłsudska
Janina Antonina Lewandowska
Jean Bird
Joanna "Jo" Mary Salter
Kafayat Sanni
Khiuaz Dospanova
Larisa Rozanova
Lettice Curtis
Lois Butler
Lydia "Lilya" Litvyak
Maguba Syrtlanova
Mandisa Mfeka
Margaret H. Woodward
Margaret Wyndham Gore
Margot Duhalde Sotomayor
Mariam Al Mansouri
Mariana Drăgescu
Marie Marvingt
Marina Chechneva
Marina Mikhaylovna Raskova
Marina Știrbei
Marion Alice Powell Orr
Marion Wilberforce
Mary de Bunsen
Mary Wilkins Ellis
Maureen Dunlop de Popp
Mohana Singh
Mona Friedlander
Nadezhda Popova
Nadia Russo
Nadia Savchenko
Nancy Harkness Love
Naomi Karungi
Natalya Meklin
Nina Raspopova
Olga Sanifirova
Olubunmi Ijelu
Pamela Rodrigues Pereira
Polina Gelman
Priya Nalgundwar
Priya Paul
Raisa Aronova
Roni Zuckerman
Rosa Garcia-Malea
Rosemary Rees
Sabiha Gökçen
Sara Stires
Serafima Amosova
Smaranda Brăescu
Sophie Alexandrovna Dolgorunaya
Tamar Ariel
Tatyana Makarova
Thokozile Muwamba
Valentina Grizodubova
Vera Tikhomirova
Violet Milstead Warren
Virginia Thomas

Yael Rom
Yekaterina "Katya" Budanova
Yevdokiya Bershanskaya
Yevdokiya Nikulina
Yevdokiya Nosal
Yevdokiya Pasko
Zoya Parfyonova
Zuleykha Seyidmammadova

Pirate/Privateer
Aethelflaed
Alfhild
Anita Garibaldi
Anna Carey
Anne Bonny
Anne Dieu-le-Veut
Catherine Hagerty
Charlotte Badger
Charlotte de Berry
Christina Anna Skytte
Elise Eskilsdotter
Elizabeth Patrickson
Flora Burn
Frances Stoddard
Grace O'Malley
Groa
Huang Pei-mei
Ingela Olofsdotter Gathenhielm
Jane Francis
Jane Randall
Jeanne de Clisson
Joanna Harris
Johanna Jungberg Hard
Julienne David
Lai Choi-san
Lu Mu
Margaret Croke Jordan
Margaret Pope
Maria Lindsey Cobham
Martha Farley
Mary Carleton
Mary Critchett
Mary Percevall
Mary Read
Mary Wolverston Killigrew
Rachel Wall
Sadie Farrell
Sayyida al-Hurra
Sela
Teuta
Zheng Yi Sao

Prisoner of War
Aafia Siddiqui
Abbakka Chowta of Ullal
Afra 'Bint Ghifar al-Humayriah
Agnes Comyn of Strathearn
Agnes Dorothee Humbert
Agueda Esteban
Agustina Raimunda of Aragon
Ahlam al-Tamimi
Ā'ishah bint Abī Bakr
Ala Gertner
Aldonça de Bellera
Amalafrida
Amy Clarke
Ana Monterroso de Lavalleja
Andrée Borrel
Ani Pachen
Anita Garibaldi
Anna Carey
Anna Henryka Pustowójtówna
Anna Jöransdotter
Anna Wajcblum Heilman
Anna Wolkoff
Anne Bonny
Anne Dieu-le-Veut
Anne Farquharson Mackintosh
Anne Holck
Anne Vere Fairfax
Anne MacLeod McKay
Annike Svahn
Antonia León y Velasco
Antonia Santos Plata
Antonia Spath Bruha
Aqualtune Ezgondidu Mahamud da Silva Santos
Arsinoë IV
Astrid Dollis Dahlgren
Bauck Poppema
Berty Albrecht
Bianca Canales
Bina Das
Blanche Arundell
Bras Piqué
Brigid Foley
Brita Olovsdotter Tott
Buffalo Calf Road Woman
Carmen Rodríguez de Gaitán
Caterina Sforza
Cecily Gordon Lefort
Chand Bibi
Chiang Ch'ing
Chiomara
Christian "Kit" Cavanagh Davies
Christina of Saxony
Cicely Arundell
Claire Phillips
Cleopatra V Selene
Cloelia
Constance Georgine Markievicz
Corba of Thorigne
Dahteste
Diana Hope Rowden
Djamila Bouazza
Djamila Bouhired
Dollis Dahlgren
Dolores Vela de Veintimilla
Du Fengyang
Ebba Gustavsdotter Stenbock
Ecaterina Cercheza
Eleanor of Provence
Eileen Nearne
Éliane Brault
Éliane Sophie Plewman
Elisabeth de la Bourdonnaye
Elisabeth Retiffe
Elizabeth Hatzler
Elizabeth O'Farrell
Elizabeth Patrickson
Ella Reno
Ellen Askwith
Else Marie Pade
Elżbieta Zawacka
Ester Wajcblum
Eulàlia Papavoine
Evota of Stirling
Faye Turney
Flora Sandes
France Bloch-Serazin
Frances Hook
Frances Stoddard
Francina Broese Gunningh
Françoise-Marie Jacquelin
Gabrielle Weidner
Gaidinliu Pamei
Genia Fischer
Germaine Tambour
Gertrud Koch
Gertrudis Medeiros
Gouyen
Gulab Kaur

Halszka Wasilewska
Hanna Stadnik
Hannah Emerson Duston
Hannah Szenes
Hela Rufeisen Schüpper
Helena Molony
Hetty Voûte
Ilona Zrínyi
Inge Weidenau Frank
Irina Burnai
Jane Francis
Jane Howard
Janina Wasiłojć-Smoleńska
Jean "Jenny" Cameron
Jeanne Merkus
Jennie D. Hart
Joan Beaufort
Joan of Arc
Johanna Stegen
Joséphine Marchais
Juana Gabriela Moro
Julia Grenan
Julienne David
Kalpana Datti
Kamala Das Gupta
Kathleen Florence Lynn
Kattalin Aguirre
Khawla bint al-Azwar
Kittur Chennamma
Kitty Grande
Kseniya Semyonovna Konstantinova
Lakshmi Sahgal
Lalla Fatma N'Soumer
Lau Mazirel
Lela Karagianni
Leontine Suetens
Leslie Joy Whitehead
Leticia Montenegro
Lidia Lwow-Eberle
Lilian Mercedes Letona
Liliane Rolfe
Lise London
Liza Ivanovna Chaikina
Lolita Lebrón
Loretta Janeta Velázquez
Louise Aslanian
Louise de Bettignies
Louise Michel
Louise-Renée Leduc
Lozen
Madeleine Damerment
Madeleine ffrench-Mullen
Madeleine Passot

Madeleine Riffaud
Madeleine Tambour
Madeleine Truel
Maeda Matsu
Małgorzata Fornalska
Mangammal
Manuela Beltran
Manuela Miranda
Manuela Sáenza
Mareta Duduyeva
Margaret Cochran Corbin
Margaret de Badlesmere
Margaret George Shello
Margaret Johnstone Ogilvy
Margaret of Anjou
Margaret of Beverley
Margaret O. Murphy
Margarita Tutulani
Marguerite Baker Harrison
Marguerite Gonnet
María Baltazara Terán Garzon
Maria Bochkareva
María de Estrada
Maria Emhart
Maria Jacoba de Turenne
María Loreto Sánchez Peón
María Luisa Cáceres Díaz de Arismendi
Maria Malko
María Miranda
Maria Olip'
María Remedios Del Valle
Maria van Spanjen
Mariana Bracetti Cuevas
Marie-Claude Vaillant-Couturier
Marie-Jeanne Schellinck
Marie Magdelaine Mouron
Marie Manuel
Marie Nordmann-Cohen
Marie Perolz
Marie Reynoard
Marie-Thérèse Figueur
Marieta de Veintimilla
Marina Lebstuck
Marinette Menut
Mariya Bayda
Marta Bindiger Cigi
Marthe Cnockaert
Mary Ambree
Mary Bell
Mary Corliss Neff
Mary Edwards Walker

Mary Parcevall
Mary Read
Marzia Ordelaffi
Matangini Hazra
Mathilde Adrienne Eugénie Verspyck
Mathilde Lucia Carré
Maud de Braose
Melchora Aquino
Milunka Savić
Mindla Maria Diament
Mollie Bean
Molly Bell
Monica Wichfeld
Monique de Bissy
Muhumusa
Nadia Savchenko
Nell Ryan
Nexhmije Hoxha
Nguyễn Thị Định
Noor-un–Nisa Inayat Khan
Nur Jahan
Nyi Ageng Serang
Okaji no Kata
Olga Bancic
Olga Alkalaj
Pauline Léon
Petronilla of Leicester
Philothey Benizelos
Razia Sultana
Regina Safirsztajn
Reina Prinsen Geerlig
Richilde of Hainault
Rita Arnould
Rosa Donato
Rose Gluck Warfman
Rose Grunapfel Meth
Roza Robota
Sada Kaur
Santi Das Ghose
Sarah Bradbury
Sarah Jane Smith
Sarah Jane Taylor
Sharifa Fatima
Shoshana Nyree Johnson
Sietje Gravendeel-Tammens
Sofia Kossak-Szczucka
Solveig Bergslien
Sonia Olschanezky
Sophonisba
Suniti Chaudhuri
Suzanne Hiltermann-Souloumiac
Sylvette Roussel Leleu

Sylvia Salvesen
Tarabai Bhosale
Tarenorrerer
Thérèse Pierre
Théroigne de Méricourt
Timycha
Toypurina
Tsola Nincheva Dragoycheva
Vahida Maglajlić
Vera Figner
Vera Leigh
Vicenta Equino
Violette Szabo
Virginia d'Albert-Lake
Winifred Carney
Yolande Beekman
Yvonne Oddon
Yvonne Rudellat
Zarema Muzhikhoeva
Zofia Kossak-Szczucka
Zofia Poznańska
Zoulikha Bekkadour

Prophet
Boudicca
Bowdash
Chief Earth Woman
Fu Jing
Hang
Hanging Cloud
Isabelle Wilhelmine Marie Eberhardt
Jingu of Japan
Joan of Arc
Kahina Dihya of Numidia
Libuše
Lozen
María de la Candelaria
Muhumusa
Nehanda Charwe Nyakasikana
Pieronne of Brittany
Scathach of Skye
T'ang Sai'er
Theodora of Vasta
Tiphaine Raguenel
Toypurina
Veleda

Raider
Aife of Alba
Anna Ivanovna Maslovskaya
Ashley White
Atha
Blanche of Castile
Breffu of St. John
Catharina Aaltjen Boekbinder
Clara de la Rocha
Dahteste
Faye Schulman
Francien de Zeeuw
Ghazāla al-Haruriyya
Gouyen Lozen
Grace O'Malley
Gwenllian ferch Gruffydd
Hanging Cloud
Hate Woman
Hatshepsut
Huang Pei-mei
Jennie D. Hart
Juana Ramona
Kalpana Datta
Lozen
Lucie Bernard Aubrac
Margarita Neri
María de la Luz Espinoza Barrera
Matangini Hazra
Nancy Wake
Pritilata Waddedar
Riet van Grunsven
Sarah Malinda Pritchard Blalock
Sedar Botan
Seh-Dong-Hong-Be
Sietje Gravendeel-Tammens
Teuta
Trinidad Peréz Tecson
Valentina Ramírez Avitia
Woman Chief

Ranger
Allene "Ally" Somera-Zyko
Ho Te Que
Janina Simmons

Rebel
Agueda Kahabagan
Agustina Mejía
Agustina Peralta
Aisha al-Hurra
Amalasuintha
Amelia of Berbice
Amelia Robles Àvila
Aminta Granera Sacasa
Ana Josefa Morales
Ana María Merchán Delgado
Ana Monterroso de Lavalleja
Andrea Ricaurte de Lozano
Angela Jiménez
Angela Maclovia Lavayen
Anna Henryka Pustowójtówna
Anna Szatkowska
Anne Vere Fairfax
Anselma Leyton
Antonia León y Velasco
Antonia Moreno
Antonia Santos Plata
Apacuana
Arsinoë IV
Asatu Bah Kenneth
Ascensión Ortega
Asma Gargoum
Atha
Axeline "Agnes" Elizabeth Salomon
Aya Virginie Touré
Azad Deylami
Baltazara Chuiza
Banu Khoramdin
Barbara Forero
Barbara Montes
Bergljot Håkonsdatter
Basina of Soissons
Betsy Gray
Bianca Canales
Bibiana Talero
Bina Das
Boudicca
Breffu of St. John
Candelaria Forero
Carlota Armero
Carlota Lucumí
Carlota Rengifo
Carmen Grimaldo de Valverde
Carmen Parra
Carmen Rodríguez de Gaitán
Carmita
Casilda Zafra
Celia Sánchez Manduley
Chen Shuozhen
Chiang Ch'ing
Chrodielde
Claire Lacombe
Clara del Rey Calvo
Clara Tocarruncho
Cleopatra II

Constance Georgine
  Markievicz
Cristina Trivulzio di
  Belgiojoso
Cubah Cornwallis
Cut Nyak Meutia
Dalla Abbazi
Delfina Torres de Concha
Delia Montero Maridueña
Deng Yingchao
Djamila Bouhired
Dolores Nariño
Dolores Salas
Dolores Vargas
Dorotea Castro
Dorotea Lenis
Dolores Usubillaga
Dolores Vela de Veintimilla
Eliska Vinccent
Elly Duncan
Engracia Salgar
Estefanía Linares
Estefanía Neira de Eslava
Estefanía Parra
Eusebia Galviza
Evangelina Diaz
Evangelista Tamayo
Fastrada
Fatima Bredan
Felicia Solano de Vizuete
Fidela Ramos
Filomena Chávez de Duque
Filomena Ganga
Funmilayo Ransome-Kuti
Gabriela Silang
Gaidinliu Pamei
Gaitana
Gao Guiying
Genoveva Sarmiento
Gertrudis Espalza
Gertrudis Vanegas
Gioconda Belli
Grace Eniola Soyinka
Gulab Kaur
Gülnar Hatun
Gwendolen of Cornwall
Herma Paschinger
He Zizhen
Hong Xuanjiao
Hor Lhamo
Ignacia Medina
India Juliana
Inas Fathy
Inés María Jiménez
Inés Osuma
Ines Peñaranda
Isabel Nariño
Isabel Roger
Isabella of France
Jackie Crookston
Jane Howard
Josefa Venancia de la Encarnación Camejo[
Joaquina Aroca
Joaquina Galarza de Larrea
Josefa Baraya
Josefa Conde
Juana Béjar
Juana Escobar
Juana Plazas
Juana Ramírez (Colombia)
Juana Rodríguez
Juana Santos
Juana Velasco de Gallo
Judon
Júlia Bányai
Juliana
Juliana Pizarro
Justina Estepa
Kaipkire
Kalpana Dartta
Kamala Das Gupta
Käthe Wanek Odwody
Kiki Latry
La Mulâtresse Solitude
Laskarina Bouboulina
Laurean Sierra
Leonarda Carreño
Leontine Suetens
Leticia Montenegro
Leubevere of Cheribert
Leymah Gbowee
Li Zhen
Lin Hei'er
Lolita Lebrón
Lorenza Avemanay Tacuri
Louise-Renée Leduc
Lu Mu
Lucia Lucumí
Lucumí Fermina
Luisa Battistati
Luisa Trilleras
Luise Aston
Mae Murray
Maire O'Ciaragain
Man Thiện
Manuela Beltran
Manuela Chuiza
Manuela Escobar
Manuela Malasaño Oñoro
Manuela Miranda
Manuela Sáenz
Manuela Tinoco
Manuela Uscátegui
Margarite Tutulani
Maria Bonita
María de la Candelaria
María de la Luz Espinoza
  Barrera
María de los Ángeles Ávila
María del Carmen Olano
María del Rosario Devis
María del Transito Vargas
María Felipa de Oliveira
María Gamarra de Hidalgo
María Gertrudis Romero
María Josefa de Lizarralde
María Josefa Esguerra
María Larrain
María Luisa Cáceres Díaz de
  Arismendi
María Mercedes Viteri
María Miranda
María of Curaçao
María Pacheco Padilla
Maria Piotrowiczowa
María Quinteras de Meras
María Rosa Lazo de la Vega
María Trinidad Sánchez
Mariana Bracetti Cuevas
Marie-Jeanne Lamartiniére
Marretje Arents
Marta Tello
Martha Christian Tijahahu
Martha Walsh
Mary Leticia Thomas
Matangini Hazra
Mathilda McBean
Matilde Anaray
Mercedes Ábrego de Reyes
Mercedes Loayza
Mercedes Nariño
Micaela Nieto
Moscho Tzavella
Muhumusa
Nanny of the Maroons
Nathalie Lemel
Nehanda Charwe
  Nyakasikana
Nelida Cabigayan
Nguyễn Thị Định
Nicolasa Jurado

Nora Astorga
Paula Contreras
Paule Mink
Pauline Léon
Policarpa Salavarrieta
Porfiria Aroca de la Paz
Presentación Buenahora
Pritilata Waddedar
Qiu Ersao
Remigia Cuesta
Rosa Collazo
Rosa Villafuerte de Castillo
Rosa Zaráte de la Peña
Rosario Carifa
Rosaura Rivera
Salomé Buitrago
Samsi
Shote Galina
Simona Amaya
Sirma Voyevoda
Sitara Begum
Sofía Moreira de Sabando
Susanna Abrahamson
Su Sanniang
T'ang Qunying
T'ang Sai'er
Taramon Bibi
Tatiana Grigorievna Solomakha
Teresa Andrade
Teresa Cornejo
Teresa Izquierdo
Teresa Magbanua
Théroigne de Méricourt
Tomasa Tito Condemayta
Tomasa Rodríguez
Toypurina
Transito Villagomez
Triệu Thị Chinh
Tringë Smajl
Trinidad Peréz Tecson
Trưng Nhị
Trưng Trắc
Tsola Nincheva Dragoycheva
Úrsula Goyzueta
Veronika Gut
Vicenta Equino
Victoria "Toya" Montou
Wu Shuqing
Yatie
Yohl Ik'nal
Zhao Pingyang

Recruiter
A-Nong
Angela Maclovia Lavayen
Aethelburg of Wessex
Aethelflaed
Agnes Primocic
Ahilyabhai Holkar
Anna Eriksdotter Bielke
Anne Farquharson Mackintosh
Archidamia
Avanti Bai Lodhi
Belawadi Mallamma Desai
Bibi Dalair Kaur
Blenda
Buffalo Calf Road Woman
Caterina Sforza
Chand Bibi
Chen Shuozhen
Chilonis
Cleopatra VII Philopator
Cockacoeske
Dandara
Dhora Leka
Djamila Bouhired
Dorotea Castro
Edith Tudor-Hart
Eliza Alice Lynch
Euphemia Leslie
Fulvia Flacca Bambula
Furra
Gertrud Koch
Gwendolen of Cornwall
Haika Grossman
Hangbe
Isabella of France
Jane Howard
Jean "Jenny" Cameron
Joan of Arc
Joanna of Flanders
Juana Azurduy de Padilla
Juana Ramírez (Venezuela)
Kaipkire
Khawla bint al-Azwar
Lady Triệu Thị Chinh
Lakshmibai
Laskarina Bouboulina
Laudomia Forteguerri
Leni Egger
Li Zhen
Loretta Janeta Valezquez
Louise Aslanian
Lu Mu
Madame Arnaud

Mai Bhago
Manuela Eras de Gandarillas
Manuela Medina
Manuela Sáenza
Margareta von Ascheberg
Margarita Neri
Maria Cameen Faxell
Maria Emhart
María Gamarra de Hidalgo
María Josefa de Lizarralde
María Larrain
Maria Flip
Marianne Feldhammer
Marianne Golz
Marie-Madeleine Fourcade
Martha Glar
Mary Hay
Matilda of Tuscany
Monica Wichfeld
Nexhmije Hoxha
Parysatis
Pelaghia Roşu
Philippa of Hainault
Prudence Cummings Wright
Richilde of Hainault
Rosa Campuzano
Sayyida al-Hurra
Sichelgaita
Sophonisba
Sugandha
Tachibana Ginchiyo
T'ang Sai'er
Telesilla
Toypurina
Trưng Nhị
Trưng Trắc
Uda Devi
Velu Nachiyar
Wanda of Poland
Wu Zetian
Xóchitl
Yaa Asantewaa
Zhao Pingyang
Yun Hui-sun

Reformer
Matilda of Tuscany
Olga of Kiev
Renée de Bourbon

Rescuer
Agnes Primocic
Alma Allen
Anna Maria Jansdotter Engsten

Antoinette Gluck Feuerwerker
Apollovna Isoltsev
Audrey Hepburn
Barbara Helen Bailey
Bindu Sebastian
Buffalo Calf Road Woman
Cecilia Rozgonyi
Celia Sánchez Manduley
Cloelia
Danielle Casanova
Delphine Aigle
Elvire de Greef
Gabrielle Weidner
Germaine Ribière
Gisela Wieberdink-Soehnlein
Gouyen
Helen Studler
Hetty Voûte
Ilona Colonist
Isabella of Lorraine
Jackey Smith
Jadwiga
Jane Lane
Janine de Greef
Jennifer M. Moreno
Kathy Piccollo
Katie Beattie
Khawla bint al-Azwar
Kseniya Semyonovna Konstantinova
Laskarina Bouboulina
Lau Mazirel
Lela Karagianni
Lise Børsum
Lucie Bernard Aubrac
Manuela Sáenz
Margaret of Attenduli
Margaret of Anjou
Maria Abrahams
María Mercedes Viterbi
Maria Wagner Plieseis
Maria Wagner Plieseis
Marie Schotte
Monica Wichfeld
Natalia Khorunzha
Nur Jahan
Olga Alkalaj
Olga Hudig
Ólöf Loftsdóttir
Qin Liangyu
Radhika Menon
Resi Pesendorfer
Rose Gluck Warfman
Sara Yehoshua Fortis
Sedar Botan
Sonia Shainwald Orbuch
Suzanne Hiltermann-Souloumiac
Tamara Long-Archeleta
Tina Buchter Strobos
Truus van Lier
Valentina Grizodubova
Vladka Meed
Wanda Hjort Heger
Willemiena Bouwman
Xun Guan
Yarden Shukron Yifrah
Yun Hui-sun
Zinaida Ivanovna Mareseva

Rustler
Gouyen
Lozen
Nancy Hart Douglas
Running Eagle

Saboteur
Aafia Siddiqui
Adele Bei Ciufoli
Andrée Borrel
Amena Sultana Bokul
Aminat Nagaev
Anna Goldsteiner
Anna Ivanovna Maslovskaya
Anne-Sofie Østvedt
Antonia Spath Bruha
Baya Hocine
Bianca Canales
Bracha Fuld
Carla Capponi
Catharina Aaltjen Boekbinder
Cecily Gordon Lefort
Cristina Luca Boico
Delilah
Djamila Bouazza
Djamila Bouhired
Elena Haas
Elizabeth Peet McIntosh
Else Marie Pade
Fana Kochovska
France Bloch-Serazin
Freddie Nanda Dekker-Oversteegen
Frieda Belinfante
Gertrud Koch
Hannie Schaft
Hassiba Ben Bouali
Hedda Lundh
Hydna of Scione
Jeanne Merkus
Juana Gabriela Moro
Juana Plazas
Kalpana Datta
Kamala Das Gupta
Katie Beattie
Klára Andrássy
Lau Mazirel
Lidia Brisca Menapace
Lina Merlin
Lise de Baissac
Lucia Ottobrini
Lucie Bernard Aubrac
Maddalena Cerasuolo
Madeleine Riffaud
Maria Lewis
María Loreto Sánchez Peón
María Parado de Bellido
Maria Teresa Regard
Mariam Tuburova
Marie-Claude Vaillant-Couturier
Marie Nordmann-Cohen
Marisa Musu
Marthe Cnockaert
Mary Jane Green
Mindla Maria Diament
Monica Wichfeld
Netiva Ben Yehuda
Odette Sansom
Olena Bilozerska
Olga Bancic
Pearl Witherington
Pritilata Waddedar
Rosa Nagaev
Rosia Altman
Samia Lakhdari
Sara Yehoshua Fortis
Sarah Jane Smith
Satisita Dzhbirkhanova
Simone Segouin
Sofija Jovanović
Sonia Olschanezky
Sonia Shainwald Orbuch
Sonya Butt
T'ang Qunying
Truus Menger-Oversteegen
Tsola Nincheva Dragoycheva
Virginia Hall
Wanda Gertz Kazik

Yvonne Rudellat
Zivia Lubetkin
Zohra Drif
Zoulikha Bekkadour
Zoya Anatolyevna Kosmodemyanskaya

Sailor
Aagt de Tamboer
Adriana la Noy
Ann Mills
Anna Alders
Anna Jens
Anna Maria Jansdotter Engsten
Anne Chamberlayne
Antoinette Berg
Artemisia II
Brita Olsdotter Hagberg
Carla Monteiro Araújo
Catalina de Erauso
Charlotte de Berry
Donna Tobias
Dorothea Maria Lösch
Faye Turney
Francien de Zeeuw
Grace O'Malley
Johanna Bennius
Johannan Pieters
John Brown
Kiran Shekhawat
Leanne Crowe
Loretta Walsh
Lumchuan
Lumke Thoole
Marcia Andrade Braga
Maria van Spanjen
Mary Anne Talbot
Mary Buick Watson
Mary Lacy
Mary Read
Nora Tyson
Radhika Menon
Sara Stires
Shannon Mary Kent
Stella Tate
William Brown

Sea Captain
Alfra 'Bint Ghifar al-Humayriah
Anne Dieu-le-Veut
Cecilia Rozgonyi
Dandara
Dorothea Maria Lösch

Hedborg
Ingela Olofsdotter Gathenhielm
Jeanne de Clisson
Oserrah
Radhika Menon
Urduja
Veborg
Visna
Wafeira

Sharpshooter/Sniper
Anna Cunningham Hamilton
Anush Apetyan
Buffalo Calf Road Woman
Clara de la Rocha
Ehyophsta
Elaine Mordeaux
Hanna Dmyterko
Irene del Carmen Morales Galaz
Jane Magre Dieulafoy
Juana Azurduy de Padilla
Kang Keqing
Klava Monakhova
Klavdiya Kalugina
Leigh Ann Hester
Li Xiu
Lozen
Lucy Matilda Thompson Gauss
Lyudmila Pavlichenko
Maddalena Cerasuolo
Margaret Skinnider
Marie-Madeleine Jarret
Mariya Semyonovna Polivanova
Martha Jane Cannary
Marusia Chikhvintseva
Milunka Savić
Nadia Lugina
Natalya Venediktovna Kovshova
Nur Jahan
Olena Bilozerska
Olena Stepaniv
Olha Basarab
Rengin Yusuf
Shoshana Nyree Johnson
Sofia Galechko
Sophia Galechko
Susan Ahn Cuddy
Sylvia Mariotti

Tanya Chernova
Tatyana Baramzina
Uda Devi
Valentina Petrova
Woman Chief
Yamamoto Yaeko
Yona Markova
Zina Gavrilova
Zinaida Andreevna Urantseva

Shieldmaiden
Alfhild of Geatland
Lagertha
Hedborg of Sle
Veborg
Visna of the Slavs

Soldier/Warrior
Acha no Tsubone
Adela Velarde Pérez
Alexandra Beiko
Amy Clarke
Ana Butinà
Ana María Mallorquí
Ana Noguera
Ana Roure
Ana Turó
Analaura Esparza-Gutiérrez
Andrea Banderlú
Andreana Druzina Ida Sabo
Andriana Susak-Arekhta
Anna Jöransdotter
Anna Maria Lane
Anne Marie Doering
Antoinette Berg
Antònia Boer y Artolà
Antònia Camprubí
Antònia Costa
Antònia Esparch
Antònia Gelabert
Antònia Mora
Antònia Pelegri
Antònia Rodrigues
Antonija Javornik
Arin Mirkan
Artunis
Ascensión Ortega
Asma bint Abī Bakr
Atanasia Vidal
Audata
Barbara Pieters Adriaens
Benita Portales
Betty L. Adams
Buffalo Wallow Woman

Caeria
Candelaria Forero
Candelaria Pérez
Càndida Jou
Casta Alvarez
Catalina de Erauso
Catalina Delà
Catalina Junquet
Catalina Pagès
Catalina Marimón
Catalina Vidal
Cathay Williams
Catherine E. Davis
Chief Earth Woman
Christian "Kit" Cavanagh Davies
Claia Casellas
Colestah
Cosme Mendoza Chavira
Deborah Squash
Deng Yulan
Dho Minde
Ding Le Tunn
Dominga Cortada
Ecaterina Teodoroiu
Ehyophsta
Éliane Brault
Elisa Bernerström Servenius
Elise Toft
Elizabeth Caroline Newcom
Eulàlia Colomer
Evangelista Tamayo
Fana Kochovska
Fannu
Fanny Wilson
Faye Schulman
Felicísima Quintana
Filomena Valenzuela Goyenechea
Flora Sandes
Frances Hook
Francijntje van Lint
Franciscà Artigas
Franciscà Barnés
Franciscà Cullel
Franciscà Eras
Franciscà Fàbrega
Franciscà Feu
Franciscà Llogar
Franciscà Marti
Franciscà Morel
Franciscà Pacul
Franciscà Payret
Franciscà Puig
Franciscà Xifreu
Franziska Scanagatta
Gerónima Amich
Gerónima Sala
Gertrudis Camps y Roger
Gertrudis Esclusa
Gertrudis Turón
Giuseppina Vandal
Halide Edib Adivar
Hang
Hanging Cloud
Helen Ruz
Her Four Blankets
Hojo Masako
Hui Po Yung
Hypsicratea
Ida Sabo
Idia of Benin
Ignacia Alsina
Ignacia Cantalosella
Ikeda Sen
Inahime
Inés Alabreda
Irena Scheur-Sawicka
Irene del Carmen Morales Galaz
Irene Miawa Vivash
Irma Bandieri
Isabel Costa
Isabel Metjà Ibanéz
Isabel of Conches
Janina Wasiłojć-Smoleńska
Jeanne des Armoises
Jennie Hodgers
Jessica Lynch
Johanna Sophia Kettner
John Brown
Josefa Amar y Borbón
Josefa de Azlor
Josefa Valls
Josefa Venancia de la Encarnación Camejo
Josephine Okwuekeleke Tolefe
Jovita Feitosa
Juana Béjar
Juana Bernagosi
Juana Galán
Juana Rodríguez
Juliana Dias da Costa
Juliana Larena
Kara Fatma
Kateryna Noskova
Kathleen Clarke
Kathleen I. Wilkes
Khutulun
Kuilix
Leslie Joy Whitehead
Lidia Lwow-Eberle
Liri Gero
Lisbetha Olsdotter
Lizzie Compton
Lori Ann Piestewa
Louisa Hoffman
Ludmilla Kornilov
Macalda di Scaletta
Maeda Matsu
Magdalena Serra
Mah Laqa Bai Chanda
Manuela Roig
Manuela Sancho
Manuela Tinoco
Marelene Clyke
Margaret George Shello
Margaret Johnstone Ogilvy
Margareta Elisabeth Roos
Margarita Carreras
Margarita Cassà
Margarita Quintana
Margarita Roig
Margarita Salabert
Margarita Tutulani
Margarita Virosta
María Abras
Maria Agustín
María Àngela Tarragó
María Bandrell
Maria Bochkareva
María Casademunt
María Cendra
María Ciurana
María Crus
María Dalmau y Mar
María de Estrada
María Esquero
María Gatell María Rafols
Maria Jacoba de Turenne
María Josefa Esguerra
María Josefa Jonama
María la Bailadora
Maria Llúcia de Puig y Quintana
María Magdalena Mir
María Marqués
María Mato
Maria Olip'
María Pascual Balet
María Pastells

Maria Quitéria
María Remedios Del Valle
María Riera
María Rocosa
María Rosa Falgueras
María Rosa Saló
María Rosa Vala
María Serra
María Sureda
María Tarrús
María Tomàs
María Vidal
María Vilanova
María Yatón
Mariana Perramón
Marie Magdelaine Mouron
Marie von Fery Bognar
Marina Bartolome Dizon-Santiago
Marta Tello
Mary Ann Berry Brown
Mary Fine Weather
Mary Galloway
Mary Greyeyes
Meaghan Frank
Michelle Thompson
Milunka Savić
Modthryth
Mollie Bean
Moving Robe Woman
Muncunchimeg Nyamaajav
Nancy Ward
Narcisa Bofill
Natalie Tychmini
Nellie Graves
Nexhmije Hoxha
Nichola Goddard
Nusaybah bint Ka'ab
Okaji no Kata
Okurakyo no Tsubane
Olga Krasilnikov
One Who Walks with the Stars
Osthryth of Mercia
Pancha Carrasco
Pantea Arteshbod
Paolina Vadala
Paula Argimont
Paula Martínez
Petra Herrera
Pieronne of Brittany
Princess Halima
Rita Banús
Rita Costa
Rita Fàbregas
Rosa Barnat
Rosa Bernagosi
Rosa Donato
Rosa Forns
Rosa Giralt
Rosa Joíre
Rosa Llobera
Rosa Martorell
Rosa Masmitjà
Rosa Massó
Rosa Planas
Rosa Rodríguez
Rosa Romani
Rosa Saura
Samanthia Griffiths
Sarah Jane Taylor
Seen by Her Nation
Serafina Vey o Vehi
Shoshana Nyree Johnson
Sofia Noti
Sofija Jovanović
Sophronia Smith Hunt
Susie Shot-in-the-Eye
Suzanne Puanani Vares-Lum
Suzanne "Sanité" Bélair
Taramon Bibi
Teresa Amat
Teresa Ametler
Teresa Andry
Teresa Comella
Teresa Cornejo
Teresa Ferrarons
Teresa Garriga
Teresa Illas
Teresa Mayol
Teresa Pascual
Teresa Pujol
Teresa Testa di Lana
Teresa Vivetas
Teresinha Gomes
The Other Magpie
Triaria Vitellia
Tulsi Gabbard
Tyonajanegen
Valeriana Nató
Virginia Hall
Virginie Ghesquière
Wanda Krahelska-Filipowicz
Wang Shaowen
Wang Yi
Yona Markova
Youtab Aryobarzan
Zivia Lubetkin
Zofia Kossak-Szczucka
Zoya Smirnow

Special Ops
Ashley White
Jennifer M. Moreno

Spiritual Crusader
Alice Auma
Isabella I of Castile
Joan of Arc
Leymah Gbowee
Margaret of Beverley
Muhumusa

Spy/Reconnaisance
Adelaide Mulheran Hawkins
Agueda Esteban
Andrea Ricaurte de Lozano
Andrée Borrel
Ann Bates
Anna Smith Strong
Anna Wolkoff
Anne Hennis Bailey
Asma Gargoum
Astrid Dollis Dahlgren
Betty Ann Lussier
Brita Olovsdotter Tott
Chen Shuozhen
Claire Phillips
Cleopatra VII
Dahteste
Dana Colvin
Deborah Sampson
Delphine Aigle
Diana Rowden
Ding Le Tunn
Dollis Dahlgren
Doris Bohrer
Edith Tudor-Hart
Ehyophsta
Elizabeth Lamb
Elizabeth Peet McIntosh
Elizabeth Ryder Maxwell
Elizabeth Sudmeier
Ella Reno
Eloise Randolph Page
Emilie Tillion
Erika Schwarze Wendt
Ethel Rosenberg
Eugenie Shakhovskaya
Francien de Zeeuw
Françoise Deprés

Freddie Nanda Dekker-Oversteegen
Gabrielle Jeanine "Gloria" Picabia Buffet
Germaine Guerin
Germaine Ribière
Germaine Tillion
Giliana Balmaceda Gerson
Gioconda Belli
Han E
Hannie Schaft
Harriet Tubman
Hélène Louise de Munck
Hetty Voûte
Hui Po Yung
Ida Veldhuyzen van Zanten
Inas Fathy
Isabella Hoppringle
Isabella I of Castile
Isabelle Wilhelmine Marie Eberhardt
Jane Horney
Jane Ryder Whorwood
Jane Sissmore Archer
Jane Wallis Burrell
Janet Pringle
Jeannie Rousseau
Jennie D. Hart
Joan Miller
Josefa Venancia de la Encarnación Camejo
Josephine Baker
Juana Escobar
Juana Gabriela Moro
Juana Ramírez (Colombia)
Júlia Bányai
Julia Child
Juliet Beyler
Kari Hiran
Karin Lannby
Kate Brown
Kiki Latry
Kitty Grande
Kitty Harris
Krystyna Skarbek
Laura Secord
Laurean Sierra
Lela Karagianni
Liza Ivanovna Chaikina
Loretta Janeta Velázquez
Louise de Bettignies
Lydia Darragh
Magdalena Leones
Manuela Escobar
Manuela Sáenz
Margaret Catherine Moore "Katy" Barry
Margaret O. Murphy
Margaret Skinnider
Margaret Utinsky
Marguerite Baker Harrison
Marian McKenzie
María Baltazara Teran Garzon
María Loreto Sánchez Peón
María Parado de Bellido
María Remedios Del Valle
Marie Leonie Vanhoutte
Marie-Madeleine Fourcade
Marina Lebstuck
marjorie Amor
Marthe Hoffnung Cohn
Mary Hay
Mary Herbert
Mary Jane Green
Mary Jane Richards Bowser
Mary Reynolds
Mathilde Lucia Carré
Mattie Winnemucca
Melita Norwood
Nancy Hart Douglas
Naomi Flores
Odette Sansom
Olga Gray
Parysatis
Pauline Cushman
Petrocinio Gamboa
Policarpa Salavarrieta
Riet van Grunsven
Rosa Campuzano
Rose Valland
Sarah Aaronsohn
Sarah Emma Edmonds
Sarah Winnemucca
Simona Josefa Manzaneda
Sitt al-Mulk
Solveig Bergslien
Suzanne Hiltermann-Souloumiac
Sylvette Roussel Leleu
Tamara Haydée Bunke Bider
Tatyana Savelyevna Marinenko
Tomoe Gozen
Truus Menger-Oversteegen
Úrsula Kuczyński
Violette Lecoq
Virginia Hall
Xi Shi
Yvonne Huynh

Squad Leader
Ana Detrell
Antònia Betlem
Eulàlia Vila
Florentina Serrats
Franciscà Ball-llobera
Franciscà Soler
Haldis Elisabeth Arentz Sveri
Magdalena Daví
Magdalena Mollera
Magdalena Teixidor
María Mato
Rita Sala
Rosa Costa
Rosa Mir
Teresa Palau
Timycha
Vicenta Tornabells

Strategist
A-Nong
Aethelflaed
Amalasuintha
Amelia of Berbice
Ameliane du Puget-Glandevès
Amina
Aminta Granera Sacasa
Ana Dara
Ani Pachen
Anna Ivanovna Maslovskaya
Apacuana
Artemisia I
Artemisia II
Arwa Al-Sulayhi
Bakwa of Turunku
Berty Albrecht
Cecilia of Le Bourcq
Charlotte Amalie
Comandante Ramona
Cristina Luca Boico
Datar Kuar
Ding Le Tunn
Doquz Khatun
Ecaterina Teodoroiu
Éliane Sophie Plowmen
Elizabeth I of England
Eurydice of Egypt
Gabrielle Weidner
Geertruida Wijsmuller-Meijer

Germaine Tambour
Ghaliyya al-Wahhabiyya
Glory of the Morning
Harriet Tubman
Hawida Shibadi
Hazrat Mahal
Hui Po Yung
Hweida Shibadi
Ingela Olofsdotter Gathenhielm
Jhalkaribai
Jindan Kaur
Joan of Arc
Joaquina Galarza de Larrea
Jozette McLean
Juliana Dias da Costa
Kaihime
Khawla bint al-Azwar
Khutulun
Kura Ocllo
Lagertha
Laodice I
Li Xiu
Lozen
Lucie Bernard Aubrac
Madeleine Tambour
Manuela Cañizares
Manuela Sáenz
Margaret Catherine Moore "Katy" Barry
Margaret of Anjou
Marguerite Gonnet
Maria Bochkareva
María Felipa de Oliveira
Marthe Cnockaert
Matilda of Tuscany
Mavia
Micaela Bastidas Puyucahua
Mimi Mingat-Lerme
Nabila Abdelrahman Abu Ras
Nancy Wake
Nancy Ward
Nandi Bhebhe
Nehanda Charwe Nyakasikana
Nell Ryan
Nyi Ageng Serang
Olga Alkalaj
Patrocinio Gamboa
Pearl Witherington
Philippa of England
Qutlugh Nigar
Rafaella Herrera
Rojda Felat
Sadie Farrell
Sarah Aaronsohn
Sarah Feely Bryant
Shajar al-Durr
Sharon T. Swartworth
Sichelgaita
Sietje Gravendeel-Tammens
Suzanne Puanani Vares-Lum
Sylvia Salvesen
Thao Sriunthorn
Thao Suranari
Thao Thesauri
Thérèse Pierre
Thyra Danebod
Tirgatao
Tomasa Tito Condemayta
Trưng Nhị
Trưng Trắc
Vera May Atkins
Xiao Yanyan
Zaynab an-Nafzāwiyyah
Zheng Yi Sao

Stretcher Bearer
Agueda Alsina
Ana Ferrer
Annie Blair
Franciscà Rexach
Gerónima N.
Josefa Barrera
Josefa Demà
Magdalena Blanch
Maria Comadira
María Rosa Falgueras
Marie-Thérèse Figueur

Supplier/Smuggler
Agueda Esteban
Aisha Gdour
Ala Gertner
Alakhai Bekhi
Alice Stopford Green
Aliquippa
Andrée Borrel
Anna Rheinholdsdotter Leuhusen
Anna Wajcblum Heilman
Anne-Marie Walters
Annie Higgins
Antonia Spath Bruha
Antonina
Berta Bergman
Bianca Canales
Bibiana Talero
Bracha Fuld
Brigid Foley
Brigida Silva de Ochoa
Bronia Klibanski
Candelaria Figueredo
Caridad Mercader
Casilda Zafra
Catharina Aaltjen Boekbinder
Cécile Rol-Tanguy
Celia Sánchez Manduley
Cleopatra VII Philopator
Concepción Mariño Carige Fitzgerald
Dahteste
Dalla Abbazi
Dorotea Castro
Effie Taafe
Eilís Elliott
Elena Barščiauskaitė
Eliza Alice Lynch
Elizabeth Lamb
Elizabeth Ryder Maxwell
Emily Elliott
Estefanía Neira de Eslava
Estefanía Parra
Ester Wajcblum
Evota of Stirling
Françoise-Marie Jacquelin
Freddie Nanda Dekker-Oversteegen
Frumka Płotnicka
Geertruida Wijsmuller-Meijer
Genia Fischer
Germaine Guérin
Gertrudis Vanegas
Gioconda Belli
Gulab Kaur
Haika Grossman
Hanna Stadnik
Hannie Schaft
Hela Rufeisen Schüpper
Hélène Studler
Henriette Maria of France
Huang Pei-mei
Ignacia Medina
Inas Fathy
Inge Weidenau Frank
Ingeborg Wallheimer Kahlenberg
Irena Adamowicz
Irena Scheur-Sawicka

Irma Bandiera
Isabella I of Castile
Jacqueline Nearne
Jane Ryder Whorwood
Jean "Jenny" Cameron
Jeanne Hachette
Joan of Arc
Johanna Jungberg Hard
Johanna Stegen
Jozette McLean
Juana Velasco de Gallo
Julia Diament Pirotte
Kamala Das Gupta
Laskarina Bouboulina
Lela Karagianni
Leni Egger
Lidia Brisca Menapace
Lina Merlin
Lise de Baissac
Liza Czapnik
Lozen
Lucie Boutillier du Retail
Luisa Trilleras
Louise Aslanian
Louise Gavan Duffy
Magdalena Avietėnaitė
Magdalena Leones
Malalai
Margaret of Anjou
Margaret Skinnider
Margaret Utinsky
Margareta von Ascheberg
Margaretha Sandra
María Agudelo de Olaya
Maria Bochkareva
Maria Emhart
María Rosa Lazo de la Vega
Marianne Feldhammer
Marianne Golz
Marie Leonie Vanhoutte
Marinette Menut
Marta Bindiger Cigi
Mary Spring Rice
Matilde Anaray
Mercedes Ábrego de Reyes
Micaela Bastidas Puyucahua
Mimi Mingat-Lerme
Mirjam Ohringer
Molly Osgood Childers
Naomi Flores
Nazik Khatim
Nichole M. Frye
Nora Astoria
Octavia Minor

Olga Bancic
Ona Šimaitė
Princess Halima
Pritilata Waddedar
Rabia Gajun
Regina Safirsztajn
Resi Pesendorfer
Riet van Grunsven
Rose Grunapfel Meth
Rosie Hackett
Roza Robota
Ruzanna "Salima" Ibragimova
Sarah Jane Smith
Şerife Bacı
Sietje Gravendeel-Tammens
Simona Josefa Manzaneda
Sofía Moreira de Sabando
Telesilla
Teresa Izquierdo
Teresa Magbanua
Tosia Altman
Truus Menger-Oversteegen
Vahida Maglajlić
Valentina Grizodubova
Varsha Kukreti
Vladka Meed
Wanda Hjort Heger
Wanda Krahelska-Filipowicz
Yael Rom
Yolande of Aragon
Yvonne Rudellat
Žamila Kolonomos
Zofia Kossak-Szczucka

Surrendered
Ada of Caria
Aisha al-Hurra
Akai Teruko
Anita Garibaldi
Anna Eriksdotter Bielke
Anne Holck
Anne Margrethe Bangs Strømsheim
Begum Samara
Belawadi Mallamma Desai
Blanche Arundell
Bùi Thị Xuân
Camilla Rodolfi
Charlotte Stanley
Christina Nilsdotter Gyllenstierna
Christina of Saxony

Christine de Lalaing of Espinoy
Cicely Arundell
Cleopatra VII Philopator
Cleophis
Ebba Gustavsdotter Stenbock
Elizabeth Dowdall
Ermengard of Provence
Fulvia Flacca Bambula
Guiraude de Lavaur
Herma Paschinger
Ilona Zrínyi
Juliane de Fontevrault
Käthe Wanek Odwody
Kong Sikhen
Laudomia Forteguerri
Lettice Fitzgerald Digby
Louise Labé
Maria Emhart
Mariotta Haliburton
Mary Hawtrey Bankes
Marzia Ordelaffi
Matilda of Ramsbury
Minnie Hollow Wood
Nelida Cabigayan
Numata Jakō
Nur Jahan
Pharantzem of Armenia
Phila of Macedonia
Richardis of Schwerin
Roxana of Bactria
Samsi
Teuta
Trưng Nhi
Trưng Trắc
Zheng Yi Sao

Switchboard Operator
Karina S. Lau

Swordfighter
Ahilyabhai Holkar
Alberte-Barbe d'Ernécourt
Amina
Ana María Martínez de Nisser
Anne Keith Smythe
Betsy Gray
Chand Bibi
Durgavati
Josefa Venancia de la Encarnación Camejo
Juana Azurduy de Padilla
Khutulun

Liu Jinding
Mammy Yoko
Manto Mavrogenous
Mary Ambree
Miyagino
Sarah Jane Taylor
Shinobu
Sichelgaita
Tomoe Gozen
Wang Cong'er
Yuenu

Tank/Truck Driver
Alexandra Beiko
Alina Tumriyeva
Anna Ivanovna Maslovskaya
Crystal Davis
Hélène Studler
Khava Barayeva
Lori Ann Piestewa
Luiza Magomadova
Mareta Duduyeva
Minnie Bendina Spotted Wolf
Miyoko Hikiji
Monica Beltran

Telegrapher/Radio Operator
Eileen Nearne
Karina S. Lau
Kitty Harris
Liliane Rolfe
Lone Morgensen Masłocha
Madeleine Damerment
Noor-un–Nisa Inayat Khan
Odette Sar Wilen
Phyllis Latour
Rita Arnould
Solveig Bergslien
Ürsula Kuczyński
Yelena Stempkovskaya
Yolande Beekman
Yvonne Huynh
Zofia Poznańska

Terrorist
Aafia Siddiqui
Ahlam al-Tamimi
Aiza Gazuyeva
Alina Tumriyeva
Aminat Nagaev
Comandante Ramona
Dzhennet Abdurakhmanova
Khadijat Mangerieva

Khava Barayeva
Lida Khildehoroeva
Luiza Magomadova
Major Anna Maria
Mareta Duduyeva
Mariam Tuburova
Markha Ustarkhanova
Maryam Sharipova
Naida Asiyalova
Netiva Ben Yehuda
Pritilata Waddedar
Roza Nagaev
Ruzanna "Salima" Ibragimova
Satisita Dzhbirkhanova
Sonia Perovskaya
Subcomandante Elisa
Mariam Tuburova
Vera Figner
Zarema Muzhikhoeva
Zinaida Aliyeva
Zulikhan Elikhadzhiyeva
Zura Barayeva

Underground Agent
Agnes Dorothee Humbert
Agnieszka Dowbor-Muśnicka
Alma Allen
Alexandra Kudasheva
Ingeborg Wallheimer Kahlenberg
Jacqueline Bordelet
Marie Marvingt
Monica Wichfeld
Yvonne Oddon

Wounded Veteran
Aafia Siddiqui
Adeline Stocking Foot
Agnes Humbert
Ahumai Te Paerata
Amelia Robles Àvila
Amina
Amy Clarke
Ana Lezama de Urinza
Angélique Duchemin Brûlon
Anna Maria Lane
Anna Sophia Detzliffin
Anne Margrethe Bangs Strømsheim
Annie Blair Etheridge
Annike Svahn
Antonija Javornik

Bowdash
Bracha Fuld
Brita Olsdotter Hagberg
Caridad Mercader
Catharina Aaltjen Boekbinder
Catherine E. Davidson
Christian "Kit" Cavanagh Davies
Christine de Lalaing of Espinoy
Claire Lacombe
Crystal Davis
Danielle Greene-Byrd
Dawn Halfaker
Deborah Sampson
Djamila Bouhired
Durgavati
Ecaterina Teodoroiu
Eleonore Prochaska
Elisabeth Someruell
Eliza Allen Billings
Esperanza Llorens
Evangelina Diaz
Fana Kochovska
Fanny Wilson
Flora Sandes
Frances Hook
Frances Louis Clayton
Francina Broese Gunningh
Franziska Scanagatta
Friederike Krüger
Geneviève Prémoy
Gregoria de Jesús
Hangaku Gozen
Hannah Snell
He Zizhen
Hela Rufeisen Schüpper
Helen Ruz
Isabel Pi
Janina Simmons
Jennie Hodgers
Jessica Lynch
Joan Beaufort
Joan of Arc
Juana Azurduy de Padilla
Juana Rodríguez
Júlia Bányai
Katherine Grandison
Kendra Coleman
Klára Andrássy
Kseniya Semyonovna Konstantinova
Kuyili

Lidia Lwow-Eberle
Lilliard of Ancrum
Lisa Jade Head
Lizzie Compton
Loretta Janeta Velázquez
Louise Michel
Lucy Matilda Thompson Gauss
Madeleine Truel
Manuela Medina`
Mareta Duduyeva
Margaret Cochran Corbin
Margaret of Beverley
Margaret Skinnider
Marguerite Delaye
María Agustín Linares
Maria Bochkareva
María Marfày Vila
María Plajas
Maria van Antwerpen
Marie-Jeanne Schellinck
Marie Magdelaine Mouron
Marie-Thérèse Figueur
Marissa Strock
Mariya Bayda
Mary Anne Talbot
Mary Brose Tepe
Mary Edwards Walker
Mary Ellen Wise

Mary Galloway
Mary Jessie Herrera
Mary Reynolds
Mercadera
Milunka Savić
Mollie Bean
Molly Bell
Nadezha Durova
Nadia Lugina
Natalie Tychmini
Nellie Graves
Nene Hatun
Netiva Ben Yehuda
Nicolasa Jurado
Nina Raspopova
Nusaybah bint Ka'ab
Olena Bilozerska
Olga Kokovtseva
Phoebe Smith Hessel
Rachel Bosveld
Rashida Salmeeva
Rawya Ateya
Riet van Grunsven
Roja Felat
Rose Barreau
Sarah Borginis
Sarah Emma Edmonds
Sarah Malinda Pritchard Blalock

Sarah Rosetta Wakeman
Shinobu
Shoshana Nyree Johnson
Sichelgaita
Sietje Gravendeel-Tammens
Sofija Jovanović
Sue Downes
Susan Sonnheim
Susan Travers
Tamar Ariel
Tammy Duckworth
Tania Chernova
Teresa Balaguer
Timycha
Tina Buchter Strobos
Tomoe Gozen
Tosia Altman
Trinidad Peréz Tecson
Valeriya Osipovna Gnarovskaya
Viktoria Savs
Vishpala
Visna
Yekaterina Ryabova
Yevdokiya Nikulina
Yvonne Rudellat
Žamila Kolonomos
Zoya Parfyonova
Zoya Smirnow

Bibliography

Primary Sources

Adams, Henry Gardiner, ed. *A Cyclopaedia of Female Biography*. London: Groombridge, 1857.

Annuaire du Conseil Héraldique de France. Paris: Conseil Héraldique de France, 1898.

Appian. *The Foreign Wars*. New York: Macmillan, 1899.

Ari the Learned. *The Book of the Settlement of Iceland*. Kendal, UK: T. Wilson, 1898.

Babur. *Baburnama*. New York: Modern Library, 2016.

Bartholomaeus of Neocastro. *Historia Sicula*. Bologna, Italy: L.A. Muratori, 1728.

Beague, Jean. *The Scots War*. Paris, 1556.

Beveridge, Henry. *The Akbar Nama*. Calcutta: Asiatic Society, 1907.

Bochkareva, Maria. *Yashka: My Life As Peasant, Exile, and Soldier*. London: Constable and Company, 1919.

Bovill, W.B. Forster. *Hungary and the Hungarians*. London: Methuen, 1908.

Bricka, Carl Frederik. *Dansk Biografisk Lexikon*. Copenhagen: F. Hegel & Son, 1887.

Buchanan, George. *Rerum Scoticarum Historia*. London: Simpkin, Marshall, 1582.

Calendar of the Patent Rolls Preserved in the Public Record Office. Great Britain: Public Record Office, 1897.

Caradoc of Lhancarvan. *The History of Wales*. London: T. Evans, 1574.

Carrey, Emile. *Refits de Kabylie*. Paris: Michel Llevy Frères, 1858.

Chambers, William, and Robert Chambers, eds. *Chambers's Journal of Popular Literature, Science, and Arts*. London: W. & R. Chambers, 1860.

Champney, Lizzie W. *Three Vassar Girls on the Rhine*. Boston: Estes & Lauriat, 1887.

Chronica Monasterii de Melsa. London, 1868.

Chronicles of Froissart. London, 1816.

Clayton, Ellen C. *Female Warriors*. London: Tinsley Brothers, 1879.

Đặng Thùy Trâm. *Last Night I Dreamed of Peace*. New York: Harmony Books, 2007.

D'Arc, Pierre Lanery. *Le livre d'or de Jeanne d'Arc*. Paris: H. Leclerc et Cornuau, 1894.

De La Nicolliere-Teijeiro, Stephane. *La Course et Les Corsaires du Port de Nantes*. Chalon-sur-Saone, France: L. Marceau, 1896.

De Pauw, Linda Grant. *Battle Cries and Lullabies: Women in War*. Norman: University of Oklahoma Press, 2014.

Deel, Derde. *Vaderlandse Historie*. Amsterdam: Johannes Allart, 1788.

Després, Françoise. *Détails Historiques sur Les Services de Françoise Després*. Paris: L.G. Michaud, 1817.

Du Pan, J. Mallet. *The History of the Destruction of the Helvetic Union and Union*. Boston: J. Nancrede, 1799.

Durova, Nadezhda. *The Cavalry Maiden*. Bloomington: Indiana University Press, 1988.

Ellis, William. *Narrative of a Tour through Hawaii*. London: H. Fisher, Son, and P. Jackson, 1827.

Fabre, Augustin. *Histoire de Marseille*. Vol. 2. Marseilles: M. Olive, 1829.

Figueur, Thérèse. *Les Campagnes de Mademoiselle Thérèse Figueur*. Paris: Dauvin et Fontaine, 1842.

Forbes, Robert. *Jacobite Memoirs of the Rebellion of 1745*. Edinburgh: William & Robert Chambers, 1834.

Forester, Thomas. *Ordericus Vitalis: The Ecclesiastical History of England and Normandy*. London: H.G. Bohn, 1853.

Fornander, Abraham. *An Account of the Polynesian Race*. London: Trübner & Company, 1880.

Frazer, J.G. *Pausanias's Description of Greece*. London: Macmillan, 1913.

Gairdner, James. *The Paston Letters*. Westminster, UK: A. Constable, 1874.

Greenwood, Grace (1854). *Greenwood Leaves: A Collection of Sketches and Letters*. London: Ticknor, Reed, & Fields, 1854.

Gribble, Francis Henry. *Women in War*. London: E.P. Dutton, 1916.

Griffith, Ralph T.H. *The Hymns of the Rigveda*. Delhi: Motilal Banarsidass, 1973.

Hale, Sarah Josepha. *Woman's Record; or, Sketches of All Distinguished Women, from "the Beginning" till A.D. 1850*. New York: Harper and Brothers, 1853.

Hansen, Thorkild. *Islands of Slaves*. Accra, Ghana: Sub-Saharan Publishers, 2005.

Harley, Lady Brilliana. *Letters of the Lady Brilliana Harley*. London: Camden Society, 1854.

Hennet, Leon. *Une femme soldat: Rose Barreau*. Albi, France: Nouguies, 1908.

Heywoode, Thom. *Gynaikeion: or, Nine Books of Various History Concerning Women*. London: Adam Islip, 1624.

Hookham, Mary Ann. *The Life and Times of Margaret of Anjou, Queen of England and France*. London: Tinsley Brothers, 1872.

Humbert, Agnes. *Résistance: Memoirs of Occupied France*. New York: Bloomsbury, 2008.

Hutchinson, William. *A View of Northumberland*. Newcastle, Eng.: T. Saint, 1776.

Ibn Battuta. *The Travels of Ibn Battūta, A.D. 1325–1354*. London: Hakluyt Society, 1994.

Jianjun He. *Spring and Autumn Annals of Wu and Sue*. Ithaca, NY: Cornell, 2021.

Johannis de Fordun. *Chronica Gentis Scotorum*. Edinburgh: Edmonston & Douglas, 1871.

Krimmer, Elisabeth, and Patricia Anne Simpson, eds. *Realities and Fantasies of German Female Leadership*. Rochester, NY: Camden House, 2019.

The Ladies Dictionary. London: John Dunton, 1694.

Lemmon, Gayle Tzemach. *The Daughters of Kobani*. New York: Penguin, 2021.

Ludlow, Edmund. *Memoirs*. Oxford, UK: Clarendon Press, 1894

Madiou, Thomas. *Histoire d'Haïti: 1799–1803*. Port au Prince, Haiti: H. Deschamps, 1803.

McCullough, Helen Craig. *The Tale of the Heike*. Stanford, CA: Stanford University Press, 1988.

Meacham, A.B. *Winema and Her People*. Hartford, CT: American Publishing, 1876.

Norton, Henry, ed. *Deeds of Daring*. Norwich, NY: Chenango Telegraph Printing House, 1889.

Oliphant, Laurence. *The Trans-Caucasian Campaign of the Turkish Army*. London: Blackwood & Sons, 1856.

Oviedo, Jose de. *Historia de la Conquista y Población de la Provincia de Venezuela*. Caracas: Biblioteca Ayacucho, 1723.

Phillips, Thomas. *A Journal of a Voyage Made in the Hannibal of London*. London: Walthoe, 1693.

Podobna, Yevgeniya. *Girls Cutting Their Locks*. Kyiv: Ukrainian Institute of National Remembrance, 2020.

Porter, Arthur Kingsley. *Lombard Architecture*. New Haven, CT: Yale University Press, 1916.

Robertson, William H. *The History of the Reign of the Emperor Charles the Fifth*. Philadelphia: J.B. Lippincott, 1876.

Rutt, John Towill, ed. *The Theological and Miscellaneous Works of Joseph Priestley*. Cambridge, MS: Harvard University, 1802.

Sandes, Flora. *An English Woman-Sergeant in the Serbian Army*. London: Hodder and Stoughton, 1916.

Schultz, James Willard. *Blackfeet Tales of Glacier National Park*. Boston: Houghton Mifflin, 1916.

Simon, Fray Pedro. *Noticias Historiales de las Conquistas de Tierra Firme en las Indias Occidentales*. Bogotá: Ministerio de Educacion Nacional, 1953.

Talbot, Mary Ann. *The Life and Surprising Adventures of Mary Ann Talbot, in the Name of John Taylor*. London: Robert S. Kirby, 1809.

Tan, Sima. *Records of the Grand Historian*. New York: Columbia University Press, 1995.

Tregellas, Walter H. *Cornish Worthies*. London: Elliot Stock, 1884.

Tremblay, Paul, ed. *Les Hommes Illustres du Département de L'Oise*. Paris: Bibliothèque du Beauvais, 1864.

Urquidi, Jose Macedonio. *Bolivianas Ilustres*. La Paz, Bolivia: Arno Hermanos, 1919.

Walker, Mary Edwards. *Hit*. North Syracuse, NY: Gegensatz Press, 1871.

Walsh, William Shepard. *Curiosities of Popular Customs*. Philadelphia: J.B. Lippincott, 1897.

Wildwood, Warren. *Thrilling Adventures among the Early Settlers*. Philadelphia: J. Edwin Potter, 1866.

Wyles, Lilian. *A Woman at Scotland Yard: Reflections on the Struggles and Achievements of Thirty Years in the Metropolitan Police*. London: Faber & Faber, 1952.

Yonge, Charlotte Mary. *Cameos of English History*. New York: Macmillan, 1899.

Articles

"Australia's Only Woman Pirate." *Sydney Morning Herald* (26 October): 21.

Beam, Beebe. "My Life as a Soldier." *San Francisco Sunday Examiner* (1 October 1900): 1.

"Brave Women." *New York Times* (8 February 1880).

Burton, R.F. "A Visit to Lissa and Pelagosa." *Journal of the Royal Geographical Society* 49 (1879): 151–189.

Carette, Captain. "Algérie." *L'Univers Pittoresque*. Paris: Firmin Didot, 1850, 30–31.

"The Chamberlaynes of Chelsea." *The Sketch* 23:287 (27 July 1898): 211–212.

Dickens, Charles. "Famous British Regiments." *All the Year Round* 234 (24 May 1873): 84–90.

Jackson, J.E. "The Eminent Ladies of Wiltshire History." *Wiltshire Archaeological and Natural History Magazine* 20:58 (1882): 26–44.

"A Lady Soldier." *Providence (RI) Evening Press* (17 September 1864): 4.

"Lieutenant Madame Brulon: A Modern Heroine." *The Lily* (16 October 1854).

"The Life of Mrs. Mary Ralphson." *Scots Magazine and Edinburgh Literary Miscellany*, 71 (1809): 569–570.

"Louise Labé," *La Belle Assemblée*. London (August 1821): 55–57.

"Mary Ellen Wise." *Pittsburgh Daily Commercial* (9 May 1864): 2.

"Siege of Girona." *Edinburgh Annual Register, 1809*. Oxford, UK: Ballantyne & Company, 1811, 768–786.

"Tuesday, September 2, 1794." *London Gazette*.

Secondary Sources

Angelov, Dimiter. *The Byzantine Hellene*. Cambridge, UK: Cambridge University Press, 2019.

Appleby, John C. *Women and English Piracy,*

1540–1720. Woodbridge, UK: Boydell Press, 2013.

Bamyeh, Mohammed A., ed. *Intellectuals and Civil Society in the Middle East*. London: I.B. Tauris, 2012.

Bartlett, Robert C. (2000). *England Under the Norman and Angevin Kings: 1075–1225*. Oxford, UK: Clarendon Press, 2000.

Bender, Sara. *The Jews of Białystok During World War II and the Holocaust*. Hanover, NH: Brandeis University Press, 2008.

Benjamen, Alda. *Assyrians in Modern Iraq: Negotiating Political and Cultural Space*. Cambridge, UK: Cambridge University Press, 202.

Bennison, Amira K. *Almoravid and Almohad Empires*. Edinburgh: Edinburgh University Press, 2016.

Bird, Dunlaith. *Travelling in Different Skins: Gender Identity in European Women's Oriental Travelogues, 1850–1950*. Oxford, UK: Oxford University Press, 2012.

Booth, Marilyn. *Infamous Women and Famous Wombs*. New York: Palgrave Macmillan, 2001.

Boris, Eileen, Sandra Trudgen Dawson, and Barbara Molony, eds. *Engendering Transnational Transgressions: From the Intimate to the Global*. London: Routledge, 2020.

Calderini, Simonetta. *Women as Imams*. New York: Bloomsbury, 2021.

Caravantes, Peggy. *The Many Faces of Josephine Baker*. Chicago: Chicago Review Press, 2015.

Chopra, Ruma. *Almost Home: Maroons Between Slavery and Freedom in Jamaica, Nova Scotia, and Sierra Leone*. New Haven, CT: Yale University Press, 2018.

Coogan, Michael E., and Cynthia R. Chapman. *The Old Testament and Literary Introduction to the Hebrew Scriptures*. Oxford, UK: Oxford University Press, 2017.

Cordell, M.R. *Courageous Women of the Civil War*. Chicago: Chicago Review Press, 2016.

Cortese, Delia, and Simonetta Calderini. *Women and the Fatimids in the World of Islam*. Edinburgh: Edinburgh University Press, 2006.

Creighton, Margaret S., and Lisa Norling. *Iron Men, Wooden Women: Gender and Seafaring in the Atlantic World, 1700–1920*. Baltimore: Johns Hopkins University Press, 1996.

Crone, Patricia. *The Nativist Prophets of Early Islamic Iran: Rural Revolt and Local Zoroastrianism*. Cambridge, UK: Cambridge University Press, 2012.

Dall, Caroline H. *The College, the Market, and the Court*. Frankfurt, Germany: Outlook, 2020.

Dekker, Rudolf M. *The Tradition of Female Cross-Dressing in Early Modern Europe*. London: Macmillan, 1989.

Dermineur, Elise M., Åsa Karlsson Sjögren, and Virginia Langum, eds. *Revisiting Gender in European History, 1400–1800*. New York: Routledge, 2018.

Din, Nazira Zayn al. *Unveiling and Veiling: On the Liberation of the Woman and Social Renewal in the Islamic World*. Toronto: University of Toronto Press, 1928.

Duncombe, Laura Sook. *Pirate Women: The Princesses, Prostitutes, and Privateers Who Ruled the Seven Seas*. Chicago: Chicago Review Press, 2017.

Ermatinger, James W. *The Roman Empire: A Historical Encyclopedia*. Santa Barbara, CA: ABC-Clio, 2018.

Faure, David, and Ho Ts'ui-p'ing, eds. *Chieftains into Ancestors: Imperial Expansion and Indigenous Society in Southwest China*. Vancouver: University of British Columbia Press, 2013.

Garland, Lynda. *'Till Death Do Us Part?': Family Life in Byzantine Monasteries*. London: Routledge, 2013.

Gates, Henry Louis, Emmanuel Akyeampong, and Steven J. Niven, eds. *Dictionary of African Biography*. Oxford, UK: Oxford University Press, 2012.

Grainger, John D. *The Galatians: Celtic Invaders of Greece and Asia Minor*. Padstow, UK: Pen and Sword History, 2020.

Greenwood, Frank Murray, and Beverley Boissery. *Uncertain Justice: Canadian Women and Capital Punishment*. Toronto: Dundurn, 2000.

Habibi, Abd al-Hayy. *The Hidden Treasure: A Biography of Pashtoon Poets*. Lanham, MD: University Press of America, 1997.

Hanna, Mark. *Pirate Nests and the Rise of the British Empire: 1570–1740*. Chapel Hill: University of North Carolina Press, 2015.

Heimerman, Cheryl A. *Women of Valor in the American Civil War*. Auckland, NZ: Pickle Partners, 2015.

Holt, Nathalia. *Wise Gals: The Spies Who Built the CIA and Changed the Future of Espionage*. New York: G.P. Putnam's Sons, 2022.

Ingbrant, Renata. *The Transgressive Agency of the Cross-Dressing Soldier*. London: Routledge, 2020.

Jackson, Peter. *The Mongols and the West: 1221–1410*. New York: Taylor & Francis, 2014.

Javlekar, Arvind. *Lokmata Ahilyabai*. New Delhi: Ocean Books, 2005.

Jestice, Phyllis G. *Imperial Ladies of the Ottoman Dynasty*. Cham, Switzerland: Palgrave Macmillan, 2022.

Kampouroglos, D.G. *'Athenaikov 'Archontoloyion*. Athens: Sideres, 1921.

Khaira, Raj Kaur. *Stories for South Asian Supergirls*. New York: Puffin, 2021.

Knight, Franklin W., and Henry Louis Gates, Jr. *Dictionary of Caribbean and Afro–Latin American Biography*. Oxford, UK: Oxford University Press, 2016.

Kurup, Pushpa. *Power Women: A Journey into Hindu Mythology*. New York: Bloomsbury, 2021.

Lampe, David. *Hitler's Savage Canary: A History of the Danish Résistance in World War II*. London: Frontline Books, 2014.

Lardinois, André. *Making Silence Speak*. Princeton, NJ: Princeton University Press, 2018.

Lavelle, Ryan. *Places of Contested Power*. Woodbridge, UK: Boydell Press, 2020.
Loud, G.A. *The Age of Robert Guiscard: Southern Italy and the Norman Conquest*. New York: Longman, 2000.
Malouf, Tony. *Arabs in the Shadow of Israel*. Grand Rapids, MI: Kregel, 2003.
Marsot, Afaf Lutfi Al-Sayyid. *A History of Egypt: From the Arab Conquest to the Present*. Cambridge, UK: Cambridge University Press, 2007.
McBurney, Christian M. *Spies in Revolutionary Rhode Island*. Charleston, SC: Arcadia, 2014.
McMahon, Keith. *Celestial Women: Imperial Wives and Concubines in China from Song to Qing*. Lanham, MD: Rowman & Littlefield, 2020.
Meri, Josef W., ed. *Medieval Islamic Civilization: An Encyclopedia*. New York: Routledge, 2006.
Mernissa, Fatima. *The Forgotten Queens of Islam*. Minneapolis: University of Minnesota Press, 1993.
Monica Porter. *Children Against Hitler*. Yorkshire, Eng.: Pen & Sword, 2019.
Moore, Kenneth Royce, ed. *Brill's Companion to the Reception of Alexander the Great*. Leiden, Holland: Brill, 2018
Moran, Sarah Joan, and Amanda Pipkin. *Women and Gender in the Early Modern Low Countries*. Leiden, Holland: Brill, 2019.
Moubayed, Sami. *Steel & Silk: Men and Women Who Shaped Syria 1900–2000*. Seattle: Cune, 2006.
Neatby, Nicole, and Peter Hodgins, eds. *Settling and Unsettling Memories: Essays in Canadian Public History*. Toronto: University of Toronto Press, 2012.
Pachen, Ani. *Sorrow Mountain: The Journey of a Tibetan Warrior Nun*. New York: Kodansha International, 2000.
Potholm, Christian P. *Hiding in Plain Sight: Women Warriors Throughout Time and Space*. Lanham, MD: Rowman & Littlefield, 2021.
Pyy, Elina. *Women and War in Roman Epic*. Leiden, Holland: Brill, 2020.
Rasheed, Abubakar, and Sani Abba Aliyu, eds. *Current Perspectives on African Folklore*. Zaria, Nigeria: Ahmadu Bello University, 2014.
Rose, Sarah. *The D-Day Girls*. New York: Broadway Books, 2019.
Sachs, Fruma, and Sharon Halevi. *Gendering Culture in Greater Syria*. New York: Bloomsbury, 2015.
Sankey, Margaret D. *Women and War in the 21st Century: A Country-by-Country Guide*. Santa Barbara, CA: ABC-Clio, 2018.
Schneider, Tammi Joy. *Judges*. Collegeville, MN: Liturgical Press, 2000.
Schwenkel, Christina. *The American War in Contemporary Vietnam: Transnational Remembrance and Representation*. Bloomington: Indiana University Press, 2009.
Scott-Douglass, Amy. *Enlarging Margaret: Cavendish, Shakespeare, and French Women Warriors and Writers*. London: Routledge, 2006.
Scroggins, Deborah. *Wanted Women*. New York: HarperCollins, 2012.
Singh, Khushwant. *Ranjit Singh: Maharaja of the Punjab*. Delhi: Penguin India, 2008.
Smith, Angela K. *The Second Battlefield: Women, Modernism and the First World War*. Manchester, UK: Manchester University Press, 2000.
Smith, Warren W. *China's Tibet?: Autonomy or Assimilation*. Lanham, MD: Rowman & Littlefield, 2009.
Speckhard, Anne, and Khapta Akhmedova. *Black Widows and Beyond*. London: Routledge, 2007.
Stockel, H. Henrietta. *Chiricahua Apache Women and Children: Safekeepers of the Heritage*. College Station, TX: Texas A&M University Press, 2000.
Surhone, Lambert M. *Umadevi*. Beau Bassin, Mauritius: Betascript, 2010.
Tate, G.P. *The Kingdom of Afghanistan, a Historical Sketch*. London: Bennett Coleman, 1911.
Todd, Ann. *OSS Operation Black Mail*. Annapolis, MD: Naval Institute Press, 2017.
Toler, Pamela D. *Women Warriors: An Unexpected History*. Boston: Beacon Press, 2019.
Turnbull, Stephen. *Samurai Heraldry*. New York: Bloomsbury, 2012.
———. *Samurai Women 1184–1877*. New York: Bloomsbury, 2012.
Tyldesley, Joyce A. *Chronicle of the Queens of Egypt: From Early Dynastic Times to the Death of Cleopatra*. New York: Thames & Hudson, 2006.
Vitiello, Massimiliano. *Amalasuintha: The Transformation of Queenship in the Post-Roman World*. Pittsburgh: University of Pennsylvania Press, 2017.
Woods, Jonathan. *Colonization, Piracy, and Trade in Early Modern Europe*. Cham, Switzerland, Palgrave Macmillan, 2017.
Yada-McNeal, Stephan D. *50 Women Against Hitler*. Norderstedt, Germany: Books on Demand, 2018.

Chapters and Book Articles

Adegbindin, Omotade. "Gender Advocacy in Africa: Insights from Ifá Literary Corpus" in *Being and Becoming: Gender, Culture and Shifting Identity in Sub-Saharan Africa*. Denver, CO: Spears Media, 2016, 235–248.
Agbese, Aje-Ori. "Preserving the Memories of Precolonial Nigeria: Cultural Narratives of Precolonial Heroines" in *The Routledge Companion to Black Women's Cultural Histories*. Londnon: Routledge, 2021, 89–99.
Bowd, Gavin. "Romanians of the French Résistance." *French History* 28:4 (December 2014): 541–559.
Carney, Elizabeth D. "Women and Military Leadership in Pharaonic Egypt." *Greek, Roman, and Byzantine Studies* 42 (2001): 25–41.
Casablanca, Luis. "The Women of 1819." *Latin American Post* (7 August 2019).
Esperdy, Gabrielle. "The Royal Abbey of Fonte-

vrault." *Journal of International Women's Studies* 6:2 (June 2005): 59–80.

Fisher, Max. "The Bizarre and Horrifying Story of the Lord's Resistance Army." *Atlantic* (17 October 2011).

Fox, Diane Niblack. "Fire, Spirit, Love, Story." *Journal of Vietnamese Studies* 3:2 (2008): 218–221.

Franceschini, Jacopo. "The Fatimids." *Medieval Warfare* 2:6 (2012): 9–13.

Garcia, Elena Fernandez. "Mujeres Sitiadas: La Compañía de Santa Barbara de Girona." *Dossiers Feministas* 15 (2011): 63–75.

Griswold, Eliza. "Islam and the West through the Eyes of Two Women." *New York Times* (27 January 2012).

Guo, Weiting. "The Portraits of a Heroine: Huang Bamei and the Politics of Wartime History in China and Taiwan, 1930–1960." *Cross-Currents* 33 (2019): 6–31

Ha, Quan Manh. "When Memory Speaks: Transnational Remembrances in Vietnam War Literature." *Southeast Asian Studies* 5:3 (December 2016): 463–489.

Haas, Mary E. "Women and War" in *Women in the Third World: An Encyclopedia of Contemporary Issues*. New York: Garland, 2014, 1716.

Hameso, Seyoum. "The Furra Legend in Sidama Traditions." *The Oromo Commentary* 7:2 (1997): 16–18.

Husn, Ma'n Abul. "Khawla Bint Al Zwar." *Al Shindagah* (May-June 2003).

Idoux, Guylaine. "Aviatrice, alpiniste, soldate, résistante ... entre vérité et affabulation, Marie Marvingt, l'héroïne oubliée." *Le Journal du Dimanche* (21 March 2022).

Jászberényi, Sandor. "The Mother Who Fought ISIS to the Death." *Wall Street Journal* (18 November 2014).

Lau, Maximilian. "Both General and lady." *Women and Violence in Late Medieval Mediterranean, ca. 1100–1500*. New York: Routledge, 2022.

"The Legend of La Adelita." *Del Rio Grande* (May 2018): 10–13.

Leigh, Devin. "The Origins of a Source: Edward Long, Coromantee Slave Revolts and the History of Jamaica." *Slavery & Abolition* 40:2 (2019): 295–320.

Loman, Pasi. "No Woman No War: Women's Participation in Ancient Greek Warfare." *Greece & Rome* 51:1 (April 2004).

Maier, Christoph T. "The Roles of Women in the Crusade Movement." *Journal of Medieval History* 30:1 (March 2004): 61–82.

Martin, Douglas. "Ani Pachen, Warrior Nun in Tibet Jail 21 Years, Dies." *New York Times* (18 February 2002): B7.

Martina, Luis Sola. "Una Mujer entre las Tropas de Marina del Siglo XVIII." *Revista Española de Defensa* (March 2018): 60–62.

Mayfield, Tyler. "The Accounts of Deborah (Judges 4–5) in Recent Research." *Currents in Biblical Research* 7:3 (2009): 306–335.

Millman-Brown, Randi. "The Search for Thor." *Norwegian American* (11 July 2019).

Mogelson, Luke. "Dark Victory in Raqqa." *New Yorker* (6 November 2017).

Niane, Djibril Tamsir. "The War of the Mulattos." *Black Renaissance* (22 June 2001).

"Nyabyinshi: The Warrior Virgin Princess, Her Journey." (Rwanda) *New Times* (29 September 2007).

Paddock, Richard C. "Day to Day Among the Viet Cong" *New York Times* (4 August 2006).

Parks, Sara. "Women and Gender in the Apocrypha" in *The Oxford Handbook of the Apocrypha*. Oxford, UK: Oxford University Press, 2021, 477.

Phan, Aimee. 2005. "A Daughter Returns Home—Through Her Diaries." *USA Today* (12 October 2005).

Rees, Owen. "Queens and Valkyries—Women as Warriors." *Medieval Warfare* 4:2 (2014): 6–8.

Ruutz-Rees, Caroline. "Renee, a Sixteenth-Century Nun." *Romanic Review* 13:1 (1 January 1922): 28–36.

Schulters, Alexandra W. "Subjectivity Politics in *Sorrow Mountain*." *Genders* 44 (2006).

Senovilla, Maria. "Pioneering Women in the Military." *Revista Española de Defensa* (April 2020): 53–57.

Van Oppen, Branko. "Amastris: The First Hellenistic Queen." *Ancient World Magazine* (22 October 2018).

Verde, Tom. "Malika VI: Sayyida al-Hurra." *Aramco World* 68:1 (January-February 2017): 34–37.

Walker, Crista. "Eyes Turn to Female Medic." *Spearhead* 2:1 (Spring 1991).

Zachs, Fruma, and Youval Ben-Bassat. "Women's Visibility in Petitions from Greater Syria During the Late Ottoman Period." *International Journal of Middle East Studies* 47:4 (2015): 765–781

Zhwak, Mohammad Saeed. "Women in Afghanistan History." *Afghan Digital Libraries* (1995).

Zwarenstein, Carlyn. "Legacy of a Zapatista Rebel." (Toronto) *Globe and Mail* (11 January, 2006).

Electronic Sources

Dube, Zorodzai. "The Ancestors, Violence and Democracy in Zimbabwe." *Verbum et Ecclesia*. http://www.scielo.org.za/pdf/vee/v39n1/40.pdf, 1–8.

"Interview with Rebel Leader Aya Virginia Touré." *BBC Outlook* (23 March 2011). Kakar, Palwasha. "Tribal Law of Pashtunwali and Women's Legislative Authority." http://www. law. harvard. edu/programs/ilsp/research/kakar. pdf (2004).

"Partisan Q&A Webcast with Sonia Orbuch." www.youtube.com/watch?v=-W4Dv EbComU (April 17, 2012).

"Random Scottish History." https://randomscottishhistory.com/2021/.

Index

Aceh Empire 1, 151, 281, 294, 437, 470
Achaemenid Empire 15, 19, 21–22, 42, 437
Aethelflaed 63–66, 482
Afghan War 283, 404–436
Afghanistan 22, 120, 136, 156, 166, 283, 316, 400–401, 405–406, 412–413, 415, 417–423, 425–426, 431, 433, 470
Afrika Korps 2, 387
Aisha 1, 4, 55
Akbar 120, 136–137, 149, 249
Aksum 67
Akwamu 187, 195, 470
Alabama 267, 272–273, 285, 412
Alaska 311, 416, 429, 490
Albania 23, 26–27, 32, 73–74, 78, 157, 208, 294, 299, 303–305, 313, 351–352, 357, 378–379, 382, 470
Alberta 281, 294, 355, 398, 472
Albigensian Crusade 87–88
Alexander III the Great of Macedon 21–25, 82, 257
Alexandria, Egypt 25–26, 29–33, 41, 91, 118, 215, 272
Alexios I Comnenos 73
Algeria 28, 58, 75, 132, 137, 257, 269, 274, 291–292, 362, 279, 392–393, 398, 470
Ali Pasha 141, 208, 234
Alice Network 300
Allenby, Edmund 304
Alliance Network 356
Al Qaeda 2, 404, 420, 422, 433
Alsace 302–303, 337, 376, 383–384
Amazons 3, 23
American Civil War 2, 261–283, 285
American Revolution 193, 196, 198–202
Amin, Idi 2, 432
amputation 45, 55, 59, 61, 140, 215, 265, 271, 274, 297, 310, 330, 338, 348, 416
Anglicanism 146, 158, 161, 199, 215
Angola 153, 163, 170, 248, 293, 438–439, 470
Anjou 68, 81–82, 86, 94, 109, 112, 115, 120, 212, 470
Antigua 188, 282, 470

Apache 253, 278, 283–285, 420
Aquitaine 72, 84, 86, 101, 319, 437, 470
Arab-Israeli War 388, 392, 440
Arabia 29, 39, 41, 43, 50–52, 54–55, 57, 143, 234, 440, 470
Aragon 75, 79, 94, 103, 104, 108–109, 118, 123, 131, 133, 148, 224, 233, 248, 292
Arapaho 274, 279–280
Arauco War 132, 146, 154
Arawak 138, 186, 195
Archer 1, 7, 10–11, 14–15, 17–18, 26, 29, 31, 33, 38, 42, 44, 48, 50–52, 55, 61–62, 69, 76–80, 84, 86–88, 90, 92–93, 95–96, 98, 100–102, 104, 112, 113, 130, 133, 135–137, 150, 155, 160, 163, 168, 197, 213, 245, 441
Argentina 149, 220–221, 225, 228, 238, 247, 276, 355, 395, 402, 470–471
Argos 3, 12, 16–17, 25, 242, 471
Arizona 252, 283, 285, 399, 407, 410, 490
Arkansas 262–263, 267, 271–274, 490
Armenia 13, 30–32, 38, 42–43, 59, 62, 80, 91, 297, 345, 406, 435, 471
Armenian genocide 304, 310
Ashanti 186, 194, 291, 271
Assyria 4, 13–14, 22, 394, 471
Ataturk 309, 320
Athens 22, 25, 29, 32, 147, 242–243, 337, 362, 381–382, 398, 471
Augustus 4, 32–34, 36, 41; *see also* Octavian
Aurangzeb 167, 172–173, 178–180, 239
Auschwitz-Birkenau 1, 293, 336, 341–342, 351, 360–361, 363, 371, 373, 379–380, 382–383
Australia 220, 328, 404, 406, 418, 433, 471
Austrasia 49, 61, 437, 471
Austria 38–39, 58, 39, 78, 141, 171, 173, 175, 178, 188–189, 191, 194, 206–209, 212–213, 217, 219, 221, 224, 243, 252–255, 268, 274, 277, 285, 298–302, 304, 317–318, 321, 334, 337–340, 364, 370, 372, 374, 385, 406, 440, 471
Aymara 202–204, 225

Azerbaijan 59, 62, 297, 301, 347, 435, 471
Aztec 124, 126

Babur 2, 120–121
Babylonia 7, 13–15
Bactria 4, 22, 471
Bali 97, 151
Bangladesh 316, 382, 396, 437
Bantu 287, 292
Barbados 176, 195, 400, 471
Barbarossa 133, 184, 339
Barbie, Klaus 331, 336, 362
Barons' War 88–89, 92–93
Bavaria 39, 101, 106, 138, 174, 188, 215, 224, 277, 302, 307, 328, 351, 471
Beijing 50, 68, 150, 160, 170, 291, 420
Belarus 195, 231, 248, 268, 293, 300–301, 327, 345, 348, 350–351, 357, 359–360, 363, 371, 375–376, 379, 381, 471
Belgium 34, 71, 98, 143, 145, 168, 172, 178, 189, 205–206, 208, 233, 254, 286, 288–289, 300–303, 319, 323, 329–330, 333, 335, 340, 342, 349, 353–354, 382, 386, 393, 398, 421, 424, 440, 471–472
Belize 400
Bengal 1, 124, 143, 197, 314–316, 328, 352–353, 396, 428, 437, 472
Benin 105, 123–124, 135, 142, 182, 207, 250, 256, 290, 472
Bergen-Belsen 350, 360
Biafra 393
Bialystok Ghetto Uprising 369
Black Death 95, 99, 100–101, 104
Black Widows 5, 404, 406, 408, 426
Blackfoot 2, 245, 250, 294, 366
Bohemia 3, 59, 360, 381, 437, 472
Boko Haram 424
Bolivar, Simon 2, 230–231, 234–235, 240–241, 243, 246–247
Bolivia 164, 202, 204, 225, 228, 230, 234, 246, 248, 283, 395, 472
Bosnia 157, 194, 279, 304, 338
Bosporus 20, 31, 34, 43, 99, 472
Botswana 244, 293, 431
Brahmanism 56, 70, 315, 396
Brazil 163, 167, 170, 178, 228, 238, 242–244, 248–249, 255, 273,

499

276, 287, 321–322, 431–433, 472, 484
Britannia 4, 10, 13–14, 36–37; *see also* Great Britain
British Columbia 250, 472
British East India Company 197, 219, 245, 249, 259
Brittany 72, 86, 99–100, 103, 108–109, 176, 193, 209, 212, 369, 437, 472
Bronze Age 4, 7–9
Brule 280
Buddhism 57, 65, 85, 107, 142, 155–156, 339, 384, 388
Buffalo Soldiers 274
Bulgaria 99, 207, 285, 295, 299, 303, 312, 337–338, 381, 391, 393, 437, 472
Burgundy 49, 61–62, 66, 74, 78, 80, 106–107, 109, 116, 127, 175, 472
Burkina Faso 77, 433, 438
Burma 134, 205, 258, 366
Burundi 386, 418
Byzantium 3, 43–45, 47–48, 52–54, 60, 67, 70, 73, 76, 83, 99, 219, 437, 472

Calamity Jane 1, 279
Cameroon 240
Canaan 11
Canada 175, 187–188, 193, 245, 262, 281, 294, 303–304, 311, 317, 319, 341, 349–355, 366, 378, 383, 389, 393, 398, 401, 404, 417, 421, 431–432, 439, 472; Alberta 281, 294, 355, 398, 472; British Columbia 250, 472; New Brunswick 262, 473; Newfoundland 69, 187–188, 228, 432, 440, 473; Nova Scotia 163, 203, 228, 389, 401, 473; Ontario 233, 265, 294, 312–313, 319, 353–354, 401, 417, 473; Quebec 175, 198, 303, 354–355, 439, 473; Saskatchewan 277, 353, 439, 473
Canadian Women's Army Corps 353, 389
Caria 18, 21, 473
Carthage 27–28, 47–48, 58, 473
Castile 75, 78–79, 93, 104, 117–118, 126–127, 130–131, 133, 195, 223, 278, 284, 287, 473
Castro, Fidel 378, 390, 395
Catalonia 1, 94, 103, 109, 173, 212, 437, 473
Catholics 68, 72–73, 103, 110, 117–118, 120, 129, 131–132, 137, 140–141, 146, 148, 161–162, 171, 175, 181, 189, 196, 205, 211–212, 216, 250, 279, 293, 322, 338–339, 342, 345, 358, 372
Celts 16, 20, 36–37, 440
Central African Republic 432
Chad 433
Chalcis 48, 337, 473
Chariot Warfare 4, 7, 9, 11, 13, 19, 27, 38, 61, 208, 443

Charles I of England 158–162
Chechnya 404–408, 411, 414, 426, 473
Cherokee 193
Cheyenne 4, 274–275, 277, 279–280, 294
Child, Julia 1, 358–359, 465, 490
Chile 132, 146, 154, 164, 201, 225, 235, 239, 247–248, 283, 333–334, 354, 473
China 2, 4, 8, 17–19, 26, 35–36, 40–42, 46, 50–51, 54–58, 67–68, 70–71, 80, 87–88, 93, 101–103, 107, 114–115, 136, 150, 160–161, 170, 176, 192, 210, 214, 222–223, 256, 258, 291–293, 295, 310, 312–314, 320, 386, 388, 397, 403, 420, 440
Chinese Women's Army 295
Churchill, Winston 323, 325–326, 335
CIA 332, 358–359, 369, 388, 390–391, 398, 439
Cilicia 13, 32–33, 60, 77, 80, 91, 474
Cleopatra VII 1, 31–33, 247, 441, 444, 460, 464, 466–467, 475
Cochise 285
Colombia 130, 142, 176, 195, 202, 228–229, 231, 235–236, 238–241, 246–247, 249, 431
Colonial wars 178–196
Colorado 250, 253, 274–275, 399, 430
Combat Terrorist Movement 342
Comet Line 309, 340–341
Communism 5, 248, 299, 311–314, 318–320, 335, 338–339, 341, 342, 345–346, 348, 351–353, 360, 362, 364, 367, 370, 374–375, 377–379, 388, 390, 394, 397
concubines 58, 91, 152, 155
Congo 186, 285–286, 340, 386, 393, 418, 433, 471, 474
Connecticut 169, 333, 398
Conquistador/Conquistadora 123–124, 130, 132, 146, 438
Constantinople 43–44, 47, 67, 73, 76–78, 99, 113, 164, 166, 241, 254, 257, 310, 438
Corfu 27, 74, 299, 304–305, 383
Corinth 17, 24, 27
Cornwall 10, 14, 144, 474
Corsica 211–213, 305, 342, 361, 371, 475
Cortes, Hernan 124, 12
Costa Rica 195, 258, 475
Counting Coup 281, 394, 438
Cree 353
Creek Tribe 193
Crete 4, 25, 27, 33, 67, 164
Crimean War 255, 257, 279
Croatia 26–27, 104, 157, 171, 253, 279, 298, 307, 338, 437, 475
Croix Rouge 386
Cromwell, Oliver 159–161, 164, 166
Crook, George 279

Crow Tribe 250, 257, 277, 279–280, 297
Crusades 1, 5, 45, 72–94, 438, 445, 464
Cuba 124, 235, 248, 250–251, 262, 276, 278, 378, 390, 392, 395, 475
Curaçao 183, 475
Custer, George Armstrong 4, 271, 277, 279–280
Cyprus 16, 18, 25, 29–31, 33, 86, 90–91, 93, 114, 433, 475
Cyrenaica 26, 58, 438, 475
Cyrene 16, 26, 33
Cyrus II the Great 14–15, 19, 38
Czechoslovakia 59, 268, 297, 307, 317, 320, 334, 338, 372, 377, 381–383, 396, 431, 440, 475

D-Day 331, 370, 377–378
Dachau 322, 331, 345, 362, 369, 372
Dahomey 182–183, 207, 256, 475
Dakota 267, 279
Danish West Indies 187
Darius I 19, 22
Darius II 15, 22–23
Day of the Colombian Woman 238
Deborah 1, 10–12, 71, 108, 227, 443, 444, 478
De Gaulle, Charles 372, 377, 379–380
Delaware Tribe 193
Denmark 45–46, 62–65, 70, 72, 76, 80, 102, 107, 110, 112–113, 115, 122–128, 166, 179–180, 184, 204, 244, 254, 282, 326, 329, 331, 375, 378, 384, 393, 421, 438–439, 475
Diraar ben al-Azwar 52–53
Djibouti 418
Donkeyman Network 365
drones 5, 402, 434, 455
Dutch East India Company 180, 184, 192
Dutch East Indies 168, 245, 279, 373, 475

Ecuador 125, 130, 154, 218–219, 227–229, 243, 246, 284, 286, 378, 382, 398, 435, 475
Edelweiss Pirates 328
Edessa 81–82, 475
Egypt 4, 8, 10–11, 14, 16, 18, 24–34, 39, 41, 43, 52, 54, 70, 75, 89–91, 93, 142, 215, 234, 243, 304, 338, 380, 387, 391–392, 400, 434, 439, 475
Eighth Crusade 92
El Salvador 229, 382, 396, 398, 476
Elizabeth I 1, 14, 138, 140, 144, 146, 151, 444, 465, 476
Elizabeth II 400, 407, 417
England 10, 14, 36, 47, 57–58, 61, 63–66, 70, 75, 79, 81, 83, 47, 57–59, 61, 63–66, 70, 75, 79, 81–83, 86, 88–89, 92–96, 98, 100–101, 103, 105–109, 111,

114–115, 125, 133–134, 138–142, 144–148, 151, 158–162, 164–165, 161, 170, 173–174, 176–177, 179, 181, 183–191, 193, 197, 207, 209, 213, 215–216, 220, 223, 230, 233, 244, 246, 249, 273–274, 288, 291, 299, 301, 303–306, 308, 310, 314–315, 317–320, 322–324, 327, 329, 332–333, 336, 338–341, 343–344, 350, 352–356, 360–362, 364, 375–378, 381–382, 384, 386, 400–402, 416–417, 419, 422–423, 425, 439–440, 474–476; see also Britannia; Great Britain
English Civil War 159–162, 164
Ephesus 19, 26, 31, 33, 82
Epirus 23, 25, 227, 208, 476
Estonia 139, 184, 439, 476
Ethiopia 34, 42, 52, 67–68, 75, 105, 287, 340, 382, 418, 477

Faisal I 311, 390
Fante 186, 194
Fascists 5, 295, 312–313, 317–319, 321–323, 326–328, 330–332, 335, 338, 342, 344–346, 352, 357–358, 364, 367–370, 374–375, 377, 379–382, 386, 439
Fatimids 69–70
FBI 389, 420
Fedayeen 407
Finland 45, 110, 118, 122–124, 139, 149–150, 182, 184, 227, 324, 386, 439, 477
First Crusade 72, 76–78, 80
First Indochina War 2, 386
Flanders 71, 76–77, 80, 84, 92, 97, 99, 101, 127, 129, 145, 191, 301, 477
Flathead 245, 281
Florida 188, 262, 285, 354, 357, 430, 490
Fourth Crusade 79
France 39, 49, 61–62, 66, 68, 71, 75, 77–82, 86, 88–91, 94, 96, 98–100, 102–103, 108–109, 112–113, 115–116, 118, 128, 133, 140–141, 147–148, 156–157, 159–160, 162–163, 165, 173, 175, 178, 181, 185, 188–189, 192, 205–209, 218, 222, 231–232, 237, 250, 266, 269, 272, 278, 291, 300–302, 306, 308, 317–323, 325, 328–329, 331–333, 335, 340–341, 348–352, 354–357, 360–365, 368–370, 372, 374–379, 383–384, 387, 391–392, 395, 398, 404, 410, 421, 433, 437–440, 477–478; see also Franks
Franks 13, 47, 49, 61–62, 66, 77, 91
French and Indian War 175, 186, 193
French East India Company 191
French Foreign Legion 387
French Red Cross 303
French Resistance 4, 303, 319, 323, 325, 332, 336, 342, 345, 348, 350, 356, 360, 362, 372, 377–378, 380, 496
French Revolution 206, 208, 211–213, 215–216, 303
Frisia 1, 71, 105, 117, 120–121, 185, 438, 478
Fulani 135, 250, 290

Gaddafi, Muammar 421–423
Galatia 20, 28, 478
Galicia 79, 132, 147, 213, 220, 298–302, 307, 438
Galilee 11, 387–388, 478
Gambia 423, 478
Geatland 4, 45–46, 61, 438, 478
Genghis Khan 4, 87–89, 93, 115, 120
Genoa 78, 99, 110, 113, 141, 188, 213, 377, 478
Genocide 89, 216, 292, 304, 310, 320, 326, 338, 359–360, 371, 380, 438, 440
Georgia (country) 87, 143, 154, 297, 309, 478
Georgia (state) 193, 199, 201, 261, 264, 266–267, 270, 272, 297, 394, 421, 423, 431, 435, 490
German South West Africa 292, 478
Germanicus 34–36
Germany 35, 39, 84, 200, 299–301, 305, 307–308, 317, 322–324, 329, 341, 343, 346–347, 349–353, 369–372, 374, 376, 379, 404, 406, 409–410, 414, 416, 419, 421, 423, 430; see also Gestapo; Nazis; SS
Geronimo 278, 284–285
Gestapo 300, 305, 321–323, 326, 328–329, 331–337, 344–346, 349, 351–353, 355–357, 360–365, 369, 371, 373–375, 377–378, 386, 438
Ghana 74, 176, 186–187, 194–195, 248, 291, 409, 418, 422, 431, 438, 478
Gibraltar 75, 131, 189, 209, 220, 333, 336, 340, 349, 352, 377
Gloria Network 335
Gold Coast 186, 248, 291, 438, 478
Goths 43–45, 47–48
Great Britain 178, 182, 209, 230, 245, 251, 318, 343, 391, 403, 406–407, 421, 434, 437; see also Britannia; United Kingdom
Great Nordic War 179–184
Great Sioux War 279
Greece 12, 17–19, 22, 24–25, 27, 29, 31–33, 39, 64, 73, 99, 114, 141, 147, 164, 207–208, 242–243, 299, 337, 362, 381–382, 398, 437, 439, 471, 478
Greenland 61, 122, 439
Grenada 235, 478
Grenadines 402
Guadeloupe 218, 479
Guam 142, 149, 292, 399
Guatemala 4, 56, 382, 398, 401, 479
Guerrilla War 4, 11, 35, 40, 43, 50, 60, 91, 103, 130, 128, 130, 146, 169, 171, 173, 178, 186, 201–202, 208, 214, 216–217, 228–231, 237, 242, 244–247, 251, 264, 266, 268, 273, 279, 281, 284, 287, 290, 294, 303, 312–314, 316, 320–321, 328, 330–331, 337–338, 344, 346, 351, 362, 364, 369–370, 377–379, 382, 388, 390, 392–397, 401, 406, 408, 414, 417, 427, 431, 438, 451
Guevara, Che 395
Guinea 1, 142, 176, 250, 438, 479
Guiscard, Robert 72–74
Gustav I Vasa 126–127
Guyana 195
Gypsies 321, 338, 340, 363, 372

Hainaut 82, 97, 101–102, 208, 479
Haiti 2, 123, 176, 187, 207, 209, 218, 251, 399, 433, 438
Han Dynasty 35, 40, 46, 50, 295
Hatshepsut 8, 458, 475
Hausa 135, 138, 142, 154, 290
Hawaii 235, 241, 290, 366, 391, 399, 411, 430, 434, 438, 490
Henry IV 73–74, 76, 111
Heraclius 52–53
Hinduism 4, 7, 20, 23, 65, 70, 91, 98, 120, 137, 156, 173, 197, 259, 396, 437, 479
Hispaniola 123, 207, 209, 218, 251, 428, 440, 479
Hitler, Adolf 317, 321–322, 326, 328, 335, 339, 346, 359, 369, 378, 382, 385
Hmong 150
Ho-Chunk 185–186
Holland 37, 94, 97, 101–102, 120, 127, 143, 145–146, 156, 160, 162, 165, 168, 172–174, 178–179, 184–185, 191–192, 204, 216–217, 220, 233–234, 237, 258, 266, 281, 294, 300, 327, 329–331, 383, 341, 349, 354, 362, 373, 381–382, 384, 393, 406, 348, 440, 479
Holy Roman Empire 73–74, 76, 81, 84, 97, 112, 123, 127, 129, 133, 157, 172, 175, 179, 191, 437, 479
Honduras 229, 382
Hong Kong 292, 310, 354, 439, 479
Hopi 407
Huguenots 137, 140–141, 147
Hundred Years' War 101, 103–104, 106, 108–110, 112, 120
Hungary 102, 104, 107, 171, 108, 243, 252–253, 255, 268, 285, 295, 298–300, 302–304, 307, 321, 327, 338–339, 370, 372, 379–380, 437, 471, 479
Hunkpapa 277
Hussein, Saddam 401, 409, 412, 415, 422

Iceland 3–4, 61, 63, 69, 115, 122, 439, 479
Idaho 250, 282, 490

502　Index

Illini 185
Illinois 196, 266–268, 271–273, 399, 413, 415, 490
Illyria 24, 26–27, 38, 479
Inca 20, 125, 130–131, 201, 203, 221, 240, 479
India 7, 13, 29, 56, 70, 83, 89, 91–92, 97, 101, 119–120, 128, 132, 134, 136–139, 143, 149, 159, 167, 170, 172–174, 178–180, 191, 197–198, 208, 213, 219, 245, 248, 258–259, 296, 315–316, 319, 322, 328, 323, 361, 366, 388, 391, 396, 399–400, 402–403, 428–429, 433, 437, 439, 472, 479–480, 484
Indiana 264, 267, 413, 490
Indonesia 56, 98, 150–151, 192, 245, 279, 294, 373, 412, 437
Inquisition 109–110, 119
Inupiat 311
Iowa 186, 271, 398, 406, 490
Iran 14–15, 17, 19, 21–23, 29–30, 32–33, 38–40, 43, 53–54, 57, 59–60, 72, 91, 129, 143, 154, 257, 345, 352, 401, 412, 419, 428, 439, 440
Iraq 5, 13–15, 22, 38–39, 41, 52, 55, 70, 310, 387, 390, 394, 399–401, 406–407, 409–411, 417–419, 421–422, 425, 427–430, 432, 439, 480
Iraq War 5, 410–411, 417–419, 421–422, 425, 428, 430
Ireland 61, 63–64, 68, 82, 86, 96, 106, 112, 137–140, 144, 149, 158–159, 173–174, 183, 185, 198–199, 209, 211, 215, 226–228, 230, 262, 266, 276, 285, 305–306, 324, 329, 352, 354, 480
Irish Rebellion of 1641 158–159
Iron Age 10–45, 65, 438
Iroquois Confederacy 1, 175, 193
ISIS 427–249, 431
Islam 4, 48, 50–52, 54–56, 58, 60, 68, 89, 118, 124, 135, 143, 154, 166–167, 185, 207, 234, 259, 290, 406, 408, 414, 418, 425, 427, 431–432, 435, 437–438; *see also* Muslims
Israel 7, 10–14, 30, 33, 52–53, 85, 293, 304, 336–337, 353, 360, 380, 387–388, 391–392, 405–417, 427, 434–438, 440, 480; *see also* Jerusalem; Jews; Zionism
Italy 16, 20, 24, 27–28, 32, 37–38, 47–48, 62, 71–74, 76, 83, 99, 103, 106, 112, 129, 174–175, 178, 188, 208, 210, 213, 215–217, 254–255, 262, 287, 327, 331, 352, 356, 358–359, 367, 374, 377, 387, 398, 400, 421, 435, 437, 440, 480; *see also* Augustus; Germanicus; Julius Caesar; Romans
Ivory Coast 422, 480

Jabin 10–12
Jael 4, 11, 46, 157, 177, 442, 478
Jainism 70, 136

Jamaica 157, 176, 184, 186, 194–195, 230, 247, 276, 289, 402, 407, 480
Japan 2, 5, 40, 55–56, 58, 84–86, 132, 136, 138–139, 142, 144–145, 148, 152–153, 155, 157, 275, 286, 290, 292–293, 298, 309–310, 318, 320, 325, 346–347, 358–359, 391, 406, 426, 437–440, 458, 481
Java 56, 97, 151, 192, 237, 245, 281–282, 340, 375, 481
Jerusalem 13, 38, 52, 70, 76–78, 80–82, 85, 90–91, 129, 304, 342, 383, 388, 391, 405, 435
Jews 1, 3, 20, 29, 38, 51, 59, 131, 242, 293, 304, 307, 311, 317–319, 321–326, 328–331, 333–343, 345–346, 348–351, 353, 356–363, 369, 371–373, 375–376, 379–384, 386, 405, 427, 435, 458
Joan of Arc 1, 108–110, 116, 133, 225, 312, 388, 442, 444, 446, 448–449, 457–458, 460, 464, 466–468, 477
Jordan 3, 11, 33, 39, 41, 53–54, 78, 386–387, 392, 405, 432, 481
Judea 12, 38, 41, 391, 435, 481
Juh 284
Julius Caesar 31–33, 37
Jutland 45, 61, 64–65, 254, 481

Kansas 253, 274, 389–390, 402
Kashmir 65, 156, 219, 239, 249, 481
Kazakhstan 15, 17, 298, 406, 434, 481
Kelantan 167, 481
Kentucky 264–266, 268–269, 415, 490
Kenya 400, 417–418
KGB 309, 312, 320
Khalid bin Walid 52–54
Khazaria 59, 481
Khoi 292
Kiowa 412
Knights Hospitallers and Knights of Malta 141
Knights Templar 91
Kongo 153, 163, 167, 170, 438, 481
Kootenai 245, 281
Korea 40, 54–56, 58, 136, 146, 150, 286, 296, 314, 357, 399, 412, 414, 440, 481
Korean War 314
Kosovo 38, 294, 313, 419, 422
Kublai Khan 87, 93
Kurds 257, 320, 394, 401, 415, 427–428, 431
Kush 4, 23, 29, 33–34, 38, 42, 67, 481
Kuwait 13, 22, 38–39, 52, 406–407, 410–412, 414, 432, 439

Lakota 277, 279–280
Laos 245–246
Latvia 139, 247, 268, 393, 433, 439
Lebanon 8, 11, 33, 41, 78, 304, 312, 339, 386, 417, 432–434, 439

Lemnos 113, 481
Lenni Lenape 193
León 78–79, 481
Leonardo da Vinci 123
Liberia 409, 422, 481
Libya 9, 16, 26, 33, 49, 47, 58, 421–424, 438, 481–482
Lithuania 108, 139, 159, 179, 195, 247–248, 252, 268, 293, 322, 324, 327, 333, 345, 380, 482
Lombardy 73, 76, 482
Lorraine 76–77, 108–110, 158, 303, 323, 384, 482
Louis IX 89–91
Louis XVI 205, 208, 211
Louisiana 176, 185, 187, 262, 272, 274, 490
Luftwaffe 1, 332, 348, 364, 367, 380–381, 385, 439
Luxembourg 97, 104, 107, 145, 188, 206, 322, 330
Lycia 3, 7, 31, 482
Lydia 14–15

Macedonia 21–25, 27, 38, 207, 285, 294–295, 299, 304–305, 312, 337, 351, 483
Madagascar 355
Madeira 400–401, 482
Magic 55, 71, 109, 186, 205, 219, 256, 288
Magna Carta 86, 89
Maine 68, 198, 252, 263–264, 490
Malacca 124, 150, 294, 482
Malaysia 48, 167, 205, 366
Mali 77, 135, 142, 433
Malta 215, 254, 306, 482
Manchu 88, 150, 160, 170, 214, 293, 295, 314, 318
Mao Zedong 313–314
Maori 220, 272
Mapuche 132, 146, 154
Maratha Empire 170–171, 173, 178, 197, 209, 213, 219
Marianas Islands 399
Marie Antoinette 205
Mark Antony 31–33
Maroons 164, 167, 170, 186, 194, 218
martial arts 1, 16, 18, 24, 35, 42, 46, 52, 54, 67, 80, 107, 119, 132, 136, 150, 157, 160–161, 170, 172, 197, 214, 217, 244, 256, 275, 291, 217, 320, 413, 429, 439, 451–452
Martyrs 1, 23, 27, 49, 60, 63, 76–77, 108, 110, 128–129, 131, 137–138, 142–143, 147, 168–169, 179, 187, 196, 201, 204, 209, 215, 218, 223, 230, 237–239, 241–242, 258, 270, 275, 304, 312, 315–316, 334, 336, 346, 348, 353, 355, 357, 369–370, 372–373, 378, 383, 386, 388, 392, 404, 406, 408, 414, 427–428, 435
Maryland 186, 265, 269–271, 309, 331–332, 335, 400, 422, 490
Massachusetts 169, 177, 198, 202,

Index

204, 233, 262, 264, 270, 305, 397, 420, 490
Mauritania 41, 75, 237, 433
Mauritius 352, 482
Maya 49, 56, 181, 401, 439
Medes 13, 15, 17, 22–23, 40
Melanesia 237
Mercia 46, 54, 57, 63–66, 110, 439, 482
Meroë 28, 34, 38, 42, 439, 482
Mesopotamia 7, 13, 15, 22, 38–39, 52, 439, 482
Mesquaki 185
Mexican-American War 252–253
Mexico 49, 65, 124, 126, 149, 181, 237, 241, 248, 252–253, 258, 278, 284–285, 290, 297, 310, 320, 313, 390, 396, 401, 409, 438–440, 482; *see also* Maya
MI5 1, 314, 318–319, 322–323, 328, 344, 354, 439
MI6 300, 318, 439
Michigan 261–262, 265, 268, 347, 355, 412, 490
Milan 112–113, 118, 121, 175, 212, 254, 377, 482
Miles, Nelson A. 280
Ming Dynasty 115, 136, 150, 160–161
Mingo Seneca 193
Minnesota 265–267, 490
Minutewomen 2, 198
Mississippi 185, 258, 264, 266–268, 271–272, 424, 490
Missouri 252–253, 257, 264, 266, 272–274, 279, 324, 347, 435, 490
Mohawk 175, 199, 233
Moldavia 165–166, 255, 307
Molucca 235, 237, 482
Mongolia 4, 8, 46, 87–89, 91, 93, 102–103, 115, 120, 144, 176–177, 429, 482
Montana 2, 4, 257, 274–275, 277, 279–281, 294, 366, 405, 490–491
Montenegro 27, 279, 287, 295, 299, 303
Moors 47, 101, 113–119, 132–133, 136, 148, 159
Moravia 67, 213, 219, 437
Morocco 74–75, 81, 118, 131–132, 148, 185, 277, 292, 325, 376, 392, 398, 482
Mozambique 397, 433
Mughal Empire 2, 120, 136–137, 149, 156, 167, 170, 172–173, 178–180, 213, 219, 239
Muhammad 4, 50–53, 55, 75, 111, 118–119
Muskogee 193
Muslims 20, 50–55, 57, 59–60, 62, 67, 70, 72, 74–78, 80–82, 85, 87, 89–91, 100, 108, 111, 113, 115, 119, 131, 133–143, 147, 150, 154, 166, 179, 208, 216, 234, 242, 248, 258–259, 279, 281, 294, 338, 352, 361, 388, 392, 404–405, 408–409, 411–412, 422, 427–429, 433, 437; *see also* Islam

Namibia 292–293
Nana 278, 284–285
Naples 48, 74, 90, 104, 106, 109, 123, 141, 175, 262, 371
Napoleon 4–5, 194, 210–235, 237, 297
Napoleonic Wars 222, 224, 233, 303
Natchez 186–187
National Guard 206, 208, 241, 278, 389, 395–396, 406, 409, 411–413, 415–416, 425–426, 430, 434–435
NATO 393, 415, 418, 421, 423–425, 433
Navarre 94, 137, 210, 483
Nazi Holocaust 292, 299, 336, 351, 358, 360, 383
Nazis 5, 293, 295, 302, 311, 313, 317, 319, 321, 323–325, 327–328, 330–338, 341–368, 370–382, 384–386, 437–439; *see also* SS
Nebraska 256, 274, 418, 491
Nelson, Horatio 215, 220
Nepal 249, 259, 388, 399, 427, 483
Netherlands 37, 94, 97, 101–102, 120, 127, 143, 145–146, 156, 160, 162, 165, 168, 172–174, 178–179, 184–185, 191–192, 204, 216–217, 220, 233–234, 237, 258, 266, 281, 294, 300, 327, 329, 330–331, 383, 341, 349, 354, 373, 381–382, 384, 393, 406, 348, 440, 479
Nevada 282, 399, 491
New Brunswick 262, 473
New France 175, 439
New Hampshire 177, 199, 202, 491
New Jersey 199–200, 267–268, 491
New Mexico 253, 274, 278, 284–285, 313, 399, 413, 491
New York 198–200, 203–204, 261–262, 265, 267, 271–272, 274, 276, 331, 335, 340, 350, 355, 360, 373, 384, 389, 394, 400–401, 404, 430–431, 491
New Zealand 220, 271, 328, 483
Newfoundland 69, 187–188, 228, 432, 440, 473
Nicaragua 195, 258, 395–396, 398, 483
Nietzsche, Friedrich 377
Niger 424, 433
Nigeria 94, 123, 135, 138, 142, 154, 156, 387, 393–394, 409, 418, 422, 424, 439, 483
Night Witches 5, 317, 344, 348–349, 364–365, 368, 385
Nili Network 304
Nine Years' War 175, 184
Normandy 72–82, 84, 86, 103, 106, 129, 165, 344, 370, 376, 378, 483
Norse 45, 61–64, 69, 439
North Carolina 185, 261, 264–266, 270–271, 366, 425, 435, 491
Norway 45–46, 62–64, 70, 119, 113–114, 122–123, 126, 155, 179–181, 183–184, 217, 321–322, 324, 329–330, 335, 345, 364, 385–386, 393, 421, 425–427, 433–439, 483
Nova Scotia 163, 203, 228, 389, 401, 473
Numidia 4, 27–28, 41, 58, 483

Octavian 31–33; *see also* Augustus
Oglala 274, 280
Ohio 193, 196, 207, 263–265, 269, 272, 286, 340, 423, 491
Ojibwa 258, 286
Oneida 175, 199
Ontario 233, 265, 294, 312–313, 319, 353–354, 401, 417, 473
Operation Barbarossa 339–340
Oregon 292, 491
OSS 1, 318, 331, 358–359, 439
Ostrogoths 47, 483
Ottoman Empire 107, 113, 122, 131, 133–134, 141, 143, 147, 157, 159, 164, 166, 172, 178, 195, 207–208, 215, 234, 242–243, 254, 257, 279, 281, 294–295, 297, 299, 304, 309–310, 312–313, 320, 438, 483

Paiute 282
Pakistan 7, 23, 65, 216, 239, 248, 391, 396–397, 404, 420, 428, 439, 483
Palestine 3, 11–12, 27, 41, 43, 53–54, 72, 76, 78, 85, 93, 254, 304, 328, 336, 359–360, 369, 379, 391–392, 405, 407, 417, 435, 483
Palmyra 41–42, 483
Pamunkey 169
Panama 407, 422, 483
Papua New Guinea 417, 483
Paraguay 2, 131, 228, 273, 276–277, 483
Paraguayan War 2, 273, 276
paratroopers 5, 318, 327–329, 333, 335, 339, 346–347, 349, 352, 355, 360, 362, 368, 370–371, 373, 375–377, 380, 382, 385–386, 388, 391–392, 394, 399, 421, 423, 425, 429–430, 433, 435, 455
Parthia 15, 17, 30, 32–33, 38–40, 62, 439, 483
Pat Line 329
Pend d'Oreilles 250
Pennsylvania 186, 193, 196, 198–200, 202, 231, 269–270, 308, 311, 491
Persepolis 19, 21–22
Persia 13–16, 18–19, 21–23, 41, 43, 48, 52, 54, 60, 62, 91, 143, 149, 166–167, 309, 437–438, 483–484
Peru 46, 125, 130, 132, 148, 154, 164, 201–203, 225, 228, 238, 242–243, 246–248, 283–284, 378, 386, 438, 484
Philby, Kim 314, 318, 329
Philip II of Macedon 23–24
Philippines 5, 100, 136, 148, 196, 288–292, 296, 310, 346–347, 397, 399, 438, 484

Picardy 109, 129, 172, 484
piracy 5, 35, 45, 61, 67, 89, 111, 115, 131, 136–137, 141, 144, 151, 154, 156–157, 164, 166, 176, 181, 183–188, 201–202, 217, 220, 222, 227–228, 241, 243, 276, 310, 320, 456
Pitcher, Molly 1, 199–200
Pizarro, Francisco 130, 132
Poland 1, 59, 139, 159, 179, 212, 222, 224, 247–248, 268, 293, 297–302, 304, 307, 309, 311, 318, 323–324, 326–327, 330, 334, 336, 341, 345–346, 348, 351, 353, 359–360, 363, 365, 369, 371, 373, 375, 379–383, 406, 438, 439–440, 484
Pomerania 107, 110, 179, 181, 184, 227, 299, 349
Ponca 256
Portugal 104, 117, 124, 127, 131–134, 136, 143, 146, 148–149, 151, 163, 167, 170, 173, 178, 180, 209, 212, 223, 230, 233, 238, 242–244, 249, 325, 329, 400, 431, 438, 484
Provence 62, 78, 83, 88, 90, 92, 322, 484
Prussia 166, 188, 194, 208, 216–217, 221–222, 224, 232–234, 254, 268, 277, 270, 298–299, 318, 321, 332, 348, 376, 381, 385, 484–485
Ptolemy I 24–25
Puerto Rico 229, 275, 389–390, 410, 485
Punic Wars 27–28
Punjab 156, 179, 208–209, 216, 239, 248–249, 295–296, 316, 428, 439, 485
Puritanism 160–162, 177, 440

Qatar 421, 432
Qing Dynasty 160, 170, 256, 258, 291, 293, 295, 297, 440
Quebec 175, 198, 303, 354–355, 439, 473
Quechua 203–204, 225

Rangers 1, 169, 269, 393, 423, 425, 430, 435, 440, 458
Ravensbrück 299, 309, 320–321, 332–334, 336, 340, 342, 345, 349–350, 352, 356, 360–361, 369, 372–373, 376
Red Crescent 311, 392
Red Cross 176, 302–303, 306, 311, 317, 329, 332–334, 339–340, 357, 361, 365, 369, 373, 384, 386, 406, 422, 426, 430, 440; *see also* White Buses
Renaissance 45, 95, 115, 121, 122–497
Rhode Island 169, 200–201, 265, 410, 491
Rhodes 21, 25, 29, 383
Rhodesia 288, 397
Righteous Among the Nations 293, 317, 322, 331, 334, 343, 345, 349, 356, 358, 361, 363, 371–372, 379, 382
Roman Empire 4, 28, 33–34, 36–44, 52, 91, 249, 437–438, 440, 485
Roman Monarchy 16, 485
Roman Nose 274–275
Roman Republic 22, 26–27, 30–33, 485
Romania 165, 253–255, 257, 281, 304, 307, 319–320, 324–325, 328, 335, 339, 348–349, 393, 437, 440, 485
Romanovs 195, 242, 247, 284, 440
Romans 2, 27–28, 32, 47, 64, 298, 438, 440
Rommel, Erwin 387
Russia 67, 139, 165, 182, 184, 194, 206–207, 217, 219, 222, 227, 231–232, 234, 242, 247, 252–253, 268, 277, 278–279, 281, 284, 299–302, 307–309, 317–319, 323–324, 329, 333, 343–344, 346–347, 350–351, 357–358, 368, 379, 386, 399, 402, 404–406, 408, 414, 425–426, 430, 434, 437–439; *see also* White Russians
Russian Empire 159, 222, 247, 293, 298, 300, 309, 311, 327, 339, 347, 350, 359, 363, 485
Russian Soviet Federation 348–349, 364–365, 367, 371, 381, 385, 485–486
Rwanda 288–289, 292, 433, 489

Safavids 143, 154, 166–167, 440
St. Croix 49, 282, 489
St. Vincent 402
Saladin 85
Samaria 13, 435, 486
Samurai 84–87, 132, 139, 142, 145, 148, 152, 157, 275, 440
San Salvador 229, 398
Sandinistas 395–396, 398
Santo Domingo 228, 251
Sardinia 90, 103–104, 141, 175, 254, 486
Sarmatia 29, 286
Saskatchewan 277, 353, 439, 473
Saudi Arabia 51, 392, 401
Savoy 74, 92, 99, 110, 114, 133, 141, 153, 175, 355, 440, 486
Saxony 23, 62, 68, 105, 122, 179, 184, 194, 225, 232, 350, 446, 486
Schleswig-Holstein 64–65, 254
Scotland 2, 39, 63, 65, 81, 95–96, 98, 101, 105, 111, 115, 125, 128–129, 133–134, 137, 139–140, 155, 158–160, 163, 166, 171, 174, 189–192, 203, 214, 220, 228, 230, 252, 264, 303, 306, 324, 333, 354–355, 364, 400, 419–420, 437, 439, 486; *see also* Britannia; Great Britain
Scotland Yard 314–315
Scythia 3, 14–15, 17, 23, 29–30, 486
Second Crusade 78, 81–83
Second Delian League 21
Seleucids 26–28, 30, 440
Semiramis 13
Senegal 75, 237, 310, 340, 386
Sengoku Period 138–139, 143–145, 152, 155, 440
Serbia 107, 207, 213, 257, 279, 285, 295, 299, 303–305, 307, 313, 337–338, 346, 436, 486
Seventh Crusade 89–90
Shaka Zulu 236
Shang Dynasty 4, 8
sharpshooter 1, 52, 158–159, 161–162, 175, 274, 277, 279, 297, 300–302, 314, 341, 364, 370, 375, 378–379, 407, 415, 462
Shawnee 193, 196, 207
Shield Maidens 2, 45–46, 62
Shogun 85–87, 138–139, 152–153, 155–15
Shoshone 275, 294
Siam 3, 9, 134, 167, 184, 205, 245–246, 486
Siberia 17, 115, 283, 301, 309, 311, 324, 347, 370, 486
Sichuan 8, 55, 102–103, 150, 170, 214, 314, 420
Sicily 20, 27, 48, 72, 78, 86, 90, 93–94, 141, 255, 359, 376, 398, 437, 486
Siena 135, 486
Sierra Leone 250, 289, 418–419, 422, 487
Sikhism 179, 208–209, 216, 219, 239, 248–249, 296
Silesia 188, 212, 293, 327, 332, 360, 363, 385, 440
Silk Road 54, 57
Sinai 8, 27, 43, 391–392
Singapore 366, 421
Sino-Japanese War 320
Sioux 256, 258, 280–281, 286
Sisera 11, 177
Sitting Bull 277, 280
Six-Day War 391–392
Skye 16, 190, 487
slavery 16–17, 47, 49, 55, 58, 65, 78, 81, 91, 95, 115, 123, 131–132, 141–142, 163–167, 170, 176, 178, 182–183, 185–187, 194–196, 203, 207–208, 216, 218, 222, 229, 232, 237, 240, 246, 250–251, 256, 263, 270–271, 274, 276, 284–285, 292–293, 314–315, 373, 383–384, 427, 438–439
Slovakia 171, 252, 307, 347, 379, 437, 487
Slovenia 117, 307, 364, 437, 487
sniper 259, 305–306, 341, 343–344, 350, 375–376, 378–379, 434–435, 438, 440, 462
SOE 331, 333, 377, 440
Solomon Islands 148–149
Somalia 8, 34, 106, 382, 418, 487
Sonderkommando Revolt 382
Song Dynasty 67–68, 71, 80, 88
South Africa 168, 184–185, 192, 235–236, 244, 265, 287, 292, 352, 424, 431, 437

South Carolina 183, 188, 201–202, 270, 412, 416, 491
South Dakota 257, 277, 279–280, 390, 491
Soviet Union 248, 311–314, 317–320, 322–324, 328–329, 333, 339–341, 343–344, 346–350, 352–353, 358–360, 363–365, 367–373, 375, 379, 381, 383–385, 389–390, 398, 437, 485, 487
Spain 4, 27, 49, 74–75, 78–79, 118, 124, 126–127, 131–132, 141, 144, 146–149, 154, 174, 178, 185, 188, 195–196, 202, 205, 212, 215, 220–421, 223–225, 227, 230, 233, 236, 242, 246, 248, 276, 317, 319, 322, 333, 335, 340, 345, 374, 377, 400, 402, 421, 437–438, 487
Spanish Armada 146, 220
Spanish Civil War 248, 319, 322, 335, 374
Sparta 17, 20, 25, 241, 489
Special Ops 327, 352, 388, 407, 414, 423, 464
Spindle Network 356
Spiritualist Network 360
Spring and Autumn Era 2, 17, 19
SS 313, 323–324, 329, 334–335, 351, 357, 361, 364, 369, 372, 375–379, 382–383, 385
Stalin, Joseph 318, 320, 323–324, 326, 335, 343, 351, 438
Sudan 8, 28, 34, 38, 42, 142, 290, 382, 404, 418, 433, 439
Suez 391–392
suicide bombing 198, 405, 408, 411, 414, 418, 431
Sumatra 56, 97, 124–125, 151, 281, 437, 489
Sun Yat-sen 293
Sweden 1, 46, 61–62, 107, 110, 112–114, 118, 122–123, 125–128, 139, 149, 154–155, 157, 166, 171, 179–184, 204, 207, 217, 227, 244, 250, 299, 321–322, 326, 329, 334–336, 346, 364, 369, 373, 378–379, 384, 431, 438–440, 489
Switzerland 119–120, 153, 206, 215–216, 223, 255, 284, 291, 317–318, 323, 333, 342, 356, 358, 363, 374–375, 382, 384, 393, 489
Syria 3, 7, 11, 14, 20, 22, 25–27, 29–30, 38–39, 41, 43, 48, 52–54, 57, 59–60, 70, 77, 80–81, 85, 90, 254, 310–312, 386–387, 392, 394, 427, 429–431, 438, 489

Taino 123, 138, 186
Taliban 404–405, 417, 419–422, 425
T'ang Dynasty 50–51, 54, 56, 58, 67
Taoism 50, 55
Tasmania 220, 246, 440
Tennessee 193, 250, 263–269, 272, 418, 421, 491
terrorism 5, 284, 312, 319, 323, 335, 341–342, 387, 393, 398, 401, 404–406, 408, 410–411, 414, 416, 418, 420–421, 423, 425–426, 429–431, 433, 435–436, 438, 468
Teton 280
Texas 250, 252, 274, 278, 297, 411, 419–421, 430, 491
Thailand 71, 205, 384, 394, 399, 414–415, 428, 431, 489
Thebes 8, 21, 29, 489
Third Crusade 84–86
Thrace 3, 21, 44, 99, 320
Tibet 47, 239, 308, 374, 388, 489
Toltec 65, 489
Tower of London 92, 96–97, 111, 115–116, 161
Transylvania 165, 171, 253–254, 440, 489
Trinidad and Tobago 230, 402, 489
Trithyrius 54
Trojan War 3, 9–10, 19
Tunisia 28, 47, 70, 292, 423–424, 489
Turin 71, 74–75, 374, 398
Turkestan 347–348, 489
Turkey 7, 9, 13, 15, 18–22, 24, 26, 28, 30–33, 39, 41, 43–44, 54, 57, 59–60, 73–74, 76–78, 80–82, 85, 87, 91, 99, 101, 107–108, 113, 133–134, 141, 143, 157, 164, 172, 195, 207–208, 215, 234, 242–243, 253–254, 279–281, 283, 285, 294, 297, 309–310, 312–313, 320, 382, 401, 424, 427, 431, 437–438; *see also* Ottoman Empire
Turkmenistan 54, 60, 438

Ubermensch 377
Uganda 163, 288–289, 399–400, 418, 431–432, 489
Ukraine 29, 105, 159, 171, 195, 247, 268, 282, 284, 298–302, 307, 311, 317, 323, 339, 341, 344, 347, 348–349, 363–365, 367, 370, 379–381, 406, 426–427, 429–430, 434, 438, 489–490
United Arab Emirates 424, 428–429, 490
United Kingdom 322, 392, 406, 431, 439
United Nations 392, 400, 422, 426–427, 431–433
United States 235, 296, 317, 332, 351, 389–391, 393, 395, 397, 404, 406–407, 410, 412, 421, 427, 431, 433–434, 437, 490
Uruguay 238, 276, 433, 492
Utah 399
Uzbekistan 120, 350, 439

Venetians 74, 102, 113, 121, 141, 164, 174, 274, 492
Venezuela 2, 138, 142, 154, 167, 228, 230, 232, 235–236, 241, 246–247, 250, 263, 382, 412, 492
Vermont 436, 491
Victorio 278, 283–284

Vietnam 3, 4, 8, 35–36, 40–41, 48, 70, 159, 217, 338–339, 374, 379, 387, 393–395, 397, 433, 439–440, 492
Vikings 1, 45–46, 61–68, 69–70, 82, 440
Villa, Pancho 297
Virginia 169–170, 185–186, 193, 199, 203, 261–263, 265–267, 269–274, 359, 398, 414–416, 491

Wahhabi 234, 404, 408
Wales 10, 13, 37, 63, 65–66, 79, 82–83, 86, 93, 97, 115–116, 160–161, 214, 220, 230, 305, 418, 420, 492
Walloons 76, 168, 173, 208
Wars of the Roses 111, 114–115
Warsaw Ghetto Uprising 2, 359, 363, 367
Washington 245, 260, 282, 416, 491
Washington, D.C. 225, 252, 258, 261, 263–264, 266–267, 272, 389, 391, 404, 409, 413–416, 418, 421, 491
West Virginia 196, 207, 264, 269, 390–392, 407, 492
White Buses 1, 329, 372, 440
White Russians 323
Wisconsin 185–186, 258, 265–266, 400, 409–410, 412–413, 492
Women's Army Corps 353, 383, 389–390, 394
Women's Auxiliary Air Force 354
Women's Auxiliary Ferrying Squadron 355
Women's Battalion of Death 301, 308
Women's Warrior Society 280
World War I 293, 295, 297–313, 318, 390
World War II 242, 248, 290, 293, 295, 297, 313, 317–386, 425–426
Wu 2, 4, 17–19, 40–41, 46
Wyoming 279–280, 359, 492

Xerxes I 13–19, 22

Yemen 3, 48, 51–52, 67, 75, 110–111
Yom Kippur War 391
Yoruba 95, 135–136, 251, 387
Yuan Dynasty 87, 93, 102–103, 114–115, 214
Yue 2, 4, 17–19
Yugoslavia 295, 297, 313, 320, 337–338, 364, 380, 481
Yunan 42, 71, 103, 170, 258

Zambia 286, 429, 492
Zapatistas 2, 297, 310, 401
Zeeland 101–102, 146, 156, 168, 195
Zegota 293, 363, 371
Zimbabwe 1, 287, 397, 492
Zionism 304, 336, 379, 387, 391, 438
Zoroastrianism 22, 60, 62

www.ingramcontent.com/pod-product-compliance
Ingram Content Group UK Ltd.
Pitfield, Milton Keynes, MK11 3LW, UK
UKHW051824310725
2551IPUK00017B/173